DETROIT

DETROIT

Race Riots, Racial Conflicts, and Efforts to Bridge the Racial Divide

Joe T. Darden and Richard W. Thomas

Michigan State University Press
East Lansing

Copyright © 2013 by Michigan State University

♾ The paper used in this publication meets the minimum requirements of ANSI/NISO Z39.48-1992 (R 1997) (Permanence of Paper).

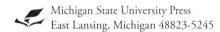 Michigan State University Press
East Lansing, Michigan 48823-5245

Printed and bound in the United States of America.

19 18 17 16 15 14 13   1 2 3 4 5 6 7 8 9 10

LIBRARY OF CONGRESS CATALOGING-IN-PUBLICATION DATA

Darden, Joe T.
Detroit : race riots, racial conflicts, and efforts to bridge the racial divide / Joe T. Darden and Richard W. Thomas.
    p. cm.
    Includes bibliographical references and index.
    ISBN 978-1-60917-352-4 (ebook)—ISBN 978-1-61186-066-5 (pbk. : alk. paper)
1. Detroit (Mich.)—Race relations—History—20th century. 2. Race riots—Michigan—Detroit—History—20th century. 3. Violence—Michigan—Detroit—History—20th century. 4. African Americans—Michigan—Detroit—History—20th century. I. Thomas, Richard Walter, 1939– II. Title.

    F574.D49N43345 2013
    305.896'073077434—dc23   2012028156

Book design by Scribe Inc. (www.scribenet.com)
Cover design by Charlie Sharp of Sharp Des!gns, Lansing, MI.

Front cover photo is of Detroit, Michigan, 24 July 1967, as 12th Street descends into chaos on the first day of civil unrest. At rear, center, the Blind Pig, whose raid by police officers sparked the conflict, can be seen behind the Economy Printing sign. In the distance a photographer snaps pictures of the scene. Detroit News Collection #318; Walter P. Reuther Library, Wayne State University. Front cover inset photo is of Mayor Coleman A. Young, as a candidate for reelection in 1977, on election night with Gladys Whitt and Joyce Garrett, 8 November 1977, Detroit News Collection #2995; Walter P. Reuther Library, Wayne State University.

Back cover photographs are of the Focus: HOPE Walk 2008, used courtesy of Focus: HOPE and Detroit Public Library Special Collections; and of the Michigan Roundtable for Diversity Youth Summit, used courtesy of Michigan Roundtable for Diversity and Inclusion.

g green press INITIATIVE Michigan State University Press is a member of the Green Press Initiative and is committed to developing and encouraging ecologically responsible publishing practices. For more information about the Green Press Initiative and the use of recycled paper in book publishing, please visit www.greenpressinitiative.org.

Visit Michigan State University Press at www.msupress.org

This book is dedicated to the people and organizations in the city of Detroit, the suburbs, and beyond who have contributed to the struggle to bridge the racial divide since the riot of 1967.

Contents

List of Tables   ix

Acknowledgments   xiii

Preface   xv

Chapter 1.   Historical Causes and Consequences of the 1967 Civil Disorder: White Racism,
             Black Rebellion, and Changing Race Relations in the Post–Civil Disorder Era   1

Chapter 2.   Conflict between the Black Community and White Police:
             Before and after the 1967 Civil Disorder   29

Chapter 3.   Racial Conflict over School Desegregation   67

Chapter 4.   Racial Conflict over Employment Discrimination   81

Chapter 5.   The Emergence of Black Political Power after 1967: Impact of the
             Civil Disorders on Race Relations in Metropolitan Detroit   93

Chapter 6.   City and Suburban Conflict over Residential Sharing of Neighborhoods   137

Chapter 7.   The Declining Auto Industry and Anti-Asian
             Racism: The Murder of Vincent Chin   155

Chapter 8.   African American and Middle Eastern American Relations after 1967   181

Chapter 9.   Old Minority and New Minority: Black-Latino
             Relations in a Predominantly Black City   199

Chapter 10. Economic Restructuring, Black Deprivation,
             and the Problem of Drugs and Crime   221

Chapter 11. Measuring the Racial Divides in Metropolitan Detroit   239

Chapter 12. Interracial Cooperation and Bridge Building in the Postriot Era   265

Chapter 13. Alternative Futures for Residents of Detroit   297

Appendix. Method of Computation of the Index of Dissimilarity   319

References   321

Index   341

Tables

Table 1.   Racial segregation of Detroit Public Schools in 1962   69

Table 2.   High schools with less than 50 percent black
             enrollment in the city of Detroit, 1970   70

Table 3.   Racial composition of Detroit schools, 1961, 1967, and 1970   71

Table 4.   Total number and percentage of students in
             Detroit by race, 1961, 1967, and 1970   72

Table 5.   Funding ratios in Detroit School District versus surrounding
             suburban school districts, 1967–1968 and 2003–2004   76

Table 6.   Percentage of students proficient on MEAP in Detroit School District and
             in the suburban districts of Wayne, Oakland, and Macomb counties, 2007   77

Table 7.   Ratios of MEAP proficiency, Detroit School District versus suburban
             districts of Oakland, Macomb, and Wayne counties, 2007   78

Table 8.   Racial, age, and unemployment characteristics of riot areas, of city of
             Detroit, and of metropolitan area, 1970 (%)   90

Table 9.   Unemployment in Detroit and the metropolitan area,
             1967 and 2005–2009, by race   91

Table 10.   Hispanic settlement in Detroit in 2010   204

Table 11.   Residential segregation trends in Detroit, 1980–2010,
             blacks, whites, and Hispanics (index of dissimilarity)   206

Table 12.   Number and percentage black and Hispanic
             populations in Detroit, 1980–2010   206

Table 13.   Occupational differences between Hispanics
             and blacks in Detroit, 1970   207

Table 14.   Occupational differences between Hispanics
             and blacks in Detroit, 2000   208

Table 15.   Differences between Hispanic and black unemployment
             rates in Detroit, 1970, 1990, 2000, and 2005–2009   209

Table 16.   Hispanic and black median household
             income in Detroit, 1970 to 2005–2009   209

Table 17.   Percentage of Hispanic and black families below
poverty level in Detroit, 1970, 2000, and 2005–2009   210

Table 18.   Percentage of black and Hispanic population of Detroit 25 years
and over with a bachelor's degree or higher, 2000 and 2005–2009   210

Table 19.   Hispanic and black MEAP scores in Detroit
Public Schools, grade 3, fall 2008   211

Table 20.   Comparison between Hispanic and black students
MEAP scores in Detroit Public Schools, fall 2008   212

Table 21.   Hispanic and black MEAP scores in Detroit
Public Schools, grade 6, fall 2008   213

Table 22.   Hispanic and black MEAP scores in Detroit
Public Schools, grade 8, fall 2008   213

Table 23.   Hispanic and black homeownership in
Detroit, 1970 to 2005–2009   214

Table 24.   Median value of Hispanic and black owner-occupied
housing in Detroit, 1980–2008   214

Table 25.   Black- and Hispanic-owned businesses in Detroit, 2002   216

Table 26.   Racial/ethnic differences in business ownership in Detroit, 2007   222

Table 27.   Business participation rates in Detroit, by race and ethnicity, 2007   232

Table 28.   Business ownership in the suburbs of Detroit, by race, 2007   233

Table 29.   Rates of violent crimes and property crimes in Detroit, 1980–2007   236

Table 30.   Black and white population in the suburbs of Detroit, 1960–2010   242

Table 31.   Black and white population of Detroit and its suburbs, 2010   243

Table 32.   Residential segregation trends in metropolitan
Detroit and the city of Detroit, 1960–2010   244

Table 33.   Residential segregation in Detroit between blacks and whites with
the same levels of household income, 2000, and change since 1990   245

Table 34.   Residential segregation in Detroit suburbs between blacks and whites
with the same levels of household income, 2000, and change since 1990   246

Table 35.   Residential segregation in Detroit between blacks and whites
with the same levels of education, 2000, and change since 1990   247

Table 36. Residential segregation in Detroit suburbs between blacks and whites
with the same levels of education, 2000, and change since 1990   248

Table 37. Race and place divide in higher education, 2008   249

Table 38. Race and place divide, median household income, 2008   249

Table 39. Race and place divide in occupational status, 2008   250

Table 40. Race and place divide in median value of housing, 2008   250

Table 41. Race and place divide, median gross rent, 2008   251

Table 42. Race and place divide in homeownership, 2008   251

Table 43. Race and place divide, age of housing, 2008   252

Table 44. Race and place divide, poverty rates, 2008   252

Table 45. Race and place divide, unemployment rates, 2008   253

Table 46. Race and place divide, percentage of households
without vehicle available, 2008   254

Table 47. Percentage of Detroit renter households paying
contract rent at various levels, 2005–2009   307

Table 48. Percentage of Detroit renter households that could
afford to live in selected Wayne County suburbs, 2009   308

Table 49. Percentage of Detroit renter households that could
afford to live in selected Oakland County suburbs, 2009   309

Table 50. Percentage of Detroit renter households that could afford
to live in selected Macomb County suburbs, 2009   310

Table 51. The average rent per month for two-bedroom apartment in selected
suburbs in Oakland, Wayne, and Macomb counties, May 22, 2011   311

Table 52. Patterns of black suburbanization in Detroit, 2000 and 2010   314

Table 53. Patterns of black-white residential segregation in suburban Detroit, 2010   316

Acknowledgments

THIS BOOK WAS MADE POSSIBLE BY THE CONTRIBUTIONS OF OTHERS. THUS, WE OWE them our sincere appreciation. Lisa Eldred provided outstanding editorial assistance for the entire manuscript. We also received assistance in bibliographic collections and data gathering from Kayla Benard, a recent graduate from Michigan State University. We appreciate her contribution. We also owe a great debt of gratitude to Andy Lee, a former graduate assistant in the Urban Affairs Program at Michigan State University, for researching newspaper accounts covering the Vincent Chin case and collecting materials from the American Citizens for Justice (ACJ) upon which chapter 7 is based. We also appreciate the assistance that the ACJ provided to Andy during his work on the project. Thanks also to Alexis Braun Marks, archivist at the Charles H. Wright Museum Archives Library, who came to our aid when we desperately needed to access the archives' collection of Mayor Coleman Young's papers. Thanks to Thomas Costello, Jr., President of the Michigan Roundtable for Diversity and Inclusion, and Matt Hoerauf, Community Development Manager of the Michigan Roundtable for Diversity and Inclusion, for their cooperation in gaining us access to the organization's papers and documents. We also thank the staffs of the Bentley Historical Library at the University of Michigan and other collections. Finally, we want to thank Julie Loehr, assistant director of Michigan State University Press, for understanding the need for such a volume as part of the MSU Press collection.

Preface

DURING THE SUMMER OF 1967, DETROIT, MICHIGAN'S LARGEST CITY, EXPERIENCED the worst race riot in the city's history and the most severe racial conflict in the entire nation. During a two-week period, which began on July 23, at least 43 people were killed, hundreds were wounded, and numerous properties were destroyed. This urban disorder would influence racial thinking and the collective memories of blacks and whites throughout the coming decades. This book examines six basic questions. What happened? Where did it happen? Why did it happen? To what extent have the conditions that caused the riots changed since the riots? What efforts have occurred since the riots to reduce racial conflicts and build bridges across racial divides? What are the alternative futures for Detroit residents?

The ideas expressed in the book are grounded in the following themes: *Place of residence matters. Spatial injustice* has been a recurring problem, and a remedy worth exploring is the *geography of opportunity.* The book is based on a comprehensive set of data sources, both primary and secondary. It draws heavily from U.S. census reports and archival documents. The Detroit riots are examined within the contexts of two landmark governmental reports by presidential commissions that focused on race: *Report of the National Advisory Commission on Civil Disorders* (the Kerner Commission Report), published in 1968, and *One America in the 21st Century: Forging a New Future,* also called the John Hope Franklin Report. Both reports were initiated under Democratic administrations, and most black Detroiters have consistently been supportive of the Democratic Party.

Our socioeconomic analysis, which revealed inequality by race and place, led to a key political question: what do these two reports and our own data and analyses tell us about the effectiveness of black political leadership in Detroit in reducing racial divides? What do the results tell us about a black politically controlled city's ability to improve the lives of the predominantly black residents? In other words, what has been the effectiveness of black political power and black demographic dominance in driving socioeconomic change in Detroit?

The spark that set off the riots in Detroit was actions by the predominantly white police toward members of the black community. This book examines the relationship between the black community in Detroit and the police. The volume also examines black-white inequality and conflict in the public schools, employment and unemployment, housing, and the sharing of neighborhoods. However, racial conflict in Detroit extends beyond just blacks and whites. Thus, this volume examines Asian-white conflict, black-Arab conflict, and black-Latino conflict. The book examines organized efforts over the years to reduce the many conflicts and bridge racial divides.

The final chapter offers alternative futures for residents of Detroit. Among the alternatives is a spatial mobility strategy within the context of a geography of opportunity for those residents who want to move to greater economic and social opportunities that lie beyond the city's borders.

As members of the team of researchers who examined the racial divide in Detroit in the volume *Detroit: Race and Uneven Development*, published in 1987, we have expanded our coverage of the various groups that have a stake in Detroit. We observe that many of the problems revealed in the earlier volume are not only still present, but have gotten much worse. Our hope is that this book will serve as an important source of information for individuals, families, neighborhood groups, nonprofit and civil rights organizations, and policymakers and administrators who want to examine alternative options and take the action necessary to enable the residents of Detroit to improve the quality of their lives.

CHAPTER 1

Historical Causes and Consequences of the 1967 Civil Disorder

White Racism, Black Rebellion, and Changing Race Relations in the Post–Civil Disorder Era

In July 1967, Detroit experienced the bloodiest urban disorder and the costliest property damage in U.S. history. When it finally ended, forty-three people had been killed—thirty-three blacks and ten whites—over one thousand injured, and 3,800 arrested (Fine, 1989: 299). Close to 5,000 people were left homeless, most of them black. More than 1,000 buildings had been burned to the ground. When the total damage was tallied, it soared to $50 million. During the riot, or "rebellion," as most black radicals called it, several white police officers deliberately shot three unarmed black men to death in the Algiers Motel. Two of the men were shot while lying or kneeling (Widick, 1972; Hersey, 1968). Race relations would never be the same. This chapter will explore the historical causes and consequences of this tragic event, and how segments of the black and white communities reacted to it.

More than forty years after the 1967 civil disorder in Detroit, people are still talking and writing about it. It remains a major historical and racial event in the collective memory of a generation of black and white metro Detroiters who either experienced the event or heard about it from older relatives and friends who lived in Detroit or the suburbs at the time. This event, more than any other in the period after World War II, left an indelible imprint on both that generation and the generations that followed. Many black and white people in metro Detroit, and particularly those whites who left because of the riot, still define the stages of their lives by the event. A white former Detroiter who was a young woman at the time recalls:

> I was 18, just graduated from high school and working at Macabee Life Insurance in Southfield. In the middle of the day I was paged to the front office and saw my dad standing there. He had come to take me home. I remembered worrying about where the rioters were in relation to my home (Six Mile/Lahser/Evergreen area) and Dad reassuring me they were far away. However, the next day I recall my Dad coming home and telling my Mom he was going to stay home for the duration. That frightened me, my Dad worked 12–14 hours a day and for him to take off work was a major event. . . . I don't recall any looter damage as far as we were but I do recall soldiers on

the streets. . . . By January my folk had sold their house and moved to South Lyon. Even though I was moving on in my life I hated leaving that fabulous neighborhood. I can't imagine growing up anywhere else. (Discuss Detroit Forums, October 27, 2006)

From this "white" perspective, the "riot" disrupted a comfortable lifestyle, forcing her family to become refugees from their "fabulous neighborhood." Even at this distance of four decades, there is little sense from this observer of what might have caused the "riot" that led to her family's "exodus" from the city to distant South Lyons.

A black teenage male had a different experience of the same event. His narrative reveals the fear of the average black family caught between the rioters and the white police and National Guard, operating at times like a hostile "occupying army."

There was a little party store right across the street on the other side of 12th, and Mom sent me out to the store to get some milk. . . . I ran out of the house and got into the middle of the street when the National Guard hollered, " Stop!" I literally froze in the middle of the street. They called me over and asked where was I going, what was I doing: and I told them . . . I live right here and my mom was just sending me to the store. They made me go back in the house, made my mom and dad come out and explain to them where I was going, and what I was going for, and then stood there and watched as I went across the street to the store and came back.

Then one night, my younger sister was just an infant at the time, and they had pinned a sniper down on the roof of the building across the street on 12th. My mom got up about eleven-thirty or twelve. The police had turned off all of the street lights up and down 12th Street, so it was pitch black. My mom got up to go downstairs to get my sister a bottle. When she turned on the light in the living room . . . the light hit like a floodlight; and she got about two steps when the National Guard and the police said over a megaphone she had about two second to turn off that light or it would be blown out because it was giving their position away and illuminating them to the sniper. She turned the lights out, and I remember how she crawled back up the steps. She was so scared. She made us sleep under our beds that night because of the gunfire. The next morning I got up, went out in the backyard, and saw spent shells. And our garage on the alley side was just riddled with bullets

At first the riots were a matter of just looting stores and people roaming. Then it got ugly. I mean, it turned more violent, where there were snipers and gunfire, and we were literally under martial law. If there was a group of four or five blacks walking down the street together they were broken up. The police would stop them, break them up, and make them go a different way. It was really scary. I remember how firemen stopped coming into the neighborhood because they were being shot at. (Moon, 1994: 373–74)

A generation of blacks and whites experienced the riot in dramatically different ways, creating sometimes historically conflicting narratives. The black narrative, which was confirmed by the Kerner Commission Report, placed the blame squarely on institutionalized racism that crippled the lives of so many blacks during the years leading up to the riot: "What white Americans have never fully understood—but what the Negro can never forget—is that white society is deeply implicated in the ghetto. White institutions created it, white institutions maintain it, and white society condones it" (National Advisory Commission on Civil Disorders, 1968: 2). George Romney, who was governor of Michigan during the riot, agreed with the report, saying, "What triggered the riot in my opinion, to a considerable extent, that between urban renewal and expressways, poor black people were bulldozed out of their homes. They had no place to go in the suburbs because of suburban restriction. They settled along 12th Street. The concentration of people on 12th Street was too great. So when that incident occurred, it was a spark that ignited the whole area" (Moon, 1994: 396). In short, white institutional racism in the form of urban renewal, expressways, and white suburban resistance were the major causes of the civil disorder, or rebellion, of 1967. But, as to be expected, black and white collective memories of the event differ.

Historian Sidney Fine, in his study of the riot, wrote, "Whites and blacks just after the riot viewed what had happened and its consequences in very different ways. As two University of Michigan political scientists put it, 'for the most part it was as if two different events had taken place in the same city, one a calculated act of criminal anarchy, the other a spontaneous protest against mistreatment and injustice'" (1989: 369). According to one community survey, when blacks and whites were asked which of three possible interpretations came closest to explaining why the riot had occurred, 69 percent of the blacks, but only 28 percent of the whites, thought it was because people were "being treated badly." Furthermore, 31 percent of whites blamed the riot on "criminals" and 37 percent believed that the riot occurred because "people wanted to take things." As for blacks, 11 percent believed the former and 18 percent the latter (Fine, 1989: 369).

There were still other sharp differences in black/white views of the social impact of the riots. In one of the above surveys, 31 percent of blacks believed the riot would "help" black-white relations, compared to only 4 percent of whites. "Three-quarters of the whites, as compared to 38 percent of the blacks, expected that race relations in Detroit would be impaired. Those who believed race relations had been helped thought that the riot has made whites understand that blacks had to be 'taken seriously' and had also led to a quest for solutions to the city's racial problems." However, "those who thought race relations had suffered stressed 'white fear, distrust, dislike, anger toward blacks'" (Fine, 1989: 369).

Four months after this survey, another one revealed that "a smaller percentage of blacks (27 percent) and a larger percentage of whites (13 percent) believed that the riot had helped black-white relations. Almost 70 percent of the white respondents now thought that blacks were pushing 'too fast' for what they wanted, and just over 67 percent believed that blacks in the central city had only themselves to blame for the fact that they had 'worse jobs, education, and housing than white people'" (Fine, 1989: 369).

This "blame the victim" view held by many Detroit whites was a classic example of how white collective memory distorted history, and was often deliberately blank, or at least benignly ignorant, of the city's racist history prior to the 1967 riots, when blacks in Detroit routinely experienced discrimination in jobs, housing, public accommodation, and education (Stolberg, 1998; Sugrue, 1996; Thomas, 1992). And, of course, most whites knew or cared little about the brutal police treatment of blacks in the city during these years that triggered the 1967 riot.

To many whites, the riot spontaneously flared up from the unruly black masses of the ghetto, whom they saw as too lazy to work and too willing to commit crimes, and much too prone to violence. There was no reason for such behavior. The riot, they felt and firmly believed, was simply a breakdown of law and order.

While a police raid on a "blind pig" (an after-hours drinking establishment) triggered the disorder, according to some observers, the black "rebellion" itself "developed out of an increasingly disturbed social atmosphere, in which typically a series of tension-heightening incidents over a period of weeks or months became linked in the minds of many in the Negro community with a shared network of underlying grievances" (National Advisory Commission on Civil Disorders, 1968: 111).

Ten years prior to the riot the housing market was so racially restricted that although blacks represented 20 percent of the population in Detroit they were living in less than 1 percent of the new houses built. This meant that those blacks who could afford to buy new houses were denied the opportunity. Thus, black ghettos became more crowded. In short, blacks were forced to live in "essentially the same places that their predecessors lived during the 1930s—the only difference [was] that due to increasing numbers, they occup[ied] more space centered around their traditional quarters" (Hoult and Mayer, 1962).

One could reasonably argue that the black anger and frustration in the 1960s that finally erupted in 1967 stemmed in no small way from the countless expressions of white hostility directed toward blacks throughout the 1950s. In 1950 Detroit veered dangerously close to another riot—the most recent one had occurred in 1943—when the Detroit Common Council held a public meeting to discuss a proposal for a cooperative housing project to be built in northwest Detroit, a stronghold of white resistance. Whites in the area wanted no part of the proposed project in their community, because three of the project's fifty-four families would be black. White leaders supporting the project made no headway at the meeting. Blacks became angry, and the mayor fired an important black leader for criticizing what he had called "the vacillating policy" of the Detroit Housing Commission. The crisis eventually led to the resignation of the director of the city's Interracial Committee (Darden et al., 1987a).

Between 1954 and 1956 there was an increase of white resistance to blacks moving into "their neighborhoods." These whites were determined to keep blacks out. In at least five separate instances large groups of whites demonstrated in front of black homes, triggering serious racial incidents. Some blacks, unable or unwilling to stay in the face of such hostility, decided to leave. In January 1956, a black man who had recently moved into a predominantly white neighborhood in northeast Detroit was informed by white neighbors that he was not welcome. Soon after, someone burned down his garage, and a few months later he found one side of his house soaked in fuel and a fire burning nearby (Darden et al., 1987).

The most hard-core resistance to the "Negro tide" was centered in the far northwest section of the city. In 1956 this bulwark of white racism contained fifty neighborhood improvement associations that blocked sales of houses to blacks, organized demonstrations in front of black homes, persuaded white brokers not to sell to blacks, and protested against public housing projects (Darden et al., 1987).

This section of Detroit was the site of one of the largest racial demonstrations over housing in the 1950s and, according to the city's Commission on Community Relations, "drew nation-wide attention." In February 1957, a white mob of about 300 people gathered in front of the home of Mrs. Ethel Watkins, a black divorcee. They objected to the presence of a black person in their all-white neighborhood. As the mob increased, police were forced to seal off the area to passing cars and pedestrians. Except for a stone thrown through one of the windows of the house one day and a snowball thrown through the front door glass another day, the mass demonstration was nonviolent but nonetheless racist. For example, a black reporter on the scene was told by a young member of the mob to take a picture of the "monkey in the cage" (City of Detroit Commission on Community Relations, 1957; *Michigan Chronicle*, February 16, 1957). Understandably, Mrs. Watkins was hysterical and felt that she could not stand much more of the mob demonstration. Under police protection she left the house and spent the night at the home of a relative, with the intention of giving up the house rather than facing hostile neighbors (*Michigan Chronicle*, February 16, 1957).

The large demonstration surprised the police and other city agencies. The mayor's Commission on Community Relations had made contact with ministers in the neighborhood, and one of them had even visited Mrs. Watkins in her home to welcome her into the community. Unfortunately, other white ministers and neighbors did not share his outlook. The white woman who sold the house to the black woman was so upset over the reaction that she offered to purchase the house back "to end all this which has affected her much as it has Mrs. Watkins" (*Michigan Chronicle*, February 16, 1957).

After talks with the black realtor who had arranged the sale and representatives of various concerned city agencies, Mrs. Watkins mustered the courage and returned to her home. However, her white neighbors persisted in their efforts to dislodge her from the neighborhood. They went so far as to send a delegation to the black realtor to buy back Mrs. Watkins's house for $1,400 more that she had paid for it. The realtor refused their offer. Seven hundred residents of the neighborhood held an emergency meeting at a local church, where with outside assistance, they formed a so-called "improvement association" and discussed techniques and methods for getting rid of Mrs. Watkins and preventing blacks from entering the neighborhood in the future (*Michigan Chronicle*, February 23, 1957).

The effects of this organized white resistance and "racial terrorism" on many black families prevented them from moving into white neighborhoods for fear of having their property destroyed or worse, their lives threatened. Instead, many black families probably decided to stay put, remaining in overcrowded, poor ghettos, which became breeding grounds for angry black youth waiting for an opportunity to explode. A generation of whites would soon forget this period of racial terrorism and see no connection between it and the resentment and anger of another generation of blacks toward "the white Establishment."

The growing black population in Detroit during the 1950s had few outlets to ease the pressure. They were squeezed in on all sides by resistance from hostile white neighborhoods on the borders of black ghettos and equally hostile suburbs; and policed by what many blacks considered to be "a white occupying army." While black housing problems were compounded by urban removal policies that uprooted the African American community of Paradise Valley and forced much of the poor black population to move to the 12th Street area, which became the epicenter of the 1967 riot or rebellion, white racial privilege paved the way for white Detroiters to move to the growing suburban communities to realize their version of the "American Dream." Once there, they quickly established a new wall of resistance against those blacks also seeking to relocate to better themselves.

Most white popular narratives of the many causes of the 1967 riots do not mention the connection between white escape to the suburbs and the walls they erected to prevent blacks from sharing the same suburban dream. These walls kept blacks locked into a declining central city, barred from decent jobs and housing, and forced them to raise their children on low wages and send them, often hungry, to shabby, run-down schools.

This suburban ring of racism was constructed and maintained by suburban officials such as the late Orville L. Hubbard of Dearborn, Michigan, a favorite of suburban racists who promised to keep blacks out of white suburbs. To many whites in Dearborn and other suburbs and white neighborhoods in Detroit, Mayor Hubbard seemed invincible in his resistance to racial integration, blacks, and the federal government. During the 1960s Mayor Hubbard's Dearborn emerged as "a symbol of the deep-rooted racism of the north," and the mayor himself was said to be one who "speaks his city's mind on the subject and the mind of many northern white suburbs as well" (Serrin, 1969: 26; *Detroit Free Press*, December 17 and 19, 1982).

While many whites in Dearborn did not share Mayor Hubbard's antiblack mania, it is interesting to note that during his tenure, no viable movement of white citizens arose in the city to effectively challenge his racist views. Perhaps the good liberal whites of Dearborn realized that although the mayor's racism was an embarrassment, it could be endured, because at least it protected their white-skin privileges. In spite of the racism, some might have argued, Dearborn was a great place to live. Few cities of comparable size delivered such benefits to its citizens: low taxes (in 1967 Ford paid 52 percent of all Dearborn's city taxes), clean streets, a free shoppers' babysitting service, fast snow removal, one of the best-endowed recreation programs in the metropolitan area, a summer camp, a police escort service for New Year's celebrants too drunk to drive, and a senior citizen high-rise located in Florida (*Detroit Free Press*, December 19, 1982).

Mayor Hubbard created a white working-class utopia that many white liberals also found satisfying. Therefore, Mayor Hubbard remained in office as an avowed, unabashed racist; because he protected white suburban privilege, he satisfied the needs of most of the white community in Dearborn. The historical cost of maintaining this racist white working-class utopia has been long-term mutual racial antagonism between many Dearborn whites and Detroit blacks and a racially segregated metropolitan community.

Dearborn was not the only suburb that created walls to maintain racial segregation. In the summer of 1967, soon after a black man and his white wife moved into their new home in Warren, angry whites gathered around the house and, for two nights, threw stones and broke windows. Someone threw a smoke bomb into the house. The Warren police hesitated to arrest members of the mob, but finally convinced them to go home (*Michigan Chronicle*, June 24, 1967; *Detroit Free Press*, June 13 and 16, 1967).

Detroit's ghettos were forced to accommodate an increasingly poor and marginalized black population. The black population density resulted in decreasing amounts of land available for public recreation; and since the black population was younger than the white, more recreation areas were needed for black children. As the Detroit Urban League reported in 1967, this lack of recreation space meant black "children and youth were growing up in areas in which the conditions were unfavorable for their development as individuals" (Detroit Urban League, 1967: 8).

Lacking the space for fruitful recreation, many black youth took to the streets and were lured into crime. More than likely, many of these youth, caught up in the cycle of poverty and alienation, took to the streets during the riot, targeting all symbols of white dominance, especially the all-pervasive white police force.

Substandard housing and racially restricted living spaces produced an unhealthy environment for education for students and teachers in Detroit's black communities. On the eve of the 1967 urban disorder, more than 50 percent of the black students (in black high schools) dropped out before graduation. Seventy-two percent of all black students went to schools that were 90–100 percent black. During the 1966–67 school year, "only 30 percent of the eligible students were assisted by the 11.2 million in Title 1 funds earmarked for inner city schools"(Detroit Urban League, 1967: 8).

Predictably, these conditions generated a high rate of unemployment among black youth. Most black youth less than twenty-five years of age in 1971 experienced a rate of unemployment between 30 and 40 percent (Widick, 1972). Many of these youth fit the profile of the typical rioter, had dropped out of school, and were slightly more educated than their peers. They also had a great deal of racial pride (National Advisory Commission on Civil Disorders, 1968).

RACIAL HYSTERIA IN THE EARLY POSTDISORDER PERIOD

After the riot, white police feared blacks even more now that they knew how volatile the racial situation was in Detroit. Their perception of the future of race relations in Detroit led them to flock into the National Rifle Association, using their membership to buy carbines in preparation for the next black rebellion. Private citizens began buying guns in record numbers, and white suburban housewives were seen on television practicing shooting handguns (Widick, 1972). The city of Warren on the northeastern border of Detroit began organizing for "trouble" by forming a militia. Mayor Cavanagh described the buying of guns by blacks and whites in anticipation of the next riot as "literally an arms race in Detroit" (Fine, 1989: 387).

Breakthrough, a white far-right organization led by Donald Lobsinger, began to attract many whites after the riot, compared to the few hundred they were able to get to its meeting before the riot. Lobsinger explained that the purpose of the organization was to "arm the whites and to keep them in Detroit because if the city became black, there would be 'guerrilla warfare in the suburbs.'" According to Lobsinger, Breakthrough was needed "because the police had failed to protect the white community" (Fine, 1989: 383). The whites who attended these meetings tended to be "enthusiastic and revivalist," middle-aged, of East European background, drawn to Breakthrough's propaganda that the riot had been a "'Communist-inspired insurrection' whose purpose was to 'terrorize blacks' to join 'the black power movement,' after which the 'entire Negro community' could 'move in on the whites.'" This claim had also been made by a John Birch Society front organization, Truth About City Turmoil (TACT) (Fine, 1989: 384).

Breakthrough's followers were urged to buy weapons and certain supplies to store up for the next "'much more terrifying' riot." The organization "suggested that they arrange for safe locations to which they could send their children when the dreaded event occurred. It advised whites to establish a 'block to block home defense system' for protection against 'bands of armed terrorists' invading from the inner city to 'murder the men and rape the women'" (Fine, 1989: 384). As for those whites who were working to heal the racial wounds from the riots, Breakthrough "cautioned its audience not to allow themselves 'to be misled once more by the do-gooders and bleeding hearts' who were proposing as measures to forestall race riots the same kinds of 'solution' as had failed in the past" (Fine, 1989: 384).

Breakthrough not only fanned the flames of postriot racial hysteria among many whites, it also engaged in its campaign the support of other organizations, such as "American Legion Posts, the Detroit Police and Firemen's Association for Public Safety, and the Chaldean Society for Preservation of Liberty" (Fine, 1989: 384). In perhaps the most shameful and racist action in its history, the National Rifle Association displayed weapons at Breakthrough's meetings that contributed to the "arms race," which worried Mayor Cavanagh.

Perhaps the most dramatic white reaction to the 1967 riot and one of the singular historical events that stands out in the current white collective memory of the riot was white flight to the suburbs. "Many whites simply fled Detroit in the wake of the riot. White flight was hardly a new phenomenon, but the rate of departure for the suburbs considerably increased in the aftermath of the riot," as Fine correctly points out. For example, "an average of twenty-two thousand whites had left Detroit each year from 1964 through 1966, but forty-seven thousands departed in 1967—it is a good guess that three-quarters of them did so after the riot—eighty thousand left in 1968, and forty-six thousand in 1969" (Fine, 1989: 384).

The racial hysteria among whites fleeing Detroit for the suburbs in the postriot period added to the greater fear and racial hysteria of whites already residing in the suburbs (Fine, 1989). Racial hysteria among some suburban communities created such a siege mentality that they hired auxiliary police to patrol their streets and organized a wave of gun clubs (Fine, 1989). Many white suburbanites felt they had to be prepared for the riot in the near future.

As whites in the suburbs were organizing and joining gun clubs and practicing pistol shooting, militant black leaders were warning blacks that the police were planning to provoke an incident as an excuse to attack them. In March 1968, one of these leaders advised blacks to "store enough food for a month in anticipation of an invasion by armed, white racist suburbanites." A month later, a black organization set up a Black Unity Day Rally "to inform blacks about defense and survival methods" (Fine, 1989: 384–85).

As could be expected during the postriot period, wild rumors began spreading in both the black and white communities, fueling the mounting tension and racial hysteria. According to rumors making the rounds in the white community, "Blacks would set fire to the expressways and shoot whites in their cars. . . . blacks would shut off the city's water supply and its public utility service. . . . there was talk of black 'killer squads' that would come from the inner city to murder children and of black maids dispatched to suburban communities to poison the residents of the households where they served. The castration of young whites by blacks was a common rumor toward the end of February 1968" (Fine, 1989: 385).

Rumors in the black community spoke of how whites would try "to provoke a race war and then would invade the inner city to murder blacks, that the police were training suburban whites to shoot (which was not that far from the truth), and that the police was anxious for a riot 'to get even' with Blacks" (Fine, 1989: 385).

The rumors mills in both black and white communities encouraged a dramatic rise in gun sales. Licenses to buy handguns rapidly rose during the first six months of 1968. More ominously, however, was the rise in sales of firearms that did not have to be registered, such as rifles, shotguns, and carbines, which "tripled after the riots" (Fine, 1989: 385). The "arms race" even extended to Ohio, where handgun laws were less restricted, giving Detroiters even more access to guns (Fine, 1989).

The courageous mayor did all he could to halt both the rumors and the "arms race." He tried in vain to persuade the Common Council to require that all sellers and purchasers of long guns be licensed, that such weapons be registered, and the sale of ammunition be restricted to legitimate gun users (Fine, 1989: 385). On March 7, 1968, Cavanagh appeared on television to calm citizens' fears and reassure them that "the police were prepared to prevent trouble and to attack the 'voices of the right and the left' that were seeking to divide the city" (Fine, 1989: 385). Unfortunately, this attempt to calm the rising tide of fear and rumor-making probably fell on deaf years in the black community. Blacks had little faith in the predominantly white police force, with its long history of racism, not to take sides in the racial crisis. The mayor had to continue his efforts, however. To check the circulation of wild rumors, the mayor ordered the establishment of a Rumor Control Center "that would check out rumors and counter falsehood with truth" (Fine, 1989: 386).

As well-intentioned and effective as the Rumor Control Center was, one scholar pointed out that it tended to serve "the white community and did nothing to deal with the discontents of the black community that led to riots. Rumors . . . do not cause riots but are rather 'part of the same process that induces collective outburst'" (Fine, 1989: 386).

UNLIKELY BEDFELLOWS FROM THE ASHES: BLACK MILITANTS, WHITE CORPORATE LEADERS, AND THE FUTURE OF RACE RELATIONS IN DETROIT

The 1967 urban disorder—or "black rebellion," according to some segments of the black community—galvanized an assortment of black leaders and organizations, ranging from black militant and separatist groups such the Republic of New Africa, to storefront community organizations such as Operation Get-Down and the Inner-City Sub-Center, to well-established old-guard organizations such as the Detroit Urban League and various churches. There could be no doubt that the riot forever changed the historical, social, economic, and political trajectory of the black community in its relationship to white metro Detroit.

No matter how various segments of the black and white community choose to describe or interpret the tragedy of July 1967—whether as an "urban disorder," "riot," or "black rebellion"—it marked the beginning of a new community identity among many blacks. As one white scholar wrote, the 1960s riots "stimulated a new burst of pride and revived belief that blacks could force changes through united efforts." "That many blacks derived satisfaction in the riot's aftermath from the fact that blacks had stood up to whites seems evident," echoed another white scholar (quoted in Fine, 1989: 371). A black friend of the *Free Press*'s Frank Angelo stated that, after the riot, he "had a feeling that Negroes in Detroit were walking taller" (Fine, 1989: 371).

To militant blacks and restless, unemployed, and recently politicized black youth, it was a defining moment in their lives. They refused to allow whites to define what happened during those bloody days in July as a mere urban disorder or riot. They decided to seize the power to define this momentous historical event that claimed so many black lives. Rather, it was a "black urban rebellion," marking a revolutionary turning point in the lives of the "Black Nation."

This process of redefining the historical meaning of "the riot" began with leaders like Detroit radical black preacher Reverend Albert B. Cleage Jr., who gave a sermon on the black struggle at a memorial service for those killed in "the rebellion." "We are engaged in a nationwide rebellion," he declared, "seeking to become what God intended that we should be—free men with control of our destiny, the destiny of black men" (Widick, 1972: 189).

Other voices soon emerged. Two black representatives of the Malcolm X Society, one of the many militant black organizations that surfaced during this period, presented a bold statement to the New Detroit Committee (to be discussed later) calling for control of black areas in the city:

We speak in the name of the Malcolm X Society, which represents the political side of the Black Revolution. We speak for the militants, not because we control or direct them—we do not—but we are both part of the same revolution . . . and we therefore understand what the goals of the revolution are, that those goals are not being achieved, and what will happened if they are not achieved. (*Michigan Chronicle*, December 2, 1967)

According to the statement, the "simple overriding goal for which Black people fought this July [was] control of our lives and all those institution which affect them. We have failed to gain control in the following areas: police . . . jobs . . . Housing . . . and economic control" (*Michigan Chronicle*, December 2, 1967). The Malcolm X Society went on to elaborate on each area that the group believed should be under black control. Regarding law enforcement, they wanted police in black areas to be under "Black command." It would be unacceptable, they argued, to have a black in the number 3 position in the Police Department if the person could not give "a single order to a line policeman." If the black community could not get a black police commissioner, then "the only acceptable approach to Black control is the creation of a Board of Commissioners to replace the single Commissioner, with each commissioner over a district and each Commissioner elected by votes in his District. This is an absolutely essential revision of police power. For the police force must cease to be a White people's army used to oppress Black people" (*Michigan Chronicle*, December 2, 1967).

This view of the police force as "a White people's army" was not limited to black militants but shared by many other segments of the black community, and was reinforced by the police and the National Guard during the urban disorder. Concerning police recruitment, the statement said that "police recruitment must be taken from the Department and placed under the normal civil service like the recruitment for other city departments" (*Michigan Chronicle*, December 2, 1967). However, radical changes in the Police Department would have to wait until the election of Coleman Young in 1973 as the first black mayor in Detroit (Ashton, 1981; Rich, 1989; Young and Wheeler, 1994).

The Malcolm X Society's statements on jobs for the black community echoed age-old concerns of preriot moderate black organizations, so they were not introducing anything new. "The power of the state must be used to create Black employment and full employment, under a Black supervisor . . . the notion of Black people waiting on the largess of good White people is absurd." A full employment program was needed and should be "time-phased, enforceable and reviewable." Government "at the state and local levels must commit itself to full employment at decent wages at a given time, list the unemployment and the underemployed, match these people with jobs on a compulsory basis, and subject the entire program to systematic in-process review by a board of Black citizens." In addition, "where jobs . . . at a decent wage no longer exist[], the government must open businesses directly to make such jobs [available]" (*Michigan Chronicle*, December 2, 1967).

As with other needs of the pre-riot black community, housing was even more of a need afterward, so it was not a surprise that it would be one of the top priorities in the Malcolm X Society's statement to the New Detroit Committee. The Society demanded that "a crash program of immediate relief for people in the rebellion area must be instituted. Hundreds are without adequate sanitation facilities, without hot water, without heat, without properly working windows and doors, and, in the case of city welfare recipients, without the means of withholding rent from landlords, since the rent is sent directly to the landlords" (*Michigan Chronicle*, December 2, 1967). On their "must items" list for housing the Malcolm X Society included housing code enforcement, minimum housing standards, and "seizure and correction of bad housing" (*Michigan Chronicle*, December 2, 1967).

The Society assured the New Detroit Committee that it was prepared to "support these charges with specific data," and expressed its concern over symbolic gestures, such as changing the names of streets in the riot areas. Such "farces as the turning of 12th Street [the main site of the urban disorder] into a Boulevard while no concrete housing plans are implemented, must be halted" (*Michigan Chronicle*, December 2, 1967).

The items mentioned in the Malcolm X Society statement were not entirely new. Throughout the long tradition of black community building in Detroit, many of these issues and concerns had been tackled, but with much less radical spin. Traditional black organizations had a long history of struggling with housing, jobs, and police brutality. The Detroit branch of the Urban League had voiced these concerns for years and tirelessly built programs around many of them (Thomas, 1987a, 1992). The crucial difference in the voicing of these concerns after the 1967 riot was that, unlike the post-1943 period, key white power brokers were more interested in the voice of black militants. Therefore, at least for a while, the Malcolm X Society had their ear.

The final item in the Society's statement focused on black economic control:

> Four million dollars are needed to start to assist Black churches, organizations, and businesses to get their economic projects off the ground between now and March 1, 1968. One-third of the money would be administrative grants; the rest, a revolving loan fund. The money must be made available on a simple and direct basis. (*Michigan Chronicle*, December 2, 1967)

As it turned out, the timing was on the side of black militants, at least for a while. White power brokers in Detroit were already setting up their own plans to address many of the same problems outlined by the Malcolm X Society; and because of their fear of more riots, they were more than eager to involve black militants. Mayor Jerome Cavanagh and the business community, reeling from the sheer devastation of the riot, realized that they needed help in rebuilding the city and that help had to come from the private sector. On July 28, just a few weeks after the riot, the Greater Detroit Board of Commerce, representing "thirty-eight hundred business, professional, and industrial interests asserted that since the riot had made it evident that the 'basic solution' for 'these problems' was jobs, its main response to the disorder would be an effort to cope with unemployment and underemployment in the city's disadvantaged areas" (Fine, 1989: 320). The Board promised to continue its support for the Career Development Center and announced the formation of a Manpower Development Committee along with other related initiatives (Fine, 1989). However, the black militants did not receive a hearing within the private sector until the establishment of the New Detroit Committee.

By far the most significant response of the business community to the riot was the establishment of the New Detroit Committee, which was formed on July 27, 1967. Mayor Cavanagh and Governor Romney led the way in the formation of the committee by convening a meeting of 160 community leaders to discuss Detroit's "current and future problems." Both men had asked Joseph L. Hudson Jr., president of the J.L. Hudson Company, Detroit's largest department store, to lead the new committee that would help rebuild Detroit's social and physical structures (Fine, 1989). Many segments of the community were represented at the meeting, but Congressmen John Conyers "complained that 'the voiceless people of the community' were missing. 'I didn't hear anyone off of 12th Street' he declared. 'Anyone poor or black. And that's what triggered this as I understand it'" (Fine, 1989: 320). Conyers was, of course, right. The voiceless people needed to be heard, which was why they had "rebelled" earlier in the month. To the great credit of the mayor and the other white leaders at the meeting, they agreed. Conyers was helping to pave the way for black militants to voice their concerns about black community building in the postdisorder period.

Mayor Cavanagh's concern, however, was how to "associate the commanding firms in the private sector with the well-being of the city to a degree that had previously been lacking. This, indeed, was the message the riot conveyed to the heads of the Big Three auto companies who Cavanagh invited to the July 2 meeting" (Fine, 1989: 320). Surprisingly, during this meeting there was an honest sense of repentance and remorse uncommon among white power elites. Instead of piling all the blame for the riot on blacks, they engaged in some obviously painful soul searching.

Of course, one could argue that they were also embarrassed by the riot because they were major figures on the world stage, and their city—with its reputation as a "model city"—had imploded on their watch. Still, their remorse was heartfelt. James Roche of General Motors declared, "We didn't do enough. . . . An extra effort is needed." Henry Ford, agreeing, confessed, "I thought I was aware . . . I guess I wasn't. This terrible thing has to wake us up." Lynn Townsend of Chrysler echoed their sentiments: "We'd better make an extra effort. Detroit is the test tube for America. If the concentrated power of industry and government can't solve the problems of the ghetto here, God help our country" (Fine, 1989: 320). Interestingly enough, Hudson felt that business leaders in the past had failed the city because they, as Fine explained, "left the city's problems to be solved by government and social workers and [believed they] had absolved their responsibilities by writing a check. Now, he said, they had to involve themselves personally in the rebuilding of Detroit's social and physical framework" (Fine, 1989: 320).

These remarks and "confessions" of remorse and guilt on the part of these business leaders were profoundly revealing. Most if not all probably remembered the 1943 race riot, and although that riot was more of a clash between blacks and whites than the 1967 riot, which was more of "rebellion" or "disorder" of some marginalized and alienated blacks, these leaders must have known that social and economic conditions of blacks had not changed that much between the 1943 and 1967 riots. Housing was still substandard, unemployment was still ravaging the Black community, and police brutality was still a problem. But as Henry Ford II, whose family had been involved with the black community since at least World War I, confessed, "I thought I was aware . . . I guess I wasn't" (Fine, 1989: 320). And if they were not aware of the smoldering fire in the belly of their precious model city, what would it take to make them sufficiently aware to make a difference? This was the challenge ahead for Hudson, and blacks, especially the black militants and Conyer's voiceless people on 12th Street, were waiting to see the results.

As anxious and repentant as the business leaders were to grapple with their past failures to address the problems that had led to the riot, Hudson realized that he needed more input than what they as leaders provided at the July 27 meeting. He was wise enough to seek other counsel outside his inner circle of white business leaders. He approached Hugh White and James Campbell, two leaders of the Detroit Industrial Mission. Hudson needed and trusted White's racial awareness and his understanding of the organizational dynamics.

White and Campbell were well aware of the tendency of leaders to create blue-ribbon committees as a substitute for real problem-solving, and they did not want the new committee to suffer the same fate. They suggested that black militants be included on the committee, with power that they could consider as meaningful. More important, and probably for the sake of racial diplomacy, they advised Hudson to consult with black community leaders to determine who should serve on the committee. He should, they advised, include leaders of organizations that the traditional black leadership was "out of touch with," such as the Inner City Organizing Committee and the WCO (West Central Organization), and militant leaders like Cleage (Fine, 1989).

For the moment this advice was on target. Some "established Negro leaders" were "out of touch" with certain militant leaders, but that did not mean that other established leaders, such as Conyers, Urban League workers, and some community church leaders were out of touch with people on the streets who had participated in the riot. Hudson took the advice, however, and involved a group of selected black militants with somewhat vague ideologies and strategies of black community building, on a committee with selected white power elites who were desperate to heal their city. These power elites had little understanding of the problems of the black community, but the riot had taught them the terrible lesson of what alienated and frustrated elements of that community could do to the peace and stability of the city.

Taking the lead in what was a new experiment in postriot social change, White and Campbell arranged a meeting in which Hudson asked some black militants to advise him on the "operation and the membership of the new committee." One well-known militant, Milton Henry, told the committee members that black nationalists should be involved in the reconstruction of the city. Reverend Cleage outlined areas in which cooperation between blacks and the committee was possible. Lorenzo Freeman, a WCO organizer, however, disagreed with the idea of an interracial committee, saying it was "passé." Not unlike similar black nationalist tendencies at the time, Freeman's ideological position was clear: White leaders should "unblock" the white community and black leaders should "take care of the black community" (Fine, 1989: 321). This was nothing more than vintage black nationalist rhetoric that often could not be translated into practical solutions. The committee needed the views of the militants, but it also needed the tested wisdom of black moderates, such as Arthur Johnson and Damon Keith, who were also at the meeting.

When the selection of the committee was completed, it had "three militants among the nine blacks . . . appointed to the thirty-nine member committee." Predictably, the inclusion of the black militants raised some reactions from some people who felt the New Detroit Committee was merely "rewarding lawlessness in adding the three militants to the committee." Hudson replied, "We are responding to complaints against injustices." Later, when the committee was accused of seeking "riot insurance" in embracing the militants, Hudson explained that there could be no guarantee that another disturbance would not occur. He argued that the voices of the black militants had to be heard. His hope was that the militants would "sensitize" and educate the whites on the committee (Fine, 1989).

Perhaps the whites on the committee were not the only ones who needed to be "sensitized." Some of the black moderates were far from comfortable with the views of the black militants. William T. Patrick, Jr., a black moderate, characterized the militants' approach to whites in the following way: "Give . . . us what we want or we'll burn your damn house down, whereas the moderates said, give us want we want because it is the morally correct thing to do" (Fine, 1989: 376).

The participation of black militants and moderates reflected a growing ideological conflict over how best to address the pressing problems of the black community during both the pre- and postriot periods. The black militant camp included Maoists, the Republic of New Africa—the most extreme of the black nationalist groups, which advocated the "creation of a separate Black nation on U.S. soil and independent Black city-states within our cities"—advocates of self-determination, and followers of Malcolm X, including the young Black nationalists and students who produced the *Inner City Voice*, among others (Fine, 1989; Ingram, 1961: 20). These groups and organizations tended to be ideological and programmatically opposed to the tradition of interracial coalition-building advocated by the moderate camp.

The black moderates included those who still had faith in integration and in traditional means of black community building. While they were well aware that the current crisis called for some rethinking of traditional approaches, they did not think that their voices should be ignored. The Trade Union Leadership Council (TULC), the Cotillion Club, the Booker T. Washington Business Association, the *Michigan Chronicle*, and the Council of Baptist Ministers, among others, had played leading roles in the black community-building process for decades (Foner, 1981; Thomas, 1987a, 1992). Given their long history of involvement in the black community, one can understand why some of these moderates black organizations felt slighted by their exclusion from the New Detroit Committee.

The Booker T. Washington Business Association saw its exclusion as an "affront." The Council of Baptist Ministers shared the feeling, particularly since they spoke for "125 ministers and 150,000 communicants." Some people wrote letters protesting that "grass roots people from the immediate affected community had been excluded." The black newspaper, the *Michigan Chronicle*, criticized the committee's selection of the three black militants, complaining that they "did not speak for the 'man on the street'" (Fine, 1989: 323).

By August two major black organizations had emerged out of the ashes of the urban disorder or black rebellion, proclaiming their own views on what should be done to address the problems of the black community. The City Wide Citizen Action Committee took the lead in seeking ways to organize the black community after the riot. At their citywide meeting on August 9, 1967, at the City-County Building, militant slogans of black revolutionary rhetoric held sway. "We must control our community or we won't have a community." Moderate Robert Tindal of the NAACP did not have a chance and was shouted down. Reverend Cleage, who had emerged as the "most influential spokesman for black militancy and black nationalism in Detroit following the riot," declared that "the Toms are out." He was elected chairman of the CCAC. One local magazine commented that the CCAC was "possibly the most broadly based Black Power organization in any city" (Fine, 1989: 373).

Savoring what would turn out to be temporary postriot influence, several weeks later the CCAC met to spell out its goals and objectives to "an overflow crowd" and received unanimous approval. Cleage told the gathering that there was no east or west side of Detroit. "We are speaking for black people all over the city." This, of course, amounted to unabashed militant hyperbole. He reported that a structure would be put together similarly to that of the New Detroit Committee. The gathering was informed that "technicians and architects from many parts of the country have offered their services so that the needs of the community, which has been articulated so many times, can finally be put into action." The CCAC, Cleage explained, was trying to "find out what other organizations are doing . . . and we're not trying to supplant them" (*Michigan Chronicle*, August 12, 1967).

During the meeting, several committees reported on their tasks. The legal committee's responsibility was to be a "nuisance" whenever it saw black people getting unequal justice in the courts. A representative of the legal committee said that the only way to stop unequal justice was to unite, saying, "We are just a part of this total revolutionary picture, all working together." The chairman of the consumer control committee reported that the black community must remove the Chaldeans from the community because they were exploiting blacks. He informed the gathering that a price index sheet would be published to show people how the corner store prices compared with prices from major stores. The chairman of the redevelopment committee mentioned that three experts in housing and development would be working with CCAC and that any plan that displaced the black community would not be accepted. Other goals and objectives were also discussed (*Michigan Chronicle*, September 23, 1967).

Although the CCAC's militant programs were at odds with the moderate approach to the black community's postriot problems, Hudson and the New Detroit Committee embraced the organization. This was consistent with their belief that some moderate black organizations were out of touch with the marginal elements of the black community, and consistent with their policy of involving militants in the work of the committee. This recognition by the committee validated the CCAC in the eyes of important segments of the larger Detroit community and no doubt encouraged Cleage to claim that for the first time in the history of the city, blacks had formed an "informal organization" that could speak for the entire community (*Michigan Chronicle*, September 23, 1967).

The CCAC was basically a black militant organization with a black nationalist self-determination approach to postriot black community building. Members of the organization ranged from those "favoring self-determination or separation" to those favoring an "all-out war." Notwithstanding their militant rhetoric, their strategies and proposed programs for addressing the problems of the black community arising from the riot were mainly funded by white sources. For example, in September the Interfaith Emergency Council contributed $19,000 to CCAC. The Interreligious Foundation for Community Development presented the organization with a check for $85,000 because it believed that the CCAC was the first "black organization in the country" that displayed "unity and determination in seeking to" control the community where black people were in the majority. Essentially, this meant that CCAC was being funded to develop a community-building strategy based upon the philosophy of black community control. In December the CCAC opened a store through its Black Star Co-op to produce African dresses, and encouraged teaching black history, culture, and languages in public schools (Fine, 1989).

Although the CCAC had been embraced by Hudson and the New Detroit Committee and had been anointed by supporters as the voice of the entire black community, another black organization emerged with a competing ideology and strategy for postriot black community building. Composed of black moderates who resented the attention the militants were receiving through CCAC as spokespeople for the black community, the Detroit Council of Organizations (DCO) formed under the leadership of Reverend Roy Allen, president of the Council of Baptist Ministers (Fine, 1989).

The moderates who joined this organization held a special resentment for Cleage, who they saw as a Johnny-come-lately to the black movement. Perhaps this was due to the fact that many of these moderates had been involved in the black community much longer than Cleage and except for the rise of black radicalism, particularly during the postriot period, might have remained in position of power and influence both in the black community and in the white community. Clearly the riot and involvement of militants on the New Detroit Committee was perceived by some moderates as a slap in the face. Thus, one could argue that the establishment of the DCO was an attempt by these moderates to reclaim their traditional leadership position and influence.

The DCO recruited middle-class and upper-class black professionals, black trade union members, community leaders, and the Democratic Party. A few months after the establishment of DCO, a host of the traditional black organizations with a history of longtime service in the black community joined the organization. Among them were the Cotillion Club, the Wolverine Bar Association, the Trade Union Leadership Council, and the NAACP. With such an array of impressive traditional black organizations with time-tested credentials of service on behalf of the black community, it wasn't long before the DCO was able to claim to be the voice of twenty-nine organizations and 350,000 Detroit blacks (Fine, 1989).

If Cleage was a Johnny-come-lately, according to moderates in the DCO, he accused them of being "the creature of the white establishment, City Hall, and the UAW" (Fine, 1989: 375). These attacks by both camps meant little in the scheme of things. Both were committed to their particular philosophy of postriot social change. Reverend Allen argued that "legal and peaceful means" could solve the problems of the black community. The DCO, he explained, was not "out of touch" with the rioters and "was not opposed to any black group, and wanted to work with the CCAC." He did, however, characterize some of the CCAC's views and approaches to the postriot black problems as "irresponsible." The DCO, for its part, did not depart from the preriot traditional moderate's belief in integration as the best possible solution to black problems. It wanted "integrated schools, open housing, the building of low-cost homes for blacks, more blacks on the police force, and improved police-community relations, and increased job opportunities for blacks" (Fine, 1989: 376). One can see how this approach might have seemed "out of touch" with the new realities and demands of the postriot crisis, and why the New Detroit Committee was seeking "new blood."

If any progress was going to be made in unifying the black community during the early stages after the riot, the CCAC and the DCO would have to find common ground for working together. James S. Garrett, a member of the Cotillion Club and the DCO, expressed his concern for unity between the two organizations, even as he recognized their "fundamental differences." In October 1967, Garrett and Cleage spoke together before the Booker T. Washington Business Association, where they continued a discussion from the previous month. Recognizing the growing tension between the two organizations, both men agreed that unity was needed for the benefit of the black community. Garrett argued that in order to achieve unity "there must be efforts on the part of all groups." He said, "I get the feeling here of antagonism that anything that the DCO might propose is going to be knocked down. There are disagreements within each organization . . . but we have got to get together: we are all seeking self-determination" (*Michigan Chronicle*, November 11, 1967). Responding to a question concerning what issues DCO and CCAC could work on together, Cleage, speaking for CCAC, said that his organization "would support any black group that makes sense. We are going to love our black brothers in spite of what they might do." Garrett, in turn, suggested that one key program on which both organizations could work would be finding a black in each precinct to help DCO to establish a civilian review board. He pointed out that DCO had met to "hear and consider CCAC's proposals" (*Michigan Chronicle*, November 11, 1967).

Both organizations were aware of the need to reconcile their differences for the sake of the black community. The riot had certainly left the black community in a traumatic state. There was too much work to be done to waste time bickering over ideologies and programs. To his credit, Garrett extended a longer olive branch than the opposing camp in an article in the *Michigan Chronicle* in December 1967 entitled "Negro Community Must Strive for Unity,

Not Division." His purpose was to explain to the black public the origins, philosophies, and strategies of the CCAC and DCO. "The riot in July of this year made a tremendous impact on the Negro community," Garrett wrote. "In essence, it was a great awakening to a vital need, the need to combine efforts to eliminate the cause and correct the conditions that brought about the explosive reaction. There was a sense of obligation and necessity permeating the air to draw closer together and work collectively toward common goals" (*Michigan Chronicle*, December 30, 1967). Commenting on how the black community responded to the riot, he continued, "Many individuals, groups and organizations made numerous attempts to provide a means in an organized manner to effectively give purpose, substance and form to these aspirations. Some meaningful success has been achieved in this regard." He mentioned CCAC as one of the "meaningful" successes.

Speaking as a moderate, Garrett demonstrated admirable generosity in his description of the origins of the CCAC. "The City-Wide Citizen Action Committee came into existence following a meeting of people who felt they could best express themselves and pursue their objectives under the leadership and concepts of their own choosing," he explained. "The Committee immediately set out to deal with grievances and problems in a manner determined as appropriate and necessary. The desire expressed was to bring about radical change in the Black areas for the primary benefit of Black people. Accomplishing these objectives meant obtaining control of the areas with respect to business, and social and structural development" (*Michigan Chronicle*, December 30, 1967).

After explaining the origins and philosophy of the CCAC, Garrett turned to the DCO, his organization. He explained how the DCO emerged at the same time as the CCAC, which "brought together organizations, groups and individuals whose ideas and attitudes were similar on methods and approaches for firm establishment of Negro citizens in the economic, social and political life of the whole community." The DCO's main objective was to assemble blacks to provide a source "for collective action in an organized fashion by its members and supporters . . . to act as a coordinating organization, to work toward the elimination of discrimination, and to carry out programs that will be basic to the specific needs of the city and the critical problems confronting the Negro community" (*Michigan Chronicle*, December 30, 1967).

Garrett conceded that both organizations desired to "improve conditions for Negroes." But there was still a major ideological divide between them. As Garrett pointed out, the "CCAC has advocated separatism. DCO does not, but rather endeavors to make Negroes an integrated part of the total community" (*Michigan Chronicle*, December 30, 1967). In short, the CCAC advocated a black nationalist, self-determination approach to the postriot black community, in contrast to the DCO's traditionalist integrationist approach. Notwithstanding their differences, however, Garrett believed that they were not so "acute that they could or should prevent them from finding a way of develop[ing] . . . means to plan together on common objectives. This would seem to be an important effort to make if the Negro community is to have some semblance of total unity" (*Michigan Chronicle*, December 30, 1967).

In his article, Garrett offered advice on how the DCO and the CCAC should cooperate. He cautioned that before matters became too serious, the two organizations should focus on "why they exist and what was intended to be accomplished for the benefit of the community. Every effort should be made to undo any damage that has been done and to start anew" (*Michigan Chronicle*, December 30, 1967).

As he summed up his article, Garrett outlined what his organization, the DCO, would do to address this "sensitive situation" with the CCAC. It would "cooperate as fully as possible where appropriate and feasible in nature and to dissuade conflict, disunity, and competition and confusion between and among organizations operating toward common objectives. . . . Whether these very important groups work together or apart, neither should interfere with the other's efforts to accomplish worthwhile objectives" (*Michigan Chronicle*, December 30, 1967).

One wonders if the CCAC and the DCO might have been better able to work out their differences over how best to address the problems of the black community during this period if New Detroit had not influenced the interaction between militants and moderates. According to some observers, certain white business leaders on the committee had become awed by the black militants on the committee and their tales of life in the inner city. Arthur Johnson, one of the black moderates on the committee, reported that the white businessmen on the committee "were really out of it." This view was echoed by one of the black militant members: "You can shock [them] by telling them what goes on for one day in a Negro's life" (Fine, 1989: 376). As one local white newspaper reported, "There was a hypnotic attraction for these middle and upper-class Whites in dealing with the Inner City for the first time" (*Detroit Free Press*, August 11, 1968, quoted in Fine 1989). No wonder a teenage black militant on the committee was able to assume the role of the "'teacher' of GM's James Roche concerning the nature of the black community" (Fine, 1989: 376).

New Detroit was experimenting with who should be "listened to" in the black community, which explains why some of the white leaders of New Detroit were not interested in listening to the DCO. From their perspective, the DCO did not represent the "real black" community. As Henry Ford put it, "The middle class black is as far removed from what's happening in the ghettoes as we are" (Fine, 1989: 376). This attitude prompted the DCO to accuse New Detroit of trying to "buy off" so-called militants and misinterpreting the mood of the black community. In the end, the DCO ended its relationship with New Detroit when it was unable to come up with matching funds for the $100,000 New Detroit had offered. Several militants left the committee, one returned, and the committee hired another, Frank Ditto, who became a trustee and its "brightest star" until he resigned several years later (Fine, 1989).

In the next few months relationships among all the parties in this drama shifted back and forth, illuminating the complex interplay between New Detroit, black militants, and black moderates over the best approach to address the problems of the black community (Fine, 1989; Gordon, 1971; New Detroit, 1968).

BUILDING FROM THE ASHES: BLACK COMMUNITY BASE ORGANIZATIONS TAKE ON THE TASK

While black militant and moderate organizations battled over who should represent the interests of the postriot black community within Detroit, two community-based organizations emerged that were destined to outlast and outperform many of their contemporaries. The Inner-City Sub-Center and Operation Get-Down were among the best examples of postriot community building that provided practical strategies for the long haul.

The Inner-City Sub-Center

The Inner-City Sub-Center (ICSC) was one of several community-based organizations that emerged during the postdisorder period. The brainchild of the Education Committee of the Association of Black Studies at Wayne State University in Detroit, it was established to address the needs of ghetto residents. The ICSC started in a storefront on the east side of Detroit the year of the riot. Popularly called "the Center," it had a big picture of Malcolm X plastered on the front of the building. Black youth in the neighborhood were immediately attracted to the Center, where they were exposed to black history and culture taught by the Center staff. Speakers were brought in for discussion groups to help raise the consciousness of black youth (Taylor, 1987; Inner-City Sub-Center, 1986).

In 1968 the ICSC was incorporated as a nonprofit organization. The following June, it received a grant from the Youth Opportunity Program that funded several programs aimed at black youth. At the end of this initial program, the organization received financial support from New Detroit that funded a one-year cultural and recreation program. The next source of funding for the ICSC came through United Community Services summer grants, Christ Church Cranbrook Grants, and community support. A big break came in 1972, when New Detroit supported a three-year development program. During the fall of 1973, the ICSC moved to the old Thomas Lutheran School on Fischer, which provided the Center more space to expand its programs to include preschool, senior citizen, and adult education programs and a food co-op. This expansion enabled the Center to provide services to more than 2,000 people a year. In 1976, almost a decade after the riot, the ICSC reached what it considered a "major turning point in its history" when, after a successful campaign, the Center was able to move to a school building on East Forest (Inner-City Sub-Center, 1986).

The ability to access grants was again crucial in this next stage of postriot black community building. The restoration of the building on East Forest was made possible through grants from Detroit's Neighborhood Service Department, the Dayton/Hudson Foundation, the Kresge Foundation, and the Detroit Development Corporation. Additional funding came from United Community Services, the State of Michigan's Neighborhood Education Authority, and the Comprehensive Youth Training and Community Involvement Program (CYTCIP) of New Detroit. Starting in January 1982 the United Foundation Neighborhood Area Project funded the Center's Youth Development Program for four years. By the fall of 1985, the Center reached another stage of its development when the United Foundation admitted the Center into its "family" as a provisionary member. The Center was then awarded funds for its Neighborhood Development Program. In 1986 the Center served more than 10,000 community residents (Inner-City Sub-Center, 1986).

Unlike some traditional black self-help organizations and institutions in Detroit and elsewhere that depended upon white financial aid that often influenced "the politics" or the basic philosophy of the enterprise, the ICSC emerged during the period when some radical black community-based organizations could at least call some of the shots. Because many of these community-based organizations came about in the period after urban disorders, they had more credibility among poor blacks, as well as among white funding sources, than the older, more moderate black self-help organization and institutions.

Paul Taylor and David Booker, codirectors of the ICSC, came out of the radical black movement of the 1960s. Twenty years later, in 1987, the ICSC had not abandoned its commitment to the cultural values of the movement. In its promotional brochure the Center's philosophy was explained: "To provide meaningful and relevant programs, services, and activities to the Black community that will serve to raise the level of Black consciousness, awareness and understanding, and promote positive Black values, pride, love, and respect among Black people (Inner-City Sub-Center, n.d.).

Consistent with this philosophy, the ICSC developed a program based upon "Seven Principles of Blackness—Nguzo Saba," created by black cultural nationalist and founder of the US organization and Kwanzaa, Maulana Ron Karenga (Brown, 2003). Below is how it appeared in an ICSC brochure:

The Sub-Center's Value System

NGUZA SABA (Seven Principles of Blackness)

1. UMOJA (Unity). To strive for and maintain Unity in the family, community, nation and race.
2. KUJICHAJULIA (Self-Determination). To define ourselves, speak for ourselves, instead of being defined and spoken for by others.
3. UJIMA (Collective Work and Responsibility). To build and maintain our community together and to make our Brothers' and Sisters' problems our problems, and to solve them together.
4. UJAMAA (Collective Economics). To build and maintain our own stores, shops and other businesses and to profit together from them.
5. NIA (Purpose). To make our collective vocation the building and development of our communities, in order to restore our people to their traditional greatness.
6. KUUMBA (Creativity). To do always as much as we can, to leave our community more beautiful and beneficial than when we inherited it.
7. IMANI (Faith). To believe with all our heart in our parents, leaders and people, and the righteousness and victory of our struggle. (Brown, 2003)

These values seemed to be the motivating principles behind ICSC's impressive range of programs. A senior citizens program included hot lunches, arts and crafts, field trips, group sessions, counseling, bus transportation, and daily exercise, among other activities. The adult program offered career counseling, an exercise class, sewing, upholstery, and GED preparation. There also was a hot breakfast program and a self-supporting co-op store that modeled economic self-help or "Ujamaa" (Inner-City Sub-Center, n.d.).

In 1987 the ICSC's youth program formed the centerpiece of the organization. Since its establishment in the wake of the 1967 riot, it had focused on the problems of poor inner-city youth, guiding them away from the streets to more socially responsible roles in the community. At the Center black youth studied African and African American history and culture, learned African dance and choir, and participated in arts and crafts, baseball, basketball, gymnastics, and music. They also learned karate, obtained tutoring and counseling, and participated on a drill team. These youth-oriented programs reflected Taylor's belief that "when it comes down to the most significant thing we can do, the main program has always been and always will be the youth program, because it's our contention that consciousness raising for the young folk . . . is the key to the struggle." If "resources get so tight that we had to scrap everything, we would scrap everything but the youth program," Taylor said (Taylor, 1987).

This commitment to the development of black youth at the Center during the postriot decades no doubt redirected some of their lives from the frustration and alienation that had led an earlier generation to riot. Instead, the Center and its values and programs provided a framework for both individual and community development. While we will probably never fully appreciate the tremendous influence that the Center had on this generation of black youth, we can applaud the role of the directors and the Center in providing them with a sense of vision and empowerment.

The Ujamaa Club

The Ujamaa boutique shop was one example of the Center's effort to empower black youth. The shop, housed in the Center, was operated by black youth between the ages of fourteen and twenty-one who were members of the Ujamaa Club. They sold clothes and candy, held bake sales, and solicited donations. The youth and the Center divided the profits. The members of the club met once a week on Thursday for a couple of hours. As one staff member said, the program was "a self-help program . . . operated by youth" (Morant, 1987).

During one of these meetings Paul Taylor gave an inspiring talk to the youth of the Ujamaa Club about how the principle of cooperative economics related to the black community. He started with an introduction to the concept of Ujamaa, explaining that Ujamaa money is used to benefit everyone. Taylor described what he considered to be the three kinds of young adults "out here." One kind is the person who needs money but does not care how he or she gets it. "He will hit people on the head, he will break into folks' homes, sell dope on the corner, and she will sell herself on the street . . . They will do any and everything because their thing is to get money by any means necessary."

The second kind of young adult understands that there are no jobs to be had, but he or she is "not going to break into people's houses, or sell dope on the corner, or sell herself on the street." This young adult will come home from school, talk on the telephone, watch TV, keep off the corner, and when he or she needs money they will ask their family or friends. This type of black young adult, according to Taylor, is the majority. "They are not going to do nothing wrong, but then again they are not going to do anything right in terms of trying to make some money or resources for themselves." These people will sit around waiting for summer jobs or their parents to give them some money.

The third type of young adult, "the one we are looking for, is not going to sell dope, or rob or sit around talking on the phone and looking at TV. This type of young adult is going to put his intelligence to work . . . is going to do something . . . to make some money for themselves." Instead they will babysit, shovel snow, mow lawns, and go to the store for people. "This young adult might be doing any number of positive things to make an honest living." This is "the kind of young adult that we are looking for to join . . . the Ujamaa Club" (Taylor, 1987).

Realizing that this generation of black youth needed to understand some basic economic facts about their community, which had steadily declined since the 1967 disorder, Taylor explained to them the nature of the sales industry and its impact on their community:

> Believe me, when I tell you everything is brought and sold . . . most anything that we can look at in this room was brought by somebody and sold by somebody. Unfortunately, historically we as black folk have been the buyers and not the sellers. We buy everything and sell nothing . . . This club . . . is designed to teach us some basic principles about sales. We want to become salespeople . . . not just consumers . . . and that is really what the club is all about. (Taylor, 1987)

Black youth of the Ujamaa Club used three methods to make money. One was by direct sales through which club members approached people to buy merchandise by first explaining to them "what we are and what we are about and asking their support." Members received commissions for each sale. The second method involved group projects. Once a month the club decided on a collective project to prevent club members from being "caught up and hung up on . . . individualism." The profits from the group projects went into the club treasury and were earmarked for the club's economic and business development programs, which helped to start businesses in the community, such as the club's Boutique Shop. The goals, according to Taylor, were to "have as many businesses as we can . . . on each corner. . . . We want to be able to control . . . the businesses in our community through cooperative ownership. . . . We are trying to get away from the ideas that 'as soon as I get . . . some money I am going to do something else.' . . . We are trying to get to 'we and us.'" The third method was through donations. Taylor believed that when people heard about what the Ujamaa Club was "doing and trying to do," they would make donations to it. Taylor reasoned that people would support the club because they would be impressed with its objectives and goals and "wanted to see a group of young adults do something positive" (Taylor, 1987).

After advising black members on the three methods of generating money, Taylor pointed out that most of the businesses in communities were either owned by nonblacks or "individualistic blacks—the latter being the opposite of Ujamaa's model of collective ownership" (Taylor, 1987). Therefore, members of the Ujamaa Club should see black businesses as community-owned.

The "nonblacks" Taylor referred to were the increasing numbers of Chaldean immigrant store owners in black communities who arrived during the early postdisorder period. This increase was caused in large part by changes in the immigration laws in the 1960s and 1980s (Sengstock, 1999). Chaldeans and other Middle Eastern grocers filled the vacuum in poor inner-city neighborhoods created by the flight of large supermarket chains in the wake of the 1967 riot (David, 2000; Sengstock, 1999). While providing inner-city neighborhoods with basic foods, these store owners created a challenge for black community organizers like Taylor who were trying to teach the younger generation the importance of black community business ownership.

Whatever one might think of the economic philosophy of the Ujamaa Club, it was certainly a vast improvement over the aimless, self-centered materialism of many black youth and adults of the generation that came of age in the period after urban disorders. It was a refreshing alternative to views held by many contemporary black business persons in Detroit, who saw blacks as consumers to be exploited instead of members of communities needing social and economic development.

Taylor's example of "materialist" black businesses could have easily been a reference to the Motown Record Company. As historian Suzanne E. Smith commented in her study of the company, by 1973, when Motown left Detroit, it was "the most successful black business in the United States, with $40 millions in sales" (Smith, 1999: 255). But what did its success mean for black community-building in Detroit? Smith convincingly argues that "the false promises of black capitalism originate in the faulty assumption that capitalism can be enlisted to remedy racial inequality. Improving the racial conditions of society has never been capitalism's primary objective" (Smith, 1999: 255).

Essentially this was the message Taylor was conveying to the generation of black youth who grew up during the golden era of Motown, which was also the period after urban disorders.

This generation needed to understand that a successful black-owned company based on the principles of capitalism alone could in fact be a deterrent to the best interests of the black community. For example, as Smith explains so well: "On a more global level, Motown's decision to leave Detroit and the community that nurtured it not only participated in the larger process of deindustrialization of the city, but ultimately created the circumstances that left the company vulnerable to corporate takeovers in years to come" (1999: 256). Helping black youth see the difference between black capitalism/materialism and black cooperative ownership was crucial in helping them understand their responsibility to the poor and underdeveloped segments of their communities.

Taylor's discussion of the three kinds of black youth was an excellent way of helping young blacks recognize that they had to take the responsibility for improving their lives and the lives of their communities. The third kind of young adult Taylor discussed was the model that he hoped all black youth would emulate. The Ujamaa Club represented an excellent first step for this postdisorder generation.

Operation Get-Down

Operation Get-Down (OGD) also was a product of the early era after the 1967 civil disorder. Incorporated in September 1971 as a nonprofit organization (Operation Get-Down, 1986) the evolution of the OGD as a black self-help organization resembled that of the ICSC. Both organizations were founded by young black radicals who were motivated by the spirit of Malcolm X and the black movement of the 1960s and energized by the militancy of the era. In addition, both organizations used white resources for some of their most important community-based programs, yet neither organization compromised its commitment to the philosophy of black self-help as a community-building strategy.

In 1970, when Detroit was still recovering from the riot, the United Methodist Church hired Barry L. Hankerson, a young black activist, to work in Detroit as a community developer. Hankerson arrived in Detroit in 1969. He was twenty-one years old and just out of college and like other young blacks of his generation was inspired by the teachings of "Malcolm X, Marcus Garvey and other Black nationalists" (Hunter, 1997: 16). Before working for the United Methodist Church, Hankerson was a substitute teacher at Post Middle School. While there he wrote plays and taught social studies. Soon he attracted attention for his ability to organize and inspire people (Hunter, 1997). Undoubtedly these were the skills for which he was recruited by Rev. Charles P. Strong of the United Methodist Church as a community liaison (Hunter, 1997).

In 1969, Bernard Parker, who with Hankerson cofounded OGD in 1971, was an eighteen-year-old student at the University of Michigan. He was a member of the Black Panther Party and the University of Michigan Black Action Movement. Encouraged by his mother to become active in the Detroit east side community where he was raised, Parker made daily commutes home to serve as the first youth director for the United Methodist Church organization (Hunter, 1997). Parker recounts how he first met Hankerson, with whom he would work for several decades:

Back in 1969, I went to a meeting at the urging of my mother, at Bethany United Methodist Church . . . that was the community where I was raised and my mother wanted me to go and hear what they were suggesting for the community. She really wanted to get me out of the Black Panther Party and other organizations I had joined at the University of Michigan, Ann Arbor. (Hunter, 1997: 16)

Parker went to a meeting where he met both Rev. Charles Strong, the minister of the church, and Barry Hankerson. "I was very impressed with what Barry was talking about," Parker later explained. "He talked about taking control of the community we lived in, the need to learn how to plan and that they were going to have a group of people come to community training classes to become leaders" (Hunter, 1997: 16). Meetings were set up that included Bernard Parker, black youth, senior citizens, college students, and families. They were held at St. Mark's United Methodist Church, which included weekly leadership classes focusing on communication skills, problem-solving techniques, conflict management, and group motivation. Hankerson played a leading role in conducting these classes. Parker credited a local white minister for teaching him and other young blacks techniques of problem solving, long-range planning, and self-development (Parker, 1987).

In June 1971, the United Community Services Summer Project Fund financed the group's first summer project, which provided services to unemployed, "unoccupied" low-income black youth. The group later adopted the language of these youth in naming the organization "Operation Get-Down." "Get-down" referred to how well one was performing a particular activity: "The brother was really getting down." Several months later, when the organization was incorporated, the members elected Barry Hankerson as chairperson and Bernard Parker and Frances Messinger as vice chairpersons (Operation Get-Down, 1986).

From the beginning, OGD viewed itself as a self-help organization. According to one source, "their guiding principle was self-help, the motivating force and motto was adopted from Malcolm X," who said, "I believe that when you give the people a thorough understanding of what confronts them and the basic causes, they will create their own programs; and with a program, you get ACTION!" (Operation Get-Down, 1986).

Much like other black community-based organizations at the time, OGD had to rely upon funding sources outside of its control. As the need for community programs increased and "funding . . . remained elusive," OGD was forced to function one day at a time. There were long periods of rejections; requests for grants were constantly turned down. It seemed that no one was willing to trust this unknown group of people from the east side (Operation Get-Down, 1986). Finally, however, the organizers came up with a solution solidly grounded in the black self-help tradition and an excellent example of community building in the postdisorder era.

This solution involved organizing a fund-raiser for sickle-cell anemia, which at the time had not gained much attention as a health risk peculiar to blacks. The effort provided city-wide exposure for OGD while addressing a serious health need in the black community. The organization received support from Dr. Charles Whitten, who was already working with the Sickle Cell Detection and Information Center at Kirwood Hospital. Operation Get-Down then approached WKBD (Channel 50) for airtime to produce a telethon for sickle cell. The TV station refused to go along with the project until OGD came up with 50,000 signatures on a petition. In addition, WKBD wanted OGD to come up with a nationally known personality to host the telethon and five well-known stars to be on the show (Operation Get-Down, 1986; Hunter, 1997).

After much hard work, OGD was able to meet these requirements. On May 28, 1972, Operation Get-Down's Sickle Cell Telethon was on the airwaves. The show ran from 6:00

P.M. to 2:00 A.M., and Sammy Davis Jr. and Nipsey Russell were the cohosts. The nationally known stars who participated were Muhammad Ali, Gladys Knight and the Pips, the Four Tops, Marvin Gaye, the Spinners, and Stevie Wonder. Other people involved in political, professional, and community life volunteered to provide technical and other assistance. The telethon proved a great success and raised more than $250,000 for the Kirwood Hospital Sickle Cell Detection and Information Center. As a result, OGD gained the needed exposure that forced the city of Detroit to recognize it as a serious and committed organization (Operation Get-Down, 1986; Hunter, 1997).

The successful telethon no doubt played a role in convincing New Detroit to award OGD a grant and also to purchase a building for the organization. In November 1972, OGD held its first open house. Larry Doss, New Detroit's president, was the keynote speaker. New Detroit's support for OGD was yet another example of its expanding role in the city's long healing process. OGD extended an invitation to the community to become involved in a range of programs, including Head Start day care, adult education (GED), a youth recreation project, and a community development program. These programs contributed to the reduction of gang violence in the 1970s and improved relationships between the black community and the police on the east side. In addition, OGD increased parent and community involvement at several Detroit Public Schools (Kettering, Burroughs, and A. L. Holmes School) and obtained recreation areas on the east side for black youth. The organization also played a key role in the establishment of the Harper Gratiot Multi-Purpose Center (Operation Get-Down, 1986).

Throughout this early period of growth and development, OGD continued to view itself as a black self-help organization. Much of black Detroit was still reeling from the emotional, social, and economic trauma of the riot, yet Detroiters were eager and willing to take charge of its future, with or without outside help. And OGD was a perfect example of this spirit. While at the same time securing funds from outside sources, it never forgot Malcolm X's advice about the role of black people in creating their own program. To this end, OGD tried to rely upon black resources as much as possible. In a 1987 interview, Bernard Parker, who had succeeded Barry L. Hankerson as OGD's executive director in 1974, said, "There are enough black dollars out here to support black programs; we just have to tap them" (Parker, 1987).

Tapping black dollars to support black programs proved very successful for OGD, particularly by focusing on black entertainers. The organization raised money through cabarets, dinner sales, and such productions as *Crack Steppin'* and *Rhythm's Blues* by playwright Ron Milner. Milner had worked closely with OGD over the years in writing, producing, and touring several plays. For example, Milner's play *Crack Steppin'* was created and written with the assistance of black youth associated with OGD. They performed in the play, which had a successful tour in Detroit and other cities. Other plays followed, demonstrating once again how blacks with imagination could build upon strength within their own community (Parker, 1987).

In 1973 OGD started a food co-op. In 1987 *Black Enterprise* magazine reported that OGD's co-op "has become the nation's largest inner-city food cooperative" (Gite, 1987). Referring again to the teachings of Malcolm X, Parker explained, "Malcolm said people who control their food control their minds . . . if people can control what they are eating, then they can control what they are going to eat, how they are going to eat where they are going to eat. There is power in that" (Gite, 1987). The 1967 rebellion also influenced the establishment of the food co-op, as explained by a member of OGD: "Initially, the program was developed as a precaution. The 1967 rebellion (riots) was still fresh in our minds and we understood the consequences of challenging authority without a source for our food supply. Certain that there was a need for change and willing to take on the task, we decided to develop a Food Co-op program. In the event of a revolution, we would be able to supply ourselves and our community with adequate food" (Hunter, 1997: 21).

The food co-op also grew out of a 1970 boycott of a store for selling poor-quality food. Fifty families pooled their money and purchased vegetables and produce in bulk at lower prices than at grocery stores. Famous vocalist Gladys Knight contributed $500 to get the project going. Detroit area residents on welfare and Social Security and the unemployed received free membership in the co-op. Others paid a membership fee of five dollars a year. Starting as a single small store, the co-op soon expanded to five other sites located in churches and Detroit Neighborhood Services Centers. In 1986, the largest of these sites was serving 1,200 people a week (Operation Get-Down, 1986).

A year earlier, OGD received another grant from New Detroit that allowed it to serve senior citizens with food vouchers that allowed them to obtain fresh food each month from the OGD food co-op system. That same year Detroit's Health Department asked to join OGD's food co-op system so that their expectant parents could obtain fresh food (Operation Get-Down, 1986). OGD's food co-op soon expanded to include 40,000 square feet of refrigeration and a fleet of trucks, vans, and cargo wagons that provided it with the capacity to receive, transport, and distribute more than three million pounds of food a year. This capacity and success resulted in OGD receiving a contract from the Michigan State Department of Social Services to supply food to twenty-two food shelters throughout Wayne County and a state grant of $748,000 to provide fresh food to 9,000 families each month through emergency shelters (Gite, 1987).

By 1976, a decade after the riot and five years after OGD started, the organization had evolved into one of the most impressive self-help black community organizations in the city. Its accomplishments far exceeded most of the black community efforts that emerged out of the disorder, and continued to hold the lead for at least a decade longer. While it still secured grants, "the organization's guiding principle of self-help continued to prevail" (Operation Get-Down, 1986).

In 1985, two years shy of the twentieth anniversary of the 1967 riot, OGD was still going strong. That year it took on a new challenge and added a program called BIRTH (Babies' Inalienable Right to Health) as a response to the rate of infant mortality and morbidity in Detroit (Operation Get-Down, 1987). The program was run as a pilot during the summer of 1986 and supported entirely by funds raised through various activities. Although BIRTH received a $20,000 grant from New Detroit in early 1987 for assistance in transporting clients back and forth between the Center and the location of their doctor's appointment (Operation Get-Down, 1987), the emphasis always was on self-help.

In 1995 OGD began collaboration with Hutzel Midwifery Services, which provided "health services such as prenatal care, post natal care, family planning, and OB/GYN services through its B.I.R.T.H. program" (Hunter, 1997: 124). The program expanded to include transportation for activities associated with the project, medical visits, field trips, shopping and food preparation instruction for healthy pregnancies, and the proper feeding of babies, along with helping clients deal with "family issues and conflict [and] mental and emotional stress" (Hunter, 1997: 124).

The problems of black youth had not been neglected in the expansion of OGD's food co-op and other programs. During the 1985–86 fiscal year, OGD organized and hosted several events aimed at black youth. These included a youth conference at Wayne State University featuring Kim Fields and Taurean Blacque as keynote speaker, which attracted more than 350 young adults; a teen resources fair at which forty-two youth-oriented human services agencies participated; and the BIRTH program (Operation Get-Down, 1986). Four teenage mothers worked as assistants in this program, which provided expectant mothers with on-site meals; prenatal care; childbirth education; medical care; individual, family, and group counseling; family planning; transportation for medical visits; and field trips (Operation Get-Down, 1987; Hunter, 1997).

By 1991 OGD had become a United Way agency with close to a $2,000,000 annual budget and a staff of about seventy people. The programs included a health clinic, emergency food programs, a program for pregnant teenagers, day care, adult education, an after-school youth program, and a homeless warming center. In addition, OGD operated "a caravan that goes out every night to feed about 400 homeless people." According to Parker, OGD was "the largest community agency of that nature in the nation" (Mast, 1994: 179).

In 1990 Parker was elected to the Wayne County Board of Commissioners, where he represented the constituency around the OGD community on the east side of Detroit. "I ran on my experiences in Operation Get-Down and said that I wanted to take that experience down to government: self-determination and helping people to solve their own problems. My campaign was very grass roots" (Mast, 1994: 179). As a commissioner, Parker was finally in a position to influence public policy. In his first year in office, Parker opened up the first community office of any Detroit commissioner. Half of his staff were placed in the neighborhood, addressing constituent concerns, such as the cutoff of their utilities and complaints about tax bills (Mast, 1994).

In 1997, the thirtieth anniversary of the 1967 urban disorder and black rebellion, Bernard Parker retired from Operation Get-Down after twenty-two years as its executive director. As one of the cofounders of OGD he became known as a strong advocate for poor blacks within the city of Detroit (Hunter, 1997). Three decades after the Detroit rebellion of 1967, the black community could boast of having produced one of the greatest community-based leaders of the era.

On the fortieth anniversary of the 1967 civil disorder, OGD was still going strong, still dedicated to the well-being of the needy in Detroit.

CONCLUSION

The 1967 riot, or rebellion, as many blacks preferred to describe it, was the result of decades of white institutionalized racism. Few whites were willing or able to connect the historical and social causes to their tragic consequences. Most blacks had no trouble doing so. It was a defining moment in the personal and collective lives of both communities. Segments of the white and black communities responded to it in vastly different ways. Many whites fled to the suburbs, and those already there armed themselves for the coming "racial war." It was a wakeup call to the white power elite as well as to some segments of the black leadership, who for some reason never saw the disorder coming and were not quite sure what to do after the flames died down. It radicalized many segments of the black community and encouraged them to look inward for their economic and social development. One of the most impressive developments during the post-1967 era was the growth of black community organizations such as the Inner-City Sub-Center and Operation-Get-Down, which emerged to meet the challenges of a distressed community still in the throes of the aftermath of the 1967 riot.

CHAPTER 2

Conflict between the Black Community and White Police

Before and after the 1967 Civil Disorder

IF AFRICAN AMERICANS IN DETROIT BETWEEN 1925 AND 1945 WERE TO NAME THE worst racial abuses they had to encounter, without a moment's hesitation they would have said "white police brutality." White police officers in the black ghettos in Detroit and throughout the country symbolized a form of unbridled racism. The racial practices of the Detroit Police Department towards the black community were a major contributor to the larger racial tension and conflict in Detroit before and after the 1967 riot.

In some ways, the white police in the black ghettos functioned as the first line of white defense against the invading "black hordes" that, if not checked, would overwhelm surrounding white neighborhoods. White police brutality, therefore, often functioned, whether deliberately or not, as an effective method of racial-social control. During this period, when the black population was rapidly increasing in Detroit and bursting through the seams of the ghettos to which black people were restricted, white police brutality could (and often did) maintain the racial status quo when all other efforts to check black movement failed or were weakening in the face of black protest.

Although Detroit's black population increased significantly between 1915 and 1920, only fifteen black officers were numbered among the 3,000 members of the police force by 1920. As the black population expanded during the 1920s, the Detroit Police Department (DPD) hired only thirty-two additional black officers. During the 1930s, the black population increased by 25 percent, compared to a white increase of 1.7 percent, but the DPD hired only sixteen more blacks during that period (Kresnak, 1980).

As crime increased in the black ghetto (largely as a result of the terrible living conditions produced and maintained by racial discrimination in housing and employment), the DPD expected these black officers to "keep their people" in line. But the major responsibility of "keeping the nigger in line" fell to the predominantly white DPD, which tended to go overboard in combating crime in black neighborhoods. Such overzealousness in the 1920s contributed to increased racial tension and conflicts between the black and white communities. A report of the Mayor's Committee on Race Relations, published in 1926, placed much of the blame for poor race relations on the police department:

There is evidence that in many cases Negroes are treated with undue severity, not to say brutality, by the police. The assumption among many police officers that Negro criminals offer a special peril to the life of the officer and that consideration of self-defense, therefore, justifies unusually precipitate action in firing upon Negro criminals is not borne out by the facts. This unjustified assumption has resulted in needless loss of life on occasion of Negro arrests. This condition will probably not be remedied without much greater vigilance on the part of the department in disciplining officers of unwarranted brutality. (Mayor's Committee on Race Relations, 1926: 7)

The committee did not accept the popular belief circulating in the black community that many of the white police working in the black districts were southerners venting their racist feelings against blacks. The committee did, however, recommend that "the police department formulate a policy of excluding from precincts in which colored people predominate, officers whose social background or previous history prompt them to an undue measure of race prejudice." Furthermore, the Committee suggested that "it might be a wise policy for the department to investigate the personal bias of officers it intends to use in colored districts" (Mayor's Committee on Race Relations, 1926: 8). However, these recommendations had little effect on the racist behavior of white policemen.

White police brutality increased as the black population expanded during the 1930s. Blacks were indiscriminately beaten, repeatedly harassed, and often killed at the hands of racist policemen for doing little more than saying the wrong thing or making a move at the wrong time. More often than not, white policemen were not punished for such racist actions. For example, in 1933, white policemen killed several blacks in rapid succession, prompting the black community, along with several concerned civic organizations, to lodge complaints against "the promiscuous shooting of Negroes by police" (*Detroit Tribune*, September 30, 1933).

Two years later, white policemen were still shooting blacks on the slightest pretense. In one case, in 1935, a white policeman fatally shot a young black man in the abdomen while he was sitting in the rear seat of a car that the officer had stopped for exceeding the speed limit. The officer claimed he thought the victim was armed. At his trial the jury could not reach a verdict despite the testimony of eyewitnesses that the shooting was unjustified (*Detroit Tribune*, June 15, 1935). Several months later, another white officer seriously wounded a sixteen-year-old black youth. The officer explained that he really shot at the rear of a garage the youth was attempting to open, and the kid "ducked into the line of fire" (*Detroit Tribune*, August 24, 1935).

In June 1935, a white policeman shot and killed a sixteen-year-old boy "for allegedly taking a sweater" from a store (*Detroit Tribune*, June 15, 1935).

These shootings prompted increased protests from the Detroit branch of the NAACP, which spent much of its resources protesting against police brutality. In July 1938, Dr. James J. McClendon, president of the branch, protested the beating of a black man by a white policeman while the former was in custody in the Canfield station. At a conference called to discuss the matter, with the participation of Mayor Richard Reading, the superintendent of police, and officials of the Canfield branch, McClendon told the mayor that "this sort of thing must stop. Officers of the Canfield station are noted for their brutality toward colored citizens and we are assembled here [to] protest against their attitudes and we are asking you, the Chief Executive of our city, to put a stop to it" (*Detroit Tribune*, July 23, 1938). The mayor responded by ordering an investigation of charges of police brutality against black citizens (*Detroit Tribune*, August 6, 1938).

Incidents of police brutality stepped up in 1939. Early in the year the president of the North Detroit Youth Council of the NAACP addressed a mass meeting at a local church organized to protest a recent killing of a black autoworker, Jesse James, by a white policemen. He declared, "Negroes are being shot down like rats and unless we put up a bigger fight such conditions will continue to exist" (*Detroit Tribune*, February 11, 1939).

Speaking at the same mass meeting, the NAACP president informed the audience that "the case will not be over until the policeman is punished for the slaying of Jesse James" (*Detroit Tribune*, February 11, 1939). The Reverend Horace White, pastor of the Plymouth Congregational Church and chairman of the Legal Redress Committee of the NAACP, informed the crowd that they "should get mad . . . and then you'll get something done" (*Detroit Tribune*, February 11, 1939). Referring to white elected officials who many blacks believed were dragging their feet on the issue of police brutality, White told the audience to "vote for one who promises to abolish police brutality." Another speaker urged concerned organizations to concentrate their efforts in a coordinated drive to achieve justice for the victim (*Detroit Tribune*, February 11, 1939).

White public officials appeared insensitive to both black victims of police brutality and black protesters. Few, if any, white policemen were punished for killing a black. Alarmed over this situation, in April 1939 the NAACP called for a conference to plan a mass protest against "the alarming increase in beatings, killings, and illegal arrest of colored citizens by police" (*Detroit Tribune*, April 8, 1939). Later in the month, organizations began planning a "Brutality Week" to protest killings by police (*Detroit Tribune*, April 22, 1939).

A week before the mass meeting one of the local black newspapers ran this editorial:

The Detroit Police Department is apparently trying to establish a national record for brutality of Negro citizens. In spite of the many protests made to those in authority, the brutality continues. . . . Since January 1, this year, the number of Negroes slain in cold blood and savagely beaten and clubbed by local police officers has steadily mounted. . . . In addition to these and other murders by Detroit policemen in recent months, many other members of our race have been brutally clubbed and beaten by officers of the law, without just cause. . . . Policemen are paid by taxpayers to preserve law and order and to protect human lives and public and private property, but they had no right to take the law into their own hands, as so many of them do. It is not their duty to act as judge, juries and executioners, in their dealings with Negroes. Policemen have no legal or moral right to let their racial or religious prejudices lead them to persecute members of our race or any other racial group, and when policemen . . . forget their duty as to indulge in such lawless acts of violence, they should be curbed, reprimanded, and in flagrant cases they should be dismissed from the Police Department and punished by the courts of justice.

Colored citizens of Detroit have been protesting for some time to those in local authority, and appealing to them to put a stop to this police brutality, but our protests thus far seem to have fallen on deaf ears. (*Detroit Tribune*, July 15, 1939)

Close to 1,500 people attended the mass meeting on police brutality held at Beth AME Church. The dominant theme was a call for removal of city officials who tolerated police brutality against black citizens. The speakers included Charles H. Houston, the famous black lawyer from Washington, D.C., and special counsel for the national headquarters of the NAACP; John P. Davis, executive secretary of the National Negro Congress; attorney Henry Fried of the Civil Rights Federation; attorney Harold E. Bledsoe; and Dr. James McClendon, president of the local NAACP and chairman of the Committee to End Police Brutality (*Detroit Tribune*, February 11, 1939).

Houston's major contribution to the meeting was in broadening the audience's understanding of the social and institutional aspects of white police brutality against black citizens. He told the audience members that they should not attribute police brutality solely to the policeman on the street when such brutality continues months and months. "Instead," he explained, "go after the City Hall Gang. . . . When a police cracks the head of a Negro," Houston continued, "he is saying, 'I don't agree with you about poor housing condition and intolerable slum environment.' To the laborer and Jew, he is saying, 'Shut up or you will get what the Nigger got'" (*Michigan Chronicle*, July 29, 1939).

Davis's talk had a special relevance because he had led the fight against police brutality in Washington, D.C. After discussing the protest campaign there, Davis pointed out that "the nightstick that cracks the Negro's head is held not alone in the policeman's hands, but in the hands of the mayor." McClendon discussed the recent wave of police brutality and the problems the committee had encountered in its attempts to obtain warrants for the arrest of officers responsible for killing and beating black men. "We intend to do something about that," McClendon warned, "if we have to vote out every person in the city hall" (*Michigan Chronicle*, July 29, 1939).

The mass meeting was not limited to speakers denouncing city officials accused of tolerating police brutalities. Petitions were circulated advocating the removal of the police commissioner (*Michigan Chronicle*, July 29, 1939).

In late August the Committee to End Police Brutality, still under the leadership of the NAACP Detroit president, Dr. James J. McClendon, staged mass protest meetings on nine playgrounds throughout the city. Speakers discussed the objectives of the meetings and listed incidents of police brutality. People were encouraged to sign petitions for the removal of the police commissioner from office. The next month the committee submitted a petition to the Detroit Common Council requesting that the Council investigate the policies and practices of the police department, an investigation that, the committee was convinced, would lead to the firing of the police commissioner. The attorney for the committee informed the Council that the committee had filed countless protests with the commissioner and the mayor, but to no avail (*Detroit Tribune*, September 2, 1939; *Michigan Chronicle*, September 2, 1939).

On the surface, the protest of the NAACP and the Committee to End Police Brutality seemed little more than periodic aggravation at white pubic officials. Below the surface of the seemingly glacial black struggle against police brutality, however, a steady and constant transformation of black self-consciousness was taking place. Those involved were fighting back against what many of them thought to be the invincibility of the white police system, which bordered at times on a form of "racial terrorism."

White police brutality continued throughout the 1940s, followed by continued black protests in which the NAACP played a leading role. Occasionally, blacks were able to get back at white public officials who tolerated police brutality. For example, when Mayor Reading refused to remove the police commissioner, the black community showed its displeasure and political muscle in the 1939 mayoral election by voting against him in his bid for reelection (*Detroit Tribune*, November 11, 1939). A year later, the Detroit NAACP led the successful fight to defeat a local judge in his reelection bid. And in case anyone had any doubts about the political power of black protest organizations in punishing public officials who tolerated police brutality, a writer in one of the local black newspapers pointed out that "The margin of his defeat was just enough to let the judge know that Negro voters defeated him" (*Detroit Tribune*, November 16, 1940).

World War II provided some white policemen more opportunities to vent their racist feelings against black citizens. The 1942 Sojourner Housing riot and the 1943 race riot were clear and blatant examples of white policemen abusing their authority as protectors of the public. During the former housing riot, a white mob attempted to stop black tenants from moving into a new housing project. The police, armed with tear gas and a riot car, made frequent runs into the melee. Scores of people, mainly blacks, were injured by the police, who tended to side with whites by arresting blacks (Capeci, 1984; Widick, 1972). Although whites in the 1943 riot numbered in the thousands, while blacks numbered in the hundreds, the police killed seventeen blacks (some were shot in the back), but not one white. On Woodward Avenue, a major thoroughfare on the edge of the ghetto, white mobs beat blacks under the very eyes of the police (Widick, 1972).

As Capeci and Wilkerson pointed out, "The police exerted ultimate unbridled force against Blacks, thereby cheapening the worth of their lives and inviting unbridled White violence against them. In contrast they employed only persuasion on White rioters" (1991: 19).

After the 1943 riot, Judge George Edwards, who became commissioner of the Detroit police department from 1961 to 1963, "believed that police malfeasance had fueled the 1943 riots" (Stolberg, 1998: 74). On the night of June 4, 1948, Leon Mosley, a fifteen-year-old black youth driving a stolen car, was beaten and then shot in the back and killed by white police officers, adding to the long list of black complaints against police brutality (Dillard, 2007). A Joint Committee for Justice for Leon Mosley was organized by community leaders and organizations, including Reverend T. S. Boone of King Solomon Baptist, future mayor Coleman Young, the NAACP, the Civil Rights Congress, the Communist Party, the Congress of Industrial Union Council, and the United Auto Workers. Although a manslaughter warrant was issued against one of the two officers involved in the shooting, in the end the commissioner "refused to have the officer arrested" (Dillard, 2007: 185).

One local black newspaper claimed that during the decade of 1943–53, police brutality "became the symbol of everything that was wrong with Detroit" (*Michigan Chronicle*, March 21, 1953). Relations between the black community and the police became so bad that NAACP officials "spent most of their time processing complaints against the police department" (*Michigan Chronicle*, March 21, 1953). The situation became so serious that the black community was forced to use the courts to clarify the use of firearms by white policemen in apprehending persons suspected of crime. Unfortunately, the problem would continue for several decades, until Mayor Young's election in 1973. In short, it took black political power to end what at times amounted to white police intimidation of the black community (Rich, 1989).

Much of the racism that existed in the police department during this period reflected the social mores of a predominantly white male department and the larger white society. Black and white policemen neither walked beats together nor rode together in squad cars. Blacks did not belong to the motorcycle squad, the arson squad, or the homicide squad. The department assigned white police to black and white districts but assigned black policemen only to predominantly black districts to "do a job with Negroes." In 1953, out of a department of 4,200 policemen, only 101 were black, of whom there were only four uniform sergeants and one detective lieutenant. No black policemen worked in administration at central headquarters or were assigned to any precinct unless they were on special duty (Kresnak, 1980; *Michigan*

Chronicle, March 21, 1953). Since at the time most blacks lived west of Woodward Avenue, this policy was obviously designed to control black communities, while at the same time keeping black policemen out of white communities.

The appointment of John Ballenger as police commissioner in 1943 was the first serious attempt to develop a sound policy of race relations between the black community and the predominantly white police department. He introduced intercultural courses in the police academy, promoted the first uniformed black sergeant, and initiated a general campaign against police brutality. Ballenger also created a policy-study commission with members from the black community, unprecedented in the history of Detroit race relations. Sadly, Ballenger was the last police commissioner before 1953 to attend a meeting of the Detroit Interracial Committee, a committee in which all police commissioners held membership as a function of their office (*Michigan Chronicle*, March 21, 1953).

Evidently, most white police officials, as well as the rank and file of the department, were not interested in improving race relations in Detroit if it meant challenging the racial status quo. Given that the racial policies of city hall were not much better at the time, the police department could not help but reflect the racial prejudice of the local government. In short, the department was really an extension of the racial policies of city hall, the enforcement arm of the policy of white racial containment and control of the black population.

Police brutality against blacks continued into the 1950s. Beating blacks in precinct stations was a common practice of many white policemen, which was why black policemen were kept outside of some police stations. A former black policeman commented on this practice, which was still common in the 1950s: "[White police officers] did it for kicks just for fun" (Kresnak, 1980: 72). Beating black citizens "just for fun" indicated the degree to which racism had infected the mentality of many white policemen by the 1950s. The practice was designed to intimidate and "terrorize" the black community into accepting white dominance.

In December 1960, the NAACP "highlighted continued police brutality in Detroit when its executive secretary, Arthur L. Johnson, described the problem in a statement for the U.S. Commission on Civil Rights." Johnson reported that Detroit provided "an impressive case study of the hard core existence of the racial problem in the North," and that police brutality "by its very nature is perhaps the most openly oppressive form of racial injustice [that] Negroes suffer here" (Stolberg, 1998: 149).

Between 1956 and 1960 African Americans in Detroit filed 149 formal complaints with the NAACP against the police (Stolberg, 1998). Two cases in the 1950s demonstrated the extent of the racist behavior of some white policemen toward black citizens:

> In one especially egregious 1957 case, a woman driving on East Jefferson was stopped for no reason by three police officers. One asked to see her license, then asked if she owned the car, and then struck her in the face while the other two officers restrained her. They drove her to the station, where the desk sergeant told them to take her to the hospital. After [she received] stitches and a shot of painkiller, the police dragged the woman to jail. The bogus charges of drinking and reckless driving were suspended the following day, and she was released. (Stolberg, 1998: 149)

In this case, the white male police officers engaged in both sexist and racist harassment. Their treatment of this black woman revealed a deep and pathological hatred of black people and disregard for and lack of respect for black women. The police behavior was meant to dehumanize her as a member of what they perceived to be a degraded race. To this extent their treatment of this black woman was firmly grounded in the prevailing racial attitude of the larger white society.

In another incident, a black couple leaving a bar was accosted by four men who yelled at the woman, "Hey baby do you want some business?" Her date asked the men why they were bothering his girlfriend. "What do you mean?"

> They responded, "That nigger bitch going along there?" Then they attacked him. When he fought back, one said: "You don't know who you're messing with, we're police officers." Another hand-cuffed him and shoved him into the back of an unmarked car between the two other policemen, who called him a "nigger" and a "monkey" as they beat him. After they arrived at the jail, they continued to strike him, and one said: "We'll give you something to tell the NAACP." The man was charged with soliciting but was later found not guilty. (Stolberg, 1998: 150)

This case, once again, revealed the pattern of white male police sexist and racist stereotypes of black women as prostitutes, but what was more revealing was the all too common beating ritual of black men by white police as a show of racial control. This reinforced their depraved sense of control over him as a black man and deprived him of any sense of his own "manhood" in protecting the women of his race. Therefore, the white police officers walked away with a revived sense of having restored, at least for the moment, white racial dominance.

Largely as a result of the local NAACP's complaints of police brutality, two studies were launched during this period. In the late summer of 1958, Mayor Louis Miriani appointed a Citizen's Advisory Committee on Police Procedures to investigate NAACP's charges of police brutality (Stolberg, 1998). The resultant committee report in March 1960 did not please Arthur Johnson, the president of the NAACP. He accused the committee of whitewashing "the wrong-doing of police officers. . . . In its evasive and indirect approach, however, the Committee did recognize that 'one of the major problem areas yet remaining in police-community relations involves complaints of police mistreatment.'" The committee report did suggest "that if the police department could not process charges more effectively, then the major should establish an independent citizen review board" (Stolberg, 1998: 150).

The same year that Mayor Miriani appointed his Citizen's Advisory Committee, the Detroit Bar Association conducted its own study of police practices. Among all the findings in the report, "the most alarming statistics . . . showed that out of 63,301 arrests in 1956, 26,696 were made without warrants" (Stolberg, 1998: 150). The investigators discovered more alarming facts when they examined 103 charges of police brutality between January 1956 and July 1957. "In most complaints, the victim said the police assaulted them, insulted them with racial epithets, and indiscriminately searched their wallets and pockets. When citizens questioned the violations of their civil liberties, police responded by beating and arresting them" (Stolberg, 1998: 150). In these situations the police were clearly expressing a long-held view among large segments of the white public that blacks had no rights that whites had to respect if granting such rights threatened their control and dominance.

How did the police explain their actions? They "insisted that the illegal arrests were necessary to control crime. Given the department's lack of money and manpower, police had no choice but to arrest suspects first, then find the evidence against them later." Furthermore, they added, "The follow-up of clues, the shadowing of suspects, etc., are methods appropriate to television drama, but the entire police force would be quickly bogged down if these methods were pursued in every case brought to police attention." The police concluded that arrests "formed a legitimate means of harassing illegal enterprises in cases where it would be impossible or time-consuming to prosecute" (Stolberg, 1998: 151).

The Detroit Bar Association did not buy the police's self-serving logic, correctly arguing that "unreasonable searches were unconstitutional, engendered disrespect for the law, and bred mistrust—especially among African Americans" (Stolberg, 1998: 151). The report could have added that the "unreasonable searches" also bred deep hatred of white police among a generation of young black males—who only a decade later would express their hatred on 12th Street, where the 1967 riot first erupted.

Johnson appreciated the manner in which the Bar Association "condemned these [police] practices with unrestrained vigor" and noted that it also "expressed the view that a determination to correct the problem did not exist in the Police Department" (Stolberg, 1998: 151). This was rooted in both the police department's culture and the support it received from the larger white society. Few white organizations were willing to stand up to the police establishment for its harsh treatment of African Americans. Only one, the Presbytery of Detroit—in March 1960—had the courage to endorse the NAACP's request for a permanent citizens' review board. It stood out as the only white civic or religious group to take a bold stand against police brutality against blacks (Stolberg, 1998).

Detroit's three white newspapers denied that police brutality existed. According to the *Detroit Free Press*—voicing the sentiments of many white Detroiters—Johnson and the NAACP were just troublemakers (Stolberg, 1998). Notwithstanding the denials of the white press and its supporters, Johnson's concerns would find an outlet at a higher national level.

In November 1961, the U.S. Civil Rights Commission put out a report based on evidence it had gathered from Johnson and other African American leaders from around the country. The report did not mince words in its criticism of police forces on both the state and local levels: "Police brutality by some state and local officers presents a serious and continuing problem in many parts of the United States. . . . Negroes are the victims of such brutality far more, proportionately, than any other group" (Stolberg, 1998: 152).

This was not a revelation to black communities. Most understood how disproportionate the white police treatment of blacks was in comparison to other groups, which could be explained by the centuries-old white obsession of "white policing of black populations" to "keep them in their place" (Hawkins and Thomas, 1991: 65).

The report stuck at the heart of the social causes of white police brutality when it attributed the problem to "the poor caliber of local police and the inadequate training they receive . . . [and] urged the federal government to help local authorities recruit better candidates." More importantly, the commission report "proposed more sweeping changes that, among other things, would have made local officials legally liable for police misconduct" (Stolberg, 1998: 152).

National efforts to curb police brutality were strengthened when, in March 1962, Attorney General Robert F. Kennedy "asked Congress to toughen federal status against police brutality by adding beatings or attempted beating to extort a confession or deliver 'summary punishment' [to that category]" (Stolberg, 1998: 152). Predictably, police department heads across the country, including Detroit, were upset over the commission report, but Congress ignored them and incorporated their recommendations into the Civil Rights Act of 1964 (Stolberg, 1998). Unfortunately, they did not help stem police brutality in Detroit.

Interestingly enough, there was a six-month period in 1962 when the Community Relations Bureau (CRB) of the Detroit Police Department—where blacks with complaints about the department could go to lodge them—"had not received a single brutality complaint"

(Fine, 1989: 105). In fact, after the huge Walk to Freedom on July 23, 1963, in which 125,000 people, led by Dr. Martin Luther King and Mayor Jerome Cavanagh, walked "in orderly fashion down Woodward Avenue" (Fine, 1989: 107), James Garrett (a member of the black leadership) "hailed the police performance [during both the six-month period and the Walk to Freedom] as 'a MASTERPIECE in police-community relations.'" He declared that "for the first time, Negroes in Detroit looked with honor and pride on our police forces" (Fine, 1989: 107).

Dr. King was sufficiently impressed with the performance of the Detroit police and wrote Police Commissioner George Edwards that his department had demonstrated to the black community that it was "a genuine protector and friend rather than an enemy" (Fine, 1989: 108).

A few days later these praises vanished in the wake of a white police slaying of a black prostitute.

THE POLICE KILLING OF CYNTHIA SCOTT, JULY 5, 1963

Eleven months after the CRB "reported that it had not received a single brutality complaint in six months," a white "notorious cop" killed Cynthia Scott, a black prostitute, setting off a firestorm of criticism from the black community. According to historian Sidney Fine, the following took place:

> On July 5, 1963, Theodore Spicher, a policeman with a poor reputation in the black community, and his scout-car partner, Robert Marshall, observed Scott, money in hand, walking with a black male. According to the police report, the two officers approached Scott and her companion to question her about the money since there had been "a lot of jack-rolling by prostitutes and pimps" in the area. Spicher told Scott, who was apparently drunk, that she was under arrest for larceny from a person and ordered her to enter the scout car. As she was about to do so, she turned on Spicher and cut him on the index finger. She turned to run, and when Spicher tried to stop her, she slashed him again. He shot her twice in the back as she fled, and when she turned and allegedly sought to slash him a third time, he shot her in the stomach, and she fell. As Marshall then sought to disarm her, she cut him on the arm. (Fine, 1989: 106)

While the Homicide Bureau investigation not surprisingly "produced some corroborative evidence," the black community accused the police of provoking the incident "by trying to make an illegal arrest, that Scott was resisting a 'police shakedown,' that the money in her hand was change her companion had returned to her after she had sent him to buy some food, and that she did not have a knife or that Spicher had removed the knife from her person only after he had shot and killed her and then used the knife to cut Marshall" (Fine, 1989: 106).

Given the history of seemingly unrestricted police brutality in the black community and Spicher's poor reputation among blacks, it was not unreasonable for the black community to believe that the two white police officers had conspired to cover up the slaying. Three days after the police slaying of Scott the prosecutor "ruled that Spicher had had a legal right to use fatal force to stop a fleeing felon" (Fine, 1989: 106). As expected, "the killing, followed by [Prosecutor] Olsen's exoneration of Spicher, ignited a firestorm in the black community" (Fine, 1989: 106).

As if matters could not get any worse, on July 12, a week after the Scott's slaying, during a car chase the police killed an eighteen-year-old black youth driving a stolen car (Fine 1989, 106). Notwithstanding the criminal activities in which these two blacks were involved, these two police slayings a week apart undermined any progress that had been made in police-community relations under Police Commissioner Edwards. As Congressman Charles Diggs, Jr., warned in a letter to Mayor Cavanagh, this progress "could be seen going down the drain" (Fine, 1989: 106).

The Scott slaying galvanized many sectors of the black community from black radical organizations like UHURU and the Group of Advanced Leadership (GOAL), to the more established NAACP as well as black political leaders. To some segments of the black community, Scott's slaying elevated her to the status of "Saint Cynthia." As historian Angela D. Dillard explains, "Saint Cynthia was no Rosa Parks . . . but the incident touched off a storm of protest. . . . The dead prostitute swiftly became a martyr" (2007: 267).

On July 13 UHURU and GOAL picketed police headquarters. UHURU then organized street rallies as follow-ups. It also led a group of protesters in a sit-in in Mayor Cavanagh's reception room, where they demanded he appoint a black police commissioner, disarm the police, and arrest Olsen. GOAL attempted to have Spicher brought to trial in addition to helping Scott's mother sue Spicher and the police department for $5 million (Fine, 1989). The NAACP demanded that police superintendent Eugene Reuter, who had been appointed by Edwards, investigate the slaying. The organization also made an appeal to Michigan's attorney general "to review the case." Congressman John Conyers, along with the Metropolitan Detroit branch of the American Civil Liberties Union, led a citizen committee that not only criticized the prosecutor but circulated petitions for his recall (Fine, 1989).

The police slaying of Cynthia Scott and her elevation to martyrdom and sainthood by the more radical segments within the black community also served the purposes of those seeking political power. In 1964 her name became a rallying cry for Henry Cleage when he was running for the office of Wayne County prosecutor on the all-black Freedom Now Party ticket. "When I am elected," he declared, "I will see to it that the case of Cynthia Scott is re-opened" (Dillard, 2007: 267).

The police slaying of Cynthia Scott would linger and smolder in the collective memory of black Detroiters for several years, adding to their hatred and mistrust of the predominantly white police force in their community during the 1967 riot.

GEORGE EDWARDS: POLICE COMMISSIONER AS REFORMER

In January 1962 Mayor Cavanagh appointed George Edwards, a white liberal with a history of working on behalf of racial justice, as police commissioner. In conversations with Edwards, the mayor knew the future police commissioner had two major concerns about race relations in Detroit: "Avoiding a [race] riot and promoting color-blind law enforcement" (Stolberg, 1998: 33). Edwards's experiences with race relations in Detroit had convinced him that "race hatred and race conflict constituted in domestic affairs, the greatest threat of all to the American dream . . . and that the police-black community problem had to be solved if 'domestic tranquility was to become a reality'" (Stolberg, 1998: 33).

Cavanagh had already demonstrated his commitment to racial equality and justice by appointing Alfred Pelham, an African American, as city controller—"the first black to fill so important position in Detroit's government" (Fine, 1989: 18). Furthermore, the mayor appointed blacks to head his Commission on Children and Youth and as secretary of the Department of Public Works (Fine, 1989). These appointments represented significant racial progress in city government and earned Cavanagh much-deserved respect from the black community. Notwithstanding these achievements in race relations, however, historian Sydney Fine argues that blacks were more pleased with the appointment of a white, George Edwards Jr., as police commissioner (Fine, 1989).

Given the history of police brutality in the black community and Edwards's reputation as a long-serving public servant working on behalf of minorities and the working class, blacks in Detroit saw him as their champion in their protracted struggle against police brutality. A biographer of Edwards pointed out that he "enjoyed an unparalleled reputation as a champion of equal opportunity for African Americans" (Stolberg, 1998: 31). This explains why the executive secretary of the Detroit branch of the NAACP compared the impact of Edwards's appointment on Detroit blacks to President Lyndon B. Johnson's later appointment of Thurgood Marshall to the United State Supremes Court (Fine, 1989).

Blacks also felt close to Edwards because many of them were his friends and had shared stories with him in "graphic detail" about police abuses. These stories of "being stopped and searched with no pretense of probable cause and generally with rudeness that doubly infuriated them" (Stolberg, 1998: 32) had outraged him. Armed with this personal knowledge of police abuse of blacks, Edwards saw his job as teaching police that "they didn't have a constitutional right to beat up Negroes on arrest." He informed the police that it was their job "to serve the citizens, not to ride herd on them" (Fine, 1989: 103).

Edwards proceeded to put his reforms in place by having notices "posted above the admitting desk of each precinct setting forth his objectives as commissioner: more vigorous law enforcement, equal protection and enforcement of the law and citizen support for law enforcement." This was his way and hope of moving "Detroit away from the possibility of serious racial strife and in the direction of a more unified and safer city" (Fine, 1989: 103). He ordered an end to what came to be called "the alley court," which was the practice of "exacting physical punishment on the street"(Fine, 1989: 103).

Predictably, the entrenched high command of the police department set out to sabotage Edwards's efforts to reform police practices (Fine, 1989). Notwithstanding the resistance, Edwards launched a massive recruitment campaign in 1962 aimed largely at blacks, which resulted in some small improvements in black assignments and promotions during his tenure as police commissioner (Fine, 1989).

The Detroit Urban League (DUL) and the NAACP were not impressed with these changes, however. The DUL claimed that the department was still assigning white officers to integrated scout cars to punish them, which the department claimed was an "absolute untruth." The executive secretary of the NAACP accused the police department of being a segregated institution with very little career opportunities for black officers (Fine, 1989).

Edwards's response to the Scott slaying offended many blacks, including some of his allies. When Edwards concluded that the white officer who shot Scott was justified in the shooting, many blacks accused him of whitewashing the case. Most of his black friends and allies did not abandon him, however. While they disagreed with his handling of the Scott case, they still supported his appointment to the federal bench (Stolberg, 1998).

In summing up Edwards's impact on black community-police relations during his two years as commissioner, Fine argues that while these relations "took a turn for the better . . . it is doubtful that the police department changed very much during his two years at the helm. His efforts at reform had been resisted from the start by the department's bureaucracy, and as a police official who headed a special squad at the time asserted, Edwards was commissioner for too short a time to have had any real impact at the 'rank and file' level" (1989: 107).

Edwards's short tenure as police commissioner was one of the major reasons that some black leaders feared that he had not done enough to ensure that his reforms would survive after his departure from office (Stolberg, 1998). His refusal to establish a civilian review board for police brutality was a constant source of controversy. For example, while Congressman Charles C. Diggs Jr. praised Edwards for the progress achieved under his "valuable leadership," he informed Edwards that he would not always be police commissioner and some machinery should be set up that would assume that after he left office, progress would continue (Stolberg, 1998).

Whatever his perceived shortcomings while a police commissioner, however, no one could doubt Edwards's deep concern for defusing racial tension between the police department and the black community by recruiting more black officers and promoting racially unbiased policing and citizen cooperation (Stolberg, 1998).

COMMUNITY-POLICE RELATIONS DURING THE 1967 RIOT

As riots exploded in cities throughout the nation in the 1960s, former police commissioner Edwards—now a federal judge—could see the connection between the racist practices in police departments and the spreading urban disorders. Two years before the riot in Detroit and in the year of the Watts riot, Judge Edwards once again commented on the volatile nature of the relations between the black community and white police:

> It is clear that in 1965 no one will make excuses for any city's inability to foresee the possibility of racial trouble. . . . Although local police forces generally regard themselves as public servants with the responsibility of maintaining law and order, they tend to minimize this attitude when they are patrolling areas that are heavily populated with Negro citizens. There they tend to view each person on the streets as a potential criminal and enemy, and all too often that attitude is reciprocated. Indeed, hostility between the Negro communities in our large cities and the police departments is the major problem in law enforcement in this decade. It has been a major cause of all recent race riots. (National Advisory Commission on Civil Disorders, 1968: 85)

In July 1967 a police raid on a "blind pig" in the black ghetto triggered one of the worst riots in U.S. history. When it finally ended, forty-three people were dead, seventeen of whom were shot by police, and the number injured exceeded one thousand; 3,800 were arrested (Fine, 1989: 299). Close to 5,000 people were left homeless—most of them black (National Advisory Commission on Civil Disorders, 1968). The most shocking occurrence of the riots, which would damage black community-police relations for decades, however, was the execution-like slaying by police of three unarmed black men in the Algiers Motel. Police shot these men to death while they were lying or kneeling (Fine, 1989; Widick, 1972).

John Hersey's book *The Algiers Motel* (1968) captured the events that led up to the killings, including the horrendous beating and racist taunting of the victims before they met their deaths at the hands of white officers who could only be described as racist psychopaths. As Hersey wrote, "It is by now, on Monday, July 31, clear that the killings in the Algiers [motel] were not executions of snipers, looters, or arsonists caught red-handed in felonious crimes in the heat of a riot, but rather that they were murders embellished by racist abuse, indiscriminate vengeance, sexual jealousy, voyeurism, wanton blood-letting, and sadistic physical and mental tortures characterized by the tormentors as 'a game'" (Hersey, 1968: 245–46).

CONFRONTATIONS BETWEEN THE BLACK COMMUNITY AND POLICE:, 1968–1969

Informed social observers and community leaders had little hope that the early postriot period would witness a decrease in tension and confrontation between the predominantly white police department and the black community. Notwithstanding the resistance of some white police officials to increasing the number of blacks in the department, 180 blacks were hired in 1968, making up about 35 percent of the total number hired that year. This was more than the total number of blacks recruited from 1962 to 1967 (Fine, 1989).

The number of blacks hired dropped to 23 percent of the total hires in 1969. Absent any racial discrimination in the department, 239 black police officers in 1968 and 241 in 1969 would have been hired (Fine, 1989). Increased numbers of black police officers would have played a vital role in reducing confrontations between the police and the black community. A predominantly white police department not only lacked racial diversity, but by its very nature nurtured a culture of white racial exclusion. As one black leader explained, "'every confrontation' between the police and blacks became 'a racial confrontation' because of the largely white complexion of the Police Department" (Fine, 1989: 412).

No wonder that in February 1968 warning signs were beginning to be raised in the still smoldering city. That month, both Mayor Cavanagh and the Michigan Civil Rights Commission were informed that the police and the black community were on a "'direct collision course' and that 'dramatic remedial action' of a kind no city had ever before undertaken was required" (Fine, 1989: 412). In April, Governor Romney received a similar warning from the Michigan State Advisory Committee to the United States Civil Rights Commission informing him that "'the greatest threat to racial peace' in the state was the manner in which law enforcement officers operated in and serviced the black community" (Fine, 1989: 412).

Police Aggression at Cobo Hall I and II and Veterans Memorial, 1968

It appeared that the above warnings went unheeded by Detroit police officials. During 1968, the police department was involved in several incidents directly related to the racial attitudes and actions of white police officers (Georgakas and Surkin, 1998). The first of several incidents occurred on May 3, 1968, several months before the first anniversary of the 1967 riot. The setting was the Poor People's Campaign led by Reverend Ralph Abernathy. According to Georgakas and Surkin, the following events unfolded: "A rally had been scheduled to be held at Cobo Hall, Detroit's Convention Center. . . . The demonstration, which was being telecast over a local channel, was peaceful and orderly until a car stalled. At that point, the police became extremely agitated and, almost without warning, mounted a cavalry charge upon the demonstrators. Nineteen people were seriously injured in action" (1998: 158).

An official of the U.S. Department of Justice who witnessed the aggressive actions of the police commented, "I saw old ladies being pushed and manhandled, grabbed by the collar and pushed outdoors. I saw young men being beaten with billy clubs . . . I saw officers ride horses into a crowd which I judged to be under control. I saw officers strike individual in that crowd for no apparent reason" (Georgakas and Surkin, 1998: 158).

What was most alarming to these U.S. Department of Justice officials was the inability of the police command officers to control their men. "[One official] asked several command officers to pull other officers back. They attempted to but were unsuccessful. In fact, one command officer was knocked down by a patrolman. . . . All of this over a stalled car well out of traffic. Police were insensitive" (Georgakas and Surkin, 1998: 158–59).

This was still another incident contributing to the tensions between the black community and the Detroit Police Department. Once again blacks and their white allies vented their anger and frustration against this latest in a series of aggressive behavior. In a not-too-veiled threat to the mayor via the black newspaper, the *Michigan Chronicle*, State Senator Coleman Young warned, "if the mayor is afraid to take on the DPOA [Detroit Police Officers Association] then we will do it for him. Otherwise this city is headed for a blood bath" (Georgakas and Surkin, 1998: 159).

Nothing of any substance emerged from the mayor's office sufficient to check future police action, which resulted in still another incident at Cobo Hall on October 29 called Cobo Hall II. Over 1,000 black and white protestors gathered to voice their opposition to George Wallace's presidential candidacy. At some point fistfights broke out, and then, according to some observers, the police revealed their "pro-Wallace sympathies." "They made virtually no attack on Wallace people and seemed to single out white anti-Wallace demonstrators for the roughest treatment. The idea of containing the violence seemed to have no priority at all. The police violence was more fragrant than during Cobo Hall I" (Georgakas and Surkin, 1998: 159).

Few were spared in the melee. "Bystanders, reporters, and photographers were beaten . . . even . . . a field investigator for Mayor Cavanagh's Community Relations Commission, who was specially assigned to observe the event, was injured by the police" (Georgakas and Surkin, 1998: 159). One incident in particular was pointed out as a glaring example of both police aggression and bias in crowd control. When a busload of "Wallace supporters threw hunks of scrap iron at a group struggling with a Wallace-ite, the people hit by the iron were attacked by the police, while no action was directed toward the bus. Numerous individuals complained of being beaten at the rally and at police headquarters afterwards" (Georgakas and Surkin, 1998: 159). Shelia Murphy, one of the organizers of the protest, would later report that one police officer told her, "We'd kill you if we thought we could get away with it" (Fine, 1989: 416).

Cobo Hall II was not the end of the confrontations between police and the black community in 1968. A far worse racial incident involving white police officers occurred outside Veterans Memorial Hall on the night and early morning of November 1–2, 1968. While the Ebenezer AME Church was sponsoring a high school dance attended by blacks on the sixth floor of the building, the off-duty white police officers were attending a dance organized by the wives of the DPOA. Two black teenagers, the sons of two prominent black families, claimed that as they entered the building they were the targets of racial slurs by white police officers. One youth stated that when the dance on the sixth floor ended and the youth were leaving, he was stopped at gunpoint just outside the building and beaten by six or eight white men, some of whom had been drinking, and none of whom identified themselves as police officers (Fine, 1989).

This youth claimed that he was chased and beaten into unconsciousness by a group of policemen, one of whom fired at least one shot. The youth's mother also stated that a group of whites choked her son in the building's parking lot. When the young men locked themselves in their car for protection, their attackers kicked in the car's fenders and dented the roof (Fine, 1989). One witness, the father of one of the youths, reported that when he arrived at the building at about 2:00 A.M., he saw several policemen in plainclothes "staggering around drunk," one with a gun in his hand (Fine, 1989: 417).

On November 4, in a display of interracial unity against police brutality, an array of black and wh\ite community groups rallied to demand an investigation of the incident. More than 400 gathered in the Central Methodist Church and organized the Detroit Task Force for Justice, an interracial organization aimed at controlling police power and one that called for the termination of the DPOA and civilian control of the police department (Fine, 1989). The *Detroit Free Press* added its editorial voice to the movement on the front page and asked, "Who's the Boss of Detroit Police?," adding that the city "faced a growing crisis over the control of its police department and policemen" (Fine, 1989: 417).

In the end, nine policemen were suspended and on November 16, 1968, a white assistant Wayne County prosecutor issued a public statement in which he stated the police attacks on the black youths were unprovoked. "The policemen, with varying degrees of participation, threatened and assaulted the Negro youths without provocation or justification. At no time did any of the police officers identify themselves, make any arrests, or make any report of the incident" (Georgakas and Surkin, 1998: 161).

The New Bethel Incident, 1969

The mounting tension between the black community and white police finally exploded on March 29, 1969, outside of a popular black church in the 1967 riot area. Two white police officers were shot, one killed and the other wounded, while they were (according to some reports) investigating some armed black men attending a meeting of the Republic of New Africa, a black separatist group, at the New Bethel Baptist Church. Police cars from four precincts soon arrived, attempted to enter the church, and claimed that they were fired upon. As police "secured" the church (some observers would say "stormed"), four people inside the building were wounded (*Detroit Free Press*, March 31, 1969).

Over a hundred people in the church were arrested and taken to the police headquarters. This mass arrest prompted black state representative James Del Rio to contact Recorder's Court judge George Crockett, "claiming suspects' civil rights were violated" (*Detroit Free Press*, March 31, 1969).

When Del Rio and Judge Crockett arrived at police headquarters, Crockett demanded a list of the people arrested. After being told there was no list, Crockett went to the police commissioner's office with a writ demanding that those arrested but not charged be released. Several hours later Judge Crockett held court on the first floor of the police headquarters and released thirty-nine prisoners. That afternoon, the judge kept two men in jail and released the remaining prisoners (*Detroit Free Press*, March 31, 1969). As a result of the release, a firestorm of white criticism encircled the African American judge and fueled more racial polarization.

Blacks and whites differed widely over the actual facts of the shooting incident and Judge George Crockett's handling of the incident as reported in the mass media (Warren, 1972). In the April issue of *Tuebor*, "The official organ of the Detroit Police Officers Association," the large-print headline read: "FULL STORY OF ASSASSINATION OF PATROLMAN M. CZAPSKI." According to the paper, the following took place:

Patrolman Michael Czapski, age 22, and patrolman Richard Worobec, 28, cruising near Linwood and Euclid observed ten to twelve men dressed in green military fatigue uniforms with leopard skin epaulet armed with rifles and carbines in front of the New Bethel Baptist Church. They immediately stopped the scout car got out to investigate. *Neither drew his gun. Upon seeing the Officers, the would-be-killers, in guerrilla fashion, turned and fired. Patrolman Czapski, fatally wounded, fell. Patrolman Worobec, although critically wounded, managed to crawl to the scout car and call for assistance.* Patrolman Czapski, brutally shot seven times, was dead upon arrival at Ford hospital. The scout car was riddled with bullets. Patrolman Worobec escaped with his life.

The assassins ran into the New Bethel Baptist Church. Patrolman Worobec's cries for help were heard over the police radio. Within seconds, supporting scout cars arrived on the scene. Black as well as White Officers responded. Fellow officers removed Czapski and Worobec while under fire from the church. *A ranking officer at the scene pounded repeatedly on the locked door of the church and demanded entry. The only answer received was gun fire.* The Officers then broke into the darkened barricaded building. Immediately they were fired upon from the center of the alter by a rifleman. The man dove for cover behind an overturned table near the pulpit. Shots were being fired from all over. Other officers came in and turned on the lights. Everyone was ordered to stand with their hands up. Slowly they began to rise as directed. One hundred forty-two (142) adults including five (injured persons, as well as five (5) juveniles were in the building.

The majority, both men and women, were wearing paramilitary fatigues with leopard skin epaulets, and combat boots, the uniform of the Republic of New Africa. Requests for information brought only silence. Not one person offered assistance or cooperation. Nine weapons, including rifles, handguns, gas ejecting spray and a quantity of ammunition was recovered from inside the church building. . . . The ranking officers at the scene ordered all those present arrested. (*Tuebor*, April 1969)

Blacks had a different interpretation of the incident. Reverend C. L. Franklin, the pastor of the church, claimed that while the incident did "'regrettably and unfortunately' involve the death of a police officer and the wounding of five other people charged that police over-reacted to the shooting" (*Michigan Chronicle*, April 12, 1969). The police overreaction involved, the pastor explained, "the wounding of four Black attendants of the affair" (public meeting sponsored by the Republic of New Africa) and "flagrant shooting into a crowd which included . . . men, women and very small children who obviously could not all have been guilty" (*Michigan Chronicle*, April 12, 1969).

Black state representative Neil Saunders, who interviewed some of the blacks arrested that fateful night, accused the police of "unnecessary rough tactics in effecting arrests of people who offered no resistance." "Women told us how their dresses were pulled up over their heads and how they were patted down—an illegal act by police officers—the women also told us how the police kicked them and their children and how they hit men who were innocent of any wrong. Men and women told how they were dragged from the floor and how they were hit over their heads and about their bodies with guns" (*Michigan Chronicle*, April 12, 1969).

Both Representative Saunders and Reverend Franklin claimed that the police did not give any "warning to the people inside the church about the shooting outside" (*Michigan Chronicle*, April 12, 1969). According to what some of the victims told Saunders, the people in the church were not told to "come out with their hands up or they would be arrested" (*Michigan Chronicle*, April 12, 1969).

Black nationalist leader Milton R. Henry, vice president of the Republic of New Africa, called the police storming of the church "uncivilized and unjustified . . . a bloody, storm trooper attack" (*Detroit Free Press*, April 1, 1969). Henry claimed the two police officers provoked the situation, citing two unidentified witnesses who said that "the two police officers got out of their car with guns drawn, provoked their assailants in some way and that the assailants fired at the officers in self-defense" (*Detroit Free Press*, April 1, 1969).

Several days after the shooting, close to 100 off-duty policemen and their wives picketed the Tenth Precinct—the home station of the two officers—to protest the handling of the prisoners taken at the church. Some carried picket signs saying "Crockett Justice? Release killers. Prosecute prosecutors. Give license to kill policemen" (*Detroit Free Press*, April 1, 1969). As the public outcry—mainly white—grew, more policemen and their wives picketed the Recorder's Court, completely ringing the building. Some police wives went to the office of the U.S. Attorney Robert Grace, where they demanded "a federal investigation of Crockett and of Detroit's city administration." Angry telephone calls into Recorder's Court were coming in "at a rate of one a minute." The majority of the calls either demanded Judge Crockett's resignation or were seeking information about how he could be removed from office (*Detroit News*, April 1, 1969).

Three days after the shooting and Judge Crockett's controversial release of the black arrestees at the church, Governor Milliken and Mayor Cavanagh added their views to the controversy concerning Crockett's decision. During his weekly news conference, the governor said that he was "extremely concerned about the allegations made with regard to Judge Crockett's handling of the matter . . . and [wanted] to strongly encourage the tenure commission to investigate the case thoroughly. This is the logical and proper approach" (*Detroit Free Press*, April 3, 1969). Milliken explained that he was not trying to prejudge Crockett but had "deep concern" over the police contentions that Crockett's release of suspects "could hamper their investigation" (*Detroit Free Press*, April 3, 1969).

Mayor Cavanagh described Crockett's decision as "highly unusual (and) to some degree questionable" and that he supported a state Judicial Tenure Commission probe of Judge Crockett. "The investigative procedures the police were following were made extremely difficult by the highly unusual, to some degree questionable, but nonetheless unusual incidents that took place, including that of Judge Crockett's participation in the case," the mayor argued. "I think Judge Crockett acted with haste in exercising what obviously are his judicial prerogatives" (*Detroit Free Press*, April 3, 1969).

The controversy over Judge Crockett's actions soon erupted in the state senate, where black and white legislators engaged in a bitter debate. After the debate, the senate adopted a resolution that asked the Judicial Tenure Commission to conduct the investigation of Crockett's actions. One white member of the house of representatives introduced a resolution to remove Crockett from the bench, accusing the judge of "unlawful and unjudicial interference" with the office of the Wayne County prosecutor. He asked the legislature to "direct Gov. Milliken to fire the Judge." State Senator Coleman Young, black Democrat of Detroit and soon to be the city's first black mayor, called the proceedings a "Senate lynching session" (*Detroit Free Press*, April 2, 1969).

Michigan's thirteen black legislators were not about to stand idly by and allow that to happen. In the midst of the Crockett controversy they did not allow the white public to forget the police storming of New Bethel Baptist Church and the resulting damage done to the $600,000 structure. After viewing the damage done to the church by police bullets, the three black senators and ten black representatives initiated a fund to repair the damage (*Michigan Chronicle*, April 12, 1969).

One black representative, Jackie Vaughn III, proposed that New Bethel Baptist Church be designated as a "shrine and place of pilgrimage for all people dedicated to freedom and civil liberty" (*Michigan Chronicle*, April 19, 1969). He suggested in a telegram to C. L. Franklin, the pastor of the church, "that March 30, the day of the shooting, be declared a 'day of infamy' in commemoration of the police 'attack' on the church" and that the church "be preserved as it was after the police had fired shots into doors, walls, furniture, the pulpit and pews" (*Michigan Chronicle*, April 19, 1969).

On the same day Milliken and Cavanagh made their public statements about Crockett, William T. Patrick (who had been Detroit's first black city council person and was now serving as president of New Detroit), along with a coalition of black groups, organized to protest what they described as a police invasion of the church. In a private letter to Judge Crockett a day after he released the prisoners, Patrick described him as "an authentic hero of these trying times" and his action as "a beacon of light" that probably prevented widespread racial confrontation throughout the city (*Detroit Free Press*, April 3, 1969). This was an obvious reference to the 1967 riot.

Patrick praised Crockett for his actions. "I view your historic actions of [Sunday] . . . as being another peak of achievement for you. Your insistence on the full utilization of the law as a servant of this community in a time of great stress was most remarkable." In another reference to the 1967 riot, Patrick wrote, "I think you may have spared our community most disastrous consequences as the result of your forthright stand" (*Detroit Free Press*, April 3, 1969).

While Patrick viewed Crockett's action as preventative of another possible race riot, Mayor Cavanagh justified the police raid on the black church and the mass arrests of blacks as the police's "only appropriate way." According to the mayor, "had any other tactics been used other than to quickly assemble a group and enter the building and try to effect the arrest of 150 people, then the chances of having maybe a full-scale riot or something equally serious were great" (*Detroit Free Press*, April 2, 1969).

The local chapter of the NAACP, with its long history of protesting police brutality in Detroit, also supported Crockett's decision to release the prisoners of the mass arrest. In a letter published in the April 12 issue of the *Michigan Chronicle*, the organization commended the judge for his "courageous action in helping to secure the release of many members of the black community who were arrested in connection with the New Bethel incident. Too often in the past, the voice of justice has been silent in order to permit certain highly questionable police procedures. That these procedures have been in derogation of the basic fundamental constitutional rights guaranteed to every citizen," the letter continued, "has meant little or nothing if the person detained was poor, black or ignorant. It is indeed comforting to know that such is not nor ever will be the case while you are Judge of the Recorder's Court" (*Michigan Chronicle*, April 12, 1969).

The letter mentioned attacks on Judge Crockett by the white news media. "We at the NAACP are well aware of the gross distortions reported by the news media and particularly the *Detroit News*, with reference to your handling of what was a potentially explosive situation. Absent your intervention, Detroit could well have been on its way to a repeat of 1967. That the news media chose to delete this from the consideration of the public is deplorable, but alas consistent with their efforts to discredit you in their hate campaign" (*Michigan Chronicle*, April 12, 1969).

The NAACP informed the judge that, by his actions, he had "helped to insure that there will be equal justice under the law for all people. We are proud that you have exhibited a fierce dedication to the principles upon which this great nation was founded in the face of the unwarranted attack by many who should support you. We are proud that you have shown us that the independence of the judiciary is essential to the concept of an orderly society. And lastly, but far from least, we are proud that you are Black" (*Michigan Chronicle*, April 12, 1969).

As hundreds of white policemen and their wives and supporters protested Judge Crockett's actions, a new black organization formed to protest the police action at the church and to support Judge Crockett. This new coalition group called itself the Black United Front (BUF) and was led by Dan Aldridge, who worked for the Detroit Commission on Children and Youth. Other members of the BUF included Black Panthers, the Wayne State University Association of Black Students, the Guardians (a black police officers group), the Eastside Voice of Independent Detroit, two black churches, and "representatives of Democratic Congressman Charles Diggs and John Conyers and State Rep. James Del Rio, D-Detroit" (*Michigan Chronicle*, April 12, 1969). The group was formed, Aldridge said, because "we are concerned with the inexcusable conduct of a police force [that] indiscriminately fired into a church and upon defenseless women and children" (*Michigan Chronicle*, April 12, 1969).

Letters to the editor of the two white daily newspapers revealed just how deeply these events had racially polarized the community. One reader wrote:

> It was with shock, anger and disgust I read of Judge Crockett's infamous behavior concerning the persons brought in for questioning in the case of two Detroit policemen. . . . When one in so high a place . . . uses his authority to exercise his personal bias, the people of Detroit should not sit idly by. This man has made a mockery of our judicial system.

Another reader had still another view of the events:

> It is small wonder that most black people in Detroit have little respect or love for the Detroit police. The latest police action in their private war against the black man was the invasion of a black church and indiscriminately shooting it up. . . . Is nothing sacred to the police? Does the fact that people are black give the police the license to kill or fire into a gathering of men, women and children under the pretext of law enforcement? There was no armed attack on the white church which sheltered a draft dodger. I wonder why. (*Detroit Free Press*, April 1, 1969)

The *Detroit News*, the more conservative of the two daily newspapers, questioned wherever Judge Crockett had abused his power. In an editorial, "An Abuse of Power?" the paper asked: "Have law enforcement and justice taken another beating from Recorder's Court Judge Crockett, Jr.? Certainly the judge owes the community an explanation of his disturbing conduct of last weekend. . . . It appears possible that in his haste to release the prisoners the judge may have stretched his own authority beyond its legal boundary" (April 1, 1969). After questioning the manner in which Crockett processed and finally released the majority of those arrested, the newspaper argued that the questions it raised, while not "all the questions by any means," were "sufficient . . . to justify an investigation into Judge Crockett's conduct by the state judicial tenure commission recently established to probe abuses of judicial power" (*Detroit News*, May 1, 1969).

In a *Detroit Free Press* editorial on Wednesday, April 2 (three days after the shooting), entitled "Let's See Each Other Instead of Stereotypes," the paper attempted to shed some light on the events. "The clamor growing out of last weekend's Linwood Avenue incident shows just how difficult it is for human beings to communicate across racial lines. It is so easy, at such a moment, to think strictly in racial stereotypes. The white man is tempted to see only a judge turning loose suspects after a policeman has been shot in cold blood. The black man is tempted to see only the invasion of a black church and the mass arrest of suspects and innocents alike" (*Detroit Free Press*, April 2, 1969). The editors then spoke to those of reason among black and white Detroiters:

The reasonable man—and Detroit can thank a kindly fate that there are still many reasonable men around—knows that the truth is more complicated. He knows that a man has been killed and five others wounded in a tragic incident. He knows that the black nationalists are peddling an empty doctrine and trying to stir up those who do not share their political views. He knows that most black citizens know this. He knows that it must have been scary beyond belief to be either inside or outside New Bethel Baptist Church. He knows and regrets deeply—that a church did get shot up and this is not the sort of thing we want to be happening.

The reasonable man knows that the police undoubtedly did swoop up some innocents . . . that the writ of habeas corpus was not intended to interfere with normal and routine investigation procedures. The reasonable man knows all these things, and he will keep the Linwood Avenue tragedy in perspective. The only further danger to Detroit from such an episode is that the reasonable men will let the stereotype-builders run away with things and drive us apart. Heaven knows we have had enough trouble understanding each other in the past.

Somewhere in human experience there must be the tools to bridge the chasm across which we so often glare at each other in righteous indignation. Somewhere there must be the wellspring of compassion that could make us weep ungrudgingly over a dead white policeman and over the injured, of whatever race.

 If we are not wary, though, this event—which should simply be an isolated human tragedy—will become larger then life. A white man's special truth will butt head on into a black man's special truth, and peace will be lost somewhere in the no-man's land between. No one has the right to feel self-righteous in this. Wrongs have been done, now and in the past. But we can—we must overcome them, do a little forgiving and try to make our city work. To paraphrase the words that are so much in the minds of Christians this week: Father forgive us, for we know not what we do to each other. (*Detroit Free Press*, April 2, 1969)

The clamor over the actions of Judge Crockett would continue in the media for some time, but meanwhile some parties were trying to educate the public as to the legality of his actions. On May 2, 1969, the New Detroit Board of Trustees adopted a report entitled, "The New Bethel Report: 'The Law on Trial,'" which emerged from a request from its Law Committee "to determine whether the administration of justice had functioned effectively in the aftermath of the tragedy" (*New Bethel Report*, 1969: 3). The report concluded, "Based upon our examination of the facts and law involved in this case, we are convinced that Judge Crockett's actions were taken in good faith with ample legal basic. We hope that this will end the matter" (*New Bethel Report*, 1969: 31). Unfortunately, it would not end the Detroit Police Officers Association's (DPOA) relentlessness (*Detroit News*, May 1, 1969; *Tuebor*, June and July 1969).

Changes in the attitudes of some of the news media played a role in ending the matter. As Warren points out, "The media coverage of events relating to the New Bethel shooting incident took on a somewhat different character following the initial controversy. The months of May and June brought several occurrences which had a potential for altering the original perceptions of the affair" (1972: 125). He referred to the *Detroit Free Press* admitting to "inaccuracies in its reporting of the incident: 'In the confusion that swirled around the courtroom proceeding that day [March 30] the facts of what took place were reported inaccurately by many media including this paper. We have since corrected these errors and we think they are human factors which explain, but the original inaccuracy cannot be excused. In part the error was ours and we regret it'" (Warren, 1972: 125).

On June 16, 1970, a jury of ten blacks and two whites voted for acquittal of the two men accused of shooting the two officers outside of New Bethel church (*Detroit Free Press*, June 17 and 18, 1970; *Detroit News*, June 16, 1970; *Michigan Chronicle*, June 27, 1970).

STOP THE ROBBERIES, ENJOY SAFE STREETS (STRESS)

A year later, the police and the black community were on another collision course.

The harsh realities of urban life in Detroit during the 1970s fostered continued racial tensions and conflicts between the growing black community and the predominantly white police department. Violence was on the rise, and as Georgakas and Surkin explain: "By 1970 the situation was clearly out of hand. There were more than 23,000 reported robberies, which meant that at least one out of every 65 Detroiters had been a victim. An army of drug addicts lived in the remains of 15,000 inner-city houses abandoned for an urban renewal program which never materialized" (1998: 167).

The worst part of this scenario was the alarming rise of gun ownership. "More than 1 million guns were in the hands of the population, and union officials estimated that half the workers came to the plants armed with one weapon or another." Add to this mix the related fact that, according to Georgakas and Surkin, by early 1971 "the atmosphere of permissiveness regarding police misconduct and the growing chaos in the streets had prepared the way for a new police unity called STRESS (Stop the Robberies, Enjoy Safe Streets). This unit was a secret, elite section of Detroit's undercover assault squads" (1998: 167).

The preferred policing method used by STRESS was the "decoy" operation, "in which one police officer acted as a potential victim in some area where a crime was likely to occur. As the decoy was attacked, other STRESS officers moved in for the arrest" (Georgakas and Surkin, 1998: 167). Most of the high-crime areas in which STRESS operated were predominantly black, which increased confrontations between the black community and the police. The decoy method, therefore, soon turned into a form of illegal entrapment, which resulted in a record number of police killing of blacks. For example, during its first year of operation the Detroit Police Department had the "highest number of civilian killings per capita of any

American police department. The Detroit police killed civilians a the rate of 7.17 per 1,000 officers in 1971. . . . More than one-third of the killings in Detroit were done by STRESS, which represented, at most 2 percent of the department" (Georgakas and Surkin, 1998: 168).

The unit was also accused of conducting 500 raids without the use of search warrants and killing twenty people within thirty months. In their own defense, STRESS officers countered that the disproportionate number of killings by their unit was because they were engaged in dangerous work fighting street crime "on the only terms that criminals understood." In fact, they felt that they deserved to be "commended for bravery rather than criticized" (Georgakas and Surkin, 1998: 168).

In its first year of existence STRESS had a checkered reputation. At the beginning the victims of crime welcomed the anticrime unit, but between January 13, 1971, and June 10, 1971, when their operation made its first report, fifteen people had been killed, of whom thirteen were black (*Michigan Chronicle*, June 10, 1972).

The worst case was the September 17 shooting death of two unarmed black teenagers, aged fifteen and sixteen, by STRESS officer Richard Worobec, who had been wounded during the New Bethel incident in 1969. Worobec claimed that he was attacked by the youths while he was acting as a drunk. He said he shot them as they fled after he identified himself as a police officer (*Benton Harbor News Palladium*, December 14, 1971; *Detroit Free Press*, December 14, 1971; *Detroit News*, December 14, 1971).

Some questioned whether Worobec volunteered for the unit because it would provide him the greatest opportunity to avenge the 1969 killing of his partner. Tom Turner, the black president of the Metropolitan Detroit AFL-CIO Council, raised the question in a letter to Mayor Gribbs concerning the STRESS program: "I do not want to prejudge Patrolman Worobec, but I do suggest that it may be a serious error of judgment to involve policemen who some believe may have old scores to settle" (*Michigan Chronicle*, June 10, 1971).

It did not take long for community groups to respond to STRESS's activities. On September 23, 1971, the State of Emergency Committee was formed to protest the killings of the two black youths. Thousands of people marched to demand the abolition of STRESS. On October 2, a memorandum by a city agency, the Detroit Commission on Community Relations, called for suspension of STRESS operations and asked that STRESS resources be transferred to other programs for citizen cooperation (*Michigan Chronicle*, June 10, 1971).

On December 13, 1971, the Michigan Civil Rights Commission held a press conference and issued the following statement:

> As a result of the expression of public concern following the September 17 slaying of two Detroit youths by a Detroit Police officer, the Michigan Civil Rights Commission directed that an investigation be conducted into the activities and procedures of . . . STRESS. . . . As of this date, eleven (11) citizens have been killed by STRESS officers. Ten of these fatalities occurred in instances where the decoy method was being employed. Ten of the eleven victims were black. . . . Our review disclosed that one officer and several of his partners participated in a total of seven of the eleven STRESS fatalities. This same officer had been involved in a relatively larger number of citizen-officer injury incidents prior to joining STRESS. Another officer was assigned to STRESS while awaiting a Trial Board Hearing on charges of mistreating a black prisoner, although he was subsequently exonerated. Police Department statistics indicate that crimes of robbery have decreased where STRESS has been assigned, but there is no indication that the decrease is attributable to the employment of the decoy techniques. (Michigan Civil Rights Commission, 1971)

As a result of its preliminary review, the Michigan Civil Rights Commission directed eight recommendations to the Detroit Police Department. The first one, "that the decoy method be immediately discontinued as a STRESS technique," and the sixth, "that the Michigan Civil Rights Commission staff will participate in human relations training programs, particularly for STRESS officers," were both rejected by John Nichols, the police commissioner (*Detroit News*, December 14, 1971).

Nichols wasted little time holding his own press conference to defend STRESS and the use of the decoy method. He said that the decoy method would be "retained because it was legal, properly managed and definitely effective." He claimed that the black community approved of STRESS "in its entirety" but said "some are falling prey to vociferous members of the community pretending to represent all black citizens" (*Detroit News*, December 14, 1971).

Not surprisingly, given the increase in crime in many black neighborhoods, some blacks agreed with Nichols's support of STRESS, but were concerned about its abuses. In his letter to the mayor, Turner pointed out that many black leaders had approved of the "innovative program," but notwithstanding their support, "he was uneasy about some aspects of STRESS." He accepted the fact that the decoy method was a "legitimate form of police protection," but he was "especially uneasy about a White police decoy in a Black neighborhood because it invites suspicion and provocation" (*Michigan Chronicle*, June 10, 1971).

Some blacks, however, did not fault STRESS, and criticized blacks who were protesting the abuses of STRESS instead of focusing on crime. In November 1971, a black columnist for the *Michigan Chronicle* described these protestors as "short on foresight." "The biggest issue in Detroit for the past four years has been crime in the streets," he wrote. "In recent months more aggressive enforcement, plus participation by citizens, has lessened the problem somewhat. The big controversy recently, of course, has been over the STRESS unit . . . the average citizen condones the STRESS operation when it isn't approached with a racist attitude" (*Michigan Chronicle*, October 16, 1971).

He reminded his readers that "there are Black officers in the STRESS unit, and according to this column's information, Blacks were there the night two youths were slain." For the writer, "law and order" was the real issue, and he "bore in mind that without law there is no order. And no matter how much havoc, hell and protest are stirred up, the police will prevail/ . . . To advocate that we abolish STRESS shows a lack of foresight on the part of many Blacks, even though they are justified in being concerned" (*Michigan Chronicle*, October 16, 1971). For this writer, "the real concern and the protest march should have been directed toward combating crime a couple of years ago. Perhaps then the young brothers would have been spared the need for STRESS decoys" (*Michigan Chronicle*, October 16, 1971). In short, the reporter's position was that the black youth were fully responsible for their slaying by a white police officer!

There is no doubt that crime in the black community was a major problem in the postriot period, but the writer seemed determined to pile all the blame upon the black community and excuse police abuse:

The civil disturbances of 1967 should remind Black people not to attempt to destroy something they can't replace. There is no merit in biting the hand that feeds you. Neither is there merit in destroying the forces that protect the community, especially when the majority of Blacks are afraid to join forces to protect themselves. . . . If you say "let the police do it," then cut out the complaining and shut up. (*Michigan Chronicle*, October 16, 1971)

In early March 1972, another confrontation between STRESS and the black community erupted, but with a complicated racial twist. In an incident called the "Rochester Street Massacre," three black STRESS officers claimed they saw a man with a gun enter an apartment building. He was later identified as a Wayne County sheriff's deputy. The STRESS unit called other police and together they entered the apartment, firing their weapons. All four were Wayne County sheriff's deputies. One man in the apartment was killed and three were seriously wounded. One deputy was shot six times as he stood with his back to the wall, and his hands in the air, holding his ID badge in his hand (Georgakas and Surkin, 1998). The deputies and the three STRESS police officers were in plain clothes. All were black (*Detroit Free Press*, March 10, 1972). In the end, three officers were indicted and acquitted (Georgakas and Surkin, 1998).

Although there were a few black police officers in STRESS, the Guardians of Michigan, an African American police officers association, demanded that STRESS be abolished. The Guardians joined thousands of blacks in an anti-STRESS march in the wake of the Rochester Street incident. Tom Moss, the president of the Guardians, argued that putting STRESS officers dressed as decoys on the street "is just like laying a $5 bill in the middle of the floor." Other members of the Guardians agreed. A former president claimed that "STRESS, by its mere existence, makes more criminal types out of members of the Black community. It uses Black people to put fear in the minds of so-called criminals" (*Michigan Chronicle*, March 18, 1972).

Notwithstanding the Guardians' position on STRESS, some black STRESS officers saw themselves as playing a vital role in fighting crime in the black community. While they did not mention the decoy method, they did see their role in STRESS as defending the black community from criminals. "'We're out here to serve the people," one black STRESS officer explained. "We all grew up in the ghetto. We know what its like to have some junkie come in and clean out your house. . . . The other day a junkie caught a lady with a baby in her arms coming out of a bank. He put a gun up to the baby's head and told the women to give him her money. Now, if he's desperate enough to do that to a baby you know what he'd do [to you]." Another STRESS officer said:

> That's why we lean on dope houses. Little six and seven year old kids tell us "that's the dope house." If you go through all the steps of the procedure to bust the cat . . . usually the worst thing that happens to him is a reduced charge of attempted possession and sale. We can't let guys like that feed off our people. So we go by and let him know we're on to him. We get a lot of "gas" from the department and we understand their point, but we're not going to let that guy operate if we can help it. . . . It's dangerous operating that way, but we get the job done. (*Michigan Chronicle*, May 20, 1972)

While some segments of the black community and liberal and radical groups were clamoring for the abolishment of STRESS, other segments—also concerned about the program's abuses—were worried about the rising crime rate in the city. A few weeks after the Rochester Street incident, the Interdenominational Ministerial Alliance of Detroit and Vicinity, which had a combined membership of 300,000, issued a statement: "The 1971 crime rate in the city of Detroit has brought to our realization the need for better protection of people and property in the city. Six hundred and ninety murders were committed in the city of Detroit last year. Of these, approximately 570 were committed by Blacks on Blacks" (*Michigan Chronicle*, April 8, 1972).

The ministers' group described the impact of the rising crime rate on their communities and families. "Our communities have been victimized to the extreme with muggings, breaking and entering, rapes, purse snatching, kidnappings and arsons," the ministers stated. They were particularly worried about the most vulnerable members of their communities and the decreasing sense of security. "Senior citizens, men, women and school children have been open prey for the criminal elements of our city. So much so, that many are afraid to go out day or night. Churches, schools, homes and places of business have all felt this menace— crime. Drug traffic is rampant in the schools, on the streets, and in the community in general" (*Michigan Chronicle*, April 8, 1972).

One of the ministers shared a story of how three black youth robbed him outside his church. "Three of them met me right outside the church doors early one evening. One had a deer rifle, and the other a handgun. They took my money, my watch and my Masonic ring. I didn't see three kids—I saw that great big deer rifle barrel" (*Michigan Chronicle*, April 8, 1972).

One would have thought that the ministers' group would have embraced STRESS unconditionally. Instead, they explained that their statement was not a "blanket endorsement of STRESS." One member of the group said, "We don't believe an honest investigation of the Rochester St. incident was conducted. We think an outside agency should investigate. We intend to ask for a grand jury investigation." Another member felt that "there should be a court case against STRESS. Let them prove themselves. We want nothing swept under the covers. There is something wrong there—all the pieces of the puzzle don't fit" (*Michigan Chronicle*, April 8, 1972).

Before the end of the year, another incident between STRESS officers and members of the black community grabbed the attention of the public. On December 4, 1972, four STRESS officers had a shootout with three young black men who, according to one source, "had been waging a private war against big-time heroin dealers in their neighborhoods" (Georgakas and Surkin, 1998: 206). While staking out a dope house that "three vigilantes" had attacked, STRESS went after the armed men instead of the dope pushers. During the resulting shootout four STRESS officers were wounded and the four armed black men escaped. Several weeks later, during a second shootout with the same black men, a STRESS officer was killed and another wounded. The armed black men escaped again (Georgakas and Surkin, 1998).

During the following weeks, "STRESS put the black neighborhoods under martial law in the most massive and ruthless police manhunt in Detroit history. Hundreds of black families had their doors literally broken down and their lives threatened by groups of white men in plain clothes who had no search warrants and often did not bother to identify themselves as police" (Georgakas and Surkin, 1998: 171).

This police action resulted in "56 fully documented cases of illegal procedure [being] brought against the department." Unfortunately, one black victim of this massive and illegal manhunt was a fifty-seven-year-old unemployed man who was killed by STRESS officers when he shot at them, believing they were a gang of robbers invading his home. On January 12, 1973, one of the black vigilantes, Hayward Brown, was finally captured. The other two were killed in a shootout with police in Atlanta (Georgakas and Surkin, 1998: 171).

The trial that followed featured the famous radical black lawyer Ken Cockrel, who, in defending his client, put STRESS on trial. In the process of defending Brown's participation in the one killing and several woundings, "Cockrel invoked the Algiers Motel, Cobo Hall I, Cobo Hall II, Veterans Memorial, New Bethel, the Rochester Street Massacre, and the whole record of STRESS and the Detroit Police Department" (Georgakas and Surkin, 1998: 171).

Brown was acquitted in 1972. He later became sort of a folk hero, speaking on radio and television. Some saw him and his companions as heroes who had "taken on a job that the STRESS squad, for all its bloody fingers, had not been able to handle" (Georgakas and Surkin, 1998).

The controversy over STRESS would not end until the election of Coleman Young, the first black mayor of Detroit, in 1973. During his mayoral campaign against John Nichols, Young focused on STRESS. "We want professionals, not Keystone Cops," he said (Rich, 1989: 104). Not surprisingly, blacks' votes for Young reflected their anger at STRESS, and three months into his first term as the first black mayor of Detroit, Young announced the disbanding of STRESS. This ended one of the bloodiest periods in black community-police relations in Detroit, but other confrontations were destined to arise as the city and the police department became more racially polarized.

THE BEATING DEATH OF MALICE GREEN, 1992–1997

Close to twenty years after Mayor Coleman Young closed down the STRESS operation, another highly racialized incident occurred. On November 5, 1992, two white police officers, Walter Budzyn and Larry Nevers, attempted to arrest a thirty-five-year-old black male named Malice Green outside a West Warren Avenue crack cocaine house. According to one newspaper report taken from police officials and witnesses, the two white plainclothes officers, in an unmarked car, stopped Green's car. They asked him for his driver's license. When he opened his door and glove box to get it, one of the officers, apparently suspicious of what was in Green's hand, asked him what he was holding and to let it go. One of the officers jumped into Green's car and started beating his hands with his flashlight while the other officer leaped into the car on the other side. By then Green, hanging half way out of his car, dropped what was his hand: a piece of paper. He was struck in the chest and, according to witnesses, appeared dazed (*Detroit News* and *Free Press*, November 7, 1992).

Soon other police arrived, including Sgt. Freddie Douglas, a black officer. According to some witnesses, "One of the arrivals, a white male officer, pulls Green off his seat and beats him with his fist in the face, chest and stomach. Another officer stands on Green's neck as handcuffs are put on. At least two other uniformed officers reportedly hit Green, who drops some keys" (*Detroit News* and *Free Press*, November 7, 1992).

The police then flagged down two EMS units. Once on the scene, one of the technicians sent a message to his supervisor, asking, "What should I do if I witness police brutality/murder?"

The incident caused Green to go into a seizure. He was rushed to Detroit Receiving Hospital, where he was dead on arrival. The Medical Examiner's Office reported that the cause of death was homicide from "blunt force trauma to the head" and that Green had sustained seventeen blows to his head, hands, and body (*Detroit News* and *Free Press*, November 7, 1992).

Budzyn and Nevers were charged with second-degree murder for their participation in Green's murder. Another white officer, Robert Lessnau, "was charged with assault to commit great bodily harm," and Freddie Douglas, the black officer, was "charged with manslaughter for allegedly failing to stop the officers" (*Detroit Free Press*, August 24, 1993).

Nevers and Budzyn were partners and were known on the streets by the nicknames Starsky and Hutch, the two characters of the popular cop TV show. Each of them had more than twenty-five citizen complaints filed against them during his career.

At the time of the fatal beating of Green, Budzyn, forty-seven, had been a policeman for nineteen years. In 1988 he was sued for an assault that cost the City of Detroit $10,000. A year earlier he had been named precinct patrol officer of the year.

Larry Nevers, fifty-two, had been on the police force for twenty-four years and had been sued "at least twice for alleged brutality." The city settled both suits. During the early 1970s he was a member of the controversial STRESS unit. According to Nevers's colleagues, however, he was a hardworking, aggressive cop. "He goes out and digs and looks for what's going on. . . . Everyone in the precinct, black and white, they want to work with Larry." Several hours after Green's death, Nevers told a *Free Press* reporter, "I must've done something wrong—a guy died" (*Detroit Free Press*, November 17, 1992).

This unfortunate incident took place in the wake of the Los Angles riots of 1992 brought about by the acquittal of white police officers who were videotaped beating black motorist Rodney King. In a city already burdened with a long and tragic history of racial conflict and racial polarization, it did not take long for the brutal murder of Malice Green by a white police officer to unleash anger and indignation within the black community. The well-known black minister Charles G. Adams wrote in his *Michigan Chronicle* column, "The high cost of racism is clearly evident in the brutal beating of Rodney King in Los Angeles and the heinous murder of Malice Green in Detroit. Look at the astronomical costs to those cities in terms of legal fees and claims! How many millions will Detroit have to pay because a few cops vented racial rage against a citizen they should have been protecting." Some white officers of the Detroit Police Department "have never accepted the fact that for almost 20 years they have had to work under the authority of African American leadership in the DPD and the city," Adams wrote. "When they saw Malice Green, they saw Coleman Young and tried their best to beat his brains out, costing the city millions of dollars in legal fees and claims" (*Michigan Chronicle*, November 18–24, 1992).

A day after the police killing of Green, mourners and protesters erected a makeshift shrine composed of posters, signs, flowers, and a soapbox where Green's death supposedly occurred. A few weeks later the shrine "began to overflow with offerings. Art work, handbills and mementos adorn[ed] the rundown building hovering over the site. Some spoke to specific business, political and other interests now hooked into the Green tragedy" (*Michigan Chronicle*, December 2–8, 1992).

As expected, Green's killing reverberated throughout the media. One writer from predominantly white Dearborn Heights wrote, "Why do the media portray the beating of Malice Green as racially motivated? Why are people in these stories described as black or white? It seems you are trying to turn this incident into something it is not." Another writer accused the media of having "done a great disservice to police officers" and shifted the blame for Green's death to Green himself. "If Green had to reach into his glove department to retrieve requested documents, he should have informed the officers of his intent. Once Green allegedly tried to hide his possession of an illegal substance from officers, and circumvent their seizure of the substance through physical resistance, any consequence resulting from his struggle lay at Green's feet alone." Reflecting an opposite view, another writer wrote, "I am appalled that two white officers beat one black motorist. This incident proves that white motorists are treated differently from black motorists by police officers." Another writer wrote, "Too often, as a European American, I forget the discrimination, unfairness and hate that many Americans put up with daily. I doubt a European American would have been treated the same way" (*Detroit Free Press*, November 17, 1992).

Soon after charges were filed against the four officers, two related issues emerged: a change of venue for the trial and the fact that few police officers in Detroit had ever been convicted of first- or second-degree murder. There was the possibility that a fight over a change of venue could happen, but according to legal officials at the time, "not since the infamous Algiers Motel incident during the 1967 riots has a major local criminal trial been removed from Detroit." They also could not recall a case "where an on-duty officer was convicted of any offense higher than manslaughter in the death of a civilian" (*Detroit Free Press*, November 17, 1992).

Blacks in Detroit had not forgotten how three young black men were shotgunned to death at close range in the motel by white police officers who also threw racial and sexual slurs at them. Nor could blacks forget how the initial police report falsely accused the victims of being snipers killed during a gun battle with police (Heresy, 1968). As if this was not enough to bear, in 1969 the black community had to endure the movement of the trial of one of the police officers charged with the murders to Mason, Michigan, a short distance from Lansing, where an all-white jury acquitted him (Fine, 1989). The lawyer for the police officer fully understood how to take advantage of the still seething postriot racial tension and conflicts at the time and admitted that he had no difficulty getting the trial moved to Mason. "It was a hot potato. The Recorder's Court was happy to get rid of it," he said. Once the trial was moved to Mason, the lawyer had no trouble getting an all-white jury. On the other hand, however, "'From the victims' perspective, and the prosecutors,' it was an uncomfortable atmosphere,'" he added (*Detroit Free Press*, November 18, 1992). Clearly this lawyer knew how to play the racial card to benefit his white client.

By 1992 the black community/police relationship had undergone radical changes. Detroit was a black majority city with blacks comprising 76 percent of its population. Community activists who had labored for decades against white police brutality could no longer claim that the DPD functioned as an occupying army. Notwithstanding these changes, there was yet some lingering doubt that the officers would be convicted of murder in the beating death of Green.

Serious questions surfaced during the preliminary examination of the four officers: "Was Green experiencing an 'adrenaline cocaine phenomenon' or were Detroit police officers overly aggressive? Did police officials wipe blood from Green's car?" (*Michigan Chronicle*, December 2–8, 1992). Green's longtime friend Ralph Fletcher, one of the last people to see him alive, testified that he saw Budzyn and Nevers "wiping blood off Green's car" and that "the car was pushed closer to the intersection" (*Michigan Chronicle*, December 16–22, 1992).

Defense attorneys wasted little time questioning "the credibility and characters of Green and . . . prosecution witnesses in the case." During cross examination by Michael B. Batchelor, a black lawyer representing Budzyn, Fletcher admitted that he permitted crack users to smoke crack in his home in exchange for cash. He also admitted that he did not witness Nevers hitting Green, but he did see Nevers swing his flashlight. It probably did not help the prosecution's case that an autopsy revealed cocaine and alcohol in Green's system. Yet when questioned by the defense attorneys, the medical examiner insisted that repeated blows to Green's head resulted in his death (*Michigan Chronicle*, December 2–8, 1992).

In late December the charge of involuntary manslaughter against Sgt. Freddie Douglas, the only black officer and supervisor present during the beating death of Green, was thrown out. The judge rejected the prosecutor's argument that Douglas could have saved Green's life had he intervened in the beating. Instead, the judge countered that the blows resulting in

Green's death could have been delivered before Douglas arrived on the scene. On hearing the judge's decision, an emotional Douglas "shuddered, rubbed his teary eyes and raised his folded hands in thankful prayer." Later he said, "I never gave up hope." The decision greatly upset Green's sister, who complained "why did they let him off. He should have stopped it. All he did was stand there and look." Douglas still faced a misdemeanor charge of neglect, however (*Detroit Free Press*, December 24, 1992).

According to Douglas's lawyer, the only reason his client was charged was because prosecutors were influenced by the beating of Rodney King and the riot that occurred in the wake of the officers' acquittal. He did not think the beating death of Green was racist, but believed that the charge against his client was racist because "the mayor and the prosecuting attorney for Wayne County decided to defuse a situation that could have been volatile and charge a black" (*Detroit Free Press*, December 24, 1992). People in the neighborhood where Green grew up and was so brutally murdered were divided over the charges against Douglas being dropped. Some argued that Douglas should have stopped the beating, while others argued that he did not hit Green and he did tell them—Budzyn and Nevers—to stop the beating (*Detroit Free Press*, December 24, 1992).

On December 23, 1992, in an attempt to settle a $61 million lawsuit over Green's death, the City of Detroit countered with a proposal of $5.1 million payment to fourteen members of his family. Less than a month later, U.S. District Court Judge Gerald Rosen blocked the settlement and on April 13, 1993, called the Green family lawyers greedy and refused to allow the city to pay the $5.1 million settlement. Legal fights over the money would continue for four more years.

For the next nine months Detroit became the center of the most intense racial drama in decades. On January 21, Judge George Crockett III, the son of the judge known for his intervention in the New Bethel incident, was selected to preside over the Recorder's Court trials. On two occasions, one in May and the other in June, Crockett denied defense lawyers' motions to move the trial out of Detroit. February brought more suspicion and drama when someone shot and killed Robert Knox, one of the witnesses to Green's beating. According to the police chief the shooting was drug-related (*Detroit Free Press*, August 26, 1993).

The trials began on June 2, 1993, with the selection of juries for Nevers and Budzyn. (Lessnau, the other white officer involved, accepted a nonjury trial to be decided by Crockett.) Eight days later, Nevers's jury selection was completed. A change of venue was requested again, and once again Crockett refused to move the trial out of Detroit. On June 16, Officer Budzyn's jury was ready to hear his case (*Detroit Free Press*, August 26, 1993).

As expected, much of the controversy surrounding the trial related to the coroner's report and the exact cause of Malice Green's death. Defense lawyers challenged Wayne Country assistant medical examiner Dr. Kalil Jiraki's testimony that Green died from fourteen blows from large flashlights. The medical experts for the defense countered that Green's death was caused by his cocaine use or, they conceded, by a combination of cocaine and the beating. One defense expert, Oakland County Chief Medical Examiner Ljubisa Dragovic, disagreed with Jiraki's autopsy. He argued that Green's brain was "wired up" from cocaine use and the police beating "triggered the massive seizure" that killed Green. After much prodding by a "relentless prosecutor," Dragovic reluctantly concluded that Green's death was a homicide (*Detroit Free Press*, July 27, 1993). Philadelphia medical examiner Haresh Mirchandani attributed Green's death to an irregular heartbeat "brought on by cocaine intoxication, blunt injuries to the head and physical and mental exertion" (*Detroit Free Press*, July 28, 1993).

On July 19 the prosecution rested its case against Budzyn, Nevers, and Lessnau. The following day, Budzyn testified, "I never hit anybody." When Nevers took the stand on August 3, he testified that he hit Green because he tried to grab Nevers's holstered gun, a claim that no doubt resonated with his supporters, who knew that Nevers had once almost been killed by a suspect who grabbed his gun (*Detroit Free Press*, August 26, 1993).

On August 9, the defense lawyers for Budzyn and Nevers saw an opportunity for mistrials because the films provided as entertainment for the jurors included *Malcolm X*, which showed scenes of the police beating of Rodney King in Los Angles. Their motions for mistrials were denied. On August 13, just four days later, the jury began its deliberation on a case that had already begun to divide the metropolitan community along racial lines. On August 23, the jury arrived at a verdict: Budzyn and Nevers were guilty of second-degree murder, Lessnau not guilty. A photo on the front page of the *Detroit Free Press* under the large headline, "IT WAS MURDER, JURIES RULE," graphically displayed the impact of the guilty verdict on the two officers: "After hearing they were found guilty, a sobbing Larry Nevers leans against the chair of a stoic Walter Budzyn in Detroit Recorder's Court on Monday" (*Detroit Free Press*, August 26, 1993).

Responses to the Verdicts

Susan Watson, an African American columnist for the *Detroit Free Press*, was moved by Nevers's display of emotion, but reserved most of her sentiment for Malice Green:

> It was hard to look at pictures of Larry Nevers and not feel a twinge of emotion. The veteran cop dropped his head into his hands and sobbed when jurors convicted him and his partner of murder in the death of Malice Green. Nevers' chest heaved, and he seemed to struggle for breath. The weight of the verdict physically overwhelmed him. It was sad, but sadder still is the fact that Malice Green is dead. I remembered that as I watched Nevers. After the verdicts were read, Nevers rose from his seat and left the courtroom. . . . As bleak as his life may seem right now, he still has tomorrow . . . he still has a chance to find some new meaning in life . . . And that's something that was denied Green when he had his encounter with a street version of the criminal justice system last November. (August 26, 1993)

Family Responses

Although Green's relatives were pleased with the verdict, they still felt a heavy sense of loss of a son, brother, father, and husband. His sister said they would not be satisfied until the officers were sentenced. Green's mother, while also pleased with the verdict, commented that it would not bring back her son. "I will never be able to see my son again. The officers' families will be able to visit them." One of Green's daughters added that the case had been "hard on all of us. They took our father away." One of the sisters reported that the most difficult part for the family was "just sitting listening to the testimony. . . . We were just praying before they read the verdict." Listening to Budyzn's testimony troubled her. "He didn't hear nothing, he didn't see nothing, and he didn't do nothing . . . I guess my brother got them 14 blow upside the head from the goddamn instrument in the car" (*Detroit Free Press*, August 26, 1993).

The relatives and friends of the convicted officers were also overwhelmed with emotion as they closed ranks around them. Budzyn's family vented their anger at the verdict. His daughter described how her father would do anything for anyone, and recalled how he used his own money to pay for hotel rooms to shelter battered women running from their attackers. Budzyn's father blamed his conviction on the jury of eleven blacks and one white. Budzyn's ex-wife rallied to his defense, saying that she thought it was "a sad day when five crack addicts can convict innocent police officers of second-degree murder." She felt that the jurors were intimidated by the possibility of a riot of the masses. "I feel that this jury found him guilty of second-degree murder to placate the masses. I don't understand what evidence they had. There was no blood on the flashlight. There was no blood on him" (*Detroit Free Press*, August 26, 1993).

After hearing the verdict Nevers went home and stayed inside, "sheltered behind blinds drawn tightly shut." He was visited by somber friends and relatives. His sister-in-law, who viewed the coverage of the verdict on television, said that they were devastated. When Nevers returned home from the court, she hugged him. "I don't think we even talked," she said (*Detroit Free Press*, August 26, 1993).

Police Response

It was expected that the verdict would have a powerful impact on police officers in Detroit and the suburbs. Given the history of racial tensions in Detroit and the dramatic change in the racial makeup of the police department during the Young administration, it was no wonder that the police reactions to the verdict reflected the social and racial fissures in the larger metropolitan society. Some officers speculated that Green's use of cocaine may have been a contributing factor to his death, echoing what medical experts for the defense had argued. Tom Schineider, a white policeman and head of the Detroit Police Officers Association (DPOA), issued a statement calling the guilty verdicts "a victory for the drug addicts, dope dealers, pimps and prostitutes," and claimed that the officers were not able to get a fair and impartial trial because of public statements by Mayor Young, Chief Stanley Knox, and the news media (*Detroit Free Press*, August 26, 1993).

Some police officers had different views on how much their colleagues' responses to the verdicts were racially based. One officer stated that "the black investigators feel the verdict was justified; the white ones feel the officers were just doing their jobs." Still another officer explained, "It definitely wasn't a black or white thing. It was a situation that got out of control, and they lost it. Every day there are blacks killing blacks in the streets of Detroit and that's the greatest injustice" (*Detroit Free Press*, August 24, 1993).

Notwithstanding the range of reactions to the verdicts among Detroit police, reflecting some racial sentiments, two newspaper writers reported that "the fatal beating of Malice Green and convictions of fired white officers Larry Nevers and Walter Budzyn have not worsened race relations in the department. In fact, some said the slaying brought officers closer together, sort of in an 'us-versus-criminal mentality'" (*Detroit Free Press*, August 28, 1993).

Predictably, the guilty verdict of the two white police officers generated much heat among letters to the newspapers. The letters revealed the vast difference—mainly racial—between those who supported the officers and those who did not. One letter writer wrote: "It is not by coincidence that the officers feel they did no wrong. They were nurtured in a society that told them they are superior to the African-American male, and their badges simply gave them a stamp of approval." Another writer felt the "trials were comparable to a black being tried before the Ku Klux Klan. The case should have been tried in Macomb or Oakland County." These were and still are mostly white areas. According to still another writer, "Malice Green was a victim of a society in which police officers are supposed to make us feel safe. The police who were supposed to protect Malice Green beat him to death. How safe does that make us feel?" Another writer blamed Green and his drug use for causing the officers to overreact and implied that the guilty verdict was motivated by the fear that a nonguilty verdict would have triggered a riot similar to the recent disorders in Los Angeles. "The officers may have used excessive force in gaining control of Malice Green, but shouldn't Green have been accountable for his actions? Without cocaine in his system would these officers have been on trial for murder? Were the verdicts rendered to prevent a riot in Detroit? Nevers and Budzyn were sacrificial lambs" (*Detroit Free Press*, August 28, 1993).

The *Detroit Free Press* can be credited with publishing a balanced editorial in the wake of yet another racial incident in the already racially polarized Detroit metropolitan community. "Justice appears to have been served by the murder convictions of two former Detroit police officers for the fatal beating of Malice Green," the editors wrote. "Although no one can properly take pleasure in the guilty verdicts, or in the horrifying events that led to them, the community can derive a measure of quiet satisfaction from the fact that its criminal justice system seems to have worked as it is supposed to work: openly and fairly." They praised the two officers for their years of service to the city and expressed sympathy for Nevers' sobbing response to the verdict. "Nevers and Budzyn were veteran officers who often distinguished themselves in tough jobs patrolling the city's mean streets. The image of Mr. Nevers burying his face in his hands and sobbing as his conviction was announced likely will prove indelible for many people who saw it." But, in balance, the editors added, "such matters in no way mitigate the officers' deadly, irreversible misconduct in the Green case. To suggest otherwise would do a disservice to all other police officers with equally dangerous and thankless jobs who do not illegally resort to fatal force to maintain public order" (*Detroit Free Press*, August 28, 1993).

The editorial did not stop there. "The Green trial suggests—again—that brutality remains a systemic, not individual, problem in the Detroit Police Department, despite marked overall improvements in police-community relations in the past 20 years. Monday's convictions will not erase that problem, and Detroit's next mayor will have to address it in a way that incumbent Coleman Young has not." The Detroit Recorder's Court juries were praised for their "diligence and patience throughout the long weeks of testimony and deliberations," and the prosecuting and defense attorneys were described as "sincere and passionate advocates for their positions." Judge George Crockett III "worked hard and generally well to manage his courtroom during the tense trials, although we disagreed with some of his harsh and peremptory orders to the news media. Other decisions by the judge are likely to be cited on appeal." Predictions of postverdict violence were overplayed, particularly given the fact that the juries were predominantly black and the judge was African American. "The verdicts in the Green case make counterproductive any extra-legal responses by Detroit—although predictions of such disturbances struck us as exaggerated. The trials were heard by an African-American judge and by juries whose composition reflected the community in which Mr. Green lived and died, bolstering the legitimacy of whatever verdicts were reached" (*Detroit Free Press*, August 24, 1993).

The editors ended with both a note of sadness and hope. "A dignified sadness would seem the most appropriate reaction to this personal and community tragedy. There is room for relief that the trails ended in a way that should inspire renewed confidence in Detroit's institutions of justice. But for the city, its police department—and especially for Malice Green and his family—the price of that renewal was unacceptably high" (*Detroit Free Press*, August 24, 1993).

The television coverage of the trial and the verdict was well balanced and avoided the temptation to exploit the situation, particularly the emotionally charged moment when the verdicts were announced. "As verdicts were rendered in the Malice Green trials, images from the courtroom were filled with a haunting, almost unbearable tension, especially when Larry Nevers was pronounced guilty of second-degree murder and emotionally unraveled before viewer's eyes." While it "was an incredibly dramatic TV slice of real life . . . to their credit, Detroit's local TV stations for the most part refused to exploit the drama." Carol Rueppel, news director of WVID-TV (Channel 4) said that they "wanted to be on top of the story, but not alarmist." Another news director, Mort Meisner of WJBK-TV (Channel 2), said, "You stay away from a lot of speculation." Even Bill Bonds, the white, "often flamboyant" anchor at WXYZ (Channel 7), reined himself in when he asked a reporter on the scene before the verdicts, "I'm not trying to hype this thing . . . but what's going on down there?"(*Detroit Free Press*, August 26, 1993).

In the wake of the verdicts expressions of joy combined with caution could be heard on Detroit's two major news radio stations, WQBH-AM (1400) and WCHB (1200), which served predominantly black audiences. After a review of the verdicts Martha Jean (the Queen) Steinberg, the very popular black WQBH radio personality, played a gospel song, "A Good Day." During her regular program of gospel music and commercials, however, she interspersed postverdict advice to her radio audience, cautioning them to "maintain calm." "I'm asking you to be real cool," she said (*Detroit Free Press*, August 26, 1993).

Talk radio WCBH provided blacks the opportunity to discuss the verdicts from their unique perspective. Most callers supported the guilty verdicts. Some accused the white media outlets of "conducting an inflammatory riot watch." For example, on the talk show the Reverend Wendell Anthony, president of the Detroit chapter of the NAACP, implied that "some in the media have done more inciting than informing" (*Detroit Free Press*, August 26, 1993). But, according to one reporter, "Local TV already had set the tone for restraint" (*Detroit Free Press*, August 26, 1993).

Protestors and Riot Prevention

In the tense moments after the verdicts were announced, several black community leaders stepped up to the plate to avert riots. As a crowd of 200 to 300 gathered around the spot where Green was beaten to death by the two convicted police officers, Rev. Darnell Taylor noticed that the crowd was growing and becoming unruly and out of control. He and others decided to take the crowd on a march. Soon Taylor was leading 150 people down West Warren toward a location where a teenager was killed by a policeman a month earlier "after allegedly pointing a gun at the officer." As Taylor led the crowd on the march, "they sang, laughed and called to spectators to join them. When they got to the site, they joined hands, formed a circle and prayed and sang. Then they dispersed—peacefully." Other community leaders as well as responsible members of the crowd also joined in to help keep the peace. As one reporter explained, "It was no accident; it was the preaching, cajoling at times, physical intervention of community leaders that kept the outpouring of emotions largely peaceful after the verdicts were announced. It was not always community activists who provided the leadership," he added, "Several times, provocateurs were restrained or shouted down by people in the crowd" (*Detroit Free Press*, August 28, 1993).

After the announcement of the verdicts, police strategy appeared to be to allow the protestors to vent their emotions. Warren Street, the site of Green's murder, was closed to traffic. Little wonder, therefore, that police chief Stanley Knox expressed his gratitude to community leaders like Taylor, "who constantly exhort[ed] the crowd to remain peaceful over a makeshift sound system rally organizers had set up. He simply drowned out rabble-rousers" (*Detroit Free Press*, August 28, 1993).

Posttrial Complications

At a news conference after the guilty verdicts were announced another drama began to unfold, adding yet another complication to the already racially tense postconviction mood of the city. The lone white member of the Walter Budzyn's jury complained that "duress" compelled him to vote to convict Budzyn of second-degree murder. "It was a very hard and difficult decision for me to make. . . . I didn't think it was proven, as far as intent," he said. While he always believed that Budzyn was guilty, he was not convinced that it was second-degree murder. It appeared that he blamed much of his duress on the pressure put on him by black jurors, claiming that after they screamed at him, he just gave in. According to this juror, there was intense discussion in the Budzyn's jury room during the last few days as the black jurors tried to convince him to side with them. "It was felt by some people, that because I was white and having an opposing view to theirs, they felt it was racial. But it definitely was not racially motivated in any way, shape or form" (*Detroit Free Press*, August 26, 1993).

The white juror claimed that racial tensions in the jury room increased after he remarked to the black jurors, "It seems like you people want to turn this into a Rodney King situation." Angry at the name-calling, he banged his hand into a door, causing bruises that were clearly visible during the news conference. Disappointed and angry because he did not hold out, he conceded that "in the end, the verdict sheet was in front of me and I just signed it, and said 'Boom, here it is.'" Although he had one last opportunity to change his mind when Judge Crocket III polled the jurors, he decided not to do so (*Detroit Free Press*, August 24 1993).

The white juror also called a WXYT-AM radio talk show to apologize for the verdict to Budzyn's lawyer, who was on the show. Later, the lawyer said, "The fact that he felt he owed an apology was an indication to me that maybe an injustice had been done." When the lawyer asked the juror if Budzyn had gotten a fair trial, the juror replied, "No." On hearing this, chief Recorder's Court judge Dalton Roberson responded, "I think he's . . . having some emotional problems with the verdict, and he needs to avail himself of our psychological counseling services." The juror turned down the offer, saying, "I don't think I am deranged or otherwise have lost my mental faculties . . . I definitely have some problems with the verdict that I came to" (*Detroit Free Press*, August 28, 1993).

The black jurors "were stunned" by the white juror's depiction of what happened in the jury room. One black juror said she and the white juror were "close, very close. We talked a lot . . . I never would have thought he would have done some of the things he is doing today."

They had sat near each other and discussed evidence together. "We didn't try to persuade him. What we did was put all the evidence before him" (*Detroit Free Press*, August 26, 1993).

Another black juror argued that race was not a factor. Instead, she claimed that the white juror tended to side with the police because of his years of military experience. She felt that he "initially put a lot of his feelings and beliefs into the decision. We kept telling him that he couldn't go by his beliefs, that you have to go by the facts and the decisions" (*Detroit Free Press*, August 24, 1993). One of the black jurors mentioned that the white juror told her that "because of the decision he made he was going to have to go home and face his people." She told him, "we all do" (*Detroit Free Press*, October 13, 1993).

The Sentencing of Budzyn and Nevers

On October 12, 1993, Detroit braced for the sentencing of Budzyn and Nevers. Before hearing his sentence, Nevers approached the bench and in an emotional voice told Judge George Crockett, "I never had the opportunity to express to the Green family my sincere apologies for the loss of their son, husband and father . . . Your honor, I did not kill Malice Green. I never intended to hurt him, to do anything to him other than to arrest him for a felony." Malice Green's stepdaughter was not moved by Nevers's apology. "He wasn't apologizing to me. He was trying to protect himself," she said.

Before he imposed the sentence on Nevers, Crockett told him, "Mr. Nevers, you were the senior officer that evening, the most experienced, the elder. Yours were the blows that resulted in the death of Malice Green. . . . What you did was excessive in the extreme" (*Detroit Free Press*, October 13, 1993).

Next it was Budzyn's turn to approach the bench before sentencing. Unlike his stoic reaction to his conviction months earlier, this time he "brushed away uncharacteristic tears and spoke quickly, almost inaudibly." He told the judge that he was sorry for what happened, that there was nothing that he could ever do to change it. "I was just doing my job and I was arresting him for narcotics. I never struck Mr. Green." When Crockett asked, "What do you mean, never?" Budzyn said, "I did not strike that man." Judge Crockett asked if he had hit Green on the knuckles and knees as he had testified at his trial. Budzyn replied that he had not, which contradicted his testimony. When asked if he had struck Green at all, he said, "No, sir." It took only a brief moment for Crockett to respond to this obvious contradiction. "Mr. Budzyn, I believe from the evidence I heard that you did in fact strike Mr. Green." In addition to striking Green and then contradicting his own testimony, Crockett held Budzyn responsible for Green's death by his inaction and failure to stop Nevers from beating Green (*Detroit Free Press*, October 13, 1993).

Seated in the front row of the courtroom, the Green family waited for the sentences to be announced. Malice Green's widow, Rose Mary Green, told Crockett, "It is time for the world to see through the excuses and face the truth—being black, unemployed and having used drugs did not kill Malice. Mr. Budzyn and Mr. Nevers killed my husband" (*Detroit Free Press*, October 13, 1993).

Judge Crockett sentenced Nevers to twelve to twenty-five years in prison, where he would have to spend no less than nine years and eight months in a maximum security prison before seeking parole. Budzyn received eight to eighteen years in prison with at least six years and five months in prison (*Detroit Free Press*, October 13, 1993).

The sentences aroused deep feelings among the families, friends, and supporters on both sides. Malice Green's father found little satisfaction in the sentence because he had lost a son forever. "No. I'm not satisfied, but what can I do? Nothing," he said. Budzyn's ex-wife had expected a lighter sentence and expressed disgust at the way in which he was portrayed. "I don't want to hear any more of this garbage. Walter Budzyn doesn't deserve this. Walter Budzyn is not going to do any eight years in jail. He's going to have people fighting for him," she exclaimed. Green's younger sister shared her family's anguish over how they had been treated since the verdicts. "We have been hurt and insulted by many who support these ex-officers and act as if my brother, who they never knew, did not have a right to live" (*Detroit Free Press*, October 13, 1993).

As expected, politicians shared their views on the sentences. A spokesman for the Macomb Coalition for Republicans—a largely white suburban organization—said, "We all watched the politicians and special interest groups in the form of Mayor Young and the NAACP railroad two people through the criminal justice system . . . this will go down as one of the saddest days in the city's history" (*Detroit Free Press*, October 13, 1993).

Judge Crockett acknowledged the conflicting and painful divisions as the result of his sentences, but voiced pride in both the city and the legal system. Before he rose to leave the bench, he addressed the courtroom:

> No one in this community will be completely satisfied with what has transpired this day. Mr. Green's family will never, ever see him again. The defendants' families will not see them. The circumstances that gave rise to the loss of life of Mr. Green touched all of us. I have abiding faith in the cool heads that live in this community, in its sense of fair justice and fair play. This trial has demonstrated this city is without peer in this nation. This is Detroit, Michigan. (*Detroit Free Press*, October 13, 1993)

Few people were surprised at the reactions to the sentences that predictably followed time-worn racial city/suburban pathways. Following the former white police officers' convictions, old racial antagonisms constantly resurfaced in the letters in newspapers and talk shows, revealing racial division between blacks and whites and city and suburban communities. Not that there had not been racial divisions before. There were still historic wounds that had barely healed from past racial conflicts going back to the 1967 riots and the days of STRESS. On October 13, the *Detroit Free Press* ran a huge headline, "Ex-cops get prison." Underneath this one ran another slightly smaller caption, "Episode tore open city's racial wounds." The writer reported that letters to newspapers showed "a deep division between black and white people, city and suburban community . . . church leaders say it's time for healing. It's time, they say, for making sure the fatal beating of Green doesn't leave a lasting rift between Detroit area black and white people" (*Detroit Free Press*, October 13, 1993).

In the midst of the storm of racial anger and frustration that followed in the wake of the sentences, there were steady voices calling for racial calm and reconciliation. These healing voices had always emerged during periods of racial conflicts. A resident of Wyandotte remarked that city and suburban residents should "stop being angry with one another and stop living in the past." Referring to the trials, verdicts, and sentences, she added, "The whole thing seems to have been made into a black and White issue rather than what it really is—people being punished for something they did. . . . People have to get past color and begin trusting each other again." The Reverend Edgar Vann, pastor of Detroit's Ebenezer Church, confessed that healing the recent rift in the community would not be easy, but believed that "if there's any entity that can heal, it's the church. . . . The church can bring stability to this community." The pastor planned to discuss the sentences in his next Sunday sermon and expected that other ministers would do the same. In his sermon he planned to make appeals for community restraint and offer prayers for the families of Green, Budzyn, and the city. Based on his firm faith in the role of the church to heal Detroit's racial wounds—particularly in the wake of the sentences—the pastor believed that churches had "a great role to play in terms of keeping people calm, of healing and of helping to disseminate the proper information" (*Detroit Free Press*, October 13, 1993).

Not everyone was convinced that Detroit's long-standing racial wounds could be healed anytime soon. Professor Lyn Lewis, chairperson of the sociology department at the University of Detroit–Mercy, said, "Before Malice Green, there was racial division, there was discrimination and there was prejudice in all sphere of life. And that stuff will remain. All we're seeing now is what has existed all along and now people have a Malice Green case around which to voice their opinions." Lewis was not convinced that the Green case would be "a forum in which people will heal the rift because people don't see themselves as being wounded. There are no politicians, no social scientist or community leader who can effectively bridge this gap" (*Detroit Free Press*, October 13, 1993).

Unfortunately, the professor was partially correct. Due to years of appeals and further legal actions, the Green case was prevented from becoming an effective forum for the healing of the racial wounds of the Detroit metro community. Instead, the opposing sides hardened their positions as the legal fight over the conviction of the two white ex-officers continued.

Retrials of Budzyn and Nevers

Both Budzyn and Nevers appealed their convictions, "alleging jury tainting, jury bias, errone-ous jury instruction, insufficient evidence and improper denial of a change of venue to lessen pre-trial media impact" (*Detroit News*, November 11, 1996). On July 31, 1997, the Michigan State Supreme Court agreed that the jury had been tainted, mainly by the showing of the *Malcolm X* film, and granted Budzyn a new trial. Their decision, however, only affected Budzyn's conviction because the evidence against him was less compelling than the evidence against Nevers (*Detroit News*, August 17, 1997). On March 19, 1998, he was retried and again found guilty, this time for the lesser crime of involuntary manslaughter. Unlike the predominantly black jury in the first trial drawn from predominantly black Detroit, accused by some Whites of racial bias, the jury for the retrial was more racially diverse, made up of eight whites, one Asian, and three blacks. This jury resulted from the merging of the Detroit and suburban Wayne County court systems ("White Ex-Officer Guilty in Black Motorist's Death," 1998). In January 1999, the Michigan Court of Appeals reinstated the earlier sentence of four to fif-teen years. Since Budzyn had already served the minimum under the first conviction, he was released (*Detroit Free Press*, January 13, 1999, April 19, 2000).

Nevers lost his 1997 appeal to the Michigan Supreme Court. However, he won his appeal in federal court, which overturned the verdict two years later. As in Budzyn's case, the court of appeals based it decision on the showing of *Malcolm X* in addition to the jury hearing about preparation for riots in case the white ex-officers were acquitted. The appeals court decision was then appealed to the U.S. Supreme Court, which allowed the decision to stand. In May

2000, Nevers was convicted of involuntary manslaughter and sentenced to seven to fifteen years in prison. Three years later, in March 2003, the state appeals court overturned this conviction. In September 2003, the conviction was upheld by the State Supreme Court. This long legal process finally ended for Nevers in 2001 (*Detroit Free Press*, September 23, 2003).

The protracted legal process weighted heavily on the families involved. During the retrial of Larry Nevers in March 2000, Malice Green's mother, Patricia Green, mentioned that the trials were causing her heart to fail and said that her doctor told her that she might not be able to sit through the trial. As a grieving mother, however, she felt very strongly that her son was murdered and that Nevers should return to prison. "This new trial just opens up new wounds," she said. "I can't get no rest and I know he's not resting" (*Detroit Free Press*, April 19, 2000).

CONCLUSION

Long before the 1967 riot, the racial practices of the Detroit Police Department towards the black community represented the single most important source of racial conflict in Detroit. In many ways it was a form of social control and intimidation that forced the Detroit branch of the NAACP to expend enormous energy processing complaints from black citizens about white police abuse.

In both the 1943 and the 1967 riots, many white police officers abused their power by brutalizing and killing black people. Police action sparked the 1967 riot. Racial conflict over police practices, for example, STRESS, played a key role in the election of Coleman Young, the first black mayor of Detroit. Yet Young's election and long tenure as mayor and his creation of a racially integrated police department did not prevent the brutal murder of a black motorist, Malice Green, by two white police officers.

CHAPTER 3

Racial Conflict over School Desegregation

THE PROGRESS OF BLACK STUDENTS TOWARDS ACADEMIC ACHIEVEMENT AND ATTAINMENT OF equality with their white counterparts is often framed within the context of the internal characteristics of the child's family or the structures of society that, regardless of family structure, may prohibit a child's mobility. This chapter examines both of these perspectives in the search for answers as to why black students did not achieve parity with white students in Detroit and the suburbs before the civil disorders of the 1960s—and have not achieved since those disorders. We first explain in more detail what each of the two positions, internal characteristics of family and structural constraints of society, suggests.

THE INTERNAL CHARACTERISTICS POSITION

The *internal characteristics* argument suggests that the individual family or student is the deciding factor in student academic achievement. A family and/or student must value hard work, a high degree of studying, and an appropriate investment of time and money, and success will follow. Moreover, any student (regardless of economic status, race, or ethnicity) can improve his or her educational performance through persistence, completing homework, and holding a passion for education (Zhou and Kim, 2007).

This view stresses a racial or an ethnic group's characteristics and behavioral patterns, including behaviors toward education, which are perpetuated from one generation to the next.

This argument is often used to explain the exceptional academic achievement of the children of Asian immigrants. Asian American children, even those from uneducated, low-skilled, and poor immigrant families and refugees, have not only exceeded children of African American and Latino families but have fared significantly better than white students in grade point averages (Zhou and Kim, 2007).

The major criticism of this argument is that it only "blames the victim," that is, the poor student and poor family, for not succeeding in school while ignoring structural constraints.

THE STRUCTURAL CONSTRAINTS POSITION

The *structural constraints* position suggests that there are differential constraints imposed on families and students that vary by class, race, ethnicity, and more importantly place *of residence*. These constraints are imposed on less powerful families (disproportionately poor black families) by the more powerful upper- and middle-class whites who control the institutions (including educational institutions). Moreover, these controlling groups shape the curriculum, the pupil assignments, the neighborhood attendance boundaries, the allocation of resources, and the race and ethnic composition of teachers. As a result, upper- and middle-class white students benefit academically at the expense of poor black students. Some researchers point out that many black students in cities such as Detroit have resided in concentrated poverty neighborhoods, that is, neighborhoods where at least 40 percent of the residents were poor (Jargowsky, 1997). These neighborhoods were also residentially segregated by race and class and excluded from the mainstream population (Darden, 2007a). They argue that these neighborhood conditions gave rise to self-defeating values and behaviors (Zhou and Kim, 2007: 2; Lewis, 1966). Instead of blaming the victim for not achieving academically, this argument attributes much of the problem *to the inequality in the public schools* by neighborhoods, resulting in disadvantages to black and Latino students in comparison to White students. These disadvantages occur throughout neighborhoods where poor black and Latino students are overrepresented in the public schools in the Detroit metropolitan area.

This chapter provides strong evidence for the structural constraints argument, resulting in the persistent inequality in the quality of schools attended by black students versus white students in the educational system. It also examines the role played by advocacy-based community organizations, such as the National Association for the Advancement of Colored People (NAACP).

RACIAL CONFLICT OVER SCHOOL DESEGREGATION
BEFORE THE CIVIL DISORDERS OF 1967

Racial conflict over school desegregation started before the civil disorders of 1967 and before Detroit became a predominantly black city. Unlike cities in the Deep South, which were experiencing de jure school segregation, that is, segregation by law, blacks in Detroit were experiencing de facto school segregation, that is, residential segregation and de jure segregation due to the actions of public officials.

As for *de facto school segregation* Detroit was highly segregated by neighborhood in 1960 (Darden, 2007c). Since students were required to attend public schools in their neighborhood, school segregation by race and class occurred. However, in some instances, school officials changed boundaries, or refused to eliminate the boundaries in order to maintain school segregation (Darden et al., 1987). To get the school board to act on desegregating the schools, the NAACP encouraged the end of neighborhood schools, and instead supported increased bussing of students, the distribution of experienced teachers throughout the school system, and citywide tests to compare educational opportunities and achievement of students in all parts of the educational system (Disbrow, 1968). It should be noted that this was before the civil disorders of 1967.

In fact, it was before 1967 that the NAACP accused school authorities of maintaining de facto segregation and called Detroit one of the United States' most racially segregated cities in respect to housing and school patterns (NAACP, 1963; Disbrow, 1968: 263). School officials denied that they had de facto segregation and pointed to their open school policy, the placement of Negro teachers in some all-white schools, and efforts to obtain better treatment of minority groups in textbooks (Detroit Board of Education, 1965; Disbrow 1968: 263).

The evidence suggests, however, that the Detroit Public Schools were racially segregated. Of the 271 schools in 1962, seventy-five (27.6 percent) were all white and eight (3 percent) were all black. Moreover, 26 percent were predominantly black public schools (table 1). According to Disbrow (1968: 244), "How local, state, and federal agencies met the problem would determine the health of the Detroit school system in the 1960s and thereafter."

In 1962, the Citizens Advisory Committee on Equal Educational Opportunities in Detroit Schools issued a report that included a recommendation to spend more money for "disadvantaged" students in depressed areas (Citizens Advisory Committee on Equal Educational Opportunities, 1962; Disbrow, 1968: 242). Thus, there was recognition that Detroit Public Schools were not equal on the basis of race or on the basis of class.

In 1962, five years before the riot, Detroit had nine administrative districts for 285,000 pupils attending 273 schools that were already racially segregated. To address the problem of de facto school segregation, the Citizens Advisory Committee on Equal Educational Opportunities recommended that existing boundary lines for neighborhood schools be retained, but kept flexible for administrative purposes. The Advisory Committee also recommended that certain pupils be allowed to attend any school in order to obtain the best possible specialized program (Citizens Advisory Committee on Equal Educational Opportunities, 1962; Disbrow, 1968: 242).

Opposition by the NAACP

The NAACP opposed the continuation of neighborhood school boundary lines, calling it *policy containment.* The allocation of black and white teachers was considered, and the Advisory Committee suggested the frequent moving of teachers into different types of socioeconomic neighborhoods (Disbrow, 1968: 242–43).

Since the *Brown v. Board of Education* Supreme Court decision in 1954, the NAACP had been urging an end to neighborhood schools in Detroit, requiring increased bussing of

Table 1. Racial segregation of Detroit Public Schools in 1962

Racial composition of school	Number of schools	Percentage of total
All white	75	27.6
All black	8	2.9
Predominantly white	29	10.7
Predominantly black	70	26.0
Racially mixed (integrated)	89	33.0
Total	271	100

Source: Computed by the authors from Disbrow (1968).

students, the distribution of experienced teachers throughout the school system, and citywide tests to compare educational opportunities and achievements of students in all parts of the educational system (NAACP, 1963).

RACIAL CONFLICT OVER SCHOOL DESEGREGATION AFTER THE CIVIL DISORDERS OF 1967

In 1968, almost two-thirds of black Detroit residents believed that blacks did not attend schools as good as those whites attended in Detroit. Schools within the city were worse in mostly black neighborhoods than in mostly white neighborhoods (Welch et al., 2001). Place of residence was a factor in school satisfaction. Among blacks and whites alike, living in the city and living in a neighborhood with a higher proportion of blacks were negatively related to evaluations of the schools (Welch et al., 2001). Despite black dissatisfaction with the schools, no action was taken to provide more resources to black schools, nor was action taken to desegregate the schools.

School Desegregation Efforts: The Legal Struggle by the NAACP

The segregation of schools clearly followed housing segregation. At the high school level, for example, in 1970 black students were in the minority (less than 50 percent of enrollment) only in schools located on the periphery of the city, adjacent to the suburbs (table 2). Also in 1970, of the thirty-seven school districts in Wayne County, thirty were 95 percent white, five were 48 percent to 82 percent white, and two were 15 percent to 22 percent white.

Therefore, on August 18, 1970, the Detroit branch of the NAACP and individual parents and students commenced action on the issue of segregation in the Detroit Public Schools. Defendants in the case were the Detroit Board of Education, its members, and its former

Table 2. High schools with less than 50 percent black enrollment in the city of Detroit, 1970

High school	*Percentage black*
Chadsey	34.2
Cody	10.7
Denby	4.2
Ford	25.0
Osborn	22.8
Redford	3.3
Southwestern	44.0
Western	45.0

Note: There were 21 total high schools, excluding Cass Technical.

Source: Michigan State Board of Education (1972b).

superintendent of schools; the governor, attorney general, State Board of Education, and the state superintendent of public instruction (Michigan State Board of Education, 1972a). Plaintiffs alleged that the Detroit public school system had been and still was segregated on the basis of race as a result of official policies and actions of the defendants and their predecessors in office. At the time the NAACP filed suit, out of a total of 308 schools, there were approximately 146 schools that were 90 percent or more black in student composition and approximately sixty-one schools that were 90 percent or more white.

Legal action commenced by the NAACP culminated in a ruling on September 27, 1971, by Judge Stephen Roth of the Eastern District of Michigan in favor of the plaintiffs. On October 4, 1971, Judge Roth ordered the State Board of Education to develop within 120 days a means by which de jure segregation might be eliminated in the Detroit Public Schools (Michigan State Board of Education, 1972a). Judge Roth described the city of Detroit in 1971 as a "conglomerate of poor blacks and poor whites plus the aged" (*Bradley v. Milliken*, 345 F. Supp. 914 (E. D. Mich. [1972]).

Thus, to desegregate the schools, on November 5, 1971, Judge Roth ordered that the Detroit Public Schools be desegregated by means of a *metropolitan plan*. He ordered that the racial proportions of each school reflect the racial proportions in the metropolitan district. At the time of the decision, the district proportion minority was 15 percent. Thus, no school population in the metropolitan school district was to deviate more than 15 percent above or 15 percent below the district percentage (Michigan State Board of Education, 1972b).

Racial Composition of Detroit Schools

At the time of the decision, of the total number of Detroit public schools, thirty were all black and eleven were all white (table 3) (Michigan State Board of Education, 1972b).

The percentage of black students to total students in Detroit in 1961 (prior to the civil disorders) was 45.8 percent, compared to 53.6 percent for the white students (Michigan State Board of Education, 1972b).

In 1970, following the civil disorders, the black student population had increased to 63.8 percent, while the white student population had decreased to 34.8 percent. The rapid increased segregation of Detroit schools in such a short time was unusual. Detroit experienced the largest percentage increase in black students of any major northern school district (Michigan State Board of Education, 1972b; see also *Bradley v. Milliken*).

Table 3. Racial composition of Detroit schools, 1961, 1967, and 1970

Number of schools with no black or no white students			
Year	No blacks	No whites	Total schools
1961	73	8	273
1967	15	16	296
1970	11	30	303

Source: Department of Intergroup Relations (1970).

The growth of the black population in the city increased racial isolation. Outside the city of Detroit, in the suburbs of the tri-county area (Wayne, Oakland, and Macomb), only 24,000 black students were enrolled in public schools, compared to 184,194 black students in the city schools in 1971.

There were eighty-seven school districts in the tri-county area. Of these districts, seventy-three had 95 percent or more white students, while Detroit had 63.8 percent black students and a decreasing white student population. The existence of racially segregated housing patterns locked black students into a segregated school system (Darden et al., 1987). (The nature of these housing patterns will be discussed in detail in chapter 6.)

The Desegregation Plan

The Detroit Board of Education submitted its school desegregation plan to the United States District Court on December 4, 1971. The Board concluded that "the only meaningful solution to the problems of racial isolation in Detroit Public Schools was the development of a metropolitan plan of desegregation" (Detroit Board of Education, 1971).

At the time, the city of Detroit had a total population of 1.5 million and a student population of 283,000. The student population had increased by 4,200 students from 1960 to 1970, although the total population had declined. Racially, however, the white student population had been steadily decreasing, while the black student population was increasing (table 4).

The Michigan State Board of Education stated reasons to oppose the Detroit school plan. It argued that a metropolitan plan (1) would accelerate white out-migration from Detroit, and (2) would not automatically bring about equality of educational opportunity (Michigan State Board of Education, 1972a). Nevertheless, because of the judge's order, the State Board of Education submitted a metropolitan school district desegregation plan (Michigan State Board of Education, 1972b).

This plan contained several alternatives and focused on the creation of a new educational authority and the abolition of thirty-seven existing school districts for the purpose of facilitating desegregation. The plan was defined to include all of the eighty-seven school districts and their student populations (exclusive of K-3 students) in the tri-county area of Wayne, Oakland, and Macomb in an activity that was designed to achieve desegregation through proportional distribution of racial populations, the reduction of racial isolation, and enhancement of the potential for improved educational quality (Michigan State Board of Education, 1972b).

Table 4. Total number and percentage of students in Detroit by race, 1961, 1967, and 1970

Year	*Black*	*%*	*White*	*%*	*Other*	*%*	*Total*
1961	130,765	45.8	153,046	53.6	1,701	0.6	285,512
1967	171,707	58.2	120,544	40.9	2,614	0.9	294,865
1970	184,194	63.8	100,717	34.8	4,832	1.4	289,743

Source: Department of Intergroup Relations (1970).

A key question was how much enhancement was to occur to improve educational quality. In addition to racially proportional representation in the schools that would reflect that the metropolitan area schools, the plan also provided for the following:

1. Equitable distribution of financial resources to all children in the region
2. A standard instructional salary schedule, thereby reducing the inequity between staff because of high remuneration in some districts
3. A higher degree of social integration
4. The opportunity for more community participation in decision-making in the school's activities
5. The opportunity for modifying the school curriculum through greater parental involvement
6. The opportunity to desegregate the teaching staffs
7. The opportunity to integrate housing in the metropolitan area. (Michigan State Board of Education, 1972a)

It is interesting that no specific mention was made of reducing the academic achievement *gap* between black and white students (Michigan State Board of Education, 1972b). Nevertheless, the plan was a positive step towards desegregating the Detroit Public Schools. However, the metropolitan desegregation plan was never implemented. The State of Michigan appealed Judge Roth's decision to the U.S. Supreme Court, which overruled the lower court in 1974.

THE *MILLIKEN V. BRADLEY* DECISION'S IMPACT ON DESEGREGATION

The *Milliken v. Bradley* U.S. Supreme Court decision in 1974 reduced bussing as an option for black students to attend predominantly white schools in the suburbs of Detroit. The Supreme Court based its decision on its view of the remedial policies of the federal courts. The court stated, "A federal remedial power may be exercised only on the basis of a constitutional violation and as with any equity case, the nature of the violation determines the scope of the remedy" (see *Swann v. Charlotte-Mecklenburg Board of Education*, 402 U.S. 1, 16 (1971). Specifically, the U.S. Supreme Court ruled:

> Before the boundaries of separate and autonomous school districts may be set aside by consolidating the separate units for remedial purposes or by imposing a cross-district remedy, it must be shown that there has been a constitutional violation within one district that produces a significant segregative effect in another district. Specifically, it must be shown that racially discriminatory acts of the state or local school districts, or a single school district have been a substantial cause of interdistrict segregation. (*Milliken v. Bradley,* 1974, 744–45)

The *Milliken v. Bradley* decision not only denied black children in Detroit and their parents the relief of interdistrict bussing, it denied them a judicial declaration that accurately described the full extent of their injury (Lawrence, 1977–78). The Supreme Court's refusal to involve white suburbs in remedying the school segregation in the city of Detroit marked a judicial retreat related to the Fourteenth Amendment in the face of strong white opposition to forced bussing (Lawrence, 1977). From the constitutional standpoint, no state shall deny to any person within its jurisdiction the equal protection of the laws. There are different ways such protection can be denied. One way is by the unequal distribution of a resource (education of equal quality via the public schools) to benefit one group (whites in the suburbs) while disadvantaging another group (blacks living in the city of Detroit) (see Estreicher, 2008: 244). The Supreme Court allowed the State of Michigan, whose principal responsibility is to produce public goods including education, to use artificial municipal boundaries as a barrier to trump equal protection for black and white students in the area of education.

It was the conclusion in the *Brown v. Board of Education* decision in 1954 that (*a*) racial segregation influences blacks by labeling them as inferior; (*b*) the existence of a racially segregated system operates to injure black students; and (*c*) once the state has successfully established and institutionalized racial segregation, the institution is self-perpetuating and need not be actively maintained (Lawrence, 1977). The evidence is overwhelming that the state, through its actions or inaction, enabled or allowed a racially segregated public school system in the city of Detroit. This resulted in *structural constraints* on the academic achievement of black students that continue to the present day.

Lawrence (1977) argues that the U.S. Supreme Court in the *Milliken v. Bradley* decision failed to accurately identify and articulate the nature of the injury inflicted by racial segregation, which is a reflection of the court's lack of commitment to achieving true equality for blacks.

Following the *Milliken v. Bradley* decision, the Detroit Public Schools became increasingly black and academically unequal compared to the predominantly white schools in the suburbs. In 1994, a civic group graded the Detroit School District's performance as a C in overall student success, a B in fiscal integrity and managerial accountability, and a C+ in community confidence. Student achievement in Detroit schools continues to lag behind that in Detroit's suburbs (Welch et al., 2001). Moreover, test scores of Detroit students on the Michigan Educational Assessment Program (MEAP) continue to be worse relative to white students in the tenth grade than they are in fourth grade, indicating that the deficit grows the longer students stay in the Detroit school system (Welch et al., 2001).

THE CURRENT CONFLICT OVER SCHOOL DESEGREGATION

In this section we examine the current conflict over the lack of school desegregation and its consequences more than forty years after the civil disorders of 1967 and more than thirty-five years after the *Milliken v. Bradley* decision of 1974.

Using comparative data we examine the racial composition of Detroit's public schools and the racial composition of public schools in Detroit's suburbs in Wayne, Oakland, and Macomb counties. We then compare the quality of Detroit's public schools with the quality of public schools in the suburbs. Data were obtained from http://greatschools.net, a national organization that rates public schools.

Racial Composition of Schools in 2008: Detroit versus the Suburbs

In 2008, Detroit's elementary schools were on average 86.3 percent black. Of the 135 elementary schools where data were provided, twenty-eight, or 21 percent of the schools, were 100 percent black. The middle schools in Detroit had an average black enrollment of 90.8 percent. Of the seventy-seven middle schools in the study, twelve, or 15 percent, were 100 percent black. Finally, Detroit's high schools were 90.2 percent black. Of the thirty-five high schools where data were available, none had a 100 percent black enrollment.

In ten of the elementary schools in Detroit, Hispanic enrollment exceeded 50 percent. Hispanics also constituted a majority in four of the middle schools and one of the high schools.

The average white enrollment was 4.4 percent in the elementary schools and 3.0 percent in the middle schools. A still lower percentage (2.8 percent) is enrolled in the high schools.

The Detroit Public Schools were clearly more racially segregated in 2008 than before, during, and after the civil disorders of 1967. While blacks constituted 86–90 percent of the school enrollment, whites represented 2.8–4.4 percent of the student body. The racial difference is a reflection of neighborhood of residence (city vs. suburbs). Whereas within the tri-county area (Wayne, Oakland, and Macomb), the majority of black students attend school in the city, the majority of white students attend school in the suburbs. The pattern of white suburbanization and the concentration of blacks in the city has been responsible for the new de facto school segregation.

More important than the racial composition of the schools in Detroit, with their overwhelming black enrollment, are (1) the degree of inequity in local funding between the Detroit Public Schools and school districts in the surrounding suburbs, and (2) the racial difference in academic achievement.

Funding Disparities between the Detroit School District and Surrounding Suburban Districts

In 1967–68, the year of the civil disorders in Detroit, data on funding in Detroit and other school districts in the state were provided by State of Michigan reports. The reports provided financial data based on state equalized valuation per resident pupil (Michigan Department of Education, 1968, 2004). The reports also provided data on general fund revenue per pupil by source (local or state). Additionally, data were provided on funding spent for total instruction per pupil and average teacher salaries per pupil.

We compared funding per pupil (local and state) and total instruction funding per pupil and average teacher salaries per pupil between the Detroit School District and the mean funding per pupil for each of the districts in the counties of Oakland, Macomb, and Wayne. We used ratios for each of the variables to compare disparities in 1967–68 and 2003–4. The results are revealed in table 5.

In 1967–68, funding from local sources in the Detroit School District exceeded the average funding for the suburban school districts in Wayne, Oakland, and Macomb. The ratio was 0.96 for local sources. However, by 2003–4, a wide funding gap between Detroit and the surrounding suburban districts had opened. Funding from local sources for suburban districts increased to more than twice the funding in Detroit. The ratio was 2.17 favoring the suburbs.

Table 5. Funding ratios in Detroit School District versus surrounding suburban school districts, 1967–1968 and 2003–2004

Year	Local sources per pupil	State sources per Pupil	Total instruction per pupil	Instruction salaries per pupil
1967–1968	0.96	1.06	0.94	0.97
2003–2004	2.17	0.84	0.81	0.82

Note: Ratios were as follows: a ratio of 1.0 = equal funding; a ratio of less than 1.0 = the funding for Detroit School District exceeds the mean funding for surrounding suburban districts; a ratio of greater than 1.0 = mean funding for suburban districts exceeds funding for Detroit district.

Source: Computed by the authors from data obtained from Michigan Department of Education (1968, 2004).

In some suburban districts, local funding per pupil was extremely high in comparison to Detroit. For example, the ratio was 6.5 in Birmingham, 4.5 in Farmington, 7.0 in Lamphere, 4.8 in Troy, 7.7 in Southfield, and 6.7 in Bloomfield Hills. The local funding disparity by district in 2003–4 ranged from .44 in Dearborn Heights (Detroit favored) to 7.7 in Southfield (suburb favored). However, state-level sources of funding per pupil between Detroit and the surrounding suburbs in 1967–68 was slightly higher on average in the suburbs. The ratio between state sources of funding per pupil was 1.06 in 1967–68 and declined to .84 in 2003–4. Thus, the Detroit School District received more state funding per pupil in 2003–4 than the surrounding suburban school districts. The Detroit School District was already receiving more funding per pupil for total instruction and instructional salaries than the suburban districts in 1967–68 and the gap in favor of the Detroit School District increased between 1967–68 and 2003–4. For example, the ratio for total instruction and instructional salaries changed from 0.94 to 0.81 for total instruction per pupil and from 0.97 to 0.82 for instructional salaries per pupil from 1967–68 to 2003–4 (table 5).

Differences in Academic Achievement between Detroit and Suburban School Districts, 2007

To assess differences in academic achievement, we compared MEAP scores. The tests were taken in October 2007. The MEAP tests reflected skills learned through the end of the previous year. MEAP scores are divided into four performance levels: advanced, proficient, partially proficient, and not proficient. Students who place in either the advanced or proficient levels are considered "proficient" in the subject. Those students who place in partially proficient or not proficient are deemed "not proficient."

Table 6 shows the mean MEAP scores for grades 3, 7, and 8 in math, reading, and writing for Detroit and the suburban districts in Oakland, Macomb, and Wayne counties. On each type of test, students in the Detroit School District scored lower, followed by students in Wayne County, followed by students in Macomb County. The highest-scoring students lived in Oakland County.

Another pattern was also revealed by the test scores. The disparity in math scores between students in the Detroit School District and the suburban school districts increased

Table 6. Percentage of students proficient on MEAP in Detroit School District and in the suburban districts of Wayne, Oakland, and Macomb counties, 2007

	Third grade			*Seventh grade*			*Eighth grade*		
	Math	Reading	Writing	Math	Reading	Writing	Math	Reading	Writing
Detroit	70.0	72.1	39.8	43.5	38.6	56.6	38.5	51.9	47.1
Oakland County	93.8	89.8	64.5	76.4	76.6	80.3	77.5	81.3	74.8
Macomb County	91.4	85.9	55.9	72.3	69.5	73.9	73.3	72.1	69.2
Wayne County	84.7	79.5	48.5	60.8	58.3	67.9	58.5	68.3	61.0

Source: Michigan Department of Education (2008).

from third grade to seventh grade to eight grade. In other words, the longer students remain in the Detroit Public Schools, the greater the academic achievement *gap* as measured by MEAP test scores.

Table 7 shows the racial disparity in academic achievement between Detroit and the suburban school districts. The mean ratio for third-grade students was 1.34 between Detroit and the Oakland County school districts. However, the mean ratio increased to 1.75 for seventh-grade students and 2.01 for eighth-grade students. A similar increase occurred between Detroit and the suburbs of Macomb and Wayne counties. A ratio of 2.01 means that students in the eighth grade in Oakland County had test scores that were twice the scores of students in Detroit.

Quality education remains a function of place. In August 2010 the state of Michigan issued its list of the ninety-two lowest-achieving schools (Michigan Department of Education, 2010). Schools with average combined reading and math proficiency rates that are among the lowest 105 of all public schools of the same type (elementary or middle) are considered low-performing. Whether a school makes adequate yearly progress and whether a secondary school has a graduation rate below 60 percent are also taken into consideration.

Of the ninety-two schools, forty-two (45.6 percent) were located in the Detroit School District. Moreover, among the 100 largest school districts in the United States, Detroit had the lowest graduation rate, at 42 percent (Greene and Winters, 2006).

Current Efforts to Address Disparities in Academic Achievement

Having failed to achieve equality in academic achievement for students in the Detroit Public Schools, despite its struggle to do so over more than forty years, the city has placed its most recent hope in charter schools. Detroit's DPS Renaissance 2012 Plan aims to transform the city's low academic achievement school system into a district that is smaller and with a "portfolio" of charter schools that are independently run (Dawsey, 2011). The DPS Renaissance 2012 Plan is a response to the continuous enrollment decline experienced by the city, especially during the years 2000 to 2010. The decline has led to the closure of 50 percent of the city's schools since 2005. More importantly, such a decline is probably related to the fact that the district continues to experience some of the worst national test scores among all large school districts (Great Schools.net, 2008, Dawsey, 2011). At the present time, there is

Table 7. Ratios of MEAP proficiency, Detroit School District versus suburban districts of Oakland, Macomb, and Wayne counties, 2007

	Third grade			*Seventh grade*			*Eighth grade*		
	Math	Reading	Writing	Math	Reading	Writing	Math	Reading	Writing
Detroit vs. Oakland County	1.34	1.24	1.62	1.75	1.97	1.41	2.01	1.56	1.58
Detroit vs. Macomb County	1.30	1.19	1.39	1.66	1.80	1.30	1.90	1.38	1.46
Detroit vs. Wayne County	1.21	1.10	1.21	1.39	1.51	1.19	1.51	1.31	1.29

Note: Ratios compare the percentage of students proficient on MEAP. A ratio less than 1.0 = suburban students scored lower than Detroit students; a ratio greater than 1.0 = suburban students scored higher than Detroit students.

Source: Computed by the authors from data obtained from the Michigan Department of Education (2008).

a lack of research-based evidence that charter schools will improve the academic achievement of students in Detroit. Instead, Frankenberg, Siegel-Hawley, and Wang (2010) argue, based on their research nationally, that charter schools have created an illusion of real choice without providing evidence of higher academic achievement for students. Moreover, an analysis of charter schools has revealed that they are more racially segregated than traditional public schools (Frankenberg, Siegel-Hawley, and Wang, 2010).

The data thus far indicate that Detroit's charter high schools underperform the city's traditional public schools. In 2009–10 just six of twenty-five charter schools had higher proficiency rates on the Michigan Merit Examination than those in Detroit's traditional public schools (*Huffington Post*, September 7, 2011). Yet the emergency manager for the Detroit Public Schools, Roy Roberts, continued in 2012 to rely on charter schools as the remedy for low academic achievement. He closed sixteen traditional public schools and converted four to charters in the spring of 2012 (Chambers, 2012).

CONCLUSIONS

This chapter examined the struggle over more than forty years for black students in the Detroit Public Schools to achieve equal academic achievement with white students in school districts within the Detroit metropolitan area. The metro area was defined as the suburban school districts of Oakland, Macomb, and Wayne. The period examined extended from the 1967 to 2011.

Efforts to raise academic achievement for black students in the Detroit metro area to the same level as white students were examined within the context of two perspectives. One perspective is the internal characteristics perspective, which attributes the lack of black academic achievement to family structure, values toward education, and lack of hard work. This perspective contributes less weight to structural barriers such as the race- and class-segregated and unequal public school system that exists in Detroit.

The other perspective is the structural perspective, which attributes greater weight to those unequal structures within the educational delivery system than to the characteristics of the black family. The evidence suggests that on most socioeconomic indicators, poverty, employment, housing, parental education, income, and occupational status, the black family is disadvantaged in comparison to the white family (Darden, Stokes, and Thomas, 2007). This disadvantaged status may play a role in the lower academic achievement of black students compared to white students in Detroit. However, the data suggest that a more important factor has been the structural barriers of a racially segregated and unequal educational system that contributes to the lower academic achievement of black students.

We have documented the extent of racial segregation in the schools and the inequity in the level of academic achievement. We have also emphasized the failure of the U.S. Supreme Court and the state of Michigan to remedy the segregation. By rejecting metropolitan school desegregation, the U.S. Supreme Court subjected black students in the Detroit Public Schools to *perpetual* school segregation and unequal academic achievement based on race. Thus, black students in the Detroit Public Schools have seen no improvement in their efforts to achieve equality since the civil disorders of 1967. Not only were black students in Detroit experiencing a racially separate and unequal educational system before and during the civil disorders of 1967, but the condition has worsened over time. Today black students in Detroit are more racially segregated than black students were before the *Brown v. Board of Education* decision in 1954, and they continue to receive an education that is separate from and unequal to that of their white counterparts.

Discussion of Options

For a period of more than forty years black students have remained in separate and unequal schools in the Detroit metropolitan area, and we believe based on past research that the future is not encouraging. There are two options. One option is to remain in the Detroit School District and put *hope* in the charter schools to raise academic achievement. As stated previously, there is little research to suggest that charter schools will actually raise the academic achievement of black students, especially those in very poor neighborhoods. The other option for black parents is to relocate to districts with high-achieving schools in the suburbs by changing their place of residence. Many choices exist for parents to select a high-achieving school district within the Detroit metropolitan area. Indeed the massive out-migration of residents from Detroit during 2000–2010 suggests that many parents have already chosen this option.

Unlike earlier decades discussed by Darden and colleagues (1987), the sharp race and income divide separating the city and the suburbs has been changing. Many suburbs have become more socioeconomically and racially diverse (U.S. Bureau of the Census, 2010; Logan and Stults, 2011). There are suburban public schools that provide opportunities for advancement that the Detroit Public Schools do not provide. They offer resources combined with a learning environment that is integrated by race and class. Research suggest such environments are more likely to raise students' academic achievement, aspirations, and expectations than schools in poor neighborhoods that are segregated by race and class (Tefera et al., 2011;

Frankenberg and Orfield, 2007). Thus, given the two options, we believe the second option is more promising.

Indeed, we believe the next major struggle for civil rights in education will be played out in the suburbs of Detroit with *place of residence* as the key remaining barrier to overcome. One example of note is the recent suit by a black family against the suburban, predominantly white school district of Grosse Pointe for kicking their children out of school in 2008. School officials said the family did not live in the district. The black family said their kids were removed because they were going to Grosse Pointe schools while black (Ashenfelter, 2011). The school district has denied the charges, stating that the district did an investigation of the residency of the black parents in 2008 and found out that the family rented a flat in Grosse Pointe Park but did not live there (Ashenfelter, 2011). Grosse Pointe Park police had been going to the black family's home and looking in their mailbox (Ashenfelter, 2011). The recent suit is the latest evidence of increasing racial conflict over school desegregation in suburban, predominantly white school districts. In 2005, parents in the district pressured the school officials to require every student to reestablish residency. Some critics of the action said it was motivated by race. Parents said they did not want nonresidents attending school in the district.

However, Governor Rick Snyder proposed a plan that would require every school district in the state to accept out-of-district students when space is available. Many white suburban residents of Grosse Pointe Park were opposed to the plan (Ashenfelter, 2011). However, we expect the conflict to continue as more black parents attempt to enroll their children in predominantly white suburban schools.

CHAPTER 4

Racial Conflict over Employment Discrimination

Rioting in Detroit provided one of the worst instances—so bad, in fact, that the events of July 24–28, 1967, will remain forever etched in my memory.

—LYNDON BAINES JOHNSON (1971: 167–68)

THE SIGNIFICANCE OF THE DETROIT RIOT

THE DETROIT RIOT WAS THE *ONLY* RIOT SINGLED OUT FOR COMMENT BY PRESIDENT Lyndon Johnson in nearly six hundred pages of detailed reflections on important political events of the 1960s (Feagin and Hahn, 1973).

The riot lasted a week. Between July 23, when the after-hours club in Detroit's ghetto was raided by the police, and August 1, when the curfew was lifted and the last government troops were withdrawn, the Detroit riot (even more than those in Los Angeles, Newark, Chicago, and Washington, D.C.) became the most serious act of collective violence on the part of black Americans in recent history (Feagin and Hahn, 1973). *Place mattered* in the location of the riot. The riot occurred in poor predominantly black neighborhoods. Black residents of riot-torn neighborhoods were sometimes joined by low-income whites in a type of integrated looting that was apparently the *first* of its kind in the recent history of urban violence (Locke, 1969). After the riot ended, forty-three people were dead and property damage exceeded $45 million (Eisenhower Foundation, 2007). Both figures were higher than in other cities where race-based riots occurred.

One of the primary reasons for the riot was *employment discrimination.* Such discrimination continues to result in racial conflict in Detroit. This chapter examines racial conflict over employment discrimination since the civil disorders by assessing the *disparity* in unemployment rates by racial group but more importantly by *place of residence* within the city and between the city and the suburbs. We argue that blacks have resided in neighborhoods where the opportunities for employment have been declining compared to the places where whites reside. In other words, blacks have continued to face what Kain (1968) termed *spatial mismatch.* This phenomenon occurred first between neighborhoods within the city and later between the city and the suburbs of Detroit. It is reasonable to hypothesize that this disadvantage in employment played a key role in the riot of 1967.

Factors Related to the Detroit Riot

We believe the riot in Detroit was related to three factors:

1. *Black concentration.* The riot occurred only in neighborhoods where blacks were in the demographic majority.
2. *High black unemployment.* The riots occurred in neighborhoods (census tracts) *where* the black average unemployment rate was significantly higher than the city average and the Detroit metropolitan area as a whole.
3. *Black frustration over the lack of change.* Blacks were increasingly demanding actions that would provide them with greater access to economic resources, that is, jobs, but their voices were not heard by those in positions of power.

SPATIAL MISMATCH AS A CONCEPTUAL FRAMEWORK

Kain (1968) was the first researcher to attribute the high rate of black unemployment to the high level of black residential segregation in the central city while jobs were increasingly relocating to the suburbs where whites had greater access. Between 1958 and 1982, Detroit lost 187,000 jobs, mostly in manufacturing and retail sectors, where blacks were disproportionately concentrated (Darden et al., 1987). A shortage of jobs in the area *where* most blacks resided contributed to higher rates of unemployment, lower wages, and greater transportation costs to blacks in their journey to work if they were employed (Ihlanfeldt and Sjoquist 1998).

Kain (1968) called the relationship between black residential segregation and a lack of black access to jobs the spatial mismatch hypothesis. Since Kain's study other researchers have analyzed black unemployment rates and residential segregation and found a correlation (Wilson, 1987; Kasarda, 1983, 1989). In 1992, Kain conducted an extensive literature review of fifty spatial mismatch studies and found that support for the hypothesis continued to be strong (Kain, 1992). In 1998, Ihlanfeldt and Sjoquist reviewed twenty-eight studies and concluded that twenty-one, or 75 percent, supported the hypothesis. More recently Stoll (2007) examined spatial mismatch between blacks, Hispanic, and whites and jobs and urban sprawl. He found that urban sprawl is positively and significantly related to spatial mismatch for blacks and to a lesser extent Latinos, but not for whites. Stoll (2007) predicted that as metropolitan areas become more sprawling, blacks and to a lesser extent Latinos will experience greater spatial isolation from employment.

THE BLACK RESPONSE TO EMPLOYMENT DISCRIMINATION

Although blacks in Detroit have responded to discrimination in employment in many ways (most nonviolent), the riot of 1967 was the most confrontational. According to Boskin (1969), the riots in Detroit and other cities were spontaneous outbursts of hostility towards ghetto conditions, that is, the neighborhood where the population lived, and towards those who were responsible for maintaining such disadvantages by denying them equal access to jobs. The two institutions that represented the white establishment, the police and businesses, were singled out for attack. Largely ignored, according to Boskin (1969), were libraries, schools, and civic buildings.

The Detroit riots revealed that black separatists tended to support violence as a means of achieving racial progress towards equality (Hahn, 1970). According to Boskin (1968), the Detroit disorders and other riots of the sixties can be interpreted as an exercise of will, the emergence of solidarity, of group consciousness. He argued that blacks expressed their hostility in violent ways because American society at large failed to allow blacks to participate as equals in a democratic nation.

According to Grimshaw (1969), as long as a subordinate group is willing to accept a lower status, an accommodative relationship between the dominant group and the subordinate group will prevail without violence. When, however, the subordinate group challenges or assaults the accommodative structure of inequality, or when the dominant group perceives that such an assault is occurring or is threatened, violence is likely to follow.

Based on surveys of residents on 12th Street and Clairmount, the core area of the Detroit riot, 86 percent of the black residents mentioned socioeconomic deprivation or racial discrimination as the underlying cause. As remedies to avert further rioting, the overwhelming majority stressed the need for programs to end discrimination, especially in employment, and to alter basic ghetto conditions (Feagin and Hahn, 1973). However, most white citizens and governmental leaders in Detroit believed the causes of the riot were outside agitators, criminals, or black extremists rather than overarching social and economic inequality based on race or the governmental structure of ghetto society (Feagin and Hahn, 1973). These different views about the causes of the riots reflect a continuing and increasing polarization of black and white perspectives on urban issues (Feagin and Hahn, 1973). They also lead to continuous racial conflict.

Most studies following the riots focused on the causes (Fogelson and Hill, 1968; Spilerman, 1970, 1971). Few studies have focused on the impact the riots may have had, the socioeconomic *changes* leading towards racial equality. This chapter expands our knowledge of that area by examining the changes in black unemployment during the period from 1967 to 2009.

To date, the studies that have examined the postriot effects have been short-run studies for the decade immediately surrounding the event (1960–1970) (Berkowitz, 1974). Our focus is on the long-term changes, if any. Berkowitz (1974) discusses the difficulties and challenges of such studies of change. Among their limitations is the lack of sufficient quantitative data to test hypotheses.

Unlike some studies that include a large number of socioeconomic variables (Berkowitz, 1974), we limit our discussion in this chapter to conflict over the *gap* between black and white unemployment by *place of residence*.

Objective

Our objective was to analyze any changes in black unemployment from 1960 (before the riot) to 2009 (i.e., almost a fifty-year period). The comparison will be made between (1) black unemployment and white unemployment, (2) unemployment in the neighborhoods (census tracts) where the riot occurred and the city as a whole, and (3) the census tracts where the riot occurred and the Detroit metropolitan area as a whole.

In terms of black unemployment, we will answer the question of whether much changed in the conditions of black unemployment following the 1967 riot in Detroit. We then examine the possible reasons for any changes or lack thereof. These may include continued discrimination in employment, deindustrialization, spatial mismatch, and a lack of a well-trained black workforce in an increasingly service-oriented economy.

We begin by examining the characteristics of the riot neighborhoods in Detroit.

THE CHARACTERISTICS OF THE RIOT NEIGHBORHOODS IN DETROIT

We argue that the characteristics of places of residence mattered in explaining why the riot occurred in some neighborhoods and not in others. Based on the report of the National Advisory Commission on Civil Disorders (1968), also referred to as the Kerner Commission Report, the civil disorders in Detroit occurred in sixty-four census tracts or neighborhoods. We compared the demographic characteristics of the neighborhoods where the disorders occurred with the city of Detroit and the metropolitan area as a whole. Any inequality by race can serve as an indicator of the possible reasons for the disorder.

According to the Kerner Commission Report, there were 215,438 nonwhites and 69,526 whites living in the riot neighborhoods. Thus, nonwhites (i.e., mostly blacks) constituted 75.6 percent of the population in the riot areas. There was little difference in the ages of the black and white working-age populations (i.e., fifteen to sixty-four). Indeed, 83.2 percent of the black population and 85.3 percent of the white population was between twenty-five and sixty-four. The younger (fifteen to twenty-four) age population constituted a small percentage among both blacks and whites. In the city of Detroit in 1970, only three years after the riot, whites still constituted a numerical majority (70.8 percent) among the total population of 1,670,144, in comparison to 24 percent in the riot neighborhoods. Thus, the overwhelming black concentration, or residentially segregated neighborhoods, were related to the riot location.

The rate of black males unemployed was 17 percent in the riot neighborhoods, slightly lower than the 18.1 percent for the city of Detroit and the metropolitan area as a whole. The key difference in unemployment was between blacks and whites. In the riot neighborhoods, the black male unemployment rate was 1.6 times the rate for white males. In the city as a whole the black male unemployment rate was 18.2 percent, or 2.4 times the rate for whites. In the metropolitan area as a whole, the black male unemployment rate was 18 percent, compared to a white male unemployment rate of only 6.1 percent. Thus, within the larger Detroit metropolitan region in 1970, racial inequality in the male unemployment rate was wide. Black males were almost three times more likely to be unemployed than white males. While black males were experiencing double-digit unemployment rates, whether in the riot neighborhoods, the city, or the entire metropolitan area, white males were experiencing unemployment rates that ranged from 10.7 percent in the riot neighborhoods to 6.1 in the metropolitan area as a whole.

Moreover, the black males who were employed were disproportionately working as laborers, service workers, and private household workers. White males were much less likely to be performing this type of low-wage work regardless of where they lived. In the riot neighborhoods, for example, 28.1 percent of black males were working in these jobs, compared to 14.8

percent of whites. Therefore, black males were 1.89 times more likely than white males living in the riot areas to be employed in low-status jobs.

In the city as a whole, the racial gap widens. While 28.2 percent of black males held these low-status jobs, only 11.6 percent of white males did, a black male–white male ratio of 2.4 in favor of white males. As one compares the metropolitan area as a whole, the gap between black and white males employed as laborers, service workers, and private household workers increases even more. While 28.6 percent of black males were employed in these low-status jobs, only 10.1 percent of white males were, a ratio of 2.8 in favor of white males. In 1970 (just three years after the riots), black males were almost three times more likely than white males to be employed as laborers, service workers, and private household workers.

In the next section we examine the extent to which racial discrimination in employment played a role in explaining (1) the racial gap in the male unemployment rates, (2) the racial gap in the representation of employed males in low-status jobs, and (3) the extent to which changes in the gaps between blacks and white occurred between 1970 and 2008.

We first examine the profile of the rioter based on the Kerner Commission Report.

THE CHARACTERISTICS OF THE RIOTER IN DETROIT

The Kerner Commission described the typical rioter in the summer of 1967 as a Negro male, unmarried and between the ages of fifteen and twenty-four. He was not an immigrant or recent migrant from another state. Instead, he was born in Michigan and was a lifelong resident of Detroit. He had attended high school. But importantly, he was more likely to be working in a menial or low-status job. This was also true, however, for those blacks who did not actually participate in the riot (National Advisory Commission on Civil Disorders, 1968). If the participant in the riot was employed, he was not working full-time, and his employment was not secure, that is, he was frequently unemployed for periods of time. Furthermore, he felt that discrimination prevented him from getting a better job. In other words, he did not feel that his unemployment, low-status employment, or irregular employment was due to his lack of training, ability, or ambition. Instead, it was because of discrimination by employers (National Advisory Commission on Civil Disorders, 1968).

Forces Related to the Geographic Location of the Riot

We emphasize that *place mattered.* The riot in Detroit was not citywide. Instead, it was localized geographically to particular neighborhoods or census tracts. Other researchers have come to similar conclusions (Berkowitz, 1974; Feagin and Hahn, 1973; Fogelson and Hill, 1968).

The Detroit riot of 1967 received a weighted index of riot intensity score of 1049 by Havlick and Wade (1969). The score was based on the length of the riot, numbers killed, injured, and arrested, and the presence of the National Guard. Thus, the Detroit riot was one of the most severe riots in the country (Berkowitz, 1974).

The Detroit Riot and Black Residential Concentration

Place of residence of the black population is very important in understanding the origin of the riot. By 1960, much of the black population had relocated to the ghettos on the east and west sides of Detroit. The concentration to the northwest became the area where the *core of the riot* occurred. This is the 12th Street and Clairmount neighborhood and is where the riot began (Herman, 2002). Most of the disturbance was geographically located in these east and west-side areas. According to Herman (2002), with few exceptions the vast majority of deaths took place in census tracts (neighborhoods) where the black population had increased by more than 20 percent from 1950 to 1960. This led him to argue that "ethnic succession was the leading explanation for the riot violence." There were thirty-three census tracts that contained a riot fatality, and those tracts had an average black population increase of 44.6 percent, compared to a 13 percent increase for the city as a whole (Herman, 2002). Thus, while the black population was increasing in the city of Detroit generally, the neighborhoods where riot deaths occurred had a significantly greater rate of black population increase. Herman (2002) points out that by 1960, tracts (neighborhoods) that had riot deaths had a significantly larger average black population percentage (63 percent compared to 26 percent) and a significantly smaller average white population percentage (37 percent vs. 74.1 percent) than city areas with no riot fatalities.

Herman's (2002) argument lends support to Spilerman's (1970, 1971) hypothesis that the rioting was associated with black population size. Herman (2002) concludes that Detroit census tracts where riot violence occurred were clearly related to the exodus of whites from the neighborhoods and the immigration of blacks into them.

In terms of economic indicators, Detroit tracts (neighborhoods) with deaths due to the riots had a significantly larger average male unemployment rate (14.6 percent vs. 10.6 percent). Thus, conflict over employment or the lack of it was a key factor in the *location of the riot*, according to Herman (2002). Not surprisingly, there was an inverse relationship between riot violence and economic well-being as measured by the percentage of black males unemployed. However, Herman (2002) found using regression analysis that the percentage of black males unemployed did not have a significant effect on the dependent variable (riot deaths) when controlling for racial composition. Thus, Herman reiterates that the *location* of riot violence in Detroit was a function of black population size (concentration of blacks, i.e., segregation by place of residence). Although blacks were in the demographic majority in certain neighborhoods, they lacked the political power to make economic changes in their quality of life. Thus, many blacks became increasingly frustrated.

The situation according to Herman (2002) can be described this way: Detroit had black majorities in some neighborhoods, but the city was still governed by white politicians and white police administrations. Jobs were rarely available (i.e., without discrimination by race), and unemployment was extremely high, especially among black males.

According to Sugrue (1996), the riot in Detroit was related to both discrimination in employment and deindustrialization (both resulting in fewer jobs available to blacks). Growing resentment, related to increasing black militancy in the black community, especially among young black males, led directly to the riot (Sugrue, 1996).

It is true that at the time of the riot in Detroit, industrial decline was evident and black workers were experiencing the effects differentially (Herman, 2002). In 1960, that is, before the riot, 16 percent of blacks across the city, but only 5.8 percent of whites, were out of work, which means that blacks were 2.7 times more likely to be unemployed than whites. In motor vehicle production, a high-paying form of work, the black/white gap was even greater. In this industry, 19.7 percent of black autoworkers were unemployed, compared to only 5.8 percent of whites, a ratio of 3.4. In other words, blacks were more than three times more likely to be unemployed than whites (Herman, 2002).

Thus, by the time of the riot in 1967, a permanent class of blacks had emerged in Detroit: the "long-term unemployed" (Sugrue, 1996). Young blacks (that is, ages fifteen to twenty-four) were the most impacted by economic restructuring, and it was they who would become the key participants in the riots (Herman, 2002). The combination of discrimination in employment and economic restructuring created barriers to upward mobility of young black men in particular. Those affected most were blacks with no postsecondary education. These blacks became increasingly angry, hopeless, and tired of waiting for the "dream of prosperity" that continued to be deferred: the ultimate outcome was the explosion in 1967 (Sugrue, 1996).

In sum, based on past research combined with data on the correlation of race with unemployment and place of residence, we argue that two factors, namely black concentration and high black unemployment, were primary factors contributing to the riot. For the remaining section of this chapter, we examine these factors in more detail.

BLACK RESIDENTIAL CONCENTRATION AND BLACK UNEMPLOYMENT

Consistent with our conceptual framework of spatial mismatch (Kain, 1968) high black concentration posed a disadvantage for blacks in the area of employment in Detroit. Kain (1968) argued that a mismatch exists between labor supply and labor demand because more employment opportunities were available in the suburbs (i.e., outside the central city), where few blacks lived (Tiggs and Tootle, 1993). The spatial mismatch problem continued after the riot.

According to Deskins (1988), new automobile plants were located beyond or on the edge of the normal commuting distance that manufacturing employees generally travel. Since most blacks resided in Detroit, the distance to work sites served as a factor in the lower representation of black workers in those suburban plants. Deskins (1988) showed that the further these new plants were located from the black population, the greater the investment in the plants.

However, some researchers argue that black unemployment has less to do with space or location of jobs than with discrimination by employers and coworkers. This means that even if blacks are located outside of concentrated areas of the central city, they still face discrimination by suburban employers and coworkers (Kirschenman and Neckerman, 1991). We agree that spatial mismatch is related to both place and race.

Data from the University of Michigan's Detroit Area Study conducted in 1993 reveal that blacks from Detroit may not have searched for work frequently in the outlying suburbs where jobs were available. There is also some evidence of skills mismatch. Some employers have stated that many black applicants do not meet their standards. Finally, there is evidence of a reluctance among suburban employers to hire black applicants. In this sense place and race both matter. Suburban employers have a preference for white workers and thus discriminate against black workers (Farley, Danziger, and Holzer, 2000). The outcome is as follows: most blacks remain concentrated residentially in the city of Detroit, while most jobs for which most blacks are qualified to be hired, such as manufacturing jobs, continue to relocate to the suburbs. Given that most blacks search for jobs close to home, they are disadvantaged. Blacks are disadvantaged again because suburban employers prefer to hire white workers (Farley, Danziger, and Holzer, 2000). Many of these white workers also reside in the suburbs rather than in the city of Detroit. Just as blacks believed immediately following the riots of 1967, most blacks in Detroit (84 percent) still believed in 1990 that racial discrimination is the primary reason for their lower status than whites (Farley, Danziger and Holzer, 2000). Most black men perceive extensive discrimination in the labor market. On the other hand, most whites believe there is some discrimination in the labor market, but much less than blacks observe (Farley, Danziger, and Holzer 2000). Although Farley, Danziger, and Holzer (2000) cite the results of surveys to assess *perceived* discrimination, another way to measure perceived discrimination is by complaints to government agencies. A weakness of complaint data, however, is that they underrepresent the actual problem because some individuals who may have been discriminated against do not file a complaint. Nevertheless, such data can serve as an indicator of a potential problem that needs attention since perception in the eyes of the complainant may be just as important as real discrimination.

Michigan had already established a civil rights commission in 1964, three years before the riot. Its mission was to protect, investigate, and secure civil rights in the fields of employment, education, housing, and public accommodations (Michigan Civil Rights Commission, 1969). The commission was charged with the constitutional and legal responsibility to investigate alleged discrimination against any person because of race, color, religion, or national origin, and in employment (and later on the basis of age or sex) (Michigan Civil Rights Commission, 1969).

Since its inception, the largest percentage of complaints received by the commission has been in the area of employment discrimination. In 1968, a year after the riots, there were 1,440 employment discrimination complaints filed in Michigan, representing 71 percent of all complaints filed with the commission that year. Employment complaints alleged discrimination in refusal to hire or to promote, and in unequal working conditions.

Racial discrimination represented the largest percentage of complaints against employers (80.3 percent). Most (two-thirds) were by blacks in the Detroit metropolitan area (Wayne, Oakland, and Macomb counties). Employment complaints followed the occupational pattern of the black occupational distribution in the labor force. Fifty-six percent of all complaints were in the operative, service, and labor occupations, with the highest percentage (29.4 percent) among operatives (Michigan Civil Rights Commission, 1969). At least 35 percent of those reporting discrimination were high school graduates, and 27 percent had achieved an educational level between ninth and eleventh grade.

Forty years later, employment discrimination complaints constituted 80.4 percent of all complaints (Michigan Department of Civil Rights, 2008), an increase from 71 percent in 1968. The percentage of complaints due to race declined, however, from 80.3 percent to 37.6 percent. The number of complaints based on race actually increased from 1,157 in 1968 to 5,612 in 2006.

The Nature of Employer Discrimination

Studies suggest that employer discrimination may be subtle and indirect and related to what employers perceive as their labor needs, and the perception of the white employer as to whether the black male applicant can meet them. In our service-oriented economy, employers are increasingly demanding "soft skills" from their workers, and many white employers perceive black men as lacking in those skills. Soft skills are social skills, as opposed to technical skills. They involve the ability to interact with customers and managers. According to Moss and Tilly (1996), the employers placing the greatest emphasis on soft skills are those most likely to have negative views of black men as workers. The authors indicated that employers' perceptions of black men are partly based on stereotypes, partly cultural differences, and partly the poor skills that many less-educated black men bring to the labor market.

In surveys conducted by Moss and Tilly (1996) in Detroit, some managers in retail stores perceived black men as difficult to control. A lot of times people are intimidated by black men, and as one respondent stated, "I am not going to hire that person" (Moss and Tilly, 1996: 261). Since employer assessments of a potential worker's soft skills are subjective, the authors suggest that the possibility of racial discrimination enters such assessments.

In addition to the perception that some black men are intimidating, there is the negative perception held by some employers that black men do not have a strong work ethic when compared to immigrant workers. According to Moss and Tilly (1996), 81 percent of the respondents in a survey in Detroit had that perception. Perception aside, Darity and Mason (1998) reveal a body of evidence on actual employment discrimination, despite the presence of antidiscrimination laws. The authors present a sampling of court cases and audit studies to document the persistence of employment discrimination against blacks.

DISCUSSION: THE POSTRIOT CHANGES

In 1967 in the city of Detroit, blacks experienced an unusual rate of unemployment that was near but not quite double digits. The black rate of unemployment was more than three times higher than their white counterparts. This disparity was evident in the city as well as in the metropolitan area as a whole (table 8). By 1971, black unemployment rates had reached double-digit levels in the city and the metropolitan area, rising to 33.5 percent in 1982 in Detroit and 33.2 percent in the Detroit metropolitan area (Fosu, 1988). This unemployment rate was higher than that for the total labor force in the nation in 1932, the depths of the Great Depression (Gregory, 1984).

Since 1982, the black unemployment rate has declined in the city and in the metropolitan area, dropping to the average rate of 20 percent. The black unemployment rate in 2009 was 23.8 percent, compared to a white rate of 15.0 percent, a ratio of 1.6 in the city. Thus, since 1967, the black unemployment rate in Detroit has increased from 9.8 percent to 23.8 percent, or by 14 percentage points. The white unemployment rate has also increased (reflecting a declining overall economy in the state) from 2.9 percent to 15.0 percent, or by 12.1 percentage points. Therefore, the racial disparity gap narrowed from a ratio of 3.4 to 1.6 between 1967 and 2009 (table 9). In the Detroit metropolitan area the black unemployment rate increased from 10.9 to 20.9, or by 10 percentage points. The white unemployment rate also increased from 3.2 to 8.9, or by 5.7 percentage points. Although both blacks and whites have experienced increases in unemployment rates since 1967, the racial disparity gap decreased from a ratio of 3.4 to 2.3. Although some progress has been made in reducing the black-white unemployment gap since the riot of 1967, blacks are still more than twice as likely as their white counterparts to be unemployed in the Detroit metropolitan area more than forty years after the riot.

Table 8. **Racial, age, and unemployment characteristics of riot areas, of city of Detroit, and of metropolitan area, 1970 (%)**

Black male	*White male*	*Black male*	*White male*	*Black male*	*White male*
Riot areas		City of Detroit		Metropolitan area	
75.6	24.4	29.2	70.8	15.0	85.0
Working age 15–24					
16.7	14.7	2.2	19.1	18.6	18.8
Working age 25–64					
83.2	85.3	97.8	81.0	81.3	81.2
Percent males unemployed					
17.0	10.7	18.2	7.5	18.0	6.1

Source: National Advisory Commission on Civil Disorders (1968); U.S. Bureau of the Census (1972).

How does one assess the changes in racial disparities in unemployment rates that have occurred since the riot in Detroit? The statistical evidence suggests that the employment situation has impacted whites and blacks differently as the economy in the city and the Detroit metropolitan area declines as a whole, slightly reducing the racial gap in unemployment rates. However, the racial gap remains wide, since the probability of a black worker being unemployed is still more than one and one-half times the rate for a white worker in the city of Detroit and more than twice the rate for a white worker in the Detroit metropolitan area. These statistics are consistent with findings of the report by the Eisenhower Foundation (2007). However, since we have argued that *place of residence* via spatial mismatch is an important factor in creating the black-white unemployment gap, we examined the gap in unemployment rates between blacks and whites in the two suburban counties outside the city of Detroit. We found that the black unemployment rate in Macomb County was 16.7 percent, that is, lower than the 23.8 percent black rate in the city but still higher than the 9.7 percent rate for whites, resulting in a ratio of 1.7, that is, not very different from the 1.6 ratio between blacks and whites in the city . A similar unemployment pattern was found in suburban Oakland County, one of the most affluent counties in the United States. Recent data show a black unemployment rate of 13.2 percent, compared to a white unemployment rate of 7.2 percent, for a ratio of 1.8. These results demonstrate that although a place of residence in the suburbs seems to lower the black unemployment rate, it does not significantly eliminate the black-white unemployment gap. Thus, it is evident that both place and race matter in explaining the black-white unemployment gap.

CONCLUSIONS

We have argued that spatial mismatch, that is, black concentration in areas where few jobs exist, compared to the *place of residence* where whites reside, contributes to the high black unemployment rates of blacks compared to whites, and that this gap contributed to the riot in Detroit. We have also argued that the spatial mismatch noted at the time of the riot has

Table 9. Unemployment in Detroit and the metropolitan area, 1967 and 2005–2009, by race

Year	Detroit			Metropolitan area		
	Nonwhite*	White	Ratio	Black	White	Ratio
1967	9.8	2.9	3.4	10.9	3.2	3.4
2005–9	23.8	15.0	1.6	20.9	8.9	2.3

*Includes Asian Americans and Native Americans. Separate data for blacks in 1967 are not available.

Source: Michigan Employment Security Commission (1967); U.S. Bureau of Labor Statistics (1967); U.S. Bureau of the Census (2010).

continued as jobs and whites moved to the suburbs, leaving behind blacks in the city where fewer jobs exist. While blacks continue to complain about such segregation and employment discrimination, it appears that blacks and whites in metropolitan Detroit differ greatly in their perceptions about racial discrimination in employment. This will make any solution to the problem more difficult. This is the essence of the racial conflict in employment. While blacks acknowledge many causes for racial disparities in employment, they emphasize discrimination as the *primary* cause. Blacks generally believe that whites favor their own race and believe that whites structure the labor market to benefit whites (Farley, Danziger, and Holzer, 2000). Whites, on the other hand, believe that while there is some discrimination today, blacks themselves are to blame for lacking diligence and work ethic (Farley, Danziger, and Holzer, 2000). Many whites feel that with hard work blacks can become employed and reduce the disparities in unemployment. Yet over more than forty years the disparity in black and white unemployment rates has fluctuated but has not closed.

Policy Implications

The best way to assess the policy implications of this chapter is to return to the recommendations of the Kerner Commission Report and ask, "What actions have occurred during the period 1967 to the present?" It is fair to say that some positive actions have occurred, that is, more training programs, short-term investments, and the creation of organizations in response to the disorders. Legislation was also passed in the Michigan legislature that may have indirectly assisted in lowering the black-white unemployment gap (Darden, 2007e).

Recently, however, negative actions have occurred that may undo whatever gains may have been made in reducing the unemployment gap. On November 7, 2006, the people of Michigan voted to accept Proposal 2, an anti-affirmative action proposal that prohibits preferential treatment to any individual or group on the basis of race, sex, color, ethnicity, or national origin in the operation of public employment, public education, or public contracting (Michigan Constitution, article 1, section 26(1). Thus, affirmative action programs that sought to improve the conditions of blacks, other minorities, and women were dealt a blow in Michigan. This anti-affirmative action may have both short- and long-term consequences on the unemployment gap between blacks and whites in Detroit and the Detroit metropolitan area.

CHAPTER 5

The Emergence of Black Political Power after 1967
Impact of the Civil Disorders on Race Relations in Metropolitan Detroit

BLACK POLITICAL POWER WAS ONE OF THE MOST HISTORICALLY SIGNIFICANT DEVELopments after the civil disorders in 1967. White flight to the suburbs paved the way for a black majority in Detroit. Radical and some moderate black leaders wanted nothing less than black political control of the city. And the time was ripe! The political zeitgeist sweeping Detroit—primarily expressed through the election of a black mayor of the city—would change race relations in metropolitan Detroit for decades.

In 1968 the Reverend Albert Cleage Jr., a leader of several black nationalist groups in Detroit during the 1960s, stressed the importance of black political power in areas where blacks were in the majority: "We can vote Black and we can control political structures in any area in which we are a majority. This is a reality, and it's exactly the same thing that Whites would do if they were Black." Blacks would soon be a majority in Detroit, Cleage stated, affirming that "by voting Black we can elect a Black mayor, a Black council and a Black school board." A black candidate's only necessary qualification, according to Cleage, was that he be "devoted to the Black nation, putting his dedication to Black people first" (1968: 18).

Cleage and other black nationalist leaders rejected the traditional biracial liberal coalition politics that had dominated black political history for decades. According to his political calculations after the 1967 "rebellion," blacks would soon control the city and whites could have the suburbs. "We would appreciate it . . . if people in the suburbs [whites] would stay in the suburbs, if they would stop trying to live in the suburbs and run our Black community, if they would stop living in the suburbs while holding . . . political offices in the cities" (Cleage, 1968: 18). Cleage's view of black political independence saw whites as playing little or no role in the future of black politics in Detroit.

With regard to the whites who still lived in a black-majority city, black nationalists such as Cleage believed they would have to accept, reluctantly or otherwise, black majority rule in the city. This political scenario did not materialize in quite the way that some black nationalists desired, however. Many black moderate activists, no less "nationalist" than Cleage and other radicals, pursued the same political goals but without the rhetoric and fanfare.

The late Robert Millender was one such moderate political activist. A brilliant political strategist, Millender contributed more to black political development in Detroit during the 1967–73 period than all the black radicals and other moderate political activists combined. He was the "kingmaker" of the period. In 1968 he engineered Robert Tindal's election to the city council. A year later he worked on behalf of the unsuccessful Richard Austin campaign for mayor in the closest race in the history of Detroit. Three years later Millender added an impressive black political victory to his record by masterminding the election of Erma Henderson to the city council to replace Tindal, who had died in office. Millender's biggest political success came in 1973, when he managed Coleman Young's campaign to become Detroit's first African American mayor. By then he had overcome his bitterness against Coleman Young for allegedly failing to marshal votes for Austin (Tyson, 1980).

In the early postriot period, as more whites were leaving Detroit for the suburbs and many of those remaining engaged in last-ditch efforts to maintain political power, the political future of Detroit became one of the major topics of discussion. In the summer of 1968, *Detroit Scope* magazine broached the racially sensitive subject, "Will Detroit's Next Mayor Be a Negro?" Interestingly enough, it linked the election of a black man as mayor to both race and gender. "Whether 1969 will be the year Detroit elects its first Negro mayor—or whether the political inevitable will be delayed until 1973—boils down to a more specific and very intriguing question: Will White women vote for a Negro?" (Mollison, 1968: 5).

The writer reasoned that if Detroit's black population "does not reach 50 percent by next year [1969], or 50 percent of voter registration, a black candidate would need White votes," and since "Detroit has 47,500 more women than men registered to vote . . . and women outnumber men in 23 of the 24 election districts, it is apparent that this dominance is bi-racial." Furthermore, "since Black women could be counted upon to vote for the Black candidate under almost any circumstance, it is the White women who could hold the balance of power" (Mollison, 1968: 5)

According to this analysis, any black who was preparing to run for mayor in 1969 would have to consider the fact that, because "Negro registration tends to lag behind White registration, and because the expanding Black population has stretched the Negro get-out-the-vote organization to the breaking point, a Negro mayor in 1969 would need White support" (Mollison, 1968: 6). White support for a black candidate, therefore, would be the challenge in 1969 and the litmus test for racial healing in the immediate postriot era.

In the spring of 1969, the *Michigan Chronicle* published an editorial entitled "A Black Mayor May be Detroit's Answer":

> A great city teeters on the brink of ruin, its life blood being sapped by a number of ills. Detroiters, in this election year, must come up with the Great Physician who can diagnose, treat and eventually cure the chronic maladies plaguing the city. We sincerely believe that a capable qualified Black man in the mayor's seat is the wherewithal for starting Detroit on the road to recovery. The time is appropriate, the need is imperative. Across the nation, Whites continue to abandon the cities to Blacks, leaving behind a legacy of woes—soaring crime rates, deteriorating race relations, substandard and insufficient housing, poor school systems, and empty tax coffers. Left behind are the apathetic and disenchanted, with no investment in the future of the city and any trust or respect for existing governments. (*Michigan Chronicle*, April 26, 1969)

The editorial writers realized that "a Black mayor is no panacea," as "Cleveland's Mayor Carl Stokes has warned." They correctly pointed out that "no one is naïve enough to believe that miracles will be wrought overnight just because a man of darker hue occupies the mayor's seat. But we believe that such a man could provide the injection to restore the interest, dedication and vitality needed to get the city moving again" (*Michigan Chronicle*, April 26, 1969). Realizing that Detroit was becoming increasingly polarized by "fear and race tension," the writers claimed that "in view of recent events its growing Black population is going to hold suspect any White administration. And along the same line, Whites who harbor fear that a Black mayor will automatically show partially to Blacks are needlessly worrying" (*Michigan Chronicle*, April 26, 1969).

RICHARD AUSTIN: THE FIRST BLACK MAYORAL CANDIDATE

In 1969, Richard Austin was the ideal black candidate for mayor. Austin was the first black in Detroit to win a mayoral primary, although he lost the final election to Roman S. Gribbs. Austin was a black moderate who not only believed in the liberal coalition but also understood the pragmatism of biracial politics as one means to achieve black political ends after 1967. Like other blacks of his generation, Austin had achieved several black "firsts." He was the first black in Michigan to become a certified public accountant (CPA); the first to achieve membership in the American Institute of CPAs; the first to serve on the board of directors of the Certified Public Accountant Association; and the first to be elected Wayne County auditor (*Michigan Chronicle*, September 6, 1969).

By any objective standard of merit Austin had the professional experience and achievements to become the first black mayor of Detroit. That he did not win election was testimony both to the irrational racism of whites, who two years after the 1967 riot were still trapped in phobias of blacks taking over the city, and to the yet underdeveloped political consciousness of certain segments of the black community.

Some blacks believed that 1969 was not the year to elect a black mayor. Earlier in the year, however, Congressman John Conyers triggered interest among Detroit blacks in the possibility of a black mayor by pushing hard for a black mayoral candidate. Initially, the choice of his old political rival, Richard Austin, for this historic achievement did not excite Conyers. In 1964, they had competed in a close congressional race in which Conyers beat Austin (Tyson, 1980). However, in the mayoral contest Conyers rallied behind his former opponent. Austin came in first in the primary election with 45,856 votes, and Wayne County sheriff Gribbs came in second with 34,650. The white vote was largely split between Gribbs and Mary Beck, a white conservative, who placed third and received 26,480 of the total votes (*Detroit Free Press*, September 10, 1969).

The primary clearly demonstrated the influence of race on local politics. Austin received most of his votes from the black community. He had hoped to get 15 percent of the white vote, but received less than 10 percent. Gribbs and Beck received tremendous support from the white community for their emphasis on "law and order" (which had become a code word among many white suburbanites for controlling black unrest in the city). Gribbs, a white moderate who believed in integration, had antagonized many black leaders when, as assistant Wayne County prosecutor in 1963, he aggressively prosecuted black protesters who participated in the sit-in at the first Federal and Loan Association. As Wayne County sheriff, Gribbs also alienated many people, particularly blacks, when he attempted to get approval for his officers to use Mace, a controversial form of pepper spray. He decided to be a candidate for mayor twenty-four hours before the filing deadline to save the city from a field of what he considered less than acceptable candidates (*Detroit Free Press*, September 10, 1969; *Michigan Chronicle*, September 6, 1969).

Given the state of racial polarization two years after the riot, there can be little doubt that many whites saw Gribbs as their last "white hope" to hold on to their beloved city hopelessly but inevitably falling into the hands of the growing black population. This explains the almost instant response from the powerful white financial community who rallied to support him. Gribbs received financial backing from executives at major banking, business, and legal establishments in the city, including General Motors. Ninety percent of Gribbs's support during the primary came from managers, executives, and lawyers. Most of his financial support was centered in the suburbs. Austin's support, meanwhile, came mainly from Detroiters, most of whom were doctors, dentists, and small business owners (*Detroit Free Press*, September 28, 1969).

This election would set the stage for understanding the political implications of the racial divide between the white suburban and black city populations, which was rapidly widening in the early postriot era. Although whites were fleeing to the suburbs in increasing numbers, claiming it as their new base of white economic and political power in the region, many still wanted to maintain control of an increasingly black city. As Reverend Cleage had commented more than a year earlier, white suburbanites should "stop trying to live in the suburbs while . . . holding political offices in the cities" (Cleage, 1968).

As the two top vote-getters in the primary prepared for the November mayoral election, everyone knew that race would be the determining factor in the outcome. For some it was the elephant in the room. The *Free Press* was not alone in recognizing the racial challenge facing Austin in his bid to become Detroit's first black mayor in a city where many whites were determined to hold on to city hall as long as possible. In September the paper commented, "Although he finished first in the primary, Austin must woo many white voters to win in November . . . on the surface it looks like a tough assignment, given the racial polarization shown by Tuesday's overall voting patterns" (*Detroit Free Press*, September 10, 1969).

Austin refused to believe that whites would not vote for a black as mayor of Detroit, but he had no illusions that race was not a key issue. Attacking Gribbs, who had denied that race was a factor, Austin told a group of students in northwest Detroit, "I wish to God he was right. Race is relevant to too many people in this election" (*Michigan Chronicle*, September 20 and November 1, 1969).

How could race not be relevant to many people in 1969 in the wake of the New Bethel incident and the controversy over the role of Judge Crockett in the events of March 1969? Race had to be a major factor to both blacks and whites, as many on both sides of the racial divide rallied for and against the judge for releasing blacks mass-arrested at the church after the killing of one white officer and the wounding of another white officer (see chapter 2). The year had been the most racially polarizing year since the 1967 riot. As much as Austin refused to believe that whites would not vote for a black and Gribbs denied that race was a factor, race loomed large and ominous over the upcoming election.

Interestingly, race seemed far more important to whites than to blacks in the city. For example, blacks pursued a voting pattern similar to the 1965 city council elections when they voted for both black and white candidates, in contrast to white voters who tended to vote only for white candidates (Lewis, 1969). Likewise, in the 1969 election many blacks once again demonstrated their belief in biracial politics by voting for both white and black candidates, while most white voters repeated their 1965 pattern. A citizen research group, the Citizen's Committee for Equal Opportunity, discovered that in the primary election "White voters in appalling numbers simply did not vote for black candidates at all, or in instances where they [considered doing so], gave them such low consideration as to virtually exclude them from serious consideration" (*Michigan Chronicle*, November 1, 1969). The committee reported that, unlike many black voters, white voters were not demonstrating a belief "in the bi-racial future of the city and in the bi-racial representation in city government" (*Michigan Chronicle*, November 1, 1969). In short, many white voters barely acknowledged black political candidates as worthy of holding certain political offices.

The 1969 elections peeled the onion of white racism by examining layer after layer of thinly veiled white racial phobias. That year, a *Detroit Free Press* survey of voters revealed that white voters were mainly concerned about welfare, crime, and "the colored taking over" (*Detroit Free Press*, September 11, 1969). One could only guess as to why so many whites were afraid of blacks having the political power that whites had enjoyed for so long.

The 1969 primary elections also revealed levels of white acceptance or tolerance for degrees of black political power. While some white voters supported blacks for seats on the Detroit Common Council, they held back on supporting a black for the top office of the mayor. One white west-side residential area made the point clearly when it gave black councilman Nicholas Hood 35 percent of its votes, but gave Austin only 10 percent. No wonder a group of white leaders supporting Austin put full-page advertisements in local newspapers asking white voters, "Can you vote for a black mayor?" (*Detroit Free Press*, November 2, 1969).

Many whites had no problem responding in the negative. Reflecting the views of many white homeowners on the northeast side of Detroit, a newspaper informed its readers that if Austin were elected as Detroit's first black mayor, it would mean the beginning of the end "for the white, tax-paying homeowner." Another paper in the same area warned its readers, "Unless the white conservative voting element in this election exhibits a sudden wave of political intelligence, the election of Negro candidate Richard Austin as Detroit's first black mayor is a foregone conclusion" (*Detroit Free Press*, October 21, 1969).

The most tragic aspect of the 1969 mayoral election was that far too many whites viewed it as a last-ditch effort to maintain white political control in Detroit instead of an opportunity to build a biracial future. As surveys repeatedly demonstrated, the vast majority of whites rejected Austin, this gentle black moderate, solely on the basis of race (*Detroit Free Press*, September 11 and 19, 1969). This grim racial reality was difficult to bear for Austin, who sincerely wanted to bridge the growing post-1967 racial gap. Because he needed white votes to win, Austin campaigned in white communities as he had done in the primary. However, the odds were running against him.

Austin's black supporters who had marshaled the black votes that won him first place in the primary were becoming increasingly frustrated by white voters' blatant refusal to vote for a qualified black candidate because of race, instead of considering merit. Such white racial attitudes reinforced the black nationalist tendencies among some of Austin's followers and eroded the black moderates' faith in the future of racial integration. In his column in the local black newspaper, black nationalist Reverend Albert B. Cleage Jr. shared his frustration: "I support Dick Austin and I feel that he should receive the total Black vote, but inasmuch as his election is dependent upon a large White vote, I see no possibility of his election" (*Michigan Chronicle*,

August 23, 1969). After criticizing the black community for not registering enough blacks, Cleage warned, "The White racist syndrome will wipe out White support for Black candidates by election day" (*Michigan Chronicle*, August 23, 1969).

Cleage may have been justified in expressing what seemed like a form of black political fatalism. If blacks failed to register to vote, how could they overcome "the white racist syndrome"? In short, white racism and black political apathy could sabotage the future of black political development in Detroit. The future of the black-white political coalition was also at stake. A writer for the *Michigan Chronicle* (September 23, 1969) explained it best when he put white liberals on notice that if blacks did not come out of the November election "with a healthy victory," there would not be any more black/white coalitions. The writer argued that, in past elections, black/white coalitions had mainly benefited white politicians, and warned that "the Black community is not going to accept the short end or the blind, lame or dead horse in the trade this time."

The black leadership supporting Austin knew all too well that white liberals were not working hard enough to get white votes for black candidates. At a meeting of the black and white liberal politicians and labor leaders, black leaders informed their white allies that "the records will show we in the Black community can deliver votes better than the White community. We are sick and tired of delivering votes for White folks and listening to their excuses later. We are going to stop delivering if you don't deliver for Dick Austin and other Black candidates we have selected" (*Michigan Chronicle*, September 23, 1969).

Black/white coalition politics had reached the first in several critical junctures in the early postdisorder era. Black political activists and strategists had long realized they could call the shots in local coalition politics. Increasingly becoming a minority faction in the coalition, liberal whites had to face the fact that as blacks became a numerical majority in Detroit, they would be less responsive to the dictates of the previously white-dominated liberal coalition. That time was certainly not in November 1969, however. Dick Austin badly needed the coalition in order to win, but the coalition could not deliver sufficient white votes to give Austin the victory and the office of the mayor. Sadly, Austin lost the election, but left his indelible mark on the political history of black and white Detroit (*Detroit Free Press*, September 19, 1969).

This was a major political defeat for the black community, but their growing numbers dictated that eventually they would prevail against the protracted political rearguard action of those whites who were determined to hold on to political power in an increasingly black city. As one very perceptive white reporter observed, "After years of fitful and sometimes explosive growth, a new politics has emerged in Detroit. It belongs not to the left or the right, but to the steadily growing black community. . . . Within a very few years, most of the burdens and benefits of local political power will rest with blacks" (*Detroit Free Press*, October 21, 1969).

Most whites—even those who feared and resisted it—realized that it would only be a matter of time before the black community had enough votes to elect a black mayor and a predominantly black common council without heavy reliance on white votes. Black political activists and strategists had always known that black population growth and white flight would eventually win the day. Veteran politician Coleman Young, sitting in the state senate, bided his time, knowing that he was destined to play a major role in the "new politics" of Detroit.

COLEMAN YOUNG: THE FIRST BLACK MAYOR OF DETROIT

State Senator Coleman Young and Richard Austin could not have been more different in their personal history and political style. Austin had a quiet and accommodating political demeanor and style that had served him well in becoming the first black in various professional and political positions. Young, in contrast, had a more rough-and-tumble, combative political demeanor and style developed in the labor and black radical movements of the late 1930s and ensuing years. Young's father had been forced to flee Tuscaloosa, Alabama, where Young was born, because he was considered to be an "uppity nigger." As Young explained in his autobiography, "my father and his brothers were ambitious, more learned than most blacks in that part of the county. . . . My father got [whites'] attention after he moved his family to Tuscaloosa . . . because he sold and circulated black newspapers like the *Pittsburgh Courier* and the *Chicago Defender*." These northern newspapers were threatening to whites "because [they] encouraged black people to read . . . and put all sorts of Northern ideas in their heads, such as voting and integrated schools and labor unions." His father was forced to take the family to Detroit (Young and Wheeler, 1994: 13).

As a young man working at Ford Motor Company, Young hit a racist foreman in the head with a steel bar and as a result lost his job. His early involvement in the labor movement and his military experiences as a second lieutenant in the famous Tuskegee Airmen—in a Jim Crow army—had a profound influence on his later political views and positions on combating racial discrimination. During World War II he was arrested along with 100 other black officers for attempting to integrate an all-white officers club at Freeman Field, Indiana (Young and Wheeler, 1994). Three years after the war ended, in 1948, Young became the Michigan chair of Henry Wallace's Progressive Party presidential campaign (Tyson, 1980).

His uncompromising radicalism continued in the 1950s when he helped organize the National Negro Labor Council (NNLC), the most radical black labor organization of that period, and became its executive director. When the House Committee on Un-American Activities (HUAC) began investigating the Detroit chapter of the NNLC, Young found himself in the national limelight. In February 1952 Young stood his ground and defiantly told the members of the committee: "I am part of the Negro people. I am now in process of fighting against what I consider to be attacks and discrimination against my people. I am fighting against un-American activities such as lynching and denial of the vote. I am dedicated to that fight and I don't think I have to apologize or explain it to anybody" (Foner, 1981; Young and Wheeler, 1994: 128).

Young was one of the first radicals, black or white, to stand up to HUAC, making it clear that he would not be a "stool pigeon." When one of the committee's southern members mispronounced "Negro" as "Niggra," Young corrected him: "As a Negro, I resent the slurring of the name of my race" (Young and Wheeler, 1994: 121). Such bold defiance of the dreaded HUAC was captured on phonograph records that soon began circulating throughout the black community, elevating Young to the status of a local folk hero (Young and Wheeler, 1994).

Predictably Young's radicalism soon caught the attention of the head of the Detroit FBI. In 1954, he wrote to J. Edgar Hoover describing Young as a "dangerous individual" who "should be one of the first to be picked up in an emergency and one of the first to be considered for future prosecution" (Thompson, 2001: 195).

In 1961 Young was elected to participate in the rewriting of the Michigan state constitution. In 1964 he was elected to the state senate and moved to the position of Democratic leader (Rich, 1989: 84–85). Four years later, he became the new Democratic leader committeeman from Michigan, becoming the first black in the nation to be elected to that position. His election to this position proved to Young that racial attitudes were changing and whites were beginning to vote for candidates based on their qualifications instead of their color. At this juncture of his political career, the future mayor still believed in the efficacy of the liberal coalition for black political development, but with qualifications: "I am a Negro first and a Democrat second," he said (*Detroit Free Press*, January 4, 1976; *Lansing State Journal*, July 7, 1968). During the black nationalist period, when black separatists talked about carving out their own country in the southern United States, Young said they were "just smoking marijuana." To Young, a coalition with liberal whites was "the only way" (*Detroit Free Press*, September 22, 1968).

Senator Coleman Young seriously considered becoming a candidate for mayor of Detroit in 1969 but was prevented from doing so by a Michigan Supreme Court ruling that barred a state legislator from running for another office before the expiration of his or her current term. Young, then a three-term senator, had wanted to run because he believed that Austin had not caught on and had failed to give "the people anything to sink their teeth into as far as what he could do as mayor." According to Young, Austin's biggest shortcoming was his failure to commit himself publicly to such issues as civilian control of the police department (*Detroit Free Press*, September 10, 1969).

Some people believed that Young was not willing to support Austin. In a 1986 interview, however, Young claimed that he was not asked to participate in the Austin mayoral campaign. "I went down to the Austin headquarters and asked to help. I didn't know they had a small room in the back where they decided strategy. I was told to get out the vote in my district. I felt it was insulting. I asked, what can you do for my district? There was no consultation. Austin lost because the numbers were not right. He also took the black vote for granted" (Rich, 1989: 96).

In 1973, four years after the disappointing defeat of Richard Austin, the black community began to rally behind Young. He was ready not only to run for mayor but, most importantly, to make control of the police department a central part of his campaign. In a speech kicking off his primary campaign, Young put the police department and Police Commissioner John Nichols on notice that STRESS was a major problem in a city divided by race. "One of the problems is that the police run the city . . . STRESS is responsible for the explosive polarization that now exists; STRESS is an execution squad rather than an enforcement squad. As mayor, I will get rid of STRESS" (*Detroit Free Press*, May 11, 1973). He added, "The whole attitude of the whole Police Department, historically, has been one of intimidation and that citizens can be kept in line with clubs and guns rather than respect. The present department under Nichols is following the old blackjack rule by terror. If elected, I would fire Nichols" (*Detroit Free Press*, May 11, 1973). The police responded by endorsing Nichols, who was also running for mayor (Ashton, 1981).

In the primary Nichols and Young came in first and second respectively in a field of five, with Nichols getting 33.8 percent of the vote and Young getting 21.1 percent. The voting patterns revealed that each candidate would have to appeal to both black and white voters in order to have a chance of winning in November (Ashton, 1981).

Young had more than a growing black political base on his side. His broad political experience in local, state, and national politics gave him an important edge over the single-issue Nichols. Notwithstanding this edge, Nichols had the advantage of exploiting white fear of black crime in the street. Young knew better than to ignore crime, but his appeal to white voters emphasized economic development for the city. He promised to lead a "business resurgence" that would produce thousands of jobs and would include "new park facilities, a stadium, rapid transit, recreational facilities and housing." Young also advised the business elite of Detroit to invest in the city instead of the suburbs. In contrast, Nichols focused on crime in the street, which he argued was the most important issue in the city (Ashton, 1981).

Although Young stressed economic programs in his campaign, he never lost sight of the need to control the predominately white police department. He explained, "With the field narrowed to Nichols and me, the election was reduced to a showdown over law enforcement policies. I regretted that insufficient attention was being paid to the matter of Detroit's reconstruction, but was pleased to have the battle waged over an issue I felt so strongly about" (Young and Wheeler, 1994). According to Young, the debate over the role of the police department was crucial to Detroit's future. Nichols had to be defeated because he represented a national trend of increased police power in postriot cities.

As Young put it, "I genuinely believed that a victory by Nichols would deliver a troubling, oppressive message to the rest of the country and goose it along toward a coast-to-coast police state. Somebody had to stop the cops." Young saw himself as that person. "At street level," Young explained, "the campaign boiled down essentially to one question: Should white officers be allowed to continue to kill black people in the name of law enforcement?" (Young and Wheeler, 1994: 58).

To their credit, both Young and Nichols tried to avoid race, but any dialogue about the police became by extension a dialogue about race. Young admitted,

> The race was about race. Everybody in the city was aware of that, despite the fact that Nichols and I tried to hold our tongues whenever the issue turned to color. For me, it was only prudent to assume a conciliatory tone, because the white voters seemed to harbor a preconception that I would run them off with guns or spears or something and turn the city into a black empire. To assuage those fears, I assured them that my hiring practices would reflect a fifty-fifty racial balance. (Young and Wheeler, 1994)

During one of the "Great Debates" between the mayoral candidates, Nichols was asked why blacks should vote for him. He said, "I would hope that if there's one white man out there who's going to vote for me simply because I am white, that he would stay home on Election Day. I don't think that the criteria should be how much we can appeal to each other's ethnic group, but rather how much we can appeal to the broad base of citizens" (Rich, 1989: 104). Referring to his opponent in the race, Nichol added, "I would hope that the senator shares this belief in that we should be selected for what we stand for and not for who we are or what our accident of birth have made us in terms of skin pigmentation" (Rich, 1989: 104).

Young responded that he didn't have any problem "with that general approach. I have said before that I'm running on a program. I espouse no position which is good for blacks which I don't consider to be good for whites and vice versa. I hope to be judged and I expect to be judged based on my program. I am not naïve," Young stated. "I know that there is polarization in this city. I'm seeking to close that polarization and to unite the differences between the races. And I believe that based upon my experience, again in the legislature, the labor movement, and across the spectrum of my public life, I have been able to appeal to all groups" (Rich, 1989: 104).

The November poll revealed that whites could only equalize the ballot by turning out at a rate 6 percent higher than blacks, "but the Nichols campaign was not generating that kind of interest among white voters" (Rich, 1989: 105). Possibly most of the 58,000 new registrants that fall were black, clearly a good sign for Young. In the end, Young won the election by "a city-wide total of only 16,741 votes" (Rich, 1989: 105), becoming Detroit's first black mayor. Two decades later, reflecting back on that historic day, Young wrote:

> On Election Day, I became the goddamn mayor of Detroit. There wasn't a single precinct in the city that was close—Nichols took the white ones and I took the black ones. . . . Afterwards, I was hard-put to place the day in perspective. On one hand—the hand in which I gripped memories of the Boblo guide who turned me away from the park, the Catholic school priest who had torn up my application, Tuskegee, Freeman Field, Walter Reuther . . . the Un-American Activities Committee, the attorney general, and all the jobs I had lost over the years—it was a preposterous, impossible dream come true, an only-in-America kind of thing. On the other hand, I knew that this had only happened because, for once in my life, I was in the right place at the right time, and that my fortune was a direct result of my city's misfortune—of the same fear and loathing that had caused all of my problems and Detroit's problems in the first place. I was taking over the administration of Detroit because the white people didn't want the damn thing anymore. They were getting the hell out, more than happy to turn over their troubles to some black sucker like me. (Young and Wheeler, 1994: 200)

At that moment in 1973 Young had won a much-coveted prize for the black community, which was still in the throes of the aftermath of the 1967 riot. The results of this historic election demonstrated the valuable lessons black politicians had learned since the disappointing Austin defeat in 1969: "They now knew how to target their appeals, and they had their man campaign in white districts, even though there was an equal risk in those areas of losing votes as there was in gaining them." This was not merely a "symbolic gesture" to get white votes, but instead "it helped to show a commitment to both white and black voters that the candidate intended to conduct a fair administration. During and after the campaign, the newly elected mayor reiterated his commitment to a 50/50 administration" (Rich, 1989: 105).

The victory did not blind Mayor Young to the need to bring the races together in a city that was half black and half white. Soon after his victory he proclaimed to his supporters, "I didn't win; we won. All of Detroit won" (*Detroit Free Press*, November 8, 1973). Although he emphasized racial unity in his inaugural address, saying, "What is good for the black people in this city is good for the white people in this city," Young and his black and white supporters could not conceal their unabashed enthusiasm for the newly emerging political order. This was a black political victory, plain and simple.

A writer for the *Detroit Free Press*, one of the two white daily newspapers, understood the significance of the moment:

> The factors that led to state Sen. Coleman A. Young's election Tuesday as Detroit's first black mayor represents a major turning point in the city's racial and political history. After half a decade of falling just short, Detroit's blacks finally have wrested the balance of power from the city's whites. Blacks now have the deciding vote in major elections, especially in ones as clearly drawn as the race between Young and the white former police commissioner, John Nichols. (*Detroit Free Press*, November 8, 1973)

A few days after the historic election, a *Detroit Free Press* editorial, "Watershed Election Offers Opportunity, Hope for City" (1973), explained another benefit of the historical election: the campaign itself. The quality of the campaign between the two men, while contentious, at times was "open beyond belief. It was not racist. It was issue-oriented. John Nichols can move on to other endeavors secure in the knowledge that he, even in losing, has made a strong contribution to the stability and health of the city that he loves." Young, on the other hand,

> brings to his new office a wealth of experience in dealing with people of varied backgrounds and philosophies. . . . In his campaign he enjoyed the support of a number of institutions and organizations with multiracial leadership, and while these did not translate into massive white support, they do at least provide him a base for building the confidence of the city's white population. (*Detroit Free Press*, November 8, 1973)

Coming out of such a close election in a racially polarized city, the *Detroit Free Press* editorial writers understood all too well the burden of race that the new black mayor would have to shoulder. "In any close election, the victor comes to office needing to overcome the doubts and fears of those who did not support him," the writers argued, "He must govern everybody. That is particularly true now, when Mayor Young will have to overcome the fears left over from this city's past difficulty in keeping race from being a problem" (*Detroit Free Press*, November 8, 1973).

Sadly, most of the "doubts and fears" were among those whites who had voted against Austin and supported Nichols strictly on the basis on race, and who now saw "their city" being taken over by blacks. Some white northeast residents interviewed late Tuesday, the day of the election, talked about blacks "taking over the city" and planned on moving out (*Detroit Free Press*, November 8, 1973). Notwithstanding this all too pervasive white racial attitude, the editorial sounded a much-needed hopeful note:

> We believed Detroit is mature enough and sophisticated enough to be able to accommodate this change, to become more stable rather than less, to provide justice and security for whites and blacks alike. It is, as the mayor-elect said Tuesday, time for Detroit to become a great city again. Detroit has had enough of division and distrust. Let us build a city that will make us proud. Let us build it together. (*Detroit Free Press*, November 8, 1973)

Two days after the election, George Romney, former governor and former secretary of U.S. Department of Housing and Urban Development, commented that Young did not have a chance of coping effectively with Detroit's critical problems. He believed that no politician could solve these problems because of the nature of the American political system. "We expect too much from the political process," Romney concluded, reflecting his belief that the American political system was incapable of solving the real ills of the nation (*Detroit Free Press*, January 3, 1973).

The *Detroit Free Press* editorial writers took issue with Romney, however. Commenting that mayor-elect Young was "setting the right tone for his administration," they wrote that Young "has an opportunity that is unique in the city's history . . . to show this city, which has suffered through two of the worst race-related riots in American history, that we can put all that behind us—that we can work together to make Detroit a less fearsome place and a more hopeful city." Referring to Romney's doomsday scenario of the future of Detroit, the writers explained that Young's mission "is perhaps as important as any that ever confronted a mayor of the city of Detroit. It is a mission that, as former Gov, George Romney glumly observed, the system will tend to frustrate. But the new mayor-elect simply cannot accept Mr. Romney's verdict that his mission is foredoomed to failure. Detroit and Michigan cannot accept it either" (*Detroit Free Press*, November 13, 1973).

The Police Reaction

Predictably, many white officers were upset over the election of Young. At police headquarters the morning after the election, "there was an undertone of disappointment, irritation—maybe even betrayal—over the fact that Detroit had elected a black mayor. Nichols had been their man. He had put 30 years in the force and worked his way up the hard way from patrolman to commissioner." Young, on the other hand, "was a constant critic of the police force. He talked of abolishing the STRESS unit and bringing more blacks into the department" (*Detroit Free Press*, November 8, 1973).

One STRESS officer with twenty-two years in the department described the postelection atmosphere: "Things were kind of gloomy around here this morning. The guys are usually clowning around, but this morning they were kind of quiet. But finally I told them, there've been mayors before and they're all politicians. What's so different about this one?" (*Detroit Free Press*, November 8, 1973). To his credit, Nichols, in his defeat, asked the city to support the new mayor, which undoubtedly influenced the attitudes of some white police officers. During his concession speech, Nichols was asked if the police department "will survive." He resounded with a laugh and said, "The police department will always survive. The police department has resilience and it has strength and it will survive" (*Detroit Free Press*, November 8, 1973).

While some white police officers lamented the future under a black mayor, others took the change in stride. As one white plainclothes officers told his gloomy partner, "Look at it this way, there's always going to be crooks in Detroit and somebody has to catch them and put them in jail. Young's not going to change that, is he?" Other white officers speculated that maybe a black mayor might help them do their job better. "Maybe now," one white officer commented, "these black kids will have somebody to look up to" (*Detroit Free Press*, November 8, 1973).

One white inspector reported that he was "completely calm and confident that either one of the candidates would have made a successful mayor." In fact, he and many other white officers were more worried about the new city charter that was approved, with its provision for an ombudsman who would investigate complaints against the police, than the election of Coleman as the first black mayor. According to the above inspector, "the charter—that's the real Pandora's Box. That part about the ombudsman is fantastic. Whoever gets that is going [to be] a real dictator" (*Detroit Free Press*, November 8, 1973). No doubt he was referring to the ten-year term and wide powers that would be given to the ombudsman by the city council to "investigate city agencies for incompetence or corruption, and to help citizens with complaints about the bureaucracy" (*Detroit Free Press*, November 7, 1973).

The police department had reason to be concerned. The city charter, which passed by 44,000 votes, eliminated the office of police commissioner and established a five-person civilian board of commissioners appointed by the mayor. The mayor, in turn, would "appoint a police chief for administrative purposes, and complaints against the department will be handled by a civilian board, an idea that is repugnant to most policemen." Furthermore, the charter provided for an ombudsman to be appointed by the city council "to handle citizen's complaints in city departments" (*Detroit Free Press*, November 8, 1973).

Some writers for the *Michigan Chronicle*, the largest black weekly newspaper in the state, tempered their enthusiasm for the historic moment with advice for the future. In an open letter to the community entitled "Young Can't Do It By Himself," one writer wrote:

> For the first time in the history of Detroit, the nation's fifth largest city, a Black man has been elected as its chief executive and jubilance abounds throughout the Black community because of that victory. The election of Coleman A. Young to the mayor's seat is a dream come true for many of us who have worked long and hard to muster enough political clout to make that dream a reality . . . [However,] amid the celebration and joy over the fact that, as Mayor-Elect Young said, "We have won our place in the sun," we are sobered by the Herculean task that faces our new mayor. . . . It is on this sobering note that we convey this open letter to urge one and all to rise to the occasion and put our collective shoulders to the wheel as we have never done before. We have a right to be joyful, but at the same time we must keep the realistic fact of life before us that the hard work and diligent efforts have just begun. So there is no time to relax in victory. (*Michigan Chronicle*, November 12, 1973)

Inauguration Day, 1974

On the morning before the inaugural luncheon in January 1974, some of Young's followers held a prayer meeting, during which the Reverend Charles Butler of the New Calvary Baptist Church, referring to Young, cited the biblical phrase "Behold this man." As one newspaper observed, although members of Detroit's power elite were present, "for the first time in Detroit the street people who knew 'Coleman' when he was down and struggling were in on things, watching from the edges of the crowd, smiling as if they had been graced by greatness" (*Detroit Free Press*, January 3, 1974).

Like other joyful but wary black leaders and observers, federal judge Damon J. Keith knew the mayor would soon be facing formidable challenges. During the prayer breakfast he presented some sage advice to the new mayor:

> Always let it be known that your administration will treat all citizens with dignity and promote self-respect. I invite your attention to the fact that all those who have reached the level of excellence are characterized by their fairness, their humility and the manner in which they deal with those who are subordinate to them. Few persons have ever attained high position and remained in those high positions very long by demeaning others . . . personal integrity is an absolute and necessary quality in our public officials, especially during these troubled times. (*Michigan Chronicle*, January 5, 1974)

Judge Keith next addressed what everyone knew would be one of the greatest challenges facing the new Young administration: crime, especially black-on-black crime, and the police:

> We must devise a means of riding this city, root and branch, of the criminals who are committing murders, rapes and assaults on the people of this city. I am aware of all the sociological reasons as to why crimes are committed and understand most of them, but I say to you that while we work

to eliminate poverty, substandard housing, inadequate education and all the evils that are the by-product of a racist society, we must also, without delay or equivocation, strive to make this city of ours a safe place in which to live, in which to raise our children, in which to enjoy the fruits of our labors and our God-given rights. (*Michigan Chronicle*, January 5, 1974)

Keith then addressed the sensitive issue of black-on-black crime. "Let us look, not with shame but with cold logic at the record. The crime problem, which has won for our city an unprecedented degree of adverse publicity, is essentially a wave sparked by Black criminals preying upon Black victims. Tragically," the judge explained, "this crime wave is aided and abetted by Black people, by an 'it's no business of mine' attitude. When police come, nobody is there who remembers seeing anything" (*Michigan Chronicle*, January 5, 1974).

Keith then turned the topic to the challenges facing the Detroit Police Department in an unjust society. "Our police today are assigned an almost impossible task. They are asked by the larger society to maintain order in an unjust society, a society which has systematically and illegally frustrated Blacks in their efforts to survive. But the police alone cannot keep order unless and until the major institutions in the larger society demand justice" (*Michigan Chronicle*, January 5, 1974).

He then turned his attention to the new mayor, saying, "It is you who can awaken every citizen, Black and White, to the truism that policemen alone cannot do the job that is the obligation of every citizen and a part of citizenship to cooperate with the police." The judge told Mayor Young, "Your call, loudly given, and responded to, can reverse the crime trend in this city and prove more than any other one thing that a Black man can run a city in an outstanding manner and bring it new honors. Thus, Mr. Mayor, you must lead a revolt of the people of this community for justice and against crime" (*Michigan Chronicle*, January 5, 1974).

Keith ended his talk by returning to the solemn purpose of the spiritual breakfast:

Let it be said as we go forth this morning, from this monumental and historic prayer breakfast, that this is one of Detroit's finest hours. In the years to come, let it be said that Coleman A. Young contributed mightily to freedom, prosperity and dignity for all people during his administration, and that this quality of freedom which we hold so precious and which is indeed so unique, will be his legacy to our city, our children and to our country. (*Michigan Chronicle*, January 5, 1974)

That afternoon, Detroit Corporate and labor leaders gathered at the Cobo inaugural luncheon to honor the new mayor. Among them were such notables as Henry Ford II, chairman of the Ford Motor Company, and Leonard Woodcock, UAW president. Ford explained the significance of the new day. "We, here in this room, represent the beginning of a new coalition of business and labor, brought together by our mutual desire to pledge our support to the newly inaugurated mayor" (*Detroit Free Press*, January 3, 1974). Ford's support would be crucial in the coming years because black political power in Detroit, personified by the new black mayor, would still need powerful and willing white allies to rebuild the city. While some of Young's black followers might have been too drunk with the wine of victory to see or want it, of necessity the "new politics" would include the biracial liberal coalition.

This was, indeed, a new and glorious day for blacks in Detroit as they and their white allies engaged in a three-day inaugural celebration and the new mayor told the criminals to hit the road (Rich, 1989). Notwithstanding the well-deserved jubilation, the harsh realities of running a troubled city were waiting in the wings for the curtain to rise on this new era of black political control:

> As the band played, singer Diana Ross performed, Judge Damon Keith spoke, and the crowd cheered for Young's success, the city was reacting to the recession of 1974. The first black mayor of Detroit had inherited a politically rich city but an economically poor one. In his first four years of office, he would have a fiscal crisis in 1975, a near riot, a police confrontation over layoffs and residency rules, and the threat to close Chrysler's Jefferson Avenue plant. (Rich, 1989: 105–6)

Continued Tensions in Detroit

One of the first racial crises of the Young's administration occurred in 1975, when a black teenager named Obie Wynn was shot in the back and killed by a white bar owner. The situation had the potential of becoming another 1967 riot. Angry black protestors looted the bar and burned its carpet before they were chased away. As soon as he was informed of the crisis, Mayor Young ordered his white police chief, Philip Tannian, to send every black officer in the department to the scene, "the idea being to merge them with white officers and make a show of racial unity on the street." When the police chief informed the mayor "that he had no way of knowing which of his officers were black," the mayor, in his well-known manner, responded: "Bullshit, I said. In about an hour, they were all there" (Young and Wheeler, 1994: 207).

When Mayor Young and a group of community leaders were unable to calm the situation, Young decided to "fight attitude with attitude." He climbed up on a car and, as he recalled years later, "spoke to the people as angrily and sternly as I dared without turning them against me, figuring that the only way to check their mood was with a passionate petition of reason." He told them that "Detroit was their city and they should not tear it apart; also, that there was a difference between justice and vigilante violence and that I, like them, was interested in the former" (Young and Wheeler, 1994: 207).

The recent memory of John Conyers being stoned when he tried to calm a mob from the top of a car during the 1967 riot was not lost on Young. "When other black leaders had stood on cars during the 1967 uprising, the community had shouted them down," he recalled. "But this time was different, because the crowd knew that my words were more than rhetoric: I was the goddamn mayor. I guess they figured they owed me one more chance to prove myself. It probably didn't hurt my case when somebody threw a rock at me, which earned me some sympathy points." Young passed this first test. He had prevented more violence and a repeat of the 1967 riot, but people were still angry, and he was criticized from both sides (Young and Wheeler, 1994: 207).

The situation worsened when a Polish baker returning home soon after Wynn's killing was pulled from his car and stoned to death. Young marshaled black and white community leaders, including the parish bishop and Polish community leaders, to ease the situation. He visited the widow and mother of the victim, assuring them that justice would be served. Reflecting back on this crisis, Young wrote: "We were probably on the verge of another major riot at that moment. But it never materialized, and I firmly believe that it was our community presence which ultimately saved the day—the cooperative effort of neighborhood leaders and black and white police officers" (Young and Wheeler, 1994: 208).

Young was clearly thankful for how things turned out and attributed the outcome to the newly instituted police reforms: "Black and white police officers—including some of the newly hired women on the force—were performing in a very professional manner despite extreme provocation in the form of bricks and the like." Given the death toll of the 1967 riot, he was quick to acknowledge that this racially integrated police presence, including women, was able to restore order without firing a single shot. "If we had gone about cracking heads in the Detroit tradition, there would have been hell to pay. It was a trial by fire for our police reforms, and thank God they worked." It would not have worked, however, if the mayor had not ordered his police chief to send all black police officers in the department to the scene. This was a race-relations stroke of genius rooted in Young's understanding of how white police departments too often have mishandled racial crises. "That may have been the first time in Detroit history that black police officers had been called upon for emergency work" (Young and Wheeler, 1994: 208).

Changes to the Police Department

The greatest evidence of rising black political power in Detroit during Mayor Young's first term in office was the radical change in the racial makeup of the police department—not an easy task, considering the resistance of many white police officers and their unions. After several years of power struggles and countless bouts of negotiations, Young made some progress in changing a predominantly white police department into one that was at least in the process of becoming more racially integrated. By the end of 1976 Detroit boasted its first black police chief and a top command structure that was half black and half white. One hundred black officers had been hired since Young's election, increasing black representation from 17 percent to 22 percent (Ashton, 1981).

The "old boy's network," which had perpetuated and maintained white male privilege in promotions for decades, was forced to give way to Young's aggressive affirmative action program. As a result of this program, blacks went from 5 percent of all officers holding the rank of sergeant to 15 percent (Ashton, 1981). As Young explained in his autobiography, the police unions fought change at every turn: "As the issues played out, the battle was joined over two policies we instituted in order to bring parity to the racial balance of the department and make it more community-oriented. First, we began to enforce the city's residency rule, under which it was mandatory for police officers and other city employees to live within the city limits of Detroit." This rule, Young points out, "had been on the books since 1914 but was largely winked at by administrations prior to mine." Therefore, he argued, "Given the prevailing 'us versus them' law-enforcement climate in Detroit, the residency rule was vital to our efforts to increase the community element in the neighborhood. Consequently, we stuck with it in spite of vehement objections from the veteran cops" (Young and Wheeler, 1994: 209).

The other policy was "the existing police promotion procedures," which was based on testing which Mayor Young believed "was culturally biased and effectively discriminated against black officers." This proved to be a major challenge to the Young administration. "Without ripping apart the system," Young claimed, "we profoundly modified it by establishing two lists of test scores—one for white officers and for black. After a qualifying mark was established as a cutoff for eligibility, promotions were made alternately by selecting the officers with the highest score from the white list, then the officer with the highest score from the black list" (Young and Wheeler, 1994: 210).

Young argued that this approach did not favor black officers because they were not promoted unless "they had passed the test." In fact, Young continued, "records show that in the oral-board portion of the test, black officers on the average have scored higher than whites." This policy was not limited to blacks and whites, but also "ensure[ed] that women, who constituted only 1 percent of the department in 1974, were hired in far greater numbers" (Young and Wheeler, 1994: 210).

As expected, white police officers did not like Young's two-list policy and filed suit against him and the city of Detroit, arguing that the policy constituted reverse discrimination. Young's attitude was, "You're damn right—the only way to arrest discrimination is to reverse it." It was a long struggle, but as Young tells the story, "The final round, resolved ten years later after it was filed, was heard by the United States Supreme Court, which upheld the appellate court's decision that our policies constituted 'a valid and permissible remedy' for past discrimination."

Another police suit "contesting the promotion of officers to sergeant" through three appeals also went the way of the city, but it took twenty years. The final ruling on the case from the Sixth Circuit Court of Appeals in Cincinnati was delivered in late March 1993. When Mayor Young heard of the decision, he told the media, "After twenty years of pursuing a persistent program of affirmative action, fighting with one hand in the courts all the way, for the first time we can say we have reached our goal. The department is truly fifty-fifty, both across the board and in command ranks, including sergeant" (Young and Wheeler, 1994: 210–11).

Young and the Carter Administration

Mayor Young ended his first term in office by helping to put Jimmy Carter in the White House. As a major black figure in national Democratic politics and in labor and business circles, Young had both the power and credibility to deliver powerful black voting blocs to Carter. Young possessed such influence that when Carter slipped during the 1976 presidential campaign, saying that he saw nothing wrong with "ethnic purity"—a statement many interpreted as advocating racial purity—Young defended the Democratic candidate, explaining that he had been misunderstood. Carter was still apologizing when he met Young at the Detroit airport. As soon as Young boarded Carter's plane, he told Carter, "Get up off your knees and keep on walking" (Tyson, 1980: 38; Young and Wheeler, 1994: 223).

In 1976 during a speech in Providence, Rhode Island, Young was asked why he supported Carter: "In my view his record as the Governor of Georgia was an outstanding one. It certainly demonstrates concern for poor people, for minorities, and support for civil rights. Coming from Georgia, I think that's an outstanding thing" (Young, 1976). When asked how he felt about Carter's reservations about bussing and whether it bothered him, Young did not hesitate to express a view at odds with many black leaders. "No, no, it doesn't bother me at all; I share his reservations. I think 'bussing' is a kind of catch-all; it's not an automatic cure-all. Putting a little White kid and a little Black kid in those schools is no chemical or magical guarantee for a quality education," he argued. "I don't give a damn how you mix up Black and White within the city of Detroit; it's still only something dividing the children. No amount of integration is going to do it: improve education" (Young, 1976). In response to another question about Carter's stance on bussing and racial code words, Young continued to defend Carter. "He fought to have Blacks admitted to the Baptist Church in Plains, Georgia, where he's a member. Now if there's anything that is more personal than school, it's church. And he does live in an integrated community" (Young, 1976).

When Carter became president, Mayor Young's political power multiplied by virtue of the leverage he now had in the White House. Carter's urban policies reflected Young's. Young's appointees ended up in the Carter administration, channeling federal money to Detroit. During the Carter administration, Mayor Young could be seen operating in the country's highest councils (Tyson, 1980).

Campaigning for Carter's reelection in Chicago on October 19, 1980, Young recounted how Detroit had suffered under President Ford and the Republicans. "We were having great difficulty in Washington with President Ford. We had two Bills passed in '76 that would have brought some money to our city, and Mr. Ford vetoed both of them," Young said. "The Republican Party had literally turned its back on the cities," he continued. "They started talking about the silent majority and middle America. And in doing so, literally wrote off the cities, blue collar workers, poor folks, and, and minorities. They said they didn't need us. . . . Reagan's coming from the same place" (Young, 1980: 1). Young reminded his audience that President Carter had fought for programs to support the survival of cities whereas the Republicans had adopted an approach that in part placed people "in a so-called silent majority—that means white suburbs—and then literally turn them against the white people that live in the cities and divide the nation along those lines." On the other hand, Carter's support had helped Detroit to reduce crime in the last three years. "That can be attributed very directly to what . . . I unabashedly call—Jimmy Carter dollars" (Young, 1980: 3). When Carter lost his reelection bid, Mayor Young and the city lost its most important supporter.

Reflections on Young's First Term: Interview with the **Michigan Chronicle**

After three years in office and on the eve of his own reelection bid, Young spoke about his successes and failures in various areas of race relations. In an interview with the *Michigan Chronicle* he was asked if his affirmative action policies were working out to his satisfaction. He replied: "No. There have been peaks and valleys. We won some and lost some. But it's mandated in the city charter and we intend to continue working for it. We've made some progress in the Police Department; we haven't done as well in the Fire Department. But we plan to continue our fight there" (*Michigan Chronicle*, January 22, 1977).

The interviewer then mentioned that Mayor Young's "chances for reelection and indeed the wellbeing and future of the city depend on the quality of race relations," and posed the question, "How do you feel about the current state of race relations in the city and what do you believe your administration has contributed in that area?" Young replied that "there is much less tension between Blacks and Whites than there was three years ago. As far as my administration is concerned, I have tried to demonstrate in my appointments which have been 50/50, that it is possible to have a fair distribution of jobs and all the other possible things among peoples of different races and creeds." Notwithstanding the ongoing challenges to his affirmative action policies, Young informed the interviewer that the policies in "the Police Department and other areas of city government . . . have resulted in good relations.

One of the best examples is the Police Department. Under Chief Hart, who is Black, that department is united, more so than it was under a White chief. Chief Hart is doing a good job and is respected" (*Michigan Chronicle*, January 22, 1977).

Young went on to mention a morning prayer breakfast he had just attended as another example of good race relations. "I was at a prayer breakfast attended by clerical and lay representatives of all denominations and persuasions, Black, White and Latino. I saw it as a possible educational experience. Everyone knows that 11 A.M. on Sunday is the most segregated hour in the week," Young said, "but I think we do a bit better here than in most places. It may seem a small thing but it's important" (*Michigan Chronicle*, January 22, 1977).

Asked about the high and low points of his term to date, Young responded, "Sometimes you can have a high point when you avoid disaster." He was obviously referring to the near riot he faced after the shooting of the black teenager. Young explained that the high point in that case occurred "when we found a police department, which had been guilty of excesses in the past, being professional and, even under provocation, not firing a single shot. We also found leaders, Black and White, who had the courage to get out there in front of angry citizens and helped keep the peace." Mayor Young then expanded on that high point in race relations, which involved avoiding another 1967-type riot. "When we emerged from what could have been even worse than 1967 without a single person being killed as a result of police action, or actions of citizens against police, that to me was significant. Because it involved people of all races and religions, it told me that Detroit has picked itself up." When asked about his biggest disappointment, he pointed to the fact that Detroit has been in a "depression for the two and a half years that [he has] been in office. That has meant that I've had my back against the wall. Most of my time has been spent putting out fires instead of going ahead with our plans for the city" (*Michigan Chronicle*, January 22, 1977).

One of the biggest questions related to race relations was "the fear of crime which has so many people in Detroit scared to death." Young reported that he had recalled all the police officers who had been laid off and planned to add more. "But," he added, "there also has to be an educational approach. We have to teach people to look out for one another, to get away from that . . . city attitude that everyone has to mind his own business. When a man's house is broken into, it isn't just that man's business. I think a change in the attitude can reduce the fear of crime." Asked about what legacy he would like to leave behind, Young answered, "A rebuilt and unified city . . . a city in which the dry rot and deterioration have been stopped . . . a city with an educational system in which our young people can get a decent education . . . a city which doesn't have the disgraceful situation of a 40 percent unemployment rate for its young people" (*Michigan Chronicle*, January 22, 1977).

In August 1977, Young's reelection campaign included addresses to both the Police Academy's and the firefighters' graduation classes. They were designed to focus attention on Young's efforts in changing the racial and gender makeup of both departments. On August 20, 1977, Young told the Police Academy graduation class, "I volunteered to do something about discrimination against Blacks. Now we are hiring, as you know, new police officers. The percentage of Blacks in the Department today . . . is now ranging about 32%." This statement was greeted by applause. Continuing, Mayor Young told the class, "This City will employ about 750 new police officers. We're over halfway there, and when we get there it will be because I have given preference and importance to Black police officers as a correcting affirmative action, in the same way folks directed me to give preference to women officers by corrective Affirmative Action." Young predicted that the police department "should be, within the next month or two months, approximately 40% Black. That's a long way from where it was four years ago" (Young, Speech, 1977a).

Young understood many of the problems this new class had faced and would face in the future as the system slowly changed. He explained that it takes "a hell of a long time to turn a bureaucracy around that's ingrained and filled with bigotry, and we're still dealing with too much of that in the Police Department." But, he assured his audience that "we will deal with it. The next four years will be a hell of a lot better than the last four" (Young, 1977a).

Mayor Young made it clear to the police graduates, however, that he would not tolerate police brutality. "I'll back you to the hilt as you enforce the law fairly and I'll hang you high if you mess over a citizen. We've had too much of that. Responding to the criticism of the police graduation class of 1977, Young told the class, "We hear of 'lack of preparation,' we hear criticism, and I know what is wrong with the class of '77: It's too damn Black and too many women. It's just that simple" (Young, 1977a).

He then addressed the women police graduates. "I did not hesitate when the Court ordered me to take corrective action," he told them; "but, I must admit that I, like almost every male, had a few misgivings on how effective they would be. And I'm sure that many of the male Police Officers felt the same." He confessed that after three years of observation and experience, "women police officers are every bit as effective as men on the street and off the street, and in many cases, more effective" (Young, 1977a). This last statement brought applause. Turning his remarks to the male police officers, he told them: "Let's face it brothers, this is the way of the future. When we say equal opportunity, it goes across the board, it doesn't stop with blacks. Our women Police Officers are playing an important role—they are protecting us. They are part of the reason that our Police Department is protecting the people" (Young, 1977a).

Since this was an election year, Mayor Young could not resist bragging about his accomplishments in expanding the police force and radically changing its racial and gender makeup. "We will have, in the next six to eight weeks at the longest, between 5700 and 5800 Police Officers on the Detroit Police force. That's the highest number in the history of this City. We will have the most integrated police force in the United States," he said, again to applause (Young, 1977a).

A week later, Mayor Young presented essentially the same message to the firefighters' graduating class. "I want our Fire Department to reflect the population of this City. For a long time, there was discrimination against people because of their color," he told them. "We are seeking now to eliminate that as quickly as we can, and you are a reflection of that effort" (Young, 1977b). Young mentioned a police case in which a federal judge had found the city guilty of discriminating against women and ordered them "to go down the list of women who tried to become police officers and to hire one woman for every man until we have exhausted every woman on that list." He said, "We have done that. The Police Department is no worse for having hired women" (Young, 1977b.)

Young then explained to the graduating class how the fire department would be undergoing similar changes. "Everyone in this class—and you might as well face it, you will be integrated with women before this next three months is over, (applause) and I don't think that's going to injure your ability to perform as a fireperson—and I say 'fireperson.'" He added, "Any person who can pass the examination and who possesses all of the needed requirements, including the physical agility—any person, regardless of race, religion, or sex, as far as I am concerned, is entitled to a job with the City of Detroit." As he had with the police graduating class, Young left the firefighters with an inspiring message about their mission. "You are, indeed, a new kind of Fire Department because you are of the people. You reflect all the people in this City" (Young, 1977b).

Mayor Young ran for reelection against black councilman Ernest Browne in 1977. He was supported by Ford Motor Company chairman Henry Ford II, UAW president Douglas Fraser, and President Jimmy Carter. This was the first general election in a mayor city in which both mayoral candidates were black. Black voters rejected Browne both in the primary and in the general election. Browne's strategy of a winning coalition of a majority of white voters and a minority of black voters failed. The campaign turned ugly when Young accused Browne of selling out blacks for political gain and Browne accused Young of using racist tactics (*Detroit Free Press*, November 7, 1977).

Young's Second Term in Office

Mayor Young had won a second term in office and fulfilled some key campaign promises during his first term by using affirmative action initiatives to steadily transform the racial makeup of various city departments, particularly the police department. In the summer of 1978, when the NAACP came to Detroit to discuss affirmative action, Mayor Young welcomed the visitors with the following statement: "Welcome to Detroit, the Affirmative Action City . . . I can't think of any recent issue that is more important to the future of minorities and women and the whole American people than the issue of affirmative action" (Young, 1978). Young started out his talk by pointing to what most of those in the NAACP gathering understood only too well, that affirmative action was often seen as reverse discrimination, "some penalty on White America." He talked about the "unfinished business of the Civil War," of blacks being denied their "forty acres and a mule," of the mistake of "burying Reconstruction in blood and reaction." He warned that "unless we recognize that [history], today, we could be on the verge of a similar attempt, and I do say attempt, cause Black folks ain't going so mildly this time" (Young, 1978).

Warming to his topic, Young expanded his talk to the global implications of racial change in the United States:

> In the interest of America, we live today in a new world in which non-White people are also important. It's no longer a White man's world. There is an ascending Africa, Asia, and South America. Non-Whites, colored people—Black, brown, yellow—are very important to the world scene. To the degree that we remain a world power, indeed, to the degree that we deserve to claimed leadership in this new world, then we must deal with the problems of minorities within our own ranks. (Young, 1978)

Young linked the problems of minorities to the achievement of unity within the United States. "Unity cannot be achieved on the basis of a continual repression and suppression of any segment of our society. We should have learned [that] in '66 and '67. I hope we are learning now." So, in fighting for affirmative action, he told the audience, "we are fighting in the best interests of all Americans—all Americans. It is just as essential to the sorriest White bigot that we have equal opportunity and unity in this country, as it is essential to the lowliest Black" (Young, 1978).

He then turned to the topic of the role of government leaders at this crucial time in the history of affirmative action following the *Bakke* decision. "The perception of defeat that exists in wide sectors of the Black community, as the result of Bakke, calls upon the leadership of America to speak out in re-affirmation of the course that we have undertaken in regard to affirmative action." That means, Young advised the gathering, that during this election year blacks "ought to measure every candidate for office, whether governor, or Congress, or state legislature, or community college candidate, on 'Where do you stand on Bakke?' That's the scale; that's the measure" (Young, 1978).

Acknowledging that there have been demands that President Carter speak out on affirmative action, Young produced a memorandum that he had just received from Washington that was to be released to the press. The memorandum was addressed to "Heads of Executive Departments and Agencies":

> Since my administration began, I have been strongly committed to a policy of affirmative action. It is through such programs that we can expect to remove the effects of discrimination and ensure equal opportunities for all Americans.
>
> With your help, this administration has been able to develop and implement meaningful affirmative action programs throughout the federal government, and as a result, minority employment has increased to its highest level in history. The recent decision by the Supreme Court in Bakke enables us to continue those efforts without interruption. That historic decision indicates that properly tailored affirmative action programs, which provide minorities with increased access to federal programs and jobs, and which are fair to all Americans, are consistent with the Civil Rights Act of 1964 and with the Constitution. I want to make certain that in the aftermath of Bakke you continue to develop, implement, and enforce vigorously affirmative action programs. I also want to make certain that the administration's strong commitment to equal opportunity and affirmative action is recognized and understood by all Americans. (Young, 1978)

The president's letter of support for affirmative action outlined a post-*Bakke* strategy in his administration. Others, however, had a vital role to play as well, as Young explained to the gathering: "Ladies and gentlemen, I believe that this is the proper basis upon which to begin these discussions. It is up to us now to police this mandate at every federal, state, and local level, to see to it that it is pursued at every level of the private sector" (Young, 1978).

Mayor Young faced even tougher issues during his second term, the worst of which was a budget crisis in 1981 that forced Detroit voters to approve an income tax hike and city officials to sell $125 million in emergency bonds (*Detroit Free Press*, January 5, 1981). Young not only had to persuade city voters to go along with his plan to save the city from bankruptcy, but he also had to convince the state legislature and twist the arms of municipal workers to accept a two-year wage freeze. Black unemployment in the city remained at 25 percent as Young prepared to run for his third term. Not even the impressive Renaissance Center complex could lift the gloom of a declining city. Times were tough in the Motor City and getting tougher, especially for many blacks who still saw Mayor Young as the "big daddy," a symbol of their power and success (*Detroit Free Press*, January 1, 1984; *Lansing State Journal*, 1981).

When Carter lost his bid for reelection it hurt Detroit and severed the ties that once provided so much financial support for the struggling city. True to his street style of politics, the change in Washington did not prevent Young from calling President Reagan "prune face" and accusing him of "lacking any compassion for urban residents and the poor." In his third inaugural address, Mayor Young told Detroiters to "circle the wagons" and to "close ranks and send a message to the President . . . [This country] can't go forward if its cities are sinkholes of poverty and starvation" (*Detroit Free Press*, January 1, 1984).

Assessing his first decade as mayor of Detroit, Young focused on black unemployment and its relationship to crime. "The primary problem that we face now is unemployment," he mentioned, "the fact that in the Black community one out of four are out of a job, and among young people we have 65 to 70 % unemployment. That's a devastating figure. There's a direct relationship between that and crime" (*Michigan Chronicle*, January 14, 1984).

Being mayor of a predominantly black city surrounded by predominantly white suburbs meant that Young could never escape the covert and overt forces of racism. Many white suburbanites could not understand Young's periodic antagonism toward the suburbs, and why, according to them, he was always talking about racism. On August 22, 1984, in a talk to the Booker T. Washington Business Association, he spoke to the topic. "Now, I can't remember any recent period in this Country, and in this State, because I think it is worse in this State than it is in most of the Country, when racism has been more open and more overt. As you know," he explained, "many people get angry, particularly white people, when I talk about racism. They get angry with anybody who talks about racism. Just because they get angry does not mean that racism does not exist (Applause)" (Young, 1984).

Young argued that racism in the city and state was at "an all-time high." He accused the suburbs of wanting to control "our water and our City." Furthermore, Young continued, "We also know that there has been a reach for our transportation system. There has been a reach for the Detroit Art Institute." This "reaching," Young claimed, was a source both of conflict between suburbs and city conflict and of racism. "As long as Detroit and its suburbs keep fighting each other, as long as this feeling among those in the suburbs is that they aren't going to stand for Black folks to run a damn thing, they are going to destroy it or control it. As long as that feeling exists, let me tell you, we will all be destroyed" (Young, 1984).

Another example of racism Young discussed related to the white press's accusation that he was not reaching out to the suburbs, that he should show some leadership. In his typical brash style, Young told his audience, "Hell, I go across Eight Mile Road every other month. Do you ever hear of those sons-of-bitches coming here? (laughter). You know me; you can reach two ways, right?" He said that he has been reaching out and that he would continue to do so. "But I want somebody, sometime, to reach in. Those damn expressways run two ways. If I can get out to Ten Mile Road, those sons-of- bitches can get down here" (Laughter) (Young, 1984).

Young understood the need for suburban-city cooperation as essential for regional growth. The city could not exist without the suburbs and the suburbs could not exist without the city. In the same way, he said, downtown could not exist without the neighborhoods and the neighborhoods could not exist without downtown. But again, he argued, suburban racism was the major barrier. "None of us can exist with the blind racism that characterizes this area, which many, many people in the suburbs would just as soon see the damn thing go down before they would help Detroit," he remarked (Young, 1984).

A year later, in his annual "State of the City" report to the Economic Club of Detroit, Mayor Young devoted more than a third of his report to crime and the need for more prison space, and mentioned that economic, social, and educational deprivation is the underlying cause of crime. Rising crime had to be addressed, and Young made it clear that he did "not approve of vigilantism, but [did] approve of citizen involvement" (*Michigan Chronicle*, February 16, 1985). He did not limit himself to the problems of Detroit, however. He noted and praised "the resiliency of the people of Detroit," whom he compared to a cat with nine lives—"always capable of rebounding in [the] face of economic setbacks." Young used this opportunity to discuss the link between the economic turnaround of the city and the surrounding metropolitan region, and called for increased cooperation between the city and its suburbs in attracting more jobs into the area. He added that he was working with the county executives in this effort (*Michigan Chronicle*, February 16, 1985).

Young's Accomplishments

As Young prepared for his fourth term as mayor of Detroit, he addressed his critics by listing many of the projects he claimed had been successful during his administration. Among these projects were the Riverfront, Millender, and Trolley Plaza apartments with close to 1,800 units. He emphasized that these apartments were "50 percent Black and 50 percent White, half come from within Detroit and half from outside." To Young, this project represented economic and racial integration. He also mentioned that in other downtown areas 7,000 to 8,000 units were "subsidized and moderate income." Some critics in the black community, however, saw this "integration" as Young's attempt to stop white flight at the expense of inner-city blacks. Young denied that he had "caved in to gentrification" like other cities. "Those cities are gentrifying Black folks out of the ghettoes," Young explained. "Whites come in, take over the area, invest a lot of money in it and it becomes a lily White area. It becomes just the reverse of what it was. That's one of the things we have avoided and one of the things I am most proud of" (*Michigan Chronicle*, November 2, 1985).

While it was undeniable that Detroit had suffered a loss of 800,000 people, Young attributed the 40 percent drop in population primarily to the deterioration of neighborhoods. As whites deserted the city in the wake of the 1967 riot, blacks moved into better housing and abandoned neighborhoods in the Linwood, Mack, and Kercheval areas. The problems were compounded by exploitive slumlords who purchased property, "drained it and then left it vacant." According to Young, this resulted in the urban sprawl that left about 40 percent of Detroit's land unused. Being the optimist he had to be, running a city in decline, Young did not waste time worrying about the problems, but instead came up with ways to correct some of the imbalances between land and people. For those critics who said that the city had deteriorated since he became mayor, Young countered, "The deterioration was well advanced before I became mayor." Linwood, Mack, and Kercheval were already decaying in 1967, the year of the riot. "All of them were damn near burned down in '67," he reminded his critics. "You asked what are we going to do about Linwood, Mack and Kercheval. What were they before? 12th Street was worse than Linwood before we rebuilt it. So was Black Bottom, [which] we rebuilt. So was Hastings, and we rebuilt it." While he admitted that he had not been able to turn all the problems around, Young said he had "turned [a] significant portion of it around" (*Michigan Chronicle*, November 2, 1985).

The 12th Street area, the epicenter of the 1967 riot, was rebuilt during Young's term in office, a project that he did not hesitate to claim as his own. "I'm the one who built 12th street back up," he said. "When I took office seven years after the riots, 12th street was still lined with cinders and burned out homes and stores. Today it's a far cry from that." He went on to list the devastated areas that had been redeveloped since he became mayor. New homes in Black Bottom had quadrupled, and the area boasted a new shopping center and community center; brand-new housing was built on both sides of the Chrysler Freeway (the old Hasting Street) extending from downtown to Farnsworth; the Warren and Chrysler centers had been built, as well as the Seven Mile–Livernois shopping center, the Seven Mile–Gratiot commercial strip, and the Kern Gardens housing project; Belle Isle underwent renovations; and there were "ongoing city lighting improvements" (*Michigan Chronicle*, November 2, 1985).

Young also included the controversial GM plant built on the foundation of Poletown as an accomplishment. Young saw this project as especially significant because it was "the only one in the nation built in a central city and it will provide as many as 6,000 badly needed jobs. It is one of the best things I have been able to do since I became mayor . . . for every thousand jobs . . . there will be 6,000 more jobs created in supplier plants" (*Michigan Chronicle*, November 2, 1985).

While Young could point to various accomplishments during this election year, critics could point to lingering problems, such as the increase in violent crime. Most alarming during this election year was the dramatic increase in black teenage violence. As one reporter described it, "Teenage violence has escalated at such a rate that as authorities arrest one teen gunman, another is committing a similar crime in another part of town. More than 200 Detroit Public School children have been shot in 1985 resulting in 24 teenaged deaths" (*Michigan Chronicle*, November 2, 1985). This had to be a heavy burden for the first black mayor of Detroit, who more than anything wanted to be a role model for black youth.

The Impact of the Beating Death of Malice Green

Mayor Young's last term in office was marred by the police beating death of Malice Green on November 5, 1992 (see chapter 2). A writer for the *Detroit News and Free Press* expressed the effect of this event on Young's mayoralty: "The foundation upon which Mayor Coleman Young built his career and his administration was rocked Thursday by the beating death of a Detroit man at the hands of Detroit police officers" (November 7, 1992). As he would later write, "nothing knocked me cold like the beating death of an unemployed father of five named Malice Green . . . I would have sworn—in fact, I probably had sworn—that it could never happen in Detroit." It was his "worst nightmare coming true." It was especially disturbing that one of the white officers involved had been a member of the STRESS unit Young had abolished during his first months in office (Young and Wheeler, 1994: 322).

This tragedy cut to the very heart of Young's two-decade-long struggle to improve relations between the black community and the police. "For nearly twenty years," he said, "I had emphasized a firm but respectful style of law enforcement. I had campaigned on that issue and fought over it with veteran cops." Changing the attitudes of the Detroit Police Department had been the first priority of his first term as mayor, and as he put it, "I was damn proud of the progress we had made since then in our relationship with the people, much of which could be attributed to the affirmative action measures we so diligently pursued for two trying decades" (Young and Wheeler, 1994: 321).

Young issued a statement after the shooting in which he said he was "shocked and sickened" at what he had learned about the role of several police officers in the death of a "citizen of the city." He "ordered an immediate, complete investigation to determine exactly what happened," and warned that

Every officer found to be guilty of any misconduct in connection with this tragic incident will be dealt with in the harshest manner possible. I have worked too long and too hard to build a community-based police department to have something like this happen. So long as I am mayor, we will not tolerate any mistreatment of the citizens of this city by the police department. (Young and Wheeler, 1994: 322)

Malice Green's beating death by two white police came on the heels of the L.A. riots following the not-guilty verdict in the trail of white police officers accusing of beating Rodney King (who fortunately did not die). Mayor Young knew all too well how volatile the situation could become. Some of Young's critics in the media attacked him for referring to the Green incident as "murder" on *NBC Nightly News*. Young retorted, "Didn't [they] understand that I had an angry city to consider? Whatever I had to say about the Malice Green incident, I had to say with the city in mind" (Young and Wheeler, 1994: 323).

Young knew that Detroit was not out of the woods when it came to riots triggered by careless and brutal police action compounded by insensitive public officials:

The people of Los Angles had just staged the most devastating riot in American history because they thought—and with damn good reason—that the authorities showed no remorse over what happened to Rodney King, were not appropriately appalled, and did not object profoundly enough to renounce it or to take even symbolic action against the perpetrators. I could not let that happen in Detroit. I was in no hurry to win back the riot championship. (Young and Wheeler, 1994: 323)

Young's mention of "riot championship" was an obvious reference to the Detroit riot of 1967, often referred to as the worst riot in U.S. history. The memory of the 1967 riot and its possible recurrence haunted black and white Detroiters for decades. Every serious racial incident had the potential—in the collective memory of Detroiters—of blowing up into another riot. Now that the L.A. riot had taken center stage in the recent history of urban riots, city officials like Young could either ignore or learn from its lessons. "My charge . . . was to convince the people of Detroit that I was on their side, Young stated, "and that I was just as outraged about what had happened as they were. My job was to learn from Los Angles; to alienate myself from any official attitude against which the people of my city might revolt" (Young and Wheeler, 1994: 323).

After twenty years as the first black mayor of Detroit, Young decided not to run again. His health was failing and, as he would later put it, "I didn't want to sleep through my last term the way Ronald Reagan did" (Young and Wheeler, 1994: 328). As he prepared to leave office, he could look back on several major accomplishments. Chief among them were "affirmative action in the police department, economic development downtown and elsewhere, and the successful management of two fiscal crises" (Rich, 1989: 265).

Undoubtedly, integrating the police department was one of Young's greatest accomplishments in the broad area of race relations. In fact, one could argue that since most of the riots of the 1960s had been provoked by practices of predominantly white police departments, Young's affirmative action policy in the police department was one of the most important contributions to racial equality and interracial cooperation in the post-1967 period. Had the police department remained predominantly white in a predominantly black city, constant conflict between the two would have been inevitable and extremely costly in lives and property.

Increases in minority hiring ranks as an equally impressive accomplishment. When Young was elected mayor in 1973, the city had granted minority contractors less than $20,000. In contrast, Young claimed, "Since 1988 we had averaged more than $125 million, the most awarded by any city" (Young and Wheeler, 1994: 329). Notwithstanding his efforts to improve minority hiring, he never abandoned his commitment to racial balance in hiring. Even though the white population was declining when Young became mayor, he promised to share political power with whites on a fifty-fifty basis. This policy on race reflected his belief that blacks and whites could live harmoniously in cities with black mayors (Rich, 1989).

Young practiced this belief throughout his years as mayor.

I've done my damnedest, in the office of mayor, to carry forward the pursuit of unity on both the intramural and extramural levels. Inevitably, my most immediate, conspicuous opportunities have occurred through the vehicle of city hiring, and I have used, as my instruments in the campaign, racial balance and affirmative action, among other means. (Young and Wheeler, 1994: 330)

He was so committed to racial balance in city hiring that whenever he could, he made sure to go "out in public with two security officers, one black, one white." Unfortunately, this display of interracial unity did not satisfy many of his critics. "Despite my record of fifty-fifty hiring," Young protested, "I have been boorishly charged over the years with 'racial politics' and 'playing the race card.' I prefer to think of it as 'equal opportunity politics' and 'playing the equality card'" (Young and Wheeler, 1994: 330). Not able to resist a jab at the suburbs, he said, "I only wish that my fellow public servants in the suburbs were held to the same standards. To the contrary, I submit that many of them would severely endanger their reelection potential if they dared to hire on a fifty-fifty basis" (Young and Wheeler, 1994: 330).

As Mayor Young was leaving office, he noted sarcastically that "the usual dignitaries paid their respect, many of them spewing forth in uncharacteristically benevolent tones—mindful of course, that I have finally loosened my grip upon the city's top office and no longer pose an institutional threat to their agendas." True to his Black Bottom roots, however, the mayor really appreciated the "flattering remark" from JoAnn Watson, then executive director of the Detroit Chapter of the NAACP, who said, "He's the only mayor I've known in my lifetime about whom the brothers stand out on the corner and slap hands and say, 'my man'" (Young and Wheeler, 1994: 330–31).

Young reflected, "That comment was especially meaningful to me in view of the fact that it was the brothers on the corner of Black Bottom, I among them, for whom I embarked on my life's work more than fifty years ago. And it was . . . with their modern counterparts in mind that, as mayor of Detroit, I bargained with presidents and collaborated with captains of industry." In the end, Young still held this street corner brothers firm in his heart. He knew that as he ended his long tenure as the first black mayor, there was another generation of black males still struggling to survive. "If, as I suspect, those brothers slapping hands are younger men out of luck, searching for human respect and a living wage—and Detroit is full of that kind, believe me—then hell yes, I'm honored to have been their man for the last two decades, and eager to continue in that capacity, however it might shake down in the years ahead" (Young and Wheeler, 1994: 331).

DENNIS WAYNE ARCHER, MAYOR OF DETROIT,
1993–2001: CITY-SUBURBAN BRIDGE BUILDER

The next black mayor of Detroit was a glaring contrast to Mayor Young. Dennis Wayne Archer became mayor at a far less racially polarized and volatile period. Those whites still in the city had grown used to living in a black-majority city. If they feared that "the colored were taking over," they either moved or adjusted. One of the greatest sources of racial tension, the predominantly white police force, had been transformed into one of the most racially integrated police forces in the nation. While many whites in the surrounding suburbs disliked and demonized Young, they were forced to recognize his powerful and defiant regional presence. They knew that he did not care what they thought of him. In fact, it took a "streetwise" tough-taking black personality like Young for many whites to appreciate Archer.

While he was a successful lawyer and a justice of the Michigan Supreme Court, Dennis Archer was by no means a product of the black upper class. In fact, his early life and struggles in rural Cassopolis, Michigan, were far more difficult than Young's somewhat middle-class upbringing in Black Bottom. Archer was born on January 1, 1942, on Detroit's east side. Before his birth his father lost his left arm in an automobile accident that left him partially disabled and limited his job opportunities. The Archer family moved to Cassopolis when Dennis was five, where his father, "in spite of his disability, managed to support his family as a caretaker of a summer home." He "mowed the lawn, washed the car and cared for the summer home, all for a paycheck of $75 every two weeks—and only $37 every two weeks during the winter months" ("Dennis Archer," n.d.-a).

At age eight, Dennis Archer began to contribute to the family well-being by working at jobs as a golf caddy, pin-setter at a bowling alley, and a bakery which required him to rise "in the dark at 3 A.M . . . walking a mile, mopping the floor, then walking back home for another hour or two of sleep before he got up for school" ("Dennis Archer," n.d.-a).

After high school, Archer moved to Detroit to find work to finance his college education. Here again, he worked a variety of jobs to achieve his goals, including painting houses, working as a stock boy in a drug store, and becoming "the first African American worker in the Henry Ford Hospital medical records department." In college, Archer continued working menial jobs to make ends meet, such as dishwashing in Western Michigan University dormitory kitchens prior to graduating with a degree in teaching in 1965 (Johnson and Henderson, n.d.).

At that stage in his life, Archer's dream was to become a schoolteacher. He moved to Detroit and worked with emotionally disabled youngsters in the public school system. While teaching, he met his wife, Trudy DunCombe, also a teacher. They were married in 1967. She encouraged him to attend law school. Later he would return the favor by encouraging Trudy to attend law school as well. Archer began his legal education by taking night courses at the Detroit College of Law, where he earned his degree in 1970. After passing the bar, he moved from teaching to the law firm of Gragg & Gardner. A year later he switched to Hall, Stone, Archer & Glen, where he was made a partner (Johnson and Henderson, n.d.).

Archer had an outstanding career as a lawyer before he ran for the office of mayor of Detroit. He was active in the Wolverine Bar Association, a predominantly black lawyer organization, which elected him president in 1979. Four years later, in 1983, the National Bar Association, the nationwide organization of black lawyers, elected Archer as its president. In 1984, the same year that *Ebony* magazine named him one of the "100 Most Influential Black Americans," he was elected president of the State Bar of Michigan. The next year, 1985, the

National Law Journal included Archer in its list of "100 Most Powerful Attorneys in the United States" and voted him as one of the "100 Most Influential Lawyers" ("Dennis Archer," n.d.-a).

The crowning accomplishment of 1985 was Governor James Blanchard's appointment of Archer to a vacancy on the Michigan Supreme Court, a position that Archer had earned after fifteen years as a trial lawyer. In 1986, Archer was "elected to an eight-year term on the Supreme Court by the people of the State of Michigan. He was the first Black to sit on that Court in nearly 20 years and only the second in Michigan's history" ("Dennis Archer," n.d.-a).

The State Supreme Court appointment could have easily lured Archer into a sense of a glorious final personal accomplishment. Not only did the appointment "seem to signal an end to Archer's political career," but as one observer put it, "It was a prestigious posting that could be expected to continue indefinitely. He was only two years away from a guaranteed annual pension of $50,000, when he decided in 1990, to step down from the bench, return to private practice of law, and seek the mayoralty of Detroit" (Johnson and Henderson, n.d.).

Archer was not a novice in politics when he entered the Detroit mayoral race in 1993. As far back as 1969, Archer was busy "stuffing envelopes, putting together advance teams and other odd jobs for Richard Austin's unsuccessful campaign for mayor of Detroit" ("Dennis Archer," n.d.-a). Politics "fascinated" Archer to the extent that he later worked as campaign manager for both George Crockett Jr.'s successful race for Congress in 1982 and Mayor Coleman Young's successful 1977 mayoral campaign. In addition, Archer "subsequently served in high positions in the campaigns of Secretary of State Richard Austin, Governor James Blanchard, and the United States Senator Carl Levin, as well as working for the election of his friend, William Jefferson Clinton, to be president of the United States" ("Dennis Archer," n.d.-a).

When Archer decided to run for mayor in 1990, he had a private meeting with Mayor Young and told him that he would like to "emulate" what the mayor had done. Young, who was very ill and in his seventies, refused to commit himself to his onetime reelection campaign manager, no doubt because he was contemplating running for a sixth term. Regardless, according to one writer, "As the months passed, Archer made it plain that he planned to run for mayor of Detroit even if it meant facing Coleman Young in a race. It was an audacious decision. Despite his failing health, Young remained wildly popular in Detroit" (Johnson and Henderson, n.d.). Those who had always supported him saw him as a "fiercely independent politician who would guard the city against the 'hostile' forces in the predominantly white suburbs" (Johnson and Henderson, n.d.)

Archer's conciliatory approach to the suburbs as a "campaign tactic" in his formal announcement in November 1992 no doubt alarmed many blacks, who had countless reasons to distrust white suburbanites. Having decided to challenge the ailing but still formidable Mayor Young, Archer decided to pull out all the stops and "fearlessly blasted Young for his style of government." He told the *Detroit Free Press*, "The days when a handful of politicians can sit in a back room and carve up this city are over. It is time for opening the window and letting fresh air into City Hall" (Johnson and Henderson, n.d.).

As could be expected, Young was offended by Archer's comment, and after deciding not to run himself for a sixth term, endorsed Sharon McPhail, a rival candidate. Young's endorsement of McPhail

> gave McPhail an instant organization and within days, at least $250,000 through a $5,000-a-head fund raiser attended by many city officials or businesspeople who were investing in their jobs or city contracts. But it also played into Archer's hands . . . [by] linking McPhail to a tired city

government that was short on services and battered by a reputation for cronyism and corruption. Young's endorsement [of McPhail] helped Archer crystallize the race as a contest between new and old, change and more of the same. (Johnson and Henderson, n.d.)

Comments from a 1992 focus group revealed a range of opinions about Archer, such as: "Heard he's always with White people. Doesn't care anything about Black people," or "[The elitist charge] is just a label. He's intelligent, articulate, educated." Several members of the focus group saw Archer as providing a "fresh attitude" and bringing "a broader base of support to the table" and a "new spirit to Detroit" ("Focus Group, Election Campaign," 1992).

While the focus group comments shed some light on how people viewed Archer, the 1993 campaign would reveal just how much the race and class card could be played in a majority-black city. As one observer explained, "From the outset of his campaign, Dennis Archer had been troubled by what he called 'the drumbeat.' It began as a whisper. Archer was upper-crust, elitist, distant by choice from the middle and lower-class blacks who made up the bulk of Detroit." To many blacks, that was bad enough, but "after he had lunch with Oakland County Executive L. Brooks Patterson, the embodiment of mean-spirited suburban racism to many black Detroiters, Archer was labeled a lackey of some vague, white power brokers who wanted to reclaim the city. Archer, in sum, wasn't black enough to be a mayor of a city that was about 80 percent African American." What had started out as a whisper from McPhail's camp "turned . . . to a roar, playing the race card early and often" (Johnson and Henderson, n.d.).

A month before the November 1993 election, at a McPhail fund-raiser the anti-Archer race-baiting got out of hand. Reverend Charles Adams, one of Detroit's most respected and well-known black ministers and community leaders, told the gathering, "They want a nice mayor. They want a mayor to shuffle when he's not going anywhere, scratch when he's not itching and grin when he's not tickled" (Johnson and Henderson, n.d.). This was an obvious reference to the repeated claims that Archer was only interested in courting powerful white interests in the suburbs.

This attack deeply hurt Archer, coming as it did from such a respectable leader in the black community. He could not allow it to go unchallenged; as he told the *Detroit Free Press*, "I wasn't born wearing the kind of clothes I'm wearing. I wasn't born driving the kind of car I'm driving. I wasn't born making the money I'm making. . . . What kind of message does that [campaign tactic] send our children? Does that mean you have to turn your hat around backward and call somebody names in order to be considered worthy of being part of the community?" Archer concluded by pointing out that he wanted to work with those who were interested in improving Detroit, black, white, Arabic, Jewish, suburban, or city dweller (Johnson and Henderson, n.d.).

To his credit, Revered Adams realized his mistake, and before a week had passed apologized by phone to Archer. Several weeks later, on the eve of the election, Adams invited Archer to address his congregation. Taking the pulpit, Archer clarified his views about Detroit and many blacks' fear of a white suburban takeover of Detroit.

It has been said throughout this campaign that "they" want to take the city back and "they" have a candidate. I hope to let you know who they are and who I represent. I represent the people who can't get their garbage picked up on time . . . their streetlights to stay on all night . . . their phone calls answered at city hall. I stand before you representing children who are more concerned about surviving the school day . . . the homeless, the disenfranchised and the working poor who want affordable housing, and a clean and decent place in which to live. (Johnson and Henderson, n.d.)

When he ended his speech, Reverend Adams hugged him (Johnson and Henderson, n.d.).

With just a few weeks remaining in the campaign, Gail Parrish, an African American and the executive director of the Race Relations Council of Metropolitan Detroit (RRCMD), in an article in the *Detroit Free Press* entitled "Stereotyping Allows Suburbs to Set Agenda for Detroit," presented some sage advice concerning racial labeling in the campaign and black fears and anxiety about white suburban influence on the election.

> There has been a great deal of concern about racial labeling in this election. One of the most troubling aspects of this labeling and stereotyping is the degree to which it is framed as a response to suburbia. This may sound naïve, but does it really matter what suburban intentions are for Detroit? (*Detroit Free Press*, October 21, 1993)

She warned her readers not to focus "too much attention on the concerns and intentions of the suburbs" because by doing so, "we Detroiters risk falling into a trap that would keep us in a powerless reactionary stance, charting a course that is anything but independent. We risk losing the opportunity to frame effectively our own vision for the future." While she acknowledged that there were some suburban interests who were racist and "ill-intentioned," some were not. Therefore, she argued, "We are handing power that is rightfully ours to others by letting suburbanites, who have no vote in this election, frame the agenda for our city" (*Detroit Free Press*, October 21, 1993).

The city-suburban issue had been a regional issue for years, so it was no surprise that it would raise its troubling head during the campaign. Several months earlier, the RRCMD had sponsored a forum to allow the mayoral candidates to answer questions related to the racial and ethnic relations of Detroit. Dennis Archer and Sharon McPhail were among the six candidates attending the forum. Unfortunately, as reported by an observer, "It was clear by the forum's end, that the big question in the minds of those attending was still unanswered: 'Who is the best person to lead Detroit into a multiculturally harmonious future?'" (Race Relations Alert, 1993).

In September, the RRCMD sponsored its first major race and ethnic relations conference, which had the uplifting title "Tear Down the Walls: A Call for City-Suburban Reconciliation." The major focus was on "bridging the mostly white suburbs and the mostly black city," and the "possibility that a new Detroit mayor could bring new cooperation between the city and the suburbs" (*Detroit Free Press*, October 21, 1993). The keynote speaker, Clarence Page, an African American columnist for the *Chicago Tribune*, reminded the participants that the upcoming mayoral contest between Dennis Archer and Sharon McPhail would revolve around two questions: "Who is going to work the hardest for urban-suburban cooperation? And is that a bad thing or a good thing?" He added that the recent pattern of blacks moving to the suburbs may have contributed to improved relations between Detroit and its suburbs (*Detroit Free Press*, October 21, 1993).

During the campaign various news and citizens' organizations sent questionnaires to Archer to obtain his views and future policies—if he were elected—related to race and ethnic relations. The Latino News Publication was concerned about the growing Hispanic population in Detroit, and asked: "Hispanics comprise a significant portion in Detroit's population.

How are you going to interact with Hispanics to bring out their voice in your administration?" Archer responded: "I began meeting with Hispanic community leaders two years ago and my advisory council, Amigos de Archer, has been an integral part of my campaign seeking the office of Mayor of the City of Detroit." Furthermore, he assured the *Latino News*, "I am committed to improving the quality of life in the areas of education, jobs, safety and security . . . and to substantially increase the number of Hispanics in all areas of city government." He promised to have more Hispanic police officers and firefighters, to "give more concentrated attention to the gangs in the community," have "members of the Hispanic community as his appointees," and to "continue to work on a regular basis with the Hispanic community" ("Dennis Archer," n.d.-b).

The *Detroit News* candidate questionnaire wanted to know what Archer "would do to bring about improved relations between Detroit and its suburban neighbors?" Predictably, Archer promised to be "personally involved in building bridges between city and suburbs and . . . actively participate in the Big Four meetings . . . and to accept speaking engagements in the suburbs." Most importantly, he said he would "look for ways to promote the many things we have in common and work to resolve the differences and misunderstandings" ("*Detroit News* Candidate Questionnaire," n.d.).

When asked in another *Detroit News* questionnaire, "What is the state of race relations in Metro Detroit today? What would you do to ease racial tension in the region," Archer admitted that race relations were not good, but said they could be improved. His administration, he promised, "will be one of inclusion, not of exclusion. My administration will reflect the ethnic diversity of our community and will work with block clubs, neighborhood and community groups to listen to and address issues of importance and concern to our residents." Furthermore, he promised to be "personally involved in reducing racial tension rather than relying solely on the efforts of the NAACP, New Detroit, ACCESS, The NCCJ and others" ("*Detroit News* Candidate Questionnaire," n.d.).

Archer won the November 1993 election with a margin of victory over McPhail of 57 percent to 43 percent. The exit polls revealed some of the underlying racial dynamics of the election. Archer "received 90 percent of the votes by white Detroiters but only 47 percent of the black vote—to McPhail's 52 percent" (Johnson and Henderson, n.d.). During his inauguration and swearing-in ceremony, Mayor Archer threw out a challenge to Detroiters to contribute their part to improving the city. "Sweep the sidewalk in front of your house . . . clean the rubbish from the storm sewers on the street. Pick up the broken glass in your alley. Go with your neighbor to cut the weeds in the lot down the way on your street." As he had promised throughout his campaign, he called for the healing of the divide between Detroit and its suburbs. "Tell our friends in Birmingham, Dearborn, Mt. Clemens and Windsor," Archer said, "we're in this together and we're in it for the long haul" (*Michigan Chronicle*, January 5–11, 1994).

Former mayor Coleman Young was prevented from participating in the program because of illness, but the new mayor and Detroit City Council President Maryann Mahaffey paid tribute to Young's five terms as mayor of Detroit. "Today as we launch a new chapter, we cannot forget the contribution of a truly monumental figure in Detroit's history—Coleman Young." Mahaffey said that the city council would present Young "with an official testimony and medallion recognizing his public service" (*Michigan Chronicle*, January 5–11, 1994).

As Archer took office, it became abundantly clear that he was serious about reaching out to the surrounding suburbs. In July 1994, at the Greater Detroit Chamber of Commerce's

Fourteenth Annual Mackinac Conference, he was a major presence and participant in the discussions about new regional partnerships, seen as a beacon of hope for the region. In a photo in the *Detroiter* magazine, Archer was even seen smiling alongside a smiling Oakland County executive L. Brooks Patterson, long considered by African Americans in Detroit as a sworn enemy of the city. As a writer for the *Detroiter* pointed out, however, "The new mayoral leadership in the city of Detroit was seen at Mackinac as the catalyst for a new partnering in Southeast Michigan." Obviously referring to the racial tensions between Detroit under Young and the present Archer administration, the writer said, "The olive branch finally has been extended across Eight Mile Road and the dust shaken out of the welcome mat between such diverse entities as Detroit and its suburbs, Southeast Michigan and state government, Metro Detroit and Western Michigan, Democrats and Republicans, and most of all, the business community and the city of Detroit" (*Detroiter*, July 1994).

There can be no doubt that Mayor Archer introduced a fresh, new approach to running a predominantly black city surrounded by predominantly white and largely hostile suburbs. Young had been on a war-footing with many elements in the suburbs for decades, and his legacy was still smoldering in the hearts of many blacks who had more than enough reasons to distrust white suburbia—and to distrust Archer for reaching out to them. Archer was not Young, however. He came with a different vision. One urban scholar explains, "At the root of his vision for Detroit was adherence to a view that to stabilize and revitalize the city required bridge-building, negotiation and compromise with the suburbs and the white business elites. It is a vision that sees cultural separatism as an economic dead end for African Americans" (Neill, 2003: 140). While "cultural separatism" had its downside, Archer's vision for Detroit had potential risks for his credibility among Detroit blacks. "The vision has been the assertion of the possibility of a multicultural city in a regional context where persistent racism makes this an uphill task, risking the charge of being 'a silk-stocking' elitist, a synonym for 'the white man's candidate'" (Neill, 2003: 140).

Black urban planners under Archer articulated this vision, which departed from the "separatist" tendency of Young's planners. "The tone of the two Planning and Development Department directors appointed under Archer was far removed from the outlook of the separatist Ron Hewitt," writes one scholar. Gloria Robinson, the first planner appointed under Archer, "pointed to how Archer had not played the 'victim card' in the manner of Young but also mentioned the 'difficulty of sending an inclusive cultural message to the suburbs when the mayor knows the reality of the racism out there driving sprawl.'" Another black planner who replaced Robinson restated this vision for Detroit as "a city where diversity is celebrated and different people can live side by side" (Neill, 2003: 140).

It could be argued that one of Archer's greatest contributions to both the economic development of Detroit as a "black city" and the limited improvement of city-suburban race relations was his success in attracting new businesses to Detroit, such as Compuware, the computer giant (Johnson and Henderson, n.d.). Prestigious white businesses coming to Detroit had the tendency to "soften" white suburbanites' view of the "black city."

During his tenure as mayor, Archer launched negotiations for the Detroit Tigers' new baseball stadium, named Comerica Park, which opened in 2000. The renaming of the stadium after the bank is interesting as a commentary on race and the city. As one writer put it, "The new stadium is called Comerica Park—ironically named after a bank in the early 1990s that changed its name from Detroit Bank and Trust in order to disassociate itself from the negative image of Detroit" (Neill, 2004: 144). Archer also paved the way for the return of the

Detroit Lions from Pontiac to Detroit with a new stadium in the fall of 2002 (Johnson and Henderson, n.d.).

Perhaps Mayor Archer's "most defining moment [was] the day when voters okayed three casinos in the city limits" (Johnson and Henderson, n.d.), a project that the late Coleman Young had supported as a means to "create jobs and bring a measure of fiscal independence to Detroit in the form of local betting taxes" (Neill, 2003: 144). Things soon turned sour, however, when none of the three casino licenses issued went to an African American, "despite the fact that a prominent African American Detroiter had experience in this area." Robinson, one of Archer's Planning and Development directors, defended her boss's decision. "The city was not interested in cronyism," she said, "but in the best bids. The economic interests of the city were put ahead of race" (Neill, 2003: 148).

Mayor Archer's casino decision was one of the major reasons behind a recall petition organized by the Black Slate, the political arm of the Shrine of the Black Madonna and the New Marcus Garvey Movement. Ron Hewitt, one of the planning directors under Young who at the time was the regional chair of the Black Slate, was driving the effort (Neill, 2003). Some of the recall leaders expressed the same time-worn racial views heard during the 1993 mayoral campaign that Archer was "not black enough" to be mayor of Detroit. For example, Hewitt said that Archer is "somebody who doesn't take into account the needs and aspirations of black people against the background of our experiences in America." Another supporter of the recall effort labeled Archer an elitist who didn't listen to the concerns of "everyday black Detroiters." "You shouldn't have to have a college degree for the mayor to stop and pay attention to people. A real black person wouldn't ignore black people" (*Detroit Free Press*, June 9, 1999).

Detroit Free Press writer Heath Meriwether described this recall attempt among certain black critics of Archer, saying, "The not-black-enough disease strikes again." She argued that the "recall attempt flies in the face of Archer's approval rating among Detroit residents, his national prominence as a co-chair of Vice President Al Gore's presidential election campaign, and his proven ability to sell Detroit as a place where you want to do business." While Archer's critics "cite a variety of issues for wanting to oust him from his job—including the enduring one of poor city services to neighborhood, the recall boils down to this: Archer somehow is not black enough to lead Detroit" (*Detroit Free Press*, June 9, 1999).

One prominent black lawyer who disagreed with the black recall attempt argued that several of Archer's projects, such as the stadium, the casinos, and Campus Martius, provided work for a range of black companies and created well-paying jobs that enabled Detroiters to invest in homes and provide college education for their children. Furthermore, the critics had to face the fact that crime and unemployment were down and "large scale development is underway" (*Detroit Free Press*, May 23, 1999). In May 1999, a *Detroit Free Press* poll, 65 percent of 350 registered voters in Detroit "said they wanted to keep Archer in office" (June 9, 1999).

In the end, the recall attempt failed. Concerned about the divisiveness the recall attempt had caused in the black community, the Rev. Wendell Anthony, head of the Detroit chapter of the NAACP, tried to build bridges between Archer and the groups leagued against him (*Detroit Free Press*, June 9, 1999).

One of Mayor Archer's last projects, designed to carry out his vision of a multicultural metropolitan community, occurred in 2001 and was itself a sad commentary on suburban commitment to the vision. As urban planner scholar William J. V. Neill describes it:

The Detroit 300 tricentennial celebrations in 2001 showcased efforts under Archer to project an image of a multicultural city alongside a Detroit civic identity which offered an inclusive invitation to join to the rest of the metropolitan area. Celebrations reached a high point in July with a free waterfront concert by Motown recording artist Stevie Wonder, a Tall Ships Visit and a musical concert. The publicity matter for the latter, part-sponsored by the *Detroit Free Press*, included the powerful logo: "D" for diversity. Banners extensively festooned from city lamp-posts proclaimed the direct message "Proud People." Suburban identification with this civic sentiment that could also be read as a cultural statement was modest as evidenced by a shameful reluctance to contribute financially to tricentennial events as put by one local politician from the suburb of Novi: "For us to say no subjects us to criticism about a white enclave turning its back on a black community, and I'm sensitive to the charge. (Neill, 2003: 148)

After two terms in office, Archer surprised his many supporters when he decided not to seek a third term as mayor (*New York Times*, April 18, 2001). As the clouds of future economic and fiscal woes began forming over the Motor City, one scholar wrote, "it is likely that Greater Detroit under Archer missed its last chance to embrace the concept of progressive multicultural regionalism" (Neill, 2003: 156). The reasons for this missed opportunity are complex, but as urban scholar June M. Thomas argues, "If Young were indeed the main cause of estrangement [between the city and its surrounding suburbs], Archer's election should have resolved all such problems. . . . In contrast, Archer was a natural diplomat. . . . White citizens and institutions would have been hard pressed to find a capable Black mayor more open to negotiation and cooperation." Unfortunately, Thomas continues, "Once elected, Archer soon found that his willingness to cooperate did not automatically eliminate suburban noncooperation. During his first year in office, battles with regional leaders—particularly over a proposed merger of city and regional transit systems—were bruising affairs" (Thomas, 1997: 205).

KWAME KILPATRICK: THE HIP-HOP MAYOR OF DETROIT, 2001–2008

Kwame Kilpatrick was born in Detroit in 1970 and raised on Detroit's west side. According to one source, Kilpatrick "knew by the fifth grade that he wanted to be mayor," which he considered his dream job. Such youthful aspirations were not unusual, given his family's political background. His mother, Congresswoman Carolyn Cheeks Kilpatrick, had been serving as state representative from Detroit's Ninth District for two years, an office she would hold for eighteen years. His father, Bernard Kilpatrick, worked in the Wayne County Executive Office (Rochelle, n.d.).

After graduating from the prestigious and selective Cass Technical High School, Kilpatrick attended Florida A&M University, a historically black college, and graduated with a BSc degree in political science in 1992 (Stevens, 2008). Before returning home to Detroit, Kilpatrick spent a short time teaching at Richards High School in Florida. Back in Detroit Kilpatrick continued his teaching career at the Marcus Garvey Academy. During his four years at the academy, Kilpatrick was more than a teacher: "He took on the role of basketball coach and the more important role of mentor" (Rochelle, n.d.). He enrolled in the Detroit College of Law and earned his juris doctorate (Stevens, 2008).

Unlike his two predecessors, Kilpatrick was primed for office by his powerful political family. When his mother was elected to the U.S. House of Representatives, her seat was available for her son. Kilpatrick succeeded her in the Michigan House of Representatives at age twenty-six. His mother went on to serve in the U.S. Congress and to become chairwomen of the Congressional Black Caucus; meanwhile, Kwame Kilpatrick was leading the Democrats in the state legislature as minority leader, the first African American to do so. During his time in the legislature Kilpatrick "brokered the Clean Michigan Initiative, which promoted urban renewal through new funding and also secured a deal to preserve healthcare funding for those on low income" (Stevens, 2008). Sixty percent of this $675 million in funds went to Detroit. Kilpatrick also played a major role in securing millions of dollars to fight lead poisoning in the city. At the time, more child-related lead-poisoning cases were reported in Detroit than in the rest of the state combined (Rochelle, n.d.).

Kilpatrick entered the national spotlight at the 2000 Democratic Convention in Los Angles when he addressed the gathering. Four years later, he spoke again at the Boston convention. At this early age, Kilpatrick was well on his way to becoming one of the most impressive black rising stars in the state and the nation. His considerable political talents and experiences were catching the eye of the national Democratic leadership: "In 2000, the Democratic Leadership Council, the modernizing faction that came to prominence under Clinton and Gore, tipped Kilpatrick as 'one to watch'" (Stevens, 2008). Just as Kilpatrick was maturing in the role as minority leader in the state house, Mayor Archer announced in April 2001 that he was not going to run for reelection, and Kilpatrick saw his opportunity to achieve his longtime dream.

As in the three previous mayoral elections, race played its part. In contrast to Archer's attempt to build bridges between the city and its suburbs, a preelection survey revealed that "suburban healing had ranked low as a quality the next mayor should have" (Neill, 2003: 155). The pendulum was swinging back to the harsh realities of city-suburban racial and inner-city intraracial politics. In the final battle between the two main candidates, both Kilpatrick and his competitor, seventy-year-old Gill Hill, president of the Detroit City Council and former mayor Young's chief homicide detective, "underplayed bridge-building and rapprochement with the suburbs characteristic of Archer's election campaign eight years earlier." Kilpatrick "presented himself as 'a son of the city' . . . to whom Coleman Young was a 'hero'" (Neill, 2003: 155). In the end, Kilpatrick defeated Hill with 54 percent of the vote to become, at thirty-one, the youngest mayor in the history of Detroit (Neill, 2003).

This would not be the last time that Kilpatrick would be forced to engage in racial politics. In 2005, when he found himself behind in the polls during the reelection fight with Freeman Hendrix, his campaign tried to focus attention on Hendrix's suburban support. In the August primary race Hendrix had beaten Kilpatrick 44 percent to 34 percent, creating a historical first by "making Kilpatrick the first incumbent mayor to finish second in a primary in at least 60 years" (Osinio, 2005). The polls showed that black voters had split their votes between the two black candidates, and a majority of white Detroit voters and other minorities, which made up 20 percent of the voting population, supported Hendrix. In desperation, Kilpatrick fell back on the old tactic of suburban-baiting. In the first of three debates with Hendrix, Kilpatrick said, "In Birmingham and Bloomfield Hills and all these places, they do more meth, they do more Ecstasy and they do more acid than all the schools in the city of Detroit" (Osinio, 2005).

As could be expected, county and school district officials were outraged at Kilpatrick's comments. Oakland County executive L. Brooks Patterson was quick to respond: "These comments insulted the residents of Birmingham and Bloomfield Hills, insulted the students and impugned the reputation of two of our finest, exemplary school districts" (Osinio, 2005). Patterson compared Kilpatrick to the former Mayor Young, saying (somewhat incorrectly) that Young had refused to cooperate with the surrounding communities. Patterson had been around long enough to understand racial politics and had contributed his share to the playbook. He admitted, however, that he and Kilpatrick had worked together. "Kwame has largely been a very affable person to work with, but once in a while he makes comments like these that really hurt relations. I'll continue to work with him because he's the leader of Michigan's largest city, but he's not going to be on my Christmas card list" (Osinio, 2005).

Recognizing he had made a tactical political error by engaging in suburban-baiting, and before the county executive had demanded an apology, Kilpatrick made a somewhat feeble attempt at damage control by issuing a statement that read: "Character issues such as drug abuse are not exclusive to Detroit Public Schools. My reference to substance abuse, not intended to focus on any particular school district, was simply used to illustrate this position" (Osinio, 2005). Patterson appeared confused about why Kilpatrick would use such "inflammatory" statements about two of Oakland County's "most prosperous communities," unless, Patterson concluded, he was doing it to win votes (Osinio, 2005). One pollster was not surprised by Kilpatrick's desperate attempt at suburban-baiting and its impact on future city-suburban relations, saying, "Mayor Kilpatrick doesn't care about suburban relations right now . . . he just cares about the election. The problem with comments like this is that they're only made for the moment" (Osinio, 2005). Falling back on the playbook used by the McPhail campaign against Archer, Kilpatrick's strategy was to create an "us versus them" mind-set by labeling Hendrix as the candidate favored by the suburbs in hopes of winning more of the black vote (Osinio, 2005).

It did not help Kilpatrick that 2005 was also the year that *Time* magazine named him as one of America's worst mayors. In an interview with *Time*, Kilpatrick acknowledged that some of his "boneheaded behavior" during his first term could be attributed to his youth and early inexperience in running a major city (Gray, 2007). Wearing an earring, hosting a hip-hop summit, and other aspects of his image that earned him the title of the nation's "first hip-hop" mayor by "cultural icon" Russell Simmons (Gray, 2007) alienated many of Detroit's black professionals. His lifestyle and attempts to "cast himself as a racial martyr sent the message," as explained Mildred Gaddis, fifty-three, one of Detroit's popular talk-show hosts, "This is our city now, and the thug life is OK . . . This hip-hop thing . . . turned off a lot of people who initially supported him," Gaddis said, herself among them (Gray, 2007).

In the November 2005 election Mayor Kilpatrick managed to survive his historic primary loss to Hendrix, and beat his opponent 53 percent to 47 percent, thus holding onto the office of the mayor. Unfortunately, more serious challenges were waiting in the wings.

Two years later, the young mayor of Detroit was fighting for his job and his political life when he was caught up in a sex scandal involving his chief of staff, Christine Beatty. Dating back to a 2003 whistle-blower trial in which Kilpatrick's police ex-bodyguard, Harold Nelthorpe, and former deputy police chief Gary Brown, claimed they were fired because of an internal investigation into the mayor's personal life. They filed a civil lawsuit against the mayor. Both Kilpatrick and Beatty denied that they had been involved in an extramarital affair. When the trial ended on September 11, 2007, with a verdict awarding the plaintiffs $6.5 million in damages, Kilpatrick once again played the race/suburban card by blaming the "wrong verdict" on white suburban jurors (Rochelle, n.d.).

Unwilling to take the blame for his obvious wrongdoing and pledging to appeal the verdict, Kilpatrick went on radio attacking the verdict, declaring that he did not receive a fair trial and unabashedly declaring that he would not be prevented from leading the city because "I believe with all my heart and my soul that God anointed me to do this. And I believe something bad would happen to me if I walked away from this blessing" (*Detroit Free Press*, September 13, 2007). Once again playing the race card, he strongly implied that the verdict against him should be seen as an attack on all black men in Detroit. "All of a sudden, you just get corrupt, ignorant, stupid, lazy and promiscuous. . . . I just think this is a reality check—not just on Kwame Kilpatrick because, you know, I'm God's guy; I'm going to be all right—I think this is for all black men right now in the city of Detroit" (*Detroit Free Press*, September 13, 2007).

Kilpatrick's race-baiting arguments were rapidly unraveling even among black men whom he had supported for high public office, such as Amos Williams. In 2006, Kilpatrick had supported Williams as the Democratic candidate for Michigan attorney general, but the former disagreed with Kilpatrick's rather transparent and contradictory arguments. "It wasn't like the jury went out and drummed up some charges. This was litigation brought by two black men who thought the mayor had misused his power to damage their careers" (*Detroit Free Press*, September 13, 2007).

The beginning of the end of Mayor Kilpatrick's political career occurred in late January 2008 when two *Detroit Free Press* investigative reporters revealed that Kilpatrick and Beatty had lied under oath about their affair in the police whistleblower lawsuit. The mayor then made a secret deal in which he agreed to settle the lawsuit for over $9 million in exchange for keeping the private text messages between himself and Beatty about their affair secret. Kilpatrick would spend months in court battles trying to keep the text messages and secret settlement documents from being released to the public, to no avail (*Detroit Free Press*, September 5, 2008).

When the text messages were finally released and made public, they revealed that Kilpatrick and Beatty had lied about not having an affair—both were married to other people—and about not intending to fire Brown. As the two investigative reporters explained, "The Kilpatrick-Beatty relationship and Brown's dismissal were central to the whistle-blower suit filed by Brown and Harold Nelthrope . . . the two cops accused Kilpatrick of retaliating against them because of their role in an internal investigation of the mayor's security team—a probe that could have potentially exposed the affair" (Schaefer and Elrick, 2008)

In January 2008, during his seventh "State of the City" address to Detroit, Kilpatrick focused on several positive changes occurring throughout the city; then, before completing the speech, he launched into the controversy swirling around him. Once again casting himself in the role of a racial martyr, he said:

In the past 30 days I've been called a nigger more than any time in my entire life. In the past three days I've received more death threats than I have in my entire administration. I've heard these words before but I've never heard them say them about my wife and children. I have to say this because it's very personal to me. I don't believe that a Nielsen rating is worth the life of my children or your children. This unethical, illegal lynch mob mentality has to stop. And it's seriously time. We've never been here before. And I don't care if they cut the T.V. off. We've never been in a situation like this before. Where you can say anything, do anything, have no facts, no research, no nothing and you launch a hate-driven bigoted assault on a family. I humbly ask members of the council, I humbly ask the religious community, I humbly ask the brothers and sisters of the city of Detroit—I humbly asked that we say "no more" together. I love this city with every part of my being. I will continue to stay focused on building the next Detroit. God Bless you, Detroit, I love you. (Rochelle, n.d.)

The address backfired badly in some quarters. Some observers felt Kilpatrick's speech amounted to race-baiting to save his political career. Even his former political advisor, Sam Riddle, described the address as a race-baiting speech, "an act of desperation," an attempt to regain his base by playing the race card. "He's gone to that well one too many times" (Rochelle, n.d.). Carmen Harlan, an African American news anchor at a local Detroit affiliate, countered Kilpatrick's characterization of the media coverage of his scandals as a baseless "hate-driven bigoted assault on a family":

Mr. Mayor, I'd like to address you directly. You were absolutely right tonight when you said that death-threats and racial slurs are wrong. I'll even go further, they're inexcusable and inappropriate, but to say that we, the media, are to blame for the mess isn't fair either. Using emotionally driven words, like the N-word, phrases like "hate-driven" and "bigoted assault," even "lynch mob mentality," stirs the very core of even my emotions. You see, I love the city too, as much as you do. Like you, we [the media] have a job to do too. I've asked you to sit down with me; explain what we don't understand and how we may have gotten it wrong. I'm still waiting for that phone call. And I quote you, "No more, I humbly ask! The Kwame Kilpatrick roller coaster has to stop." (Rochelle, n.d.)

Notwithstanding his fading light brought on by recent criminal charges associated with the text message scandal, Kilpatrick refused to resign and fully accept blame for the millions of dollars his actions had cost the city. In February 2008, during a morning radio show he was asked if he would be willing to repay taxpayers the $8.4 million for the (secret) settlement that the city paid to the two officers. Uncontrite as ever, Kilpatrick responded: "I pay it back every day. When I go out and do an economic stimulus package for hundreds of millions of dollars. When I go find a way to do a deal on the tunnel for $75 million dollars. When I go and bust my butt every day from six in the morning to ten–eleven o'clock at night. . . . I work every day to make sure the city gets what it's owned" (WWJ AM, Detroit, February 28, 2008).

Despite the heavy burden of shame and money Kilpatrick had cost the city, he still had many supporters who refused to abandon him, or for that matter press him to resign. They became his blind enablers, willing to forgive and forget their young "hip-hop" mayor's moral failings. Kilpatrick knew this and played upon it. In March 2008, the mayor's supporters packed a church where they rallied to the chants of "I can make it through the storm" augmented by the rousing choruses of a gospel choir. Kilpatrick assured the crowd that he would not resign. When Kilpatrick, standing behind the pulpit, told them, "I will humbly serve you till the day I die," the crowd exploded in deafening applause (*Detroit Free Press*, March 28, 2008). Seeking to minimize the seriousness of his misdeeds, the mayor claimed that the text message scandal involved more than that since other people had done worse things and did not lose their freedom. He then changed the subject to one sure to elicit even more sympathy from his supporters. The real issue, he said, was really about Detroit's future and resources. "We're at a time when the most precocious resource in the world is not oil, it's water," he said. He was referring to the fact that since Detroit owns and operated the water system that supplies water to most of southeast Michigan, the suburbs that had been fighting for years to have some control in its operation (*Detroit Free Press*, March 28, 2008).

As if he did not have enough controversy, Kilpatrick's use of the N-word compounded his trouble and further eroded his credibility among some former supporters. A year earlier he had joined with the NAACP at its Ninety-eighth Annual Convention to effectively bury the N-word in an event "billed as the funeral for the racial slur that has been used against blacks for more than a century" (Sieh, 2008). Yet even this controversy was the least of his troubles. As a result of the text messages that revealed that Kilpatrick and Beatty had been involved in a love affair and had in fact committed perjury, both were charged with "obstruction of justice, conspiracy, misconduct in office and perjury" (Rochelle, n.d.)

For some strange reason, Mayor Kilpatrick refused to accept the terms of the bond in his perjury case requiring that he inform the court before leaving the city. Perhaps the heady arrogance of power and status was too much for Kilpatrick when in July he decided to violate his bond and travel to Canada on a business trip. His actions forced the hand of the county prosecutor's office to request that he be punished. Kilpatrick apologized to the court, saying, "I've been living in an incredible state of pressure and scrutiny." His apology was not sufficient. On August 6, 2008, District Court Judge Ronald Giles informed Mayor Kilpatrick that he would receive the same treatment as any other defendant and sent him to jail for the night ("Detroit Mayor Ordered Jailed," 2008). The next morning, he made history by "becoming the first sitting mayor in Detroit's 307-year history to spend a night behind bars" (Elrick and Swickard, 2008).

As his legal battles mounted, a chorus of voices began calling for his resignation. In early August *Detroit Free Press* readers shared their frustration, anger, and sadness over the troubles the mayor had brought both upon himself and the city he so often claimed he loved (*Detroit Free Press*, August 10, 2008). One reader wrote, "I am sad for our city that has lost a bright young mayor to his ego. It happens. He should resign for his own good and that of the city he loves." Another reader reminded fellow Detroiters, "Remember, my fellow citizens, that we, not any politician, are the city, and this all will pass. I hope the churches that have supported him will speak out and encourage him to resign." According to one reader, "The legacy of Coleman Young and Dennis Archer, two principled mayors who did their best for the City of Detroit, has been trashed one more time by the Hip-Hop Mayor. Somehow, Mayor Kilpatrick doesn't think the rules apply to him" (*Detroit Free Press*, August 10, 2008).

One reader blamed Kilpatrick for setting back race relations in the city and embarrassing the black community, especially black men:

> As a black man, I view Mayor Kwame Kilpatrick as the new black man's burden. Shame on the city of Detroit for putting up with this sham. . . . I can't think of any case that is more embarrassing or detrimental to African Americans everywhere than the Kilpatrick situation. It fans the glowing embers of racism and leads many non-blacks to ask: "What in the hell is wrong with you people? How can you allow this?" How indeed? (*Detroit Free Press*, August 10, 2008)

By this time, some city leaders and some of Kilpatrick's main supporters were beginning to realize that they had to cut bait in order to salvage what was left of the city's reputation. The court battles and legal challenges were bogging the city down in an ongoing legal morass. In August 2008, the influential Council of Baptist Pastors of Detroit and Vicinity abandoned its earlier reluctance to call for the mayor's resignation and issued a statement through its president saying, "We humbly urge the mayor to consider resignation from his office." The president added that "resignation would be an act of good faith that the mayor has the best interest of the city at heart . . . there is an uncertain time line for resolution of charges against the mayor . . . The legal process threatens to mire the city in a mess for an indefinite period." As a result Kilpatrick's ability to lead had been "rendered ineffective" (*Detroit Free Press*, August 10, 2008).

On September 4, 2008, after the city had endured months of regional, national, and international embarrassment, shame amid the public spectacle of legal wrangling, Mayor Kwame Kilpatrick pled guilty to two felonies and no contest to a charge of assaulting a police officer in July who was in the process of serving papers on one of the mayor's best friends. As part of the settlement Kilpatrick agreed to resign as mayor of Detroit, repay $1 million in restitution to the city, give up his law license, hold no public office for five years, spend 120 days in jail, and serve five years probation (Saulny and Bunkly, 2008; *Detroit Free Press*, September 5, 2008).

The news soon spread around the nation and the world. As quoted in the *Detroit Free Press* (September 5, 2008), the British Broadcasting Company reported the sad end of Mayor Kilpatrick: "A prominent African-African who was elected mayor at the age of 31, Mr. Kilpatrick had been considered one of the rising stars of the Democratic Party." The *Wall Street Journal* pointed to the racial tensions between the city and the suburbs produced by Kilpatrick's troubles. "The mayor's troubles exposed the long-standing resentments between the largely African-American city and its white suburban population. Many of the city's residents support the mayor and consider his legal troubles an attack on him from his political enemies. Suburban residents, many of whom left the city after the 1967 riot, called for his resignation" (*Detroit Free Press*, September 5, 2008). The *New York Times* argued that Kilpatrick's "refusal to resign delighted a certain segment of the city's mostly poor, mostly black population, who felt pride in Mr. Kilpatrick's rise from the Detroit Public Schools to the mayor's office. But others here found Mr. Kilpatrick arrogant and stubborn" (*Detroit Free Press*, September 5, 2008). *Time* magazine, quoted in the *Detroit Free Press*, assessed the costs of Kilpatrick's problems on the city. "The cost to Detroit taxpayers for Kilpatrick's abuse of power has been high—over $10 million so far, including legal fees and an $8.4 million confidential settlement paid to whistle-blowers . . . the same sum could put several hundred new police officers on the streets of the country's most violent city. Or knock down more than a thousand of the abandoned buildings that dot Detroit's streets and breed crime" (*Detroit Free Press*, September 5, 2008).

It would be difficult to imagine that all this attention was lost on the mayor. If he felt any remorse over the enormous burden he had laid on the city, he did not express it at the news conference after he pled guilty. Instead the ex-mayor could not resist yet another gesture of empty bravado, pledging to overcome his conviction and heaping blame on the media and Governor Jennifer Granholm "for damaging his marriage and career." Worse still, he issued yet another sad and tragic pledge to the gathering, "Y'all done set me up for a comeback." A month later, at his sentencing, the ex-mayor showed little remorse, "shaking his head as the judge chastised him for his crime, smiling at family and friends, at time clowning with the prosecutors who helped put him behind bars." He maintained his defiance even in the face of Wayne County Circuit Judge David Groner, who scolded him for his arrogance and sentenced him to 120 days in jail. Upset over Kilpatrick's comments at the news conference, the judge told him, "The community expected to hear a message of humility, remorse and apology. Instead, we heard an arrogant and defiant man who accused the governor, among others for his downfall.

Your statements were incredible given the fact that you had just pled guilty" (*Detroit Free Press*, October 28, 2008). Then as he was led away, Kilpatrick waved at his family and friends and said, "Y'all take it easy" (*Detroit Free Press*, October 28, 2008).

Kilpatrick had the potential to become a major leader and model for a new generation of youth, especially black youth in Detroit, who sorely needed a model beyond reproach. This "hip-hop" generation looked up to him, and for good reason: he was smart and charismatic and had accumulated an impressive list of accomplishments at a young age. Notwithstanding the scandal that brought him down while in office, Kilpatrick did accomplish some goals worthy of mentioning: he relocated some businesses downtown, including Home Depot, Borders, and Quicken Loans, revised "the development agreement with Detroit's three casinos so that permanent casinos/hotels would actually be built . . . [and] successfully closed the deal for the $180 million renovation of the historic Book-Cadillac Hotel" (Sternberg, n.d.). To his credit, he made efforts to revitalize neighborhoods by establishing "the Detroit Riverfront conservatory to redevelop Detroit's riverfront . . . [and] he also established Next Detroit, a 5-year project aimed at enhancing 6 neighborhoods through improved maintenance and new investment" (Sternberg, n.d.). The opening of career centers "to provide job retraining in high-demand areas" was certainly a key accomplishment. Other accomplishments could be added to the list as well, such as building "upon the success of 2005/2006 sporting events to attract other events, such as the National Association for the Advancement of Colored People (NAACP)'s 98th annual National convention and 2009 NCAA Men's Basketball Final Four" (Sternberg, n.d.). As one writer said, "Mayor Kilpatrick has style, presence, confidence and enthusiasm, qualities that help investors believe in his vision for Detroit" (Sternberg n.d.). He also had the political experience to resume bridging bridges across the city-suburban divide.

In spite of all this potential for greatness, he squandered it for show and sex. Among the tragic consequences of his transgressions—besides destroying the trust of the black community—was the grist he provided for the anti-Detroit mill. Black Detroiters did not need more negative press about its leaders or its city. Furthermore, the image of Detroit as a black majority-run city was damaged beyond measure by Kilpatrick's conduct while in office. No other black leader in Detroit's history has brought such shame and humiliation on a community in a constant struggle to do its best in the midst of poverty, crime, and violence.

History would not only credit him with being the youngest mayor elected as mayor in Detroit but unfortunately the only mayor in the history of Detroit to be charged with a felony while in office (Rochelle, n.d.).

CONCLUSION

The growth of black political power was the most significant development in the black community after 1967. White flight to the suburbs in the wake of the disorders made possible the growth of a black-majority city determined to take control of city hall. The election of Coleman Young as the first black mayor of Detroit signaled the end of white political control of the office of the mayor, and the beginning of the era of black mayors as the symbol of black political power. This development also contributed to the racial divide between the white suburbs and the black city. Mayor Young was the pioneer of this era of black mayors. While he was often a well-deserved thorn in the side of white suburbia with its unabashed history of racism, there can be no doubt that he made his greatest contribution to race relations by disbanding STRESS and radically changing a predominantly white police department into a racially integrated one. Mayor Archer was the brilliant lawyer and bridge builder between the white suburbs and the black city, after the suburban/city racial tension of the Young era. Sadly, Mayor Kilpatrick, the youngest of the three black mayors to be elected, brought great shame on the city of Detroit.

CHAPTER 6

City and Suburban Conflict over Residential Sharing of Neighborhoods

At the time of the riot in 1967 blacks in metropolitan Detroit were highly segregated from whites residentially. According to the index of dissimilarity (a measure of the unevenness in the spatial distribution of blacks and whites over census tracts, i.e., neighborhoods), few blacks and whites shared residential space. The index of dissimilarity in 1960 was 87.1 (Darden, 2007b). The typical black person in the city of Detroit (including the riot area) lived in a neighborhood that was more than 60 percent black in 1960 (Farley, Danzinger, and Holzer, 2000).

BLACK-OCCUPIED HOUSING AT THE TIME OF THE RIOT

The National Advisory Commission on Civil Disorders (1968) reported that in the black ghetto, grossly inadequate housing was a critical problem. In Detroit, 27.9 percent of nonwhite-occupied housing units in 1960 were classified as deteriorating, dilapidated, or lacking full plumbing. The percentage (53.1 percent) was much higher in the predominantly black areas, that is, the ghettos where the riot occurred (U.S. Bureau of the Census, 1963).

Blacks on average occupied much older housing than whites. Moreover, black-occupied housing was overcrowded. For example, in metropolitan Detroit, 17.5 percent of black-occupied housing units had 1.01 or more persons per room, compared to 8.6 percent for whites. Moreover, blacks were forced to pay higher rent for the same quality of housing as whites (National Advisory Commission on Civil Disorders, 1968). For example, in Detroit, whites paid a median rent of $77 per month, as compared to blacks, who paid $76. Yet 27 percent of black-occupied units were deteriorating or dilapidated, compared to only 10.3 percent of all white-occupied units (National Advisory Commission on Civil Disorders, 1968; U.S. Bureau of the Census, 1963).

This type of racial discrimination, that is, paying higher rent for lower-quality housing, is referred to as a "color tax." It contributed to conflict over housing and the anger and frustration among blacks in the riot area. Discrimination in housing led to a more limited supply of housing in the metropolitan area, forcing blacks to pay high rent even though they had lower incomes than whites. In the Detroit metropolitan area in 1970, 40.5 percent of nonwhite-occupied housing units had households that were paying 35 percent or more of their income for rent. On the other hand, only 21.2 percent of white-occupied housing units had households paying 35 percent or more of their income for rent.

Discrimination in housing prevented blacks access to many nonslum areas in the city and in the suburbs. By restricting the neighborhoods where blacks could live, housing discrimination made it profitable for landlords to divide large rooms in apartments into smaller ones to accommodate the black demand for housing. This process often hastened the deterioration of apartment buildings (National Advisory Commission on Civil Disorders, 1968). Also, discrimination kept prices and rents high even though the buildings were deteriorating. Whites, on the other hand, were not subjected to the limited housing market in the slum areas. They could therefore shop for lower-price rentals with higher quality.

At the time of the riot, housing programs serving low-income residents in Detroit were concentrated in the ghetto. Nonghetto areas, particularly areas in the suburbs, were opposed to low-income rent supplements or below-market interest rate housing. Thus, such housing was effectively banished from the suburbs.

SOCIOECONOMIC AND RACIAL CHANGE IN THE RIOT AREA: 1970 AND 2005—2009

The question "What socioeconomic and racial changes occurred in the riot area over a period of more than forty years?" is an important one. We examine over time the core geographic area where the riot occurred.

Fine (2007) described the core riot neighborhood as an area that was formerly occupied by Jews in the 1930s but had followed a traditional pattern of racial/ethnic residential succession. As blacks moved into the neighborhood after World War II, the Jews moved out (Fine, 2007: 4). The first blacks to move in were middle class. Fine (2007) further notes that after five years more lower-class blacks started to move into the neighborhood. That is when the neighborhood started to change in socioeconomic status. Some commercial establishments changed from businesses that were respected in the neighborhood into pool halls, pawn shops, and liquor stores. Blind pigs (after-hours drinking establishments) increased and became a common type of business in the neighborhood.

By 1970, according to the U.S. Census Bureau (1973), the population of the riot neighborhood (census tract 185) stood at 3,633. Blacks constituted 98 percent of the total population. Only 1.5 percent was white. There were wide racial disparities in the characteristics of the populations of blacks and whites. For example, whereas only 9 percent of the black population twenty-five years and older had a bachelor's degree or higher, 42 percent of the white population had such a degree. The whites residing in the area were primarily older. Indeed, 86 percent were no longer in the labor force. In the riot neighborhood, no whites in the labor force were unemployed. However, the black unemployment rate was 10 percent. No white families were in poverty. However, 18 percent of all black families were poor. Most residents, whether black or white, owned their homes. The homeownership rate in the neighborhood was 53 percent. However, 88 percent of the homes in the neighborhood were built in 1939 or earlier. The average value of the owner-occupied homes was $18,268.

By 2005–9, the total population of the riot neighborhood was 2,886, a decline of 20.6 percent since 1970 (U.S. Bureau of the Census, 2010). The total population had declined to 2,532 by 2010 (U.S. Bureau of the Census, 2011), a decrease of 30.3 percent since 1970. The black population was 92 percent. However, a small number of whites (4 percent) remained in the neighborhood.

Since the 2010 socioeconomic data was not available at the time this chapter was written, we used the 2005–9 American Community Survey (2010) to examine the extent of black and white inequality. The data revealed that 19 percent of the total population had a bachelor's degree or higher, reflecting an increase since 1970. As in 1970, no whites in the riot neighborhood were unemployed. However, 25 percent of blacks were unemployed, up from 10 percent in 1970. Homeownership declined only slightly, from 88 percent in 1970 to 82 percent in 2005–9. The neighborhood was still an area where old housing was predominant. The median year the structures were built was 1939. However, the median value of owner-occupied housing was $160,600 and the gross rent in the neighborhood was $836 per month. Whereas the poverty status of whites remained unchanged since 1970—that is, no whites were in poverty—21 percent of blacks were poor, an increase from 18 percent in 1970.

Black Housing and Neighborhood Distribution: City versus Suburbs

In 1960, before the riot, blacks consisted of only 3.7 percent of the population in the suburbs. By 1970, the black percentage had dropped slightly, to 3.6 percent, and by 1980 had increased to 4.2 percent (Darden, 2007b).

Prior to 1970, suburbanization of Detroit was primarily a white population process. Only starting in 1970 (only three years after the riot in the city) did blacks in significant numbers begin residing in the suburbs. In 1970, the number of blacks in each municipality in the suburbs remained small. Excluding the industrial suburbs of Inkster and Pontiac and the municipal enclaves of Hamtramck and Highland Park, only Clinton Township, Romulus, Port Huron, Mount Clemens, and Westland had more than 1,000 blacks in 1970 (Darden et al., 1987).

Because the number of blacks in most suburbs in 1970 was very small, most change during the following decade (1970–80) was due to black movement *into* the suburbs. The pattern of black suburbanization varied from an increase of 6,739 percent in Southfield, a growing suburb bordering Detroit in wealthy Oakland County, to a low of 3 percent in Mount Clemens, a declining suburb in Macomb County, nine miles from the city of Detroit. The movement of blacks to declining, older suburbs constituted the most representative pattern of black suburbanization. Older suburbs are those with more than 50 percent of their housing stock built before 1969. Newer suburbs are those where more than 50 percent of the housing stock was built after 1969 (Hanlon, 2009). Many of these older, inner suburbs are experiencing the negative effects of deindustrialization, an aging housing stock, foreclosures, and severe fiscal problems. Many are experiencing population decline and increasing poverty (Hanlon, 2009). Some are also experiencing increasing unemployment and declining incomes as the manufacturing jobs, especially those related to the auto industry, continue to disappear. As more blacks and Hispanics moved to the inner, older suburbs, the white population moved to the outer, newer suburbs at greater distance from the city of Detroit (U.S. Bureau of the Census, 2010). In the older, declining suburbs, few new housing units were being built and blacks were primarily replacing whites in existing housing units (Darden et al., 1987).

White Suburbanites' Resistance to Racial Residential Integration

Among the key factors explaining why blacks moved into some suburbs more than others are (1) spatial proximity of the suburb to the city and (2) white resistance to black entry into the suburban municipality. As we will see later, the income level, educational level, and occupational status of the suburbs were not major factors that prevented blacks from moving into a particular suburb. We will see later that racial discrimination in housing was a major factor.

Prior to and during the riot in Detroit, there was no fair-housing legislation to address the exclusion of blacks from predominantly white areas in the city and in the suburbs. However, by 1970 (two years after the federal Fair Housing Act), supporters of opening up the suburbs to blacks were demanding that all federal funds be withdrawn from suburbs that were all or overwhelmingly white and yet were contiguous to the city (Darden et al., 1987).

In 1970, the chairperson of the U.S. Civil Rights Commission, Reverend Father Theodore M. Hesburgh, described the suburban system of racial exclusion as the apparently hopeless encirclement of black central cities by impenetrable coils of indifferent or hostile white suburbs (*Detroit Free Press*, August 29, 1970). The commission arrived at the position after holding two public hearings on the alleged systematic exclusion of blacks from the suburbs, based on 1970 census data, which showed that the suburbs had become the nation's major residential location of the white population, while most blacks still resided in the city of Detroit.

Following passage of the 1968 Fair Housing Act and Michigan's Elliott-Larsen Civil Rights Act, blacks started to move outside the city of Detroit (Darden, 2007b). Blacks in Detroit felt the acts were clearly needed. In 1968, 69 percent of black respondents to a racial attitude survey said that there were either many or some places in the city of Detroit where an African American could not buy a house because of racial discrimination (Bledsoe et al., 1996).

At the time, there were no gender differences among African American perceptions about discrimination in housing. In 1968, younger African Americans were more likely to perceive group discrimination in housing and to feel its effects personally. Also, perceptions of personal victimization of discrimination in housing were significantly more common among upper-income African Americans than among lower-status blacks. However, there was no difference along social status levels in African Americans' perceptions of housing discrimination against blacks in general.

In 1969, only two years after the riot, about half of the whites in a survey of racial attitudes in Detroit thought African Americans were discriminated against to a significant degree in housing (Bledsoe et al., 1996). In 1969, surveys of white perceptions about sharing residential space with blacks revealed fear, as indicated by 64 percent of respondents to a survey (Bledsoe et al., 1996).

Race, Not Class Motivated White Resistance

In 1969, upper-status whites were concerned about blacks moving into white neighborhoods, with 70 percent of whites saying that problems would arise. Upper-status whites were just as likely as lower-status whites to move from their neighborhoods when blacks entered (Bledsoe et al., 1996).

We focus on three suburbs to demonstrate white suburban resistance to black entry. Those suburbs are Warren in Macomb County, Dearborn in Wayne County, and Southfield in Oakland County.

We first examined the research on housing affordability to see if blacks had the economic means to live in the three suburbs. Such an analysis was done in 1973 by Hermalin and Farley. The authors examined each suburb of 25,000 or more in the Detroit urbanized area, including Warren, Dearborn, and Southfield. They examined the total number of occupied housing units and the actual and expected housing units occupied by blacks. For Warren, the actual number of black-occupied housing units in 1970 was thirty-eight. For Dearborn, the number was only two and for Southfield, the actual number of black-occupied housing units was twelve. The authors then determined the proportion of housing units occupied by blacks in each economic category throughout the Detroit urbanized area. They next considered the spatial distribution of owned and leased housing by value in each suburb and ascertained how many blacks would be in that particular suburb if they were there in each value of housing in the same proportion that they were throughout the entire urbanized area. Similarly, they determined how many whites would be expected in each suburb if whites occupied housing there in each economic category in the same proportion that they did throughout the entire Detroit urbanized area. The number of blacks and whites *expected* in each suburb adds up to the total number of households occupied by blacks and whites in that suburb.

Based on housing value, the expected number of black households in Warren was 4,876, a far larger number than the thirty-eight that actually existed there. In Dearborn, the expected number of black households was 4,670, a much larger number than the two found there. In Southfield, the expected number of black households was 996, which was larger than the twelve black households that actually existed there. Note, however, that the gap between actual and expected number of black households was greater in Dearborn and less in Southfield. For example, in Warren, the actual proportion of black-occupied housing units was 0.1 compared to an expected proportion of 10. In Dearborn, the actual proportion of black occupied housing units was < 0.1, compared to an expected proportion of black occupied housing units of 13.5. Finally, in Southfield, the actual proportion of black-occupied housing units was 0.1, compared to an expected proportion of 4.9.

Similar calculations were made using family income as a criterion for black *expected* representation. In Warren, the expected black proportion was 14.9. In Dearborn, the expected proportion of black families was 15.9. In Southfield, the expected proportion of black families was 12.1 (Hermalin and Farley, 1973). The implication of this research is that neither the cost of housing nor the inability of blacks to pay for housing outside the city of Detroit were the primary reasons that so few blacks lived in the suburbs of Detroit in 1970 (three years after the civil disorder in the city).

WARREN: A BLUE-COLLAR SUBURB WITH A HISTORY OF OPPOSITION TO RESIDENTIAL INTEGRATION

White suburbanites in Warren, a blue-collar, working-class suburb, had resisted black entry for some time. With a total population of 89,000 in 1960, there were only nineteen blacks, or 0.2 percent of the suburb's total population. Most whites in Warren wanted to keep it that way. Moreover, some whites in Warren turned to violent means to carry out those wishes.

One of the first well-documented actions of racial harassment occurred in June 1967 when Corado and Ruby Bailey moved into the "Wishing Well" suburban subdivision on Warren's west side. Corado, a skilled worker, was black, and Ruby, his wife, was white. They had two children. For several nights after the Baileys moved into the white neighborhood, an angry crowd of whites numbering as many as 200 assembled in the front yard of an adjoining house. At various times over the next few months, rocks and stink bombs were thrown at the Bailey house (Riddle, 1998). In October 1967, a cross was burned on the Bailey's front lawn. Although the family was constantly harassed, they did not move.

By 1970, the black population had increased to 132. The reason so few blacks moved to Warren was related to Warren's resistance to blacks. For example, the city residents were incensed at what they perceived to be government intrusion into their community, or worse, government support of "forced racial integration." Some whites who now lived in Warren had once lived in Detroit and departed once blacks started to move into their neighborhood. They moved to Warren in the hope of escaping racial integration. They were now ready to forgo federal grant funds in order to maintain their preference for excluding blacks (Darden et al., 1987).

In June 1970, in a city council session, tempers flared over the issue of federal fair housing and urban renewal funds. To receive the funds, the council had to comply with fair-housing legislation. Opponents of the fair-housing measure argued that it would mean giving in to federal control. Those who supported fair housing in Warren called Warren a closed city and accused the opponents of the measure of trying to keep the city closed (*Detroit Free Press*, August 29, 1970).

All hell broke out two months later after a tense council meeting in which was discussed an article in the *Detroit News*, "U.S. Picks Warren as Prime Target in Move to Integrate All Suburbs (and How Warren was Picked for Integration)" (August 22, 1970). What whites read in the *Detroit News* was the following:

> Detroit suburbs prevent an unparalleled opportunity for the application of fair housing strategy. Nowhere else in the Midwest, perhaps nowhere else in the country, is there a combination of a large central city (Detroit) with a substantial black population . . . surrounded by large white suburbs which may use Housing and Urban Development programs in which there is extensive black employment and a great deal of middle class housing. It is proper for the Department of Housing and Urban Development to use its resources to loosen the "white noose" surrounding the city. (*Detroit News*, August 22, 1970)

At the time, Warren's total population was 99 percent white; 30 percent of all workers in the Warren auto plants were black but living in Detroit in large part due to discrimination in housing. Since their wages were comparable to whites, they could presumably afford to live in Warren where they worked, thereby eliminating the cost of transportation (Darden et al., 1987).

Yet Warren's city council members resented the Department of Housing and Urban Development's demands for fair housing. Warren's mayor, Ted Bates, accused HUD of wanting to use Warren as a "guinea pig for integration experiments" and warned that he would not tolerate such a policy even if it meant losing urban renewal funds. Instead, he would meet with other Detroit suburbs receiving HUD funds to organize support "to fight this forced integration" (*Detroit News*, August 22, 1970).

Several weeks later, George Romney, secretary of Housing and Urban Development, told the Senate Select Committee on Equal Opportunity that Warren obviously practiced racial discrimination in housing and that at the very least it would have to establish a genuine human relations commission to qualify for additional urban renewal funds. Warren would not get the funds, Secretary Romney told the committee, if it did not comply with the requirements (Romney, 1970). In early November 1970, Warren became the first municipality in Michigan to vote to drop the urban renewal program rather than meet the requirement of racial integration (Darden et al., 1987; *Detroit Free Press*, August 29, 1970). Warren would remain an exclusive, white, blue-collar suburb even though it paid the price of no federal housing funds for the next ten years (Riddle, 1998).

Fear caused many whites in Warren to support the decision to give up federal funding. Their main fear was neighborhood instability and loss of control. In other words, they feared neighborhood instability if blacks were allowed to move into Warren and loss of control over decisions. Specifically, they feared that the federally funded urban renewal projects on Warren's southern boundary with Detroit would become "beachheads for a black invasion of Warren" (Riddle, 1998: 34).

According to Riddle (1998), Warren clearly needed the federal funds. But the factor of race, that is, fear of black in-migration, was much stronger than economic need. Thus, Warren continued to exclude blacks.

By 1980, there were only 297 blacks living in Warren, representing 0.18 percent of the total population of 161,000. Warren was not only the largest Detroit suburb, but it was the third largest municipality in Michigan. Of the blacks living in Warren, most were restricted to only four census tracts (neighborhoods). These four tracts represented only 10 percent of all census tracts in the municipality. Although only a few blacks resided in Warren, they were highly segregated residentially. Warren had an index of dissimilarity of 65.9, a high level of black residential segregation from whites.

By 1990, the black population had increased to 1,033, representing 0.71 percent of the total population of more than 140,000. The blacks who lived in Warren in 1990 had a higher level of education than their white counterparts. Almost a third (32 percent) of the blacks had a bachelor's degree or higher, compared to only 10 percent of whites. Yet most blacks remained highly residentially segregated from whites. In 1990, the index of dissimilarity was 57.9, a decline from 65.9 in 1980. By 2000, there were 3,676 blacks residing in Warren, representing 2.6 percent of the total population of 138,247. However, the blacks remained highly residentially segregated from whites. The index of dissimilarity between blacks and whites in 2000 was 56.8, reflecting a 1.1 percentage point decline over the decade of 1990–2000 (Frey and Myers, 2001). Based on the most recent census data, the black population increased to 18,123 (393 percent) between 2000 and 2010. In 2010, 13.5 percent of Warren's population was black, up from 2.7 percent in 2000. The data also show a white population decline of 16.7 percent, from 126,204 in 2000 to 105,088 in 2010. whites were 78.4 percent of Warren's total population in 2010, down from 91.3 percent in 2000. More importantly, residential segregation between blacks and Whites declined substantially, as revealed by an index of dissimilarity of 32 (Logan and Stults, 2011).

DEARBORN: A SUBURB WITH A CONTROVERSIAL RACIST HISTORY

Dearborn borders the city of Detroit on the southwest. Downtown Detroit is only fifteen minutes away by car. Many firms now in Dearborn were once located in the city of Detroit (Darden et al., 1987). Sometimes job opportunities have been greater in Dearborn than in Detroit. Yet in 1970, the Dearborn suburb had only thirteen blacks. Over the years, blacks have been slow to move to Dearborn. That is because the city had a racist mayor who kept blacks out of the city. Mayor Orville Hubbard ruled the city of Dearborn for thirty-six years, from 1942 to 1977, one of the longest serving mayors in the nation. He was known in the predominantly white suburbs, the state of Michigan, and even in the nation as the mayor who provided excellent municipal services, recreation, and the exclusion of blacks from Dearborn (Gavrilovich and McGraw, 2000). Hubbard was very much like the former segregationist governor of Alabama, George Wallace. Like Wallace, he favored racial segregation and racial exclusion of blacks. During the 1960s, Mayor Hubbard emerged as the symbol of the deep-rooted racism of the North. Concerning integration, Mayor Hubbard said, "I don't believe in integration. When it happens, along comes socializing with the whites, intermarriage, and then mongrelization" (*Detroit News Magazine*, June 28, 1967). Hubbard did not just express his racist views—he translated them into public policy. He regularly posted his antiblack, anti-integration views in the city hall so that blacks would know that they were not wanted in the city. By excluding blacks and providing white working-class residents with good services and low taxes, the mayor pleased most whites, who continued to reelect him to public office. Thus, the bordering suburb of Dearborn has a racist past that has continued to live in the memory of most blacks in Detroit.

In the aftermath of the Detroit riot, Dearborn passed Michigan's first municipal "stop and frisk" ordinance in 1968. The ordinance permitted police to search "suspicious" persons, a code word for blacks. According to Good (1989), although the ordinance did not indicate "race" specifically, that was clearly on Mayor Hubbard's mind when the ordinance was proposed.

Although Hubbard died in 1982, the antiblack spirit he had instilled into Dearborn lived on. For example, three years after Hubbard's death, the city council proposed an ordinance that would restrict the use of the city's parks for residents of Dearborn only. After rejection of the ordinance by a four-to-three vote, the ordinance was placed on the November ballot by a petition drive and was approved by a vote of 17,790 to 13,976. Dearborn's two largest parks, Ford Field and Civic Center Park, along with a park adjacent to the town hall, were exempted. Backers of the ordinance denied that it was racially motivated (*Detroit Free Press*, July 17, 1985). Joseph Madison, national director of the National Association for the Advancement of Colored People Voter Education Project stated that "we are not dealing with an overt form of racism in Dearborn. What we are dealing with here is a much more sophisticated method of discrimination" (*Michigan Chronicle*, October 11, 1986). He asked, "Was it truly that the parks were overcrowded, or was it a way to send a message to blacks that they were simply not wanted in Dearborn?" (*Detroit Free Press*, July 17, 1985).

After hearing testimony at a trial in which evidence was presented documenting via newspapers that Dearborn had a practice of racial exclusion for many years, NAACP attorney Robert Sedler told the judge that Dearborn has a history of bigotry, possibly unparalleled in any city in America. According to Sedler, "white supremacy" and racial discrimination were rampant when city voters approved the ordinance banning nonresidents from most of Dearborn's parks (McGraw, 1986).

In October 1986, Judge Marvin R. Stempler of the Wayne County Circuit Court struck down the ordinance that restricted parks to residents only (*Michigan Chronicle*, October 11, 1986). Judge Stempler's conclusion was that persons enforcing the nonresident provisions of the Dearborn ordinance would be empowered to exercise totally unguided discretion as to when and where stops would be made and as to whom they would stop. This was an unreasonable intrusion to a Dearborn park user's privacy and liberty, which are protected by the Michigan and the U.S. constitutions. Up until the court decision, the NAACP had led blacks in a boycott of Dearborn businesses.

However, the city of Dearborn appealed the decision to the Michigan State Court of Appeals. On December 21, 1988, the State Court of Appeals ruled in a three-to-zero decision that the ordinance violated constitutional bans on racial discrimination and unreasonable police searches ("Court Voids Curbs on Park Use," 1988). After the ruling, Howard Simon, the American Civil Liberties Union's executive director, stated, "I am absolutely grateful for this kind of Christmas present from the courts that will hopefully put an end to one of the most racially divisive issues in Southeastern Michigan" ("Court Voids Curbs on Park Use," 1988).

In spite of the perceived racial hostility, a larger number of blacks moved to Dearborn over the years. However, those blacks who resided there were highly residentially segregated from whites. In other words, there was little sharing of residential space.

Based on the index of dissimilarity between blacks and whites, the level of segregation increased from 50.2 in 1970 to 72.8 in 1980. However, between 1980 and 1990, black segregation declined to 55 as the 490 blacks who resided in Dearborn became more dispersed. By 2000, the number of blacks had increased to 1,225 and the level of residential segregation dropped from an index of 55 to 52.6 (Frey and Myers, 2001). An index of above 50 is considered a high level of residential segregation by social scientists (Massey and Denton, 1993). The high index is due to the fact that most blacks resided in only a few neighborhoods. By 1990, for example, a third of blacks resided in the Cherry Hill community and a fifth of blacks resided in Fairlane (City of Dearborn, 1994). The Cherry Hill community is dominated by single family developments. Most (79 percent) were constructed during the forties and fifties (City of Dearborn, 1995). Fairlane was a growing community where new condominium and apartment developments were built between 1980 and 1990. It also had the highest median values of owner-occupied homes in Dearborn in 1990 (City of Dearborn, 1994).

The reasons why blacks in Detroit have continued to avoid Dearborn in the search for suburban housing was addressed by two Detroit area studies—one in 1976 and the other in 1992.

Between 1976 and 1992, both blacks and whites thought that an increasing proportion of blacks could afford to live in Dearborn. In 1976, 38 percent of whites and 48 percent of black respondents believed that blacks could afford housing in Dearborn. By 1992, the percentage of whites who thought that blacks could afford housing in Dearborn had increased to 50 percent. Among black respondents, the percentage declined slightly to 45 percent (Farley et al., 2000).

Despite the sizable percentage of black respondents who thought that blacks could afford to live in Dearborn, due to Dearborn's history of racial hostility 90 percent of black respondents reported that Dearborn's white residents would react negatively if a black family moved into the suburb. This percentage was virtually unchanged from the 92 percent of black respondents who felt that way in 1976 (Farley et al., 2000). Such a history of racial hostility in Dearborn may also explain in part why in 2000, Dearborn's black population was only 1 percent (U.S. Bureau of the Census, 2002). Based on the most recent U.S. Census data (2011) the black population reached 3,965, or 4.0 percent of Dearborn's total population, in 2010 (U.S. Bureau of the Census, 2011a). This reflected a 218 percent increase in the black population. More blacks moved to Dearborn during 2000–2010 than at any time in Dearborn's history. This may indicate that the city may be overcoming its controversial racist history.

We argue that the resistance of whites to blacks residing in Dearborn was based on race, not class. In 1990, for example, the occupational status of blacks in Dearborn was higher than the status of whites. For example, in 1990 56 percent of all the blacks in Dearborn were professional or managerial workers, compared to 32 percent of all whites. In other words, blacks were 1.75 times more likely to be professional or managerial workers than whites (U.S. Bureau of the Census, 1993). blacks also had a higher median income than whites in Dearborn. By 1990 the black median income was $36,190, compared to a white median income of $34,898, a difference of $1,292. By 2000, the white median income had increased to $46,247, while the black median income had increased to $39,688, resulting in a difference of $6,559 in favor of whites (U.S. Bureau of the Census, 2002). By 2009; however, the black median household income had once again exceeded the median household income of whites. Based on the most recent U.S. Bureau of the Census American Community Survey data, the black median household income in Dearborn was $50,859, compared to a white median household income of $48,160, a difference of $2,699 (U.S. Bureau of the Census, 2010).

However, blacks in Dearborn were paying higher rent and lived in higher-value housing than their white counterparts. In 2000, the median gross rent paid by blacks was $719, compared to $646 per month paid by whites, a difference of $73. The houses owned and occupied by blacks had a median value of $159,700, compared to $129,300 for whites, a difference of $30,400 (U.S. Bureau of the Census, 2002). Thus, the evidence is clear that the blacks who resided in Dearborn in 2000 were not living in low-rent or low-value housing and that race and not class was the major reason so few blacks resided there. More significant, however, is the decline in residential segregation between blacks and whites, from an index of dissimilarity of 52.6 in 2000 to 35.3 in 2010 (Logan and Stults, 2011).

SOUTHFIELD: THE RACIALLY PROGRESSIVE SUBURB

Located on the border of the city of Detroit and incorporated in 1958, Southfield is considered suburban Oakland County's downtown. It grew as a separate nucleus to the city of Detroit. Southfield's growth was related to the location of several Fortune 500 corporations that built their world, national, or regional headquarters there (Ieka, 1983). Southfield has been known as a suburb that rivals the city of Detroit in office space (Darden et al., 1987). But the real contribution to Southfield's growth was its suburban expansion from 1950 to 1970.

Such expansion was synonymous with white population growth. In 1960, only thirty-four blacks lived in Southfield, compared to 31,435 whites. Only in 1970 did blacks start to move into Southfield in significant numbers. By 1970, the suburb had 102 blacks. However, from 1970 to 1980, Southfield experienced the largest percentage black increase (6,739 percent) of any suburb in metropolitan Detroit. The black population increased from 102 to 6,976 (Darden et al., 1987). The blacks who resided in Southfield in 1980 lived in owner-occupied housing and paid higher rent than whites. For example, the median value of black-occupied housing was $74,000, compared to $66,300 for whites, a difference of $7,700. The blacks who rented paid on average $379 per month compared to $366 per month for whites, a difference of $13 (Darden et al., 1987).

Due to the large increase from 1970 to 1980 of blacks residing in Southfield, it was the only suburb bordering Detroit to grow during the decade. Unlike some other bordering suburbs such as Warren and Dearborn, which over the years have demonstrated hostility and resistance to blacks, Southfield decided not to engage in the mass white racial hysteria and bigotry. Instead, Southfield took a more racially progressive path to racial integration. Southfield is the exceptional suburb in metropolitan Detroit. Observing Southfield's diverse population of Orthodox Jews, Chaldeans, Koreans, Asian Indians, and blacks in the 1980s, one reporter noted that Southfield had managed the stress test of racial/ethnic integration and managed it well (Zurowich and Stoehl, 1983).

One of the best examples of Southfield's commitment to residential integration occurred in the wake of the 1967 Detroit riot. Some residents in Southfield heard rumors that masses of whites were starting to flee Southfield to escape blacks from Detroit who were moving in. Property values would fall (Zurowich and Stoehl, 1983). Southfield dismissed the rumors and fears and used its planning approach to address concerns. The suburb via a neighborhood association persuaded residents who desired to sell to agree not to put up for-sale signs on their property. The plan worked. Throughout the 1970s racial integration of Magnolia, a subdivision in Southfield, proceeded with dignity (Darden et al., 1987). In 1976, Southfield officials decided to implement a strong housing program that would enable Southfield to maintain a stable community, to show increasing housing values, and to demonstrate that it was an excellent community in which to live, work, and raise a family. Finally, Southfield thought that it must combat the insidious practices of racial steering and blockbusting (City of Southfield, 1977). In 1981–82 Southfield amended its fair neighborhood practice code to make it more effective in combating racial discrimination in housing, racial steering, and blockbusting (City of Southfield, 1981, 1982; Darden et al., 1987: 148). Throughout the 1980s Southfield officials provided progressive leadership in the area of racial integration by implementing programs aimed at reducing white hysteria in racially changing neighborhoods (Darden et al., 1987).

By 1992, 88 percent of blacks named Southfield as a desirable place to live. Yet only 61 percent of blacks viewed Warren as a desirable place to live and only 37 percent viewed Dearborn as desirable (Farley et al., 2000). These differential percentages were related to the differential racial climate in Warren, Dearborn, and Southfield (Farley et al., 2000). Thus, blacks continued to move to Southfield. By 2010, Southfield's black population was 50,432, or 70 percent of the city's total population. Whites were only 24.5 percent. However, the two racial groups continued to share residential space. The index of dissimilarity was only 26.6, lower than either Warren or Dearborn. Southfield also played a role in trying to reduce residential segregation in other municipalities in Oakland County.

The Oakland County Center for Open Housing

As more blacks moved to Oakland County, the pattern of black residential location was not even. In 1990, 80.7 percent of the 77,480 blacks in Oakland County were concentrated primarily in three suburban municipalities—Pontiac, Southfield, and Oak Park. On the other hand, only 11 percent of Oakland County's white population lived in these same three municipalities. Such an uneven spatial pattern between the races did not occur by chance. Instead, race-conscious intervention to segregate the races by means of racial steering and other forms of racial discrimination in housing were occurring, thus denying blacks equal access to housing throughout Oakland County.

It was recognized that if left unchecked, the denial of equal access to all housing in Oakland County would result in further segregating blacks and whites in the county. Such recognition led to the establishment of the Oakland County Center for Open Housing in 1990. The center's major purpose was to provide housing information, counseling, and incentive loans to home seekers interested in making pro-integrative moves within Oakland County. A pro-integrative move is one where a family moves to an area (census tract) where his or her own race is underrepresented. Based on the black and white percentages in Oakland County in 1990, any movement of a black family into a census tract that was not over 17.4 percent black, or any movement of a white family into a census tract that was not over 82.6 percent white, was considered a desegregative or pro-integrative move. The center was funded and administered by the city of Southfield (Darden, 1990).

Once the basic representation criterion had been satisfied, the areas (census tracts) were prioritized based on (1) the extent of black underrepresentation as defined by the percentage of blacks residing in the eligible areas, and (2) the rate of white population change between 1980 and 1990 in each eligible area. Based on the stated criteria, the eligible and priority areas for pro-integrative moves for blacks and whites in Oakland County were established (Darden, 1992).

Evaluation of the Program

From January 1990 to December 1993, the Oakland County Center for Open Housing (OCCOH) engaged in counseling designed to encourage pro-integrative moves within Oakland County. From January to June 1994, an incentive loan program was added. The goal of the center was to encourage pro-integrative residential choices among home seekers and renters through counseling and financial incentives. The incentives were in the form of low-interest loans designed to expand the housing options for all families within Oakland County.

From January 1990 to December 1993, the center provided services in the form of housing information and counseling to 1,703 home seekers. Of the total, 76 percent were black or African American, 15 percent were white, 7 percent were interracial, and the remainder was comprised of other races. Of the total home seekers, 762, or 45 percent, had an interest in purchasing a home. Among the potential home purchasers, 624, or 82 percent, were black, 74, or 10 percent, were white, and the remainder were either interracial or a member of a racial group other than black or white (Darden, 1994).

Based on the center's housing activity, a total of eighty-eight purchasers made pro-integrative moves between July 1990 and September 1994. Virtually all those home seekers who made such moves did so with the assistance provided by OCCOH.

Of the total home purchasers who made pro-integrative moves, 84 percent were black, 8 percent were white, and the remainder were either racially mixed or a member of a racial group other than black or white. A total of seventeen municipalities were impacted. Two-thirds of the black home seekers made pro-integrative moves in three municipalities—Southfield, West Bloomfield, and Farmington Hills. The remainder of blacks located in such places as Bloomfield Hills, Novi, Oak Park, and Troy. On the other hand, 71.4 percent of the white home seekers made pro-integrative moves in Southfield. The remainder of whites located to Auburn Hills and Lathrup Village.

Pattern of Population Distribution and Impact of Incentive Loans

From January to June 1994, the center introduced an incentive loan program as a tool to further pro-integrative activity. Although the actual number of loans made to white applicants was small, the demand was focused predominantly on Southfield, where 71.4 percent of the loans to white applicants were made. It is important to emphasize that pro-integrative moves often have a "ripple effect" on population change. Once a family of a particular race moves into an area where their race is underrepresented, a stream is often created resulting in other members of the same race moving into the same area. Thus, incentive loans that result in pro-integrative moves have an impact that is often far greater than what the mere *number* of loans would suggest. Equally important is the racial composition of the geographic area where each loan is made.

The majority of the loans went to black home seekers who made pro-integrative moves in Southfield (36.1 percent), West Bloomfield (17.5 percent), and Farmington Hills (12.1 percent).

It is fair to conclude that OCCOH engaged in very effective counseling of home seekers who moved into areas where their own race was underrepresented. The center's activities influenced population mobility into areas that may not have occurred without such counseling. The financial incentives that were added over the period January to June 1994 further enhanced the center's effectiveness (Darden, 1994).

The black demand for the housing services of the center (including counseling and incentive loans) far exceeded the demand by whites. Thus, white applicants received about 8 percent of the loans. The differential demands for OCCOH's services, however, is not surprising given the continued existence of racial discrimination in housing that restricts the housing choices of blacks. Nevertheless, since maintenance of racial residential integration involves the continued movement into an area by both white and black population groups, more attention must be paid to increasing white demand. It is important to note, however, that those white applicants who were served by OCCOH disproportionately demanded Southfield as a place to live, thereby reducing to some degree the net white population loss experienced by that municipality.

Southfield: A Place of Geographic Racial Equality[stop

By 2000, Southfield had become a place of geographic racial equality. This is a racially progressive status that very few municipalities in metropolitan Detroit have achieved. Geographic racial equality is defined as those places (i.e., municipalities) that have been incorporated and have a low level of racial residential segregation (i.e., scores below 50 percentage points) and where the racial minority group (blacks in this case) has achieved *parity* with whites in educational attainment, income, and occupational status. Of the seventy-one incorporated places in metropolitan Detroit, only four municipalities were places in 2000 where blacks had achieved geographic racial equality; Southfield was one of those four (Darden, 2009a). The other places of geographic racial equality were Farmington Hills and Rochester Hills (also located in Oakland County) and East Pointe (formerly East Detroit), a working-class suburb in Macomb County. Southfield was the only place of geographic racial equality that was also predominantly black (53.3 percent).

Blacks in Southfield exceeded the percentage of whites with a bachelor's degree or higher level of education by two percentage points, that is, 37 percent of all blacks compared to 35 percent of all whites had reached this level of educational attainment. Black median household income exceeded white median household income by $13,559, at $57,526 for blacks and $43,967 for whites. Blacks continued to exceed whites in median household income from 2000 to 2009. In the most recent U.S. Bureau of the Census American Community Survey data, the black median household income was $54,577, compared to a white median household income of $48,094, a difference of $6,483 (U.S. Bureau of the Census, 2010). Black median household income declined compared to white median household income from 2000 to 2009 in the three other places of geographic racial equality—Farmington Hills, Rochester Hills, and East Pointe—removing them from the category of places of geographic racial equality. Southfield, on the other hand, maintained its status as a place where blacks shared an equal or higher socioeconomic status with whites. Despite the sharing of residential space between blacks and whites in Southfield, racial discrimination in housing has not disappeared in metropolitan Detroit.

MOST RECENT EVIDENCE OF RACIAL DISCRIMINATION IN HOUSING IN METROPOLITAN DETROIT

Despite some exceptional cases of black access to housing and racial equality in the suburbs, the overwhelming evidence seems to suggest that blacks still face racial discrimination in housing and/or racial steering.

A Detroit area study has examined questions of perceptions of discriminatory practices by individuals, real estate agents, and lending institutions in the Detroit tri-county area. When black and white respondents in Wayne, Oakland, and Macomb counties were asked how much discrimination existed in the tri-county area that makes it hard for blacks to rent or buy housing wherever they want, there was agreement between whites and blacks. A high 85 percent of black respondents in 1992 replied "a lot" or "some" discrimination compared to 80 percent of whites (Farley et al., 1993). However, there was an important difference in the perceptions about trends in housing discrimination. Most blacks (63 percent) believed that housing discrimination against blacks was "about the same" or "even more" than ten years earlier, but most whites (57 percent) believed that there was less housing discrimination in 1992 than ten years earlier. Thus, it was the white population in the tri-county area, but not the blacks, that saw housing discrimination on the decline (Farley et al., 1993).

However, studies also suggest that most African Americans do not perceive themselves personally as victims of housing discrimination. Researchers using surveys to detect perceived discrimination in housing have had to consider the phenomenon of "discrepancy between personal and group perceived discrimination." Respondents often perceive a higher level of discrimination directed at their group as a whole than at themselves as individual members of that group (Taylor et al., 1990)

African Americans were about half as likely to report discrimination against themselves as to perceive, more broadly, that such housing discrimination existed (Bledsoe et al., 1996). Bledsoe et al.'s findings are consistent with the extensive study done by Sigelman and Welch (1991). Both concluded that there is no difference along age or social status lines in the perceptions African Americans hold about discrimination against African Americans generally.

Thus, these studies reveal a clear racial divide concerning the perceptions of housing discrimination trends. Such differences can be explained in part because of the high level of residential segregation that characterizes the Detroit metropolitan area. Different residential locations often shape different realities as experiences. According to Bledsoe et al. (1996), these different realities in turn shape or frame the racial perceptions of blacks and whites. Thus, people's perceptions differ in large measure because the realities differ. The perceptions of blacks and whites are unlikely to grow more similar until realities do so (Bledsoe et al., 1996).

The Detroit area study also asked whether blacks miss out on good housing because of discrimination by white owners, because of practices of real estate agents, or because banks and lenders do not make loans to blacks. The results showed that whites and blacks agree that blacks often miss out on good housing because white owners will not rent or sell to blacks. Indeed, 82 percent of whites and 88 percent of blacks thought that such discrimination occurred "very often" or "sometimes" (Bledsoe et al., 1996; Farley and Frey, 1994).

Differences between white and black *perceptions* of discriminatory practices increase when the question focuses on real estate agents and lenders. Blacks saw much more institutionalized discrimination than whites. Indeed, 86 percent of black respondents in the study believed that blacks miss out on good housing because real estate agents discriminate, while only 61 percent of whites believed that (Farley and Frey, 1994).

When lenders were assessed, 89 percent of black respondents believed that banks discriminate compared with 56 percent of whites. In sum, the findings revealed that despite fair housing laws, most whites and an overwhelming majority of blacks believed that blacks in the Detroit tri-county area faced discrimination in the housing market from real estate brokers and from lenders (Farley et al., 1993). Reports of discrimination in the tri-county area can also be found in Arellano and Ghannam, 1992; Blossom, Everett, and Gallagher, 1988; Darden, 2004; Gillman, 1992; Gillmor and Gallagher, 1993; and Gordon, 1993.

The perception of discrimination, however, is a weaker measure than actual behavior (Darden, 2004). The best method of determining whether discrimination against blacks is still occurring in metropolitan Detroit is the audit or paired test method. This method has been used by HUD since 1977 (Turner and Ross, 2005; Turner and Wrenk, 1993). Paired testing or the audit method is the most powerful tool for measuring *actual* discriminatory behavior. In paired testing, two matched home seekers—one white and the other black or another racial minority—visit a real estate office or apartment at different times. Both testers are equal socioeconomically (income, education, and occupation) and are trained as testers. They individually and at different times express the same home preferences and offer the same financial qualifications (Turner and Ross, 2005). The audit method, which originated as a tool to enforce fair housing laws, remains a powerful tool to detect and document discrimination. For example, systematic differences in treatment can be measured when the black tester is told no apartment is available but the white tester is told that an apartment is, in fact, available (Turner and Ross, 2005).

The information given to each auditor about the availability of housing and the terms of the conditions for rental or sale offered to each are then compared, usually by a coordinator, in an attempt to detect any differential treatment. If differential treatment is found, it serves as a measure of discrimination, since all other factors are controlled (Turner, Struyk, and Yinger, 1991).

The most recent study using the audit method to measure discrimination in housing in metropolitan areas including Detroit was conducted by Turner and colleagues (2002) for HUD. The results were based on a significant sample of 4,600 paired tests in twenty-three metropolitan areas nationwide. Because a previous study funded by HUD was conducted in 1989, the study was able to reveal that housing discrimination declined against blacks seeking to buy a home between 1989 and 2000 (Turner et al., 2002). There was also a modest decrease in discrimination toward blacks seeking to rent an apartment. The report, however, also concluded that while discrimination is downward, it remains at very high levels. Blacks most often encounter discrimination when they inquire about renting a unit. More importantly, the type of differential treatment, blacks continue to face is "racial steering," which unlike discrimination in housing, is on the increase (Turner et al., 2002).

The study revealed three types of steering, which involved information, segregation, and class. These types of steering were examined at three spatial levels, that is, census tract (which is equivalent to a neighborhood), place (a municipality), and school district. Steering was achieved through a process of recommending, inspections, and editorializing. The study revealed that differences occurred that suggest all three types of steering were occurring but that steering was strongest at the census tract or neighborhood levels for black and white home seekers in Detroit (Turner et al., 2002).

Editorializing was the most prevalent mechanism used to steer blacks and whites. Agents encouraged white home seekers to choose areas with more whites and fewer poor households. Thus, there is evidence to suggest that steering may be playing an important role in continuing to influence the sharp racial and class segregation in metropolitan Detroit. In 2000, for example, more than a quarter (26.6 percent) of all whites in metropolitan Detroit (Wayne, Oakland, and Macomb) lived in very high socioeconomic status neighborhoods. On the other hand, only 4 percent of all blacks in metropolitan Detroit resided in such neighborhoods. Instead, most blacks (55 percent) lived in neighborhoods with very low socioeconomic characteristics, compared to only 2.6 percent of all whites (Darden et al., 2010).

CONCLUSIONS

The Kerner Commission documented in 1968 that blacks and whites in metropolitan Detroit were living separate and unequal lives in neighborhoods of different racial compositions. Blacks on average occupied much older and more dilapidated houses than did whites. The poor housing quality was more severe in the predominantly black neighborhoods where the riot occurred. Yet blacks, due to discrimination, were forced to pay more rent than whites for poor quality housing. Discrimination in housing at the time of the riot prevented blacks from many nonslum areas and areas that were not predominantly black. More importantly, the tendency of white real estate agents and apartment managers to exclude blacks from predominantly white areas, whether in the city of Detroit or in the suburbs surrounding the city, continued after the riot and throughout the decades from the 1960s to the present.

Today, racial discrimination has slightly declined, but racial steering of blacks and whites to separate neighborhoods has continued despite federal and state fair housing laws. Thus, intervention into the housing market for the purpose of racial segregation and the prevention of the sharing of residential space in metropolitan Detroit contributes to metropolitan Detroit's uneven development and race- and class-based neighborhood socioeconomic inequality. Therefore, little measurable change has occurred in the sharing of residential space since the riot.

In 1970, only two years after the riot, the index of dissimilarity between blacks and whites in metropolitan Detroit was 88.9. In 2010, that is, forty years later, the index had declined by 14.9 percentage points to 74.0 (Darden et al., 1987; Logan and Stults, 2011). We should note however, that the index for 2010 includes the counties of Lapeer, Livingston, and St Clair in addition to Wayne, Oakland, and Macomb (Logan and Stults, 2011), whereas the index for 1970 includes Wayne, Oakland, and Macomb only. Thus, they are not entirely comparable. Our data seems to suggest that although the level of black-white residential segregation in metropolitan Detroit is declining but remains quite high, at the municipal scale racial integration in selected suburban areas is more promising. Housing choices of home seekers are primarily influenced at this scale. That is because this is the geographic level at which land-use policies are established, zoning regulations are implemented, and local tax and fiscal policies are created. Such policies vary from suburb to suburb, as does public service delivery (e.g., crime prevention, garbage collection, and snow removal). Most important is school quality, which also varies from municipality to municipality and has a great influence on home seekers with children. These factors are among the most influential in determining neighborhood choice among households, race and class notwithstanding.

Whites have been leaving the city of Detroit in search of such factors since 1950, a trend that increased substantially after the riot. We expect many more blacks in the city of Detroit to exercise their right to move to those suburban municipalities that offer the amenities they seek, thereby increasing racial residential integration. Such increases in racial integration will be slow and will vary from suburb to suburb, with the inner suburbs experiencing a greater share of this influx than the outer suburbs. We come to that conclusion after years of studying race, class, and population movements from the city into the suburbs. Such movement of more blacks to the suburbs could be enhanced by bold actions against housing discrimination and racial steering and programs that provide incentives for racial and class integration. To start, we have listed both the Kerner Commission's recommendations in 1968 and the recommendations of the Michigan Civil Rights Commission in 2006 as a way of highlighting their similarities. These recommendations address problems that contributed to the riot of 1967.

What the Kerner Commission Recommended for Housing, Segregation, and Racial Inequality, 1968

1. The supply of housing suitable for low-income families should be expanded on a massive basis.
2. Areas outside of the ghetto neighborhoods should be opened up to occupancy by racial minorities via the enactment of national comprehensive and enforceable open occupancy laws.

3. Expand and diversify the public housing program. Not only increase the number of units but change the structure of the units from high use in the slums to scattered sites. (National Advisory Commission on Civil Disorders 1968)

What the Michigan Civil Rights Commission Recommended for Housing Segregation and Racial Inequality, 2006

In 2006, the Michigan Civil Rights Commission convened a civil rights summit. Among the findings were that segregation in schools and housing is a major obstacle to social and economic parity between minorities and whites. Among the recommendations to address these problems were these:

1. Adopt plans that will promote racial integration of Michigan's communities and schools.
2. Advance legislation that requires the State of Michigan and its political subdivisions to prepare and make public a "racial impact" analysis before using state funds for new road construction, public transportation systems, sewer, water, gas, and electricity extensions and other attributes that contribute to sprawl.
3. Adopt and implement plans requiring the State of Michigan and its political subdivisions to ensure that a certain percentage of new housing built in communities is affordable and available for low-income residents.
4. Establish additional human rights commissions in cities, counties, and townships. (Michigan Department of Civil Rights, 2007)

Notice that the commission recommended no *specific* legislation or policies to promote racial integration in Michigan's communities and schools. This is a major shortcoming of the commission and a missed opportunity for summit participants to draft recommendations that would finally bring a reduction in the racial divide in the Detroit metropolitan area.

CHAPTER 7

The Declining Auto Industry and Anti-Asian Racism

The Murder of Vincent Chin

DURING THE ECONOMIC RECESSION OF THE EARLY 1980s, DETROIT'S DECLINING auto industry became the source of anger and hatred against Japanese-made cars. Eager to shift the blame from poor-performing American cars to better-performing Japanese cars, some angry Detroiters went so far as to shoot at passing Japanese-made cars (*Economist*, February 1, 1992). As late as 1992, at the North American International Show in Detroit, a few individuals took hammers to Honda cars (*Economist*, February 1, 1992). Before long, Japan bashing became popular among politicians like Congressman John Dingell, who blamed "little yellow men" (Wu, 2002) for the industry's economic woes. "Buy American" campaigns soon morphed into ugly, malicious forms of anti-Asian racism, which, in a city already marred by a long history of racism capped by two race riots, could ill afford it. This anti-Asian racism claimed the life of Vincent Chin and shamed a city and a nation.

THE LIFE AND DEATH OF VINCENT CHIN

On June 19, 1982, Vincent Chin, twenty-seven, a draftsman at an Oak Park engineering firm, and three friends went into the Fancy Pants Tavern in Highland Park to celebrate a special upcoming event: Chin's marriage to Vickie Wong of Mt. Clemens. The couple had met three years previously, and within two years decided to get married and start a family. The upcoming wedding generated much anticipation among their friends. One of Wong's friends and coworkers mentioned that Vickie "came to work wearing a very huge diamond" and that "for the better part of a year, they'd been looking for a house." The wedding was scheduled for a Monday "because many of their friends worked in Chinese restaurants, which are usually closed on Monday. That way everybody could be there" (*Detroit Free Press*, July 1, 1982). Vickie's friend said that Vickie had planned to wear two wedding gowns, "an American one at the wedding and a Chinese one at the reception." The couple planned to honeymoon in Aruba. One of Vincent's friends reported that "he was real excited about that" (*Detroit Free Press*, July 1, 1982).

After Chin and his friends entered the Fancy Pants Tavern, a scuffle broke out between Chin and Ronald Ebens, forty-three, a white autoworker from East Detroit who was there with his stepson, twenty-three-year-old Michael Nitz. According to a twenty-four-year old dancer at the tavern, Ebens, who thought Chin was Japanese, made some remark about Japanese foreign imports. "I heard the father (Ebens) say, 'Because of you, little motherf . . . , we're out of work.'" Vincent countered, "I'm not a little mother . . . " Then, the dancer reported, Chin "got up and pushed [Ebens] and they both picked up chairs . . . they were swinging them at each other" (*Detroit Free Press*, May 9, 1983). In the scuffle, Nitz was hit by a chair. "He got a big gash because he was dripping a lot of blood" (*Detroit Free Press*, May 9, 1983). A bouncer intervened, broke up the fight, and told the men to leave the bar. One witness said, "Ebens went to his car and got a baseball bat," and then chased Chin several blocks and hit him several times in the head. Chin was rushed to Henry Ford Hospital, where he died four days later. The day after he was supposed to marry Vickie Wong, Vincent Chin was buried (*Detroit Free Press*, July 1, 1982).

THE SENTENCING OF EBENS AND NITZ

As tragic as the beating death of Vincent Chin was to family and friends, what followed next deepened and extended their pain and cast a long shadow over the criminal justice system in the city. Robert Ebens, who beat Chin to death, and his stepson, Michael Nitz, who joined in the chase and held Chin during the beating, pleaded guilty to manslaughter after they were first charged with second-degree murder. Then came the decision destined to be heard around the country—and later the world: Judge Charles Kaufman sentenced Ebens and Nitz to only three years probation and a $3,000 fine each (*Detroit Free Press*, March 18, 1983).

Kaufman had not heard any testimony when the men pleaded guilty, but argued that "court documents showed Chin started the confrontation in the bar." Explaining his decision, he said, "The only report I saw indicated that Mr. Chin threw the first punch . . . while this certainly wasn't a case of self-defense, it was the continuation of a fight that Mr. Chin apparently started. Now Mr. Ebens and Mr. Nitz went beyond what was necessary for self-defense. If it had been a case of self-defense, they would not be guilty of anything." Kaufman's rationale for giving Ebens and Nitz such light sentences was based upon their lack of any previous criminal record and their stability in the community. "We're talking here about a man who's held down a responsible job with the same company for 17 or 18 years and his son who is employed and is a part-time student," Kaufman explained. Further justifying his decision, Kaufman said that "these men are not going to go out and harm somebody else. I just didn't think that putting them in prison would do any good for them or for society. You don't make the punishment fit the crime; you make the punishment fit the criminal" (*Detroit Free Press*, March 18, 1983).

On April 24, the *Detroit Free Press* expressed its concern over Judge Kaufman's sentencing in an editorial entitled "Vincent Chin: The Outcome Made Life Cheap and Justice Elusive." The editorial started out with a quote from Kaufman, saying, "If people feel no one should get probation for manslaughter, then they should go to the legislature to change the law." The editorial noted, "The Wayne County Prosecutor's Office has acted first, however, by decreeing that persons charged with second-degree murder, as Mr. Chin's assailants originally were, will no longer be permitted to plead guilty to a reduced charge of manslaughter." This would be a major policy change, as "a manslaughter conviction opens the way to a sentence of probation instead of prison. A conviction of second-degree murder, in contrast, mandates a prison sentence of a least a one year to life in prison" (*Detroit Free Press*, April 24, 1983).

In the end, what did all this mean?

> The change in policy will not bring Mr. Chin back to life, or restore him to his family or to the young woman he was to have married a few days after his beating. Even had the new rule been in effect last summer, it is unlikely that it would have deflected the horrifying progression of events that left Mr. Chin battered and bleeding on a sidewalk . . . [but] the policy changes might have affected the court's response to his death and spared the community the sense of outrage and injustice that the episode has aroused. (*Detroit Free Press*, April 24, 1983)

The editorial acknowledged that courts have to have "reasonable flexibility in sentencing," but argued that "the overall handling of the Chin case seems disturbingly casual. Evidence presented at the sentencing hearing was limited. Plea bargaining had already reduced the murder charges to manslaughter. No assistant prosecutor was present at the hearing to argue for a stiffer sentence." Comparing practices in Oakland County to Wayne County, the editorial explained that in the former, "prosecutors are always present at such hearings, but that is not the practice in understaffed Wayne County. Judge Kaufman disregarded the pre-sentence report's recommendation for prison terms for the assailants and handed down some of the lightest possible sentences" (*Detroit Free Press*, April 24, 1983).

The editorial concluded that the "result was a process that made Vincent Chin's life seem cheap and the criminal justice system either callous or perverse. It is not clear if there are legal grounds for reopening the question of the sentences. It is clear that police, courts and the prosecutors have to be wary of the inattention, sloppiness or jaded attitudes that might produce such questionable results again." The editorial reminded its readers that "trust in the justice system and respect for law are badly eroded when a case leaves so many people feeling what Vincent Chin whispered as he lay dying: 'it's not fair'" (*Detroit Free Press*, April 24, 1983).

THE IMPACT ON CHIN'S FAMILY

Judge Kaufman's light sentences for the two white men who had killed Chin and his reasons for doing so placed an additional emotional burden on Chin's grieving mother. Lily Chin had raised Vincent from the time she and her husband adopted him as a six-year-old orphan from China. Her husband succumbed to kidney disease in November 1981 (*Detroit Free Press*, September 9, 1987). She was still suffering from the shock of her son's brutal death when "she was jolted by the news that Wayne County Circuit Judge Charles Kaufman had set the convicted killers free. She now cries herself to sleep" (*Detroit Free Press*, May 9, 1983).

Mrs. Chin had waited patiently for nine months to see justice done for her son. Four days after the beating death of her son, Ebens and Nitz were arrested and charged with second-degree murder. Expecting due justice and desiring to put Vincent's terrible death behind her, she purchased a plane ticket to China to visit her mother "for solace in her grief." After the disappointing sentence, Lily Chin was determined to stay and seek justice. "I want to (stay) and fight . . . I lost everything. How can I live in America with that kind of law? My son is beaten like an animal and, and the killer is not in jail," she said. "If this happened in China,

[Ebens and Nitz] would be put in [an] electric chair. This is freedom and democracy? Why isn't everybody equal?" (*Detroit Free Press*, May 9, 1983).

Lily Chin lost both her son and her respect and love for America as the "Promised Land." A newspaper writer explained it best when he wrote: "She never imagined that the promise and hope of her adopted country could be shattered in a Woodward Avenue street fight, then in the marble and oak-paneled court room of Judge Kaufman" (*Detroit Free Press*, May 9, 1983).

Lily Chin's story of coming to America was not so different from millions of other immigrants. She was born Lily Yee in 1920, in Canton, China, "the only child of a prosperous merchant." She recalled her father's business being like the old Hudson department store (now demolished) in downtown Detroit, and her childhood as very happy. Lily was part of a large urban extended family of aunts, uncles, and grandparents.

World War II ended her good fortune, at least for a while. As the *Detroit Free Press* (July 7, 1983) reported, "Japanese air raids and ground troops ravaged Canton, one of China's principle seaports, in the 1930s. She remembers being roused in the pre-dawn darkness before the morning bombing raids in the mountains in the countryside with other frightened school children." Canton suffered twice from Japanese aggression, which Mrs. Chin remembered destroyed the city. Her family survived but "lost everything; her father's business was shattered."

Her life changed when she met her husband, Hing Chin, in 1947. "His mother and Lily's grandmother had been neighbors in the same village. He had come to America in 1922 at 17, living first in Seattle, then moving to New York, and finally settling in Detroit. He enlisted in the Army when war broke out and returned to China in 1947." Previously, Lily had known Hing "only through a picture his mother carried." They were married the next year. Lily came to America in 1948, despite her father's objections, which were probably motivated by his memories of his father, who experienced racial oppression as a laborer on the transcontinental railroad and returned home with "tales of bigotry and persecution." However, she could not remain in China, where she had witnessed so much violence. She promised her father she would return soon for a visit. In 1949, the Chinese Communists seized power and Mrs. Chin "was cut off from her family for years" (*Detroit Free Press*, July 7, 1983).

The Chins moved to Highland Park, Michigan, in 1948. "The early years in their new country were hard but happy. They were isolated, with no Chinese neighbors, but went to Chinatown every weekend to buy Chinese groceries. They worked in a laundry and made 'only a few dollars a week,' yet they managed to get by" (*Detroit Free Press*, July 7, 1983). Mrs. Chin did not speak much English, but she had many American friends.

The only thing missing was a child. Mrs. Chin lost her first baby in 1949, and later, after an operation, was told by a doctor that she would not be able to bear children. Their desire to have a child led the Chins to investigate adoption. Their search for "a suitable child" to adopt involved "a bureaucratic process that took years. . . . Mrs. Chin studied many photos of children in Hong Kong and Chinese orphanages before she saw a snapshot of a pudgy boy who lingered in her memory. 'I showed it to my husband and said, I like this boy.'" The Chins adopted six-year-old Vincent in 1961. They lived in Highland Park, which had undergone severe economic decline, until he turned sixteen (*Detroit Free Press*, July 7, 1983). In 1971, after Hing Chin was beaten and robbed, they moved to Oak Park.

The Chins adored their adopted son. The American promise was just beginning to bear fruit in their lives. What they were unable to accomplish in their lives was now possible through their son. "Like many families, the Chins had made a lifetime investment in their son. They lived their lives for and through him, buying his clothes and saving his tuition with their salaries from service jobs in Detroit's laundries, factories and Chinese restaurants." Mrs. Chin kept photos of Vincent housed in a large envelope that traced the stages of his short but meaningful life. They showed "a cheerful boy, always formal and proper in a jacket and tie. At seven or eight, he stands proudly before a tinsel-decked Christmas tree, his father behind him in a dark suit, his mother in an Oriental robe. At 10, he smiles for a school portrait in the optimistic attitude of one who sees a bright future before him." By the time, he had reached his teens, "he has grown tall and slim and wears dark bangs. The last picture show him in a tuxedo, escorting his fiancée down a church aisle as best man at a friend's wedding" (*Detroit Free Press*, July 7, 1983).

Always ambitious, Vincent had hopes of becoming a writer, lawyer, or veterinarian. His mother recalled that she discouraged him from these professions, probably because she wanted to protect him from failure and ensure his success in other fields. When he told her he wanted to be a writer, she said he could not make money as a writer; when he wanted to be a lawyer "because he liked to talk," she said, "Oh, you're Chinese, nobody will believe you"; then she discouraged him from becoming a veterinarian, telling him "you can't do that. You can't open up the animals, you're scared of blood." At twelve years old, Vincent worked as a busboy in a Chinese restaurant. Soon after graduating from Oak Park High School, he enrolled in the architectural department of the Lawrence Institute of Technology in Southfield, where he developed a keen interest in the design of European cathedrals. Before his death he had a full-time job as a draftsman with Efficient Engineering of Oak Park and a part-time waiter job, where he usually worked seven days a week. The two jobs enabled him to both support his widowed mother and save for his upcoming wedding (*Detroit Free Press*, July 7, 1983).

The day Vincent was killed, business at the restaurant was slow, and so he left early for that fateful bachelor party with several friends. After the chain of tragic events, his mother "received the late-night knock on the door, the visitor bearing news of Vincent's beating, and the surgeons at Ford Hospital who held out no hope to the grieving mother" (*Detroit Free Press*, July 7, 1983). Judge Kaufman's fateful decision had the impact of adding insult to injury.

Mrs. Lily Chin's outrage at the decision echoed around the country. "I'm a Chinese," she said. "This happened because my son is Chinese, not American. If two Chinese killed a white person, they must go to jail, maybe for their whole lives. But only the skin's different. The heart (of a Chinese) is no different than an American." She struggled to understand how this could happen in her adopted country. "My husband fought for this country. We always paid our taxes and worked hard. We never had any trouble. Before I really loved America, but now this has made me very angry. Something is wrong with this country" (*Detroit Free Press*, July 7, 1983).

COMMUNITY BACKLASH

Many Chinese Americans expressed their anger and dismay in the *East/West: The Chinese-American Journal*, based in San Francisco. On April 6, 1983, in a letter to the editor of the publication, one reader wrote:

I am angered and frustrated that this kind of going on still exists so openly. I wonder if Judge Charles Kaufman was or is out of his mind or he himself is a racist? In this day and age there is no room for this kind of blatant racism. Has this judge Kaufman forgotten what happened in the Holocaust of Hitler's Germany? Maybe he is just callous? If there is no satisfaction for those two racists to get what is coming to them, then use the law against them. The recourse for the survivors of Vincent Chin is to sue the pants out [*sic*] of them and more. ("Reader Angry over Injustice," 1983)

Chinese Americans around the country rallied behind the Chinese Americans in the Detroit metropolitan area as they began orchestrating a national protest movement reminiscent of the humble but dynamic beginnings of the civil rights movement. Elis Choy Lee of Ann Arbor, for example, requested that *East/West* disseminate a petition that "the state of Michigan open a public inquiry into this case" ("Michigan Reader Sends Petition," 1983).

In the April 20, 1983, letters to the editor, Helen Y. Zia, president of the American Citizens for Justice (ACJ), based in Royal Oak, Michigan, sent an upbeat letter to *East/West* on the progress of the movement in Detroit, stating, "Things are really picking up here [on the Vincent Chin case]. I've sent a set of informational material to the Asian Law Caucus, which includes the legal briefs that have been filed. If you can think of any West Coast groups or publications who should get a copy, let me know" ("Interest Up in Chin Case," 1983). She also informed *East/West* readers that the "local media [Detroit] is beginning to really pick up on this [case]. The NAACP is supporting [us]. A big spread is coming out Sunday in both dailies. Since we gave the prosecutors a deadline the showdown is near" ("Interest Up in Chin Case," 1983).

Three months later, *East/West* encouraged readers to support Lily Chin's upcoming speaking tour. "Mrs. Lily Chin, mother of the slain Detroit-area draftsman, Vincent Chin, is in town this week to talk to local supporters and to help with fundraising efforts in the area. This brave woman desires our attention and respect," the editorial said. It reminded readers, "She is not only dealing with her personal mourning but also with the heavy responsibility of helping to mobilize the community to fight against racism" ("East/West Supports Chin Efforts," 1983).

African American leaders and organizations rallied behind Mrs. Chin in her search for justice and provided her with a forum from which to share her pain and sorrow. In an interview with the *Michigan Chronicle*, the largest African American weekly in Michigan, Mrs. Chin criticized Judge Kaufman's statement that Ebens and Nitz were not the "kind of people you send to jail," because neither had previous criminal records. "If you had been good, and you killed someone, does that mean that you don't go to jail? Does this mean we all can kill and don't have to go to jail? Then why do we have jails? Why do we tax ourselves to support the prisons?" Talking through a translator, she said, "In my country, you don't kill and still walk the streets. These men wanted my son to die. They did not hit him in the body. They hit him in the head . . . they wanted to kill him, and they should be in prison for at least 35 years" (*Michigan Chronicle*, May 7, 1983).

African American leaders in Detroit, such as council president Erma Henderson and veteran labor leader Horace Sheffield, were early supporters of the efforts to obtain justice for Vincent Chin. In his weekly column, "As I See It," Sheffield expressed his heartfelt feeling about the case: "On its face, this appears to be about as horrible an instance of gross miscarriage of justice that one could possibly imagine. And in saying that—let me make it clear—it's not my intent in any way to impugn the integrity of Judge Charles Kaufman," he writes. "It's just simply that I cannot possibly understand how a man can beat another man to death with a baseball bat and not serve one day's time, especially when it was done under the undisputed circumstances that prevailed in the case" (Sheffield, 1983).

Sheffield participated in the predominantly Asian American rally on April 17, which was held in the Cafeteria of the Ford World Headquarters in Dearborn, Michigan. He noted, "There is no question but that the Chin case has brought the Oriental community together." Local black organizations opened their doors and hearts to Asian Americans seeking support for the Chin cause. Sheffield reported:

> Dr. Marira Chang, vice president of the American Citizens for Justice, discussed the case at the April 16 meeting of the Detroit Association of Black Organizations (DABO) House of Delegates meeting and was enthusiastically received. The same kind of response greeted the group's attorney, Lisa Chan, when she spoke to the monthly membership meeting of the Detroit NAACP in the Downtown YWCA the next afternoon. (Sheffield, 1983)

On May 9, 1983, hundreds of angry demonstrators bearing signs, "We Want Justice," "Cahalan Where Were You" (William Cahalan was the Wayne County prosecutor), and "It's Not Fair" rallied at Kennedy Square to protest Judge Kaufman's lenient probation sentence and fines for the murderers of Vincent Chin. The rally was organized by ACJ to "put pressure on the Justice Dept. to convene a grand jury to further investigate the case and to urge Wayne County Circuit Court Judge Charles Kaufman to resentence Ronal Ebens and Michael Nitz, convicted of the killing" (*Michigan Chronicle*, May 14, 1983).

The demonstrators were multiracial, including Chinese Americans, African Americans, white Americans, and other Asian Americans. Bill Roundtree, a national board member of the All People Congress for Human Rights, reflected, "The fact that Blacks, Asians, Whites and many different nationalities are out here protesting shows that many people are concerned," he said. Mrs. Chin gave a tearful appeal, begging for justice for her son. Supporters who also spoke included NAACP executive secretary Winston Lang, city council president Erma Henderson, New Detroit public safety and justice director Robert McClinton, and Kin Yee, president of ACJ, which was the organization representing Mrs. Chin in the case. Yee told the gathering, "We are here because a double tragedy has taken place—a double crime, if you will, because the criminal justice system that is supposed to teach our children right from wrong has allowed these murderers to walk the streets among us" (*Michigan Chronicle*, May 14, 1983).

Yee's organization was accused of waging a campaign of character assassination against Judge Kaufman. "That is not true," Yee countered. "In fact, we have stated repeatedly that we believe this case was mishandled by the criminal justice system from the very beginning, and we feel that much of the responsibility for the outrageous leniency of this sentence falls directly on the shoulders of Prosecutor William Cahalan." While Judge Kaufman was certainly not blameless, Yee believed Cahalan played a major role in Kaufman's flawed decision. "How a crime, a killing, that has clear elements of first degree, premeditated murder could be watered down to manslaughter and receive a sentence of probation is a question which must be answered by William Cahalan" (*Michigan Chronicle*, May 14, 1983).

The demonstrators continued their protests at the U.S. Court House, where they presented a letter to U.S. Attorney Leonard Gilman and to Cahalan's office. "There is strong sentiment that, as Chief Prosecutor, you failed to protect the interests of the victim, Vincent Chin, his family, and thereby failed to protect the interests of the people," the letter argued. "Of course, your office could still act to bring this outrage to an end, even though doing the right thing is sometime the more difficult option." Based upon his earlier position that his office had no further authority to act on the case, Cahalan refused to comment on the rally or the letter (*Michigan Chronicle*, May 14, 1983).

Judge Kaufman and Chief Prosecutor William Cahalan probably had no idea how their actions would trigger a firestorm of reactions around the country and in various parts of the world. At the same time that demonstrators in Detroit held their rally, Victor J. Yan, a photojournalist with the *China Times*, based in Long Island, reported that a similar rally was being held in New York. Shin Hyung Ken, a member of the North American Coalition for Human Rights, who just happened to be visiting from out of town, was moved to join the protest. "I felt I had to come out," she explained. "I am committed to the struggle for human rights. I wish more people would come out to protest this injustice" (*Michigan Chronicle*, May 14, 1983).

In late May 1983, the Detroit branch of the American Civil Liberties Union (ACLU) issued a report that placed the blame for the lenient sentences by Judge Kaufman on the Wayne County Prosecutor's Office. According to the report, "the real failure was the prosecutor's failure to make sure the judge was fully informed about what actually happened" (*Detroit Free Press*, May 28, 1983). Instead, Ebens and Nitz were able "to plead no contest to a reduced charge of manslaughter, which carries a maximum penalty of 15 years in prison." And, adding insult to injury, no one from the Prosecutor's Office was present at the sentencing. "As a result," the ACLU argued, "the sentencing judge had before him only the pre-sentence report and statements made on behalf of the defendants by defense counsel. . . . Unfortunately, the effect of . . . the sentences . . . has been to create the impression the law confers a $3,000 license to murder Chinese-Americans." While the reports suggested that public officials should acknowledge that the sentences were a mistake, they realized that resentencing Ebens and Nitz would "constitute double jeopardy and set a dangerous precedent." In an effort to avoid similar problems in the future, the ACLU recommended that prosecutors be present at sentencing or at least review presentence reports so as to be aware when "a special case warrants an appearance." In cases where that would not be possible, then the victim or his or her kin should be present at the sentencing, "to put something else besides the defendant's side of the case before the court" (*Detroit Free Press*, May 28, 1983).

An "offer of payment" of $20 was supposedly made by Ebens and Nitz to a man named Jimmie Perry to help them find Vincent Chin during the chase. In April, Liza Chan, an attorney from the suburban Detroit suburb of Southfield representing the Chinese Welfare Council of Detroit, "cited the offer of payment as further evidence of 'various and numerous material facts and errors' upon which Wayne County Circuit Judge Charles Kaufman relied in imposing a sentence of probation and fines on the convicted killers of Vincent Chin of Oak Park." Chan and the ACJ, which had been formed in the wake of the killing and the sentences, requested Judge Kaufman void his original sentence and send the men to jail. Chan and the ACJ filed a formal request with the court to have a hearing on April 29, 1983. Chan then told a press conference, "We have urged the prosecutor to ask the court to reconsider the sentence and for resentencing. We have asked the prosecutor to take the appropriate actions . . . . We have not heard from the prosecutor nor do we know what action [he plans]." The spokesperson for the Office of the Prosecutor reported that it would not comment on the request by Chan and the ACJ (*Detroit Free Press*, December 19, 1983).

THE BATTLE OVER JUDGE KAUFMAN'S DECISION

On April 29, 1983, approximately 100 protesters gathered in the courtroom of Judge Kaufman. They applauded when the attorneys asked the judge to put Ebens and Nitz in jail for the killing of Vincent Chin. Bruce Saperstein and Edward Khoury, the attorneys for Ebens and Nitz (who were not in court), argued against the motion, which asked Judge Kaufman to "appoint a special prosecutor, to allow Lily Chin and Henry Lee, who represent Vincent Chin's estate, to intervene in the case, and to throw out the probation sentence and send the men to jail." Daniel Hoekenga, an attorney representing the protest group, argued that because the prosecutor failed to appear at the sentencing, the defense lawyer was able to misrepresent the facts to Kaufman by "claiming that Chin started the fight that led to a four-block chase and beating." He pointed out that "our motion is not prompted by a desire for revenge . . . but because we believe errors in fact were presented to the court at sentencing." Saperstein countered: "I did not misconstrue facts in this case and stand on the facts I presented." Khoury "argued that the law does not allow a judge to change a valid sentence—one Saperstein called 'fair and reasonable'" (*Detroit Free Press*, April 30, 1983).

Since the lawyers for the protest group put most of the blame for the light sentences on the Prosecutor's Office, the latter was obligated to refute the charges. An assistant prosecutor informed Judge Kaufman that "the prosecutor's office was 'satisfied' with the convictions because manslaughter 'offered an adequate range of sentencing discretion." He argued that "Whether we agree with the sentence or not, there is no legal authority under which we can request this court, to amend or alter its sentence to increase its severity." In a dramatic display of emphasis that the court spectators applauded, Hoekenga concluded his argument: "Talk about crime. We have a man beaten to death with a baseball bat . . . and that man (Ebens) walks the streets and Vincent Chin is in the ground. We ask that these men be put behind bars" (*Detroit Free Press*, April 30, 1983).

Kaufman decided to study the arguments concerning changing the probation sentences he gave the defendants. At the end of the arguments, the judge admitted that "this is a very emotional and volatile issue." He refused to comment on the case after the hearing but promised that his written opinion would be ready within three weeks. This was good news for the attorneys for the protest group. One of the attorneys, Liza Chan, said, "I feel very positive. This is a case we feel should be corrected. I'm glad that the judge feels that it is serious enough to study further." The protest group's other attorney, Hoekenga, added, "Obviously, this is the first encouraging support for the community, which is so outraged by this situation."

At the end of the hearing, the protestors gathered outside the City County Building, carrying signs and shouting slogans. Lily Chin was among them, but the emotionally charged atmosphere proved too much for her. She almost fainted and had to be taken away in a wheelchair (*Detroit Free Press*, April 30, 1983).

On June 2, 1983, Judge Kaufman in a written statement ruled that there was no legal basis to invalidate the sentences he had given Ebens and Nitz. He also included in his written statement that the ACJ did not have the legal right to intervene, but he considered their arguments, because he was "satisfied that the interest expressed . . . is real and sincere." In addition, he wrote that he recognized the "petitioners . . . consist of representatives of the family of (Chin) and community groups who seek to express, by their collective voice, discontent with the sentence of the court and the alleged inaction of the prosecutor. The concern and interest expressed . . . are understandable." Kaufman argued, however, "While sympathizing with the family and community of the victim, it is the obligation of the court to decide the matter submitted in accordance with the mandates of law. The court being convinced that no error appears [to invalidate] the order of probation previously rendered, these orders will not be disturbed" (*Detroit Free Press*, June 3, 1983). Kaufman also argued in his written statement that the lack of a prosecutor did not invalidate the sentence, noting that "in Wayne County, the prosecutor appears at sentencing less than one percent of the time."

As expected, the lawyers for the two convicted killers of Chin were pleased. Nitz's lawyer, Ed Khoury, called the judge "a principle guy," and said, "He's not going to subvert the law in response to public pressure" (*Detroit Free Press*, June 3, 1983).

Understandably, the lawyers for ACJ were upset. At a press conference in Detroit's Chinatown called after Judge Kaufman's announcement, Liza Chan accused him of compounding "a miscarriage of justice" by his refusal to reverse his probation sentence. Kaufman "completely failed to recognize what we have here, which is a gross misappraisal of the court of all the facts," Chan said, stating that Kaufman refused to reverse his decision because of "a little bit of pride." He would have gone down in American history as the first judge to reverse a sentence because of a misrepresentation of facts at a sentencing. The group said it would request that the Michigan Court of Appeals reverse Judge Kaufman's sentences. During the press conference, Mrs. Lily Chin, seated at the side of one of the Chinese American organizers, could be seen crying (*Detroit Free Press*, June 4, 1983).

Judge Kaufman's decision, while disappointing, did not dampen the spirit of the nationwide movement for justice for Vincent Chin. Several weeks after Kaufman's decision and the press conference, close to 100 people came together on a Sunday afternoon at Central United Church "to start a five-day period of remembrance for Vincent Chin and to pray for his family." It was sponsored by ACJ, a predominantly Asian American organization responsible for making Chin's death a national cause. A spokesperson for the group said his death "is important for all of us to remember, not just Chinese-Americans." Meanwhile, rallies protesting the killing and sentencing were held in Los Angeles, San Francisco, and Windsor, Ontario, and one was planned for New York City. In L.A. close to 300 Asian Americans rallied at City Hall to hear speakers, including Tom Bradley, the city's first African American mayor, who "urged an end to 'racial scapegoating' and blasted Kaufman for not sentencing Ebens and Nitz to prison" (*Detroit Free Press*, June 20, 1983).

Uncovering and Understanding the Origins of the Anti-Asian Causes of Vincent Chin's Death

As protestors rallied around the country and interest spread to several countries, Ronald Takaki, a well-known Japanese American scholar and professor of ethnic studies at the University of California, Berkeley, wrote a stirring and thought-provoking article in the September 21, 1983 *San Francisco Examiner* entitled, "Who really killed Vincent Chin?" Takaki probed some of the underlying causes of the senseless and horrible murder.

> The anger propelling the movement for justice for Vincent Chin has led many people to ask a deeply political question: Who killed Vincent Chin? They know that Ebens and Nitz are only the obvious killers. They point out that the corporate executives of the auto industry must also be held

accountable for Chin's death: the auto manufacturers should have been designing and building fuel efficient cars 20 years ago, and now they are blaming Japan for Detroit's massive unemployment. (Takaki, 1983)

A UAW member in Fremont agreed. "Unemployment is not caused by foreign competition . . . it is the result of mistakes and poor planning of the multinational corporations—and General Motors is one of the biggest of them" (Takaki, 1983).

Takaki also quoted Jim Shimoura, another Asian American writer, who wrote:

It is significant that Ebens was employed as a supervisor at an auto assembly plant. In that setting, being constantly indoctrinated about the "evils" of the Japanese automobile industry . . . is it mere coincidence that the built up anger against Asians was unleashed when Ebens came upon Vincent Chin? (Takaki, 1983)

This is a crucial point in understanding the anti-Asian motives behind Eben's taunting and eventual killing of Vincent Chin and the role that U.S. auto companies played in seeding those motives. As Takaki (1983) elaborates: "In their television commercials and their promotional campaigns to 'Buy American,' U.S. automakers have contributed to the racist hysteria pervasive among white American workers and to the proliferation of bumper stickers which read: 'unemployment made in Japan.'" Few auto workers bothered to take the time to investigate the real causes of their plight. To some white workers like Ebens it was easier to blame the "racial other" for their plight instead of confronting the self-serving propaganda of the U.S. automakers. Takaki noted, "As they cutback production in Detroit and as they close plants in places like Fremont and Milpitas in California, U.S. automakers scapegoat Japan for the misery of American workers, directing the rage and frustration felt by whites like Ebens toward Japan and away from the structural ills of the auto industry."

Lest readers forget the history of anti-Asian racism, Takaki quoted George Wong, who put the killing of Chin in historical perspective:

What disturbs me . . . is that the two men who brutally clubbed Vincent Chin to death in Detroit in 1982 were thinking the same thoughts as the lynch mob in San Francisco Chinatown one hundred years ago: "Kill the foreigners to save our jobs! The Chinese must go!" When corporate heads tell frustrated workers the foreign imports are taking their jobs, then they are acting like an agitator of a lynch mob. (Takaki, 1983)

Other leaders, supporting "buy American" attitudes, also played a role in creating anti-Asian attitudes—however unintentionally—that formed the context for Vincent Chin's death. As Frank Wu later explained, "The tensions of that time in the Motor City are hard to recall, but the context made race central to everything about the Chin case. Congressman John Dingell—whose father, also a member of the House of Representatives, had called for the internment of Japanese Americans during World War II—gave an angry speech in Congress blaming 'little yellow men' for the economic woes of American automakers, whose products were facing unprecedented competition from efficient and economical Japanese imports" (Wu, 2002: 70).

Dingell was not alone in the sentiment described by the *Detroit Free Press*. Unfortunately, "It took the slaying of . . . Vincent Chin by a disgruntled autoworker in 1982 to awaken

Detroit to the ugliness and danger of anti-Asian racism" (*Detroit Free Press*, October 27, 2009). Senator Donald Riegle (D-Mich.) "compared the Japanese decision to ship more of their cars to the United States to 'an economic Pearl Harbor.'" Chrysler chairman Lee Iacocca "warned a Democratic caucus that the Japanese 'are in the backyard taking over the country.'"

The UAW also played a major role in contributing to the anti-Asian racism in the Detroit area before the death of Chin:

> A sign in the UAW headquarters parking lot urged drivers to "Park your import in Tokyo." A bumper sticker on the guard shack showed a Pac Man figure chasing slanted-eyed quarry. Some UAW locals battered Japanese cars with sledgehammers on Labor Day. (*Detroit Free Press*, October 27, 2009)

The UAW eventually got rid of the sign and bumper stickers and "discouraged the car-bashing activities," but according to one UAW official, "they reappear occasionally" (*Detroit Free Press*, October 27, 2009).

National leaders reinforced the anti-Japanese hysteria sweeping the Motor City. House Speaker Thomas O'Neill Jr. "said that if he were president he'd fix the Japanese like they've never been fixed before." And Democratic presidential candidate Walter Mondale "told [a] New York electrical worker that if you try to sell an American car in Japan, you better have the United States Army with you when they land on the docks" (*Detroit Free Press*, October 27, 2009).

The Struggles Continues

Determined to continue the struggle for justice for her murdered son, Mrs. Lily Chin and her supporters went to Washington, D.C., in June to appeal to the U.S. Justice Department. On June 29 Assistant Attorney General William Bradford Reynolds, head of the U.S. Justice Department's Civil Rights Division, met with Mrs. Chin and informed her that he considered the case "a brutal incident that was treated with apparently way too light a sentence" (*Detroit Free Press*, July 1, 1983). Attorney General William French Smith had already received a letter in May from Rep. Norman Mineta (D-Calif.) and six other members of Congress mentioning "the widespread belief that the entire case would have been handled differently by local officials if (Chin) had not been of Chinese background. We are very concerned about this case and respectively request your personal attention to it" (*Detroit Free Press*, July 7, 1983).

During the same period the U.S. Department of Justice Civil Rights Division, Criminal Section, received a document from the attorneys for ACJ and the Asian Pacific American Legal Center of Southern California, entitled "Confidential Report: The Vincent Chin Case," which detailed the history of the case, and contained profiles and statements of eyewitnesses to the killing, among others (American Citizens for Justice and Asian Pacific American Legal Center of Southern California, 1983).

Fortunately for the Chin supporters, the Justice Department guidelines allowed Reynolds to bring a case involving civil rights violations of U.S. civil rights laws before a grand jury "even if a defendant's case has been tried in a state court" (*Detroit Free Press*, July 1, 1983). A spokesperson for the Justice Department mentioned that the FBI was engaged in a "comprehensive investigation" of the Chin killing. The FBI began investigating the case in the wake of protests in several cities. "I don't know of a case," Reynolds said, "that has generated as much interest or as much correspondence. If the facts bear this out and the legal technicalities permit, this would be something the federal government ought not to leave as it has been left." The FBI investigation was a "high priority case," he added. His hope was that he could decide on bringing the case to a grand jury before summer ended (*Detroit Free Press*, July 1, 1983).

Several weeks later the U.S. Justice Department ordered the Detroit FBI to "renew its investigation of possible civil rights violations in the baseball beating death of Vincent Chin." Some sources revealed that the FBI had been ordered to question some witnesses in the case "to determine if the attack was racially motivated." Charles Moy, a spokesperson for ACJ, mentioned that the incident including Chin's beating death, Kaufman's probation for his killers, and the judge's refusal to reconsider his sentences "has aroused the Asian community as well as concerned people throughout the country . . . we're all worked hard on this to see that justice is done, not justice for Vincent Chin, but for all Americans" (*Detroit Free Press*, July 1, 1983).

In early September a federal grand jury began its inquiry (*Detroit Free Press*, September 8, 1983). In November, the grand jury indicted both Ebens and Nitz on civil rights charges. They were "charged with conspiracy to deprive Chin of his civil rights and with beating him to death with a baseball bat because of his race." The first count of the indictment stated that both men conspired to "injure, oppress, threaten and harass" Chin during his bachelor celebration party at the Fancy Pants club. The indictment also mentioned that Ebens and Nitz started the argument with Chin. They called him "'Chink,' a 'nip,' and other obscenities." Once outside the club, the indictment continued, the men chased Chin with a baseball bat and then recruited and paid a local youth $20 to help them "catch a China man." Both men "aided and abetted" each other in the beating death of Vincent Chin (*Detroit Free Press*, November 3, 1983).

Mrs. Chin's response to the news of the indictment was bittersweet. "I'm grateful and hopeful, but happy I am not," she said. "My son is gone forever. [The indictment] makes me feel that there's still hope for justice in this land." The president-elect of ACJ said, "We feel this is sort of the first step in possibly seeing justice. It's sort of a culmination of eight months of hard work trying to convince the Department of Justice and the American people that not only was a murder committed, but it was a serious violation of Vincent Chin's civil rights" (*Detroit Free Press*, November 3, 1983).

In an editorial called "Convening Grand Jury Good," *East/West* (1983) praised the efforts of the ACJ for the major role it played in rallying support for the cause. "Under the leadership of the Detroit-based coalition, many people in the Asian American and non-Asian community alike have rallied to support the nationwide efforts to secure justice for the slain man." A special thanks went to the people "who sent letters to the Justice Department and to their Washington, state and local lawmakers to support the efforts of ACJ. E/W is proud to have been a part of the news network which helped to spread the news about the beating and resulting sentences."

To Edward Khoury, Nitz's lawyer in the state court, the federal indictment was a "surprise and a bit of a shock because it doesn't comport with our finding of facts. There were no racial overtones here." Ebens's wife told reporters that the indictments were all "politics and you know it." Helen Zia, the president of ACJ, did not deny that politics played a role in the indictments. "Clearly politics had something to do [with the indictments]. If we have not gone on a nationwide campaign—writing letters even to President Reagan—this case would not have gone anywhere," she said. The assistant director of public affairs for the Justice

Department, however, denied that politics had any influence on the indictments. "I've been in this department for 15 years and I hear charges of politics in everything we do through every administration," he said. "That is simply incorrect. We filed those charges because a grand jury found evidence of deprivation of rights" (*Detroit Free Press*, November 3, 1983).

Judge Kaufman agreed that political pressure from Asian Americans and not his sentences of probation prompted the federal civil rights investigation of the beating death of Vincent Chin. "But whatever the grand jury did was not political," he said. "I'm sure what they did was based on evidence presented to them." He stood firm that his sentences of the two convicted killers were legally proper and fair, stating that the federal indictment of the two men was a civil rights issue that "was never before me." In a remark that seemed rather insensitive to the feelings of the Asian Americans whose efforts had led to the Justice Department's investigation and the eventual grand jury indictments, Kaufman said, "the Asian community owes me some gratitude, for bringing their community together under one cause" (*Detroit Free Press*, November 4, 1983).

The two men responsible for the death of Vincent Chin pleaded not guilty to charges of violating Vincent Chin's civil rights by beating him to death with a baseball bat in 1982 because he was Asian American. Because of the tension around the case the arraignment was held three hours before the scheduled time for security reasons. The FBI confirmed reports that threats were made against the lives of the two men, Judge Kaufman, and a police officer. The threat came as a letter from Chicago that was signed in the name of a Chinese street gang. The FBI, however, would only confirm that "an organization claiming to have written the letter has ties to Chicago" (*Detroit Free Press*, November 19, 1983).

In May 1984, the new lawyers for Ebens and Nitz failed in their attempt to have the jury sequestered in the upcoming trial. The lawyers told U.S. District Judge Anna Diggs Taylor that the publicity had hurt their clients' chances of getting a fair trial. The government lawyers countered that sequestering would be an unnecessary burden on the government and jurors, calling it "a procedure of last resort." The judge rejected the motion, saying that she would only sequester the jury during its deliberation at the end of the trial instead of during the trial. In explaining her decision, she said, "this could result in jurors becoming hostile toward the defendants and the whole process. It's a cruelty we couldn't impose" (*Detroit Free Press*, May 10, 1984).

The trial began on Tuesday, June 5. On one side of the court room sat four Detroit lawyers assigned to Ebens and Nitz. They argued that Chin's murder resulted from a bar brawl and was not racially motivated, and that Chin had provoked the brawl. On the other side, the government lawyers argued that Ebens and Nitz tried to "threaten, intimidate and assault Vincent Chin because of his race and national origin and because he had been enjoying the accommodation of the Fancy Pants lounge, a place of entertainment open to the public." If the defendants were found guilty, they could get a maximum sentence of life imprisonment (*Detroit Free Press*, June 3, 1984).

Because of the tremendous publicity of the case the judge and the lawyers questioned the potential jurors concerning their views ranging from Japanese imports to nude dancing. The judge questioned each juror individually to determine if he or she had hidden prejudices that would hinder arriving at a fair verdict (*Detroit Free Press*, June 6, 1984). Three weeks later, a federal jury composed of seven women and five men deliberated for over twelve hours before reaching a verdict. They said that Evens, who held the bat in the fatal beating of Vincent Chin, was guilty of violating his rights, and that he did so because of Chin's ancestry. Nitz faced the same charges, but was acquitted on both counts. On hearing the verdict, Ebens showed no emotion, while Nitz "buried his head in his hands." They later hugged after the jury left the courtroom. Obviously pleased with the verdict, Helen Zia of the ACJ said, "We think we got a fair trial, and I think we got a fair hearing on the facts. Yes, I think justice was done" (*Detroit Free Press*, June 29, 1984).

However pleased Zia was with the verdict, Mrs. Lily Chin was not. She cried when she heard that Nitz was acquitted. He was in fact the one who held Vincent Chin while Ebens beat him to death. Speaking at a press conference, she expressed her deep sorrow and anger over the verdict. "How come the son is not guilty? Both killed him. How come he's not guilty? I don't understand that. One is not guilty. If both were guilty I would feel better. One is not fair . . . two killed my son. It's not fair that one is guilty" (*Detroit Free Press*, June 29, 1984).

On September 18, 1984, U.S. District Judge Anna Diggs Taylor sentenced Ronald Ebens to twenty-five years in prison. He was allowed to remain free for thirty days on personal bond while he attempted to raise $20,000 cash or a bond to appeal his conviction. Ebens told the judge that he wanted "'to reiterate one more time' his regret and remorse. 'I'm sorry for what happened.'" During the trial Ebens testified that he had been drinking the night he killed Chin. "Too much to drink, too dumb to think," he told the jury. As to the harsh sentence of twenty-five years, Ebens told reporters that he had expected it.

One of the defense attorneys said, "I'm shocked. Anytime two judges can look at the same set of facts and one comes up with probation and the other come up with 25 years, our courts are in trouble." But the U.S. Attorney Leonard Gilman disagreed. "This is an eminently fair sentence for the circumstances of a brutal killing," he said. "I wish I could be optimistic and say that this would have some deterrent effect on such future behavior. It's a sad commentary, but I don't think it will." The executive director of the ACJ was satisfied with the sentence. "On its face, it seems to me we feel as though he will be punished for the death of Vincent Chin . . . 25 years seems like a fair sentence for the brutal murder of a man" (*Detroit Free Press*, September 19, 1984).

In a summary of the trial, a writer for *Justice Update*, a publication of ACJ, covered most of the major points of the trial for its readers, but alerted them to the fact that "of course, the legal proceedings in this case are far from over, with motions to appeal the federal case already filed, and our state appeal of the manslaughter sentence still pending." The writer reported that "many people are dismayed that in spite of the verdict and sentence, Ebens remains free after posting 10% of his bond; and Nitz was acquitted on both charges." Yet, the writer added, "ACJ will continue in its pledge to see this case to the end. In the meanwhile, we seek to use the experience that we have collectively gained to help others and to try to prevent such injustice from happening again. We hope that those of you who have supported this case so willingly and selflessly will agree that this is a worthwhile legacy to leave for the next generation" (American Citizens for Justice, 1984).

FURTHER ACTIONS OF ACJ

By the time the verdict against Ebens was announced, ACJ—which was largely responsible for building a nationwide movement to pressure the Justice Department to act—had grown into an organization with "4,000 members and 30 chapters and [was] the largest civil rights organization for Chinese Americans in the nation" (*Detroit Free Press*, September 19, 1984). In the "President's Message: ACJ: The Critical Next Step," Zia addressed those people who had "done what everyone said was impossible. Not only did we seek justice in the Chin case, but we brought together people of all nationalities and races in [a] nationwide effort that became an international issue." But, she told her readers, "now that the federal civil rights trial has finally ended, pending an appeal that is at least a couple of years away, it is time for all of us in and affiliated with ACJ to take a hard look at what is yet to be done, and what we are willing to do" (American Citizens for Justice, 1984).

At this juncture of their struggle, ACJ members, affiliates, and supporters were faced with some critical choices concerning their future direction. Would they just congratulate themselves and return to their former lives, rest on their laurels, allow the bank balance to increase interest, make "token appearances at events," or "keep on paving the road we set out upon to protect the civil rights of Asian Americans, though at a slower pace"? As Zia explained, the choice of what to do was clear: "If we don't continue to protect and advance the small gains we made with this case, we will slowly sink back to the level of ignorance that existed before the Chin case. Then the far-reaching impact of our work would have been in vain" (American Citizens for Justice, 1984).

Zia's advice could not have come at a more urgent time during the rise of anti-Asian racism in both Detroit and the nation. In November 1984, the Chin slaying was still a strong memory in many peoples' minds when a twenty-seven-year-old white Wayne State University law student won a Halloween pumpkin carving contest with a pumpkin "carved with Oriental facial features and with a baseball bat bashed through it" (*Detroit Free Press*, November 16, 1984). The contest took place at the law school's Board of Governors' Halloween party, and sadly enough, the student won based on the "applause and cheers of 30 to 40 students at the party." The student said that his carving was a commentary on the "entire Vincent Chin situation" and was not intended maliciously. He later apologized and admitted that the carving was in poor taste. "I did something in poor taste and I'm sorry. If I had any idea that I would offend people, or if I thought it would bring the school into disrepute I would have never done it . . . I may have terrible taste, but I am not a racist" (*Detroit Free Press*, November 16, 1984).

James Shimoura, a member of ACJ, was not so sure. He felt the carving was not only in extremely poor taste but "totally insensitive to the racial motivations underlying the killing of a human being." "I find it extremely outrageous, " he said, "to reduce the victim of a killing to a joke and treat it as a lighthearted and comical matter . . . you can never ridicule death, and you can't make a mockery of human life so tragically lost." The dean of the law school also agreed that the incident was "tasteless" and that he did not endorse "such black humor about such a tragic incident." The dean spoke to the student about the matter but did not pursue it (*Detroit Free Press*, November 16, 1984).

Auto World Controversy

In November 1984 the ACJ's Anti-Asian Sentiment Task Force released a photo of a poster at the "Life, Courtesy of the Automobile" exhibit at the Six Flags Auto World Theme Park in Flint, Michigan. The photo contained a buck-tooth, slanted-eyed automobile dropping bombs on an aircraft carrier with Detroit written on its flight deck against a background of a Japanese flag. Three weeks after the ACJ protested the exhibit at the "federally-assisted" theme park, the anti-Asian poster was removed. The ACJ wanted to send a clear message to the sponsors. "Though we stressed ACJ's support of Auto World's entry into Michigan's tourist industry, and that we did not seek to embarrass anyone, we stated strongly in letters and phone calls that this poster should be removed since it promoted the kind of antagonism that led to the killing of Vincent Chin" (American Citizens for Justice, 1984).

Auto World's Public Relations Department had to be pressured before it removed the offending poster. The ACJ task force contacted a network of groups and individuals who supported civil rights and Asian Americans. U.S. Congressman Robert Matsui was among the political leaders who contributed to the effort. He "sent blistering letters to Auto World and HUD, which provided Auto World with a UDAG grant" (American Citizens for Justice, 1984). Governor Blanchard also wrote a letter to Zia, criticizing the poster in the display.

> I appreciate being informed of your concern about the racial connotations in displays at Auto World in Flint. This is the first I have heard about the display you mentioned. There are of course, legal, financial and ethical considerations in any display available to the general public. I would not want to comment on those legal implications without further review. However, I want you to know right now, and unequivocally, that I adamantly oppose "humor" that depends on racial, ethnic, sexual, or regional slurs. (American Citizens for Justice, 1984)

In an obvious reference to the Auto World public relations coordinator, the governor said, "A response which justifies one such slur by pointing out that others are being slurred as well is incomprehensible to me." He added, "I had hoped that reliance on demeaning stereotypes was a form of bigotry that had become extinct in this age of raised consciousness. Perhaps my optimism is premature." In conclusion, he assured ACJ's president that he would have the matter checked out carefully. "If there is anything that I can do to eliminate such vestiges of prejudice, be assured that I will do so. Thank you again for your letter and for raising your concerns. I am pleased that American Citizens for Justice are so vigilant in informing me of problems to eliminate prejudice and discrimination" (American Citizens for Justice, 1984).

One of Senator Don Riegle's staff members also contacted Auto World. Former UAW president Doug Fraser helped focus on the issue by referring the matter to the union's civil rights division. Religious groups weighed in as well, including the representative of the Greater Detroit Roundtable of Christians and Jews, who informed the Flint Human Rights Commission of the racist poster on display (American Citizens for Justice, 1984). In the end, ACJ could count the removal of the poster as a significant milestone in its struggle to build an effective civil rights organization.

Detroit TV Show **Charlie Rum**

The Task Force on Anti-Asian Sentiment also took on another racial stereotype in a television show broadcast on Detroit's Channel 20 entitled *Charlie Rum*, about a stereotypical Chinese character played by a white actor named Jim Harper. According to the task force, "Jim Harper . . . a blonde, blue-eyed white male . . . appears on Channel 20's Martial Arts Theatre with his hair colored black, his eyelids painted to make them appear slanted, and a long Fu Man Chu mustache dangling from his face." Furthermore, the task force reported, the white actor "hunches over, squints his eyes, and delivers his introductions in Pidgin English, mispronouncing . . . every other sentence, and talking through buck teeth like a fortune cookie version of Charlie Chan. He could not have picked more stereotypes if he tried; and he apparently has" (American Citizens for Justice, 1984).

As with Auto World, Harper and Channel 20 did not see such stereotyping as racist. Harper at the time was a Detroit radio disc jockey who claimed the character of Charlie Rum helped his career, never mind that in the process it demeaned Asian Americans. The management agreed to meet with ACJ, but ACJ was already preparing a write-in and telephone campaign directed at the advertisers of Channel 20. ACJ notified its membership and supporters that if they saw the Channel 20 program, to "call up any companies advertising on the show and tell them that their ad on the program offends you. Also write letters to the General Manager of Channel 20." In addition, if they "are interested in stopping the program," ACJ asked them to send them to the next ACJ General Meeting (American Citizens for Justice, 1984).

EBENS'S CONVICTION OVERTURNED

In September 1986, as the ACJ was preparing for the next stage of the Vincent Chin case as it made its way through the appeal process, and engaging in building a civil rights movement to protect the rights of Asian Americans, a three-judge panel of the U.S. Sixth Circuit Court of Appeals in Cincinnati issued an unanimous opinion overturning the conviction of Ronald Ebens. The judges said that Judge Diggs Taylor "erred by refusing to allow Ebens' lawyers to introduce taped interviews of key prosecution witnesses." Ebens's lawyers claimed the witnesses were "improperly coached by a pro-Chin lawyer." Judge Diggs Taylor also erred, the panel wrote in its thirty-seven-page opinion, "in permitting federal prosecutors to introduce testimony by Willie Davis, a black man, who said that a white man he tentatively identified as Ebens had cursed him with a racial slur in a 1974 incident." Ebens's lawyer was relieved by the decision, saying that he was convicted "because the trial wasn't fair" (*Detroit Free Press*, September 12, 1986). This was yet another blow to Lily Chin, who was obviously very upset by the judges' decision. To her this was yet another example of how the American justice system had failed to bring her son's killers to justice. James Shimoura, now president of ACJ, could not contain his anger and disappointment. "What is very outrageous is that Ronald Ebens has already pleaded guilty to manslaughter charges over three years ago and he has yet to spend a day in jail" (*Detroit Free Press*, September 12, 1986).

For four years the ACJ and their followers and most of the public had described Ronald Ebens's killing of Vincent Chin as a horrendous example of a racist crime. They had succeeded in pressuring the Department of Justice's Civil Rights section in pursuing the case and won a federal grand jury indictment of Ebens, and eventually saw him sentenced to twenty-five years in jail for violating Chin's civil rights. Throughout the long campaign, in countless rallies, news accounts, and several trials, Ebens was the symbol of racial hatred. Several days after his conviction was overturned, Ebens said that he was not a racist, and that he was sorry for the crime and "pays for it 'every day of his life.'" Speaking at a news conference Ebens admitted his killing of Chin had been a "grievous wrong." But he stood firm that racism was not the reason for his actions and that his case should not have been tried in federal court. "I've never been a racist. I've never had anything against anyone in this whole world. And with God as a witness, that's the truth" (*Detroit Free Press*, September 17, 1986).

Meanwhile, Ebens's lawyer was calling for a U.S. Justice Department investigation of the ACJ for "improperly influencing witnesses" based upon the Court of Appeals' decision, detailing "efforts to orchestrate the testimony" of several of Chin's friends by Liza Chan, a lawyer and one of the founders of ACJ. "If the Justice Department has any integrity, as the Court of Appeals had integrity, they will abandon [Ebens's prosecution] because the case has been tainted by witnesses who were influenced," the lawyer said. James Shimoura, ACJ's president at the time, disagreed, calling the charges of witness coaching "absolutely ridiculous," adding that Ebens should be retried on civil rights charges (*Detroit Free Press*, September 17, 1986).

On September 19, 1986, barely a week after the court overturned the conviction of Ebens, the U.S. Justice Department announced that he would be retried on the same charges. Ebens had remained free on a $20,000 bond since his conviction over two years earlier. On the same day as the Justice Department's announcement, Lily Chin cried at a new conference as she asked for a new trial. "Please tell the government," she pleaded, "Do not drop this case" (*Detroit Free Press*, September 20, 1986).

In February 1987, U.S. District Judge Anna Diggs Taylor moved the trial to Cincinnati, Ohio, because, as she explained, Ebens "cannot obtain a fair and impartial trial" in the Detroit metropolitan area because of the "saturation of publicity which has surrounded this case for five years and continues." Before the first trial, Ebens's lawyer had asked the judge for a change of venue, but she had refused. According to the lawyer, the public figures in Detroit who were calling for a new trial for his client were "essentially a lynch mob . . . maybe now he'll have a chance for a fair trial." The change of venue did not come as a complete surprise to the ACJ president, who commented that it "was not totally unanticipated" (*Detroit Free Press*, February 24, 1987).

The defense lawyers for Ronald Ebens opened their case by calling several witnesses, including Ebens's stepson, Michael Nitz. Nitz said he never heard Ebens aim any racial slurs at Chin. He did concede, however, that because he was drinking his memory was vague. One of Chin's three friends who was with him at the bar testified that he remembered the fight between Ebens and Chin, but he did not remember any racial slurs. Chin's two other friends testified that Ebens started the fight when he yelled "chink" and "nip" at Chin. The dancer at the bar testified that she heard Ebens direct the following remarks at Chin: "It's because of you little mother**** that we're out of work" (*Detroit Free Press*, April 29, 1987).

During the trial, two witnesses who said they heard Ebens hurl racial slurs at Vincent Chin the night before he was killed denied that they were coached by Liza Chan. Unfortunately, on one tape, Chan was heard urging three of Vincent Chin's friends who were with him at the club to "all remember our lines, OK?" (*Detroit Free Press*, April 24, 1987). This would prove to be devastating evidence for the defense. The assistant U.S. attorney's opening remarks accused Ebens of beating Chin to death with a baseball bat "because he was a Chinese-American and enjoying entertainment in a public bar." The government would prove, he said, that Ebens had racial motives and that his remarks were made to intimidate and embarrass Chin. Ebens's lawyer said "that he will show that the killing was not racially motivated and that statements about race in this case have been made up" (*Detroit Free Press*, April 23, 1987).

In their closing arguments Ebens's defense attorneys once again told the federal court jurors that their client was not a racist. One of the attorneys took pains to convince the jurors that this was not a civil rights issue. "This is not a lunch counter in Atlanta. This is not a bus in Montgomery. This is a girlie club in Highland Park. There is not evidence that this homicide is racial," he said. The assistant U.S. attorney, however, countered that Ebens's baseball-bat beating of Chin "was racially motivated." He told the jurors that "because he was Chinese, Mr. Ebens thought Vincent Chin was less than a person. . . . He (Ebens) was so outraged that this Chinese person, this Asian had the gall and audacity to confront him for making these remarks—that this person, who was less than a human being and not supposed to respond to him—that he grabbed a chair and attempted to do serious bodily harm to Vincent Chin" (*Detroit Free Press*, May 1, 1987). On May 1, 1987, close to three years after he was sentenced to twenty-five years in prison—but never spent a day in jail—a federal court jury composed of ten whites and two blacks decided that Ronald Ebens was not guilty of violating Vincent Chin's civil rights because of his race when he beat him to death with a baseball bat in 1982 (*Detroit Free Press*, May 3, 1987).

The not-guilty verdict shook the Asian American community to its core. James Shimoura of the ACJ expressed the outrage of many Asian Americans when he said, "I think every American of Asian descent has probably shed a tear today. This was a racial murder. There's still an ongoing problem with racism against Asians, even though the jury refused to accept that" (*Detroit Free Press*, May 2, 1987). Shimoura feared that "with another recession, history could repeat itself very easily." If that should happen, "we will see the Japanese car-bashing, the anti-Asian bumper stickers, and the vitriolic rhetoric that reinforce latent racism." Ron Wakabayashi, director of the Japanese Citizens' League in San Francisco, said, "The decision will only encourage the most backward element in this country. It suggests a relaxing of law enforcement for this kind of racial violence." His concerns were echoed by James Tso, president of the Washington-based Organization of Chinese-Americans, who added that the case reflected what many Asian Americans saw as an increasing problem of racism and violence targeting them because of the country's trade deficit. "People view Asian-Americans as foreigners and not Americans" (*New York Times*, May 6, 1987).

The day after the acquittal of Ebens, the ACJ issued the following statement:

Today marks one of the darkest days in the history of Asian-Americans. The racist killer of Vincent Chin, Robert Ebens, who brutally beat him to death with a baseball bat on June 19, 1982 will NEVER SPEND A SINGLE DAY IN JAIL! For all Asian Americans and anyone who believes in justice and equal treatment under the law, there is great sadness and moral outrage. Make no mistake . . . Ronald Ebens killed Vincent Chin! Although a jury in Cincinnati, Ohio acquitted him of federal charges, this fact will never change. He pled guilty to manslaughter and admitted to the brutal killing.

Despite the countless contributions Americans of Asian ancestry have made to our society, our judicial system still treat us as second class citizens. The acquittal should NOT be considered as a signal that racism, discrimination, and bigotry have ended against Asian Americans. To the contrary, it gives our community a clear indication that we have only begun the fight for justice! The ACJ and the Asian American community are committed to the cause of seeking the affirmation of our rights as American citizens.

Despite the loss of the civil rights prosecution, we view yesterday's setback as only temporary. Asian Americans have lived in this country for over 125 years. The Vincent Chin case only proves there are many challenges we face in order to reach our goal to be fully entitled members of society. The Vincent Chin case has been the focus of a nationwide consciousness raising by all Asian Americans and concerned citizens. The ensuing dialogue and recognition of the problem of the dramatic increase in anti-Asian attitudes and violence through the Vincent Chin case has made our 4-year fight for justice worth all the struggle our group and community has endured. We are only at the early stages of our agenda to become first class citizens. People of conscience in the Detroit area, the state of Michigan, the United States, and internationally, have recognized the significance of the Vincent Chin case and rallied behind the cause.

For the many groups and individuals who have supported Mrs. Lily Chin's struggle, you have our eternal gratitude. Mrs. Chin has asked us to extend her personal thanks to her supporters for these past 5 years.

We must never forget the circumstances which gave rise to the brutal killing of Vincent Chin. Throughout history, whenever society has had economic, social, or political difficulties, the typical reaction has been to target a group of people to blame for that problem. Time and time again, Americans of Asian ancestry have been the scapegoat for the ills of society. THIS MUST NEVER HAPPEN AGAIN!

The Vincent Chin case is NOT an end; it is just the beginning of the Asian American community's effort to take our position as fully recognized members of society. There IS NO WAY we can bring Vincent Chin back to life. He has made the ultimate sacrifice in order to uphold human dignity. However, the inspiration the seeking of justice has given the Asian American community hope for the future . . . For that, the fight for JUSTICE FOR VINCENT CHIN will never end. (American Citizens for Justice, 1987)

Non-Asians were also appalled at the verdict as expressed in letters to the *Detroit Free Press*. "I am a 73 year old white woman, and in my 73 years I have never heard of such an injustice. It doesn't matter if Chin's rights were violated, he was killed. If you steal and get caught you go to jail; how can this happen?" Another wrote, "We, the American people, deserve all the crime, drugs, and violence in the schools and in the streets to which we are being subjected. We have made a mockery of justice and the law." She asked, "How can kids learn to respect the law and expect justice when they see such a prostitution of justice as the Chin case? Ronald Ebens was on trial for depriving Vincent Chin of his civil rights. Doesn't depriving him of his life count? What good are civil rights when you're dead?" One writer, however, was not inclined to show sympathy for either Vincent Chin or his mother's five-year struggle to obtain justice for her slain son. "One fact has emerged in these last five years; Lily Chin will not be satisfied with the judicial system until it hands her own baseball bat" (*Detroit Free Press*, May 6, 1987).

LILY CHIN "GIVES UP ON AMERICA"

Lily Chin did not want a bat, however. For five years she had only desired simple justice for her slain son. In a September 9, 1987, article in the *Detroit Free Press* entitled "DEATH OF A DREAM: Vincent Chin's Mother Gives Up on America," Lily Chin shared her deep disappointment. "I want to say, very, very sorry to my son. If it wasn't for me bringing him to America, he wouldn't die so young. China is poor. But at least he would eat, and he would not die so early," she said. After forty years in the United States and becoming a naturalized citizen in 1955, Mrs. Chin began making plans to return to China. "I have many friends here. I don't believe I leave this country after 40 years. I don't like to leave this country But now, I live here, I remember too much—just hurts my heart" (*Detroit Free Press*, September 9, 1987).

As terrible as the murder of her son had been, Mrs. Chin might not have given up on America if justice had been served. As she said, "If they were sitting in prison today, I wouldn't leave this country. But they're not in prison. This country just hurts my heart." The long struggle and the final disappointing outcome not only destroyed her faith in American justice but also sorely tested her faith in God. "Before I believe in God, but now, I don't believe. I think even God in heaven won't help me. I am one good person; I've never done anything bad. I ask God, 'How make me like this?'" (*Detroit Free Press*, September 9, 1987).

Before leaving for China in 1987, Mrs. Chin was awarded a $1.5 million settlement in a civil case in Cincinnati in which Ebens agreed to "pay the Chin estate $200 a month for the next two years, and $200 a month or 25 percent of his net income, whichever is more, after that." Ebens remarked that he would have to live to be 672 in order to pay off the entire debt. Understandably, the money meant little to Mrs. Chin. "If you give me $100 million, just talk, only paper. The money won't make me happy," she said. She viewed the settlement as her final effort to exact some payment from Ebens for killing her son. In her mind and heart, the monthly payments would be monthly reminders to Ebens that he took a life. While the settlement could be seen as a small but symbolic victory, being present at the settlement increased Mrs. Chin's grief as she watched Ebens's family congratulate him. That sight filled her with envy and jealousy. "He had family, I have nothing," she lamented. After the settlement, Ebens's lawyer told Mrs. Chin that his client wanted to apologize to her. She declined the offer. "Just feeling sorry is not enough . . . no use. I would not face him," she said (*Detroit Free Press*, September 9, 1987). Moreover, according to a June 2002 public statement by Helen Zia, former president of ACJ, Ebens "successfully evaded making payment despite efforts of community groups to enforce the judgment" (Zia, 2002b).

Before returning to China, Mrs. Lily Chin shared more of her sorrow with a reporter. "I have nothing to call home. I leave here, looking forward to going to China, so hopefully maybe feel better . . . not so much pain, I hope. But I think I never forget Vincent. I always have his picture in my mind," she lamented. "Sometime I hear noises, I look to the window, I hope Vincent come back. Sometime sit home alone, forget he's dead, sometimes wonder where he is, why he not home. Then I hit my head. No he never come back, he never come back" (*Detroit Free Press*, September 9, 1987).

VINCENT CHIN'S IMPACT ON ASIAN AMERICAN STUDIES

The Asian American community was determined that Vincent Chin's death would not be in vain. Over the years Asian American scholars, graduate students, and activists retold the story of Chin's murder, the failure of the American system of justice, and the emergence of a national Asian American civil rights movement. For example, in 1988, Karen Inouye wrote a M.A. thesis in speech communication at California State University, Northridge, entitled "A Thematic Analysis of Asian American Discourse in Response to the Murder of Vincent Chin." Inspired by the Vincent Chin case, Inouye wrote that the purpose of her study was "to examine Asian American patterns of discourse that attempt to address anti-Asian sentiment. The murder of Vincent Chin is the specific incident serving as the focus of this study, inasmuch as it represents a prime example of racially motivated activities against Asian Americans." Among the major themes she listed was that "anti-Asian sentiment is used as a means of diverting attention from the real cause of our country's economic problems" (Inouye, 1988).

The year 1988 was also the year when the film *Who Killed Vincent Chin* was first released. According to Bill Nichols, "*Who Killed Vincent Chin?* is the most important political documentary of the 1980s" (Nichols, 2002: 160). This film educated an entire generation about the murder, and kept the fires burning around the issues of anti-Asian racism.

Irwin Ai-Bong Tang, in his 1995 M.A. thesis, not only placed the tragic events of the Chin case in historical perspective, but also highlighted the role it played in the politicalization of the national Asian American community. "Before Vincent Chin was murdered in 1982, there was a long and consistent history of racist violence against Asian Americans . . . dating back to the first years of substantial Chinese migration in the mid-1800s. Since the murder of Vincent Chin in 1982, this consistent violence against Asian Americans has continued," Tang argued.

The continued violence against Asian Americans would never be the same after the death of Vincent Chin, however.

What makes the Vincent Chin case a watershed in the history of anti-Asian violence is the consistent and intense political organizing efforts around the issue of anti-Asian violence that have occurred in the United States since that well-publicized murder. In this way, the murder of Vincent Chin was more than a spark for Asian American activism; it was an explosion. Not only did it launch national Asian American organizing efforts on the issue of racist violence, it marked a lift-off of national Asian American organizing in general and around a variety of issues. (Tang, 1995)

To those who were still shocked, hurt, and disappointed with the verdict, Tang and others could see a tiny but growing light at the end of the dark tunnel of Chin's tragic death: "The murder of Vincent Chin nevertheless galvanized the national Asian American community perhaps for the first time this century. The Vincent Chin issue left a trail of Asian American organizations in its wake and a national sense of Asian American pan-ethnicity" (Tang, 1995). In addition, and of great historical significance, "the way that the Chin case was handled also became both a model and a lesson for future organizing around cases of anti-Asian violence and hate crime. Organizers and scholars learned from the case what should be done, what should not be done, and what should have but was not done" (Tang, 1995).

In 2001, Mrs. Lily Chin returned from China to Michigan for medical treatment. After a long illness, she died on June 9, 2002, at the age of eighty-two, at the Farmington Hills Health Center (Zia, 2002a), almost exactly twenty years after her son's death. In her eulogy for Mrs. Chin, Helen Zia described her as "the Rosa Parks of Asian Americans" because "she stood up and refused to accept what was handed to her. Her courage rang through her grief, touching all who could hear. For me and hundreds and thousands of others, it was a call heard far and wide, uniting Asian Americans and people of conscious across the country."

[Mrs. Chin's] dignity, strength and bravery stood in sharp contrast to those who said that nothing could be done, that we had to accept another "Chinaman's chance." Mrs. Chin stood up to show millions of Americans that something could indeed be done. I'm sure Mrs. Chin never imagined that she would become the symbol of moral courage to a civil rights movement that would reach around the world. (Zia, 2002a)

Remembering Vincent Chin on the Twentieth Anniversary of His Death

The "Rededication to Justice: Vincent Chin 20th Year Remembrance" program in Detroit during the weekend of June 21–23, 2002, was a reminder to those who had fought the good fight for so long that Vincent Chin's death would not be in vain. The event was a "Civil Rights Teach-In Program," sponsored by ACJ/Asian American Center for Justice. Mominic Pangborn, the president of ACJ, explained the purpose of the program: "2002 marks the 20th anniversary of the tragic death of Vincent. Milestones—both glorious and tragic—are very important. They bring us together. They create the time and space to reflect upon these seminal events. And, they are an opportunity for us to share our past with the younger generations." He then addressed Asian Americans:

> While Asian Americans have enjoyed tremendous freedom and unparalleled opportunity, the murder of Vincent Chin illustrates that we have also been the victim of being different. However, as we think about this anniversary and what it represents, I urge each of us to look inside, too. As a community of Asian Americans, do we stereotype even those within our group? Are we always open to the ethnic, religious, and social diversity of this country? Do we see the value and strength that each community brings to the fabled American mosaic? (Pangborn, 2002)

He ended his message with a warning. "As we examine our own behavior, we must not forget that we are all vulnerable at times—even in the United States. This anniversary gives us and every other American the opportunity to remember and to grow together" (Pangborn, 2002).

Maryann Mahaffey, president of the Detroit City Council, wrote a letter to Roland Hwang, vice president of ACJ, in which she shared her feelings on the Vincent Chin Twentieth Year Remembrance. "This weekend of commemoration of the Vincent Chin murder and the coming together of the Asian Pacific American Community in our area is of great historical significance to all of us regardless of our background, race or ethnicity," she said. "In our country, we have believed in the concepts of equality, justice and the beauty of diversity. But our actions as a nation have often belied this." Mahaffey then recounted the history of racial bigotry in the United States. "In the past, we have had slavery, Jim Crow, the Asian Exclusion acts, the imprisonment of Japanese Americans in concentration camps in World War II, the recent case of Wen Ho Lee, and the profiling of Arab Americans." Referring back to the Japanese import-bashing and anti-Asian racism that contributed to the slaying of Vincent Chin, Mahaffey wrote:

> Twenty years ago, it was easier to blame the Japanese for making cars popular with American buyers, than to blame our manufacturers for ignoring the market for smaller, more efficient cars. And always, there are those who blame individuals, who "profile" and resort to violence to solve problems. We see it today in the Homeland Security measures, reducing civil liberties and profiling Arab-Americans. . . . So it was magnificent, to observe and in small ways participate as a City Councilmember in the demonstrations of protest 20 years ago. (Mahaffey, 2002)

Mahaffey ended her letter to Hwang praising the unity of the Asian Pacific American communities. "Most important than now is the unity growing within the Asian Pacific American communities as evidenced in ACJ. Long live diversity and the commitment to justice and equality in our nation. May ACJ continue on its mission with all of us supporting it (Mahaffey, 2002).

Helen Zia could not attend the commemoration because of family commitments, but sent a moving statement for the event that had the virtue of both historical perspective and personal reflection. "I can hardly believe that 20 years have passed since that warm summer's night when Vincent Chin was fatally attacked during his bachelor party. The Fancy Pants bar and even the McDonald's on Woodward are gone now, but the events of that night have changed our community, and America, forever," she wrote. Zia referred to the anti-Asian racism that had been sweeping the country for years prior to the slaying of Chin. "Every Asian American in Michigan has a vivid memory of knowing that this was far more than 'just another murder'—as many people said back then, dismissing our concerns. For several years, the Midwestern and national mood had been thick with the hatred against Japan, and anyone who by their race or ethnicity served as a reminder of that hatred. Vincent, a Chinese American, was one of those reminders." But, she declared, "Vincent did not die in vain. The injustice that followed his slaying set off shockwaves in Asian American families across America, even across the Pacific" (Zia, 2002b).

And Detroit, with its long history of interracial civil rights struggles against racism, was just the place to take on still another struggle for racial justice. As Zia explained, "Detroit was the epicenter of a new civil rights movement, as Asian Americans of every ethnicity recognized immediately that any one of us could have suffered Vincent's fate. An army of volunteers came together across racial, ethnic and religious lines to draw attention to a hate crime against an Asian American" (Zia, 2002b).

After Chin's slaying, there appeared to be a reluctance to see it as a "civil rights crime." Zia criticized this thinking. "This was a civil right crime that many government officials, political leaders, constitutional law professors, journalists and even the Michigan ACLU and the National Lawyers Guild refused to accept, because they preferred to think of us as the 'model minority' and did not want to extend their understanding of civil rights law beyond their narrow thinking." Fortunately, this thinking did not prevail due to the tireless efforts of the ACJ. As Zia wrote, "the important legacies of the campaign for justice for Vincent Chin was argued by the fledging American Citizens for Justice and this new civil rights movement: That Asian Americans should be protected by federal civil rights law. Their efforts resulted in a broader view of how civil rights are applied, of who is included under hate crimes law" (Zia, 2002b). She reminded her readers:

> Today, a federal hate crimes bill, "Local Law Enforcement Enhancement Act of 2001 (S.625/ H.R.1343)," offers hate crime victims federal protections on the basis of perceived gender, sexual orientation, and disability. This is an important civil rights bill for all Americans—and I believe that the Vincent Chin campaign 20 years ago, led by Asian Americans, played a significant role in the efforts toward inclusion in civil rights law.
>
> This legacy is especially meaningful today, as people who "look Middle Eastern" or "look Muslim" are targets of hate crimes. And yet the legacy of Vincent Chin continues to be challenged. A few years ago at a showing of the play about Vincent Chin by Cherylene, "Carry the Tiger to the Mountain," the sponsors printed a statement by Ronald Ebens' attorney—in which he claimed that Vincent died as a result of hitting his head on the pavement—not from four swings of his client's baseball bat! Such an outrageous and despicable lie. (Zia, 2002b)

In the conclusion of her statement Zia gave yet another reminder that "the underlying question of who is a real American in this post September 11 world should serve as a reminder to all of us that the work begun 20 year ago is not over." Zia then shared a heartfelt testimony of how her life was affected by involvement in the Vincent Chin case. "Like so many who joined the campaign for justice, I did not know Vincent when he was alive, but my life was inexorably changed by what happened to him. His mother, Lily Chin, continue to inspire me with her courage and her love, and I ask that each of you send her your best wishes. I hope that everyone who was touched by Vincent Chin's legacy will join me in rededicating ourselves to the cause of justice, equality, and peace" (Zia, 2002b).

CONCLUSION

The bashing of Japanese-made cars in the early 1980s created a mood of anti-Asian racism in Detroit that contributed to the brutal beating death of Vincent Chin at the hands of two white men, one of whom was an autoworker from East Detroit. Even more tragic was the fact that his killers escape punishment and his mother lost faith in American justice. His death was not in vain, however. It attracted worldwide attention and gave birth to a nationwide Asian American movement for social justice. The Vincent Chin case inspired a generation of Asian American writers, scholars, and activists to dedicate their lives and work to his memory. Detroit's collective memory of how Japan bashing can get out of hand probably prevented the spread of the protectionist vandalism that occurred at the 1992 North America International Auto Show in Detroit when a few individuals "took hammers to Honda cars" (*Economist*, February 1, 1992).

Figure 1. July 23, 1967. Buildings along 12th Street are consumed by fire during the first day of the civil unrest of 1967 in Detroit. Detroit News Collection #26471; Walter P. Reuther Library, Wayne State University.

Figure 2. July 24, 1967. A bird's-eye view as the block at 12th Street and Linwood is reduced to rubble by fires during the second day of the civil unrest of 1967 in Detroit. Detroit News Collection, #26473; Walter P. Reuther Library, Wayne State University.

Figure 3. UNDATED. UNIDENTIFIED VICTIMS OF POLICE BRUTALITY, DETROIT. NATIONAL ASSOCIATION FOR THE ADVANCEMENT OF COLORED PEOPLE (NAACP) COLLECTION #24852; WALTER P. REUTHER LIBRARY, WAYNE STATE UNIVERSITY.

Figure 4. April 28, 1973. Anti-STRESS (Stop the Robberies, Enjoy Safe Streets) rally at Kennedy Square in Detroit. Detroit News Collection #811; Walter P. Reuther Library, Wayne State University.

Figure 5. May 13, 1976. Coleman A. Young, mayor of Detroit, with James Earl "Jimmy" Carter. Detroit News Collection #2957; Walter P. Reuther Library, Wayne State University.

Figure 6. APRIL 27, 2008. KWAME KILPATRICK ADDRESSES AN AUDIENCE OF 10,000 AT THE 53RD ANNUAL NAACP FIGHT FOR FREEDOM DINNER IN DETROIT. DALE RICH COLLECTION #28062; WALTER P. REUTHER LIBRARY, WAYNE STATE UNIVERSITY.

Figure 7. FEBRUARY 1, 1994. DENNIS ARCHER, MAYOR OF DETROIT, AND JESSE JACKSON, CIVIL RIGHTS WORKER. SPECIAL COLLECTIONS, DETROIT PUBLIC LIBRARY.

Figure 8. UNDATED. VINCENT CHIN, MURDER VICTIM. CONVICTED KILLERS GIVEN PROBATION. DETROIT NEWS COLLECTION #13027; WALTER P. REUTHER LIBRARY, WAYNE STATE UNIVERSITY.

Figure 9. UNDATED. COLEMAN YOUNG WITH ARAB AMERICAN WOMEN AT THE 1977 CONVENTION OF AAUG . NUMBER 2003.31.04J ARAB AMERICAN NATIONAL MUSEUM COLLECTION.

Figure 10. MAY 5, 1990. ROSE UVIISTA AND HER DAUGHTER MAYRA ENJOY DETROIT'S CINCO DE MAYO CELEBRATION. DETROIT NEWS COLLECTION #28281; WALTER P. REUTHER LIBRARY, WAYNE STATE UNIVERSITY.

Figure 11. AUGUST 1980. YOUTHS PAINT A MURAL ON A WALL ALONG VERNOR HIGHWAY IN SOUTHWEST DETROIT. THE MURALS REPRESENT CHICANO AND BLACK PRIDE IN DETROIT AND WERE SPONSORED BY THE LATINO OUTREACH COMMUNITY SERVICE CENTER. DETROIT NEWS COLLECTION #28282; WALTER P. REUTHER LIBRARY, WAYNE STATE UNIVERSITY.

CHAPTER 8

African American and Middle Eastern American Relations after 1967

WHILE THE RACIAL DIVIDE BETWEEN INNER-CITY BLACKS AND SUBURBAN WHITES HAS been widening since the 1967 riot and still remains the worst of the racial divides in the Detroit metropolitan region, other racial divides also have emerged during this period. For example, tensions and conflicts between Middle Eastern merchants and African American customers and between African Americans and Latinos have created new racial divides that complicate and compound the old black/white racial divide (Arellano, 2001; Sengstock, 1999). This chapter will seek to understand how and why racial/cultural tensions and conflicts between Middle Eastern merchants and African American customers have emerged. Our ultimate purpose is to understand what role leaders of both communities played in seeking solutions to the problems.

Few observers of the state of race relations in Detroit during the early period after the 1967 riot could have predicted the gradual shift from predominantly black/white tensions and conflicts to black/Middle Eastern conflicts and tensions. The bipolar black/white paradigm dominated the study of relations throughout the twentieth century, and with good reason. The conflicts between these two groups over housing, jobs, neighborhoods and education largely influenced how generations of scholars, policymakers, and the general public thought about race in Detroit (Capeci and Wilkerson, 1991; Darden et al., 1987b; Lee and Humphrey, 1943; Locke, 1969; Shogan and Craig, 1964; Stolberg, 1998; Sugrue, 1996).

The waves of southern blacks moving into Detroit during and between two world wars, their protracted struggles for decent housing and jobs, and their expanding community, met with relentless forces of white racial control, which was the foundation of their racialized identity. Blacks challenged and fought against this white racial control and, in the process, forged their own racialized identity (Sugrue, 1996; Thomas, 1992). In the shadow of the ongoing battles between these two major racial combatants, smaller but no less significant racial and ethnic groups, such as Latinos and Middle Easterners, tended to be overlooked. This situation would change, however.

THE SOCIAL AND HISTORICAL ROOTS OF THE BLACK/MIDDLE EASTERN RACIAL DIVIDE

In the 1960s and 1970s a convergence of global and domestic social and economic forces forever changed race relations in metropolitan Detroit. During these years blacks in Detroit overtook whites as the dominant racial group in the city, gaining political power, and engaging in struggles over school segregation, fair housing, police brutality, white suburban hostility, and drug-related youth crime and violence in economically depressed black neighborhoods (Darden et al., 1987; Lewis, 1969; Rich, 1989; Taylor, 1990; Tyson, 1980).

These struggles, especially in the wake of the 1967 race riot, intensified the racial identity of an entire generation of blacks. Radical black organizations such as the League of Revolutionary Black Workers and the Republic of New Africa and the black literary productions of Dudley Randall's Broadside Press were among those that contributed to this heady black power movement dedicated to black self-determination (Georgakas and Surkin, 1998; Thompson, 2005).

Meanwhile, changes in the U.S. immigration laws in 1965 resulted "in a considerable increase in migration into the Chaldean community," which was part of a large wave of immigrants that dramatically increased the Middle Eastern population in metropolitan Detroit, from 70,000 in 1974 to 92,000 in 2004 (Sengstock, 1999; U.S. Bureau of the Census, 2004). The 1965 immigration law that allowed more Asians and Middle Eastern immigrants to enter the United States was followed by the Refugee Act of 1980 and other legislation in 1986 and 1990 (Immigration and Nationality Act of 1965; Refuge Act of 1980; Immigration Reform and Control Act of 1986; Immigration Act of 1990; Liebowitz, 1983).

As these developments unfolded, the stage was slowly being set for a realignment of historical racial tensions and conflicts in the post-1967 era.

Prior to the increased outbreak of tensions and conflicts between blacks and Chaldean merchants in poor black neighborhoods, little contact or understanding existed between the two groups. Few blacks or whites, for that matter, knew much about the history of Chaldeans in the United States.

Chaldean immigrants come from what is now the modern nation of Iraq. The Chaldean community in Detroit dates back to 1910. The 2000 U.S. Census estimated that 31,322 foreign-born Iraqis resided in metropolitan Detroit. The majority of Chaldeans live in the Detroit metropolitan area and originate in Telkaif, "a Northern Iraqi village near the ruins of the ancient city of Nineveh . . . the home of the ancient Assyrians and Babylonians, whom the modern day Chaldeans claim as their ancestors" (Sengstock, 1983: 137). After World War II most Chaldean immigrants were those who had been born or had lived part of their lives in Baghdad or other Iraqi cities (Sengstock, 1983).

In 2008, there were 8,649 Arabs actually living in the city of Detroit, constituting only 1 percent of the city's total population (U.S. Bureau of the Census, 2009a). Chaldeans are often identified as belonging to the Arab community. Many Chaldean do not accept this identity, however. According to one scholar:

> The Chaldeans exhibit two major differences from the Arabs and their culture. The differences have to do with the Chaldeans' ancestral language and their religion. . . . There are the village and regional differences which existed in Iraq, the perception shared by many Chaldeans that they have suffered discrimination at the hands of the Arabs . . . With regard to religious differences,

one should not underestimate the importance of the Christian religion in the lives of Chaldeans. Chaldeans in Detroit take extreme pride in their status as Christians, as Catholics, and as members of the Chaldean Rites of the Catholic Church. (Sengstock, 1983: 137)

The rapid growth and size of the Chaldean community in metropolitan Detroit has enabled it to exert its influence on various aspects of life in the area. For example, as pointed out in a 1978 study of Chaldean students in Detroit's suburban high schools:

Even though Chaldeans have been members of the Detroit community for many years, public school personnel, particularly in the suburbs, are just now becoming aware that they must serve a group of students who do not share the same values and beliefs as do the administration, teachers, and counselors, as well as the overwhelming majority of students. The reality of serving a large influx of Chaldeans, combined with the growing acceptance of the philosophy of cultural pluralism, which tends to enhance tolerance for difference in culture, has caused administrators of suburban school districts to express considerable interest in understanding their Chaldean students so that the school can better fulfill their needs. The bilingual programs are evidence of this concern. (Doctoroff, 1978: 23)

This same study points out, however, that in Detroit Chaldean parents sent their children to white, working-class, Latin rites parochial schools: "In as much as the student bodies of the Catholic schools were homogeneous in terms of religion, race, and social class, the Chaldean parents were happy with their children's education" (Doctoroff, 1978: 4). When these schools closed, forcing these students into the public schools, Chaldean parents became fearful that black students would attack their children and started pulling them out of school, particularly the girls, "as soon as it was legally permissible" (Doctoroff, 1978: 18–19). This might well have been one of several areas in which African Americans and Chaldean Americans in Detroit first encountered one another and where each group formed racial generalizations about the other, contributing to the racial divide between the two groups.

Any analysis of the historical, economic, and social origins of the black/Chaldean racial tensions and conflicts in the postriot period would have to include the following factors: the increase in the influx of the Chaldean community in the 1960s and 1980s; the flight of white capital in the form of large supermarket chains that left the inner city in the wake of the 1967 riot, creating the vacuum that attracted Chaldean stores to poor black inner-city neighborhoods; and persistent residential segregation that created and maintained black inner-city ghettos where the majority of Chaldean stores were located (Farley, Danzinger, and Holzer, 2000; Sengstock, 1999).

These combined factors created the historical and social context in which many Chaldean store owners and their black customers collided, causing cultural misunderstandings, tensions, conflicts, and unfortunately in extreme cases, injuries and deaths. At an earlier time and place some of these same social and economic factors created similar problems between blacks and Jews (Kaufman, 1997), and, in other cities at the same time, blacks and Koreans (Umemoto, 1984).

Racial tensions and conflicts between Chaldean store owners and their black customers in poor neighborhoods preceded the 1967 race riot, but grew worse during that disturbance when black rioters burned and looted many Chaldean stores located in black communities

(Fine, 1989; Doctoroff, 1978). The declining economic conditions and social isolation of poor, black, crime-infested neighborhoods where Chaldean stores located after the riot did not bode well for improved relationships between these two groups.

The Chaldean merchants were moving into black neighborhoods of economically marginalized, desperate, alienated, and angry people who had been beaten down by white institutional racism and largely abandoned by the black middle and upper classes. To many poor blacks struggling to survive and maintain some pride in themselves, Chaldeans represented another racial threat. In the 1970s and 1980s, as Detroit was becoming more "black" and the black community was occupying more seats of power, poor blacks could not but notice that most of the stores in their neighborhoods were owned by what seemed to them a strange and culturally alien people. It did not help their sense of racial pride—what little pride they had, given their poor circumstances—that they had to depend on these strange people for their basic food. These strangers not only controlled the food supply of the community, but they also took money out of the black community and seemed uninterested in hiring black people. Black customers at Chaldean stores complained about being charged higher prices, arguing that the store owners cheated them. No doubt some of them did. On the other hand, Chaldean store owners "defend[ed] their position by asserting that shoplifting, pilfering, and holdups cause a need to hire security and pay high insurance premiums" (Doctoroff, 1978: 15–16).

Black customers and Chaldean owners viewed each other through cultural, racial, and class filters. Given the complex historical and social context of their interaction, they could not help but misunderstand each other. Few blacks in these poor neighborhoods understood why Chaldeans tended to hire only their own kind. Through the eyes of their collective history, poor blacks could only see the ever present demon of job discrimination.

Black youth gangs in these economically depressed and socially isolated neighborhoods expressed their own brand of anger and frustration at the ubiquitous presence of Middle Eastern stores in their community. One interviewer was able to get at the heart of the gangs' anti-Arab, anti-Chaldean feelings:

> The a-rabbs own all the stores in our hood. They hire the cuties to work the lotto tickets and won't give no dudes nothing but flunkey jobs. The a-rabbs sell shit way too high . . . and they all be dissing bloods, talking real fucked-up to us bloods. Our crew has to check some of them a-rabbs who think they got big juice 'cause they got guns. Some of them are real down with some rollers. They talk bad to us and then give the police free pops and other shit and tell lies on us after they done dissed us. . . . Ain't no store hiring nobody from my crew. One time a a-rab pulled his gun on me and some of the fellas in his store. We left because they were not bullshitting. They will cap a blood over some potato chips. But later we'll fix them punk-ass a-rabb. How come they come into our hood and start stores acting like all the bloods ain't shit. So if somebody robs or beats on people, maybe they shouldn't go to the a-rabbs' store [laughing]. (Taylor, 1990: 70)

Most Chaldean store owners had very little understanding of the plight of poor blacks in the neighborhoods in which their stores were located: "At a time in which unemployment was high and jobs were difficult to find, there was considerable anger in the black community when Chaldean stores hired primarily Chaldean employees." And most black customers did not understand that the Chaldean employees "were probably members of the storeowner's family and were paid little (or even nothing)" (Sengstock, 1999: 99). Such mutual misunderstanding in the historical and cultural context of the time widened the racial divide not only between Chaldean store owners and their black customers, but their respective larger communities as well.

BLACK/MIDDLE EASTERNER VIOLENCE

Robberies and attempted robberies leading to injuries and deaths of both African Americans and Chaldeans further intensified tensions and conflicts between the African American and Chaldean communities. In 1972, the majority of the 278 Chaldean-owned grocery stores in the Detroit metropolitan area were located in the inner city, and, as one scholar of the Chaldean community argued, the location of these stores posed "dangers for those working in them. Inasmuch as approximately twenty Chaldeans thus far have been killed in hold-ups, some owners are quitting their businesses or reestablishing them in a growing Chaldean community near San Diego, California" (Doctoroff,1978: 15). One Chaldean store owner remarked that during his twenty-four years in Detroit he had been held up eight times and experienced twenty break-ins (Gebert, 1980).

Two incidents in 1980 further strained relations between these two communities. That July, James Douglass, a nineteen-year-old black male, was shot and killed at a party store owned by two Chaldean brothers. Three months later, Nabil Zoma, a Chaldean store owner, was killed in his Hamtramck party store in an aborted attempted robbery by three black males. In response to the murder of Douglass, a black group attempted to organize black boycotts of stores owned by people from the Middle East. The murder of Zoma upset the Chaldean community and retail grocers (Gebert, 1980).

BLACK BOYCOTT OF ARAB AMERICAN GAS STATIONS

In late July 2001, the Michigan Chapter of the Reverend Al Sharpton's National Action Network announced a thirty-day boycott of all Arab American–owned gas stations in metropolitan Detroit. Reverend Horace Sheffield III, president of the organization, explained that the goal of the boycott was to have Detroiters shift from buying from Middle Eastern gas stations to buying from African American gas stations as part of the "B-Gas Campaign." Part of Sheffield's plan was to get African American and Arab/Chaldean American leaders representing the civil rights and business communities to discuss the issues dividing the communities (Angel, 2001). There were some doubts as how effective this boycott would be; most certainly it was not intended to bridge the divide between African American customers and Arab/Chaldean gas station owners.

Shortly after the boycott had been launched Arab/Chaldean American store owners, employees, and leaders denounced it. An Arab American employee at an Amoco station in Detroit called it unfair, saying the employees at the station respected their customers and that the business had even donated money to neighborhood organizations, including Sheffield's church. While Sheffield commended the station for being an example of how Arab/Chaldean American businesses should treat customers, he took the position that all Arab/Chaldean stations had to be boycotted because, as he reasoned, it would force some stations to pressure others to comply (*Detroit Free Press*, August 1, 2001).

Predictably, Arab American leaders accused Sheffield of contributing to the tensions between the communities. Nassar Beydoun, executive director of the American Arab Chapter of the Chamber of Commerce, told the *Detroit News* that Sheffield "is taking a few bad incidents and playing on the anxieties and emotions of people in trying to build a name for himself" (*Detroit Free Press*, August 1, 2001). Arab American leaders were concerned that a black boycott would contribute to increased tensions and conflicts between the communities. While this argument was valid from their perspectives, the Arab leaders failed to take into consideration the African American boycott-protest tradition out of which Sheffield was operating. It was not the best approach to the problem, but it was probably the best that he and his supporters could come up with at the time.

Beydoun's characterization of Sheffield's motive as self-serving did little to contribute to improving the relationship between African American and Arab/Chaldean leaders. The frustration and hopelessness of these leaders in struggling to address tensions and conflicts were obviously moving them to say and do things that were widening the racial divide between the two communities.

The print media was seldom much better in smoothing the relationship between the two communities. Brian Dickerson, a white writer for the *Detroit Free Press*, described the boycott as "a marvel of unabashed bigotry. . . . Other African American leaders cannot afford to indulge Sheffield's mischief a second longer. They may embrace his message of economic empowerment, but they must denounce his boycott against the Arab American entrepreneurs for what it is: old bigotry in new bottles, and a dagger at the throat of new Detroit" (Dickerson, 2001).

Much of the historical, social, and cultural causes of the tensions and conflicts between African Americans and Middle Eastern Americans remain, but fortunately, so have the brave and dedicated souls in both communities working to build bridges across the racial and cultural divides.

EFFORTS TO BRIDGE THE RACIAL DIVIDE BETWEEN AFRICAN AMERICANS AND ARAB/CHALDEAN AMERICANS

Any effort to bridge the racial divide between African Americans and Arab/Chaldean Americans had to consider a host of complex historical, social, economic, and cultural factors. As mentioned earlier, the tensions and conflicts between these two communities extended far beyond the black/white paradigm that had dominated race relations interventions in Detroit for most of the twentieth century, and particularly since the 1943 race riot (Thomas, 1987b). The 1967 riot and a range of black/white tensions and conflicts involving open housing, bussing, white flight, black community/white police relationships, and hostility between white suburbs and black Detroit, among other issues, kept the black/white paradigm at center stage of the race relations intervention discourse. As a result, New Detroit and Focus: HOPE, both born out of the ashes of the 1967 riot, rightly saw their primary mission in terms of black and white. Both organizations, however, would become more diverse in their intervention programs (Focus: HOPE, 1999a; New Detroit, 1992).

Given the constant state of tensions and conflicts between blacks and whites in the Detroit metropolitan area, few leaders noticed the global and demographic changes that were destined to change traditional race relations paradigms and call into question their efficacy in framing and resolving racial problems surfacing in low-income black neighborhoods between Arab/Chaldean merchants and their customers.

Both communities found themselves on a historical, social, and cultural collision course bought on by complex global and domestic changes beyond their comprehension and control. As William Julius Wilson notes, "Changes in the global economy have increased social inequality and created situations that enhance antagonism between racial groups" (Wilson, 1999: 123).

Economically depressed and racially and socially isolated black neighborhoods, battered by crime, drugs, and youth violence, became the major new front for racial tensions and conflicts after the 1967 riot, the era of deindustrialization in Detroit. African American residents of these neighborhoods and Arab/Chaldean merchants were pawns in the larger drama of global, social, and economic changes being played out in hundreds of locations throughout the Detroit area. These were the challenges facing African Americans and Arab/Chaldean leaders searching for new paradigms of race relations to address the ongoing tensions and conflicts between members of their communities.

There has been no lack of effort on the part of some African American and Arab/Chaldean American leaders to bridge the gap between their two communities, although as Sarafa mentioned, "the leaders of the trade groups and community organizations will certainly get along . . . but nothing that New Detroit, Inc., the Michigan Food and Beverage Association or any other well-intentioned group does or says retroactively ever really helps much" (Sarafa, 1999).

Sarafa was referring to a pattern that tended to be reactive instead of proactive. Task forces had been set up after several major conflicts between Arab/Chaldean merchants and African Americans. For example, a task force had been set up in April 1980 after the racially charged deaths of Douglass and Zoma. The cochairmen of the task force, Arab American Edward Deeb, executive director of the Associated Food Dealers (AFD) and African American Walter Douglas, president of New Detroit, expressed guarded optimism that the task force was producing some important results. Deeb acknowledged that the killing of the Chaldean store owner had "upset the Chaldean community as well as the retail grocers. But it has not and will not detract from the good progress our task force committees are making" (Gebert, 1980).

Jerry Yono, a member of the task force's Complaints and Concerns Committee, viewed the killing of the party store owner as a big setback and said that many of Chaldean grocers and party store owners in the inner city had threatened to sell their business and leave. Notwithstanding his concerns, Yono wanted the task force to continue operating. "The task force is not in vain. It had to keep going. We must work in the various communities for those who won't or can't pull out. Also, think what'll happen to the city's tax base and those neighborhoods which rely on the stores. The big chain store super markets are gone. What'll be left?" (Gebert, 1980).

The task force's report to Mayor Coleman Young revealed that the main approach taken to address the problem was to investigate complaints, which included communication barriers between store owners and customers, overpricing, pilfering, robberies, and cost of store security. The task force focused on the achievements made in lessening communication barriers between black communities and Arab/Chaldean store owners. According to Douglas, "This is one of the most effective things that the task force has done. There has [*sic*] to be meetings, and candid discussions. We started talking. We've released some steam and we are relieving tensions" (Gebert, 1980). Douglas declared that Detroit was big enough for everyone and he did not believe that Arab/Chaldean merchants "will walk away from significant investments." He added that the task force also must focus on financial and job training programs for African Americans (Gebert, 1980).

Three years later, concerned organizations and groups were still trying to "defuse what has become the most explosive issue in Detroit" (Wilson, 1983a). In March 1983, members of the Concerned Citizens Council and other organizations met to try to find a solution to the persistent problems between African American customers and Middle Eastern merchants. They followed a pattern of conflict resolution that would come to dominate future meetings. Lonnie Peek, an African American community activist and one of the coordinators of the meeting, felt that it included pointed disagreements and an important forum for pressing issues. "In the first part of the meeting there was a lot of ventilation and folk didn't know what was going to happen," Peek explained. "But after a while people started to calm down and started to think about solutions" (Wilson, 1983a).

Some of the major issues at this meeting included hiring of neighborhood people by Middle Eastern merchants; merchants' lack of respect for their African American customers—especially women and children—and merchants' attitudes and behavior. Larry Joseph, president of the AFD, agreed to convene a subcommittee to study the situation. The members of the committee included Winston Lang of the NAACP, John Knowles, representing the Black Grocers Association, and Susan Peek of the Concerned Citizens' Council (Wilson, 1983a).

The meeting devoted time to sensitizing Middle Eastern store owners. One of the lessons was that they and African American grocers shared the same problems, but Peek explained, "Black grocers have learned to deal with these problems." Detroit deputy chief James Bannon commented that some merchants overreact. According to Peek, "In four of the last five incidents, the store owner has seen fit to carry the problems on out into the street after the person has gone out of the door" (Wilson, 1983a).

Obviously Bannon's and Peek's comments at this meeting were not intended to explain the full range of causes for the violence between African American customers and Middle Eastern merchants. Deeb argued that Middle Eastern store owners had spent a lot of time working hard to understand the African American community. He said the feeling among some merchants was that their efforts had not been reciprocated. Deeb did understand that Middle Eastern merchants had a role to play in defusing tensions and conflicts between themselves and their African American customers, however. He said, "It does not make any sense to shoot or beat somebody up over 20 cents" (Wilson, 1983a).

By this time, task forces created to address African American customers and Middle Eastern merchants' violence were becoming routine patterns of reaction. Since tensions and conflicts between the two groups continued, critics again questioned the effectiveness of these task forces. It was understandable that leaders of both communities were becoming frustrated with task forces and meetings after every incident involving Middle Eastern merchants and African Americans, yet these efforts had kept lines of communication open and provided some hope for building bridges and nursing relationships between concerned representatives of both groups.

New Detroit had been involved in many task forces, and had drawn the fire of critics. For example, in the fall of 1983, following the aforementioned meeting, a writer for the *Detroit News* criticized New Detroit's plan suggesting that Chaldean grocers should just hire unemployed African Americans, and that would solve the problem. The writer referred to a paper by Mary Sengstock, an expert on Chaldeans in Detroit, in which she criticized the premises of the plan as "hopelessly flawed" because the Chaldean grocery is a family economic unit (Canton, 1983). Sengstock obviously was looking at the problem from the angle of the Chaldean community. Perhaps seen from the angle of the African American community that was providing the income for the Chaldean's family unit, the premises might not have been as "hopelessly flawed."

Racial Tensions during the Gulf War

During the Gulf War in 1991, when anti-Arab national and regional sentiment was reaching a boiling point, the *Michigan Chronicle* published an article aimed at African Americans in the city, entitled "Black Detroiters: Arab/Chaldeans Aren't Our Enemies." The writer understood how the tension generated by the war contributed to Arab/black conflict in the area. "The United States' bombing of Iraq is now causing tensions to mount in the metro Detroit area noted for its burgeoning Arab American population. But that tension has also caused Arabs and African Americans to forge a coalition that may serve to bolster understanding long after the war is over" (Wimberly, 1991).

Michael Wimberly wrote that JoAnn Watson, executive director of the NAACP, reported that the majority of callers to the NAACP expressed support for the Arab American community. "The comments have been around people of color in solidarity," Watson said (Wimberly, 1991). Wimberly also quoted Jumana Elsheick, associate director of urban affairs for Michigan Bell and a spokesperson for the Arab and Chaldean American community, who said, "The relationship between the African American and Arab Chaldean community is important. Because of our historic and current situations, we should stick together" (Wimberly, 1991). The writer also noted that the "Arab Chaldean Council, the Chaldean Federation, and other organizations are all part of the coalition working with Black organizations" (Wimberly, 1991).

Black support for the Middle Eastern community in metropolitan Detroit during the 1990–91 Gulf War was critically important at a time when this community was being both demonized and threatened by anti-Arab voices in the Detroit metropolitan area. According to Wimberly (1991), "The statement of support the NAACP is receiving in connection with the Persian Gulf crisis is kinder than many some Arabs are getting." In short, notwithstanding the history of tension and conflict between elements of the African American and Arab/Chaldean communities, African Americans appeared not to be part of the rising chorus of anti-Arab sentiments.

Middle Eastern workers in Detroit's East Seven Mile road area, a center of Iraqi-owned stores and homes, were fielding calls that were threatening "to blow up businesses and break windows" (Wimberly, 1991). Iraqis throughout the city reported that they were "experiencing antagonism." The *Michigan Chronicle* writer reported that the police and FBI were questioning Arab Americans and reported that in one case—probably indicative of many others—they "stormed his house, searching for weapons and explosives. The man refused to give his name for fear of reprisal" (Wimberly, 1991). The regional director of the Arab American Anti-Discrimination Committee expressed what had to be the feelings and concerns of most Arab/Chaldean Americans in the area during this time: "We are demoralized by the whole situation. It is just very sad" (Wimberly, 1991).

The Persian Gulf crisis, therefore, tested the struggling relationship between the progressive elements in the African American and Arab/Chaldean American community working to promote unity between the two groups. The calls of support for the Arab/Chaldean community, from African Americans to the NAACP and a writer from the city's major black newspaper, was tangible proof that decades of bridge building between the two communities had not been in vain.

The Death of Kalvin Porter

Not withstanding these bridge building efforts, tensions and conflicts between Middle Eastern merchants and blacks continued. In May 1999, they reached a new high when Kalvin Porter, a thirty-four-year-old black man, was killed in a struggle with two men of Yemeni descent outside of an Arab-owned gas station on the east side of Detroit. According to reports the fight resulted from an insulting remark made about the twelve-year-old daughter of Porter's fiancée. The two men were employees of the owner of the station (Hackney, 1999).

Porter's death triggered months of demonstrations by African Americans and rekindled accusations of mistreatment of black customers by Middle Eastern store owners. One black picketer carried a sign calling for the closure of the station. One side of the sign said: "Don't burn it down, shut it down." The other side declared: "Family first, respect my people." The picketer then voiced a common black complaint expanded to include the recent incident: "Why should they be able to economically benefit from the Black community and the community in general when they so blatantly break the law?" (Elrick, 1999).

Soon after the incident a meeting was held between African American leaders and Arab American business owners. Ed Deeb, a leader in the Arab American community and president of the Michigan Food and Beverage Association, which sponsored the meeting, argued that the incident was not racially motivated. Deeb, speaking on behalf of his group, expressed the position that while the situation was tragic, "we feel this is not a racial incident but a criminal issue and should be resolved by courts of law and the criminal justice system, so that both parties may be able to be heard fairly" (Hackney, 1999). Mary McClendon, an African American woman, countered, "There was racism and prejudice was involved. As long as earth exists, there's going to be racism and prejudice and hatred. Well, I say an eye for an eye and a tooth for a tooth" (Hackney, 1999).

The gathering was emotionally charged as decades of tensions, conflicts, accusations, and cultural misunderstanding between members of the two communities erupted. Reverend Gary Hunter, president of Families United for Non-Violence, told Arab American business owners, "You're only hiring two types of people from our community: the women you can hit on and the drunks who will clean around your store. We want our women, children, and men respected" (Hackney, 1999).

Fortunately, cooler heads prevailed, as spokespersons from both communities, while regreting the tragedy, argued that it was not racially motivated. They were especially saddened by the negative impact the tragedy was having on African American and Middle Eastern American relationships. Michael Sarafa, a Chaldean lawyer, a board member of the Arab Community Center for Economic and Social Services (ACCESS), and a lifetime member of the NAACP, wrote:

The killing was wrong, and those who did it must be punished to the full extent of the law. . . . [However,] the media's focus on racial issues surrounding the incident is the height of irresponsibility and poor judgment. While it cannot be denied that tensions exist between some members of the black community and some Arab/Chaldean business people, the fact remains that the relationship of the two groups has been overwhelmingly positive and mutually beneficial. (Sarafa, 1999)

Sarafa also pointed to the tendency of some people to

inject the suspects' ethnicity into their actions and then expect the entire Arab/Chaldean community to answer for it. The accusation of a few exploitation artists that the killing was racially motivated does not make it true or newsworthy. . . . I am tired of task forces, meetings, forums, and the like that are held ad nauseam to deal with these issues. I sat on two committees set up respectively by the two major papers in town that were organized to help sensitize the media to ethnic and racial perspectives. What's the point if they never get it? (Sarafa, 1999)

What is needed, Sarafa advised, is "the development of mutual respect that comes from positive, daily interactions—the things that happen thousands of times a day in Detroit between Arabs and blacks, business people and customers, employees and employers, friends and neighbors" (Sarafa, 1999). In addition, Sarafa pointed out that it would be better for all people to "focus on the overall crime situation in Detroit, rather than one terrible incident. Crime remains an impediment to the neighborhood stability and the city's growth" (Sarafa, 1999).

The question of crime being a major problem in Detroit was certainly undeniable. However wide the racial divide between Arab and black communities over Kalvin Porter's death, both communities realized that the persistence of crime—much of it black-on-black—affected the social fabric of many poor inner-city neighborhoods. The communities, however, did not share the same depth of understanding of the complex relationship of racial segregation, social isolation, and black poverty that were often the root causes of crime. The Middle Eastern merchants who set up shop in poor, black, crime-infested neighborhoods were probably unaware of the potentially explosive mix of black poverty, crime, violence, and cultural misunderstanding, and black leaders fresh out of the trauma of the 1967 riot and struggling to lead and guide in the midst of a declining economy, no doubt did not anticipate that black/Arab or Chaldean conflict would become a pressing racial problem.

Sarafa concluded his article with a balance of sensitivity and understanding of the hurt and pain both communities had experienced in the past and still experience in the present, which is essential to building bridges between two peoples:

Meanwhile, only the Porter family and the others like them who have experienced the loss of loved ones because of violence can know what it is like to have a family torn apart by such a senseless act— others like my wife, whose father was gunned down in his business 25 years ago . . . her father was murdered by a man who happened to be African American. He was caught, jailed for a time, and released many years ago, free to go about his business and maybe even celebrate Father's Day next month somewhere with his kids. This Father's Day for the Porter children, like the last 25 for my wife and her two brothers, will be filled with nothing but hurt. No amount of apologies, excuses, task forces or protests will matter to them. Nor will the race of their father's killers. (Sarafa, 1999)

Several weeks after the Porter killing, while protesters were marching nightly at the gas station, "vowing that it will reopen only under black ownership," Mayor Dennis Archer made his first public statement on the issue. He expressed deep concern that the killing was being called a racial crime. He mentioned the killing of Jamal Akrawi, a forty-nine-year-old restaurant owner of Middle Eastern descent, and three others, including his twelve-year-old son and a black teenager on Easter Sunday morning by robbers who did not want to leave any witnesses. "Despite the horrendous nature of this tragedy, there was no effort to disparage a whole group of people or pit members of one group against another" (Oguntoyinbo, 1999a). Understandably, in such a volatile situation involving both communities, the mayor appreciated the efforts of African Americans and Middle Eastern groups that had joined together as a result of Porter's death "in hopes of healing the racial divide" (Oguntoyinbo, 1999a).

Similar to Sarafa's approach to the Porter killing, Archer was trying to deracialize the situation and to separate the crime from the race of the perpetrator by focusing upon victims from both races. Both were well aware of the dangers of disparaging an entire racial or ethnic group by the negative actions of an individual of that group. They also understood the potential of Porter's murder for widening the racial divide between the two communities, which were separated by a history of cultural misunderstanding, anger, and pain. Attempts to surgically deracialize such complex situation by separating the crime from the race of the victim, while rationally sound and an essential first step in the process of building bridges, were simply not sufficient to heal the deep emotional wounds of those segments of the African American and Arab/Chaldean communities locked in conflict.

A year after Kalvin Porter was killed, both of his killers—the Yemeni gas station attendants—were freed. Porter's fiancée, Barbara Ann Wright, accused the court of letting two murderers go: "You've just signed a death warrant for all black men. When you go into one of their stores, you better go in there prepared to die" (Bailey, 2000). Five women and seven men, including one African American, sat on the jury that freed the two men. One newspaper reported that "people familiar with the case said the testimony of defense witness L. J. Dragovic, chief medical examiner in Oakland, was a strong influence on the jury. Dragovic testified that Porter's heart was damaged from longtime cocaine use and was exhausted during the fight ("Tense Verdict Not Guilty," May 23, 2000). In the 1990s a similar argument was used by defense experts during trial of the two white police officers accused of beating Malice Green, also a drug user, to death.

The acquittal reinforced the negative image of African American males in Detroit as merely drug addicts in contrast to men of Middle Eastern descent as hardworking immigrants pursuing the American Dream.

Tensions and conflicts continued between African American customers and Arab/Chaldean store owners, some of which led to more violence. One such incident occurred in July 2001 in Southfield, where a man of Middle Eastern descent from Sterling Heights was charged with assaulting a thirteen-year-old black youth he thought was stealing from his gas station. Another incident occurred when a black woman at another Arab American gas station accused the manager of attacking her; he in turn accused her of attacking him (*Detroit Free Press*, August 1, 2001). These incidents formed part of an ongoing pattern of tensions and conflicts between segments of the African American and Arab/Chaldean communities that seemed unending and unsolvable.

Black–Middle Eastern Relations, Post-9/11

The tension and conflict between segments of the black and Middle Eastern communities did not abate during the post-9/11 period. The Kalvin Porter murder in 1999 and the black boycott that followed in its wake raised questions about the viability of African American/Arab/Chaldean American solidarity. Unlike the show of support for Arab Americans during the Persian Gulf War, several months after 9/11 black writer Trevor W. Coleman's (2001) article "Why Arab Community Can't Take Black Support for Granted" appeared in the *Detroit Free Press*. It was in sharp contrast to the 1991 black show of support article and a barometer of blacks' changing attitudes toward Arab Americans as they faced another national crisis.

"It seems the proverbial chickens are coming home to roost for metro Detroit's Arab American community," Coleman began his article. "Years of contentious relationships between Arab American service station and store owners and their African American customers are taking a toll as Arabs seek black support for civil liberties protection following the Sept. 11 attacks by Middle Eastern terrorists" (Coleman, 2001).

Coleman mentioned a memo that Heaster Wheeler, executive director of the Detroit branch of the NAACP, sent to an attorney with the Michigan chapter of the American Civil Liberties Union, responding to a third request from the ACLU attorney to "sign yet another coalition statement on behalf of the Arab American community" (Coleman, 2001).

In the memo Wheeler reminded the ACLU attorney that the NAACP did sign a coalition statement sent on September 21 to Northwest Airlines expressing deep concern regarding racial profiling of four Northwest passengers of Middle Eastern descent. But after the third request, the NAACP director "felt compelled to remind [the ACLU lawyer] of the still very serious unresolved issues between Blacks and Arabs in metro Detroit." While pointing out that "there is no question as to where we (the NAACP) stand on the issues of racial profiling, the question is where so many of the others do stand?" (Coleman, 2001).

In what appeared to be a burst of pent-up frustration with these "serious unresolved issues," the NAACP executive reminded the ACLU attorney that "just two weeks prior to September 11, African Americans, Arabs and Chaldeans were arguing (on Channel 7 television) over respect, service quality and business issues regarding gas stations and grocery stores in Detroit. African American children of families patronize their stores . . . and few of these merchants provide scholarships or support Little League or even provide safe passage in and out of their business. Where was this coalition in response to African American frustration?" (Coleman, 2001).

Coleman recognized the delicate and even explosive nature of the NAACP memo. Most certainly it was in sharp contrast to the NAACP's seemingly unconditional support for Arab Americans during the 1991 Persian Gulf War. As Coleman wrote, however, "Such a stand may seem insensitive or at least impolitic in the current climate, but the Rev. Wendell Anthony, president of the Detroit NAACP, said Wheeler's memo was not only on target, but necessary" (Coleman, 2001).

If the executive director's memo seemed "insensitive or at least impolitic," the statement of the NAACP president was off the charts regarding the state of African American and Arab/Chaldean relations. "We cannot spend all of our energy concerned with our Arab American brothers when at the same time they do not express the same concerns about us . . . I believe we do have more in common than differences. However, it is only going to be resolved when leaders of the African American and Arab communities sit around a common table and address those issues" (Coleman, 2001).

The NAACP's views were similar to those of Sheffield, who had become one of the black community's most vociferous critics of some Arab merchants' "contemptuous attitudes" toward their African American customers, and had initiated the thirty-day boycott of Arab-owned gas stations the month before the terrorist attacks.

After 9/11 and the ACLU request for African American support for Arab Americans, Sheffield expressed the view, as the *Detroit Free Press* writer put it, that "there is too much bad history for African Americans leaders simply to extend unqualified support." Sheffield argued that "there needs to be some earnest evaluation of whether this collaboration will continue after their threat has passed . . . what they are facing is something that is new to them, something that has come upon them recently. But what we have experienced has been our experience since we've been here. We want people to partner with us and to continue to deal with us, not just because they need us, but because they respect us" (Coleman, 2001).

An Arab American activist understood the reasons behind African American feelings toward her community. "Blacks perceive the Arabs as economically exploitive of their community and disrespectful . . . and Arabs believe blacks as people will steal from them or even kill them." She disagreed with Sheffield's approach, however.

"People like Horace Sheffield come in and instead of saying, 'How do we get to know each other?' they like to divide and conquer. It doesn't help anyone. But having said that, . . . shame on us in the Arab community who see something wrong in the African American community and do not say anything" (Coleman, 2001).

Coleman concluded his provocative article explaining that "the issue here is not the shared disdain for racial profiling or the coalition's objectives of justice and fairness for Arab Americans. This is about the principles of reciprocity and simple respect. The NAACP, Sheffield and others have decided their support is no longer going to come easily. And what is wrong with that?" (Coleman, 2001).

THE HARMONY PROJECT

Some African American leaders continued their efforts to overcome what Sheffield called "too much bad history." In 1995 an African American activist, Toni McIlwain, president of the Ravendale Community organization, established the Harmony Project "to promote discussions and understanding between merchants and their customers" (Oguntoyinbo, 1999b). The incident that sparked the need for the program occurred in August 1992 when Raffael Dent, a young African American man, was shot to death by Imad Hussein Cheatio, a Middle Eastern gas station clerk. Cheatio claimed self-defense in an attempted robbery (Oguntoyinbo, 1999b).

Matters grew worse in the wake of the Wayne County Prosecutor's Office initial decision not to "bring charges against Cheatio because of what it deemed insufficient evidence of criminal intent." The decision was later overruled by the Wayne County prosecutor and Cheatio was charged "with manslaughter and felony possession of a firearm." He later escaped while on bond (Oguntoyinbo, 1999b).

Predictably, the shooting triggered mass protests, once again conjuring up images of young

African American males being shot by Middle Easterners that "became a rallying cry for many Detroit blacks who saw themselves as being mistreated by store owners (Oguntoyinbo, 1999b). Cheatio's escape fueled suspicion throughout the black community that he was helped by segments of the Middle Eastern community.

This was the boiling pot that Mcllwain decided to step into. "I kept thinking about the situation and about taking the negative and getting something positive out of it . . . I said the problem had to be related to communication. I went to the block club I had formed and said we needed to talk about it. We met with the store owners for about nine months, breaking bread together, learning each other's culture." One merchant in the neighborhood echoed Mcllwain's hope and spirit when he said it "brings us closer together. They begin to feel that we're helping them, supporting them. It's kind of like a family." His faith in Mcllwain and the process was confirmed "when three men robbed his store at gunpoint and [he] got Mcllwain's assistance in persuading police to pursue the case aggressively . . . the men were later caught" (Oguntoyinbo, 1999b).

Both merchants and customers were encouraged to seek assistance from the project. Before long, the Harmony Project attracted the attention of the staff at the Center for Peace and Conflict Studies (CPCS) at Wayne State University, who worked with Mcllwain in implementing it in other Detroit neighborhoods (Oguntoyinbo, 1999b).

On one occasion in 1998, a liaison person with the project was called to a store to mediate a dispute over a bad check. After the liaison talked to both parties, the dispute was resolved without police intervention (Oguntoyinbo, 1999b). This process helped Middle Eastern merchants develop trust in their resident liaisons. For example, in the wake of the Kalvin Porter killing in May 1999, staff members of the CPCS discussed the possibility of starting a similar project with the police and people living close to the gas station where Porter was killed. One of the key strategies of the project was to equip community people with pagers so they could be called upon to assist in mediating disputes while they were occurring (Oguntoyinbo, 1999b).

Middle Eastern merchants had a responsibility in the project as well. They were expected to "post a 12-point pledge in their stores, agreeing among other things to hire neighborhood residents and speak only English in the presence of customers. In turn, residents pledge to provide employable residents to the merchants" (Oguntoyinbo, 1999b).

Of particular importance was the fact that the Harmony Project gained support from leaders of Middle Eastern descent with a history of involvement in conflicts between African American and Arab/Chaldean communities. Nassar Beydoun, director of the American Arab Chamber of Commerce, considered it a "good project. I like the interaction between business owners and the community and the understanding on both sides" (Oguntoyinbo, 1999b). While it did not end the tension and conflict between merchants of Middle Eastern descent and their African American customers, the Harmony Project was a welcomed improvement in the long and agonizing efforts to bridge the racial and cultural gaps between these elements of their respective larger communities.

The development of mutual respect became the best investment both communities could make for the betterment of future relationships. There would be ups and downs, more tensions and conflicts, but there were always enlightened and visionary community leaders, individuals, writers, and others in both communities willing to "keep hope alive." These "bridge builders" played a vital role in maintaining coalitions designed to support one another in time of crises.

SEASON OF UNITY: FORGING BONDS OF UNITY BETWEEN ARAB
AMERICAN WOMEN AND AFRICAN AMERICAN WOMEN

Notwithstanding the understandable reluctance of certain African American male leaders to give "unqualified support" to the Arab American community in the post-9/11 period because of "serious unresolved issues" and "too much bad history," some African American women did not hesitate to offer support to Arab women. In autumn 2001 the International Awareness Committee of the Inkster Alumnae Chapter of the Delta Sigma Theta Sorority was in the process of planning a town meeting on "the oppression of women in Afghanistan," but decided to change its focus after the September 11 attack. Genarda Wright, president of the chapter, explained: "In light of the racial profiling that Arab Americans have had to endure in recent months, we really wanted to show our solidarity with Arab women. . . . Our community knows how it feels to be stigmatized and we wanted to offer our support" ("Sorority Explores Black/Arab Relations," 2001).

The event was sponsored by both the Delta Sigma Theta Chapter and the Arab Community Center for Economic and Social Services (ACCESS). Presentations at the gathering focused on "the importance of ethnic and religious tolerance." Lubna Aboose, an Arab American cultural arts outreach coordinator for ACCESS, discussed the great ethnic, language, and religious diversity within the Arab world. Participants were challenged by Connie Byrd, a Michigan State University diversity facilitator, "to examine their own biases and break down stereotypes." Some of these stereotypes included "Why aren't Arab American women more friendly? Why aren't African American women less lazy?" ("Sorority Explores Black/Arab Relations," 2001).

Members of both groups expressed their gratitude for what they learned from the event. Maha Freiji, chief financial officer for ACCESS, said that "it was such an eye opener for me about being more sensitive . . . you go into an event like that and you think you are so progressive and know everything, but you find out you have no clue." Her views were shared by Lorraine Hurst, chairwomen of the Delta chapter's International Awareness Committee. "When it started, we all had preconceived notions about each other and I think I really was able to put myself in their shoes" ("Sorority Explores Black/Arab Relations," 2001).

Other topics also were discussed at this event. In the months after 9/11, one of the most important topics for the Arab American women present was the controversial federal antiterrorism legislation and racial profiling that were threatening their community. Given the still unresolved issues between both communities, as articulated by the black male leaders, the participants discussed "the Black community relationship with Middle Eastern shopkeepers and gas station operators" ("Sorority Explores Black/Arab Relations," 2001).

For example, one African American participant reported that "there were some uncomfortable moments. A few of us worried that some might interpret our attempt to reach out as a blanket pardon for the sometimes-appalling behavior African Americans have encountered in Arab American owned gas stations and party stores." But the black women did not "back away from the issues raised by the recent 'buy black gas' campaign. In fact, black women at the event dived right in with [their] grievances. Instead of defensiveness, we got eye-opening answers to our questions" (Trent, 2001).

The event was not limited to discussions, however; it "also featured a dinner . . . of Middle Eastern and traditional African American cuisine" ("Sorority Explores Black/Arab Relations," 2001). To accommodate the Muslim women's desire to break their Ramadan fast as soon as possible, the event started with dinner, which stimulated some cross-cultural conversation that eased "the hard work ahead" (Trent, 2001).

At the end of the event, the planners had hopes that the groundbreaking event would be "only the beginning of a dialogue between Arab and African American women in western Wayne County." Maha Freiji, one of the Arab American participants, explained why women are so important to the forging of bonds between the African American and Arab American communities. "I really believe that women are extremely honest. If they believe in a mission, they go all the way . . . it's not about ego. With women, if they put their minds and hearts in it, it will go places. I really believe that if we do organize ourselves we can do something really positive with this" ("Sorority Explores Black/Arab Relations," 2001).

Trent agreed:

While men traditionally have been ambassadors, generals and presidents, women have always quietly gone about the business of effecting social change. It's impossible to imagine the abolition, civil rights and suffrage movements without the contributions of women of every ethnic background. As our sorority president, Gwendolyn E. Boyd, likes to say: "the rooster crows, but the hen delivers." (Trent, 2001)

CONTINUING EFFORTS TO BRIDGE THE RACIAL DIVIDE

Other efforts to build bridges and strengthen relationships between the African American and the Arab/Chaldean communities included an annual essay contest honoring the legacy of Dr. Martin Luther King Jr., supported by the American Arab Anti-Discrimination Committee. In February 2001, Imad Hamand, regional director of the committee, explained the purpose of the contest: "We see Dr. King's message in all of us. His message is beyond race and color and origin. This is where we feel his legacy should be appreciated and people should learn more about it" ("Essays Link Arab American Students with Dr. King's Dream," February 5, 2001).

The contest was open to Arab American and Chaldean high school seniors, who were asked to write about "what King's message means to them." The winners of the contest were given scholarships. Interestingly enough, judging from the picture of the essay winners in a *Detroit Free Press* photo, all the winners were Arab and Chaldean senior high school young women. They were all honored at the Second Annual Scholarship reception. Along with honoring the winners, the event featured a presentation by Detroit's Gardener Elementary Glee Club, composed of forty Arab American and African American students ("Essays Link Arab American Students with Dr. King's Dream," February 5, 2001).

The essay contest represented an excellent opportunity for Arab and Chaldean American youth to learn about King's legacy and in the process to strengthen relationships between African American and Arab/Chaldean American communities. Along with other efforts, the annual contest also demonstrated that forward-thinking leaders and organizations of both communities were dedicated to investing in and mapping the future rather than to dwelling on the past.

CONCLUSION

The post-1967 civil disorder period exposed another racial/cultural divide in Detroit, long dominated by white/black racial tensions and conflicts. The most recent tensions and conflicts between Middle Eastern merchants and primarily poor black customers were rooted in the deteriorating social and economic conditions in black neighborhoods in which these merchants were forced by circumstances to find their niche. Cultural misunderstanding between the two often turned into insults and violence. The black crime wave that ravaged black communities and victimized black people also claimed the lives of Middle Eastern merchants and their workers. In turn, Middle Eastern merchants and workers also killed blacks.

Most black and Middle Eastern leaders attempted to defuse the conflict, with limited success. The murder of Kalvin Porter in May 1999 by two men of Yemeni descent created a firestorm of anger within the black community leading to protests. Other conflicts triggered calls by some black leaders to boycott Middle Eastern businesses.

However, many black leaders did not abandon the Middle Eastern communities during the periods of anti-Arab hysteria during the 1991 Persian Gulf crisis and over 9/11. At the present time, the relationship between blacks and Middle Eastern Americans in the Detroit areas is a work in progress with great promise.

CHAPTER 9

Old Minority and New Minority

Black-Latino Relations in a
Predominantly Black City

BETWEEN 1970 AND 1980, DETROIT'S BLACK POPULATION INCREASED FROM 43.7 percent to 63 percent, becoming a majority black city for the first time in its history (Darden, 2009b). Detroit elected its first black mayor, Coleman Young, in 1973. Within six years of the riots, Detroit had changed from a prosperous, predominantly white city to a poor, majority black one, but with a majority black administration (Boyle, 2001). The rioting, according to Fine (1989), was born of hope, not of despair—the hope that improvement would follow the disorder in the streets.

According to Salas and Salas (1974), although most of the burning and looting of 1967 occurred in the black neighborhoods, there was also riot activity in the Mexican "barrio." Mexicans took advantage of the opportunity to vent their anger and frustration. This led to the development of Latino activism and political action to obtain the Latinos' share of any funds that the black-controlled administration might allocate to blacks.

This also led to the creation of Latin Americans for Social and Economic Development (LASED), a nonprofit corporation completely controlled and operated by the Chicano (Mexican) community. LASED (which, written as "la sed," translates as "thirst") is the oldest nonprofit organization serving the Latino community in southwest Detroit. It was created to address the changing needs of Latinos in the city. Over time, LASED established senior and youth centers, a foster care program, and other helpful services for the Latino community in the southwest. LASED also assist new immigrants to overcome barriers to assimilation (Johnson, 2010).

Originally established in 1965, the first four years of LASED were funded by the Archdiocese of Detroit. According to Salas and Salas (1974), it was the first Chicano institution in Detroit to successfully compete for program funds. At the same time that both Hispanics and blacks were competing for their share of funds, the city faced economic hardships with the election of the first black mayor, Coleman Young. Young was seen as a liberator and symbol of hope by many blacks in Detroit after decades of neglect and mistreatment by white officials and the police (Gavrilovich and McGraw, 2000), but as far as having the ability to provide much-needed assistance, Young's victory was in a sense a "hollow prize." By the time Young took office in 1974, angry whites had repeatedly defeated millage votes, leaving Detroit's public schools nearly bankrupt, and white flight of the middle class had eroded the city's tax base (Boyle, 2001). Job loss was on the rise, and by 1975, just one year after Young took office, the unemployment rate surged to 18 percent (Boyle, 2001). By the late 1970s, the city's finances were in collapse, federal aid to cities had declined, and Detroit's unemployment rate continued to climb. Thus, the relationship between Hispanics and blacks in Detroit increasingly became one best described as two racial/ethnic minorities competing for an increasingly declining resource base controlled by neither—but by powerful corporations (Boyle, 2001).

We assess what significance a majority black city had on the characteristics of the place of residence, socioeconomic status, and mobility of Hispanics. More significantly, did blacks in general exceed Hispanics in Detroit's social, economic, and spatial structure? Did the social and economic conditions of Hispanics decline within the majority black city?

We begin by examining the residential patterns of Hispanics (a majority of whom have been Mexicans). The words "Latino" and "Hispanic" will be used interchangeably.

THE EMERGENCE OF THE LATINO SETTLEMENT IN DETROIT

Based on the works of past researchers, there is disagreement as to (*a*) when Latinos arrived and settled in Detroit, (*b*) the precise geographic location of their settlement, (*c*) how many Latinos were residing there in 1970, a few years after the civil disorder of 1967, and (*d*) the appropriate name that best characterizes the settlement.

Time of Arrival and Source Regions

According to Skendzel (1980), most Latinos were of Mexican origin, and they arrived in Detroit at the end of the great immigration after World War I. There was also a record phase of Mexican immigration to Detroit during World War II. Skendzel (1980) states that the chief reason for settling in Detroit was for employment in the auto industry.

According to Badillo (2003), Detroit's Latinos were predominantly of Mexican origin, but there were also Puerto Ricans, Cubans, and Latinos from the Caribbean. Although Mexico was a major source region, many arrived from elsewhere in Michigan, especially from Texas and other states in the Southwest.

Badillo (2003) notes that Mexicans arrived in Detroit around 1917, when several hundred were observed, and 3,000 were in Detroit by 1920, increasing to 15,000 by the end of the decade.

The Geographic Location of Detroit's Latino Settlement in 1970

Disagreement over the precise location of Detroit's Latino settlement has been prevalent among researchers. According to Skendzel (1980), the first Mexican settlement was located on Third Avenue near Plum Street, an area occupied by the Detroit Edison Company after World War I. With the passage of time, Skendzel argues, the Mexican settlement moved from its original location to an area around Holy Trinity Church in a section of Detroit known as Corktown. Since the 1940s, the largest concentration of Mexicans has been in the zone between Fort Street and Vernor Highway and from Holy Trinity Church to several miles westward along Bagley Avenue to East Grand (Skendzel, 1980).

According to Badillo (2003), southwest Detroit became Michigan's largest Mexican settlement. That section of Detroit had long served as an entry point, that is, a gateway for Mexicans and Caribbean immigrants. Badillo (2003) also notes that the settlement lacked defined boundaries.

According to Baba and Abonyi (1979), the first Mexican settlement was located on the near east side of downtown Detroit in the vicinity of Lafayette and Congress streets. By 1940, most foreign-born Mexicans in Detroit lived primarily in the area from Mt. Elliot on the near east side to approximately Central Avenue on the west side, bounded on the south by the Detroit River and on the north by the Edsel Ford Freeway.

Baba and Abonyi (1979) point out that by 1970, the east side Mexican settlement had virtually disappeared, but a new settlement emerged on the west side of Detroit between Wyoming and Southfield, stretching from Lyndon on the north southward across the city limits into Dearborn. Geographically, the Latino settlement in Detroit in 1970 was the area extending from the Ambassador Bridge to Springwells, bounded on the north by Vernor Highway and on the south by the Detroit River (Baba and Abonyi, 1979). In this area, the second-generation Mexican Americans joined the foreign born in the southwest section of Detroit (Baba and Abonyi, 1979).

According to Knoll (1974), the Mexican settlement was located west of Detroit's central business district and was bounded by heavy industry on two sides.

Weeks and Spielberg (1979), using census data, stated that the Mexican settlement was located directly to the southwest of downtown Detroit. The authors defined the geographic extent of the Mexican settlement as comprising census tracts 0005, 0007, 0008, 0067, and 0068. This was the first time to our knowledge that past researchers identified specific census tracts to determine the location of the Mexican/Latino settlement in Detroit. For the geographic location of this area, see Map 1.

We examined the demographic composition of these five tracts in 1970. Our results reveal that the settlement had 15,029 people, a land area of 1.3 square miles, and a population density of 11,941 people per square mile. As a group, the tracts comprised a population that was 29 percent Hispanic (U.S. Bureau of the Census, 1972). Hispanics did not constitute a majority in any of the tracts. However, their percentage reached 47.2 percent in tract 7. Racially, the tracts as a whole were 90 percent white.

The Latino Population in 1970

As we indicate in the previous section, the census reports 15,029 Hispanics in the geographically defined settlement in 1970. Still, some researchers have questioned the low figures and instead have stated that many more Hispanics lived in Detroit than the number the census reported. Knoll (1974) stated, for example, "the estimated number of Spanish speaking people (including Mexicans, Spaniards, Puerto Ricans, Cubans, and South Americans) living in Detroit was 70,000." Knoll does not indicate the source for this estimate, which we believe is too high. According to the 1970 U.S. Census of Population and Housing there were only

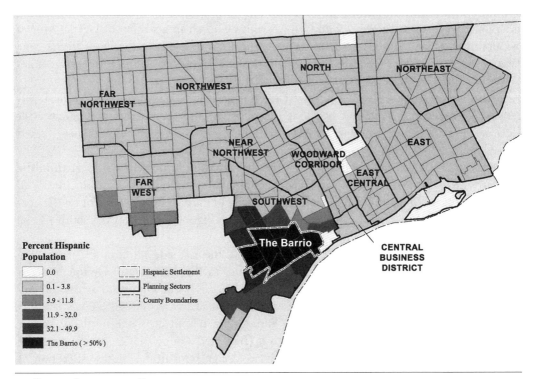

THE HISPANIC POPULATION IN DETROIT IN 2000.

27,038 persons of Spanish origin or descent living in Detroit in 1970 (see U.S. Bureau of the Census, 1972).

On the other hand, Salas and Salas (1974) also state that there were 70,000 Latino residents in the city in 1970 and that the number of Mexicans in Detroit was not reported accurately by the census of 1970. To be sure, undercounts of minority groups are common by the U.S. Census Bureau. Salas and Salas (1974) argue that many Mexicans and Puerto Ricans, especially those with light skin, checked the census category "white" to identify the group in which they belonged and did not check the option box to write in their own ethnic group.

This may be true in some instances. Without definite documentation of the numbers involved, however, we have based our analyses of the Latino population in Detroit on the data provided by the U.S. Census Bureau from 1970 to the most recent census of 2010 (U.S. Bureau of the Census, 2011a). Such data enables a comparison of the Hispanic and black population, which is the overriding objective of this chapter.

The Latino Settlement in Detroit: Its Name and Characteristics

The name of a *place* is important. A name creates perceptions of a place that may be positive or negative. The name may also convey something about the image of the people who reside there.

Our investigation reveals that agreement did not exist among researchers on what name should be used to best characterize the Mexican settlement in Detroit. Among the authors who have conducted research on the area, all but one call the settlement a "barrio," even though they acknowledged that the Mexican population constituted a minority within the geographically defined settlement (Baba and Abonyi, 1979; Badillo, 2003; Knoll, 1974; Salas and Salas, 1974; Weeks and Spielberg Benitez, 1979).

In the 1970s the Mexican "barrio" was often compared with the black ghetto. However, the black ghetto was a place where blacks constituted the numerical majority (Darden, 1981). The Mexican barrio in Detroit was less like the black ghetto than like the European ethnic enclaves described by Philpott (1978) and Peach (1996). According to Philpott, many European ethnic groups lived in concentrated areas that were identified as the "place of residence" of their particular ethnic group, although they rarely constituted a majority of the population in those areas. Philpott concluded that, in Chicago in the 1930s, among European groups, only the Polish Chicago population had a majority of Poles living in Polish neighborhoods (census tracts). Other European ethnic groups did not have a majority of their group residing in census tracts. This led Peach to conclude that such neighborhoods were not "true ghettos" in the tradition of black ghettos. Therefore, we conclude that the Mexican settlements in Detroit in 1970 most closely resembled European ethnic enclaves, which have been defined as concentrations with 30 percent (Peach, 1996) or 40 percent (Allen and Turner, 2009) of the population of the census tract comprised of a single ethnic group.

Based on the characteristics of the Mexican settlement in Detroit, Skendzel (1980) disagrees with the ethnic enclave label. The author instead prefers to call the Mexican settlement a "colony" because unlike other immigrant settlements, according to Skendzel, the Mexican settlement was not a geographically formed "Little Mexico" with definite, clearly defined quarters of the city, nor did it have its own national churches and schools and social institutions or its own exclusive commercial establishments (Skendzel, 1980). It was also not a closely knit social organization. In other words, it was not like a "Little Italy" or "Little Poland" (Skendzel, 1980).

Following the civil disorders of the 1960s, the application of the concept "internal colony" to define ghettos and barrios was widely discussed (Blauner, 1969) as an appropriate label due to the area's powerless relationship with the larger, predominantly white society. In describing the characteristics of the "colony," Skendzel (1980) stated that the settlement was lower working class with few professionals (doctors, attorneys, journalists, and business owners). There were medical, dental, and legal clinics. There were two public schools, two private high schools, four newly established community service agencies, and several active churches (Pop and Steider, 1970). Among the retail stores were restaurants, bakeries, bars, dance halls, record shops, barbershops, tamale and tortilla factories, and a movie theater (Knoll, 1974). Knoll (1974) noted that in the past, there was little evidence of community leadership and cohesiveness, but in 1970, a small number of residents started to identify the "community" as an entity.

The Mexicans who settled in Detroit had many handicaps to achieving social mobility. They spoke little English, had a limited amount of education, and were not familiar with white urban middle-class values. According to Skendzel (1980), unlike white European ethnic groups, because Mexicans are of mixed race Indian and white and called "mestizo," they experienced discrimination from whites due to their race. In this sense, the author argues that Mexicans were as much a victim of injustice as were blacks in Detroit. However, due to their smaller population, racial discrimination was not as strong as it was against the blacks

(Skendzel, 1980). According to Blalock's (1967) theory of minority group relations, the size of a minority group does matter in explaining the severity of majority group discrimination toward the minority group.

Skendzel (1980) also notes that discrimination against Mexicans varied by skin color, that is, the darker-skinned Mexicans faced the greatest amount of discrimination in housing (Skendzel, 1980). On these points, we think the author makes a very credible argument. The penalty for darker skin color has also been found in the labor market. Hersch (2008) examined data from the New Immigrant Survey for 2003 to determine whether immigrant workers with darker skin color have lower pay than their counterparts with lighter skin color and whether the pay difference was due to labor market discrimination. Hersch (2008) controlled for Hispanic ethnicity, race, country of birth, education, family background, occupation in the source country, English proficiency, visa status, employer characteristics, and current occupation. Hersch (2008) found that immigrants with the lightest skin color earn on average 17 percent higher wages than comparable immigrants with the darkest skin color. More importantly, the analyses of the data revealed that the difference in pay could not be explained by characteristics related to labor market productivity and personal background. Instead, the penalty for darker skin color was due to color discrimination in the U.S. labor market. Other studies (Darden, 1989, 2009b) have also found that the degree to which racial minorities have been discriminated against has been related to differences in skin color and size of the minority group. Usually, the larger the size of the minority group, the greater the "threat" to the status of the white majority and the greater the resistance to equal employment opportunities, housing integration, and access to equal neighborhoods (Darden, 2009b).

The Location of Detroit's Hispanic Settlement, 2010

In 2010, the location of Detroit's Hispanic settlement was still in the southwest region of the census tracts in Map 1 (table 10). All of the tracts are more than 50 percent Hispanic and

Table 10. Hispanic settlement in Detroit in 2010

Tract number	Total population	Number Hispanic	Percent Hispanic
5211	2,080	1,067	51.3
5231	1,648	1,032	62.6
5233	3,326	2,554	76.8
5234	2,720	1,411	51.9
5240	2,985	2,258	75.6
5241	3,942	2,760	70.0
5257	5,004	3,624	72.40
Total	21,705	14,706	67.7

Note: In this table "Hispanic" refers to Hispanics or Latinos of any race.

Source: U.S. Bureau of the Census (2011a).

would therefore qualify as a Hispanic "ghetto" under the definition used to describe majority-black concentrations (Darden, 1981; Peach, 1996).

In 2010 this area had a total population of 21,705 people, of whom 14,706, or 67.7 percent, were Hispanic. Moreover, of the 48,679 total Hispanic population of Detroit, 30 percent resided in this area of the city in 2010 (U.S. Bureau of the Census, 2011a).

The remaining sections of this chapter will shed more light on the differences and similarities between Hispanics and blacks in the city of Detroit. Of the total Hispanics in the city, 75 percent are of Mexican origin. We begin with the differences in the extent of residential segregation.

HISPANIC AND BLACK RESIDENTIAL SEGREGATION IN DETROIT, 1980–2010

This chapter uses indexes based on the most common methods of measuring residential segregation, that is, the index of dissimilarity. The index ranges from 0, or no residential segregation, to 100, or complete residential segregation. (For the method of index computation, see the appendix). The index is a summary measure of the spatial distribution of two population groups over census tracts. It can be interpreted, for example, as the percentage of total blacks and the percentage of total Hispanics who would have to change census tracts to make the population distribution even, or nonsegregated, throughout the city.

Since at least 1980, after Detroit became a majority black city, Hispanics (largely Mexicans) have been *less* residentially segregated from whites than from blacks. In 1980, the index of dissimilarity between Hispanics and blacks was 67.5, and 52.3 between Hispanics and non-Hispanic whites. In 1990, the black versus Hispanic index increased to 75.1, while increasing to 54.0 between Hispanics and whites. By 2010, Hispanics residential segregation from whites had increased slightly, from 58 in 2000 to 59.4.

On the other hand, blacks became less residentially segregated from whites. The black-White index declined from 63.3 in 2000 to 59.2 in 2010, thus matching the level of Hispanic-white residential segregation. Hispanics also became even more segregated from blacks. The index had increased from to 67.5 in 1980 to 81.6 in 2000. From 2000 to 2010, the index increased to 82.2.

From 1980 to 2010, the Hispanic population of Detroit increased by 68 percent, from 28,970 in 1980 to 48,679 in 2010. The percentage of Hispanics increased from 2.4 percent to 6.8 percent (table 11). On the other hand, the number of blacks in the city declined by 22 percent, from 754,274 in 1980 to 586,573 in 2010 (U.S. Bureau of the Census, 2011a). Blacks constituted 82 percent of Detroit's total population in 2010 (table 12).

Table 11. **Residential segregation trends in Detroit, 1980–2010, blacks, whites, and Hispanics (index of dissimilarity)**

Year	Black vs. white	Hispanic vs. white	Black vs. Hispanic
1980	67.4	52.3	67.5
1990	64.8	54.0	75.1
2000	63.3	58.3	81.6
2010	59.2	59.4	82.2

Note: In this table "Hispanic" refers to Hispanics or Latinos of any race.

Source: Darden, Stokes, and Thomas (2007); Logan and Stults (2010); U.S. Bureau of the Census (2011a).

Table 12. **Number and percentage black and Hispanic populations in Detroit, 1980–2010**

Year	Number black	Percent black	Number Hispanic	Percent Hispanic
1980	754,267	63.0	28,970	2.4
1990	774,529	76.0	28,473	2.8
2000	782,837	81.5	47,167	5.0
2010	596,963	82.2	48,679	6.8

Note: In this table "Hispanic" refers to Hispanics or Latinos of any race.

Source: Darden, Stokes, and Thomas (2007); Logan and Stults (2011); U.S. Bureau of the Census (2011a).

DIFFERENCE BETWEEN HISPANIC AND BLACK SOCIOECONOMIC STATUS, 1970–2010

Occupational Status

Only three years after the riots, evidence of inequality existed between blacks and Hispanics. Within the occupational structure, Hispanics had a higher percentage of workers (11.5) than blacks (7.8) in professional, technical, and kindred jobs. Compared to blacks, Hispanics also had a higher percentage of workers in managerial and administrative positions (4.5 percent compared to 2.4 percent). These were the highest-status positions in the city, and Hispanics were more likely than blacks to be represented in them.

Among blue-collar workers, Hispanics had a higher percentage (13.8 percent) in crafts-man, foreman, and similar positions than blacks . Blacks were only 9.6 percent of workers in these positions. Instead, blacks were more represented than Hispanics in such low-end positions as service workers and private household workers (table 13). The index of dissimilarity, when measuring unevenness in the distribution of blacks and Hispanics over occupational categories was 8.8 in 1970.

By 2000, the percentage of Hispanics in management, professional, and related occupations declined to 11.9 percent, from 16 percent in 1970, whereas the percentage of blacks in these occupations increased from 10.2 percent in 1970 to 20.9 percent in 2000. Thus, blacks exceeded Hispanics in the most prestigious occupations in 2000 by nine

Table 13. Occupational differences between Hispanics and blacks in Detroit, 1970

Occupation	Number Hispanic	% total Hispanic workers	Number black	% total black workers	Absolute difference in percentages
Professional, technical, and kindred workers	1,001	11.5	17,527	7.8	3.7
Managers and administration, except farm	388	4.5	5,416	2.4	2.1
Sales workers	377	4.3	6,586	2.9	1.4
Clerical and kindred workers	1,403	16.1	37,536	16.8	–0.7
Craftsmen, foremen, and kindred workers	1,200	13.8	21,396	9.6	4.2
Operatives, except transport	2,246	25.8	62,769	28.0	–2.2
Transport equipment operators	371	4.3	10,733	4.8	–0.5
Laborers, except farm	601	6.9	14,528	6.5	0.4
Farm workers	N/A	N/A	N/A	0.0	0.0
Service workers except private household	1067	12.3	39,128	17.5	5.2
Private household workers	49	0.6	7,580	3.4	–2.8
Total	8,703	100.0	223,909	100.0	23.2[*]

[*]Index of dissimilarity = $1/2$ (23.2), or 11.6.
Note: In this table "Hispanic" refers to Hispanics or Latinos of any race.

Source: Computed by the authors from data obtained from U.S. Bureau of the Census (1972).

percentage points. In service occupations, there was no difference in the representation of blacks and Hispanics.

However, in construction, extraction, and maintenance occupations, Hispanics exceeded blacks (20 percent compared to 6 percent). Hispanics also had a higher percentage than blacks in production, transportation, and material moving occupations (29.9 percent compared to 22.8 percent).

The index of dissimilarity measuring the occupational inequality between blacks and Hispanics in all occupations increased from 11.6 in 1970 to 22.6 in 2000 (tables 13 and 14).

Table 14. Occupational differences between Hispanics and blacks in Detroit, 2000

Occupation	Number Hispanic	% total Hispanic workers	Number black	% total black workers	Absolute difference in percentages
Management, professional, and related	1,915	11.9	55,431	20.9	–9.0
Service	3,546	22.0	58,502	22.0	0
Sales and office	2,306	14.4	74,480	28.0	–13.6
Farming, fishing, and forestry	242	1.5	277	0.1	1.4
Construction, extraction, and maintenance	3,245	20.2	16,212	6.1	14.1
Transportation and material moving	4,807	29.9	60,383	22.8	7.1
Total	26,061	100.0	265,285	100.0	45.2*

*Index of dissimilarity = $\frac{1}{2}$ (45.2) = 22.6.
Note: In this table "Hispanic" refers to Hispanics or Latinos of any race.

Source: Computed by the authors from data obtained from U.S. Bureau of the Census (2002).

For 2008, we present the percentage of Hispanics and the percentage of blacks in managerial and professional positions only. These positions are at the top of the status hierarchy. We found that 21.7 percent of blacks held these positions, compared to only 5.7 percent of Hispanics, a difference of sixteen percentage points, or a ratio of 3.8. Thus, blacks were more than three times more likely than Hispanics to hold managerial and professional positions in Detroit in 2008. Thus, the occupational *gap* between blacks and Hispanics at the highest, most prestigious level had increased since 2000.

Unemployment and Median Family Income

In 1970, the Hispanic unemployment rate was 8.5 percent, compared to 10.3 percent for blacks. Over the decades the rate of unemployment increased for both groups, reaching its peak in the 1980s and 1990s. By 2000, the Hispanic unemployment rate was 13.2 percent, compared to a rate of 14.7 percent for blacks. Thus, the gap in the unemployment rate narrowed from a ratio of 0.82 in 1987 to 0.93 in 2000, where a ratio of 1.00 would be equality (table 15). It is important to note, however, that throughout the entire period of 1970–2000, the Hispanic unemployment rate remained lower than the black unemployment rate despite the fact that Detroit was a predominantly black city. By 2005–9, the unemployment rate for Hispanics had increased to 18.0 percent, while the black unemployment rate had increased to 24.0 percent.

Table 15. Differences between Hispanic and black unemployment rates in Detroit, 1970, 1990, 2000, and 2005–2009

Year	Hispanic	Black	Difference ratio
1970	8.5	10.3	0.82
1990	20.4	22.2	0.90
2000	13.2	14.7	0.93
2005–9	18.0	24.0	0.75

Note: In this table "Hispanic" refers to Hispanics or Latinos of any race.

Source: U.S. Bureau of the Census (1972, 1990, 2000, 2010).

As the relative unemployment rates might suggest, Hispanic household income continued to be higher than black median household income between 1970 and 2009. In 1970, the median household income of Hispanics was $9,672, compared to $8,645 for blacks, a ratio of 1.12. By 2005–9, the median household income of Hispanics had increased to $31,378, while black median household income increased to $29,128, resulting in a ratio of 1.07. Thus, black and Hispanic income differences persisted over the decades and income equality had not been reached by 2009. Thus, blacks still earned less than Hispanics by an average of $2,250 (table 16).

Table 16. Hispanic and black median household income in Detroit, 1970 to 2005–2009

Year	Hispanic	Black	Difference ratio
1970	$9,672	$8,645	1.12
1980	$16,195	$15,403	1.05
1990	$20,164	$17,767	1.13
2000	$30,108	$29,408	1.02
2005–9	$31,378[*]	$29,128[*]	1.07

[*]Inflation-adjusted dollars for 2009 median household income.
Note: In this table "Hispanic" refers to Hispanics or Latinos of any race.

Source: U.S. Bureau of the Census (1972, 1980, 1990, 2000, 2010).

Poverty Rates

Consistent with a lower unemployment rate and higher median household income, Hispanics also had a lower poverty rate than blacks in 1970. The poverty rate for Hispanics was 11.1 percent, compared to 18.7 percent for blacks for a ratio of 0.59. However, over the decades, the poverty rate among Hispanics increased to 27.8 percent by 2000, whereas the poverty rate among blacks increased to 26.4 percent. Thus, by 2000 the Hispanic poverty rate exceeded the black poverty rate (table 17). However, by 2005–9, the gap between the Hispanic and black poverty rate had changed in favor of Hispanics as the black poverty rate increased more than the Hispanic poverty rate. The Hispanic poverty rate increased to 31.1 percent, compared to an increase in the black poverty rate to 33.5 percent, for a ratio of 0.93.

Table 17. Percentage of Hispanic and black families below poverty level in Detroit, 1970, 2000, and 2005–2009

Year	Hispanic	Black	Ratio*
1970	11.1	18.7	0.59
2000	27.8	26.4	1.05
2005–9	31.1	33.5	0.93

*A ratio less than 1.0 = Hispanics have a lower rate of poverty; a ratio greater than 1.0 = Hispanics have a higher rate of poverty.
Note: In this table "Hispanic" refers to Hispanics or Latinos of any race.

Source: U.S. Bureau of the Census (1972, 2010).

Educational Attainment

Over the entire period of 1970 to 2005–9, blacks exceeded Hispanics in the level of educational attainment as measured by the percentage of each group's population attaining a bachelor's degree or higher level of education.

By 2000, the percentage of Hispanics that had attained a bachelor's degree or higher was 5.7 percent, compared to 9.8 percent for blacks, for a ratio of 0.58 (table 18).

Table 18. Percentage of black and Hispanic population of Detroit 25 years and over with a bachelor's degree or higher, 2000 and 2005–2009

Year	Hispanic	Black	Ratio*
2000	5.7	9.8	0.58
2005–9	5.3	10.6	0.50

*A ratio of less than 1.0 = Hispanics have lower educational attainment.
Note: In this table "Hispanic" refers to Hispanics or Latinos of any race.

Source: U.S. Bureau of the Census (2004, 2010).

In 2005–9, the percentage of Hispanics with a bachelor's degree or higher declined to 5.3 percent, compared to an increase among blacks to 10.6 percent, for a ratio of 0.50. This change left Hispanics twice *less* likely than blacks to have a bachelor's degree or higher level of education (table 18). Does the lower level of Hispanic bachelor's degree holders suggest that Hispanic students in Detroit have a lower level of academic achievement than black students?

Academic Achievement among Hispanic and Black Students in Detroit, 2008

Research suggest that Hispanics and blacks lag behind whites and Asians in academic achievement (Roscigno, 2000). Indeed, racial disparities in achievement at both elementary and high school levels persist. According to Roscigno (2000), the lower academic achievement is in part related to the fact that black and Hispanic students are more likely to attend schools in cities that are highly segregated from whites and are also poorer.

Since both blacks and Hispanics experience lower levels of academic achievement, the focus of this section is to determine whether in a predominantly black city, with a predominantly black school board and administrators, Hispanics have achieved a level of academic achievement equal to that of blacks in Detroit, a poor, highly racially segregated city.

The source of data to answer that question is the Michigan Department of Education's Michigan Educational Assessment Program (MEAP) tests for 2008. The scores for blacks and Hispanics were compared in the fields of math, reading, and writing for grades 3, 6, and 8, and science for grade 8 only.

The results revealed that for grade 3, in math, Hispanic students scored higher than black students. The percentage of black students that met or exceeded the standards for math performance was 73.6 percent, compared to 82.7 percent for Hispanic students, for a gap of 9.1 percentage points (tables 19 and 20).

On the other hand, black third-grade students scored higher than Hispanic students in reading and writing. The percentage of black students that met or exceeded the standards for reading was 72 percent, compared to 68.4 percent for Hispanics, for a gap of 3.6 percentage points. In writing, 38.2 percent of black students met or exceeded the standards, compared to 36 percent for Hispanics, for a gap of 2.2 percentage points (tables 19 and 20).

In grade 6 math, 56.7 percent of Hispanics met or exceeded expectations, compared to 53.5 percent of black students, for a gap of 3.2 percentage points. In reading, 56.6 percent of black students met or exceeded the standards, compared to 52.4 percent for Hispanics, for a

Table 19. Hispanic and black MEAP scores in Detroit Public Schools, grade 3, fall 2008

Group	Subject	Average score, city	Average score, state	% met/exceeded standards
All students	Math	315	331	75
Black	Math	315	317	74
Hispanic	Math	316	322	83
All students	Reading	317	331	72
Black	Reading	317	319	72
Hispanic	Reading	313	321	68
All students	Writing	294	303	38
Black	Writing	294	296	38
Hispanic	Writing	293	298	36

Note: In this table "Hispanic" refers to Hispanics or Latinos of any race.

Source: Computed by the authors from data obtained from Michigan Department of Education (2009).

Table 20. Comparison between Hispanic and black students MEAP scores in Detroit Public Schools, fall 2008

	Grade 3	*Difference in % met/exceeded standards*
Math	9.1	Hispanics favored
Reading	3.6	Blacks favored
Writing	2.2	Blacks favored
Grade 6		
Math	3.2	Hispanics favored
Reading	4.2	Blacks favored
Writing	2.7	Hispanics favored
Grade 8		
Math	7.9	Hispanics favored
Reading	11	Hispanics favored
Science	14.4	Hispanics favored
Writing	8.4	Hispanics favored

Note: In this table "Hispanic" refers to Hispanics or Latinos of any race.

Source: Computed by the authors from data obtained from Michigan Department of Education (2009).

gap of 4.2 percentage points. However, in writing, 54.9 percent of Hispanics met or exceeded the standards, compared to 52.2 percent for black students, for a difference of 2.7 percentage points (tables 20 and 21).

Among eighth-grade students, in math, the percentage of Hispanic students who met or exceeded the standards was 53.6 percent, compared to only 45.7 percent for black students, for a gap of 7.9 percentage points. In fact, in reading, science, and writing, the percentage of Hispanics who met or exceeded the standards was higher than the percentage for black students. In reading, for example, 64 percent of Hispanics met or exceeded the standards, compared to 53 percent for blacks, for a gap of 11 percentage points. The academic achievement gap was widest between black and Hispanic students in science. While only 47.6 percent of black students met or exceeded the standards, 62 percent of Hispanics did, for a gap of 14.4 percentage points. The percentage who met or exceeded the standards in writing was 60.7 percent for Hispanics, compared to 52.3 percent for blacks, for a gap of 8.4 percentage points (tables 20 and 21).

In sum, only at the third-grade level do black students achieve at a higher level than Hispanic students in two subject areas—reading and writing. On the other hand, Hispanic students achieve at a higher level than black students in math at grades 3, 6, and 8. Moreover, eighth-grade Hispanic students achieve at a higher level than black students in all four subject areas (tables 20 and 21).

It appears that in the city of Detroit, a predominantly black city with a predominantly black school board and administrators, Hispanic students still achieve academically at a higher level than black students. It is also important to note that both Hispanic and black students, and indeed white students in the Detroit Public Schools, generally score lower on MEAP tests in all subjects than students in the state as a whole (tables 20, 21, and 22).

Table 21. Hispanic and black MEAP scores in Detroit Public Schools, grade 6, fall 2008

Group	*Subject*	*Average score, city*	*Average score, state*	*% met/exceeded standards*
All students	Math	605	624	54
Black	Math	605	609	54
Hispanic	Math	606	614	57
All students	Reading	605	625	56
Black	Reading	605	610	57
Hispanic	Reading	603	614	52
All students	Writing	601	610	53
Black	Writing	600	603	52
Hispanic	Writing	601	605	55

Note: In this table "Hispanic" refers to Hispanics or Latinos of any race.

Source: Computed by the authors from data obtained from Michigan Department of Education (2009).

Table 22. Hispanic and black MEAP scores in Detroit Public Schools, grade 8, fall 2008

Group	*Subject*	*Average score, city*	*Average score, state*	*% met/exceeded standards*
All students	Math	800	819	47
Black	Math	799	802	46
Hispanic	Math	803	809	54
All students	Reading	803	820	54
Black	Reading	803	805	53
Hispanic	Reading	808	810	64
All students	Science	801	820	49
Black	Science	800	802	48
Hispanic	Science	807	810	62
All students	Writing	801	811	53
Black	Writing	801	802	52
Hispanic	Writing	804	806	61

Note: In this table "Hispanic" refers to Hispanics or Latinos of any race.

Source: Computed by the authors from data obtained from Michigan Department of Education (2009).

Homeownership and Housing Value

The homeownership rate among Hispanics and blacks has fluctuated since 1970. In 1970, the Hispanic homeownership rate was 26.6 percent, compared to a black homeownership rate of 24.7 percent. By 1980, the rates were essentially the same (24 percent). By 2000, the Hispanic homeownership rate slightly exceeded the rate for blacks (54.9 percent compared to 53.4 percent) (table 23). By 2005–9 the Hispanic homeownership rate had declined to 48.7 percent, thus falling behind the 54.1 percent rate for blacks (table 23).

Table 23. Hispanic and black homeownership in Detroit, 1970 to 2005–2009

Year	Hispanic	Black	Ratio[*]
1970	26.6	24.7	1.07
1980	24.2	24.3	0.99
1990	46.3	49.0	0.94
2000	54.9	53.4	1.02
2005–9	48.7	54.1	0.90

[*]A ratio less than 1.0 = Hispanics have lower rate of homeownership; a ratio greater than 1.0 = Hispanics have higher rate of homeownership.
Note: In this table "Hispanic" refers to Hispanics or Latinos of any race.

Source: U.S. Bureau of the Census (1972, 1980, 1990, 2000, 2010).

Housing value of Hispanic-occupied housing has consistently been below the housing value of black-occupied housing over the decades. In 2000, the median value of Hispanic-occupied housing was $45,700, compared to $65,100 for black-occupied housing (table 24). Finally, in 2008, the value of Hispanic-occupied housing increased to $79,800 and the value of black-occupied housing increased to $89,600, for a ratio of 0.89. This is one of the socioeconomic indicators where Hispanics have not done as well as blacks over the entire study period (1980–2008) (table 24).

Table 24. Median value of Hispanic and black owner-occupied housing in Detroit, 1980–2008

Year	Hispanic	Black	Difference ratio
1980	$19,400	$22,400	0.86
1990	$18,300	$27,100	0.67
2000	$45,700	$65,100	0.70
2008	$79,800	$89,600	0.89

Note: In this table "Hispanic" refers to Hispanics or Latinos of any race.

Source: U.S. Bureau of the Census (1972, 1980, 1990, 2004, 2009b).

Differences in Business Participation Rates, 2002

Like other factors discussed in this book, *place matters* in business participation rates. Thus, the characteristics of a place are key to understanding business participation by Hispanics and blacks. Blacks have dominated the city of Detroit in population size since at least 1980. There is some evidence that suggests that *demographic dominance* can be a substitute for social capital, creating economic benefits to the black majority, including self-employment. Citing the historical case of the great migration north, several scholars contend that the black increase in population in certain sections of cities, coupled with racial solidarity, did indeed lead to an increase in rates of black self-employment from the turn of the century to the Great Depression (Butler, 1991; Kusmer, 1976; Marable, 1983; Walker, 1998).

Studies have also shown that black mayors (a product of black demographic dominance and political solidarity) were responsible for the initial opening of the government-procurement market to black-owned businesses (Bates, 1997; Woodard, 1997). For example, in cities with black majorities, policies were passed that increased financial support for black business expansion. Such policies included loans, technical assistance, set-aside programs, and training (Bates, 1997). Black business participation has also been enhanced by black mayors who advocated policies and practices that ensured the inclusion of minorities and women in the bidding process for city contracts (Gavrilovich and McGraw, 2000). Because blacks usually have limited financial and/or social capital compared to immigrant groups (Light and Gold, 2000), black demographic dominance and black political control may serve as an effective alternative to traditional social capital, thus influencing the rate of black business ownership.

Social scientists have advanced at least four theories to explain minority business ownership in general. One is the *cultural theory*, which argues that there exists a cultural element within the minority group that predisposes its members to engage in entrepreneurial activities (Light, 1980). A second theory is the *middleman theory*, which states that minority groups, especially immigrants, are often constrained by the elites and forced to occupy the position of middleman by playing the role of conduits to the masses for the delivery of goods and services usually controlled by the elites (Bonacich, 1973). A third perspective is the *disadvantage theory*. It argues that self-employment is a survival strategy that evolves when minorities encounter impenetrable barriers in the formal labor markets (Light, 1980). Finally, there is the *opportunity structures theory*. It argues that minority business ownership is a function of structural constraints (related to race, ethnicity, and *place*) such as market conditions, discrimination, residential segregation, and group size. Such structural conditions provide a protected market niche in a *place* that serves to enhance minority business ownership by catering to the particular needs of the minority group population (Aldrich and Waldinger, 1990; Brimmer, 1968; Light, 1972).

Hispanics under Black Demographic Dominance

This section examines whether black *demographic dominance* in the city of Detroit has hindered Hispanic business ownership by providing advantages to black-owned businesses, thereby contributing to Hispanic versus black inequality in the business sector. In other words, have Hispanics been disadvantaged in business ownership within a predominantly black city? The results may contribute to a better understanding of how disadvantages operate among two minority groups, both with a history of discrimination against them (Gold, 2004), and where one group has *demographic dominance* and political control in the city.

Our data were obtained from the U.S. Bureau of the Census 2002 Survey of Business Owners: Black Owned Firms (2006a) and Hispanic Owned Firms (2006b) and the U.S. Census of Population and Housing for 2000 (2002).

Results

Although Detroit is a majority black city, Hispanics have been more successful than blacks in the area of business ownership with paid employees. In 2002, blacks owned 19,530 total firms, which resulted in a business participation rate (BPR) of 25.17. On the other hand, Hispanic owned firms numbered 955, which resulted in a BPR of 20.25. Only 6.1 percent of all black-owned firms had paid employees, however, compared to 15.3 percent of all Hispanic-owned firms.

When employer firms, that is, firms with paid employees, are examined, blacks had 1,199 firms for a BPR of 1.55. On the other hand, Hispanics had 146 firms for a BPR of 3.10, that is, twice the BPR of black-owned firms (table 25).

Table 25. **Black- and Hispanic-owned businesses in Detroit, 2002**

	Black	*Hispanic*
Population	775,772	47,167
Total firms	19,530	955
Total firms BPR	25.17	20.25
Employer firms	1,199	146
Employer firms BPR	1.55	3.10
Number of employees	11,706	1,268
Nonemployer firms BPR	23.63	17.17
Average receipts per firm (all firms)	$81,085	$196,172
Employer firms average receipts per firm	$1,113,117	$1,231,973
Nonemployer firms average receipts per firm	$13,582	$9,230
% of firms that are employer firms	6.1	15.3

Note: In this table "Hispanic" refers to Hispanics or Latinos of any race. BPR (business representation ratio) is the number of black- or Hispanic-owned firms divided by the total black or Hispanic population in Detroit multiplied by 1,000. Employer firms are defined as firms with paid employees.

Source: Computed by the authors from data obtained from U.S. Bureau of the Census (2006a, 2006b).

HISPANICS' STRUGGLE FOR GREATER REPRESENTATION IN THE MAJORITY BLACK CITY: THEIR RELATIONSHIP WITH NEW DETROIT

Why were blacks less successful than Hispanics in ownership of firms with paid employees even in a majority black city with a majority black administration? The answer may be related to political activism of Hispanics to ensure their share of the resources and support, if not from the city, from influential nonprofit organizations that grew out of the riots of 1967.

Hispanics actively complained over the years about a lack of political representation on such boards as New Detroit—a coalition of urban leaders organized after the Detroit riots of 1967. The urban coalition was composed of industrial leaders, state and local elected officials, community organizational representatives, labor officials, and educators (Darden, Stokes and Thomas, 2007). Back in 1981, Augin Arbulu, the chairperson of the Hispanic Business Alliance, complained that the urban coalition had only two Hispanics on its seventy-two-member board, which included twenty blacks, and the coalition gave inadequate attention to the "Spanish speaking community" (Gebert, 1981a). Arbulu also charged that New Detroit's annual allocation of funds for the Inner City Business Improvement Forum primarily served black entrepreneurs (Gebert, 1981a).

The Hispanic alliance, composed of Hispanic business and professional leaders, called for at least 20 percent representation on New Detroit's board (Gebert, 1981a). It also called for at least one Hispanic to be appointed to its management team as vice president, more Hispanics appointed to its staff, and earmarking of at least 20 percent of its budget for Hispanic programs (Gebert, 1981a).

New Detroit denied that there was anti-Hispanic bias. Walter Douglas, the president of New Detroit in 1981, angrily denied that New Detroit favored blacks and gave only "token attention" to the city's Hispanics. Douglas stated that "although blacks are the dominant group in the city, New Detroit does not favor blacks over any other group. Instead, it expresses concerns for all minority groups and encourages business and industry to assist them whenever possible" (Gebert, 1981b: 1). At the time, there were no Arabs or Chaldeans on New Detroit's board, although they also were part of the city's business community and general population (Gebert, 1981a, 1981b).

Douglas responded to the Hispanic Alliance's demand that New Detroit appoint a Hispanic to the organization's management team by saying, "I reserve the right as president to select persons who are best for the management team. That has nothing to do with ethnicity" (Gebert, 1981a, 1981b). Douglas also denied that New Detroit's annual allocation of more than $300,000 to the Inner City Business Improvement Forum served primarily black entrepreneurs.

The pressure for more Hispanic representation and influence had come from the Hispanic Business Alliance and not the Latino Caucus, a group New Detroit created in 1973. Douglas considered the Hispanic Business Alliance a "narrow self-interested group" that was not representative of Detroit's Latinos (Gebert, 1981a, 1981b). Douglas instead preferred to listen to the Latino Caucus, composed primarily of Hispanics who participated in the various operating committees of New Detroit. The goal of the Latino Caucus was to review the activities of New Detroit and ensure that those activities positively impacted the Hispanic community in Detroit. The role of the caucus was one of *advocacy* within New Detroit. It assisted both in identifying Hispanics for appointments to various committees and in monitoring and reporting the implementation of the Hispanic Leadership Program, whose objective was to identify, train, and place potential Hispanic leaders on the city's boards, committees, and private/non-profit agencies (New Detroit, 1983a).

Yet in May 1981, the Latino Caucus of New Detroit filed a complaint of racial discrimination with the Michigan Department of Civil Rights, charging New Detroit with systematically excluding Hispanics except for a token few (Lamarre, 1981).

The core of the complaint between Latinos and blacks in a majority black city was "trust." Horatio Vargas, director of New Detroit's Latin Affairs Division, stated, "I don't think that at this point Hispanics trust Blacks or Blacks trust Hispanics" (Wilson, 1983b: 1). The lack of trust seemed to center around the belief by some Hispanics that blacks wanted to monopolize the struggle for civil rights without recognizing that the struggle for Mexican American civil rights was occurring at the same time in the Southwest as the black struggle in the South. On the other hand, some blacks believed that most Hispanics consider themselves "white," and therefore may have acted as such toward blacks (Wilson, 1983: 1).

But where there was mistrust, some Hispanics and blacks concluded that it was usually fueled by a lack of information and pessimism, which became roadblocks to a coalition of blacks and Hispanics. Because of the fragility and lack of trust that exists in the formative stage of a coalition, Dr. Charles Wright, a Detroit physician, advised the two groups to start off slowly with things such as cultural activities (Wilson, 1983b).

Following the complaint in 1981, later that year New Detroit submitted a proposal to the Dayton Hudson Foundation to create a Hispanic Leadership Development Project. The proposal was funded to develop the leadership skills of Hispanics in the Detroit tri-county area (New Detroit Now, 1981). The total cost of the project was $120,000, the funds supplied by contributions from New Detroit and the J. L. Hudson Company (New Detroit Now, 1981). Detroit was one of three cities in the United States to receive funding from the Dayton Hudson Foundation for a Hispanic Leadership Development program. New Detroit acted as fiduciary for the program and provided placement assistance, program instruction, the funding of speakers, and other resources.

New Detroit also assisted Latino outreach in linking up with the K-Mart Corporation, which in 1984 donated a building to house New Detroit's mental health, job placement, and youth and senior citizens programs, and office space for the organization's displaced homemakers program (New Detroit, 1985).

The coalition, then, was finally formed. The Hispanic Caucus was the primary link between the Hispanic community and New Detroit. In 1987–88, the Hispanic Caucus united with New Detroit's education, racial, and economic justice governmental affairs committees in opposition to federal and state efforts to make English the official language of the United States and the State of Michigan (New Detroit, 1988). In order to assist those undocumented immigrants who qualified for legalization under the 1986 Immigration Reform and Control Act, New Detroit helped draft a series of public service announcements that subsequently aired on television and radio (New Detroit, 1988).

Thus, although the success of Hispanic businesses compared to businesses owned by blacks may be attributed to many factors, one factor that also played a role was Hispanic activism and struggle for a share of the limited resources.

CONCLUSIONS

This chapter has examined the question of whether Hispanics in a majority black city are able to achieve an equal socioeconomic status with blacks, or if the socioeconomic status of Hispanics declined relative to the status of blacks after blacks became the demographic majority in Detroit. We used data from the U.S. Bureau of the Census for the period of 1970–2010, including the most recent American Community Survey data (2005–9). We also used Michigan's Department of Education MEAP downloadable data files for 2008 and the U.S. Bureau of the Census (2006a, 2006b) 2002 Survey of Business Owners, Black Owned and Hispanic Owned Firms.

We found that, on some socioeconomic indicators, Hispanics not only maintained equality with blacks, but exceeded them.

Hispanics maintained a higher median household income than blacks from 1970 to 2005–9. Their unemployment rate was also lower than the rate for blacks over the same time period. The Hispanic poverty rate was lower than the rate for blacks. Hispanics also have higher business participation rates than blacks, with Hispanics owning a higher percentage of businesses with paid employees.

Finally, Hispanic students exceed black students in academic performance in the Detroit Public Schools as measured by the Michigan's MEAP tests. Specifically, Hispanic students perform better than black students in third-, sixth-, and eighth-grade math. They also exceed black students in sixth-grade writing. Moreover, at the eighth-grade level, Hispanic students perform better than black students in all subject areas—math, reading, science, and writing.

The social and economic indicators where Hispanics have not achieved equality with blacks are in postsecondary educational attainment and occupational status as measured by the percentage of professional and managerial workers. Hispanics have consistently lagged behind blacks in the percentage of those twenty-five years and older who had a bachelor's degree or a higher level of education. Hispanics also have a lower percentage of workers in the highest-status occupation, that is, professional and managerial occupations.

In the area of housing, Hispanics have not achieved equality with blacks. Hispanics have lower homeownership rates and lower housing values than blacks. Moreover, although black residential segregation from whites has been decreasing since 1980, Hispanic residential segregation from whites has been increasing. As a result, by 2010, Hispanics and blacks had virtually the same levels of residential segregation from whites. Hispanics were even more segregated from blacks in 2010 than they were in 1980. It appears that as the Hispanic population in Detroit has increased substantially since 1980, the increase is occurring disproportionately in the Hispanic barrio, creating higher levels of residential segregation from both whites and blacks.

Based on all of the indicators explained, we conclude that the socioeconomic status of Hispanics has not necessarily been hindered due to their *place of residence* in a majority black city. On some indicators, Hispanics not only maintained equality with blacks but exceeded them. On the other hand, Hispanics lagged behind blacks and even became more unequal based on other indicators such as higher education, occupational status, and homeownership and housing value. Further study is needed to explain the major reasons for the differential patterns between Hispanics and blacks in the city of Detroit.

CHAPTER 10

Economic Restructuring, Black Deprivation, and the Problem of Drugs and Crime

THE PROCESS *OF ECONOMIC RESTRUCTURING* RESULTS IN A FUNDAMENTAL CHANGE TO the American economy. It involves a decline in manufacturing employment (which pays high wages) and an increase in service employment (which pays lower wages). This change has consequences both for employment opportunities for lower skilled workers and for the ability to earn an income to support a household. Such *economic restructuring* has severely impacted blue-collar workers in general and black workers in particular. The social and economic consequences of *economic restructuring* in the Detroit metropolitan area and the role played by *race and place* are the focus of this chapter.

RACE, SPACE, AND DECLINING EMPLOYMENT OPPORTUNITIES

Many blue-collar jobs that had, since World War II, constituted the economic backbone of Detroit and provided employment opportunities for Detroit's residents had, by the 1980s, either vanished or moved to the suburbs (Kasarda, 1989). Thus, since the riots of 1967, newer and better job opportunities were located further away from black neighborhoods in Detroit, forcing black families to spend more time and money commuting to work or looking for work outside of black neighborhoods (Darden, 1986).

Given that blacks in Detroit have more restricted residential location choices than whites, the cost associated with distance reduces access to some jobs. The net effect of these imposed travel costs is to reduce the effective wage that black city workers receive relative to suburban residents. Another cost imposed by the spatial separation of jobs and residences is that which central city blacks incur when searching for suburban employment, particularly in view of the limited information available about potential job opportunities. In addition, there is a tendency for employers to hire workers who reflect the racial character of the *place of residence* in which they are located—that is, there may also be an indirect effect of housing segregation on employment opportunities (Kain, 1968).

The problems of black residents in the city of Detroit are intensified by the fact that employment opportunities in blue-collar, semiskilled, and low-skilled jobs moved to the suburbs so rapidly that a surplus of labor in these categories had developed in the city by 1980 (McDonald, 1981). In other words, there has been a substantial shift in the occupational mix of jobs in Detroit, like other central cities (Kasarda, 1989; Wilson, 1987). There has been a decline in craftsman, operative, and laborer categories, while professional, sales, clerical, and service employment has increased proportionally in the city (Wilson, 1987). This decline of jobs in central cities has been most pronounced in Detroit and other cities in the north central region.

The City of Detroit's Share of the Metropolitan Region's Employment, 1967–2002

In 1967, Detroit had 35.8 percent of the region's retail employment. The city also had 57.9 percent of the wholesale employment and 60.5 percent of the service jobs. However, by 2002, Detroit's share of manufacturing employment had plummeted to 13.5 percent. Retail trade had fallen to 7.2 percent. Moreover, wholesale trade employment in Detroit dropped to 11.4 percent and Detroit's share of service jobs decreased from 60.5 percent to 12.9 percent (table 26).

The primary reason blacks have been impacted most severely economically is segregation, both occupational and residential. Black workers tend to be concentrated in production jobs, which is where the biggest industrial losses have occurred. Black production workers tend to be concentrated in older industrial plants, which are the ones most frequently closed (Darden et al., 1987).

Indeed, the suburbs were clearly *places* of economic opportunity, as evident by the locations of both establishments and jobs. Compared to the city, the percentage of establishments ranged from 81.4 percent for health care and social assistance to 91.6 percent for administrative support and waste management. The percentage of total paid employees ranged from 56.5 percent for arts, entertainment, and recreation to 92.9 percent for retail trade.

Table 26. Racial/ethnic differences in business ownership in Detroit, 2007

	# of all firms	# of all employer firms	# of employees	% of total ownership all firms	% of total ownership employer firms	% of total employees
Total	50,911	6,554	69,894			
White	15,668	4,957	55,471	30.7	75.6	79.4
Black	32,483	968	9,813	63.8	14.8	14.0
Hispanic*	316	70	374	0.6	1.1	0.5
Mexican	763	94	1,820	1.5	1.4	2.6
Asian	1,151	448	2,327	2.3	6.8	3.3
American Indian/ Alaskan Native	530	17	89	1.0	0.3	3.3

*In this table "Hispanic" refers to Hispanics or Latinos of any race, excluding Mexicans (since Mexicans are listed separately).

Source: U.S. Bureau of the Census (2011a).

Race, Population Distribution, and Economic Opportunities

There is a high correlation between the residential distribution of whites in metropolitan Detroit and the location of economic establishments and job locations. For example, 97.4 percent of all whites live in the suburbs. On the other hand, only 23 percent of all blacks reside in the suburbs. Thus, there is a specific difference in the location of economic opportunities and the residential location of blacks in metropolitan Detroit. This difference has been called *spatial mismatch*, a term coined by Kain (1968) based on data from Detroit and Chicago.

Kain's (1968) work on the distribution and movement of jobs and industry documented the widespread suburbanization of jobs, a pattern that was evident in the 1960s. At the same time that whites were moving from the central cities to the suburbs to be closer to jobs, because of discrimination in housing most blacks were restricted to the central city ghettos. As a result of discrimination, blacks (compared to whites) pay more on average for rent and consume less housing (Kain and Quigley, 1970). Further, because of constraints on movement to the suburbs, blacks live in different locations than whites (segregation) and also away from most white employers (spatial mismatch) (Kain and Quigley, 1970, 1972).

Kain (1968) believed that distance between black workers and jobs reduces black employment. Thus, black employment would rise, Kain believed, with distance from the black ghetto. Suburbanization of jobs, therefore, hurt black prospects for employment. Since the late 1960s there has been a continuing decentralization of jobs. Black workers, however, remain centralized, much as they were in the 1960s. While some researchers have debated the extent to which distance from jobs alone restricts black employment, in general, most researchers agree that spatial mismatch is a reality that continues to impact blacks differently (Glaeser, Hanushek, and Quigley, 2004). That is because the decentralization of jobs noted by Kain continues, and the effect on black employment is presently evident.

Katz (2004) noted that despite clear signs of renewal in many central cities, close examination of 2000 census data shows that the decentralization of jobs and economic activity remains the dominant growth pattern in the United States. New suburbs—built since the 1970s on the outer fringes of metropolitan areas—are capturing most of the employment and population growth (Berube, 2002).

Kain (1968) argued that the spatial distribution of black employment and the reduced job opportunities of urban blacks were the combined effects of housing segregation, caused by racial discrimination in housing (Moore and Laramore, 1990). Kain mentioned four reasons why housing market segregation may affect employment.

1. The distance to and difficulty of reaching suburban places may impose costs on blacks high enough to discourage them from seeking employment there.
2. Blacks may have less information about and less opportunity to learn about jobs distant from their place of residence or those of their friends. To support the second reason, Kain argued that few jobs are located from newspaper advertisements and employment offices. Workers most frequently learn about jobs from friends and other casual associations. Since blacks have few associations with white areas, the chances of blacks learning about distant job opportunities may be significantly lessened.
3. Employers located outside of black residential areas may discriminate against blacks.
4. Employers located near black areas may discriminate in favor of blacks.

A number of regression models were used to test the hypothesis that the central location of the Chicago and Detroit black concentrated areas and limitations on black residence outside these areas affect the location of black employment.

Kain (1968) concluded that housing market segregation clearly affects the distribution of black employment. However, its effect on the level of black employment and unemployment was more complex. Kain's view was that housing market segregation may reduce the level of black employment, thereby contributing to the high unemployment rates of metropolitan blacks, and that employment dispersal may further undermine their socioeconomic position. However, the results were too complex to be definitive at the time.

Other researchers have tested the spatial mismatch hypothesis, not only for effects on employment but also the effects on earnings and later workforce participation (Ellwood, 1986; Ihlanfeldt and Sjoquist, 1991). These studies and others have been reviewed by Holzer (1991), who evaluated twenty years of empirical research on the spatial mismatch hypothesis. Holzer focused on the effects of racial residential segregation of blacks in metropolitan areas, differential white versus black suburbanization, and differential suburbanization versus central city employment. He also examined the issue of "access" as measured by travel time. The preponderance of the evidence suggested that spatial mismatch was still relevant in explaining black/white employment differences, although the magnitudes of the effects remained unclear.

Holzer's (1991) review revealed that blacks in central city areas had less access to employment than blacks or whites in the suburbs, where access was measured by the ratio of jobs to people within neighborhoods and by average travel times. Employed blacks generally had higher commute times on average than employed whites (Holzer, 1991). As to the central issue, the extent to which spatial mismatch explains the lower wages or earnings of black males relative to white males, Holzer concluded that the empirical evidence remains very contradictory (Bound and Freeman, 1992).

Thus, the last half of the 1980s saw renewed interest in the spatial mismatch between jobs and residential location within metropolitan areas. The meta-reviews of authors who each covered twenty to fifty studies indicate that the empirical evidence in the 1990s continued to suggest that spatial mismatch is evident in longer commutes to work for blacks than for whites; lower wages on average for black workers than for white workers; and higher rates of unemployment for blacks than for whites (Holzer, 1991; Jencks and Mayer, 1990; Kain, 1992).

In 2000, metropolitan Detroit ranked second after metropolitan Ann Arbor among the metropolitan areas with the highest index between sprawl and mismatch. The index for metropolitan Detroit was 90.7. It was 98.1 for metropolitan Ann Arbor (Stoll, 2007). The white spatial mismatch index for the Detroit metropolitan area, on the other hand, was 36.5 (Raphael and Stoll, 2002). No other group was more physically isolated from jobs than blacks.

The spatial mismatch problem has been most severe for black teenagers who are least educated or skilled, which creates not only a spatial mismatch but a skills mismatch problem as well. Thus, the lower wages of black youth may be due to the shift in demand for low-wage jobs, and even these jobs are disproportionately located in the sprawling suburbs (Lemieux, 2006). Metropolitan areas with the highest levels of black-white residential segregation exhibited the highest degree of spatial mismatch between blacks and jobs. Metropolitan Detroit was the most residentially segregated area in the United States in 2000 with an index of dissimilarity of 85.9 (Logan and Stults, 2011). (For a discussion of the method of computation of the index of dissimilarity, see the appendix.) Although black residential segregation declined to an index of 79.6 by 2010, the Detroit metropolitan area still tied with Milwaukee as the most residentially segregated area in the country (Logan and Stults, 2011).

Blacks in metropolitan Detroit are also the most isolated among the fifty largest metro areas with large black populations. Blacks in 2010 had an isolation index of 80.9 (Logan and Stults, 2011). This means that the average black person in metropolitan Detroit lives in a census tract that is 81 percent black, which is similar to the isolation experienced by blacks in metropolitan Detroit in 1980 (Logan and Stults, 2011). Such uneven spatial distribution and spatial separation by race continues to place most blacks away from economic opportunities. Suburbs dominate employment growth as well as population growth. Employment decentralization has become the norm in American metropolitan areas. Across the largest 100 metro areas, an average of only 22 percent of people work within three miles of the city center, and more than 35 percent work more than ten miles from the central core. In Detroit, however, employment patterns have been radically altered, with more than 60 percent of the regional employment now located more than ten miles from the city center. The American economy is essentially becoming an "exit ramp economy," with new office, commercial, and retail facilities increasingly located along suburban freeways (Katz, 2004).

The residential movement of blacks to the suburbs where most of the jobs are contributed to the slight decline since 2000 in residential segregation, isolation, and spatial mismatch. Such movement may have other benefits, such as an increase in housing quality, school quality, and other amenities, in addition to fostering greater interracial contact (Raphael and Stoll, 2002). As the next chapter will show, housing quality, overall neighborhood quality, school quality, and other amenities all increase as one moves from the city of Detroit to the suburbs of Wayne and Oakland counties.

The evidence suggests that the location of most blacks in the predominantly black city contributes to spatial disparity between the city and the metropolitan area as a whole. In chapter 11, we examine this disparity in detail.

In sum, racial discrimination is a primary contributor to housing segregation. Housing segregation limits blacks' information about and access to suburban jobs, which hold the promise of stability, on-the-job training, decent pay, and socioeconomic advancement.

Racial discrimination in employment contributes to blacks' inferior rates of employment and wage levels. This occurs both directly and through discrimination's effect upon occupational segregation. Segregation of blacks into occupations associated with low pay, minimum on-the-job training or chances for advancement, and cyclical instability intensifies interracial economic disparities and enhances the probability of racial conflict (Darden, Duleep, and Galster, 1992).

Thus, by limiting the physical access to work, the means by which people become productive workers, and the occupations through which economic success is promoted, discrimination and segregation in housing and employment systematically create and perpetuate a host of socioeconomic inequalities between blacks and whites. These disparities manifest themselves in many ways, but perhaps most dramatically in higher black rates of poverty and unemployment and lower school and labor force participation (Darden et al., 1992).

These economic and social inequalities reinforce the stereotypes held by some whites and serve as a rationale for continuing white supremacy (Darden, 2009b). They legitimize white prejudices about the "undesirable characteristics" supposedly possessed by all members of the black population.

Such reinforced prejudices make it more likely that white households will want to perpetuate dimensions of segregation. Some may be unwilling to remain in their neighborhoods once blacks begin to move in or attend local schools. When seeking different accommodations, they may be reluctant to search in areas where blacks live or go to school. These actions directly reinforce housing segregation. Finally, white employees' hostility toward potential black workers might encourage employers to discriminate for the sake of maintaining workplace tranquility, or they may discriminate due to their own ideology of white supremacy (Bonilla-Silva, 2001). Their actions encourage the formation of informal networks for recruiting white employees (Darden et al., 1992).

Black households bear crushing costs from the perpetuation of this vicious cycle. One study estimated, for example, that if we could reduce housing segregation by 50 percent, the median income of black families would rise 24 percent (Galster and Keeney, 1988). Such low median black income puts a higher percentage of blacks than whites in concentrated poverty.

THE SPATIAL CONCENTRATION OF POVERTY: CHANGES OVER TIME

Concentrated poverty is defined as poverty rates of 40 percent or higher among a metropolitan area's poor in each racial category living in census tracts (neighborhoods) (Jargowsky, 1994). Researchers continue to debate whether the spatial concentration of black poverty is new or a continuing trend. Wilson (1987) argues that the concentration of black poverty is not only a post–World War II phenomenon, but it occurred in the 1980s as civil rights laws provided new opportunities for middle- and working-class blacks to move out of the ghetto in large numbers, leaving behind an isolated and truly disadvantaged black poor population lacking the institutions and human resources necessary for success. Massey and Denton (1993), on the other hand, have taken the opposite view. They argue that the geographic concentration of poverty is not new—poverty was just as concentrated in the ghetto of the 1930s as in the black underclass communities of the 1970s. They also do not attribute black poverty concentration to civil rights laws. Instead, they argue that black poverty is to a high degree the result of residential segregation from the rest of society and a great deal of hardship stemming from the economic restructuring (Massey and Denton, 1993).

Whatever the cause, several studies in the 1980s suggested a growing trend in the number of poverty areas. Kasarda (1993) analyzed census tracts in the 100 largest central cities and found that the percentage of all central city poor persons living in extreme poverty areas increased from 16.5 percent in 1970 to 22.5 percent in 1980 to 28.2 percent in 1990. Moreover, the spatial concentration of blacks was the most severe among racial groups. Variation in poverty areas by region revealed that extreme poverty was greatest in Midwestern cities such as Detroit.

Using 1990 census data, Jargowsky (1994) analyzed changes in ghetto poverty among blacks from 1980 to 1990. Defining "very poor" to mean census tracts with poverty rates in excess of 40 percent, Jargowsky concluded that ghetto poverty among blacks increased both in terms of number of blacks living in ghettos and as a percentage of the black population. Moreover, the black poor became increasingly isolated in ghettos, with nearly half of the black poor in metropolitan areas living in a ghetto neighborhood. He also noted that the physical size of ghettos expanded even in some metropolitan areas where the percentage of blacks living in ghettos declined. The largest increases in ghetto poverty occurred in the Midwest and Southwest.

Whether the concentration of ghetto poverty was a new or a continuing fact of black life in Detroit and other cities, it is clear that the National Advisory Commission on Civil Disorders (1968) recognized its existence in the late 1960s and warned white Americans to act to avoid a permanent separation along the lines of race and class. Since most white Americans ignored the warnings, by the end of the 1970s many large American cities were populated by an increasingly black unemployed and poorly educated population with single-parent households forced to live in the endless poverty with no hope of social mobility (Darden, 2001).

Observing this phenomenon, researchers coined the phrase "the urban underclass" (Katz, 1993). Although researchers disagreed over what constituted an "urban underclass" and whether it was growing, the concept in its most general form referred to a population that was highly segregated and poor with few tools or skills to change the condition. A feeling of hopelessness was a common characteristic (Jencks, 1991; Ricketts and Sawhill, 1988; Ruggles and Marton, 1986). Several authors attributed the black underclass directly to white racism, residential segregation, and discrimination and the systematic failure of white American institutions to address the needs of poor blacks in America's cities (Glasgow, 1980; Massey and Denton, 1993).

Researchers and policymakers became concerned over the growing underclass during the 1970s and 1980s. Ricketts and Sawhill (1988), for example, characterized the underclass as a population dominated by behaviors that were at variance with the mainstream American behaviors, characterized by high levels of joblessness, single female parents, school dropouts, households dependent on public assistance, men not attached to the labor force, and crime. Ricketts and Mincy (1990) used U.S. census tract data to document a growing underclass in Detroit and other central cities during the 1970s and 1980s. Such growth confirmed the belief among many researchers and policymakers that the social and economic conditions of central cities were getting worse, with the increase in underclass areas and concentrated poverty (i.e., census tracts where at least 40 percent of the residents are poor). Such patterns reflected the *economic restructuring* during this period.

However, between 1990 and 2000, several changes in the economy occurred in part due to policy changes at the federal level. First, the economy grew. There was an Earned Income Tax credit for the poor, and real wages for low-income workers rose, reducing overall poverty. There was greater participation in the labor force among men in the central cities, and crack cocaine use declined (Jargowsky and Yang, 2006). As a result, the census data revealed a decline in both underclass tracts and concentrated poverty (Jargowsky, 2003; Kingsley and Pettit, 2003). According to Jargowsky and Yang (2006), the Detroit metropolitan area led the way with declines of more than sixty underclass census tracts (neighborhoods) between 1990 and 2000. The number of tracts went from 99 in 1990 to 38 in 2000, a decline of 62 percent.

Despite the decline of concentrated poverty in the city of Detroit, businesses and industries continued to relocate to the suburbs. Of special significance is that out-migration included black-owned businesses as well.

THE CHANGING LOCATION OF BLACK-OWNED BUSINESSES: CITY VERSUS SUBURB

Many black-owned firms in the city of Detroit at the time of the riot were suffering from limited market size. In other words, most black-owned businesses relied on black consumers to remain in business (Collins, 1983; Wilson, 1975). Such racially restrictive markets were due in part to the restriction of the black-owned businesses to the central city, racial residential segregation, and discrimination. As Bates (1993) noted, white merchants were allowed to open stores in black neighborhoods, but black merchants were historically kept out of white areas. The typical black business was a small business concentrated in the city in the center of black neighborhoods where the customers were also poorer than customers in other neighborhoods (Young and Harding, 1971). Fischer and Massey (2000) have argued that some geographic concentration (residential segregation) is probably beneficial for certain types of businesses, that is, enterprises catering to the tastes of the minority groups. However, the authors suggest that higher levels of residential segregation are likely to be detrimental to business ownership because of the tendency for residential segregation to concentrate poverty. This is especially true in the case of blacks (Massey and Denton, 1993), and blacks in the city of Detroit were no exception (Gold and Darden, 2010).

Because the intended location of many black-owned businesses in the city was in segregated black neighborhoods, potential black business owners had a higher loan denial rate than potential white owners, even after controlling for differences in creditworthiness and other factors (Cavalluzzo, Cavalluzzo, and Wolken, 2002). Black business owners were also required to pay higher interest rates or put down more collateral than white business owners who located outside of segregated areas (Fairlie, 1999; Fairlie and Robb, 2004; Meier, 2006).

Limited access to capital influenced the size, location, and type of black-owned businesses. It is well documented that firms in construction, manufacturing, and wholesale trade usually required a larger amount of capital than small personal service businesses and retail establishments (Ong, 1981). Thus, fewer blacks were represented in these types of firms.

The limited access to capital forced blacks into the types of businesses with higher turnover rates, such as small retail and services (Reynolds and White, 1996). Fewer individual blacks could obtain the larger supply of capital to open manufacturing and wholesale trade businesses, which have lower turnover rates (Bates, 1997). Past research show that black-owned firms were more likely to be found in personal service type operations, which usually had worse outcomes on average than other firms (Fairlie and Robb, 2004).

Civil Rights, Set-Aside Legislation, and Minority and Women Business Development Programs

As a consequence of the civil rights movement and in the wake of the urban riots in Detroit and other cities in 1967, federal, state, and city governments undertook a wide range of affirmative action programs to provide resources to groups subject to historical discrimination on the basis of ethnicity, race, and gender. These programs sought to provide these disadvantaged groups with resources and opportunities long denied them so that they might experience rates of upward mobility associated with populations not subject to such discrimination.

The most visible of these involved providing access to education and government employment. In addition, however, affirmative action programs also sought to provide groups characterized by low rates of self-employment, including blacks, with various resources that would increase their involvement in entrepreneurship.

Shortly after taking office, President Richard M. Nixon emphasized the importance of minority business ownership as part of his urban and race relations policy (Perlstein, 2008):

> To foster the economic status and the pride of members of our minority groups we must seek to involve them more fully in our private enterprise system . . . both in the areas where they now live and in the larger commercial community—and not only as workers, but also as managers and owners. . . . Not only to share the economic benefits of the free enterprise system more broadly, but also to encourage pride, dignity, and a sense of independence. In order to do this, we need to remove commercial obstacles which have too often stood in the way of minority group members—obstacles such as the unavailability of credit, insurance, and technical assistance. (Nixon, qtd. in Wooley and Peters, 2008)

Even prior to Nixon's election, in 1967, an amendment was made to the Economic Opportunity Act (EOA) that directed the Small Business Administration (SBA) to emphasize the growth of small businesses owned by low-income persons or those located in areas of high unemployment (Bates, 1997). Gender was added as a criterion shortly thereafter.

A wide variety of minority business development programs were put into effect. In general, set-asides were the most effective means of assisting disadvantaged businesses because rather than simply encouraging the formation of businesses by women and minority group members, set-asides directly provided employment and income to such businesses. Further, once such businesses received contracts to provide goods and/or services to governmental entities, they became good credit risks and were thus able to obtain credit from banks and establish preferential agreements with suppliers, subcontractors, and the like, thereby obtaining the capital needed.

Starting in 1969, the SBA 8(a) "set-aside" program awarded $8.9 million in contracts to disadvantaged businesses, a figure that grew to $4.3 billion during the Carter administration. The city of Detroit benefited greatly from Carter's administration. This was due in part to the fact that Coleman Young, the black mayor of Detroit, was a Carter supporter and a major figure in national Democratic politics. Young was able to deliver a strong black voting block to Carter (Darden et al., 1987). As a result, "many small and Black-owned businesses stabilized and grew" (Woodard, 1997: 29). The 1977 Public Works Employment Act had a similar impact, requiring all large general contractors bidding for public works projects to allocate at least 10 percent of their contracts to ethnic minority subcontractors without regard to the size or disadvantaged status of the enterprise.

Following this governmental initiative, large corporations also established set-aside programs of their own. In 1982, through the National Minority Supplier Development Council, companies purchased $5.3 billion in goods and services from minority-owned businesses.

The Emergence of Anti-Set-Aside Initiatives

However, during the 1980s such programs came under attack and were challenged in the courts. The U.S. Supreme Court decision *City of Richmond v. Crosen* in 1989 challenged the constitutionality of minority business set-aside programs at the state and local levels.

The Court struck down as unconstitutional a Richmond, Virginia ordinance that required 30 percent of each construction contract to be awarded to a minority business. The Court ruled that a state or local government must produce specific evidence of racial or ethnic discrimination against the group targeted for assistance and the remedy selected must be "narrowly tailored" to address the types of discrimination found to exist in the jurisdiction (*City of Richmond v. J.A. Croson Company*). Before the decision, black mayors often ensured that black businesses were not overlooked in securing access to set-asides. After the decision, set-asides were suspended all over the country (Walker, 1998). Thus the degree of political influence to enhance black-owned businesses has declined since the *Richmond v. Croson* decision.

During the early 1990s, "a variety of other challenges to the set-aside requirements of government programs began to emerge" (Lowry, 2005: 8). In reaction, some government entities developed strategies that sought equal opportunity and diversity without focusing on gender, race, or ethnic origins (Insight Center for Community Economic Development, 2007). While private sector programs took important measures to support minority enterprise, the economic downturns that occurred after 2000, together with "escalating pressure on government to dismantle set-asides," created a climate which "would confound even the largest and most prolific businesses," let alone struggling minority start-ups. Accordingly, both governmental and private sector support for minority businesses became scarce (Lowry, 2005: 8).

Emergence of State Anti-Affirmative Action Propositions

During the late 1990s, and extending over a decade, activists established a legislative program to ban affirmative action through state elections. The first of these was Proposition 209, passed in California in 1996. Similar proposals were approved in Washington in 1998 (Initiative 2000) and Michigan in 2006 (Proposal 2). Having successfully promoted anti-affirmative action propositions in these states, the American Civil Rights Institute, led by California businessman and former University of California Board of Regents member Ward Connerly, made plans to expand the program to several more states (Fullbright, 2006).

The state-based anti-affirmative action proposals have received only limited support from major political actors, large corporations, and other progressive influential organizations. They regard such efforts to make it more difficult to increase and maintain minority college enrollment, business participation. and public sector employment as detrimental to an increasingly diverse and globalized society. For example, in Washington, Eddie Bauer, Microsoft, and Starbucks funded opposition to the campaign for Initiative 2000 (Stein, 2008). The coalition opposing Michigan's Proposal 2 received significant funding from Ford Motor Company, the Dow Chemical Company, and Detroit's Greektown Casino, and the coalition was endorsed by the League of Women Voters, the United Auto Workers, and the Arab-American Institute (Schmidt, 2006; Stein, 2008). Moreover, Proposal 2 was opposed by both Democratic and Republican gubernatorial candidates who were seeking office in the same election.

However, the anti-affirmative action proposals have significant appeal to white (and especially male) voters, which is why Connerly's organization promotes the anti-affirmative action cause through state initiatives rather than legislatures, which might alter outcomes. "Indeed, as evidenced in the public opinion polls, whites overwhelmingly object to government assistance targeted at blacks. Whereas eight out of every ten African Americans believe that the government is not spending enough to assist black people, only slightly more than three of every ten white Americans feel this way" (Wilson, 1999: 20).

Outcomes of Anti-Affirmative Action Propositions

Michigan's anti-affirmative action proposition is relatively recent. Accordingly, there is little data on the impact of the law on black-owned businesses. However, the California law has been on the books over ten years, so some data on its effects are now becoming available. A study evaluating the impact of a California Department of Transportation (Caltrans) program that directed purchasing to women- and minority-owned businesses determined that only a third of the state's certified Minority Business Enterprises (MBEs) were still in existence ten years after Proposition 209 went into effect. In addition, MBEs received only half of the awards and contracts from Caltrans that they had accessed prior to the law; African American–owned and women-owned contractors suffered the most adverse impacts after Proposition 209; and many of the MBE contractors still in existence "could not have initially succeeded or maintained their success" without incentives that helped them gain equal access (Discrimination Research Center, 2006: 3).

Analysis by the Insight Center for Community Economic Development found that women- and minority-owned businesses were less likely to expand in the years immediately after passage of the anti-affirmative propositions in California and Washington than were WBEs and MBEs in Oregon and Maryland, somewhat comparable states that did not change their affirmative procurement policies between 1996 and 2001 (Insight Center for Community Economic Development, 2007).

Harper and Reskin (2005) concluded after a review of the impact of affirmative action that governmental programs are increasingly challenged by activists and the courts. However, major institutions, including universities and corporations, remain committed to the goal of increasing access to underrepresented groups in schools and the workplace, even if the broad, government-based mandate for it has weakened (Harper and Reskin, 2005). Further, despite the mobilization against affirmative action purchasing programs, since 2003, while seven states have curtailed inclusive business programs, fourteen states have either initiated or enhanced inclusive business programs.

BLACK BUSINESS REPRESENTATION IN DETROIT AND SUBURBS

Black business representation is assessed using the most recent U.S. Bureau of the Census Survey of Business Owners, conducted in 2007(U.S. Bureau of the Census, 2011a). We analyzed the extent of racial and ethnic disparities in business ownership in the city and the suburbs (Wayne County excluding the city plus Oakland and Macomb counties). Our analyses show that while blacks owned 63.8 percent of all businesses and whites owned 31 percent, blacks owned only 14.8 percent of all employer businesses while whites owned 75.8 percent. The employer businesses are the large firms that require large amounts of capital to start. More importantly, these are the businesses that impact employment in the city. It is interesting to note that while whites constitute a small percentage of Detroit's total population, they own three-fourths of the employer firms (table 26). Thus despite the demographic dominance of blacks in Detroit, the black population is largely dependent on white-owned businesses for employment.

We noted in previous chapters that among the grievances mentioned by some blacks who participated in the riot was the lack of black business ownership, especially in the predominantly black neighborhoods. It appears that more than forty years later the extreme underrepresentation of black ownership of employer firms remains an issue in Detroit (Gold and Darden, 2010). The disparity in representation of businesses by race and ethnicity is best determined by using the business participation rate (BPR). It is measured by the number of firms or businesses per 1,000 persons of a specified racial/ethnic group. Table 27 shows the business participation rates for blacks, Hispanics (excluding Mexicans), and Mexicans (excluding other Hispanics). Again, we analyzed separately ownership of all firms and employer firms. While the black business participation rate is 54.4 for all firms in Detroit, the rate declines to only 1.6 percent for employer firms. The Hispanic business participation rate is 6.5 for all firms but declines to 1.4 for employer firms. The Mexican business participation rate is 15.6 for all firms but drops to 1.9 percent for employer firms. However, the racial/ethnic disparity is most evident when the white business participation rate is compared to other groups. For all firms it is 282 and the rate for employer firms is 89.1. Clearly those businesses that create and sustain jobs in Detroit are owned by whites—not blacks. whites owned 60 percent of the manufacturing firms; 66.3 percent of all wholesale firms, and 61.6 percent of all retail firms. Black-owned firms exceeded white-owned firms only in construction and services. Blacks owned 53 percent of all construction type firms and 80.4 percent of all service type firms. Examples of service type firms include professional and technical services, educational services, health care and social assistance, along with food services.

Place matters in business ownership and racial and ethnic disparity. Table 28 shows that in suburban Detroit, whites owned 91.6 percent of the employer firms in 2007, while blacks owned only 1.7 percent. Thus, although place matters in business ownership, it appears that the low percentage of black ownership of employer firms is consistent whether in the city or the suburbs. It is interesting to note, however, that black demographic dominance and black political control are no longer significant factors influencing black ownership of employer firms. That is because the black business participation rate for employer firms in the city of

Table 27. Business participation rates in Detroit, by race and ethnicity, 2007

Black (all firms)	54.4
Black (employer firms)	1.6
Hispanic* (all firms)	6.5
Hispanic* (employer firms)	1.4
Mexican (all firms)	15.6
Mexican (employer firms)	1.9
White (ALL firms)	282.0
White (employer firms)	89.1

*In this table "Hispanic" refers to Hispanics or Latinos of any race, excluding Mexicans (since Mexicans are listed separately).

Source: U.S. Bureau of the Census (2011a).

Detroit, which was 1.6 percent in 2007, is even lower than the 1.7 percent rate in the suburbs, which has a much smaller black population.

The lack of differences in black Business ownership rates in the city compared to the suburbs may be due to the greater difficulty of operating a successful business in Detroit (Gold and Darden, 2010). It appears that if black businesses are to grow and survive, they must give more weight to *location* in the suburbs rather than the city. Many Detroit black business owners are avoiding the co-ethnic retail sector in the central city and instead providing business services to a larger multiracial, multiethnic clientele in the Detroit suburbs, where economic growth is more prevalent (Bates, 1997). Most population growth is also occurring in Detroit's suburbs. The structural and demographic characteristics of a *place rather than race* are increasingly important to successful black business ownership in the Detroit region. We also observed that despite the discriminatory barriers that remain in suburban housing, more and more blacks have been moving out of the city of Detroit since at least 1980. (We discuss such black suburbanization in detail in chapter 11.)

The Decreased Influence of Detroit's Status as a Majority Black City

Traditionally, black businesses have been strongly dependent on the black population for success. Studies have shown that black mayors (a product of black demographic dominance and political solidarity) were responsible for the initial opening of the government procurement market to black-owned businesses (Bonds, 2007; Boston and Ross, 1996; Chen, 1993; Christopher, 1998). Furthermore, many cities headed by black mayors with majority black city councils aggressively sought to ensure equity in the distribution of city contracts by including minority- and women-owned businesses in the bidding process during the 1970s and 1980s as well as providing training programs for minorities and women (Bates, 1997; Woodard,

Table 28. Business ownership in the suburbs of Detroit, by race, 2007

	# of all firms	# of employer firms	# of employees	% of total ownership all firms	% of total ownership employer firms	% of total employees
Total	273,999	61,786	686,981			
White	236,019	56,608	622,654	86.1	91.6	90.6
Black	20,651	1,041	12,001	7.5	1.7	1.7
Hispanic*	1,600	290	4,125	0.6	0.5	0.6
Mexican	2,030	335	5,730	0.7	0.5	0.8
Asian	12,125	3,349	41,159	4.4	5.4	5.9
American Indian/ Alaskan Native	1,574	163	1,312	0.6	0.3	0.2

*In this table "Hispanic" refers to Hispanics or Latinos of any race, excluding Mexicans (since Mexicans are listed separately).

Note: The suburbs include Wayne County (outside Detroit) plus Oakland and Macomb counties

Source: U.S. Bureau of the Census (2011a).

1997). Majority black cities also more readily made provisions for loans to enhance black-owned businesses (Cohn and Fossett, 1996; Gold and Light, 2000). The anti-affirmative action Proposal 2 will probably weaken the influence of black mayors even more in the future. Finally, the typical black-owned business in the suburbs is not retail, but health care and social assistance.

RACE, POVERTY, AND CRIME IN DETROIT

So what are the social and economic consequences of job and business relocation from the city of Detroit to the suburbs, leaving behind a population that is disproportionately poor and black? The National Advisory Commission on Civil Disorders (1968) noted that concentrating the poor in certain sections of cities may lead to rising crime. Moreover, segregating the poor and the black in large cities leads to personal and property insecurity in neighborhoods where the poor are most highly concentrated. In America's largest cities, the most concentrated poor population is disproportionately black. Blacks reside in areas where crime rates have been historically higher than anywhere else (Darden, 2001).

The National Advisory Commission on Civil Disorders (1968) mentioned two facts that are still true today: (1) most crimes in these impoverished, inner-city areas are committed by a small number of the residents; and (2) the principal victims are the residents themselves. In terms of race relations, most everyday crimes committed in America's largest cities are not crimes committed against a member of another race. Throughout America's metropolitan areas, most crimes committed by blacks involve other blacks as victims, just as most crimes committed by whites involve other whites as victims.

Such crimes, however, do have implications for race relations. Although most crimes in the black ghetto are committed by a small percentage of black males (primarily those ages fourteen to twenty-four), they have a tendency to create fear in the minds of many whites, that is, fear of blacks in general and black males in particular. Such fear reduces interracial interaction and the opportunity for productive race relations. Moreover, high black crime rates provide a rationale for those whites who wish to rationalize segregation by any means necessary. Such individuals ignore evidence pointing to concentrated poverty as a causal factor in the rising crime rate. The key focus is on "keeping the blacks in their place." Many blacks, however, view the relationship between blacks and crime with a much broader and different meaning, which inevitably speaks to the racially unequal, unjust, and oppressive American metropolitan system (Darden, 2001).

The concept that these concentrated areas of poor blacks were analogous to white-controlled internal colonies emerged following the civil disorders of the 1960s. Staples (1975), for example, viewed black crime as a function of a group's power to define what behavior can be classified as criminal or legitimate.

In a society like that of the United States, blacks share many of the characteristics of natives in colonial countries, such as political and economic oppression, cultural subjugation, and control of their community by an alien group. Within the context of such an internal colony, crimes that are primarily committed as a result of poverty caused by differential access to the society's resources and goals are defined as a threat to the maintenance of law and order, while similar crimes of theft and violence committed by whites escape the same degree of punishment as a result of their power, as members of the ruling class, to define what activities are criminal and how serious those crimes might be. Racial differences in crime rates are viewed as a representation of the black ghetto resident's lack of control and therefore disproportionate representation in the criminal justice system (Darden, 2001). Massive brutality against the black citizenry by white police officers and inequalities in the arrest and detention of blacks, with lengthier jail sentences for blacks vis-à-vis whites who have committed similar crimes, often occur (Holmes and Smith, 2008).

For example, while blacks and whites use drugs at approximately the same rate, blacks were arrested for drug offenses at approximately five times the rate of whites during the height of the drug war in the 1980s (Darden, 2001). Moreover, possession of crack cocaine, which is used disproportionately by blacks, receives a significantly more severe sentence than the possession of powdered cocaine, which is used disproportionately by whites. Moreover, white-collar crimes, which are mostly committed by the white population, are rarely or lightly punished (Darden, 2001).

Race is a predominant factor in explaining why nearly one in four young black men in the United States were in prison or jail or on probation in 1990 (Mauer, 1990). Five years later, the proportion of black men in their twenties who were imprisoned or on probation or parole had risen to one in three. Mauer warned that if one in three white men were under criminal justice supervision, the nation would declare a national emergency (Butterfield, 1995).

Miller (1992), who has studied the damaging impact of the U.S. criminal justice system on blacks, considers the pervasive criminalization of black youth today as analogous to the white slave owners' practice of crippling young black male slaves to prevent them from escaping to freedom. The real relationship between crime and race is the systematic exploitation of blacks, reducing them to levels of poverty below the standard of living of most whites, a situation that produces a disproportionate number of economic crimes among the black population. Blacks in prison are sometimes defined as "political prisoners" because their status is determined by the economic conditions imposed upon them by the political state, not their criminal activity. By defining the problem of crime as one arising from the functioning of internal colonialism, the solution can be more correctly defined as decolonization. This means community control of the police, a jury trial by one's peers, and proportional representation of blacks on the legal staff and bench. Given the continued "significance of race" in the criminal justice system, a key question is why all-white juries are still allowed.

As long as blacks remain segregated and denied equal opportunity to leave poor areas of cities, the potential for violent racial conflict is always present. Although there are periods of remission, such areas remain potential powder kegs ready to explode (Darden, 2001).

Race and Crime in Detroit, 1980–2007

Some statistics suggest that the trend in the rate of crime can be an important measure of the trend in economic opportunities in a city. It is hypothesized that fewer opportunities result in more crimes. We examined crime data from the Federal Bureau of Investigation's Uniform Crime Reports. The most accurate number of crimes reported are those involving death. The least accurate is the number of rapes reported (Disaster Center, 2008). We present both violent crime rates and property crime rates from 1980 to 2007. The crime rate is defined as the number of crimes per 100,000 people.

The results revealed that murder/manslaughter rates declined in the city of Detroit from 46.2 in 1980 to 45.5 in 2007, a difference of 0.7 percentage points (table 29). Rape and robbery also declined. For example, the rate of rapes declined from 109.7 in 1980 to 39.6 in 2007, a decline of 63.9 percent. The rate of robberies dropped from 1,121.6 in 1980 to 763.7 in 2007, or 31.9 percent. On the other hand, the rate of aggravated assaults increased from 668.1 in 1980 to 1,440 in 2007, an increase of 115 percent. Also, the rate of total violent crimes increased from 1,945.5 in 1980 to 2,289 in 2007, or 17.6 percent.

The rate of property crimes for burglary, larceny/theft, and vehicle theft declined from 1980 to 2007, as did the total rate of property crimes. The rate of total property crimes, for example, dropped from 8,697.1 in 1980 to 6,771.7 in 2007, or by 22.1 percent (Federal Bureau of Investigation, 2007). It appears from the data that the total violent crime rate increased slightly after 1980, and the total property crime rate was much higher in the eighties (during the recession) than from 1995 to 2007 (table 29).

Drug Use: Detroit Students versus Students in the United States

Some residents within the metropolitan Detroit area believe that crime rates are related to drug use. Since crime and drugs are associated more with youth, we examined drug use among Detroit public school students in grades 9–12 and compared their drug use with students in the United States as a whole.

Detroit students attend schools in some of the most deprived neighborhoods in the metropolitan area. Thus, there is reason to suspect that drug use is much higher among

Table 29. Rates of violent crimes and property crimes in Detroit, 1980–2007

Violent crimes					
Year	Murder/ manslaughter	Rape	Robbery	Aggravated assault	Total
1980	46.2	109.7	1,121.6	668.1	1945.5
1985	59.6	144.4	1,537.6	635.0	2,376.6
1995	48.5	110.7	1,010.3	1,238.9	2408.5
2005	41.4	65.5	757.7	1,496.8	2361.3
2007	45.7	39.6	763.7	1,440	2289
Property crimes					
Year	Burglary	Larceny theft	Vehicle theft	Total	
1980	3,411.6	3,429.8	3,429.8	8,697.1	
1985	3,703.1	4,219.2	4,219.2	1,1374.7	
1995	2,242.7	4,353.3	4,353.3	9,531.2	
2005	1,699.7	1,931.7	1,931.7	6,004.0	
2007	2,063.6	2,429.6	2,278.5	6,771.7	

Note: Figures are number of crimes per 100,000 people.

Source: Federal Bureau of Investigation (1980, 1985, 1995, 2005, 2007).

youth in Detroit than in the country as a whole. To test this assumption, we examined 2007 data from the Youth Risk Behavior Study (National Center for Chronic Prevention and Health Promotion, 2009). More recent data were not available at the time this chapter was written. The survey focuses on risk behaviors that contribute to the leading causes of death, disability, and social problems among youth and adults in the United States. The national YRBS is conducted every two years during the spring semester and provides data representative of ninth- through twelfth-grade students in public and private schools throughout the United States. The Detroit YRBS is also conducted every two years and provides data representative of ninth- through twelfth-grade students in public schools in Detroit. The results presented here compare students in the United States with students in Detroit to determine whether Detroit students are at less, equal, or greater risk from drug use.

In terms of lifetime alcohol use, Detroit students are at less risk than all United States students, since Detroit students have a 66 percent use rate compared to 75 percent for all students. Detroit students also currently use alcohol less (26.7 percent) than students in the United States overall (44.7 percent). Moreover, a smaller percentage of Detroit students (9 percent) engage in episodic heavy drinking (i.e., five or more drinks within two hours) compared to all U.S. students (26 percent).

There is no statistically significant difference in the lifetime use of marijuana among Detroit students and all students. Among Detroit students, the percentage is 39.1, compared to 38.1 percent for all students.

Detroit students have a lower percentage of lifetime use of cocaine (2.6 percent) than all students (7.2 percent). Cocaine is defined here as any form, including powder, crack, or freebase, used one or more times over the life span. Detroit students also have a lower lifetime methamphetamine use (2 percent) than students nationwide (4 percent).

Finally, Detroit students have a lower percentage than students nationwide of lifetime inhalant use (8 percent compared to 15 percent). Inhalants include glue, aerosol spray cans, or paints, sniffed or inhaled to get high.

While Detroit students have less risk compared to all students of using alcohol and other drugs, they have greater risk than students overall of being offered, sold, or given illegal drugs by someone on school property (33 percent compared to 22 percent) (National Center for Chronic Disease Prevention and Health Promotion, 2009). It appears that Detroit students are victimized by the deprived neighborhoods where they must attend school. They are more exposed to drug dealers than other students. Yet despite this exposure, the students in Detroit public schools have a lower rate of drug use than students in the United States as a whole.

CONCLUSIONS

This chapter has demonstrated how economic restructuring, which meant a decline in auto manufacturing in Detroit, had a differential impact on residents of the city of Detroit, who were mostly black, as jobs relocated from the city to the suburbs. Unlike most blacks, most whites followed the economic opportunities to the suburbs of Detroit, but most blacks were restricted, until very recently, from such suburban municipalities. Such spatial mismatch resulted in fewer opportunities for blacks in the city, which impacted their earnings and employment and increased their poverty.

More than forty years after the riot, blacks in the city of Detroit still rely on white-owned employer firms for jobs, despite residence in an overwhelmingly black city. Not only have most businesses left the city since the riot but, but black-owned businesses have also become more attracted to the suburbs. The population left in the city has become more disproportionately black and poor compared to the population in the suburbs. Thus, exposure to crime and drugs became more prevalent as the economic conditions declined; concomitantly, crime rates improved as economic conditions improved. Moreover, despite the *place of residence* in deprived neighborhoods, students in the Detroit Public Schools have a lower risk of drug use than students in the United States as a whole. Instead, the greatest risk faced by Detroit public school students is the continued exposure to drug dealing in deprived neighborhoods. Policymakers must pay special attention to the characteristics of neighborhoods where black youth reside when implementing policies to address the problem.

CHAPTER 11

Measuring the Racial Divides in Metropolitan Detroit

IN 1987, TWENTY-FIVE YEARS AFTER THE RIOT, WE MADE AN IMPORTANT PREDICTION about the state of race and class in metropolitan Detroit:

> If present trends continue, racial polarization between Detroit and its suburbs is likely to increase along with the class gap between the poor in the central city and the affluent in the suburbs. Central city financial problems are likely to worsen, and the city's political influence in the region will continue to decline. (Darden et al., 1987)

We also predicted that Detroit's population would continue to decline:

> Most who leave Detroit will continue to be white and affluent. But a sizable number of middle class blacks will also migrate to the suburbs. The geographical line between black and white will still be rigidly drawn. Those remaining in the city will be mostly black and mostly poor. (Darden et al., 1987: 4)

Present data suggest that these predictions have been accurate. The trends have indeed continued. The purpose of this chapter is to document the results by using the most recent data available to measure the extent of the racial and place divides in metropolitan Detroit.

To recapture what occurred in metropolitan Detroit since the 1967 civil disorders and what was reiterated in our predictions of 1987, we note that the ideology of white supremacy, racial stereotypes, and racial discrimination in housing produced separate and unequal neighborhoods between blacks and whites and other racial/ethnic groups (Darden, 2009b). Over the years, white neighborhoods and municipalities within metropolitan Detroit received a disproportionate share of economic investment, which led to differential commercial and industrial growth between the city and suburbs. While most whites moved to the suburbs, most blacks were excluded.

The results have created a predominantly black city, a very high level of racial residential and school segregation, concentrated poverty in the city, and concentrated affluence in the suburbs. Race and class apartheid is better represented by metropolitan Detroit than by any other place in the United States. *Place of residence* is a key factor impacting the quality of life of residents. It influences housing, education, and access to jobs, shopping (e.g., grocery stores with

WHITE POPULATION 2000
METRO DETROIT

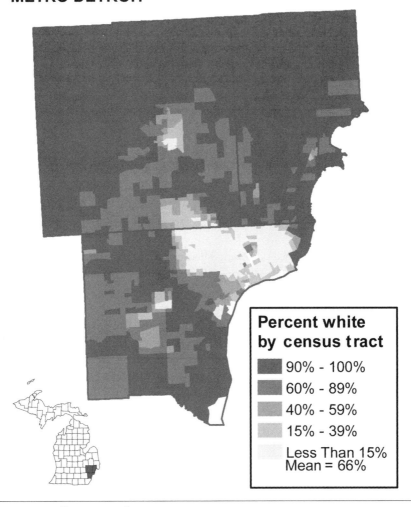

Percent white by census tract

- 90% - 100%
- 60% - 89%
- 40% - 59%
- 15% - 39%
- Less Than 15%

Mean = 66%

THE WHITE POPULATION IN METROPOLITAN DETROIT IN 2000.

fresh fruit and vegetables), health care, recreation, safety, and other public services. When place of residence is segregated by race and class, it has differential social and economic consequences.

We begin by highlighting some of the racial and economic trends since 1960, followed by a detailed assessment of the race, class, and place divide using the most recent data.

BLACKS AND WHITES IN THE SUBURBS OF DETROIT, 1960–2010

As the auto industry started to relocate to the suburbs, white workers tended to leave the city of Detroit and relocate to the suburban communities near the plants (Darden, 2009b). Most blacks could not. Such barriers to black suburbanization imposed by whites occurred not because blacks

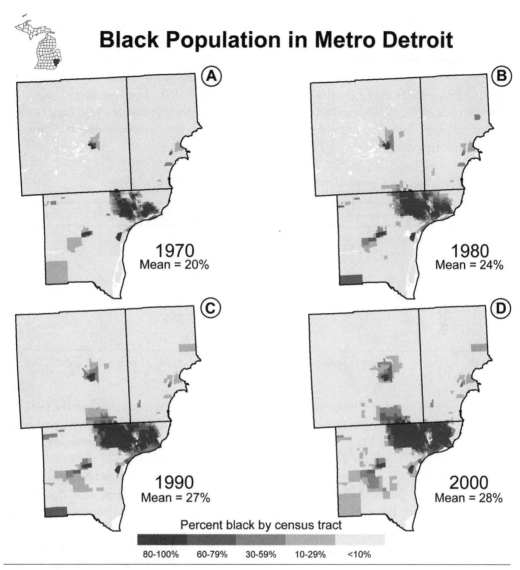

Black Population in Metro Detroit

(A) 1970 Mean = 20%

(B) 1980 Mean = 24%

(C) 1990 Mean = 27%

(D) 2000 Mean = 28%

Percent black by census tract

80-100%　60-79%　30-59%　10-29%　<10%

THE BLACK POPULATION IN METROPOLITAN DETROIT IN 2000.

could not afford the housing in the suburbs, but because of racial discrimination (Darden and Kamel, 2000; Farley, Danzinger, and Holzer, 2000). Such discrimination included restrictive covenants. Black (1947) revealed that racially restrictive covenants were quite common in the city of Detroit as a tool to maintain racial residential segregation. In fact virtually all of Detroit's new subdivisions included racially restrictive covenants (Black, 1947; see also Sands, 1972). Discrimination also included the refusal to sell or rent to blacks by white brokers and apartment managers; racial steering; exclusionary zoning; the denial of Federal Housing Administration insured mortgages; and the denial of mortgage loans by banks (Darden et al., 1987; Farley et al., 2000). Thus, blacks within the Detroit metropolitan area faced barriers to movement to the suburbs that have not been completely removed, despite the passage of antidiscrimination legislation in the 1960s. Therefore, most blacks have remained concentrated in the city of Detroit and segregated in the metropolitan area during the entire period (1960–2010).

However, a small number of blacks were able to move to the suburbs despite the discriminatory barriers. Table 30 shows that in 1960, only 76,647 blacks resided in the suburbs, representing 3.7 percent of the total suburban population. Although the Fair Housing Act was passed in 1968, the black population had increased only slightly to 96,655 by 1970, representing 3.6 percent of the total suburban population. Since 1970, however, there has been a steady increase in the black suburban population to more than 100,000 by 1980, representing 4.2 percent of the suburban population, and to 384,518 by 2010, representing 12.2 percent (more than forty years after the civil disorders) (table 30).

Table 30. **Black and white population in the suburbs of Detroit, 1960–2010**

Year	Number white	Percent white	Number black	Percent black
1960	2,012,402	96.2	76,647	3.7
1970	2,580,843	96.0	96,655	3.6
1980	2,962,565	94.1	131,478	4.2
1990	2,980,960	91.4	163,224	5.0
2000	2,667,422	86.3	235,266	7.6
2010	2,523,063	80.0	384,518	12.2

Source: Computed by the authors from U.S. Bureau of the Census (1963, 1972, 1980, 1992, 2002, 2008, 2011c).

However, compared to whites, blacks remain extremely underrepresented in the suburbs and overrepresented in the city (table 31). Such underrepresentation in the suburbs, and overrepresentation in the city has implications for residential segregation. Some observers believe that the significance of race as a factor in residential segregation has declined since the passage of the Federal Fair Housing Act of 1968, which declared racial discrimination in housing illegal (Wilger, 1988). This belief may be related to (1) the change in white attitudes toward the principle of open housing, and (2) the decline (although small) in residential segregation from 1970 to 2010 (Logan and Stults, 2011).

Both the metropolitan area and the city of Detroit experienced slight declines in the index of dissimilarity from 1990 to 2010 (table 32). The percentage of whites who agreed that "black people have a right to live wherever they can afford" rose from 65 percent to 88 percent between 1965 and 1976 (Schuman, Steeh, and Bobo, 1985).

Wilger (1988) attributes the decline in residential segregation to the construction of new housing and argues that as more new housing is built to replace existing housing, and as continued suburbanization of blacks occurs, residential segregation will continue to decline.

Our view is closer to that of Massey and Gross (1991), who argue that, although white racial attitudes did indeed shift during the 1970s following passage of the Fair Housing Act, such attitudes

Did not change enough to bring about meaningful residential integration in metropolitan areas where most Blacks live. As a result, discrimination did not decline significantly in urban areas with large Black populations, and the decline in racial segregation that occurred only serves to underscore the continued salience of race in the United States, since they occurred almost entirely in cities with small Black populations, where White preferences for limited interracial contact are not threatened by racial desegregation. (Massey and Gross, 1991: 15)

Table 31. Black and white population of Detroit and its suburbs, 2010

	Detroit		Suburbs	
	Number	Percent	Number	Percent
White	75,758	2.9	2,523,063	97.1
Black	590,226	60.5	384,518	39.4
Total	665,984		2,907,581	

Source: Computed by the authors from data obtained from United States Bureau of the Census (2011c).

Massey and Gross (1991) based their conclusions on the premise that, although they may endorse open housing as a general principle, many whites do not accept its implications in practice. Indeed, surveys of neighborhood racial preferences suggest that most whites prefer segregated neighborhoods (Darden, 1987). The preference of whites for segregation can be fulfilled in areas where the black population remains small, and where open housing practices can occur without threatening white preferences for limited black-white contact (Massey and Gross, 1991). However, in an area with a relatively large number of blacks, implying a high degree of potential black-white contact, racial segregation is generally maintained. Furthermore, when the metropolitan area has a central city that is predominantly black, the factor of race becomes even more significant because the political boundaries separating the city from the suburbs become rigid racial boundaries. Negative images whites may have of the predominantly black city are often transferred to the black individual.

The movement of blacks from central city to suburban political boundaries results in strong white resistance. According to the customer-prejudice hypothesis of the cause of discrimination, white real estate agents tend to discriminate most against lower-income blacks, who are more likely to upset their white customers (Yinger, 1995). However, race is so important to many white residents that socioeconomic status differences between black home-seekers become blurred, resulting in a high level of black segregation from whites, regardless of black socioeconomic status.

This section addresses whether, in the case of metropolitan Detroit, the high level of residential segregation is caused by differential socioeconomic status between blacks and whites. We measure the trends in black-white residential segregation and test the socioeconomic/racial residential segregation hypothesis using 2000 census data for the Detroit Standard Metropolitan Statistical Area (Wayne, Oakland, and Macomb counties).

According to theorists of human ecology, as minority groups move up in socioeconomic status, they tend to seek housing in higher-income areas—that is, the suburbs. This movement may result in a greater degree of residential integration (Massey and Denton, 1993). Of interest in this section is the extent to which African American socioeconomic status contributed to African American residential integration in metropolitan Detroit.

PATTERNS OF RACIAL RESIDENTIAL SEGREGATION
AND THEIR CONSEQUENCES

Despite passage of the Federal Fair Housing Act of 1968 and Michigan's Elliott-Larsen Civil Rights Act, metropolitan Detroit remains highly segregated by race. As used in this chapter, residential segregation is defined as the overall unevenness in the spatial distribution of two racial groups over census tracts within metropolitan areas. The degree of residential segregation presented here was measured by the index of dissimilarity. The index value ranges from 0, indicating no segregation, to 100, indicating total segregation. The higher the index, the greater the degree of residential segregation. Whatever the value of the index, it reflects the minimum percentage of either group that would have to move from one tract to another to achieve an even spatial distribution throughout the metropolitan area.

The black population has remained highly residentially segregated from whites in the metropolitan area with only a slight decline since 1960 (table 32). In 1960, the index of dissimilarity for metropolitan Detroit (Wayne, Oakland, and Macomb) was 87.1. The index reached its peak of 88.9 in 1970 and declined to 79.6 in 2010 (table 32). Yet the Detroit metropolitan area still remained one of the two most racially segregated metropolitan areas in the United States. According to Logan and Stults (2011), metropolitan Milwaukee also had an index of dissimilarity of 79.6, the highest levels among metros with the largest black populations. The level of residential segregation within the city limits of Detroit declined from an index of dissimilarity of 80.4 in 1960 to 59.2 in 2010 (table 32). Such an index, however, has less significance within a predominantly black city than in the predominantly white metropolitan area, with its rigid separation by race between city and suburbs.

Table 32. Residential segregation trends in metropolitan Detroit and the city of Detroit, 1960–2010

Year	Index of dissimilarity, metropolitan Detroit	Index of dissimilarity, city of Detroit
1960	87.1	80.4
1970	88.9	78.2
1980	85.8	67.4
1990	87.4	64.8
2000	84.7	63.3
2010	79.6	59.2

Note: For an explanation of the index of dissimilarity, see the appendix.

Source: Darden, Stokes, and Thomas, 2007; Logan and Stults, 2011.

RACE, CLASS, AND RESIDENTIAL SEGREGATION
IN METROPOLITAN DETROIT

The following analysis is designed to evaluate whether blacks and whites with the same incomes are residentially integrated in the same neighborhoods. Table 33 examines blacks and whites with comparable incomes in the city of Detroit in 2000 and the change since

1990. The income categories range from $14,999 and less to $75,000 and more. The results reveal that blacks and whites earning less than $14,999 had an index of dissimilarity of 63. These groups can be considered "poor." The results also revealed that blacks and whites earning $75,000 or more (that is, middle-class blacks and whites) were no less segregated. In fact, these groups had an index of dissimilarity of 64.2. When blacks and whites at each income level are examined, the results suggest that blacks and whites in the city of Detroit are residentially segregated when the two groups have the same incomes. Regardless of comparable incomes, blacks and whites have, on average, an index of dissimilarity of more than 60. Poor blacks and poor whites are as residentially segregated as middle-class blacks and whites (table 33). On average, 63.6 percent of black households would have to move to another neighborhood within the city to achieve even spatial distribution with white households at the same income level.

However, the 2000 figures show some progress toward residential desegregation between blacks and whites in all income levels. The dissimilarity index for 2000 was on average 1.9 percentage points lower than the index in 1990. The greatest decline in residential segregation occurred between blacks and whites earning $15,000–$34,999. The index decreased by 3.2 percentage points for this income group.

According to the ecological theory and the spatial assimilation process, when a minority group moves to the suburbs, there is an expectation of a lower level of residential segregation than what was experienced in the city, yet table 34 shows that blacks in the suburbs of Detroit with the same incomes as whites are even more segregated than blacks in the city. The average level of segregation is 70.9, which was 7.3 percentage points higher than the average segregation experienced by blacks in the city. Poor suburban blacks and whites were slightly more segregated, with an index of dissimilarity of 73.3, while affluent blacks and whites had an index of dissimilarity of 68.5. At each comparable income level, blacks and whites in the

Table 33. Residential segregation in Detroit between blacks and whites with the same levels of household income, 2000, and change since 1990

Income level	White		Black		Index of dissimilarity		
	Number	Percent	Number	Percent	1990	2000	Percentage point change
≤$14,999	13,288	26.91	74,121	27.42	64.7	63.0	−1.7
$15,000 to $34,999	14,961	30.30	79,108	29.27	66.2	63.0	−3.2
$35,000 to $74,999	15,001	30.38	80,351	29.73	66.4	64.1	−2.3
≥$75,000	6,121	12.40	36,712	13.58	64.9	64.2	−0.7
Total households	49,371	100.00	270,292	100.00			
Mean					65.5	63.6	−1.9

Source: Computed by the authors from data obtained from the U.S. Bureau of the Census (1992, 2002); Darden (2007d).

suburbs of Detroit were more residentially segregated from each other than were blacks and whites in the city of Detroit (Darden, 2007d).

Nevertheless, the figures for suburban Detroit reveal some degree of progress toward residential desegregation. At each income level, the index of dissimilarity was lower than the index of dissimilarity in 1990. On average the index declined by 7.8 percentage points over the decade. The greatest decline was between blacks and whites earning $35,000–$74,999. Among this group, the index declined by 9 percentage points (table 34).

Residential Segregation between Blacks and Whites with Comparable Education Levels

Table 35 shows that most blacks and whites with the same level of education do not share residential neighborhoods in the city of Detroit. The average index of dissimilarity for blacks and whites at all educational levels was 59.1. However, the indices of dissimilarity declined from a score of 66.6 among blacks and whites with no high school to 54.1 among blacks and whites with graduate or professional degrees.

More importantly, blacks in the suburbs with levels of education comparable to that of suburban whites experienced higher levels of residential segregation than blacks in the city of Detroit at each comparable educational level. Similar to the patterns in the city, suburban blacks experienced a decline in the level of segregation as the level of education increased. For example, the index of dissimilarity among blacks and whites with no high school diploma was 72.5. On the other hand, blacks and whites with graduate or professional degrees had an index of dissimilarity of 65.9, which is 6.6 percentage points lower. Overall, however, the average level of residential segregation between blacks and whites of comparable levels of education in the suburbs was 69, compared to 59 among blacks and whites in the city, a difference of ten percentage points.

Table 34. Residential segregation in Detroit suburbs between blacks and whites with the same levels of household income, 2000, and change since 1990

Income level	*White*		*Black*		*Index of dissimilarity*		
	Number	Percent	Number	Percent	1990	2000	Percentage point change
≤$14,999	95,620	8.97	15,766	18.02	82.1	73.3	–8.8
$15,000 to $34,999	213,097	19.99	20,397	23.32	77.7	72.1	–5.6
$35,000 to $74,999	392,788	36.85	29,622	3.86	79.0	69.9	–9.1
≥$75,000	364,339	34.18	21,695	24.80	76.1	68.5	–7.6
Total households	1,065,844	100.00	87,480	100.00			
Mean					78.7	70.9	–7.8

Source: Computed by the authors from data obtained from the U.S. Bureau of the Census (1992, 2002); Darden (2007d).

Table 35. Residential segregation in Detroit between blacks and whites with the same levels of education, 2000, and change since 1990

Education level	White		Black		Index of dissimilarity		
	Number	Percent	Number	Percent	1990	2000	Percentage point change
No high school	29,847	35.27	128,512	28.58	66.7	66.6	–0.1
High school	42,759	50.53	278,364	61.90	64.8	60.4	–4.4
College degree	6,739	7.96	29,321	6.52	62.0	55.3	–6.7
Professional degree	5,275	6.23	15,918	3.50	56.1	54.1	–2.0
Total households	84,620	100.00	452,115	100.00			
Mean					62.3	59.1	–3.2

Source: Computed by the authors from data obtained from the U.S. Bureau of the Census (1992, 2002); Darden (2007d).

However, like blacks and whites with similar incomes, blacks and whites with similar educational attainment became less residentially segregated between 1990 and 2000 in the suburbs and the city. Moreover, the decline in residential segregation in the suburbs was greater. Overall, the index of dissimilarity fell from 78.6 to 69.0, a decline of 9.6 percentage points, compared with a drop of 3.2 percentage points in the city. The decline was greatest between blacks and whites with no high school diploma (11.2 percentage points) (table 36).

In sum, the results reveal that most blacks and whites with comparable incomes and education do not live in the same neighborhoods in the city or in the suburbs. Poor blacks and poor whites are segregated; so are middle-class blacks and whites. In fact, blacks in the suburbs of Detroit with the same income and education as whites are even more segregated than blacks in the city of Detroit (Darden, 2007d).

Thus, contrary to ecological theory and the spatial assimilation process, black residential segregation seems to occur independently of socioeconomic status. These findings, based on 2000 census data, present further evidence that ecological theory and the spatial assimilation process are insufficient to explain the high level of black residential segregation in America's most racially segregated metropolitan area. Instead, these findings reconfirm the importance of *place stratification* as defined by Alba and Logan (1993). In this model, regardless of socioeconomic status, blacks, because of racial steering and/or discrimination, are not able to fully convert their socioeconomic status into the same neighborhoods as whites.

However, because racial discrimination declined between 1989 and 2000, more blacks and whites in all income and educational levels became less residentially segregated from 1990 to 2000 in both the city and the suburbs (Darden, 2007d; Turner et al., 2002). Such decline in residential segregation has been due to black movement into formerly all-white neighborhoods, especially in the suburbs of Detroit. Indeed, evidence suggests that blacks continued

Table 36. Residential segregation in Detroit suburbs between blacks and whites with the same levels of education, 2000, and change since 1990

Education level	White		Black		Index of dissimilarity		
	Number	Percent	Number	Percent	1990	2000	Percentage point change
No high school	259,718	14.19	25,812	18.21	83.7	72.5	−11.2
High school	1,084,640	59.25	84,990	59.96	80.8	70.9	−9.9
College degree	310,035	16.94	19,180	13.53	75.8	66.7	−9.1
Professional degree	176,319	9.63	11,763	8.30	74.1	65.9	−8.2
Total households	1,830,712	100.00	141,745	100.00			
Mean					78.6	69.0	−9.6

Source: Computed by the authors from data obtained from the U.S. Bureau of the Census (1992, 2002); Darden (2007d).

to move to predominantly white suburban municipalities between 2000 and 2010, yet there remained a race and class divide in metropolitan Detroit.

THE RACE AND CLASS DIVIDE IN METROPOLITAN DETROIT IN 2008

In this section we present analyses based on the most recent census data of the extent of the racial and place divide between those living in the city of Detroit and those residing in Wayne, Oakland, and Macomb counties. We limit our focus to blacks, whites, and Hispanics in order to enable a comparison of the racial divide in 2008 and the racial divide at the time of the riot more than forty years previously.

Higher Education

Table 37 reveals the extent of the higher education gap between blacks, whites, and Hispanics in the city of Detroit and in the suburbs. The most recent census data indicate that in the city of Detroit a higher percentage of whites (15.4 percent) had at least a bachelor's degree or higher level of education than did blacks (10.6 percent). However, the gap in educational attainment was widest between non-Hispanic whites and Hispanics. Whites were three times more likely than Hispanics to have a bachelor's degree or higher.

The racial gap is smaller between Hispanics and whites in affluent Oakland County. The educational attainment level was much higher for all three groups. In Oakland County 30.8 percent of blacks had a bachelor's degree or higher, which was almost three times the 10.6

percent found in Detroit. For Hispanics, 26.3 percent had a bachelor's degree or higher, that is, five times the percentage in the city of Detroit. With a ratio of 1.0 indicating equality, blacks compared to whites in Detroit had a ratio of 0.68. The ratio between Hispanics and whites in the city was 0.32. It is clear that black and Hispanic college graduates were not only more represented in suburban Oakland County, but the black-white and Hispanic-white educational gap was also lower. The ratio between blacks and whites was 0.73 and the ratio between Hispanics and whites was 0.62.

Table 37. Race and place divide in higher education, 2008

	Detroit	*Wayne County*	*Oakland County*	*Macomb County*
Black	10.6	11.2	30.8	16.7
White	15.4	23.9	41.8	20.9
Hispanic*	5.0	12.7	26.3	

*"Hispanic" refers to Hispanics or Latinos of any race.

Note: The figures are the percentage of the population with four or more years of schooling beyond high school as a percentage of the total population 25 years or older. In tables 37 to 46, data are not available for Hispanics in Macomb County because the group does not reach the 20,000 threshold.

Source: U.S. Bureau of the Census (2009a).

Median Household Income

The median household income was generally low for blacks ($29,243), Hispanics ($30,071), and whites ($30,667) in Detroit (table 38). It is interesting to note, however, that in a majority black city, both whites and Hispanics had median household incomes that exceeded the median household income of blacks. The highest incomes of blacks and whites occurred in suburban Oakland County. The median income of blacks was $50,037, the median income of whites $71,935. In terms of income inequality, the income of blacks was only 0.69 the income of whites. Thus, blacks in suburban Oakland County earned 1.7 times more than blacks in Detroit, but the income gap between blacks and whites was much larger (table 38).

Table 38. Race and place divide, median household income, 2008

	Detroit	*Wayne County*	*Oakland County*	*Macomb County*
Black	$29,243	$30,705	$50,037	$42,863
White	$30,667	$55,551	$71,935	$57,272
Hispanic*	$30,071	$41,742	$48,158	

*"Hispanic" refers to Hispanics or Latinos of any race.

Source: U.S. Bureau of the Census (2009a).

Occupational Status

The third socioeconomic indicator is occupational status. Like education and income, occupational status was higher for all three groups in the suburbs, especially Oakland County.

We measure occupational status by the percentage of managerial and professional workers aged sixteen years and older. In the city of Detroit, whites had a higher percentage (27 percent) of managerial and professional workers than blacks (21.7 percent) (table 39). However, the racial inequality gap was much larger between Hispanics and whites in Detroit. Only 5.7 percent of Hispanics were managerial and professional workers, which was only 0.21 times the percentage of whites. In Oakland County, more than a third of blacks (35.4 percent) were managerial and professional workers, compared to 45.5 percent of whites, for a ratio of 0.77. The racial inequality gap was wider between Hispanics and whites in Oakland County at 0.62.

Table 39. Race and place divide in occupational status, 2008

	Detroit	*Wayne County*	*Oakland County*	*Macomb County*
Black	21.7	22.2	35.4	22.5
White	27.0	33.1	45.5	32.9
Hispanic*	5.7	18.2	28.4	

*"Hispanic" refers to Hispanics or Latinos of any race.
   Note: Figures are the percentage of managerial and professional positions held by workers 16 years and older at the top of the occupational hierarchy based on the occupational classification system used by the Bureau of the Census in 2000.

Source: U.S. Bureau of the Census (2009a).

Median Value of Housing

Unlike education, income, and occupational status, where whites exceeded blacks in Detroit, blacks resided in housing that exceeded the value of housing occupied by whites ($89,600 to $80,400). Hispanics in the city resided in the lowest-valued housing ($79,800) (table 40).

As with socioeconomic indicators, the housing with the highest median value was located in suburban Oakland County, and whites occupied housing with the highest median value ($227,200) compared to housing occupied by blacks ($179,800) and Hispanics ($171,200). Thus, the ratio was 0.79 between blacks and whites and 0.75 between Hispanics and whites.

Table 40. Race and place divide in median value of housing, 2008

	Detroit	*Wayne County*	*Oakland County*	*Macomb County*
Black	$89,600	$93,400	$179,800	$159,500
White	$80,400	$156,200	$227,200	$169,000
Hispanic*	$79,800	$115,700	$171,200	

*"Hispanic" refers to Hispanics or Latinos of any race.
   Note: Figures are the median value of specified owner-occupied housing units. The value is the respondent's estimate of how much the property would sell for if it were for sale. It includes only one-family houses on less than ten acres without a business or medical office on the property.

Source: U.S. Bureau of the Census (2009a).

Median Gross Rent

Table 41 shows that blacks in the city paid a higher median rent ($741 per month) than whites in Detroit ($693 per month). Hispanics also paid higher gross median rent than whites ($717 per month). Interestingly, blacks in suburban Oakland County also paid higher rent than whites ($880 per month compared to $842). Thus, the ratio was 1.06 in favor of blacks in Detroit and 1.04 in favor of blacks in suburban Oakland County.

Table 41. Race and place divide, median gross rent, 2008

	Detroit	*Wayne County*	*Oakland County*	*Macomb County*
Black	$741	$744	$880	$761
White	$693	$757	$842	$737
Hispanic*	$717	$730	$798	

Source: U.S. Bureau of the Census (2009a).

*"Hispanic" refers to Hispanics or Latinos of any race.

Homeownership

In the city of Detroit, whites had a higher homeownership rate (64.2 percent) than either blacks (54.0 percent) or Hispanics (47.9 percent). The homeownership ratio between blacks and whites was 0.84 and 0.74 for Hispanics and whites in Detroit.

Table 42. Race and place divide in homeownership, 2008

	Detroit	*Wayne County*	*Oakland County*	*Macomb County*
Black	54.0	52.4	46.9	40.0
White	64.2	80.2	81.5	82.6
Hispanic*	47.9	61.5	61.1	

*"Hispanic" refers to Hispanics or Latinos of any race.

Note: Figures are the percentage of all housing units that are owner occupied, even if the unit is mortgaged or not fully paid for.

Source: U.S. Bureau of the Census (2009a).

Age of Housing

The age of housing is measured here by the percentage of housing built in 1939 or earlier (the oldest housing) and housing built in 2000 or later (the newest housing). A higher percentage of Hispanics (55.2 percent) in Detroit live in the oldest housing, followed by whites (46.5 percent). The percentage was lowest for blacks (30.2 percent) (table 43). Thus, the black/white age of housing ratio was 0.64 in favor of blacks. A lower percentage of blacks than whites in suburban Oakland County reside in older housing (5.0 percent compared to 8.3 percent).

However, a higher percentage of whites (8.1 percent) than blacks (6.0 percent) reside in housing built in 2000 or later (table 43).

Table 43. **Race and place divide, age of housing, 2008**

	Detroit	*Wayne County*	*Oakland County*	*Macomb County*
Black				
1939 or earlier	30.2	27.0	5.0	4.0
2000 or later	1.7	3.3	6.0	13.7
White				
1939 or earlier	46.5	12.9	8.3	4.0
2000 or later	1.5	5.9	8.1	11.1
Hispanic[*]				
1939 or earlier	55.2	34.0	8.3	
2000 or later	2.1	4.9	8.1	

[*]"Hispanic" refers to Hispanics or Latinos of any race.

Source: U.S. Bureau of the Census (2009a).

Poverty Rates

Disparities in poverty rates are related to marital status as well as *race* and *place of residence*. Female-headed households have higher poverty rates than married couple households regardless of race or residential location in the city or the suburbs. In the city of Detroit, the highest poverty rates (54.8 percent) are experienced by Hispanic female-headed households. There was essentially

Table 44. **Race and place divide, poverty rates, 2008**

	Detroit	*Wayne County*	*Oakland County*	*Macomb County*
Black				
Married couples	10.3	9.5	3.3	3.5
Female households	40.2	39.5	19.3	31.5
White				
Married couples	16.0	4.3	2.2	3.5
Female households	41.9	22.4	16.4	17.5
Hispanic[*]				
Married couples	23.4	13.3	11.4	
Female households	54.8	42.9	30.6	

[*]"Hispanic" refers to Hispanics or Latinos of any race.

Source: U.S. Bureau of the Census (2009a).

no difference between the percentages of white (40.2 percent) and black (41.9 percent) poverty rates among female-headed households (table 44). Thus, the ratio of poverty among Hispanic and white female-headed households was 1.3, reflecting more poverty among Hispanics.

The lowest poverty rates were among white married couples in Oakland County (2.2 percent). The poverty rate was also low among black married couples (3.3 percent), but black married couples were still 1.5 times more likely to be in poverty than white married couples. Compared to Hispanic married couples in Oakland County, black married couples experienced much less poverty. The poverty rate for Hispanics was 11.4 percent, which was five times the rate for white married couples.

Unemployment Rates

Unemployment rates were highest among blacks in the city of Detroit (22.2 percent) compared to whites (15.7 percent). Thus, blacks were 1.4 times more likely to be unemployed than whites. Hispanics, on the other hand, were only slightly more likely to be unemployed than whites (16.0 percent). While whites experienced double-digit unemployment only in the city of Detroit, blacks experienced double-digit rates of unemployment in all three suburban counties of Wayne (21.2 percent), Oakland (12.4 percent), and Macomb (14.0 percent) (table 45). Blacks were 2.3 times more likely to be unemployed than whites in Wayne County and 1.9 times more likely to be unemployed than whites in Oakland County.

Households with No Vehicle Available

In metropolitan Detroit, where a rapid transit system does not exist and public transportation in general is limited, the automobile is an absolute necessity to get to work, shop, and travel to other places without restrictions. Blacks in the city of Detroit are most impacted by the absence of a vehicle available. According to the most recent census, 22.1 percent of black households had no vehicle available, compared to 17.3 percent of white households. Thus, black households were 1.3 times more likely to have no vehicle available than white households. (It is worth noting that the percentage of Hispanic households with no vehicle available was 14.7 percent, i.e., lower than blacks and whites.) Even in affluent suburban Oakland County, 8.0 percent of black households had no vehicle available, which was twice the rate of 4.2 percent for white households (table 46).

Table 45. **Race and place divide, unemployment rates, 2008**

	Detroit	*Wayne County*	*Oakland County*	*Macomb County*
Black	22.2	21.2	12.4	14.0
White	15.7	9.3	6.5	8.9
Hispanic[*]	16.0	14.9	8.4	

[*]"Hispanic" refers to Hispanics or Latinos of any race.

Source: U.S. Bureau of the Census (2009a).

Table 46. Race and place divide, percentage of households without vehicle available, 2008

	Detroit	*Wayne*	*Oakland*	*Macomb County*
Black	22.1	20.8	8.0	9.5
White	17.3	6.5	4.2	5.1
Hispanic*	14.7	10.1	6.4	

*"Hispanic" refers to Hispanics or Latinos of any race.

Source: U.S. Bureau of the Census (2009a).

However, the largest gap between black and white households was in Wayne County, where black households were 3.2 times more likely than white households to have no vehicle available.

BLACKS, HISPANICS, AND PLACE OF RESIDENCE

In order to further assess the significance of place of residence for black and Hispanic households in metropolitan Detroit and for the quality of place of residence for all renters and owners in the city and suburbs, we calculated the percentage of total households residing in certain areas using the most recent 2009 American Housing Survey data for metropolitan Detroit.

The data address the quality of housing, households, and neighborhoods and were a direct outgrowth of the riots of 1967. In the early 1970s, the recently created Department of Housing and Urban Development (HUD) envisioned a database that would assess the quality of the housing stock, analyze its characteristics, and monitor how housing units changed over time. With funding from HUD, the U.S. Census Bureau launched its first American Housing Survey in 1973. It captured what the quality of life was like for residents by *race and place* immediately after the riot.

In this section, we rely on the most recent American Housing Survey data (U.S. Bureau of the Census, 2009c) to inform us of quality of life more than forty years after the riot. Since owners have experienced a higher quality of life in general than renters, we divide comparisons between these two groups.

The data allow us to compare the quality of place of residence and neighborhood for black and Hispanic renters and owners residing in the total geographic area of Detroit, Wayne County (excluding Detroit), and Oakland County. They also allow a comparative analysis of the quality of housing and neighborhoods for all renters and owner households residing in these three areas. Our method was to calculate the renter households separately from the owner households by race (black vs. Hispanic) and then by place of residence for all renter and owner households in these three areas.

Our final objective was to assess the cost of living in the city of Detroit compared to the suburban areas of Wayne and Oakland counties. Such comparison reveals that *place of residence and its neighborhood characteristics* have economic and social consequences.

Household Distribution by Race and Place of Residence

As we have documented in the previous chapters, the spatial distribution of households in metropolitan Detroit varies greatly by race and place of residence. The most recent data show that 75 percent of all black households resided in the city of Detroit. Only 10 percent of blacks lived in Wayne County outside of the city, and 15 percent resided in Oakland County.

Hispanics had a less concentrated spatial distribution. That is, 31.2 percent of Hispanics resided in the city of Detroit, 29.8 percent lived in Wayne County outside of the city, 26.8 percent resided in Oakland County, and 12.2 percent resided in Macomb County.

White households, on the other hand, were overwhelmingly suburbanized. Only 6 percent of households resided in the city, compared to 45.5 percent in Wayne County outside of Detroit and 48.5 percent residing in Oakland County. As we will see, such differences in residential location are related to differences in characteristics.

THE CHARACTERISTICS OF BLACK AND HISPANIC HOUSEHOLDS IN METROPOLITAN DETROIT, 2009

Comparing black and Hispanic households, first we note that black renters had a higher percentage of bachelor's degree holders (14 percent) than Hispanic renters (5 percent). However, Hispanic homeowners had a much higher percentage (36 percent) than black owners (17 percent), making Hispanic owners more than twice as likely as black owners to have a bachelor's degree.

Black renter households had a lower percentage of married couples (18 percent) than Hispanic renter households (24 percent). Indeed, almost three in four (73 percent) of black renter households were female households, compared to 69 percent for Hispanic renter households.

The percentage of married couples was much higher (44 percent) among black owners. However, Hispanics lived in married couple owner households at almost twice the rate for blacks (80 percent). Moreover, even among owner households, the percentage of black female households was more than three times the percentage for Hispanics (40 percent compared to 12 percent).

Black owner households had a lower median income than Hispanics ($34,473 compared to $42,000).

Like the social and economic characteristics of the families, black housing was of lower quality and value than that of Hispanics. The median housing value for blacks was $70,000, compared to $100,000 for Hispanics. The median year black household property was purchased was nine years earlier than that of Hispanic households (1992 compared to 2001). The median purchase price was $45,000 for black households and $70,000 for Hispanic households. Finally, blacks were less likely than Hispanics to be homeowners (51 percent compared to 73 percent).

In sum, black and Hispanic households in metropolitan Detroit are different, with Hispanics having a higher socioeconomic status than blacks. Such differences in the SES level of households are related to differences in the neighborhoods where the two groups reside.

Perception of Neighborhood Characteristics of
Black and Hispanic Renter Households

Among renter households, a higher percentage of blacks (22 percent) perceive their neighborhood as the worst neighborhood in metropolitan Detroit to live in compared to only 10 percent of Hispanic households. However, 73 percent of black renter households, compared to 80 percent of Hispanic renter households, perceive their neighborhoods as the best place to live.

A higher percentage (29 percent) of black renter households than Hispanic renter households (25 percent) reported experiencing serious crime in their neighborhood in the past twelve months. Finally, a lower percentage of black renter households (71 percent) than Hispanic renter households (90 percent) reported no other problems in the neighborhood.

Perception of Neighborhood Characteristics of
Black and Hispanic Owner Households

Among owner households, 23 percent of blacks perceive their neighborhood as the worst neighborhood to live in, compared to 18 percent of Hispanic owner households. Although there was little difference between the percentage of black renters and black homeowners in their opinion of neighborhood quality, there was a large difference in the percentage of Hispanic renters and Hispanic owners in their opinions of their neighborhood. A higher percentage of Hispanic homeowners (18 percent compared to 10 percent of black renters) indicated that they lived in the worst neighborhood. Like renters, a lower percentage of black owners than Hispanic owners indicated that they lived in the best neighborhood (72 percent compared to 80 percent).

Interestingly, there was little difference in the percentage of black and Hispanic owners who reported that they experienced serious crime in their neighborhood over the last twelve months (38 percent for blacks and 41 percent for Hispanics).

However, while black owner households were also bothered by other problems in the neighborhood (37 percent), only 15 percent of Hispanic owner households were bothered by other problems.

Assessment of Elementary Schools as Satisfactory or Unsatisfactory

black renter households were less likely to be satisfied with the public elementary school in their neighborhood than Hispanic renter households. Whereas 69 percent of black renter households indicated that they were satisfied, 86 percent of Hispanic renter households were satisfied. Almost 20 percent of black renter households were dissatisfied, compared to 15 percent of Hispanic renter households.

Like renter households, a lower percentage of black owner households (67 percent) were satisfied with their elementary neighborhood school than Hispanic owner households (89 percent). This is a large difference and may be related in part to the greater likelihood that Hispanic owner households will have children in suburban schools.

Assessment of Public Transportation

Among black renters, 89 percent (compared to 60 percent of Hispanic renters) have public transportation, and 36 percent of black renter households use public transportation regularly for commuting to school or work, compared to only 8 percent of Hispanic renter households.

Among black owner households, 88 percent have public transportation in the neighborhood, compared to 62 percent of Hispanic owner households. Whereas 11 percent of black owner households use public transportation regularly to commute to school or work, only 4 percent of Hispanic owner households use public transportation regularly to commute to school or work.

Perceptions of Neighborhood Shopping: Grocery or Drugstores within Fifteen Minutes

Among renter households, 87 percent of black households, compared to 95 percent of Hispanic renter households, were satisfied with the proximity to grocery stores and drugstores. On the other hand, 12 percent of black renters, compared to only 5 percent of Hispanic renters, were dissatisfied.

Among owner households, 87 percent of blacks, compared to 97 percent of Hispanics, were satisfied, and 11 percent of blacks, compared to only 3 percent of Hispanic households, were dissatisfied.

Perception of Police Protection

Fewer black renter households were satisfied with police protection in their neighborhood (74 percent) than were Hispanic renter households (80 percent). Among owner households, 67 percent of blacks were satisfied, compared to 87 percent of Hispanics.

Households with Trash, Litter, or Junk on Streets or Any Property within 300 Feet

Among black renter households, 67 percent experienced no trash, litter, or junk on the streets or on property in their neighborhood, compared to 95 percent of Hispanic households. Among owner households, 70 percent of both blacks and Hispanics indicated none of the items were found in their neighborhood. This is one of the few questions where no difference existed in the percentage of black and Hispanic households.

In sum, Hispanic households generally experience a higher quality of neighborhood characteristics than black households. Hispanics are also more satisfied with their neighborhoods than blacks. This may be related in part to the higher percentage of Hispanic households residing outside the city of Detroit.

We turn now to compare the characteristics of the place of residence to document the geographic fact that *place matters*. We compare first the characteristics of households (renter and owner) in Detroit, Wayne County without Detroit, and Oakland County.

CHARACTERISTICS OF PLACE OF RESIDENCE IN
DETROIT AND SELECTED SUBURBS

Among variables discussed in this section of the chapter, we note a spatial pattern in which social and economic characteristics of households and neighborhoods improves as one moves from the city of Detroit to Wayne County (excluding Detroit) to Oakland County. Again, we separate renter households from owner households.

Education and income are two indicators of socioeconomic status. The American Housing Survey data show that the percentage of renter households with bachelor's degrees or higher increased from 10 percent in Detroit to 17 percent in Wayne County (excluding Detroit) to 31 percent in Oakland County. Among owner households, the percentage of households with bachelor's degrees or higher increased from 15 percent in Detroit to 33 percent in Wayne County (excluding Detroit) to 46 percent in Oakland County.

There is also a large difference in the family structures by place of residence. Among renter households, the percentage of married couple households increases from 19 percent in Detroit to 31 percent in Wayne County (excluding Detroit) to 40 percent in Oakland County. Thus, renter married couple households are twice as likely to live in Oakland County as in Detroit.

Of more importance in terms of family structure (since it is strongly related to income) is the percentage of renter households that are female-headed households. The percentage decreases from 72 percent in the city of Detroit to 54 percent in Wayne County outside of Detroit to 38 percent in Oakland County.

Among owner households, the percentage of married couple households increases from 40 percent in Detroit to 76 percent in Wayne County outside of Detroit to 81 percent in Oakland County. The percentage of female households decreases from 43 percent in the city of Detroit to 17 percent in Wayne County outside of Detroit to only 11 percent in Oakland County. It appears that married couple households are more likely to be owners and more likely to reside in the suburbs of Detroit, whereas female households are more likely to be renters and to reside in the city of Detroit.

There is usually an association between the concentration of female households and lower median household income. That relationship is reflected in the pattern of median household income among households in Detroit compared to the suburbs. Among renter households, the median household income was $12,000 in Detroit, which doubles to $24,272 in Wayne County (excluding Detroit) and increases to $33,780 in Oakland County. Thus, among renter households, the median income in Oakland County is almost three times the median income among households in the city.

Owner households, as expected, have a higher median household income than renters. It was $27,600 among households in the city, which more than doubles to $60,800 in Wayne County outside of Detroit and increases to $69,755 in Oakland County.

Similar to the pattern of income, the percentage of homeownership increases from 54 percent among households in Detroit to 77 percent among households in Wayne County outside of Detroit to 80 percent in Oakland County.

The median housing value follows a similar spatial pattern. It increases from $50,000 in Detroit to $112,000 in Wayne County outside of Detroit to $150,000 in Oakland County. The median purchase price was $27,000 in the city, increases to $102,000 in Wayne County excluding Detroit, and increases further to $135,000 in Oakland County.

Perception of Characteristics of Neighborhoods

Among renter households, a higher percentage of households in Detroit (28 percent) perceived their neighborhood as the worst neighborhood to live in, compared to 11 percent in Wayne County (excluding Detroit) and 8 percent in Oakland County. Among owner households, 34 percent of households in Detroit perceived their neighborhood as the worst neighborhood to live in, compared to 7 percent of households in Wayne County outside of Detroit and only 5 percent of households in Oakland County.

Such variation in perception of neighborhood quality may be related to the seriousness of neighborhood crime, the quality of the public schools, and police protection.

Perception of Neighborhood Crime and Other Problems

Among renter households, 39 percent indicated that their neighborhood had experienced serious crime in the past twelve months. This compares to 25 percent in Wayne County outside Detroit and 19 percent in Oakland County. Among owner households in Detroit, 50 percent of households indicated that their neighborhood had experienced serious crime in the past twelve months. This compares to 23 percent in Wayne County outside of Detroit and 17 percent in Oakland County.

A higher percentage of household renters in Detroit (39 percent) than in the rest of Wayne County (13 percent) and Oakland County (11 percent) indicated that they also were bothered by other problems in the neighborhood. Among owner households, 46 percent in Detroit, compared to 20 percent in Wayne County outside Detroit and 14 percent in Oakland County, indicated that they were also bothered by other problems.

Perceptions of the Public Elementary Schools

A higher percentage of renters in Detroit than renters in Wayne County outside of Detroit and Oakland County were unsatisfied with the public elementary school in their neighborhood. In Detroit, 28 percent of renter households were unsatisfied, compared to 19 percent in Wayne County outside of Detroit and 9 percent in Oakland County. Among owner households, 20 percent were dissatisfied in Detroit, compared to 5 percent in Wayne County outside of Detroit and 7 percent in Oakland County.

Perceptions of Public Transportation

In Detroit, 97 percent of renter households have access to public transportation in their neighborhood, and 45 percent use public transportation regularly for commuting to school or work. This compares to 71 percent of households with access to public transportation in Wayne County and 15 percent that use public transportation regularly to commute to school or work. In Oakland County, 61 percent of households have access to public transportation, and 7 percent use it regularly to commute to work or school. Among owner households,

92 percent in Detroit have access to public transportation, and 13 percent use it regularly to commute to school or work. This compares to 56 percent of households in Wayne County outside Detroit that have access to public transportation and 4 percent that use it regularly to commute to school or work. Owner households in Oakland County had the lowest percentage (45 percent) with access to public transportation, and only 2 percent use it regularly to commute to school or work.

Satisfaction with Neighborhood Shopping in Grocery Stores and Drugstores

The lack of satisfaction among renter households in Detroit with grocery stores or drugstores within fifteen minutes of the home was 18 percent. Such dissatisfaction declined as one compares renters in Wayne County (excluding Detroit) and Oakland County. Among renter households in those suburban areas, the percentage that was not satisfied dropped to 2 percent in both locations.

Among owner households, 15 percent in Detroit were not satisfied with neighborhood shopping in grocery and drugstores, compared to 2 percent of owner households in Wayne County outside Detroit, and less than 1 percent of owner households in Oakland County.

Dissatisfaction with Police Protection in the Neighborhood

The percentage of renter households that was dissatisfied with police protection in the neighborhood declined from Detroit, where it was 33 percent, to Wayne County outside Detroit (4 percent) and Oakland County (3.7 percent). Among owner households, 40 percent were dissatisfied with police protection in Detroit, compared to 2 percent in Wayne County (excluding Detroit) and 3 percent in Oakland County.

Households with Trash, Litter, or Junk on the Streets on Any Property in the Neighborhood

Among renter households, the percentage indicating that none of the households experienced trash, litter, or junk in the neighborhood or on any property increases from 58 percent in Detroit to 83 percent in Wayne County outside of Detroit to 90 percent in Oakland County. Among owner households, the percentage indicating that none of the households experienced trash, litter, or junk in the neighborhood increased from 59 percent in Detroit to 93 percent in Wayne County outside Detroit to 94 percent in Oakland County.

In sum, the characteristics of households and neighborhoods *vary by place of residence* along with the level of dissatisfaction with the quality of the neighborhood where persons reside. The American Housing Survey data clearly revealed that the quality of the neighborhoods in Detroit was lowest, followed by the quality of the neighborhoods in Wayne County outside Detroit, with households residing in Oakland County experiencing neighborhoods of the highest quality.

Such neighborhood characteristics were related to the level of dissatisfaction among the households, which declined from the highest percentage households reporting neighborhood dissatisfaction in Detroit, followed by Wayne County outside Detroit, with Oakland County experiencing the lowest percentage of dissatisfied households (renter and owner).

Given such differences in the quality of neighborhood characteristics between the city of Detroit and the suburbs (Wayne and Oakland counties), a key question we raise is what is the cost of living in Detroit? Is it an inexpensive place to live compared to living in the suburbs?

The Cost of Living in Detroit

In this section we first examine the cost of living among black and Hispanic households. Although we do not distinguish the place of residence of the two groups, we have already indicated that black households overwhelming reside in the city of Detroit, whereas slightly less than half of Hispanic households reside in Detroit. Whether black households pay more than Hispanic households is not a simple question to answer. Comparing median monthly costs paid by owner households, Hispanics pay $1,072, compared to $943 paid by black owner households, a difference of $129. However, black households pay on average $126 per month for electricity, compared to $101 paid by Hispanic owner households, a difference of $25. On the other hand, black households pay less than Hispanic households for piped gas—$86 compared to $120, a difference of $34 in favor of black households. However, black households pay more than Hispanic households for water: $50 compared to $42, a difference of $8 per month in favor of Hispanic households. Finally, black households pay more on average than Hispanic households in taxes per $1,000 value ($29 compared to $21, a difference of $8).

In sum, there is no clear pattern of difference in cost of living among black and Hispanic households in Detroit and selected suburbs. When all owner households are compared in Detroit, Wayne County outside of Detroit, and Oakland County, the cost varies. The median monthly cost paid by households was $812 in Detroit and increases to $1,059 in Wayne County outside of Detroit and to $1,285 in Oakland County. However, households in Detroit pay more on average for electricity ($146) than households in Wayne County ($97) and households in Oakland County ($93). On the other hand, Detroit households pay less for piped gas ($82 per month) than households in Wayne County ($86) and Oakland County ($118). Detroit households pay more for water ($50 per month) than households in Wayne County excluding Detroit ($42) and Oakland County ($40). Finally, residents of Detroit pay more taxes per $1,000 value ($32) than households in Wayne County outside of Detroit ($21) and Oakland County ($19).

In sum, given the lower quality of the neighborhoods in Detroit, one would expect lower costs to live there than in the suburbs. However, Detroit residents pay more for three of the five items discussed. These items include electricity, water, and real estate taxes.

CONCLUSIONS

We began this chapter with a prediction made in 1987 about racial polarization between Detroit and its suburbs as well as the race and class gap between the poor in the city and the affluent in the suburbs (Darden et al., 1987). Our data and analysis of the race and class divide in 2008 have demonstrated that this polarization has continued. The predominately black city had an increase in its percentage black population and a decline in its percentage white population. The high level of residential segregation declined slightly in the metropolitan area and in the city but has remained high over the decades.

Although only a few (76,647) blacks resided in the suburbs in 1960, the black suburban population gradually increased to 384,518, representing 12.2 of the suburban population in 2010. Blacks, however, remained highly underrepresented in the suburbs and overrepresented in the city.

The *Detroit News* noted in 2007 that some blacks even feel isolated. Although one black couple found the white and wealthy suburb of Bloomfield Hills in Oakland County to be safe with first-rate services, life in Bloomfield Hills was hard on them in other ways. Since only one other black family was in their neighborhood, "They felt isolated. Also, their children were ostracized in middle school" (Rodriguez, 2007).

Nevertheless, a *Detroit News* poll conducted in July 2007 found that 81 percent of blacks still preferred racially mixed neighborhoods in the Detroit metropolitan area, compared to only 49 percent of whites (Rodriguez, 2007). The driving force behind the preference of blacks was for the best school district they could afford. The poll found that while only 33 percent of blacks were somewhat or very satisfied with their local schools, 70 percent of whites, most of whom lived in the suburbs, were satisfied (see chapter 3).

Given that most whites in the metropolitan area do not prefer residential integration, increased black migration to the suburbs, according to the *Detroit News*, is starting to mirror the dispersal of the white suburban population to the outer suburbs, that is, "white suburban flight from suburban residential integration" (Rodriguez, 2007). White flight was indeed operating in the demographic change in suburban Southfield as the municipality changed from predominately white to predominately black in twenty years (see chapter 6). Thus, blacks in the suburbs can expect to be pioneers and/or isolated for some time as whites continue to move outward. Such underrepresentation in the suburbs contributed to the overall level of black residential segregation, which has declined slightly since 1970. Despite the decline, blacks in metropolitan Detroit remained the most racially segregated group, that is, more segregated than Hispanics, Asians, or Native Americans (Darden, 2009b).

Moreover, such high levels of residential segregation were not due to the differential level of incomes or education. Blacks and whites with comparable incomes and education were highly residentially segregated.

The race and class divide was evident in unemployment rates, as blacks in the city experienced an unemployment rate of 22.2 percent, compared to 15.7 percent for non-Hispanic whites. Every racial group living in the city of Detroit experienced double-digit unemployment rates in 2008. The rates were much lower in the suburbs. However, blacks experienced double-digit unemployment rates even in the suburbs.

A racial gap was also maintained when measured by median income in the city and between the city and the suburbs.

The race and place divide based on marital status revealed the significance of married couple households and female-headed households in the city and suburbs. Female-headed households, a group most represented in Detroit, had the highest percentage of its population in poverty.

Prospects of a Widening Gap

At the time this chapter was written, Michigan and the nation were coming out of the worst recession since the Great Depression. Therefore, we predict that the unemployment rate gap between blacks and whites and between Detroit and its suburbs will remain for some time. That is because it usually takes blacks longer than whites to recover from a recession. There will also be an increase in the poverty rate gap between blacks in the city and whites in the suburbs because this recession impacted blacks more than whites.

For example, during the year 2008, nearly 20,000 black autoworkers had lost their jobs by November, a 13.9 percent decline in employment since the recession began in December 2007 (Chapman, 2008). This compares to a 4.4 percent decline for all workers in manufacturing. Over the years, many blacks in the Detroit metropolitan area have depended heavily on the auto industry to provide them with a middle-class lifestyle. But since 1969 in particular, the auto industry has declined dramatically, forcing black workers to seek other employment (Jacobs, 2009). Historically, the auto industry has been one of the best sources of jobs for workers without a college degree (Chapman, 2008).

Given the recession and the persistent out-migration of Detroit's middle-class black and white populations, the race, class, and place of residence divide will not only remain, but may actually expand, at least over the next decade.

CHAPTER 12

Interracial Cooperation and Bridge Building in the Postriot Era

DESPITE ITS LONG HISTORY OF RACIAL DISCRIMINATION (INCLUDING TWO TRAGIC race riots in less than a quarter of a century, constant white suburban/black city hostilities, and newly emerging racial and cultural diversity, which created even more tension and conflict between old and new minorities), many Detroiters continued to believe that their city could overcome its racial challenges. Every racial crisis in Detroit produced its very own disciples of hope, climbing stubbornly out of the ashes of despair to heal wounds and bind people together in one loving and caring multiracial community. People and organizations, old and new, preriot and postriot, refused to give up on the city.

INDIVIDUAL EFFORTS

One of the most urgent tasks was to repudiate the insane arms race. One group distributed signs stating, "This home is not armed," which soon appeared in windows and doors throughout the Detroit metropolitan area. In Warren, one of the suburbs known for its white working-class racism, 2,500 whites signed a newspaper advertisement to encourage a racially mixed family to remain in the city after they were harassed by whites. One white resident of Warren organized a fund-raising drive that produced $11,000 for the purpose of improving interracial understanding. The organizers gave $2,500 to help a black adult educational program in Detroit develop a black history library (*Lansing State Journal*, July 7, 1968).

After the 1943 Detroit riot the white power elite had placed most of the blame on so-called "black agitators" and had largely ignored institutional racism in planning ahead. In contrast, after the 1967 riot a few key white leaders in the public and private sectors began focusing on long-neglected root causes of urban racial unrest. Recognizing the historical conflict between Detroit's black community and the police department, Mayor Cavanagh ordered increased recruitment of blacks. The Michigan National Guard also began a recruitment program among blacks in Detroit. Fifteen Michigan cities (including Detroit) passed open housing ordinances following the 1967 riot. A statewide law banning racial discrimination in most real estate transactions was passed by the legislature and signed by the governor (Thomas, 1987b).

EFFORTS OF RELIGIOUS ORGANIZATIONS

A few white religious leaders in Detroit had always been at the forefront of the struggle for racial equality. It did not take a riot to get their attention, but the riot of 1967 and the subsequent publication of the Kerner Commission Report in March 1968 encouraged these leaders to take bolder actions.

Before the riot was twenty-four hours old an Interfaith Emergency Center was organized by concerned representatives of the local Council of Churches, the local archdiocese, the Jewish Community Council, and the all-black Interdenominational Ministerial Alliance (Gordon, 1971).

This interfaith interracial organization set up shop in the general riot area within sight of the fires, sniping, and police and army patrols. According to one writer, "Catholic and Protestant churches and the one synagogue in the widespread riot area were activated to serve as distribution points for medical and food needs" (Gordon, 1971: 19). This rapid organizational response to the riot would not have been possible or very effective without prior developments.

Archbishop John F. Dearden, representing the Roman Catholic Archdiocese of Detroit and 1.5 million Catholics in an eight-county area (including the city), pledged $1 million for a "campaign designed to root out white racism, to win home acceptance for Negroes, and to bring direct help to those trapped by ghetto life" (Thomas, 1987b: 148). About a month before the first anniversary of the 1967 riot, the Michigan Catholic School Superintendents' Committee decided that black history would be integrated into all subjects taught in Michigan's 675 Catholic schools. The committee also made plans to begin in-service training programs for Catholic school principals and teachers to provide them with a "better understanding of the problems facing inner-city children" (quoted in Thomas, 1987b: 148).

The Metropolitan Detroit Religion and Race Conference, 1962–1967

Prior to the riot, the Metropolitan Detroit Religion and Race Conference was formed to provide "an organizational structure and ongoing interreligious communication base." The next stage was "the emergence of the Interfaith Emergency Center during the riot crisis," followed by "the development of an ongoing Interfaith Action Council as a direct outgrowth of the IE Center's activities." It was this very vital latter phase that "resulted in an ongoing, functioning, interreligious unit designed to serve in a catalytic role by operating between the inner-city ghetto and established leadership" (Gordon, 1971: 19).

Why is understanding these developments so important for understanding religious efforts to bridge the racial divides during the post-riot period? As Gordon (1971: 19) explains, these events "directly influenced the nature of the religious leadership response during and after the riot when the IEC (IAC) operations were set up." This point cannot be overemphasized. Having an organizational setup in place "during and after the riot" most certainly contributed to the healing process.

The Metropolitan Detroit Religion and Race Conference emerged in the early 1960s as part of the legacy of the interracial efforts in the wake of the 1943 race riots. An array of social forces was at work, including (as excerpted from Gordon, 1971: 19):

- "the external pressures of the civil rights movement";
- "multiple internal religious social forces involved in moving the separate Catholic, Jewish, and Protestant establishments to act together";
- "the traditional activities of the Jewish community relations network, always operating on the principle of working with social allies whenever possible"; and
- "the emergent Protestant concern with a growing black constituency in Detroit that was highly discontented."

Gordon (1971) argued, however, that the "most dynamic development was the emergence of Vatican II and the Ecumenical Movement under the influence of Pope John XXIII." This led to the establishment in 1962 of the Detroit Archbishop Committee on Human Rights, "whose Director, Father James Sheehan, initiated communications with representatives of the local Council of Churches and the Jewish Community Council" (Gordon, 1971: 19).

These internal religious forces were developing alongside "a rising tide of civil rights activity and growing inner-city discontent." There were demonstrations for better housing, jobs and education, culminating at one historic point in the June 1963 march involving 100,000 people led by Dr. Martin Luther King Jr. An increasing number of people were looking to more radical organizations (such as CORE and the "Saul Alinsky–advised West Central Organization") to address their needs (Gordon, 1971: 20). These developments posed a serious challenge to some of the "early operational assumptions" of the Metropolitan Detroit Religion and Race Conference.

The first operational assumption that was challenged by events was that "racial divisiveness in the community could largely be overcome by reminding people of their respective religious teachings" (Gordon, 1971: 20). Therefore, raising moral issues and educating people would do the trick. The problem with this assumption was that it was based on the feeling that the majority of whites in the three religious communities "deeply felt the moral dilemma on race that Gunnar Myrdal postulated in the 1940s in his encyclopedic *An American Dilemma*" (Gordon, 1971: 20).

Sadly, they discovered that "for most whites no serious moral dilemma existed. A majority of whites simply opposed equality of opportunity for Negroes, even after an intensive educational effort was made in churches and synagogues and in the community generally to oppose a specific segregation ordinance" (Gordon, 1971: 21).

Another assumption held by the white religious leadership was they "could operate unilaterally on racial justice without a working relationship with Negroes" (Gordon, 1971: 21). This became quite apparent during the Religion and Race Conference's first program, the formation of an Open Occupancy Conference in the fall of 1962.

The issue of black participation was raised "parenthetically" by the white religious leaders (including the Detroit Council of Churches, the metropolitan Detroit Archdiocese, and the Jewish Community Council), but they were operating on the moral principle that "since it was whites who were keeping blacks from the open housing market, it was the job of whites to teach other whites their moral duty" (Gordon, 1971: 22). Notwithstanding their reasoning, prominent black leaders threatened to boycott the conference unless they were involved in both the planning and the program. To their credit, the white Conference Executive Committee agreed. Reverend Charles W. Butler of the Interdenominational Ministerial Alliance was selected as a featured speaker. Willie Baxter, a black labor negotiator and a future member of Mayor Jerome Cavanagh's administration, was selected as a member of the executive committee, and Arthur Johnson, the Michigan executive secretary of the NAACP, was placed on the Committee on Conclusions and Recommendations (Gordon, 1971).

With these issues resolved to the satisfaction of black leaders, the Open Occupancy Conference went ahead on schedule in January 1963. Soon after the conference, the organizers changed the name to the Religion and Race Conference and added the Greek Orthodox Diocese and several black Protestant lay members, including Lawrence Washington, a black auto executive. In 1964, two other black leaders were added: Reverend Joseph Pelham, "first suburban Negro minister . . . and Horace Sheffield of the United Auto Workers Union hierarchy" (Gordon, 1971: 23).

While the inclusion of these black leaders represented some degree of progress in interracial cooperation, Gordon correctly points out that "it was not then clearly perceived by members of the Religion and Race Executive Committee what the Kerner Commission highlighted, that is, that establishment black leadership never had a large following in the Negro community." Worse still, he argued, was the fact that the members did not recognize "the depth of social disorganization and feelings of alienation and free-floating hostility, accentuated by the civil rights movement" (Gordon, 1971: 23).

Considering the harsh reality that, as sociologists at the time reported, "while the middle-class black community was closing the gap, the masses of blacks in the lower socioeconomic levels were falling relatively farther behind" (Gordon, 1971: 23), between 1962 and 1967 the program of the Religion and Race Conference was way off base. During this period, the focus was on "reducing interracial tensions by a 'challenge to conscience'" aimed at the white middle-class, and "an effort to assist middle-class blacks to move into the larger community. The inner-city ghetto areas per se were not a programmatic focus" (Gordon, 1971: 23). This misguided focus ignored the worsening conditions of blacks in the inner-city ghetto, which would soon explode into a bloody riot.

Notwithstanding its misreading of the impending ghetto crisis and its lack of a programmatic approach to inner-city ghetto conditions during this period, the Conference did develop "close informal as well as formal communication links established by [its] various religious organizational staff and lay representatives . . . over a five year period of regular meetings," links that were activated during the crisis (Gordon, 1971: 24). As a result, "The rapport developed in this process was directly related to the speed with which the Interfaith Emergency Center was operationally set in July of 1967" (Gordon, 1971: 24).

As Detroit descended into darkness on that fateful summer day in July, religious leaders in Detroit could at least take pride in its "one substantive accomplishment" of having "establish[ed] the kind of communication links not evident in reports of other riot-torn cities" (Gordon, 1971: 26).

The Interfaith Emergency Council

While the 1967 riot was devastating in its overall impact on the Detroit metropolitan region, it forced the Conference's religious leaders to change their approach to race relations. The IEC emerged to address the immediate medical and food needs in the wake of the riot—a radical departure from the traditional focus upon "moral education" (Gordon, 1971: 26).

Several weeks after the riot, this new approach was dramatically reflected in a statement from one of the working committees of the IEC, which in part said:

We, of the Interfaith Emergency Council, serve two constituencies: The inner-city community and the outer-city suburban community. . . . The white constituency, being generally middle-class and relatively privileged, does not understand the meaning of the riot because it does not yet understand Negro needs, aims, and frustrations any more than it understands the plight of the poor in American society. (Gordon, 1971: 26)

This statement alone was revelatory! Instead of a call for "law and order," the working committee issued an urgent call for social action from metropolitan area religious leaders: "We . . . must seek to speak to both constituencies—inner-city and outer-city/suburban—but our first responsibility is to interpret the riot to our white constituencies as it throws light on the whole constellation of urban problems" (Gordon, 1971: 27). This "first responsibility" would be difficult given the white suburban racial hysteria of the immediate postriot period. The next related responsibility was to the black inner-city community. The working committee stressed the need to "strive to make demonstrably clear that religious groups actively support them in their effort to be free men and to enjoy the rights of life and citizenship in an affluent society. Our role is supportive" (Gordon, 1971: 27).

In terms of specific action steps, the working committee focusing on three major problems: "An adequate supply of good housing for all income levels and along with this, an open housing market throughout the metropolitan area; many more jobs at all levels of management and all degrees of skill or professionalism, plus retraining hard-core jobless persons," and, of particular importance, "quality education for all children of the Detroit area, which means in realistic terms, substantially more revenue to enable the schools to do as good a job as educators can be trained to provide" (Gordon, 1971: 27).

Along with the above, the working committee recommended as an immediate step "that Suburban Action Centers be established in the North, Northwest, West and Southwest sections of our metropolitan areas. These centers, with full-time staff and supporting clerical personnel, would provide a stimulus for a massive expansion of church and community human relations information, educational, and attitudinal change programming" (Gordon, 1971: 27).

As mentioned above, the working committee's statement to the IEC was a radical departure from the approach to race relations taken by the traditional religious leadership. What stood out was the "wider range of specific proposals in the areas of housing, jobs, and education. The second was a new, clear concern with the underclass of the black community." In short, the "religious leadership in Detroit had begun for the first time to look at the core issues in black-white relations" (Gordon, 1971: 27).

It should be kept in mind that the religious community had a long history of working together in addressing problems related to race and poverty. Over the years members of various faith communities had developed contacts and working relationships and, as already mentioned, during 1963 and 1964, had formed the Metropolitan and Race Conference, later renamed the Council for Race and Human Rights. They were actively involved in the early stages of the civil rights movement, but had been rendered ineffective by the black militant stage of the movement. However, they did manage to set up a Monday morning "interfaith hotline" among themselves that would prove very effective during the riot (Forrest, 1971).

According to one writer, "Every Monday morning at 8:00 A.M. the conference is held with a loose agenda allowing each member to contribute what he feels is important. Discussions run from how the churches could aid Negro families who move into all-white neighborhoods, to the Kodak conflict with . . . CORE . . . in Rochester, New York" (Forrest, 1971: 89). Understandably, most of the discussion focused on sharing information concerning poverty and race in Detroit. These Monday morning discussions generated invaluable confidence and understanding among the members of the hotline, which in turn contributed to the establishment of the Interfaith Action Council and the Interfaith Emergency Center. As explained by one member, "The fact that we all knew each other well enough so that when we sat together Monday afternoon we didn't have to say now who is this guy, can I trust him? I mean there had been a band of confidence built up that we immediately could move together" (Forrest, 1971: 89).

The Monday morning hotline participants were not the only means by which members of interfaith communities interacted. For example, the Detroit Council of Churches, the Interdenominational Ministerial Alliance (an African American minister's association), and the Jewish Community Council (among others) eventually gravitated toward each other to seek a remedy to the crisis. Regardless of their respective motives, they determined that "what is important in understanding the emergent process [of the IFC] is that having had previous contact with one another these individuals sought out each other to find some meaning to the crisis and to arrive at a course of action" (Forrest, 1971: 90).

One of the member organizations, the Episcopal Society for Culture and Racial Unity (ESCRU), drawing upon its experiences from the 1965 Watts riot, played a key role in the ongoing process by drawing up "a set of plans which detailed suggestions as to the role the church could play in a civil disturbance" (Forrest, 1971: 91). This would prove to be very crucial because the "plan called for an interfaith response which would refrain from offering gratuitous calls for law and order, while trying to see what creative things could be done" (Forrest, 1971: 91). In addition, the plan suggested that an information center be set up to "collect and dispense information related to the disturbance" (Forrest, 1971: 91).

In relation to the plan, one Episcopal official at the gathering wisely suggested that the group should put off for the moment any interpretation of the event. In short, it should "refrain from making statements calling for law and order." Instead participants would "remain neutral in whatever role they were to perform. Once [it had] been decided, the next step was to commit those present to a given course of action" (Forrest, 1971: 91).

The next step in that course of action came out of the ESCRU plan and was suggested by the Episcopal official: "that an information center be formed." The group voted to establish the Interfaith Emergency Center. The Episcopal Diocesan Center volunteered space to house it (Forrest, 1971: 91).

The first challenge facing the newly founded IEC was to introduce the center to the public, with radio and television acting as mediators. The public was informed that the IEC had "come into existence to aid individual citizens requesting information." The role of mass media was essential for "providing IEC with the necessary minimum legitimacy so that it would be recognized by individuals and other organizations within the community" (Forrest, 1971: 93). Given the fact that most of the welfare and community emergency agencies, for example, Red Cross and Civil Defense, "were not responding in an effective manner," mainly because of the citywide curfew, many people who had heard of IEC preferred it to the red tape associated with welfare agencies (Forrest, 1971: 93).

No sooner had the IEC been established than calls began streaming in. Surprisingly, most of these calls were not for information about the riot but from people asking for help and those volunteering their help (Forrest, 1971). According to one source:

The response was so great that they had to turn volunteers away. Instead of calling into the center—which was extremely difficult to do—volunteers converged at the center, filling hallways and adding to the general confusion that already existed. Since a general city-wide curfew had technically closed down the city, individuals were freed from their normal employment duties to be able to volunteer their time. (Forrest, 1971: 99)

Just a few days after the media announced its existence, the IEC began receiving calls from suburban churches offering to "collect food and clothing" and calls from urban churches "volunteering their services as centers for distributing food and clothing" (Forrest, 1971: 92). Before long, the Wayne County AFL-CIO (UAW) offered to provide transportation services between the city and its suburbs. "Using volunteer truck drivers and trucks donated by major companies in the greater metropolitan area, the union established a distribution department dispatching drivers to 25 collection centers and 21 distribution centers" (Forrest, 1971: 92).

The problems associated with the riot demanded that the IEC be able to adapt to changing demands. Between July 30 and August 4, the IEC gradually began to phase out its collection and distribution services in preparation for "a whole new set of problems [facing] individuals who had suffered from the disturbance. These new problems became the basis for the continuance of IEC" (Forrest, 1971: 92).

Among these "new sets of problems" were families "who were separated from one another by arrests now [seeking] to reunite themselves" and "homeless families that had been taken in by friends or relatives during the disturbance [and] now were obligated to find more permanent housing. And families who normally could make ends meet suddenly were faced with bills they were unable to pay because of the loss incurred during the disturbance" (Forrest, 1971: 103).

The IEC continued to operate until November 1967 as a model of interfaith bridge-building in a time of crisis (Forrest, 1971).

NEW DETROIT, 1968–2007

New Detroit, Inc. (NDI) and Focus: HOPE have become two of the premier bridge-building organizations in the post–civil disorder period. For example, in the wake of the 1967 riot NDI made its first effort at bridge building across race and class by appointing members from different backgrounds. Joseph L. Hudson, the first chairperson of the NDI, actively sought out aggressive grassroots blacks to be voting members of NDI in an effort to reach out to the alienated and marginal people. This decision to involve black militants created some conflict, but their involvement in the NDI gave it the credibility it otherwise would not have had. Before long, however, the militants became disillusioned with the NDI's approach to the problem (*Detroit Scope*, May 11, 1968).

For the next three decades, New Detroit, Inc.—originally called the New Detroit Committee—was one of the two premier race relations bridge builders in the Detroit metropolitan area. During this period, NDI's bridge-building projects included city-suburban high school exchanges, one of its most successful race relations efforts; bridge-building conferences; workshops and forums for city and suburban leaders; support for African American and

Hispanic cooperation; and efforts to diffuse African American and Arab/Chaldean conflicts (Thomas, 2002).

In 1994, as a result of the changing racial, cultural, and ethnic demographics of the Detroit metropolitan area, NDI embarked on a more ambitious and complex bridge-building project, the Cultural Exchange Network. This project involved thirty-three ethnic communities "ranging from Korean and Native American to members of the Hmong and Pakistani communities" (Thomas, 2002).

Bridge building in NDI became the dominant approach to the race problem in the Detroit metropolitan area during the early 1980s. In 1982 NDI's Anti-Racism Committee initiated a series of city-suburban forums designed "to reach ordinary city and suburban residents and to establish a better understanding between the City of Detroit and its suburbs" (New Detroit, 1982). The following year the Anti-Racism Committee of NDI changed its name to the Racial and Economic Justice Committee:

> Committee and Board members felt that the name "Anti-Racism" sent out a somewhat negative confrontational message rather than one of bridge building, the central concern of the coalition process. It was felt that the overall attempt of the Committee's work is to ensure racial and economic justice for all citizens realizing that if such were the consequences for Blacks and other ethnic minorities, the general society would be enhanced. (New Detroit, 1983b)

Based upon this bridge-building approach, the Racial and Economic Justice Committee presented "the first three of six city-suburban forums, designed to foster understanding of common concerns and promote cooperative problem solving between Detroit and suburban residents." These forums involved prominent policymakers in the public and private sectors, including General Motors chairman Roger Smith, who spoke at the first forum; Wayne County executive William Lucas; Oakland County executive Daniel Murphy; and Macomb County commissioner Patrick Johnson, who discussed data from the Southeast Michigan Council of Governments showing how city and suburban residents interact and work together. First Lady Paula Blanchard, special advisor to the Michigan Department of Commerce, was the featured speaker. She spoke about jobs and commerce in Michigan, emphasizing products made in Michigan. Reflecting the Racial and Economic Justice Committee's emphasis on city-suburban bridge building, the subtitle of this series of forums was appropriately named "Partners in Community Progress" (New Detroit, 1983b).

New Detroit's efforts at bridge building between city and suburbs continued into the 1990s. In December 1991, NDI's race relations committee presented a "Building Bridges" forum in which a panel of municipal and community leaders discussed "strategies to increase contact and understanding between city and suburban groups . . . and evaluated the efforts of various suburban and city organizations who already have been working to overcome the barriers that exist between their communities" (*New Detroit Now*, Spring 1992). Interestingly enough, this particular bridge-building conference was inspired by the great popularity of the city-suburban high school exchanges by NDI started in the 1980s (*New Detroit Now*, Winter 1989–90).

New Detroit's City-Suburban High School Conference and Exchange Day was one of the most successful bridge-building projects in the history of the organization. During the 1980s and 1990s, hundreds of suburban and inner-city students gathered in two-day sessions for "an opportunity to explore their differences and commonalities." The sessions involved suburban students visiting urban schools and urban students visiting suburban schools. The coordinator of the 1987 Conference and Exchange Day expressed the feelings of other like-minded bridge builders when she commented, "It is heartening when you see students from all over Metro Detroit, some of whom have never had any real or meaningful contact with one another, begin to break down racial barriers" (*New Detroit Now*, April 1987). Seeing them in the social context of the racially polarized Detroit metropolitan community, New Detroit vice president David F. Smyrna described the Conference and Exchange Days as "important first steps in achieving understanding among all of metro Detroit residents" (*New Detroit Now*, April 1987).

At the Fifth High School Conference and Exchange Day, students came from fifty-three schools. Most of the schools were in Wayne, Oakland, and Macomb counties, as well as Brighton and Howell. Some suburban students attended the conference over objections from their parents who did not want them to mingle with inner-city students. One black parent from Detroit voiced concern over her son visiting a northeast suburb "perceived as dangerous for blacks." "Don't you know," she asked her son, "they'll lynch you out there?" She asked, "Why does my son have to be the experiment?" Her son reminded his mother that the purpose of the conference was to eliminate such misperceptions (*New Detroit Now*, Winter 1989–90).

Consistent with previous Conference and Exchange Days, the students attended workshops designed to help them understand racial issues and exchanged schools to expand their experiences. Over forty teachers, counselors, and principals came along with students to the conference where they participated in their own workshops.

Given the long history of racial isolation, stereotypes, and discrimination, many people in the Detroit metropolitan area were unwilling to accept the idea of suburban and inner-city students building bridges across the racial divide. The postconference publicity covering the students' positive experiences with racial harmony triggered harassing and threatening phone calls to the conference organizers (*New Detroit Now*, Winter 1989–90). These calls reflected the fears and anxieties of many people in the metropolitan community who had a stake in maintaining the racial status quo and felt threatened by a conference of white suburban and black inner-city students determined to become bridge builders to a new multiracial social order.

Throughout the 1990s the City-Suburban High School Conference and Exchange Day programs sponsored by NDI continued to provide the main bridge-building link between suburban and inner-city students (*New Detroit Now*, Spring 1992). No other NDI race relations project held such promise for bridging the racial and class divide between Detroit and its suburbs and breaking the decades-old cycle of hostility between these two most racially segregated regions in the state.

In the 1980s NDI expanded its bridge-building programs to include more racially, culturally, and ethnically diverse populations. During 1988–89, NDI's Minority Cultural Exchange Program sponsored two major entertainment events oriented around families as a continuation of NDI's intercultural exchanges among Asian Pacific Americans, African Americans, Middle Eastern Americans, Native Americans, and Hispanic Americans. The program was based upon the belief that "intercultural understanding and cooperation is important to the social, political and economic empowerment of people of color" (New Detroit, 1988–89).

Other programs emerged during the 1990s, expanding NDI's bridge-building efforts. In February 1990 NDI sponsored "Cultural Agenda 2000," which featured presentations from five panels representing Michigan's five major minority groups: African Americans,

Arab and Chaldean Americans, Asian Pacific Americans, Hispanic Americans, and Native Americans. The participants met in small multiracial/multiethnic groups where they not only discussed relevant racial and ethnic issues, but made recommendations "for long and short term improvements" (*New Detroit Now*, Spring 1991).

In the late 1980s, NDI's Race Relations Committee created the Cultural Exchange Network to "bring together artists and audiences from diverse cultural backgrounds to explore their common artist heritage." For the next six years the network sponsored an annual series of cultural events. By 1995 the network was composed of representatives from nearly forty community-based organizations representing the five major racial and ethnic communities in the metropolitan Detroit area. In 1995, the network sponsored five cultural events to promote unity among Michigan's major minority groups. These events included the Communities of Color Leadership Reception, to "invite the leadership of the five major racial and ethnic communities to share and network with each other"; the Concert of Colors, to "celebrate the cultural diversity of Michigan's five minority communities and explore areas where the musical tradition of these communities find common ground"; the Poetry of Color Clinic; and the Dance of Color Program (*New Detroit Now*, 1995).

The musical events were not seen as separate cultural programs. According to the Race Relations Committee, "Artists from diverse cultural backgrounds will collaborate to present traditional, contemporary and crossover music of African, Arab, Latino, Asian and Native American Roots" (*New Detroit Now*, 1995). This was bridge building at its artistic best! As the Race Relations Committee pointed out in its 1995 fact sheet, "The Race Relations Committee feels that the best way to provide for better race relations in the metropolitan Detroit area is to give people from different cultural backgrounds the opportunity to come together and share positive experiences" (*New Detroit Now*, 1995).

In 1995, NDI started another multicultural bridge-building program, the Multi-Cultural Immersion Program. According to its 1999 fact sheet, the intent was "to highlight the history, culture, and community issues of each of the communities of color . . . from their perspective in their communities" using "an innovative approach to bridge communication gaps and to promote better understanding and appreciation among participants."

In addition to the five major racial, ethnic, and cultural groups in the region, the Multi-Cultural Immersion Program also involved a cross-section of the community, including business, civic groups, education, health services and community-based organizations (New Detroit, 1999). At the dawn of the new century, NDI was still engaged in exploring new ways and consolidating old ways of building bridges among racially, culturally, and ethnically diverse communities.

FOCUS: HOPE, 1968–2008

Among the many brave and dedicated souls who would arise to heal the wounds of the 1967 riot, few were as dedicated and long-serving as Eleanor Josaitis, a white housewife from Taylor, Michigan, and William Cunningham, a white Catholic priest and English teacher at Sacred Heart. They "went to view the devastation with their own eyes," unlike many white "hawkers" and curious "sight seekers" who wanted merely to view the results of the riots as confirmation of their long-held and nurtured racial stereotypes of inner-city blacks.

"The priest and the housewife were friends, drawn together by faith and a shared view that the world could be made better, that seemingly intractable problems like racism, economic segregation, social inequality were not necessarily carved in stone" (Martelle, 2008).

Forty years later, Josaitis recalled, "The tanks were going up and down the streets. Buildings were on fire. The helicopters were flying above." She and her priest decided, "We have got to do something" (Martelle, 2008). In March 1968, after months of planning, Focus: HOPE was born, "an organization aimed at bridging race and class divides to keep the riots from rekindling." According to Josaitis, "The real name was Focus: Summer Hope," because "everybody thought there was going to be a riot in '68, so we were trying to bring people together" (Martelle, 2008). They adopted the following mission statement on March 8, 1968:

Recognizing the dignity and beauty of every person,
we pledge intelligent and practical action
to overcome racism, poverty and injustice.
And to build a metropolitan community where all people
may live in freedom, harmony, trust and affection.
Black and White, yellow, brown and red
from Detroit and its suburbs
of every economic status,
national origin and religious persuasion
we join in this covenant

—Adopted March 8, 1968

Focus: HOPE came on the scene just before the assassination of Dr. Martin Luther King, Jr. on April 4, 1968. Fortunately, Detroit did not erupt as it did a year earlier, providing Focus: HOPE with just enough breathing space to begin operating with its pledge to take "intelligent and practical action to overcome racism, poverty, and injustice" ("1960s–1970s," n.d.). That same year, Focus: HOPE responded to a study of racial discrimination by the *Detroit Free Press* and the Urban League and "organized a search for evidence of widespread discrimination in food and prescription drug prices" (Focus: HOPE, n.d.-a). They recruited white suburbanites and black urbanities to go on shopping trips. "We found that folks in the city were paying 30 percent more for their groceries, and the [chain] stores were delivering old meat and fruits from the suburbs in the city." Focus: HOPE found the same pattern of racial discrimination over prescription drugs (Martelle, 2008).

Focus: HOPE understood, as did many other observers of the 1967 riot, that this form of widespread institutional discrimination contributed to the anger and frustration of blacks. Besides enlisting the help of black urbanites and white suburbanites to document regional patterns of price discrimination, Focus: HOPE also enlisted "professionals from local universities, city departments, corporations, and organizations" (Focus: HOPE, n.d.-c). The next step was to publish its own study, entitled, "Hope '68," which "was the first to offer definitive proof of systematic discrimination in food pricing." Notwithstanding this important finding, "the impact of the study went far beyond exposing the conditions believed to behind much of the violence of 1967. Hope '68 laid the foundation for Focus: HOPE's entire approach to resolving the effects of discrimination" (Focus: HOPE, n.d.-c).

Three years later, in 1971, "after gathering scientific evidence of the effects of hunger and malnutrition on the critical early development of infants, Focus: HOPE designed a supplemental food program for children up to age 6, and for pregnant and post-partum women" (Focus: HOPE, n.d.-c). This was truly remarkable and represented one of the most impressive community programs in the early postriot period. It was a bedrock effort to address the most vulnerable populations in the city. The program was later extended to cover senior citizens and "was the first and remains one of the largest Community Supplemental Food Programs in the country, with food provided through the U.S. Department of Agriculture to 43,000 women, children and senior citizens each month in the Detroit metropolitan area" (Focus: HOPE, n.d.-c).

Notwithstanding the success of their food program, Focus: HOPE's "long term objective" was to eliminate the need for such programs "by providing opportunities for all people to enter the economic mainstream." The organization defined civil rights as economic opportunity and embarked on the mission of developing education and training programs such as the Machinist Training Program (MTI), which opened in 1981 "to provide skills development in precision machining and metalworking." By 2009 opening, the program had graduated 2,740 machinists (Focus: HOPE, n.d.-c).

The Automobile Club of Michigan

One of Focus: HOPE's longest legal battles against institutionalized racism was fought against the powerful Automobile Club of Michigan (AAA). In 1970 the City of Detroit was shocked to discover via a suburban newspaper article that AAA was considering a move to the suburbs. Given the flight of people and jobs to the suburbs since the 1967 disorder, the city was understandably worried about the potential loss of 1,200 jobs. In an attempt to convince the company to remain in Detroit, Mayor Roman Gribbs, along with the newly established Detroit Renaissance Committee, proposed six sites in Detroit suitable for the company's stated needs. To sweeten the deal, the city offered to build a $4 million parking structure on or near any city site the company chose (Focus: HOPE, n.d.-b).

To the despair of the city, AAA rejected the offer and announced its decision to take an option on a thirty-acre parcel of land located in Dearborn. The company refused to budge on its decision even after Focus: HOPE and other civil rights organizations explained that the move would have an adverse effect on the AAA's minority employment. Focus: HOPE reported that "When the Automobile Club was located downtown, 70 percent of all applicants were Black; in Dearborn, less than 18 percent are Blacks. The number of Black employees has also dropped" (Focus: HOPE, n.d.-b).

Focus: HOPE formed an ad hoc coalition, the Detroit Action Coalition (DAC), to oppose the decision of AAA to relocate its headquarters from the city of Detroit to a predominantly white suburb with a black population of less than 0.02 percent. The DAC argued that "AAA's racism inspired its move." Focus: HOPE "formed that ad hoc coalition to stop the Automobile Club of Michigan's move and to save the jobs of Black employees present and future" (*Focus: HOPE News*, August 1982).

The DAC sent letters to AAA documenting its "long history of racial exclusion in membership, insurance and employment . . . going back to the original articles of incorporation which opened membership to 'any White male person over the age of twenty-one years, and of good moral character'" (*Focus: HOPE News*, August 1982). According to the DAC, the AAA's efforts to improve its image "masked the real intent of the Club: the elimination of minority employee by moving to segregated Dearborn" (*Focus: HOPE News*, August 1982).

Cunningham argued that "research shows that joblessness in urban centers directly relates to the prior removal of White residents to exclusive suburban communities. Subsequently, White-owned corporations and industries followed the path of their executives and rebuilt in suburban areas or out of state" (*Focus: HOPE News*, August 1982).

> In many instance, the effect has been more clearly to follow the White labor pool, and flee the Black labor pool. In every instance, the effect has been discriminatory. Black and other minorities have been left behind in deteriorating urban economies, without transportation access to the new job markets, or access to housing in the areas of job development. Detroit areas studies dramatize the wide difference between unemployment figures in the city when compared to suburban communities. (*Focus: HOPE News*, August 1982)

Despite all efforts and appeals, in 1974 AAA moved its headquarters and 1,200 jobs to the nearly all-white suburb of Dearborn (Focus: HOPE, n.d.-b).

AAA's move to Dearborn could be linked to its historic pattern of racial and sexual discrimination. For example, AAA engaged in discriminatory hiring practices. In 1963 and 1964 the Congress of Racial Equality (CORE) along with other civil rights groups picketed the company for discriminating against blacks. "As of 1964, the company had, in its fifty-year history, hired only 20 Blacks" (Focus: HOPE, n.d.-b). The civil rights groups demanded that the company hire more blacks. In part in response to the pressure, AAA's black employment increased (Focus: HOPE, n.d.-b).

Although some hiring of blacks occurred, race still influenced company decisions. For example, in 1966, AAA's board of directors' minutes revealed that management began voicing concern over what they felt was the declining quality of their workforce and saw the solution as a relocation to the suburbs where they would be able to "attract more qualified applicants." Until 1976, the company's personnel department "used a code to indicate race on employment applications . . . and . . . acquiesced, through the late Sixties, with requests from company managers not to send them Black applicants" (Focus: HOPE, n.d.-b).

In 1972, as the result of abortive negotiations with AAA, Focus: HOPE decided to support the struggle of the black AAA and women employees in a class action lawsuit against the powerful corporation, charging it with race and sex discrimination. Two years later, the class action suit was split, "with the original plaintiffs now representing over 3,000 Black workers," and the sex discrimination suit of four women, "two Blacks and two Whites, represented a class of over 7,000 women charging the Auto Club with sex discrimination." By this time, the case was already in the process of setting a precedent as the first case "in which a federal judge has ruled that relocation by an employer could be a violation of the 1964 Civil Rights Act as it relates to employment" (Focus: HOPE, n.d.-b).

The Auto Club fought a long and fierce battle against Focus: HOPE in an attempt to undermine its support of the black and women workers. Several times the company subpoenaed Focus: HOPE's records as a delaying tactic to prevent the discrimination cases from going to trial. Father Cunningham understood the tactic. "This is not the first attack on Focus: HOPE. It's the old strategy of divide and conquer. If the Auto Club isolates Black workers from our support, it can bring the full weight of a multi-million dollar corporation down on them" (Focus: HOPE, n.d.-b).

AAA went so far as to ask a company that had solicited funds from Focus: HOPE "to find out how the organization used its contributions." In still another attempt, AAA directed its attention to "whether Focus: HOPE employees who were working directly as paralegals for the black workers' attorneys could have access to company records or be present during proceeding" (Focus: HOPE, n.d.-b). The court supported the black workers on the issue (Focus: HOPE, n.d.-b).

AAA's tactics also included obstructing access to its records, which led Judge Charles W. Joiner to rule that the company had done so to delay the progress of the race discrimination class action suit. He also ruled that AAA officials misrepresented the existence of company documents. In response to the 1972 charge of racial discrimination in hiring, wages, and promotion, AAA officials had testified that they did not have any records identifying black employees prior to 1971 and that all the documents related to the relocation to Dearborn had been made available. It was soon discovered, however, that the AAA personnel department had maintained a "Book of Blacks—a virtual thesaurus on the employment history of the defendant's black work force" (Focus: HOPE, n.d.-b). They added that the document contained records dating back to 1956, and that the personnel department had "failed to produce for the plaintiffs a binder labeled 'Reasons for the Move'" (Focus: HOPE, n.d.-b). According to Focus: HOPE, Auto Club officials had repeatedly denied the existence of both documents (Focus: HOPE, n.d.-b).

The judge's ruling left no doubt that the company's delays and misrepresentations were designed to block AAA's black workers from obtaining information about its past and present black employees. Cunningham praised the judge for his "studied and courageous" findings, and accused AAA of "using delay as a general tactic, in the hope that we'll run out of money to continue the case, leaving the Black workers without support in a fight against a multimillion dollar company. The idea is to out-cost us" (Focus: HOPE, n.d.-b).

AAA's officials began their delaying tactics as soon as the lawyers for the black workers filed their lawsuit in December 1972 and asked the company for "the racial identification of all current and former employees." AAA officials claimed that the company did not keep records identifying the racial identity of its employees prior to 1971. Four years later, the Auto Club's lawyers, in an effort to prevent plaintiffs from identifying the company's workers and salaries, offered to identify the race of all employees for the court records. The lawyers for the black workers opposed the offer, pointing out that the company had claimed earlier that the information did not exist. The Auto Club's lawyers' next move was to claim that the company had no knowledge of the racial identity of employees who had left the company prior to 1971. They suggested that "the only source of race information would be to telephone or visit them, assuming their telephone numbers or addresses haven't changed since their employment ended. The magnitude of the task indicates the impossibility of it being performed" (Focus: HOPE, n.d.-b).

AAA's lawyers had thrown out a seemingly impossible challenge to Focus: HOPE and the black plaintiffs, but they were up to the task. Focus: HOPE's army of volunteers, working under the black plaintiffs' lawyers, "spent over 324 hours in a manual search of thousands of company documents in order to match them with employment applications which the company had racially coded" (Focus: HOPE, n.d.-b). Contrary to the claims of the Auto Club's officials and lawyers, the plaintiffs uncovered records that dated back to 1956 listing "all Black employees, including their date of hire, department, job title and pay scale." Furthermore, the testimony "taken after the discovery of the 'Book of Blacks' showed that the information was updated regularly, usually on a monthly basis" (Focus: HOPE, n.d.-b).

Shifting blame to the black workers' lawyers, AAA's lawyers claimed that they knew about the "Black books" (Focus: HOPE, n.d.-b). Judge Joiner was not convinced. He ruled that AAA had misled both the black plaintiffs and the court. As a result, he also decided that AAA "would not be able to dispute the information contained in the 'Book of Blacks' at trial" (Focus: HOPE, n.d.-b). This ruling represented "the final chapter in a four-year struggle to obtain information about the Auto Club's relocation to Dearborn. In February 1974, Judge Joiner ruled against the powerful, multimillion dollar company and gave it "90 days to comply with all requests for information concerning the move" (Focus: HOPE, n.d.-b).

Six months after the deadline, AAA received another court order for requests for information. By July 1975, during the next stage of the discovery process, it became clear that the company had not released many key records, such as "21 three-inch thick, three-ring binders maintained by Treasurer Robert Alkema" that company lawyers had delayed producing claiming that there was nothing "particularly new" in them. Yet when the plaintiffs finally gained access to the materials, they found one binder called "Reason for the Move." Another binder labeled "Presentation to the Board" revealed the calculating and insensitive reasoning behind the Auto Club's decision to relocate to the suburbs. As they saw it, the advantage of the move "outweighed the political and public relations consequences of the move" (Focus: HOPE, n.d.-b). AAA lawyers had spent an entire year hiding the three-ring binder labeled "Minority Census Report" that Judge Joiner called "The Book of Blacks." Judge Joiner fined the company $52,000 (*Detroit Free Press*, February 14, 1983).

Although the 1972 suit was filed on behalf of both black and women employees, the judge ruled in 1974 that the class action be split between the groups. Therefore, each group was required to file a separate suit against the company (*Detroit Free Press*, February 14, 1983). At the time, the original plaintiffs represented over 3,000 black workers. Two black and two white women represented "a class of over 7,000 women charging the Auto Club with sex discrimination" (Focus: HOPE, n.d.-b). Focus: HOPE continued to support both groups.

The sex discrimination suit against the Auto Club went to trial in 1979 and the court ruled in favor of the plaintiffs. In January 1982, the case was settled without appeal. The Auto Club agreed to "pay $3.75 million in damages to women workers and to provide affirmative relief, including accelerated placement of women at all levels of the company until female representation reached 50 percent" (Focus: HOPE, n.d.-c). A year later, after twelve years of time-consuming and costly research, delays and negotiations, the company settled with the black workers through a consent agreement. The Automobile Club agreed to

pay $3 million in damages to current and former Black employees and applicants; to place Black workers at various levels within the company at specified rates under an eight-year Court-monitored affirmative action plan; and to establish a trust fund of $1.7 million to assist Black employees to attain or continue employment at any AAA facility in Michigan through low interest auto and housing loans. Through November, 1992, forty-four mortgages worth $3.3 million and forty-eight auto loans valued at $387,510 were issued. (Focus: HOPE, n.d.-c)

Winning this case represented a great historic victory for Focus: HOPE and the nearly 12,000 blacks covered by the settlement. In a joint statement, Father William T. Cunningham, director of Focus: HOPE said:

We are heartened by the AAA's proposal to be a leader in equal opportunities for both women and black employees. . . . This settlement is not only the largest involving discrimination in Michigan history, it also is highly innovative. The trust fund will allow current and future black AAA employees to exercise the same housing choices as white AAA employees." (*Detroit News*, February 8, 1983)

Jack Avignone, the Auto Club president, remarked, "This agreement contains many of the employment practices already in effect as a result of the sex-discrimination case. It reinforces our commitment to affirmative action and equal opportunity" (*Detroit News*, February 8, 1983).

By the end of the lengthy legal battle against AAA, Focus: HOPE had established itself as one of the leading interracial organizations for racial and social justice, both in the metropolitan Detroit area and in the nation. More impressive work would follow, however. Some of Focus: HOPE's most impressive efforts after the 1967 riot have been in the areas of education and training. We have already mentioned the Machinist Training Institute that opened in 1981. In 1989, Focus: HOPE established the Fast Track program. This "program upgrades academic skills and disciplines of high school graduates and GED holders. In seven weeks, individuals reach an education level needed to enter the Machinist Training Institute or Information Technologies Center" (Focus: HOPE, 1999). In 1993, the Center for Advanced Technologies was established. It "integrates hands-on manufacturing training and academic learning within a production setting and educates advanced manufacturing engineers-technologists at world-competitive levels" (Focus: HOPE, 1999). Six years later, in 1999, Focus: HOPE introduced still another program, the Information Technologies Center, to "provide a broad range of industry-certified training programs concentrating on Network Administration; System Administration; Database and Application Administration; and Telecommunications" (Focus: HOPE, 1999). These and other programs enabled many minorities and women in Detroit to gain access to many occupations from which they were excluded or for which they were not trained.

One final (but not the least important) feature of Focus: HOPE's more than forty years of dedicated work in race relations and community development is the annual Focus: HOPE Walk, which began in 1970. This walk, symbolized on banners and pins by a black hand and a white hand reaching toward each other with the word "Hope" inscribed above and below, soon became Detroit's most popular post-1967 celebration of interracial harmony. Nine years later, one article reported, "Brotherhood and sisterhood is not a dead cause as evidenced by thousands of men, women, both Black and White, who participated in Focus: HOPE's ninth annual civil and human rights celebration" (*Focus: HOPE News*, July 1979).

Continuing, the article described the spirit of the walk. "Focus: HOPE placards decorated the routes as metro-Detroiters came from four directions—north, south, east and west—together once more in a symbolic demonstration of racial harmony at the State Fair Grounds. As one small child's sign indicated, 'We have not forgotten King's Dream.' Several Detroit area entertainers, friends of Focus: HOPE, were at the Fair Grounds to greet the marchers, and to lead everyone in songs of brotherhood" (*Focus: HOPE News*, July 1979). The walk was not just a "visible sign of people sharing their feelings on racial justice." In addition, it was "one of the major funding sources of Focus: HOPE. People carried their sponsors list of pledged contributions reminding them that tired feet shouldn't threaten completion. Pledges are coming in the daily mail bag" (*Focus: HOPE News*, July 1979).

Focus: HOPE's Walk, with its symbol of black and White hands reaching out to each other, was a yearly reminder that hope was being kept alive in postriot Detroit. People marched because they believed in the vision and work of the organization. For example, those who participated in the 1982 walk shared their reasons. A social worker from the Detroit suburb of Grosse Pointe Park wrote:

I walk because I support Focus: HOPE as an organization. It does more than talk; it realistically supports people in the community. Focus: HOPE insists on holding families together by serving as a resource. . . . I'm a clinical social worker . . . dealing with foster children. Focus: HOPE has always helped in getting food to moms and children. (*Focus: HOPE News*, August 1982)

A pastor from East Detroit commented, "I think the WALK represents an expression of solidarity bringing people from all parts of the metropolitan area in a public statement of unity. We are brothers and sisters in a sometimes divided society." A business owner from the Birmingham/Troy suburban community joined in the walk because, as he explained,

I'm a business resident of Troy and I live in Birmingham, but my heart is in Detroit. I see Detroit as a melting pot of people that I want to be a part of . . . The WALK is one of my favorite, most inspiring things to do. We need more people who are willing to stand up for civil rights and be counted. It is easier to be inconspicuous or quietly send in a financial donation, which is alright. But by walking, I may give other people confidence to show publicly their concern for civil rights. (*Focus: HOPE News*, August 1982)

The walk also inspired people to play a key role in promoting racial harmony and cooperation in metropolitan Detroit in the future. A teenager in the 1982 walk said,

I like the spirit of everyone and the feeling of community. It's one time to really feel free to talk to everyone because everyone is there for a single purpose; there is a single topic to talk about. I also feel I contribute to Focus: HOPE's statement of racial harmony—about people working and living together. Someone needs to make a statement. (*Focus: HOPE News*, August 1982)

In the 1990 Sixteenth Annual Walk for Justice on a Sunday in October, record numbers participated. According to one report, "Close to 6,000 walkers, and several hundred volunteers, participated in the 12-kilometer (8 mile) trek" (*Focus: HOPE News*, December 1990). Among the VIPs on hand for the occasion were "Senator Carl Levin; Congressmen John Conyers Jr. and Sander Levin; Michigan Senators Jackie Vaughn III and John Engler; Detroit City Council President Maryann Mahaffey and member Mel Ravitz; Detroit Archbishop Adam Maida; and Detroit Free Press publisher, Neal Shine." After the walk, "foot-weary walkers and volunteers celebrated the more than $60,000 raised by enjoying hot dogs and refreshments" (*Focus: HOPE News*, December 1990).

Fifteen years later, Focus: HOPE Walk 2005 celebrated diversity. That year's walk took on more meaning because of some recent acts of racial intimidation in metropolitan Detroit. Eleanor Josaitis, CEO and cofounder of Focus: HOPE, cautioned that "we still have a long ways to go. Our work is needed as much today as it was 38 years ago. We have to stop this racial hatred. We all must stand up and say that racism is not acceptable" (*Hope in Focus*, Holiday 2005).

Nothing could discourage the annual walk, however. "As people of all races, religions and ethnic backgrounds walked together on a beautiful day, Josaitis noted that Focus: HOPE is striving to build a community of respect. . . . 'Our whole intent is to bring people together'" (*Hope in Focus*, Holiday 2005).

MODEL OF RACIAL UNITY CONFERENCES, 1994–2000

Following a long tradition within the American Baha'i community of promoting unity among racially diverse people, and especially between blacks and whites (Thomas, 1993), in 1993 the Baha'i Spiritual Assembly of Detroit "created a task force to carry out a faith-based mandate to promote racial unity" (Model of Racial Unity, 1998c). Two years later the task force became a non-profit organization, called "The Model of Racial Unity, Inc" (Model of Racial Unity, 1998c).

In keeping with the interfaith tradition of both the larger Baha'i community as well as that of the Detroit metropolitan community, the task force expanded its membership to include members from the Episcopal Diocese of Detroit and the Catholic Youth Organization (CYO). Both organizations made major contributions to the functioning of the new interfaith organization, Model of Racial Unity. "Two representatives from Episcopal Diocese of Detroit participated in the conference planning, and the Catholic Youth Organization provided staff support and other resources to their efforts which addressed the anti-racism work in the areas served by the CYO" (Model of Racial Unity, 1998c).

The task force launched its first conference on June 11, 1994, in Cobo Hall "to promote unity among the diverse populations of the Detroit Metropolitan area by bringing together people of different racial and ethnic backgrounds, in an atmosphere of cooperation and mutual respect" (Model of Racial Unity, 1998c). A day before the conference, the *Detroit Free Press* explained that "the Baha'i Faith Community of Greater Detroit is a main sponsor of the conference, which is an outgrowth of the religion's guiding principles: unity across racial and ethnic lines" (*Detroit Free Press*, June 10, 1994).

The task force invited over thirty civil, social, and business organizations and groups throughout the metropolitan area to participate in the conference, which included sixteen workshops focusing on themes such as "Conflict Resolution in the Schools," "Effective Responses to Racial/Ethnic Remarks," and "Conquering Fear and Reaching across Cultures" (*Detroit Free Press*, June 10, 1994).

Among these participants were several Baha'i speakers and scholars in the field of race relations. Professors June and Richard Thomas from Michigan State University were keynote speakers, focusing on "race relations in metro Detroit." Psychologist Michael Rogell, a Baha'i of Jewish background, conducted a session on "Identifying and Overcoming Obstacles for the White Male in the Quest for Racial Unity" (*Detroit Free Press*, June 10, 1994). "What I try to do is to get white men to see that doors open to them because they are white men," Rogell explained. "We don't see those doors opened; only the people for whom they are closed see that. . . . There is this invisible dynamic of power that we deny" (*Detroit Free Press*, June 10, 1994).

The Second Annual Model of Racial Unity Conference demonstrated how far the organization had progressed since the first conference. General Motors Corporation was now the major corporate sponsor. Smaller but no less dedicated corporate sponsors included Azar's Oriental Rugs, Michigan Food and Beverage Association, Mag-Co Investigation, and the Eastern Market Association. The owners of Azar's Oriental Rugs and Mag-Co were also members of the metropolitan Baha'i community. The former was Iranian-American and the latter African American. There were over thirty cosponsors covering a vast array of racial, ethnic, cultural, religious, and regional groups (Model of Racial Unity, 1995).

Given the increasing racial and ethnic diversity in the Detroit metropolitan area, racial and ethnic cosponsorship of the Model of Racial Unity Conference was a crucial barometer of its legitimacy and acceptance. This was particularly important at a time when ongoing conflicts were still festering between certain groups, such as African Americans and Arab/ Chaldeans. Therefore, the extent to which diverse groups bought into the conference vision was the extent to which they, hopefully, were willing to participate and carry on the work of promoting unity throughout the year. The Chaldean Federation of America, Latino Family Services, the Detroit Chapter of the Arab Anti-Discrimination Committee, the Michigan Regional Office of the Anti-Defamation League, and the Asian American Center for Justice (of the American Citizens for Justice) were among the racial and ethnic cosponsors (Model of Racial Unity, 1995).

Another group of cosponsors were from predominately white (and some very affluent) suburbs. Their involvement in the conference demonstrated that they had not lost hope in the possibility of building bridges between the predominately black inner-city and the predominantly white suburbs, particularly at a time when residential racial segregation was increasing. While suburban whites committed to bridging suburban-city racial divides were among the minority in their suburban communities, they were among the torchbearers of hope. These included the Farmington–Farmington Hills Multi-Cultural/Multiracial Community Council, Birmingham/Bloomfield Task Force on Race Relations and Ethnic Diversity, People of Livonia Addressing Issues of Diversity (PLAID), Lake Area Council for Diversity–West Bloomfield, and the Racial Justice Center of Grosse Pointe (Model of Racial Unity, 1995).

The real work of the annual conferences occurred in the workshops. The workshops not only provided information about pressing and ongoing racial issues, but engaged the participants in developing problem-solving skills. For example, one of the morning workshops ("How to Achieve Racial Harmony," conducted by James Lee, assistant vice president for equal opportunity and neighborhood relations at Wayne State University, City of Detroit neighborhood service commissioner, and a member of the NAACP) "was designed to identify issues which oppress individuals and groups from living in harmony. Each aspect of disharmony will be discussed and analyzed. The end result is to develop new and workable solutions to remedy oppression and to promote peace" (Lee, 1995).

Other workshops covered a range of topics related to race and diversity. "Why We Have a Race Unity Conference" was conducted by Paul Harrison, Susan Harrison, and Oliver Thomas, three Baha'is of the Model of Racial Unity Conference task force. This workshop was designed as "an opportunity for the people who helped organize the 'Model of Racial Unity Conference' to talk directly to conference attendees" (Harrison, Harrison, and Thomas, 1995). The purpose of the workshop on "Personal Recovery from Racism," conducted by Father Clarence Williams, pastor of St. Anthony's Church of Detroit, a black Catholic priest, was to lead "participants through the various stages of recovery, and allow discussion of the concepts and an experiences of the recovery model presented in the keynote" (Williams, 1995). The workshop on "Healing Racism in America" was concerned with "learning what we as individuals and members of institutions can do to heal racism in America and move toward becoming active participants in building allies among people of color and white people" (Jordan and Waslawski, 1995). The Baha'i Youth Workshop and the Catholic Youth Organization conducted a "Workshop on Youth's Response to Racism" that addressed "racism in the educational system, the superiority behavior of white instructor and student, and the inferiority behavior that is projected on non-white students" (Baha'i Youth Workshop and the Catholic Youth Organization, 1995). Robert Arcand, executive director of the Greater Interfaith Roundtable, led a workshop on "Practical Programs to Promote Diversity," in which "existing efforts promoting diversity will be discussed with specific opportunities for involvement or patterning in your own community" (Arcand, 1995).

June M. Thomas, professor of urban and regional planning at Michigan State University, conducted a workshop on "Social Justice in the City." The workshop explored "spiritual writings concerning relationship between unity and social improvement in the metropolitan areas." Participants were expected to "develop criteria for bringing about social justice in the metropolis" (J. M. Thomas, 1995).

Richard Thomas, professor of history and urban affairs at Michigan State University conducted a workshop on "Unifying Racially Polarized Groups." The purpose of the workshop was "to explore visions, methods, and techniques of promoting multiracial unity in racially polarized communities" (R. W. Thomas, 1995).

The professional expertise and insight of psychologists and social workers proved invaluable to the conference's aim of promoting unity among racial groups. For example, in the workshop entitled "US and THEM: The Challenge of Diversity," two psychologists and a social worker explored the idea that "being part of a group provides many benefits, ranging from increased self-esteem to physical survival. Racial pride, patriotism and ethnic identity are reflections of group loyalty. People tend to emphasize good within their own group, danger and bad in others. As our world shrinks, will this tendency help us to survive? Our technology may require a new psychology" (Fabrick, Myers, and Barakat, 1995).

Because of the recent history of conflicts between the Arab/Chaldean Americans and African Americans, the "Chaldeans in Our Society" workshop was critically important to the conference. Conducted by the Chaldean Federation of America,

> the workshop will focus on two areas in which the Chaldean Federation of America and the Chaldean community have worked to promote racial and ethnic unity: (1) by working with surrounding communities where Chaldean businesses operate. (2) By sponsoring weekend retreats and seminars between Chaldean Americans and African Americans to encourage positive communication and promote cultural and racial understanding. (Chaldean Federation of America, 1995)

Native American and Mexican American perspectives also were presented at the conference. In a workshop entitled "Racism from an Indigenous People's Point of View," Angie Reyes and Andrea White addressed "the impact of 500 years of genocide of the indigenous peoples of America." Both women came from a rich professional, community, cultural, and ethnic background that greatly contributed to the diversity of the conference (Reyes and White, 1995).

There were other workshops as well, all devoted to the singular purpose of addressing issues related to promoting unity among racially and culturally diverse peoples and communities in the Detroit metropolitan region.

A day after the conference, the *Detroit News* shared some of the impressions of a few of the participants:

> Detroiter Lila Cabbil looked around at 200 people of different races, cultures and religions who had gathered at Cobo Center on Saturday. Then she smiled. It's events like the second annual Model of Racial Unity Conference, she said, that invigorates her work as an anti-racism consultant. . . . "If I didn't see all these people who are making an effort to fight racism, I would not feel so inspired and

energized to do the work I do . . . this keeps me focused. I feel like I'm part of a collective journey." (*Detroit News*, May 21, 1995)

The reporter pointed out that "More people seem to be joining that journey, organizers said, because attendance at the conference jumped to 200 people this year from 120 last year." Quoting Father Clarence Williams, the African American Catholic priest, the reporter wrote, "After the event . . . attendees can serve as 'catalysts' of racial unity when they return to their communities" (*Detroit News*, May 21, 1995).

As a fitting tribute to the organizers, workshop presenters, cosponsors, and the more than 200 participants of "different races, cultures and religions," Mayor Dennis W. Archer designated May 20, 1995, as "Model of Racial Unity Day":

Despite much positive advancement over the last few decades towards the goal of greater interracial understanding, racial prejudice is still an active, destructive attitude in our nation.

People of every racial, ethnic or religious background must make a concerted effort to overcome conscious or subconscious feelings of prejudice in themselves and in the larger community.

It is not sufficient to simply be aware of the negative effects and destructive processes of racial prejudice. Instead, Americans and Detroiters must recognize the positive alternative and encourage existing models of interaction which promote racial unity.

However, the goal of achieving racial unity must not be a task left to the next generation of Americans. Individuals today must actively work and commit themselves to achieving the goal.

The Baha'i Faith Community of Greater Detroit, the Catholic Youth Organization and the General Motors Corporation are to be saluted for their commitment to this goal. These three organizations, along with 30 other civic, religious and business organizations as co-sponsors, are the major sponsors of the Second Annual Model of Racial Unity Conference.

Therefore, I, Dennis W. Archer, Mayor of the City of Detroit, issue this Proclamation designating May 20, 1995 as Model of Racial Unity Day in the City of Detroit. I commend the efforts of these organizations and their commitment and leadership to this cause. (Archer, 1995)

The Third Annual Model of Racial Unity Conference occurred on May 18, 1996, in Cobo Hall. The theme was "Transformation of the Metropolitan Area: Moving from Diversity to Racial Unity." As before, the major sponsors were the Baha'i Community and the Catholic Youth Organization of Detroit. General Motors and the Cranbrook Peace Foundations were the major financial contributors. They were joined by an array of smaller cosponsors, some of whom had been cosponsors of the first two conferences. The featured speakers were Barbara Love, professor at University of Massachusetts and author of "several publications on Multiculturalism, Diversity, and Internalized Oppression," and Nathan Rutstein, author of the book *Healing Racism in America* and a founding member of the Institute for the Healing of Racism. The conference had three primary objectives:

(1) To inspire and empower individuals and organizations already involved in Racial, Religious and Ethnic unity activities; (2) To encourage and promote individuals and groups to move from a stance of problem identification to proactively implementing solutions; (3) To create a low-cost, quality event that addresses issues of racial unity and is accessible to everyone. (Model of Racial Unity, 1996)

Like the proceeding conferences, this conference offered workshops and youth participation (Model of Racial Unity, 1996).

In 1998, Sharon N. Campbell, the president of the Board of Directors of the Model of Racial Unity, welcomed participants to the Fourth Model of Racial Unity Conference.

Today, you will join with others, who are also facing the challenges of promoting racial unity, in activities which will result in a shared vision of racial unity. You will not only develop a vision for the whole of the metropolitan area, today's activities will also produce a plan of action including an implementation and accountability strategy. (Campbell, May 2, 1998)

The Local Spiritual Assembly of the Baha'is of Detroit (LSA), as one of the main sponsors, also included a welcome message in the 1998 conference booklet in which it mentioned a statement of racial unity produced by its national body in 1991:

The Vision for Race Unity, a document created by the governing body of the Faith states that "healing the wounds of racism and building a society in which people of diverse backgrounds live as members of one family is the most pressing issue confronting America today." . . . This document also suggests that if a peaceful solution to racism is not found, both the internal order and national security of the United States may be disrupted. As we harbor a bias toward someone who is different, we automatically eliminate opportunity for enrichment and prevent others from knowing us as well. (Local Spiritual Assembly, May 2, 1998)

Those who participate in this conference, the LSA explained, "will begin the exploration of the vision of racial unity within civic groups in Detroit, gain some new insights and/or tools . . . see a new methodology of discussion or consultation which is free of threat allowing full disclosure of pertinent ideas. One may experience some level of personal transformation." In addition, the LSA continued, "One may experience a sense of community which holds a promise of support and belonging. Whatever it is you are able to give and take from your participation, we hope it will be manifested in a plan of action" (Local Spiritual Assembly, May 2, 1998).

The Fourth Model of Racial Unity Conference had its own distinctive quality and focus: "the envisioning of the characteristics of racial unity; the identification of issues to be addressed in achieving this vision; and, the initiation of planning for achieving racial unity in this metropolitan area" (Fourth Model of Racial Unity Conference, 1998). This departure from earlier conferences was reflected in its theme: "Vision to Action-Strategies for the 21st Century." According to the Model of Racial Unity's newsletter, "People who believe in the oneness of humanity, from civic groups, religious communities, education, human services, government and business joined to create a shared vision of racial unity and strategized how to make it a reality. This was an assembly of people who are facing the challenges of transforming metropolitan Detroit, building a multiracial society based on justice, interracial unity, harmony and love" (Model of Racial Unity, 1998a).

The hallmark of this conference was the way in which it structured sessions around "communities of interest"—government and law enforcement; business; housing and neighborhoods; youth; and health (Model of Racial Unity, 1998a). The real work was accomplished in these interest groups by "skilled facilitators" (Model of Racial Unity, 1998a).

According to the 1998 conference report, the vision and strategies followed the following steps: the vision; what needs to change; how do we make these changes; and immediate action steps. Just a few examples should suffice to show how this process was fleshed out.

The "vision" of the Local Government Interest Group was "Fewer local governments; political campaigns are less racist; government licensing is more racially unifying; more communities are racially mixed; people are more trusting of governments; less driven by commercialism."

Next, in terms of "what needs to change," the Local Government Interest Group aimed to "develop regional government strategies; more dialogue of urban and rural/suburban governments; recognition that people are more important than a particular government's monetary interest; more local government input on industry decisions to move out."

For the big question, "How do we make these changes," this interest group came up with the following: "Equitable services available in every community to 'remove' the reason to move for better services; destroy rundown houses; change tax policies to have a racially neutral impact; make local governments accountable for implementing effective diversity strategies."

Lastly, for "Immediate Action Steps," exploring how to make these changes happen, the group decided to "discuss these possibilities with local governments and their agencies; regional planning groups SEMOG should be more involved in these issues; educate and license realtors to be 'Fair Housing Advocates'" (Model of Racial Unity, 1998b).

Given the impact of race on youth of all racial, ethnic, religious and cultural background in the Detroit metropolitan area, the Youth Interest Group had an impressive and inspiring vision statement: "We take responsibility for loving, nurturing, and educating all children equally because they are our own" (Model of Racial Unity, 1998b). Their vision emphasized that "children learn what they live; it take a whole village to raise a child; youth feel connected to society and have the ability to affect change; youth have a greater sense of hope; youth are putting down guns and picking up books; history written and taught to, by . . . (all people); living in a multicultural world." In terms of "where are we now," the interest group reported: "Too many White children—'I deserve it and you don't' (youth learn this early); People are 'Whited'; Difficult to know how to—where to—start" (Model of Racial Unity, 1998b).

In order to accomplish their vision, the Youth Interest Group came up with the following strategies: "Need for education about racism versus multicultural diversity. Increase awareness of the impact of White privilege. Equity—healing not possible without it. Reparations—economic. Raise children with recognition of racism as a disease. Listen to youth and follow their leadership. Build upon (celebrate) the human shades of life. Provide opportunity for students to develop knowledge, creativity, self-determination and nobility" (Model of Racial Unity, 1998b).

The "Action Steps" were "Love each other while we change. Provide extracurricular activities for youth. Greater interaction between youth of all shades of life across city/suburb borders. Educate about contributions of Whites to the struggle. Make every day racial unity day. Education year round with opportunity for applied learning. Attend and monitor school PTA meetings. Serve as resources to school, whether or not they have children . . . (retirees)" (Model of Racial Unity, 1998b).

Sadly, the worlds of the majority of inner-city black youth and the majority of suburban white youth are literally miles apart. More often than not, poverty, inadequately funded schools, and crime and violence-infested neighborhoods characterize the lives of black youth in the city. This is a life that most suburban white youth could never comprehend. Therefore, unity among them would never occur until this divide is crossed.

These were only a few of the interest groups at the Fourth Model of Racial Unity Conference in 1998. The board of directors compiled the results of discussions from the interest groups in a conference report "intended to be part of a process by Model of Racial Unity to promote continuing, systematic, harmonious, long-term visioning, planning and implementation of the conditions for achieving the ultimate goal of racial unity in the Detroit metropolitan area" (Model of Racial Unity, 1998a).

The Fifth Model of Racial Unity Conference, on March 27, 1999, built on the work of the final report of the 1998 conference. Moving forward with the vision of that conference, the 1999 conference adopted the theme "Planning and Implementing Practical Steps Forward" (Model of Racial Unity, 1999a). The 1999 conference focused on "'practical steps' to move racial unity forward in Detroit metropolitan area." The 1999 conference organizers decided that "last year's interest groups will be the focus of the March 27 [1999] Conference efforts to develop 'practical steps'" (Model of Racial Unity, 1999a).

Some of the "practical steps" produced by the 1999 conference included those of the Housing Interest Group. These were of particular relevance because of the long open housing struggle and the increasing residential segregation in the Detroit metropolitan area. Among the barriers to housing diversity, which the practical steps were developed to overcome, were lending, crime, value of homes/unit, unclean streets and neighborhoods, and quality of public schools (see chapter 11). The "Practical Action Steps" included "Become a tester for fair housing. Learn the realities of real estate discrimination. Create a list of home-buying educators and flexible lenders. Be part of a changing community. Go to neighborhood meetings on schools and crime prevention. Don't have more 'meetings.' Have socials, cookouts, and block clubs. Schedule meetings in your neighborhood. Establish a relationship with local police. Attend your precinct meeting" (Model of Racial Unity, 1999b).

The Faith Communities Interest Group started the process of coming up with its "Practical Action Steps" by asking, "Where are we now? Where do we want to go?: Obstacles/opportunities and practical action steps" (Model of Racial Unity, 1999b).

The list of where the Faith Communities Interest Group wanted to go logically led to what were the opportunities and obstacles to getting there. The opportunities included the interest group; the Internet; tools available for analysis of racism; resources and people available; growing consensus that racist acts are bad. The obstacles included limited opportunities for interaction; concentration on obstacles rather than opportunities; inability to listen; quick easy answers; unwillingness to share resources; media sensationalism of the negative aspect of the problem rather than problem solving.

The last and most important step in this group process was coming up with "Practical Action Steps." For the Faith communities Interest Group, these included organization, recruitment, developing an advocacy group, networking, active collaboration among faith communities in providing for safe dialogue and confrontation, and identifying roles that existing organizations (e.g., Models of Racial Unity, NCCJ) can play in accomplishing these priorities (Model of Racial Unity, 1999b).

The 1999 Model of Racial Unity Conference inspired several organizations to begin "collaborating on an extensive cultural exchange program between suburban and Detroit school districts at the middle school level." The organizations involved in this effort were the Charles H. Wright Museum of African American History, the National Conference for Community and Justice, the Detroit Empowerment Zone, Garden City Public Schools, Detroit Public Schools, and the Wayne County Regional Educational Services Association (Model of

Racial Unity, 1999a). Garden City's Memorial Elementary and Garden City Junior High and Detroit's McMillan Dual Multi-Cultural School were among the participating schools. The organizations launched their collaboration on September 23 at the Charles H. Wright Museum and made plans to "place students in teams to work cooperatively in overcoming an outdoor Adventure Challenge Course Wayne County RESA" (Model of Racial Unity, 1999a).

The Sixth Model of Racial Unity Conference was held on May 20, 2000, with the theme "Diversity Happens—Unity is a Choice." This would be the last Model of Racial Unity Conference. According to the conference organizers, this phase "helps individuals think about the choices they make when forced to look at the harsh reality of their own prejudices and misconceptions of other races" ("Racial Unity Conference, May 20 at Cobo Hall," 2000).

The conference program included three segments:

- Diversity cameos: Learn what you were always afraid to ask about one of six ethnic or religious groups
- Skills training workshops: Learn how to handle a racial joke or what to do if you are the victim of discriminatory workplace bias
- Interest group collaboration workshops: Your chance to share your racial unity activities and build allies with similar interests in education, health care and four other fields. (Model of Racial Unity, 2000)

The keynote speaker's talk befittingly reflected the theme of the conference: "Welcoming People into our Kitchens" (Model of Racial Unity, 2000).

Further Work of the Metropolitan Detroit Baha'i Community.

Baha'is in metropolitan Detroit did not limit their work in race relations to the annual Racial Unity Conferences. In 1992, Ted Amsden and his wife, Ruth Rydstedt, a white Baha'i couple living in Grosse Pointe, joined with Laurence and Winifred White, an African American couple from Detroit, and "launched a monthly series of family-room talks that brings diverse groups together to promote positive ideas and a greater understanding of each other" (*Detroit News*, January 29, 1993). Amsden explained that they view the effort as "a service. . . . We are not asking speakers to address the Baha'i point of view. We are attempting to bring a diverse group of people together to achieve a more positive sense of unity" (*Detroit News*, January 29, 1993).

For nearly a decade, a long and impressive list of speakers was invited to speak on a wide range of topics related to the promotion of "interracial understanding and dialogue" (Amsden and Rystedt, 1992, 1993, 1994, 1995, 1998, 1999, 2001). Among these were Desiree Cooper, program director, community education, Center for Urban Studies, Wayne State University, who spoke in April 1993 on "Economic Power and Race Relations: A Simulation" (Amsden and Rystedt, 1993). The next month, L. Rod Toneye, a consultant with Training Resources in Detroit, and Ron Aramaki, a consultant with Ann Arbor Counseling Associates, addressed the topic of "Promoting Dialogue Among African Americans and Asian Americans" (Amsden and Rystedt, 1993).

In January 1994, Sidney Bolkosky, professor of history at the University of Michigan, Dearborn, spoke on the "Implications of the Holocaust for Our Time" (Amsden and Rystedt,

1994). One of the key topics of 1995 was a talk by Jane Shallal, president of the Chaldean Federation of America, on "Getting to Know the Chaldean Community" (Amsden and Rystedt, 1995). In June 1998, Professor Michael Naylor, chairman of the Department of Performing Arts, Washtenaw Community College, discussed "Overcoming Black and White Dualism: The Creolization of Music in America (Amsden and Rystedt, 1998).

This effort was yet another example of how the Baha'is of metropolitan Detroit applied their belief in the unity of humankind to the racial and cultural challenges of a divided Detroit after 1967. As a result of their efforts, the Baha'i-sponsored "talk series was awarded a 1993 'Detroit Principles Award' by the Race Relations Council of Metropolitan Detroit and was featured in Chuck Stokes' 'Spotlight on the News' on Channel 7 in 1998" (Amsden and Rystedt, 1999).

THE DETROIT ROUNDTABLE OF CATHOLICS, JEWS AND PROTESTANTS/ MICHIGAN ROUNDTABLE FOR DIVERSITY AND INCLUSION, 1941–2011

The Detroit Roundtable of Catholics, Jews and Protestants grew out of the Detroit Council of Catholics, Jews and Protestants, founded in 1941. It is the oldest of the organizations that has been involved in race relations in Detroit. The organization was a response to "the growth of totalitarianism abroad and divisions within the Detroit community inflamed by such preachers/politicians as Gerald L. K. Smith and Father Coughlin. The aim of the Roundtable was to foster religious and racial brotherhood and to counter those who would divide the community or religious or racial lines" (Michigan Roundtable, n.d.-b). The organization carried out this aim by conducting and sponsoring seminars, workshops, lectures, dinners, and annual Brotherhood Week observances (Michigan Roundtable, n.d.-b).

Throughout its long and distinguished history of combating discrimination and promoting religious and racial harmony, the Roundtable has changed its name several times, "reflecting changes in scope and objectives." First, it was the Detroit Roundtable, then it became the Greater Detroit Roundtable of the National Conference of Christians and Jews, next it became the Greater Detroit Interfaith Roundtable, the National Conference for Community and Justice of Michigan, and in 2006, it changed its name to the Michigan Roundtable for Diversity (Michigan Roundtable, n.d.-b).

The 1943 riot brought the so-called "Negro Problem" to the forefront of the Roundtable's agenda, "so that the organization which began as a mediator of religious differences grew into a strong organ of human relations" (*Detroit Free Press*, December 12, 1965).

Even before the riot, the Roundtable engaged in efforts designed to foster good relations with the African American community. For example, in October 1942, it announced, "On October 29 . . . outstanding leaders of the Negro community will be present at a luncheon meeting of [the] National Association of Colored People at the Lucy Thurman YWCA." It also mentioned that a team of speakers from the DRT would be addressing the gathering (*Detroit Times*, October 24, 1942).

Several years after the 1943 Detroit race riot, the Roundtable participated in the Interracial Workshop Conference sponsored by the City of Detroit Interracial Committee. Reverend Joseph Q. Mayne, the executive secretary of the Roundtable, expressed a rather radical view when he suggested the "churches were not as active as they should be in fostering harmonious group living and proposed that all places of worship be thrown open to all persons regardless of color" (*Detroit News*, June 2, 1946)

During this period, the Roundtable played a key role in sponsoring and supporting major African American leaders and organizations, such as the October 1947 visit to Detroit of Father Herman A. Porter, of the Society of Priests of the Sacred Heart of Jesus, "the thirty-first Negro Priest in the United States" (Detroit Interracial Council, October 4, 1947).

By the end of the decade, the DRT had established itself as a leader in promoting harmony among racial, religious, cultural, and economic groups with an increasing focus on racial issues. One of its most impressive efforts was its work with students from Detroit area high schools. During the summer of 1949, the organization sponsored a gathering of students from twenty-five high schools "to discuss how to get along with high school neighbors" (*Detroit Free Press*, June 4, 1949). According to one report, "More than 250 delegates from Detroit, Ferndale, Royal Oak, Birmingham, Grosse Pointe, Inkster and Mt. Clement will meet . . . at Highland Park High School" to discuss "ways of breaking down barriers among students of differing racial, religious, cultural and economic groups." The gathering was "the largest of its kind for teen-agers" (*Detroit Free Press*, June 4, 1949). While much more remained to be done, the Roundtable was at least preparing the next generation to take up the important work of addressing racial problems in the city.

The persistence of racial discrimination over other forms of discrimination in Detroit clearly indicated a need for the Roundtable to focus more attention on the former. As Frank J. Wurtsmith of the Roundtable said, "Racial prejudice is still Detroit's most serious problem. Much more attention must be given to the need for adequate housing and job opportunities than has been given in the past" (*Detroit Free Press*, February 19, 1950).

In 1957, in the wake of the nationwide publicity of the desegregation of Central High School in Little Rock, Arkansas, which prompted President Eisenhower to send in federal troops (Franklin and Moss, 1998), a Mumford High School senior working with the Detroit Roundtable proclaimed, "I want to find out about prejudice and everything that goes with it—not in little Rock, but here in Detroit" (*Detroit News*, December 28, 1957).

The student was a member of a group called Teens Quiz the Experts that interviewed Richard Marks, director of the Detroit Commission on Community Relations. The teens asked Marks the following questions:

- How can young people of Detroit better understand minority groups?
- Is it true that modern youth has begun to overcome racial prejudice?
- How can we combat the subtle attempts at discrimination made by Detroit restaurants when they refuse service to those of minority groups? (*Detroit News*, December 28, 1957)

Mark's response to the students was instructive: "Suppose you went into a restaurant with a group of Junior Roundtable members and the waitress refused to serve two of the members because they were Negroes. Would you ever go back to that restaurant? I don't think so" (*Detroit News*, December 28, 1957).

By 1960, the Roundtable had earned a reputation for its teacher scholarship program that since 1941 "had encouraged 401 Michigan residents . . . to increase their efforts to better their community climate." Sara Colvin, educational director of the Roundtable, praised the work of the teachers who had received the scholarships. "Their influence in the fight against misunderstanding among people of different faiths, races and national backgrounds has been felt by thousands of school children, PTA groups and youth groups" (*Grosse Pointe News*, June 10, 1960).

Five year later, and two years before the 1967 riot, the Roundtable had contributed more than its share to the promotion of racial harmony. Its Junior Roundtable group brought students together from eighty-one public, parochial, and private schools. The group had also spent thirteen years sponsoring an annual Rearing Children of Good Will Border-Cities Conference dedicated to stamping out "prejudice before it takes hold of children's minds" (*Detroit Free Press*, December 12, 1965). The Roundtable awarded close to forty tuition scholarships to summer workshops in human relations at Michigan colleges every year and contributed to training programs for police in "handling community tensions involving racial and religious problems." Furthermore, the Roundtable's Speaker's Bureau assisted community organizations in obtaining expert speakers to address human relations issues and made available at its office an "extensive library of booklets and films on racial and religious problems" (*Detroit Free Press*, December 12, 1965). In explaining the purpose of the efforts, an official of the Roundtable commented that he had seen a lot of progress over the years, and that he was optimistic. "People don't like to hear bigoted cracks any more, and getting past that is a good sign" (*Detroit Free Press*, December 12, 1965).

Unfortunately, while the Roundtable's decades of efforts were sincere and noteworthy, they fell far short of understanding and addressing the core issues that resulted in the 1967 riot. The following winter, Nate S. Shapero, a leader of many civic and charitable projects, essentially expressed this view when he was honored by the Roundtable at the Seventeenth Brotherhood Dinner in Cobo Hall. "I believe no one of us tonight needs to be told that a cure for racial strife may be the first order of business before us. . . . we have the first ingredients for such a cure in our hand," he said. Shapero added, "How can we in good conscience, not accept the responsibility of finding solutions to the problems that brought mobs howling through our streets?" He told them, "Be the leader in this movement. We have in this Roundtable the brains, the talent and the money to find and implement any program we chose to establish. I suggest we can find out why Twelfth Street went up in smoke, why some of our brothers believe we have abandoned them and why they seek brutal and undemocratic revenge." He then reminded the Roundtable, "We were instrumental once in conquering hate and fear and we can do it again" (Michigan Roundtable, n.d.-b).

The Roundtable could indeed conquer "hate and fear" again during the post-1967 era, much as they had attempted to do, albeit with limited success, during the post-1943 riot. Three years after the riot (amid the lingering conflicts and tension between the black community and the Detroit Police Department), the Roundtable received "the Civilian Award of the Detroit Department for its key role building police-citizen relationship in the city" ("Detroit Roundtable Receives Police Commissioner's Civilian Award," 1970).

In the 1980s the Roundtable engaged in a range of activities around issues of social justice and intergroup cooperation and harmony. In the early 1980s, it supported the efforts of the Chinese American community to gain justice for Vincent Chin (Roundtable Responds to Vincent Chin Case, Fall 1983).

In its annual report and newsletter of 1984–85, the Roundtable reported that "A major part of our work . . . is 'looking for trouble,' trying to identify situation which can lead to conflict and hatred among different groups." Once the observers "locate trouble," they "engage in trouble shooting, trying to create understanding where there is hostility and get people of good will to work positively on constructive solutions to conflict (Greater Detroit Round-table, 1984–85).

An example of such "trouble shooting" occurred during the conflict between blacks and Jews during the presidential primaries as a result of Reverend Jesse Jackson's derogatory remarks about Jews as "hymies" and New York City as "Hymie Town" (*Washington Post*, February 13, 1984). The Roundtable in cooperation with the Pontiac Urban League cosponsored a forum at Oakland University to defuse the tension that erupted from that situation. It also provided "resources, materials, help and advice to a group of people from both minorities who met for over six months at Marygrove College to study the problem." The study group concluded "that while there were 'valid reasons' for the recent tensions, both Jews and Black people 'have more that unities them than divide them'" (Greater Detroit Roundtable, 1984–85). The group pledged to "defuse tensions as they erupt," to "encourage organizations within the two communities to tackle the more long range tasks of creating and enhancing general understanding, and to work together on a 'common human agenda' to make our city, state and nation more economically viable, compassionate, and . . . more 'open' dealing with the frustrations which lead to prejudice" (Greater Detroit Roundtable, 1984–85).

In 1990, the Roundtable prepared to troubleshoot yet another issue, "the skinheads." It published an article in its newsletter, "Our Answer to the Skinheads—Taking Back the Future," in which it stated: "It was not too long ago that we believed that prejudice was declining [and] and the new generation saddled with antiquated hatreds. Such hopes were dashed by Klan recruiters in the 70s, the rise of the skinheads in the 80s, and overt acts of brutality in the 90s" (Greater Detroit Roundtable, 1990).

In keeping with its long history of challenging religious and racial hatred, the DRT decided to take action against this new wave of racism. "To protect the next generation from the burden of bigotry, the Greater Detroit Interfaith Roundtable is meeting this challenge by bringing together the large number of constructive youth organizations working for good will in the Detroit metropolitan Area," it wrote (Greater Detroit Roundtable, 1990). To counteract youth racism, with a grant from the Skillman Foundation the DRT started "The Youth for Unity program," which helped youth organizations "publicize their activities in the general community and make them known to each other, so they can help each other and work together on joint projects" (Greater Detroit Roundtable, 1990).

The Roundtable's annual Anytown, USA Retreat youth program was another way of protecting "the next generation from the burden of bigotry." Each summer for one week, young people from the tenth, eleventh, and twelfth grades met in a program "where they have the opportunity to express themselves and their own heritage and to appreciate others of different backgrounds through communication, sharing, and closeness." During the summer of 1990, the group of young people "decided to continue keeping the experience alive by continuing to see each other and holding periodic meetings to spread what they have learned to other young people in the Detroit area" (Greater Detroit Roundtable, 1990).

In November 2006, the Detroit Interfaith Roundtable announced a name change: Michigan Roundtable for Diversity and Inclusion. "We . . . are celebrating a new name! What's in a Name Change? Some people would say not much . . . but we have been burdened with a name that people could not remember and could not connect with our mission," they explained. "Now, if you understand the importance of both Diversity and Inclusion, you will get it! You'll remember and know the organization to call for help with your school congregation or business of racism or sexism or religious discrimination or any other of the cultural 'isms' [that] raises its ugly head" (Michigan Roundtable, 2006).

The new name reflected the organization's dedication to the new challenges facing the city, state, and nation. An official of the MRT took note of these new challenges when he lamented the passage of Proposal 2 in November 2006, which outlawed affirmative action in municipal, regional, state government, and higher education designed to "redress long-standing discrimination against women and people of color." He mentioned the surprise of some people over the "overwhelming defeat" of affirmative action. "Sometimes," he said, "those of us who spend time with leaders of human relations board members who 'get it,' and corporate foundation leaders, may forget how ingrained prejudice and discrimination are in this country. Thus, the passage of Proposition [*sic*] 2 sent an undeniably clear message to human relations advocates and groups across Michigan. A large majority of voters have strong biases and prejudices against helping women and people of color" (*MRDI News*, Spring 2007).

The official then listed the lessons learned from the passage of Proposal 2: "Discrimination is alive and well among many individuals and institutions. The private sector (e.g. business and faith communities) will need to take the lead if racism, sexism, and religious discrimination are [to be] significantly reduced. Outstate areas are the most deficient in terms of institutional and individual bias" (*MRDI News*, Spring 2007).

According to the official, the Roundtable's programs "are ideally suited to create change in those outstate areas," noting that most of the eighty-three counties in Michigan "voted against affirmative action, including some with significant numbers of Hispanic and African Americans." Therefore, he continued, "Michigan must face the fact that not only are we in a state of economic distress, we are a state now known as one of the most segregated" (*MRDI News*, Spring 2007).

Notwithstanding the sad state of race relations in the region, the official did see hope in the ability of the Roundtable to made a difference. "The Michigan Roundtable knows how to change both attitudes and behaviors found in traditional forms of bias and discrimination against Jewish, African, Catholic, Asian, Americans, among others" (*MRDI News*, Spring 2007). He cautioned, however, that "change takes long periods of struggle . . . too often in Southeast Michigan, we have bought into some slogans or simplistic solution to create racial harmony." This approach obviously had not worked in the past. "With the defeat of affirmative action, we have to recognize that attitudinal change takes serious dialogue with those who are different, a longstanding commitment to learn about different cultures, and a willingness to change the behavior of our institutions. Simple solutions are a pipe dream" (*MRDI News*, Spring 2007).

The official claimed that the Roundtable's programs work and that their evaluations "speak to serious change." He argued that the organization had "witness[ed] major shifts in attitudes and behavior at companies, schools, and even some historically racist communities like Howell which are rapidly making changes" (*MRDI News*, Spring 2007).

These changes inspired MRT's continual efforts to take on more challenges—in short, to troubleshoot more pressing and difficult racial and cultural issues. "This is why," the official pointed out, "we are seriously considering expanding the Michigan Roundtable programs, providing services and training outstate and in counties that traditionally have not welcomed people who are different." The official acknowledged that such changes will take time, but warned that "Michigan will not prosper as a state if we do not become more diverse and more inclusive" (*MRDI News*, Spring 2007).

On February 5, 2007, the second in a series of community conversations, "Bridging the Racial Divide," represented one of the Roundtable's most promising cosponsored projects during the year. The other cosponsors included New Detroit, Kingsberry Productions, and Detroit Public Television/Channel 56. This community conversation took place in seven metropolitan Detroit locations and was a follow-up to an identical one in 2006, which involved participants' responses to a documentary *The Cost of Segregation*, the creation of Kingsberry Productions (*MDRI News*, Spring 2007).

Dan Krichbaum, the Roundtable's president, explained, "The racial divide in our community may involve geographic boundaries, as well as interpersonal barriers such as race, religion, or ethnicity." Therefore, the project "helps create a new level of understanding between the participants in our conversation groups, as well as spur greater community dialogue in Southeast Michigan" (*MRDI News*, Spring 2007).

A diverse gathering of fifty to sixty adults took part in the program at sites across southeast Michigan. After the showing of the film, Roundtable staff facilitated group discussion. Later that evening, Channel 56 (PBS) aired the documentary for the public (*MRDI News*, Spring 2007).

In the program of the Roundtable's Sixty-first Annual Humanitarian Tribute on November 6, 2008, just a few days before the historic 2008 presidential election, Thomas Costello, president and CEO, wrote: "As we watch an historic election, one thing is clear: Race is still an important factor in our lives. The survey research and focus group data is showing that even if you are a Harvard educated U.S. Senator, to an embarrassingly large group of people you are still and foremost, an African American and therefore unworthy to be President" (Michigan Roundtable, 2008).

This sad but very real fact did not deter the Roundtable. Costello proclaimed that the "Michigan Roundtable is preparing to confront this reality, and push hard to get Michigan to recognize it has a serious problem when it comes to race—a problem that affect our economy, our government and our very social fabric." Costello announced that the Roundtable "was about to engage in an exciting new effort to engage our community and our state in a process of recognition and reconciliation: Recognizing that our segregated community is not the result of accident, but explicit actions by leaders in our state, followed by reconciliation that will involve addressing diversity and inclusion in a variety of ways" (Michigan Roundtable, 2008).

As the first African American president was being elected, the Roundtable was preparing a new generation of youth to participate in a more diverse world culture. "The future of our region lies in the ability of our young people to work and live in a diverse world culture," the organization declared. It would accomplish this goal by building "leaders, prepared with the skills to engage those who are different and to collaborate in productive relationships" (Michigan Roundtable, 2008).

In 2008 the Roundtable's Youth Program planned to "use the internet to provide a forum for on-going dialog on issues of diversity and inclusion . . . and provide resources, recognition and support to student groups doing diversity and Inclusion work." The Roundtable's Leadership in the New Century (LINC) program, through its annual Connection Conference, played a key role in the improvement of race relations among students throughout the region. In 2008 the Roundtable reported that "Over 400 students attended the conferences which promote action for diversity and inclusion in schools. These activities provided a foundation for creating a positive youth culture, leading to a more inclusive society" (Michigan Roundtable, 2008).

In 2011, the Roundtable was still working to promote diversity and inclusion in the region. As it says in its current mission statement: "We work to address inequity throughout our region through a process of recognition, reconciliation and renewal. We strive to build relationships that create social justice and build sustainable inclusive communities."

> We believe that achieving trusting interpersonal relations, which bridge racial, religious, ethnic, and other cultural boundaries is critical to building diverse inclusive communities. In our commitment to this cause, we seek to demonstrate the highest standards of interpersonal and institutional conduct through honesty, dignity, fairness, and respect. (Michigan Roundtable, n.d.-a)

CONCLUSION

We can be thankful for the generation of people, groups, and organizations who arose before, during, and after the Detroit civil disorder of 1967 to calm the minds and heal the wounded bodies, hearts, and souls of a divided population. New Detroit and Focus: HOPE were among the first of several organizations to rush to the rescue of the shattered city. They remain the two longest-serving organizations in the post-civil disorder period, and they built a lasting legacy of multiracial/cultural community building across an often racially contentious metropolitan community. In the 1990s, the Baha'i Spiritual Assembly of Detroit, inspired by their long tradition of interracial unity work of the American Baha'i community, founded the Model of Racial Unity Conferences. The spirit and the purpose of the conferences inspired many civil, social, and business organizations and groups to become cosponsors. The annual conferences provided workshops representing a range of racial, ethnic, and cultural groups and organizations reflecting the rich diversity of the Detroit metropolitan community. Although the MRUC did not last as long as New Detroit and Focus: HOPE, it made a valuable contribution to multiracial unity in the Detroit metropolitan community during the post-1967 period. The Michigan Roundtable for Diversity and Inclusion, under various previous names, is one of the oldest human rights organizations in Detroit, going back to before the 1943 race riot. Over the years it expanded from being an organization largely confined to building bridges between Catholics, Protestants, and Jews to one embracing more diverse and inclusive interests. To its great credit, the Roundtable has adjusted to the rapid social changes and difficult challenges of the region by developing effective programs geared not only to combatting all types of discrimination but to building and sustaining a diverse and inclusive community. It has been both a leader and a cheerleader in this noble effort for over six decades.

CHAPTER 13

Alternative Futures for Residents of Detroit

On October 27, 1961, *Time* magazine published the following:

> Detroit's decline has been going on for a long while. At the depth of the recession, when Detroit really began reeling, 20 percent of the city's workforce was unemployed. Blight is creeping like a fungus through many of Detroit's proud, old neighborhoods. During Detroit's decay, much of the city's middle class packed up and headed for the suburbs.

Compare that to this statement, published in the *Detroit Free Press* on November 29, 2009:

> Detroit's economic and social problems are staggering. A general fund deficit of $300 million, nearly 80,000 vacant buildings, an official unemployment rate of 30 percent, continuing population losses of more than 10,000 residents a year, a land mass that is one-third empty, public high school dropout rates of 70 percent, more than a third of the city living in poverty, and one of the nation's highest homicide and crime rates.

As the quotes above and the preceding chapters indicate, Detroit has gotten worse, not better, since the riots. We have documented the many challenges for residents of Detroit since 1967.

Many residents, organizations, and others have struggled to change the city in order to make it more livable for the population by increasing employment opportunities, the educational quality of the public school system, and the overall quality of housing and neighborhoods.

Despite the many efforts, the evidence is overwhelming that the conditions have *worsened* over time. So what are the future alternatives for the residents? Some may want to continue the struggle for many more years in the hope that somehow improvement in their quality of life will occur, that their children will somehow receive a quality education, and that jobs will somehow return to the city. This is the "stay where you are" option. Some residents will exercise it. However, if past behavior of those who promised to change Detroit, its school system, its ability to provide employment, and to improve the quality of housing and neighborhoods is the best predictor of future behavior, then this option may not be best for those Detroit residents who are tired of waiting. To them we offer the "spatial mobility" option. We will devote the rest of this final chapter to explaining it and what it has to offer the residents of Detroit.

WHY SPATIAL MOBILITY IS A VIABLE ALTERNATIVE FOR DETROIT RESIDENTS

Migration theory argues that residents often move due to push and pull factors (Greenwood, 1985). The push factors impacting residents of Detroit include (1) the low quality of education provided by the Detroit Public Schools, (2) the lack of jobs in the city, resulting in high unemployment rates, and (3) the lack of quality housing and neighborhoods at a competitive price.

EDUCATION IN THE PUBLIC SCHOOLS

We have documented in chapter 3 the struggle of many residents and organizations in Detroit to create a quality educational system equal to that of the quality of education in the suburbs. Yet during the entire period of 1967–2009, the quality of education received by students in the Detroit Public Schools did not improve at a level that reduced the inequality. Instead, the quality of education worsened.

The most recent study of the failure of Detroit's public schools to offer a quality education revealed that students in grade 4 in the city school district scored the lowest in math among all of the United States' large cities. The score for Detroit students in grade 4 math was 200. The national average was 239, and for all large cities, the average score was 238 (National Center for Education Statistics, 2009).

Detroit's students also performed poorly in eighth-grade math, scoring only 238. The average score was 271 for large cities and 282 for the nation as a whole (Arellano, 2009b; National Center for Education Statistics, 2009). The results of the study, which consisted of a national comparison of Detroit's students with other students in large public school districts and students in the nation as a whole, convincingly demonstrate that students in the Detroit Public Schools are not achieving at the level of their peers in other public school districts. The worsening of public schools in Detroit is related to increasing poverty, high unemployment rates, racial residential segregation, declining property values, shrinking government revenues, increasing crime, and neighborhood blight (Borowy, 2009).

The evidence is clear, and should be assessed by parents who want a quality education for their children. Should they remain in the city of Detroit and subject their children to the continuous failure of the Detroit school system (public and charter) to provide them with the quality of education their children deserve?

In Detroit as in other urban school districts, the gap in test scores between the city and suburbs begins in kindergarten and increases as grade levels increase. It is no surprise that many parents in Detroit are not satisfied with the quality of education their children are receiving. Indeed, some are angry and appalled following the results of the National Assessment for Educational Progress (NAEP) report denoting Detroit's poor performance. On December 19, 2009, over 500 upset members of the Detroit Parent Network met to discuss the "poor performance" problem with Robert Bobb, the school district's financial manager. One parent stated, "Someone needs to go to jail for the deplorable state of our public schools" (Buckman, 2009). This heated remark was widely interpreted as if parents were calling for the imprisonment of the teachers and administrators for the failure of the city's education system. However, the parents merely thought that someone should be held accountable. Those culpable, according to the executive director of Detroit Parent Network, Sharlonda Buckman, included officials, teachers, and parents who neglect their responsibilities (Buckman, 2009).

Buckman's op-ed in the *Detroit Free Press* stresses that parents must take responsibility too, and some in the city do not. Although families in the city confront enormous challenges—unemployment, unsafe neighborhoods, illiteracy, and a struggling school district—there is no excuse for ignoring a child's education (Buckman, 2009).

Buckman (2009) calls for the legislature to institute badly needed education reform, including policies that would transfer the authority of the Detroit Public Schools to the financial manager, Robert Bobb. Buckman also urges reforms that would enable Michigan to compete for the more than $400 million federal dollars in the Race to the Top legislation. To be competitive for the federal grants, the state legislature must bring reforms to Michigan's classrooms (*Detroit Free Press*, November 29, 2009).

In December 2009 the Michigan Senate passed Senate Bill 981 by a vote of twenty-three to eight, establishing a process by which no more than ten failed schools could be converted into charter schools, and existing charter schools that meet high standards could be converted into "school of excellence" charters, allowing thirty charters in total. By the 2011 school year, the Detroit School District had established twenty-five charter schools, and by February 2012 it had added four more (Chambers, February 9, 2012).

The bill also authorized the creation of two statewide cyber-schools, require school districts to adopt some form of merit pay, eliminate the current Algebra 2 high school graduation requirement, increase the compulsory school attendance age from sixteen to eighteen, and mandate the certification of school administrators. The Michigan House passed a companion bill 981 by a vote of eighty-two to seventeen (*Lansing State Journal*, December 27, 2009).

The Michigan Senate also passed House Bill 4787 by a vote of twenty-three to eight. This bill creates a state school reform/redesign officer with power to impose school intervention models on failed public schools, either (1) closing the school, (2) imposing new management and personnel, or (3) contracting with a charter school manager. This reform/redesign officer would have the power to revise teacher seniority and work rule provisions in an existing collective bargaining agreement, but could not change the pay scales or benefits.

House Bill 4787 passed the House by a vote of sixty-five to thirty-three (*Lansing State Journal*, December 27, 2009). This legislation prohibits privatizing noninstructional services in a public school unless the current union employees are given an opportunity to bid on the contract. The bill also amends the school union law to accommodate the powers of a new state school reform/redesign officer created by House Bill 4787.

Finally, House Bill 5596 provides an alternative teacher certification. The bill, which passed the House by a vote of seventy-four to twenty-five and the Senate by a vote of twenty-seven to three, authorizes an "interim teaching certificate" for individuals who have a college bachelor's degree with at least a 3.0 grade point average, and who are taking a twelve-credit-hour alternative "intensive" teaching program that meets the standards defined in the bill.

The Legislative Requirements for Real Reform

Under the legislation the existing alternative public schools would have to exhibit 90 percent proficiency in math and science, or 75 percent if at least half of the students came from low-income households (*Detroit Free Press*, November 29, 2009). One cannot help but note the lower academic expectations for districts with low-income households. The "reform legislation" would also enable high schools with 80 percent proficiency in student learning and high rates of graduation and college attendance to qualify for "schools of excellence" status (*Detroit Free Press*, November 29, 2009).

Michigan will use student achievement data to measure teacher performance for the first time. In other words, only through pressure and the prospects for federal dollars is Michigan moving for the first time in its history toward a more performance-based education system. Under the new system, student progress will be tied to teacher evaluations, pay bonuses, and tenure (*Detroit Free Press*, November 29, 2009).

The "reform legislation" does not give academic control of the Detroit Public Schools to Robert Bobb, the district's emergency financial manager. The legislation also does not give control to Detroit's mayor.

While these legislative efforts to reform the state's public schools move in a positive direction, based on the numerous attempts to improve the schools of Detroit over a forty-year period, we believe the reform legislation is too little, too late. Responsible parents should look for alternatives for educating their children outside of the Detroit School District. We will return to discuss the benefits of such an alternative education in one of many suburban districts. Now we discuss the second push factor, that is, a lack of jobs in the city of Detroit, resulting in a very high rate of unemployment.

THE SPATIAL MISMATCH FACTOR

Residents in Detroit continue to experience spatial mismatch. This concept, first noted by Kain in 1968, describes the effects of having jobs disproportionately located in the suburbs, while blacks are disproportionately located in the city. This lack of sufficient jobs in the city results in very high rates of unemployment.

In chapter 4, we discussed the continued struggle of many workers in Detroit to find the job opportunities in the city where they reside. However such jobs are disproportionately located in the suburbs. Over the years, city residents have witnessed a continual decline in jobs at a rate disproportionately high compared to the suburbs. This absence of jobs has been reflected throughout the period from 1967 to 2009 in differential unemployment rates.

By the end of that period, figures show, the city of Detroit was in a state of economic depression. According to the U.S. Bureau of Labor Statistics, Detroit's unemployment rate peaked at 30 percent in September 2009 and remained above 25 percent in February 2010, which was the rate of unemployment for the nation as a whole during the Great Depression (U.S. Bureau of Labor Statistics, 2010). The rate for metropolitan Detroit (reflecting largely the suburbs) was 14 percent. Thus, spatial mismatch, which we discussed in chapter 4, continues to be an economic problem for residents of Detroit.

When John Kain first coined the concept of spatial mismatch based on data from Detroit in 1968, he considered the source of the problem to be the disproportionate location of job opportunities in the suburbs while blacks were disproportionately confined to residential neighborhoods in the city. Predominantly black neighborhoods in Detroit also suffer from disinvestment at a level much higher than comparable predominantly white neighborhoods

(Darden, 2009b). The evidence is clear that job growth has been highest in the suburbs, which are usually overwhelmingly white. Researchers have documented spatial mismatch and job sprawl for some time now (Stoll, 2007).

We will return to the employment alternatives in the suburbs that residents of the city may want to consider as a way to improve their social mobility via movement out of the city to the suburbs. Next, however, we discuss the third push factor, that is, lack of quality housing and neighborhoods in the city at a competitive price compared to housing and neighborhoods in most suburbs.

HOUSING CHARACTERISTICS AND NEIGHBORHOODS

Earlier in the text we documented the struggle for quality housing and neighborhoods of residents of the city for a period of more than forty years. Yet inequality remains between what the city has offered and the alternative in the suburbs. The U.S. Department of Urban Development's American Housing Survey, conducted by the Census Bureau, has assessed the physical characteristics of housing and neighborhood characteristics since 1973. As a result of the 1967 civil disorders, the Douglas Commission on Housing (also called the Kaiser Committee) and the Presidential Advisory Commission on Civil Disorders (also called the Kerner Commission) were set up to study the causes of the problems. These commissions recommended an annual housing survey in order to assess the seriousness of housing needs and track progress of the national housing production goals (Housing Statistics User Group West, 2003). The survey assesses the type of structure, year built, place of structure, city/suburb rent, characteristics of occupants (race/ethnicity), educational level, income level, choice of present neighborhood, overall opinion, and problems in the neighborhood—crime, noise, traffic, trash, litter, junk on streets and properties, housing deterioration, poor public services, undesirable commercial institutions, and industrial facilities.

Data from the U.S. Department of Housing and Urban Development's American Housing Survey (2009) suggest that neighborhoods in the city of Detroit are more likely than neighborhoods in most of Detroit's suburbs to have crime, noise, housing deterioration, poor public services, undesirable commercial, institutional, and industrial facilities, and trash, litter, and junk on the streets (chapter 11). Thus, we argue that one proven way to improve residents' condition and quality of neighborhood, as well as employment prospects and educational quality, is to exercise the option of *spatial mobility*.

THE BENEFITS OF SPATIAL MOBILITY

The benefits of city-to-suburb spatial mobility have their roots in movement of white ethnic/ immigrant groups who moved to the suburbs in large numbers after 1950. The benefits have been demonstrated for nonwhites since the 1960s by the Gautreaux public housing desegregation case in Chicago, originally filed in 1969. It was later settled by the U.S. Supreme Court in 1976 (*Gautreaux, et al., v. Chicago Housing Authority, et al.*, 1967; *Hills v. Gautreaux*, 425 U.S. 1976). It was ruled that a metropolitan remedy would be appropriate to end the concentration of the poor in high-rise developments in black areas in the city of Chicago. The use of vouchers became part of the metropolitan remedy.

The Remedy: The Tenant-Based Section 8 Housing Voucher Program

The Section 8 voucher program was seen as a policy tool not only to enable families to choose better-quality housing consistent with their preference, but also to address spatial mismatch directly by facilitating the families' access to employment (Johnson, 2001).

Following the *Gautreaux v. Chicago Housing Authority* court decision, a settlement was negotiated under which HUD agreed to implement a Section 8 rent-subsidy program throughout the six-county Chicago metropolitan area, and to fund the nonprofit Leadership Council for Metropolitan Open Communities to manage it. A 1981 consent decree required HUD to continue the program until 7,100 black, low-income families had been placed in low-poverty areas where less than 30 percent of the population was black (Gallagher, 1994). By 1994, the Council had helped almost 5,000 families find housing outside of poverty areas. More than half moved to the suburbs, where jobs are more plentiful and education is usually of higher quality.

Researchers generally agree that the Gautreaux spatial mobility program was a success (Rosenbaum, 1995). By changing their environment, that is, moving from the city to the suburbs, households had increased employment, higher efficacy levels, and better residential conditions, and their children had higher high school graduation rates (Rosenbaum, 1995; Rosenbaum, Reynolds, and DeLuca, 2002; Rubinowitz and Rosenbaum, 2000).

Since the 1976 Supreme Court ruling in the *Gautreaux* case, public housing authorities have been under increasing pressure to provide deconcentrated residential options for poor, minority tenants. The options have been carried out with a Section 8 certificate and voucher program or scattered-site housing (Briggs, Darden, and Aidala, 1999).

As policymakers came under increased pressure to find ways to improve the well-being of disadvantaged children and families, the link between residential mobility and social mobility received increasing attention. Indeed, Henry Cisneros, former secretary of Housing and Urban Development, embraced spatial mobility programs as a cornerstone of his push for fair housing (Gallagher, 1994).

During the 1970s and 1980s, Detroit and other northern cities lost large numbers of manufacturing and other low-skilled jobs, many of which were relocated to the suburbs, leaving unemployed blacks and Hispanics in central city locations. Such a changing American economy, with its emphasis on deindustrialization and job dispersal, has continued. The impact has led to increased concentrations of poor blacks and Hispanics, with high rates of unemployment, teenage pregnancies, out-of-wedlock births, single-parent households, increased crime, increased school dropout rates, and above all, a general lack of economic self-sufficiency (Wilson, 1987).

Residential mobility has been a crucial avenue for attaining economic self-sufficiency in America. It is the way in which most white ethnic groups obtained economic advancement—through better jobs, better neighborhoods, and better schools. Such residential mobility has led to *generational socioeconomic gains* for the children of white ethnic groups. Yet because of racial barriers to residential mobility, this normal avenue for economic self-sufficiency has been largely closed to many poor blacks and Hispanics (Comers, Briggs, and Weismann

2008). Indeed, some researchers feel so strongly about the benefits of spatial mobility that they have argued that improving the housing in a bad neighborhood may actually be counterproductive (Shlay, 1993). For example, Shlay (1993) argues that by spatially concentrating poverty and thereby limiting access to those human-capital-generating resources that are requisite for attaining economic self-sufficiency, housing can thwart economic achievement. The Department of Housing and Urban Development took the same position in 1973, when it concluded that there was a disproportionate concentration of poverty in central cities. Therefore, improvements in the physical condition of this housing may worsen the situation by reducing the migration of the poor out of an unsuitable environment (U.S. Department of Housing and Urban Development, 1973).

The Moving to Opportunity Program (MTO)

In order to measure the impact of neighborhoods on the lives of poor and minority residents and how their well-being might change if families moved to nonpoor, nonminority neighborhoods, Congress funded a Moving to Opportunity (MTO) demonstration program in 1992. The MTO program was designed to answer questions about what happens to poor families when they are given the opportunity to move out of distressed public housing in the poorest neighborhoods of five very large American metropolitan areas—Baltimore, Boston, Chicago, Los Angeles, and New York. Congress provided $70 million in Section 8 rental vouchers, with additional vouchers allocated by participating housing authorities.

The results from the MTO program were not as clear and dramatic as the results from the Gautreaux program, and may be appropriately characterized as mixed. However, the results did show some positive impact for households who moved great distances from their original place of residence. In other words, those who moved to low-poverty suburban neighborhoods experienced lower unemployment rates, increased feelings of safety in the neighborhood, and improved mental health for adults and female youth (Basolo and Nguyen, 2009; Goering and Feins, 2003; Orr et al., 2003; Kling, Ludwig, and Katz, 2005).

The key problem with the MTO program was that less than half (47 percent) of the families assigned to the experimental groups, that is, the groups required to relocate to a low-poverty neighborhood (i.e. less than 10 percent) actually did so (Comers, Briggs, and Weismann, 2008). Instead, most of the experimental group families moved to other predominantly minority neighborhoods in the central city and inner suburbs, not racially integrated areas in more affluent outer suburbs at greater distances from the central city, as the more successful Gautreaux families did. Thus, the MTO families may not have experienced the full benefits of living in a low-poverty, racially integrated neighborhood (Comers et al., 2008).

It is fair to conclude that the MTO program has not lived up to its full potential. The research suggest that most MTO families never left their original urban school district and did not move very far from their old neighborhood, and that their children never really had access and experience living in a high-performing suburban school district (Engdahl, 2009). This led some critics of the program to conclude that poor black families cannot or will not move to distant neighborhoods (Basolo and Nguyen, 2009; Clampet-Lundquist and Massey, 2008; Engdahl, 2009; Ludwig et al., 2008). Another issue that has been debated is whether the suburban communities will reject the families based on race (Turner et al., 2002). The fact that many poor blacks did not move to distant suburbs helps to explain the results of the final

MTO report (U.S. Department of Housing and Urban Development, 2011). MTO spatial mobility programs did improve the quality experienced by families who relocated in terms of housing, poverty, and aspects of disadvantage based on safety and physical and mental health. However, MTO programs did not appear to improve educational outcomes, employment, or earnings (U.S. Department of Housing and Urban Development, 2011). A reanalysis of the MTO data by Burdick-Will et al. suggests that a neighborhood's effects on a child, including educational outcomes, may be contingent on factors such as exposure to violence or relative disadvantage of the neighborhood in which the child lives. Children living in very disadvantaged neighborhoods may experience stronger effects than those living in moderately disadvantaged areas. In high-poverty neighborhoods in Chicago and Baltimore, the MTO data showed improvement in test scores when students and parents moved to a less disadvantaged neighborhood. In Boston, Los Angeles, and New York, where neighborhoods are comparatively less disadvantaged, the researchers did not find clear test score improvements.

The research suggests that low-income African American families face both race and class barriers when moving to predominantly affluent white neighborhoods (Kissane and Clampet-Lundquist, 2005). These barriers are exacerbated by gender, as low-income African American single mothers are more often stigmatized and are more likely to also face gender discrimination as a single parent (Mendenhall, 2005).

However, a recent evaluation of the Baltimore spatial mobility program suggests that none of the arguments are valid.

Background on Baltimore's Spatial Mobility Program

The Baltimore Housing Mobility Program originated as a partial settlement of the 1996 landmark *Thompson v. the U.S. Department of Housing and Urban Development* public housing desegregation case. For more than six years, the Baltimore Housing Mobility Program has been moving families into lower-poverty, less racially segregated neighborhoods (Engdahl, 2009). According to Engdahl and Tegeler (2009), the benefits for the more than 1,500 families moving to new neighborhoods under the program underscore the need to encourage many more families to move to less segregated, higher opportunity areas.

Data and Analysis

The study uses administrative data, surveys of participants, and interviews with program staff and participants to provide the first comprehensive evaluation of families in the spatial mobility program.

Among the reasons for participating in the program, 86 percent of the respondents wanted to move to a better and safer neighborhood and 67 percent wanted better and safer schools. While some families found what they preferred in the city, 89 percent used their rental voucher to move to suburban neighborhoods.

On average, the neighborhoods that the families moved from were 80 percent African American. The unemployment rate was 17 percent, the poverty rate was 33 percent, and there was a median household income of $24,182. Only 61 percent of the adults had a high school diploma, and only 6.3 percent had a bachelor's degree.

On the other hand, the neighborhoods the families moved to had on average an African American population of 21 percent, an unemployment rate of 4.4 percent, a poverty rate of 7.5 percent, and a median household income of $48,318. Eighty-five percent of the neighborhood residents had graduated from high school, and 19 percent had a bachelor's degree (Engdahl, 2009).

Almost all (95 percent) of the new movers surveyed said their new neighborhood was better or much better than the neighborhood they left behind in the city. Overall, those surveyed reported improved quality of life and educational opportunity, as well as better employment opportunities in their new neighborhoods. In their new neighborhoods, participants said they felt safer, healthier, less stressed, and more confident in their future and the future of their children. Most parents reported that their children were doing better in school, and 93 percent reported that they were satisfied or very satisfied with the schools in their new community. Their satisfaction appeared to be related to the fact that there was less crime and drugs in the neighborhoods. Moreover, their neighbors were friendly. School quality was a major factor. Quantitatively, in the new neighborhoods' elementary schools, 69 percent and 76 percent of students scored proficient or higher on state math and reading tests compared with 44 percent and 54 percent in the city schools they attended before moving to the suburbs (Engdahl, 2009). A high percentage (89 percent) of the parents who moved to the suburbs said their children appear to be learning better or much better in their new schools. The schools were better resourced, had fewer dropouts, and were high performing.

SPATIAL MOBILITY: AN ALTERNATIVE REMEDY FOR RESIDENTS IN DETROIT

Based on lessons learned about spatial mobility programs elsewhere and the encouragement from the success of the program in Baltimore, we now introduce an alternative for those residents who are not satisfied with their present neighborhood, its housing and schools. We make this proposal based on the research related to (1) differences in neighborhoods and school quality between Detroit and its suburbs, (2) the research related to household preferences (absent constraints) and (3) the research related to the spatial distribution of rent levels in selected suburbs of the metropolitan area (i.e., affordability).

The data and research have consistently shown that the best schools are located in the suburbs of metropolitan areas (Sander, 2006). Moreover, the quality of the public schools has traditionally been a push factor away from the city and a pull factor to the suburbs for the white middle- and upper-class populations.

School quality in Michigan, like most other states, is directly related to location (city vs. suburbs), property values, and the overall economic prosperity of municipalities (Bayoh, Irwin, and Haab, 2006; Zahirovic-Herbert and Turnbull, 2008). Moreover, school quality is among the leading factors of household choice decisions traditionally exercised by the middle and upper classes (Figlio and Lucas, 2004). Our argument is that such options should and could be exercised by residents of Detroit who want a better-quality school environment. Research has shown that school quality, as measured by the average combined math and English scores, has the largest marginal effect on household choice probabilities (Bayoh et al., 2006). To influence that choice, many apartment managers and real estate agents include information about the quality of the public schools in the district where the apartment or house is located (Zahirovic-Herbert and Turnbull, 2008).

Thus, school quality has continued to influence where families choose to live. It influences business decisions and job location. Since parents with fewer constraints (white and middle class) have often made the decision earlier, they have been traditionally more likely to take advantage of the location of the higher-quality schools. Such schools are also located in districts with high public expenditures. Households that have had few constraints have sorted themselves out based on public expenditures that appeal to their preferences. Thus, households with children "theoretically chose to live in a community that spends a lot on public schools," according to Tiebout (1956). It is worth emphasizing, however, that Tiebout includes only those households without race and class constraints. It has been the location decisions of the households with few constraints who presently reside overwhelmingly in the suburbs that have been the most powerful force driving disparities in the public schools (Hoxby, 2000). We argue for extending Tiebout's choice model to those who have heretofore been residentially immobile. In other words, we encourage them to also exercise the push-pull factors in location decision-making.

For unsatisfied parents in Detroit, we suggest the mobility option because charter schools have not been an effective alternative to improve the quality of education in Detroit. There is little evidence in Detroit that charter schools have performed better than traditional public schools (Arellano, 2009a, 2009b). It should be emphasized that a household does not just buy or rent the property at a particular location, but the household buys or rents the neighborhood with all of its characteristics and its public school district. Choosing a quality public school district is one of the most important decisions a parent can make because education is an important determinant of social mobility. It will also determine to a great extent an adult's future socioeconomic status (Rouse and Barrow, 2006).

The Affordability Factor

It has been well documented that it is not the lack of affordable housing that best explains blacks' underrepresentation in the suburbs (Farley, Danzinger, and Holzer, 2000). Residential segregation, where most blacks reside in the city and most whites reside in Detroit's suburbs, is not primarily due to income differences, occupational differences, or educational differences between blacks and whites (Darden and Kamel, 2000). If households were assigned to neighborhoods based strictly on income, metropolitan Detroit would be very integrated racially (Darden, 2007d; Farley et al., 2000). Instead, the research suggests that blacks and whites may have different knowledge of the geography of the housing market. Blacks more often than whites may overestimate the cost of rent in the suburbs and therefore do not look for apartment vacancies in such neighborhoods based on the quite possibly inaccurate belief that they cannot afford to live there. According to Farley, Danzinger, and Holzer (2000: 179):

> A few people may do library research to investigate property values, crime rates and the test scores of children attending the local schools but those individuals are rare exceptions. When a person contemplates moving or staying, he or she normally relies on information and misinformation

provided by friends, relatives, coworkers, and neighbors. Over time we develop images of where we would like to live and where we would like to avoid.

Using data from the University of Michigan's Detroit Area Survey for 1976 and 1992, the authors concluded that both blacks and whites believed that most blacks could afford to live in Detroit's suburbs (Farley, Danzinger, and Holzer, 2000). Our more recent data and analysis confirm such beliefs about affordability. We use two sources of data: (1) the most recent American Community Survey for Detroit (U.S. Bureau of the Census, 2010) and (2) data from Apartments.com published in *Detroit Free Press*'s advertisement of vacant apartments on May 22, 2011, for Detroit and selected suburbs.

Based on analysis of American Community Survey data for 2005–9, 1.3 percent of Detroit renter households paid contract monthly rent at levels as low as $100 per month to levels ranging from $1,250–$1,499 per month (0.6 percent). The majority (56 percent) of Detroit renter households paid contract rent at levels ranging from $400 to $699 per month (table 47).

Table 47. Percentage of Detroit renter households paying contract rent at various levels, 2005–2009

Monthly rent	Percentage of total households
Less than $100	1.3
$100–$149	1.5
$150–$199	4.1
$200–$249	2.1
$250–$299	3.0
$300–$349	4.2
$350–$399	6.2
$400–$449	9.0
$450–$499	10.7
$500–$549	12.0
$550–$599	8.0
$600–$649	9.0
$650–$699	7.3
$700–$749	5.5
$750–$799	4.8
$800–$899	5.6
$900–$999	3.5
$1,000–$1,249	1.7
$1,250–$,1499	0.6
Total	100.0

Source: Computed by the authors from data obtained from U.S. Bureau of the Census (2010).

To determine the percentage of Detroit renter households that could afford to live in selected suburbs outside Detroit given the level of rent they were paying to live in Detroit, we calculated the percentage of Detroit renter households paying a rent amount that equaled or exceeded the median contract rent amount for a selected group of suburbs in Wayne, Oakland, and Macomb counties. We found that the percentage of Detroit renter households that could afford to live in the various suburbs of Wayne County ranged from 11.7 percent in Northville to 46.1 percent in Belleville, Flat Rock, Lincoln Park, and Melvindale (table 48).

Table 48. Percentage of Detroit renter households that could afford to live in selected Wayne County suburbs, 2009

Suburb	Percent	Median contract rent
Belleville City	46.1	544
Canton	16.5	753
Dearborn	22.0	702
Dearborn Heights	16.5	759
Flat Rock	46.1	521
Harper Woods	16.5	733
Lincoln Park	46.1	556
Livonia	22.0	726
Melvindale	46.1	532
Northville	11.7	831
Plymouth	22.0	693
Riverview	29.3	652
Southgate	22.0	664
Taylor City	29.3	634
Westland	22.0	671
Woodhaven	29.3	628

Note: Affordability is based on the percentage of households paying a rent amount that is equal to or higher than the median contract rent of the respective suburban municipality.

Source: Computed by the authors from data obtained from the U.S. Bureau of the Census (2010).

The percentage of Detroit renter households that could afford to live in selected suburbs in Oakland County ranged from 0.9 percent in West Bloomfield to 46.1 percent in Holly (table 49).

In Macomb County, the percentage of Detroit renter households that could afford to live in the various suburbs outside Detroit ranged from 22 percent in Shelby Township and Sterling Heights to 46.1 percent in the city of Fraser (table 50).

In the final analysis, we examined the available apartments in these selected suburbs and in Detroit and the advertised monthly rent requested on May 22, 2011. We limited the analysis to two-bedroom apartments. Table 51 shows that the average monthly rent for a two-bedroom

Table 49. Percentage of Detroit renter households that could afford to live in selected Oakland County suburbs, 2009

Suburb	Percent	Median contract rent
Auburn Hills	16.4	742
Birmingham	2.6	980
Bloomfield Township	6.1	888
Clawson	29.3	647
Farmington	16.4	735
Farmington Hills	6.1	811
Holly	46.1	542
Madison Heights	29.2	629
Novi	6.1	817
Oak Park	16.4	721
Rochester	22.0	699
Rochester Hills	6.1	850
Royal Oak	16.4	719
Southfield	6.1	817
Troy	6.1	872
Walled Lake	16.4	737
Waterford	29.2	619
West Bloomfield	0.9	1,146
Wixom	38.0	558

Note: Affordability is based on the percentage of households paying a rent amount that is equal to or higher than the median contract rent of the respective suburban municipality.

Source: Computed by the authors from data obtained from the U.S. Bureau of the Census (2010).

apartment in the city of Detroit was $974. Thus the Detroit apartment seeker could rent a two-bedroom apartment at a *lower* rate in the following suburbs of Oakland County:

- Auburn Hills
- Bloomfield Township
- Clawson
- Farmington
- Farmington Hills
- Holly
- Madison Heights
- Novi
- Oak Park
- Rochester
- Rochester Hills
- Royal Oak

- Southfield
- Troy
- Walled Lake
- Waterford
- Wixom

In Wayne County, all of the sixteen suburbs listed in table 51 advertised apartments at a lower monthly rate than the rate advertised for the city of Detroit. Finally, all nine suburbs in Macomb County advertised apartments at rent levels lower than the levels for Detroit.

Table 50. Percentage of Detroit renter households that could afford to live in selected Macomb County suburbs, 2009

Suburb	*Percent*	*Median contract rent*
Clinton Township	29.3	630
Fraser	46.1	561
Harrison Township	29.3	641
New Baltimore	38.0	586
Roseville	29.3	626
Shelby Township	22.0	691
Sterling Heights	22.0	676
Utica	38.0	595
Warren	29.3	635

Note: Affordability is based on the percentage of households paying a rent amount that is equal to or higher than the median contract rent of the respective suburban municipality.

Source: Computed by the authors from data obtained from the U.S. Bureau of the Census (2010).

To be sure, there may be apartments that rent for less than those that happened to be advertised in the *Detroit Free Press* on May 22, 2011, in Detroit and selected suburbs. Our purpose here was to demonstrate that apartments for rent are not necessarily lower in Detroit and higher in the suburbs, and that those renters who can afford to pay $974 per month for a two-bedroom apartment in Detroit have several selected options to rent apartments at a lower monthly rate in several selected suburbs in Wayne, Oakland, and Macomb counties. Thus, we conclude that the lack of ability to afford apartments in the Detroit suburbs is not the primary barrier preventing renters in Detroit from moving to selected suburbs.

Movement to Suburban Detroit

What we are advocating is an alternative for Detroit residents (especially parents) to choose not just another school but another neighborhood. In this regard we take a different approach from those researchers who focus only on providing vouchers to students in low-achieving schools to attend private schools (Robinson, 2005). Not surprisingly, the most recent research suggests little difference in the achievement of students who remain in their poor neighborhoods but attend private schools. Indeed, results from the city of Milwaukee's twenty-one-year-old school choice program revealed that students in the school choice program performed worse than or about the same as students in Milwaukee's public schools in math and reading on the latest statewide test (Richards and Hetzner, 2011). The Milwaukee parental choice program was intended to improve the achievement of poor city children in failing public schools by allowing them to attend higher-performing private schools with publicly funded vouchers. In the voucher program, 55.2 percent of students scored proficient or better in reading, while 34.4 percent of students scored proficient or better in math. However, in the Milwaukee public schools, 59 percent scored proficient or better in reading and 47.8 percent of students scored proficient or better in math (Richards and Hetzner, 2011).

We believe that private schools do not necessarily improve academic achievement for low-income students as long as the student remains in a poor neighborhood environment.

What we advocate instead is a change in the municipality, which will bring a change in the school district where the student attends. A change in the district can provide many options for the student to attend high-achieving public schools (Hoxby, 2001).

A change in municipality can also provide higher-quality public services, garbage collection, police protection, greater access to health care, and supermarket shopping facilities. Moreover, such amenities can be obtained at a lower tax rate compared to the tax rate in the city.

Thus, given affordability and the knowledge of municipalities that offer such alternatives and a declining discriminatory housing barrier, we can expect more residents from Detroit to take advantage of the alternative. Indeed, many residents have already started the residential mobility process.

Table 51. The average rent per month for two-bedroom apartment in selected suburbs in Oakland, Wayne, and Macomb counties, May 22, 2011

Oakland County		
Suburb	Number available	Rent
Auburn Hills	4	693
Birmingham	3	1,190
Bloomfield Township	1	810
Clawson	1	645
Farmington	6	803
Farmington Hills	11	873
Holly	1	499
Madison Heights	5	566
Novi	12	942
Oak Park	1	830
Rochester	7	738
Rochester Hills	6	883
Royal Oak	6	691
Southfield	11	827
Troy	9	819
Walled Lake	2	702
Waterford	5	561
West Bloomfield	4	1,316

Table 51. The average rent per month for two- bedroom apartment in selected suburbs in Oakland, Wayne, and Macomb counties, May 22, 2011 (*continued*)

Wayne County		
Suburb	**Number available**	**Rent**
Belleville	5	689
Canton	10	933
Dearborn	4	854
Dearborn Heights	9	717
Detroit	**8**	**974**
Flat Rock	1	669
Harper Woods	2	727
Lincoln Park	1	599
Livonia	2	805
Melvindale	1	660
Northville	4	931
Plymouth	9	772
Riverview	1	650
Southgate	3	633
Taylor	3	603
Westland	14	683
Woodhaven	4	613
Macomb County		
Clinton Township	12	697
Fraser	1	595
Harrison Township	4	707
New Baltimore	1	550
Roseville	2	650
Shelby Township	3	846
Sterling Heights	13	763
Utica	1	830
Warren	2	734

Source: Computed by the authors form data obtained from *Detroit Free Press* advertisements of vacant apartments, May 22, 2011.

POPULATION INCREASES IN SUBURBAN DETROIT, 2000—2010

From 2000 to 2010, the total population of Detroit declined from 951,270 to 713,777, or by 25 percent (U.S. Bureau of the Census, 2011b). Among those who left the city, 185,874, or 80 percent, were black. While we do not have the data on where all of the blacks who left Detroit relocated, it is reasonable to hypothesize that an overwhelming majority relocated to the various suburbs in Wayne, Oakland, and Macomb counties. We test this hypothesis by examining the black population increase in various Detroit suburbs. Of the thirty-eight suburban municipalities examined, the black population increased substantially between 2000 and 2010. The following Detroit suburbs increased in population by more than 10 percent over the decade (table 52):

- Eastpointe
- Farmington
- Farmington Hills
- Ferndale
- Grosse Pointe Park
- Melvindale
- Roseville
- Taylor
- Warren
- Wixom

Indeed, while the city of Detroit experienced a large-scale black decline, all of the thirty-eight Detroit suburbs of 10,000 or more experienced black population increase. Such increases changed Oak Park to a majority black suburb with a black population of 59.1 percent. Southfield, which was 55.4 percent black in 2000, became 71.7 percent Black in 2010 (table 52).

Patterns of Black-White Residential Segregation in Suburban Detroit, 2010

Unlike blacks who remained in the city of Detroit in residentially segregated neighborhoods, those blacks who reside in the suburbs live in racially integrated neighborhoods. Of the thirty-eight suburban municipalities examined, only one suburb—Wixom—had a relatively high level of black-white residential segregation as revealed by an index of dissimilarity of 59.9 (table 53). In all the remaining suburbs, the index of dissimilarity (which measures the unevenness in the spatial distribution of blacks and whites over census tracts) ranged from a low of 6.8 in Fraser to 46 in Taylor. The mean level of black-white suburban residential segregation was 24.6. The low level of black-white residential segregation compares to 59.2 in the city of Detroit. A low level of residential segregation ensures racial integration of the public schools, which provides black students with an equal opportunity to attend high-achieving public schools, which are more represented in suburban Detroit than in the city.

While the data suggest that many residents of Detroit have already been moving to the suburbs, others may wish to move but may need assistance in the housing search process. We discuss the type of assistance that might be the most useful.

The Benefit of Assistance in the Housing Search Process

Like the residents of the successful spatial mobility programs, the research suggests that greater success occurs if those seeking housing in the suburbs have assistance from a metropolitan-wide, nonprofit housing organization. Indeed, based on previous research, an unassisted apartment search in the suburbs is usually a limited search geographically (Comers et al., 2008). However, to keep those who are searching for housing from being steered by some agents in the private housing market or discriminated against outright by others (Turner et al., 2002), we recommend that a fair housing organization provide such assistance. Ideally, in Detroit the organization with the skills, the knowledge, and experience is the Fair Housing Center of Metropolitan Detroit.

An Expanded Role for the Fair Housing Center of Metropolitan Detroit

Since 1977, the Fair Housing Center of Metropolitan Detroit has been investigating complaints of discrimination in housing in metropolitan Detroit. Under the effective leadership of Clifford C. Schrupp, its executive director, paired testing has been an effective tool to detect where any discrimination in housing has been occurring through a systematic gathering of information. Such testing, also called the audit method, is the strongest and most effective method of measuring housing-related discrimination. Its strength is based on the fact that the

Table 52. Patterns of black suburbanization in Detroit, 2000 and 2010

Municipality	*Total population, 2010*	*Number black, 2000*	*Percent black, 2000*	*Number black, 2010*	*Percent black, 2010*
Allen Park	28,210	241	0.8	696	2.5
Auburn Hills	21,412	2,742	13.8	4,229	19.8
Berkley	14,970	137	0.9	544	3.6
Beverly Hills Village	10,267	352	3.4	746	7.3
Birmingham	20,103	208	1.1	691	3.4
Clawson	11,825	129	1.0	287	2.4
Dearborn	98,153	1,390	1.4	4,296	4.4
Dearborn Heights	57,774	1,358	2.3	4,892	8.5
Eastpointe	32,442	1,725	5.1	9,990	30.8
Farmington	10,372	298	2.9	1,259	12.1
Farmington Hills	79,740	6,040	7.4	14,436	18.1
Ferndale	19,900	930	4.2	2,200	11.1
Fraser	14,480	175	1.1	675	4.7
Garden City	27,692	389	1.3	1,133	4.1
Grosse Pointe Park	11,555	430	3.5	1,313	11.4
Grosse Pointe Woods	16,135	132	0.8	791	4.9
Harper Woods	14,236	1,523	10.7	6,711	47.1

Table 52. Patterns of black suburbanization in Detroit, 2000 and 2010 (*continued*)

Municipality	Total population, 2010	Number black, 2000	Percent black, 2000	Number black, 2010	Percent black, 2010
Hazel Park	16,422	443	2.3	1,954	11.9
Lincoln Park	38,144	926	2.3	2,577	6.8
Livonia	96,942	1,105	1.1	3,609	3.7
Madison Heights	29,694	638	2.0	2,158	7.3
Melvindale	10,715	603	5.6	1,260	11.8
Novi	55,224	1,036	2.2	4,785	8.7
Oak Park	29,319	14,004	47.0	17,321	59.1
Rochester	12,711	247	2.4	507	4.0
Rochester Hills	70,995	1,819	2.6	3,516	5.0
Roseville	47,299	1,413	2.9	6,165	13.0
Royal Oak	57,236	1,045	1.7	2,795	4.9
Southfield	71,739	43,412	55.4	51,445	71.7
Southgate	30,047	685	2.3	1,843	6.1
South Lyon	11,327	53	0.5	145	1.3
Sterling Heights	129,699	1,853	1.5	7,213	5.6
Taylor	63,131	6,181	9.4	10,671	16.9
Trenton	18,853	106	0.5	323	1.7
Troy	80,980	1,850	2.3	3,595	4.4
Warren	134,056	4,204	3.0	19,443	14.5
Wixom	13,498	370	2.8	1,577	11.7
Woodhaven	12,875	319	2.6	779	6.0

Source: Logan and Stults (2011).

participants are matched on all relevant characteristics except race, ethnicity, or national origin. Thus, the results of the tests show that actions by apartment managers are the direct result of discrimination due to race, ethnicity, or national origin. This is the only method thus far that measures direct behavior instead of sentiments, or what landlords or apartment managers say they believe (Darden, 2004).

The Fair Housing Center of Metropolitan Detroit has been a key player in the Public/Private Partnership for Fair Housing since its creation. It has been able to effectively assist complainants, resolving complaints through its own negotiations or an administrative process in which it has referred complainants to administrative agencies, including HUD, or to court via private attorneys (Fair Housing Center of Metropolitan Detroit, 2009).

The Fair Housing Center believes, and we concur, that the increased black movement to the suburbs and the low levels of black residential segregation may be due to changes in the

Table 53. Patterns of black-white residential segregation in suburban Detroit, 2010

Municipality	Index of dissimilarity
Allen Park	27.1
Auburn Hills	21.9
Berkley	14.2
Beverly Hills	20.8
Birmingham	19.2
Clawson	8.4
Dearborn	35.3
Dearborn Heights	29.2
Eastpointe	25.2
Farmington	31.6
Farmington Hills	20.3
Ferndale	17.3
Fraser	6.8
Garden City	15.7
Grosse Pointe Park	25.3
Grosse Pointe Woods	25.5
Harper Woods	13.8
Hazel Park	10.7
Lincoln Park	31.8
Livonia	32.1
Madison Heights	22.5
Melvindale	14.2
Novi	24.4
Oak Park	41.3
Rochester	12.2
Rochester Hills	26.6
Roseville	31.2
Royal Oak	20.0
Southfield	26.6
Southgate	40.2
South Lyon	8.1
Sterling Heights	22.8
Taylor	46.0

Table 53. Patterns of black- white residential segregation in suburban Detroit, 2010 (*continued*)

Municipality	Index of dissimilarity
Trenton	40.7
Troy	20.1
Warren	32.0
Wixom	59.9
Woodhaven	16.0
Mean	24.6

Note: The index of dissimilarity ranges from 0 to 100. The higher the index, the higher the level of residential segregation. See the appendix for details.

Source: Logan and Stults (2011).

behavior of housing providers who are now serving black home-seekers that they had previously denied. The Fair Housing Center notes that many of those home seekers, especially prior to 2000, were denied housing opportunities because of race (*Fair Housing News*, May 2011). The Center also notes that fair housing training of housing providers (rental, sales, and mortgage lending) has increased dramatically over the last fifteen years. The Center believes that such increase in training has been related to the damages (more than $11 million) paid by housing providers to plaintiffs in the more than 400 housing discrimination lawsuits that were assisted by the Fair Housing Center (*Fair Housing News*, May 2011; see also Meyer, 2007).

Given its long history in working in metropolitan Detroit to combat unlawful housing discrimination, no other organization is better informed about the places (municipalities) that may be hostile and the places (municipalities) that may be more hospitable to residents of Detroit. The Fair Housing Center is also more informed than other organizations about the fair housing practices of apartment managers and real estate brokers throughout the metropolitan area.

Thus, by expanding its activities (which may require additional funding) to serve potential apartment seekers in their geographic search throughout the metropolitan area, the placement of Detroit residents who wish to relocate to the suburbs can be effectively achieved.

For those parents who may not be able to move to a high-achieving school district in the short run, we believe the governor's proposal that would mandate all of the state's 551 school districts to enroll students who live outside their districts if they have room is an excellent proposal that would provide greater opportunities for those who stay in the city (Angel, 2011). It would remove the geographic barriers to all students achieving equal educational opportunity by providing them an option other than the failing schools in their neighborhood district. The proposal making schools of choice mandatory was expected to be drafted by the fall of 2011 (Angel, 2011). At the time of this writing, however, no legislative action had been taken.

Method of Computation of the Index of Dissimilarity

THE INDEX OF DISSIMILARITY IS BASED ON CENSUS TRACTS. THE INDEX OF DISSIMIlarity D is defined as the overall unevenness in the spatial distribution of two racial groups. It is stated mathematically as:

$$D = 100 \left(\frac{1}{2} \sum_{i=1}^{k} x_i - y_i \right)$$

where:

x_i = the percentage of a minority population living in a given census tract

y_i = the percentage of the non-Hispanic white population (or other majority population) living in the same census tract.

The index of dissimilarity is equal to one-half the sum of the absolute differences (positive and negative) between the percentage distributions of the minority population and non-Hispanic white population (or other majority population) in the city of Detroit.

The value for the index of dissimilarity D can range from 0 (indicating no residential segregation) to 100 (indicating total segregation between the minority and the majority group). The higher the index of dissimilarity, the higher the level of residential segregation.

References

Adams, G. 1992, November 18–24. "The High Cost of Racism." *Michigan Chronicle.*

Alba, R., and J. Logan. 1993. "Minority Proximity to Whites in Suburbs: An Individual Level Analysis of Segregation." *American Journal of Sociology* 98, 1388–1427.

Aldrich, H., and R. Waldinger. 1990. "Ethnicity and Entrepreneurship." *Annual Review of Sociology* 16, 111–35.

Allen, J. P., and E. Turner. 2009. "Ethnic Residential Concentrations with Above-Average Incomes." *Urban Geography* 30(3), 209–38.

American Citizens for Justice. 1984, November. *Justice Update* (newsletter).

———. 1987, July. Press conference official statement. *Justice Update* (newsletter).

American Citizens for Justice and Asian Pacific American Legal Center of Southern California. 1983. Confidential report on Vincent Chin case. Report to U.S. Department of Justice, Civil Rights Division.

Amsden, T., and R. Rystedt. 1992. Invitation to monthly discussion in Detroit. Document in possession of the authors.

———. 1993. Invitation to monthly discussion in Detroit. Document in possession of the authors.

———. 1994. Invitation to monthly discussion in Detroit. Document in possession of the authors.

———. 1995. Invitation to monthly discussion in Detroit. Document in possession of the authors.

———. 1998. Invitation to monthly discussion in Detroit. Document in possession of the authors.

———. 1999. Invitation to monthly discussion in Detroit. Document in possession of the authors.

———. 2001. Invitation to monthly discussion in Detroit. Document in possession of the authors.

Angel, C. 2011, July 24. "Pointes Take Pulse on Schools." *Detroit Free Press.*

———. 2001, August 1. "Gasoline Boycott Initiated." *Detroit Free Press.*

Arcand, R. 1995, May 20. "Practical Programs to Promote Diversity." Workshop presentation at the Second Annual Model of Racial Unity Conference, Detroit.

Archer, D. 1995, May 20. Model of Racial Unity Day. Office of the Mayor, City of Detroit.

Arellano, A. 2001, August 16. "Hispanic Community Makes Its Voice Heard." *Detroit Free Press.*

———. 2009a, December 15. "Detroit Charter Schools: New Accountability Movement Targets Low-Performing Charter Academies." *The Detroit News.*

———. 2009b, December 8. "Detroit Hits Educational Bottom." *The Detroit News.*

Arellano, A., and J. S. Ghannam. 1992, December 29. "U.S. Alleges Bias in Housing." *Detroit Free Press.*

Ashenfelter, D. 2011, July 10. "Parents Sue Grosse Pointe Schools." *Lansing State Journal.*

Ashton, P. J. 1981. *Race, Class and Black Politics: The Implications of the Election of a Black Mayor for the Police and Policing in Detroit.* East Lansing: Michigan State University.

Associated Press. 1987, April 23. "Lawyer: 1st Chin Trial Was 'Rigged.'" *Detroit Free Press.*

Baba, M., and M. Abonyi. 1979. *Mexicans of Detroit.* Detroit: Wayne State University Press.

Badillo, D. 2003. *Latinos in Michigan.* East Lansing: Michigan State University Press.

Baha'i Youth Workshop and the Catholic Youth Organization. 1995, May 20. "Workshop on Youth's

Response to Racism." Workshop presentation at the Second Annual Model of Racial Unity Conference, Detroit. Bailey, R. 2000, May 18. "1 Freed in '99 Killing in Detroit." *Detroit Free Press.*

Basolo, V., and M. T. Nguyen. 2009. "Immigrants' Housing Search and Neighborhood Conditions: A Comparative Analysis of Housing Choice Voucher Holders." *Cityscape* 11(3), 99–126.

Bates, T. 1993. "Black Businesses and the Legacy of Racism." *Focus* 21(6), 5–6.

———. 1997. *Race, Self-Employment, and Upward Mobility: An Illusive American Dream.* Baltimore: John Hopkins University Press.

Bayoh, I., E. G. Irwin, and T. Haab. 2006. "Determinants of Residential Location Choice: How Important Are Local Public Goods in Attracting Homeowners to Central City Locations?" *Journal of Regional Science* 46(1), 97–120.

Berkowitz, W. 1974. "Socioeconomic Indicator Changes in Ghetto Riot Tracts." *Urban Affairs Quarterly* 10(1), 69–94.

Berube, A. 2002. *Gaining but Losing Ground: Population Change in Large Cities and their Suburbs in the 1990s.* Washington, D.C.: Brookings Institution.

"Better Than Expected." 2009, December 20. *Detroit Free Press.*

Black, H. 1947. "Restrictive Covenants in Relation to Segregated Negro Housing in Detroit." M.A. thesis. Wayne State University.

"Black Legislators Decry New Bethel Damage." 1969, April 12. *Michigan Chronicle.*

Blalock, H. 1967. *Towards a Theory of Minority Group Relations.* New York: Capricorn Books.

Blauner, R. 1969. "Internal Colonialism and Ghetto Revolt." *Social Problems* 16, 393–408.

Bledsoe, T., M. Combs, L. Sigelman, and S. Welch. 1996. "Trends in Racial Attitudes in Detroit, 1968–1992." *Urban Affairs Review* 31, 508–28.

Blossom, T., D. Everett, and J. Gallagher. 1988, August 4–12. "The Race for Money." *Detroit Free Press.*

Bonacich, E. 1973. "A Theory of Middleman Minorities." *American Sociological Review* 38, 583–94.

Bonds, M. 2007. "Looking beyond the Numbers: The Struggles of Black Businesses to Survive: A Qualitative Approach." *Journal of Black Studies* 37, 581–601.Bonilla-Silva, E. 2001. *White Supremacy and Racism in the Post–Civil Rights Era.* Boulder, Colo.: Lynne Renner.

Borowy, T. 2009. "Attributes of Place Associated with School Quality: A Michigan Case Study." Michigan State University.

Boskin, J. 1968. "Violence in the Ghettos: A Consensus of Attitudes." *New Mexico Quarterly* 37, 317–34.

———. 1969. "The Revolt of the Urban Ghettos, 1964–1967." *Annals of the American Academy of Political and Social Science* 382, 1–14.

Boston, T. D., and C. L. Ross. 1996. "Location Preferences of Successful African-American Owned Businesses in Atlanta." *Review of Black Political Economy* 24(2), 337–57.

Bound, J., and R. B. Freeman. 1992. "What Went Wrong? The Erosion of the Relative Earnings and Employment of Young Black Men in the 1980s." *Quarterly Journal of Economics* 107, 201–32.

Boyle, J. 1987, April 24. "Witnesses in Chin Slaying Trial Say Lawyer Didn't Coach Them." *Detroit Free Press.*

———. 1987, April 29. "No Slur Heard from Ebens, Court is Told." *Detroit Free Press.*

———. 2001. "The Ruins of Detroit: Exploring the Urban Crisis in the Motor City." *Michigan Historical Review* 27(1), 109–27.

Bradley vs. Milliken, 1972. 345 F. Supp. 914, c.e.d. Michigan.

Briggs, X. D. S., J. Darden, and A. Aidala. 1999. "In the Wake of Desegregation: Early Impacts of Scattered-Site Public Housing on Neighborhoods in Yonkers, New York." *Journal of the American Planning Association* 65(1), 27–49.

Brimmer, A. 1968. "Desegregation and the Negro Leadership Crisis." In E. Ginsberg, ed., *Business Leadership and the Negro Crisis*. New York: McGraw-Hill.

Briscoe, S. 1992, December 2–8. "In Memory of Malice Green . . . ?" *Michigan Chronicle*.

Brown, N. 1973, November 12. "Open Letter to The Community: Young Can't Do It By Himself." *Michigan Chronicle*.

Brown, S. 2003. *Fighting for Us: Maulana Karenga, the Organization, and Black Cultural Nationalism*. New York: New York University Press.

Buckman, S. 2009, December 20. "In Detroit Schools, Adult Complacency Should Be Criminal." *Detroit Free Press*.

Burdick-Will, J., J. Ludwig, S. Raudenbush, R. Sampson, L. Sanbonmatsu, and P. Sharkey. 2011. "Converging Evidence for Neighborhood Effects on Children's Test Scores: An Experimental, Quasi-experimental, and Observational Comparison." In G. Duncan and R. Murnane, eds., *Whither Opportunity? Rising Inequality, Schools, and Children's Life Chances*. New York: Russell Sage Foundation.

Butler, J. S. 1991. *Entrepreneurship and Self-Help among Black Americans*. Albany: SUNY Press.

Butterfield, F. 1995, October 5. "More Blacks in Their 20s Have Trouble with the Law." *The New York Times*.

Campbell, S. N. 1998, May 2. Conference program. Fourth Model of Racial Unity Conference, Detroit.

Canton, G. 1983, September 10. "Chaldean/Black Solutions Won't Work." *The Detroit News*.

Capeci, D. J., Jr. 1984. *Race Relations in Wartime Detroit: The Sojourner Truth Housing Controversy of 1942*. Philadelphia: Temple University Press.

Capeci, D. J., Jr., and M. Wilkerson. 1991. *Layered Violence: The Detroit Rioters of 1943*. Jackson: University Press of Mississippi.

Castine, J. 1983, May 9. "A Bat, a Gavel, a Question of Justice." *Detroit Free Press*.

———. 1983, June 3. "Judge Refuses Any Changes in Chin Death Case Sentences." *Detroit Free Press*.

———. 1983, June 4. "Another Chin Case Appeal." *Detroit Free Press*.

———. 1983, November 4. "Chin Judge Says Politics Stirred Case." *Detroit Free Press*.

Cavalluzzo, K., L. Cavalluzzo, and J. Wolken. 2002. "Competition, Small Business Financing, and Discrimination: Evidence from a New Survey." *Journal of Business* 75, 641–79.

Chaldean Federation of America. 1995, May 20. "Chaldeans in Our Society." Workshop presentation at the Second Annual Model of Racial Unity Conference, Detroit.Chapman, M. 2008, December 30. "Black Workers in Auto Plants Losing Ground." *New York Times*.

"Challenge to Young from Judge Keith." 1974, January 5. *Michigan Chronicle*.

Chambers, J. 2012, February 9. "DPS to Close 16 Schools, Offer 4 Others for Charters." *The Detroit News*.

Chen, G. M. 1993. Minority business development: Where do we go from here? *Review of Black Political Economy* 22(2), 5–10.

Chong, L. 1987, September 9. "Death of a Dream: Vincent Chin's Mother Gives Up on America." *Detroit Free Press*.

Christopher, J. E. 1998. "Minority Business Formation and Survival: Evidence on Business Performance and Viability." *Review of Black Political Economy* 26(7), 37–72.

Citizens Advisory Committee on Equal Educational Opportunities. 1962. Findings and recommendations. Box 11, Cavanaugh Collection, Wayne State University Archives.

City of Dearborn. 1994. "Population Characteristics, 1990." City Planning Commission, Dearborn, Mich.

———. 1995. "City of Dearborn Consolidated Plan, 1995–2000." Economic and Community Development Department, City of Dearborn, Dearborn, Mich.

City of Detroit Commission on Community Relations. 1957. Annual report.

City of Southfield. 1977. "Implementation of Housing Program." Clerk records, Southfield, Mich.

"Civil Rights Group Urges 30 Day Boycott of Arab American Gas Stations." 2001, August 1., *Detroit Free Press.*

Clampet-Lundquist, S., and D. Massey. 2008. "Neighborhood Effects on Economic Self-Sufficiency: A Reconsideration of the Moving to Opportunity Experiment." *American Journal of Sociology* 14, 107–43.

Cleage, A. B., Jr. 1968. "Black Power—an Advocate Defines It." *Public Relations Journal* 24(July), 81.

Cohn, S., and M. Fossett. 1996. "What Spatial Mismatch? The Proximity of Blacks to Employment in Boston and Houston." *Social Forces* 75, 557–72.

Coleman, T. W. 2001, November 8. "Why Arab Community Can't Take Black Support for Granted." *Detroit Free Press.*

Collins, S. M. 1983. "Making of the Black Middle Class." *Social Problems* 30, 369–81.

Comers, J., X. S. Briggs, and G. Weismann. 2008. *Struggling to Stay Out of High Poverty Neighborhoods: Lessons from Moving to Opportunity Experiment.* Washington, D.C.: Urban Institute.

"Convening Grand Jury Good." 1983, August 10. *East/West: The Journal of Chinese Americans.*

"Court Voids Curbs on Park Use." 1988, December 21. *New York Times.*

Darden, J. T. 1981. "Definitions of Ghetto: Consensus versus Non-consensus." In J. T. Darden, ed., *The Ghetto: Readings and Interpretations.* Port Washington, N.Y.: Kennikat Press.

———. 1986. "Accessibility to Housing: Differential Residential Segregation for Blacks, Hispanics, American Indians, and Asians." In J. Momeni, ed., *Race, Ethnicity and Minority Housing in the United States.* Westport, Conn.: Greenwood.

———. 1987. "Choosing Neighbors and Neighborhoods: The Role of Race in Housing Preference." In G. Tobin, ed., *Divided Neighborhoods: Changing Patterns of Racial Segregation.* Newbury Park, Calif.: Sage.

———. 1989. "Blacks and Other Minorities : The Significance of Color in Inequality." *Urban Geography* 10, 562–77.

———. 1990. "Racial Residential Segregation and Discrimination in Housing: The Evidence from Municipalities in Three Michigan Counties (Oakland, Wayne, and Macomb): 1970–1990." City of Southfield, Southfield, Mich.

———. 1992. "Population and Methodology for the Development of an Incentive Loan Program in Oakland County." City of Southfield, Southfield, Mich.

———. 1994. "Evaluation of the Impact of the Oakland County Center for Open Housing." City of Southfield, Southfield, Mich.

———. 2001. "Race Relations in the City." In R. Paddison, ed., *Handbook of Urban Studies.* London: Sage.

———. 2004. *The Significance of White Supremacy in the Canadian Metropolis of Toronto.* Lewiston, N.Y.: Edwin Mellon Press.

———. 2007a. "Residential Apartheid American Style." In R. Bullard, ed., *The Black Metropolis in the Twenty-first Century: Race, Power and Politics of Place.* Boulder, Colo.: Rowman and Littlefield.

———. 2007b. "The Housing Situation in Metropolitan Areas of Michigan." In J. T. Darden, C. Stokes, and R. Thomas, eds., *The State of Black Michigan, 1967–2007.* East Lansing: Michigan State University Press.

———. 2007c. "Residential Segregation of Blacks in Metropolitan Areas of Michigan, 1960–1990." In J. T. Darden, C. Stokes, and R. Thomas, eds., *The State of Black Michigan, 1967–2007*. East Lansing: Michigan State University Press.

———. 2007d. "Changes in Black Residential Segregation in Metropolitan Areas of Michigan, 1990–2000." In J. T. Darden, C. Stokes, and R. Thomas, *The State of Black Michigan, 1967–2007*. East Lansing: Michigan State University Press.

———. 2007e. "Assessment of the Michigan Legislative Response to Past Recommendations and Future Actions Needed." In J. T. Darden, C. Stokes and R. Thomas, eds., *The State of Black Michigan 1967–2007*. East Lansing: Michigan State University Press.

———. 2009a. "Geographic Racial Equality in America's Most Segregated Metropolitan Area: Detroit." In J. Frazier, J. T. Darden, and N. Henry, eds., *The African Diaspora in the United States and Canada at the Dawn of the 21st Century*. Binghamton, N.Y.: Global Academic Publishing.

———. 2009b. "Race Matters in Metropolitan Detroit." In R. Schaetzel, J. T. Darden, and D. Brandt, eds., *Michigan Geography and Geology*. Boston: Pearson Custom Publishing.

Darden, J. T., H. O. Duleep, and G. Galster. 1992. "Civil Rights in Metropolitan America." *Journal of Urban Affairs* 14, 469–96.

Darden, J. T., R. Hill, J. Thomas, and R. Thomas. 1987. *Detroit: Race and Uneven Development*. Philadelphia: Temple University Press.

Darden, J. T., and S. Kamel. 2000. "Black Residential Segregation in the City and Suburbs of Detroit: Does Socioeconomic Status Matter?" *Journal of Urban Affairs* 22, 1–13.

Darden, J. T., M. Rahbar, L. Jezierski, M. Li, and E. Velie. 2010. "The Measurement of Neighborhood Socioeconomic Characteristics and Black and White Residential Segregation in Metropolitan Detroit: Implications for the Study of Social Disparities in Health." *Annals of the Association of American Geographers* 100(1), 1–22.

Darden, J. T., C. Stokes, and R. Thomas, eds. 2007. *The State of Black Michigan, 1967–2007*. East Lansing: Michigan State University Press.

Darity, W. A., and P. L. Mason. 1998. "Evidence on Discrimination in Employment: Codes of Color, Codes of Gender." *Journal of Economic Perspectives* 12, 63–90.

David, G. C. 2000. "Behind the Bulletproof Glass: Iraqi Chaldean Store Ownership in Metropolitan Detroit." In N. Abraham and A. Shryock, eds., *Arab Detroit: From Margin to Mainstream*. Detroit: Wayne State University Press.

Dawsey, C. P. 2011, June 9. "DPS Slows Plan to Change Schools to Charters." *Detroit Free Press.*

"Dennis Archer." N.d.-a. Vol. Black Biography. Burton Historical Collection, Detroit Public Library.

"Dennis Archer." N.d.-b. Latino News publication, candidate questionnaire. Vol. Campaign Endorsements, 1993. Burton Historical Collection, Detroit Public Library.

Department of Intergroup Relations, Michigan Department of Education. 1970. "Racial-Ethnic Distribution of Students and Employees in the Detroit Public Schools." Library of Michigan, Lansing.

Deskins, D. 1988. "Michigan's Restructured Automobile Industry: Its Impact on Black Employment." *The State of Black Michigan*. Annual report. Michigan State University Urban Affairs Programs.

Detroit Board of Education. 1965. Detroit Public Schools teacher integration and placement. Box 13, Detroit NAACP Collection, Wayne State University Archives.

"Detroit Charter High Schools Underperform Public Counterparts, Analysis Shows" 2011, September 7. *The Huffington Post*. Retrieved from http://www.huffingtonpost.com/2011/07/08/detroit-charter-high-schools-underperform_n_893327.html.

———. 1971, December 3. Resolution, Central Board of Education. Walter P. Reuther Library, Wayne State University.

Detroit Interracial Council. 1947, October 4. Invitation: To Dear Friends, from Charles L. Rawling. Scrapbook 12, Greater Detroit Roundtable of the National Conference of Christians and Jews, Michigan Roundtable for Diversity and Inclusion Records, Bentley Historical Library, University of Michigan.

"Detroit Mayor Ordered Jailed for Violating Bond." 2008, August 7. *MSNBC.com.* Retrieved March 30, 2011, from http://www.msnbc.msn.com/id/26073538/.

"*Detroit News* Candidate Questionnaire. Dennis Archer." N.d. Vol. Campaign Endorsements, 1993. Burton Historical Collection, Detroit Public Library.

"Detroit Roundtable Receives Police Commissioner's Civilian Award." 1970, January 5. Letterhead. Box 5, Michigan Roundtable for Diversity and Inclusion Records, Bentley Historical Library, University of Michigan.

Detroit Urban League. 1967. *A Profile of the Detroit Negro: 1959–1967.* Detroit: Detroit Urban League.

Dickerson, B. 2001, August 6. "Gas Boycott Fills Air with Bigotry." *Detroit Free Press.*

Dillard, A. D. 2007. *Faith in the City: Preaching Radical Social Change in Detroit.* Ann Arbor: University of Michigan Press.

Disaster Center. 2008. *Index of the State of Michigan Uniform Crime Reports, 1985–2005.*

Disbrow, D. 1968. *Schools for an Urban Society.* Lansing: Michigan Historical Society.

Discrimination Research Center. 2006. *Free to Compete? Measuring the Impact of Proposition 209 on Minority Business Enterprises.* Berkeley, Calif.: Discrimination Research Center.

Discuss Detroit Forums. N.d. "1967 Race Riots." Retrieved August 4, 2009, from http://atdetroit.net/forum/messages/6790/85964.html?1233694687.

Doctoroff, A. M. 1978. "The Chaldeans: A New Ethnic Group in Detroit Suburban High Schools." University of Michigan, Ann Arbor.

Dodson, J. 1983, June 20. "Services Held to Remember Vincent Chin Slaying Case." *Detroit Free Press.*

"East/West Supports Chin Efforts." 1983, July 13. *East/West: The Journal of Chinese Americans.*

Eisenhower Foundation. 2007. *What Together We Can Do: A Forty Year Update of the National Advisory Commission on Civil Disorders.* Eisenhower Foundation.

Ellwood, D. T. 1986. "The spatial Mismatch Hypothesis: Are There Teen-age Jobs Missing in the Ghetto?" In R. B. Freeman and H. J. Holzer, eds., *The Black Youth Employment Crisis.* Chicago: University of Chicago Press.

Elrick, M. L. 1999, May 17. "Gas Station Closes for 2nd Day." *Detroit Free Press.*

Elrick, M. L., J. Schaefer, and J. Swickard. 2008, October 28. "Off to Jail: Mayor Kilpatrick Leaves with a Wave." *Detroit Free Press.* Retrieved June 30, 2011, from http://www.freep.com/article/20081028/NEWSSO1/81028100/OFf-jail.

Elrick, M. L., and J. Swickard. 2008, August 7. "Jailed Mayor Faces More Charges Friday for Allegedly Shoving, Berating Officers." *Detroit Free Press.* Retrieved March 30, 2011, from http://www.freep.com/article/20080807/NEWS01/80807034/.

Engdahl, L. 2009. *New Homes, New Neighborhoods, New Schools: A Progress Report on the Baltimore Housing Mobility Program.* Baltimore: Baltimore Regional Housing Campaign.

Engdahl, L., and P. Tegeler. 2009. Regional housing mobility: A report from Baltimore. *Poverty and Race,* 18(6): 1–2, 6.

"Essays Link Arab American Students with Dr. King's Dream." 2001, February 5. *Detroit Free Press.*

Estreicher, Samuel. 2008. "The Non-preferment Principle and the 'Racial Tiebreaker Cases.'" New York University School of Law Public Law and Legal Theory Research Paper Series, Working Paper no. 08-02.

Fair Housing Center of Metropolitan Detroit. 2009. "275,000,000 and Counting: A Summary of Housing Discrimination Lawsuits That Have Been Assisted by the Efforts of Private, Non-profit Fair Housing Organizational Members of the National Fair Housing Alliance." Fair Housing Center of Metropolitan Detroit.

Fairlie, R. 1999. "The Absence of the African-American Owned Business: An Analysis of the Dynamics of Self-Employment." *Journal of Labor Economics* 17(1), 80–108.

Fairlie, R., and A. Robb. 2004, September. "Why Are Black Owned Businesses Less Successful Than White Owned Businesses? The Role of Families, Inheritances, and Business Human Capital." IZA Discussion Paper no. 1292. Retrieved February 15, 2012, from http://www.IZA.org/publications/dps.

Fabrick, S., M. Myers, and Y. Barakat. 1995, May 20. "us and them: The Challenge of Diversity." Workshop presentation at the Second Annual Model of Racial Unity Conference, Detroit.

Farley, R., S. Danzinger, and H. Holzer. 2000. *Detroit Divided.* New York: Russell Sage Foundation.

Farley, R., and W. Frey. 1994. "Changes in the Segregation of Whites from Blacks during the 1980s: Small Steps towards a More Racially Integrated Society." *American Sociological Review* 59, 23–45.

Farley, R., C. Steele, T. Jackson, M. Kryan, and K. Reeves. 1993. "Continued Racial Residential Segregation in Detroit: Chocolate City, Vanilla Suburbs." *Journal of Housing Research* 4(1), 1–38.

Feagin, J., and H. Hahn. 1973. *Ghetto Revolts: The Politics of Violence in American Cities.* New York: Collier-Macmillan.

Federal Bureau of Investigation. 1980. *Crime in the United States: Uniform Crime Reports.* Washington, D.C.: U.S. Department of Justice.

———. 1985. *Crime in the United States: Uniform Crime Reports.* Washington, D.C.: U.S. Department of Justice.

———. 1995. *Crime in the United States: Uniform Crime Reports.* Washington, D.C.: U.S. Department of Justice.

———. 2005. *Crime in the United States: Uniform Crime Reports.* Washington, D.C.: U.S. Department of Justice.

———. 2007. *Crime in the United States: Uniform Crime Reports.* Washington, D.C.: U.S. Department of Justice.

Figlio, D. N., and M. E. Lucas. 2004. "What's in a Grade? School Report Cards and the Housing Market." *American Economic Review* 94(3), 591–604.

Fine, S. 1989. *Violence in the Model City: The Cavanagh Administration, Race Relations, and the Detroit Riot of 1967.* Ann Arbor: University of Michigan Press.

———. 2007. *Violence in the Model City: The Cavanagh Administration, Race Relations, and the Detroit Riot of 1967.* East Lansing: Michigan State University Press.

Fischer, M., and F. Massey. 2000. "Residential Segregation and Ethnic Enterprise in U.S. Metropolitan Areas." *Social Problems* 47, 408–24.

Focus: HOPE. 1999. "Programs. Detroit." Focus: HOPE Resource Center, Detroit.

———. n.d.-a. "Focus: HOPE." Retrieved August 23, 2009, from http://www.focushope.edu.

———. n.d.-b. The Case against AAA. Box 14, Focus: HOPE Collection, Archives of Labor and Urban Affairs, Wayne State University.

———. n.d.-c. Press release. Box 14, Focus: HOPE Collection, Archives of Labor and Urban Affairs, Wayne State University.

"Focus Group, Election Campaign." 1992. Dennis Archer Papers. Burton Historical Collection, Detroit Public Library.

Fogelson, R. M., and R. B. Hill. 1968. "Who riots? A Study of Participation in the 1967 Riots." In *National Advisory Commission on Civil Disorders, Supplementary Studies.* Washington, D.C.: Government Printing Office.

Foner, P. S. 1981. *Organized Labor and the Black Worker.* New York: International Publishers.

Forrest, T. R. 1971. "Emergent Communal Response." In L. Gordon, ed., *A City in Racial Crisis: The Case of Detroit Pre- and Post- the 1967 Riot.* Dubuque, Iowa: W. C. Brown.

Fosu, A. 1988. "Michigan Black-White Unemployment Patterns, 1971–1986: Differences by Gender." *The State of Black Michigan.* Annual report. Michigan State University Urban Affairs Programs.

Frankenberg, E., and G. Orfield. 2007. *Lessons in Integration: Realizing the Promise of Racial Diversity in American Schools.* Charlottesville: University of Virginia Press.

Frankenberg, E., G. Siegel-Hawley, and J. Wang. 2010. *Choice without Equity: Charter School Segregation and the Need for Civil Rights Standards.* Los Angeles: Civil Rights Project, UCLA Graduate School of Education and Information Studies. Retrieved February 15, 2012, from http://civilrightsproject .ucla.edu/research/k-12-education/integration-and-diversity/choice-without-equity-2009-report/ frankenberg-choices-without-equity-2010.pdf.

Franklin, J. H., and A. A. Moss. 1998. *From Slavery to Freedom.* New York: McGraw Hill.

Frey, W., and D. Myers. 2001. "Analysis of Census 2000." Social Science Data Analysis Network.

"Full Story of Assassination of Patrolman M. Czapski." 1969, April. *Tuebor.*

Fullbright, L. 2006, December 14. "Connerly Gearing Up for Wider Crusade: Affirmative Action Foe Considers Launching Campaigns in 9 States." *San Francisco Chronicle.*

Gallagher, M. L. 1994, July 12–13. "HUD's Geography of Opportunity." *Planning.*

Galster, G., and M. Keeney. 1988. "Race, Residence, Discrimination and Economic Opportunity." *Urban Affairs Quarterly* 24, 87–117.

Gavrilovich, P., and B. McGraw. 2000. "The Detroit Almanac." *Detroit Free Press.*

Gebert, A. 1980, October 26. "Store Slayings Fuels Tensions." *The Detroit News.*

———. 1981a, January 28. "Latinos Critical of New Detroit." *The Detroit News.*

———. 1981b, January 29. "New Detroit Denies Anti-Hispanic Bias. *The Detroit News.*

Georgakas, D., and M. Surkin. 1998. *Detroit: I Do Mind Dying.* Updated ed. Cambridge, Mass.: South End Press.

Gillman, D. 1992, December 11. "Landlord Pays for Bias Talk." *Detroit Free Press.*

Gillmor, D., and J. Gallagher. 1993, January 22. "For Blacks, Loans More Often Denied." *Detroit Free Press.*

Gite, L. 1987, March. "Feeding the Masses." *Black Enterprise.*

Glaeser, E. L., E. A. Hanushek, and J. M. Quigley. 2004. "Opportunities, Race, and Urban Location: The Influence of John Kain." National Bureau of Economic Research Working Paper no. 10312.

Glasgow, D. 1980. *The Black Underclass: Poverty, Unemployment, and the Entrapment of Ghetto Youth.* New York: Vintage.

Goering, J., and J. Feins, eds. 2003. *Choosing a Better Life: Evaluating the Moving to Opportunity Social Experiment.* Washington, D.C.: Urban Institute Press.

Gold, S. 2004. "From Jim Crow to Racial Hegemony: Evolving Explanations of Racial Hierarchy." *Ethnic and Racial Studies* 27, 951–68.

Gold, S., and J. Darden. 2010. "Ethnic Merchants in a Black Majority City: The Case of Detroit." In S. Gold, ed., *The Store in the Hood.* Boulder, Colo.: Rowman and Littlefield.

Gold, S., and I. Light. 2000. "Ethnic Economies and Social Policy." *Research in Social Movements, Conflicts and Change* 22, 165–91.

Good, D. 1989. *Orvie, the Dictator of Dearborn.* Detroit: Wayne State University Press.

Gordon, G. 1993, June 20. "Feds: Area Is Biased in Renting." *Detroit Free Press.*

Gordon, L., ed. 1971. *A City in Racial Crisis: The Case of Detroit Pre- and Post- the Detroit Riot.* New York: William C. Brown.

Gray, S. 2007, September 20. "Can Kwame Kilpatrick grow up?" *Time*. Retrieved March 30, 2011, from http://www.time.com/time/nation/article/0,8599,1663791,00.html.

Greater Detroit Roundtable. *GDRTNCC Annual Report and Newsletter*. 1984–85. Box 1, Michigan Roundtable for Diversity and Inclusion Records, Bentley Historical Library, University of Michigan.

———. 1990. *Greater Detroit Interfaith Roundtable Newsletter*. Box 1, Michigan Roundtable for Diversity and Inclusion Records, Bentley Historical Library, University of Michigan.

Greene, J., and M. Wunters. 2006. *Leaving Boys Behind: Public High School Graduation Rates*. New York: Manhattan Institute for Policy Research.

Greenwood, M. J. 1985. "Human Migration: Theory, Models and Empirical Studies." *Journal of Regional Science* 25, 521–44.

Gregory, K. 1984. "The Economic Status of Blacks in Michigan." *The State of Black Michigan*. Annual report. Michigan State University Urban Affairs Programs.

Grimshaw, A. 1969. *Racial Violence in the United States*. Chicago: Aldine.

Hackney, S. 1999, May 21. "Blacks, Arabs Split on Motive in Killing." *Detroit Free Press*.

Hahn, H. 1970. "Black Separatists: Attitudes and Objectives in a Riot-Torn Ghetto." *Journal of Black Studies* 1, 35–53.

Hanlon, B. 2009. *Once the American Dream: Inner-Ring Suburbs of the Metropolitan United States*. Philadelphia: Temple University Press.

Harper, S., and B. Reskin. 2005. "Affirmative Action at School and on the Job." *Annual Review of Sociology* 31, 357–79.

Harrison, P., S. Harrison, and O. Thomas. 1995, May 20. "Why We Have a Race Unity Conference." Workshop presentation at the Second Annual Model of Racial Unity Conference, Detroit.

Havelick, J. R., and M. Wade. 1969. "The American City and Civil Disorders." *Urban Data Service* 1 (January), 1–31.

Hawkins, H., and R. W. Thomas. 1991. "White Policing of Black Populations: A History of Race and Social Control in America." In E. Cashmere and E. McLaughlin, eds., *Out of Order: Policing Black People*. New York: Routledge.

Hermalin, A., and R. Farley. 1973. "The Potential for Residential Integration in Cities and Suburbs: Implications for the Busing Controversy." *American Sociological Review* 38, 595–610.

Herman, M. 2002. "Ethnic Succession and Urban Unrest in Newark and Detroit during the Summer of 1967." Joseph C. Cornwall Center for Metropolitan Studies, Newark, N.J.

Hersch, J. 2008. "Profiling the New Immigrant Worker: The Effects of Skin Color and Height." *Journal of Labor Economics* 26, 345–86.

Hersey, J. 1968. *The Algiers Motel Incident*. New York: Bantam Books.

Holmes, M. D., and B. Smith. 2008. *Race and Police Brutality: Roots of the urban dilemma*. New York: SUNY Press.

Holzer, H. J. 1991. "The Spatial Mismatch Hypothesis: What Has the Evidence Shown?" *Urban Studies* 28(1), 105–22.

Hoult, T. F., and A. J. Mayer. 1962. "Race and Residence in Detroit." Urban Research Library, Wayne State University.

Housing Statistics User Group West. 2003, September 25. "American Housing Survey." University of California, Berkeley.

"How the Case Unfolded." 1993, August 24. *Detroit Free Press*.

Hoxby, C. M. 2000. "Does Competition among Public Schools Benefit Students and Taxpayers?" *American Economic Review* 90, 1209–38.

———. 2001. "How School Choice Affects the Achievement of Public School Students." Koret Task Force Meeting. Hoover Institution, Stanford University.

Hunter, R. L. 1997. "Urban Warriors: The History of Operation Get Down." Operation Get Down, Inc., Detroit.

Ieka, D. 1983, August 1. "Southfield 2001: The City Matures but Still Finds Much to Congratulate Itself About." *Detroit Free Press.*

Ihlanfeldt, K. R., and D. L. Sjoquist. 1991. "The Role of Space in Determining the Occupations of Black and White Workers." *Regional Science and Urban Economics* 21, 295–315.

Ingram, J. 1961, May 31. "The Republic of New Africa: Is It a Serious Threat?" *Detroit Scope.*

Inner-City Sub-Center. 1986. Seventeenth Annual Souvenir Booklet. Inner City Sub-Center, Detroit.

———. N.d. "Inner-City Sub-Center, Inc. is about Helping People."Inner City Sub-Center, Detroit.

Inouye, K. M. 1988. "A Thematic Analysis of Asian American Discourse in Response to the Murder of Vincent Chin." California State University, Northridge.

Insight Center for Community Economic Development. 2007. "The Evolution of Affirmative Action." Insight Center for Community Economic Development, Oakland, Calif.

"Interest Up in Chin Case." 1983, April 20. *East/West: The Journal of Chinese Americans.*

Jacobs, A. J. 2009. "The Auto Industry and The manufacturing Sector." In R. Schaetzel, J. T. Darden, and D. Brandt, eds., *Michigan Geography and Geology.* Boston: Pearson Custom Publishing.

Jargowsky, P. A. 1994. "Ghetto Poverty among Blacks in the 1980s." *Journal of Policy Analysis and Management* 13, 288–310.

———. 1997. *Poverty and Place.* New York: Russell Sage.

———. 2003. *Stunning Progress, Hidden Problems: The Dramatic Decline of Concentrated Poverty in the 1990s.* Washington, D.C.: Center on Urban and Metropolitan Studies.

Jargowsky, P. A., and R. Yang. 2006. "The 'Underclass' Revisited: A Social Problem in Decline." *Journal of Urban Affairs* 28, 55–70.

Jencks, C. 1991. "Is the American Underclass Growing?" In C. Jencks and P. E. Peterson, eds., *The Urban Underclass.* Washington, D.C.: Brookings Institution.

Jencks, C., and S. E. Mayer. 1990. "Residential Segregation, Job Proximity, and Black Job Opportunities." In L. E. Lynn Jr. and M. G. H. McGeary, eds., *Inner-City Poverty in the United States.* Washington, D.C.: National Academy Press.

Johnson, A. J., and A. N. Henderson. N.d. "Dennis Archer." Retrieved October 16, 2009, from http://www.answers.com/topic/dennis-archer.

Johnson, L. 1971. *The Vantage Point: Perspectives of the Presidency, 1963—1969.* New York: Holt, Rinehart and Winston.

Johnson, M. 2001. "Decision Support for Family Relocation Decisions under the Section 8 Housing Assistance Program Using Geographic Information Systems and the Analytic Hierarchy Process." *Journal of Housing Research* 12, 277–306.

Jordan, D. and J. Waslawski. 1995, May 20. "Healing Racism in America." Workshop presentation at the Second Annual Model of Racial Unity Conference, Detroit.

Kain, J. F. 1968. "Housing Segregation, Negro Employment and Metropolitan Decentralization." *Quarterly Journal of Economics* 82, 175–97.

———. 1992. "The Spatial Mismatch Hypothesis: Three Decades Later." *Housing Policy Debate* 3, 371–460.

Kain, J. F., and J. M. Quigley. 1970. "Measuring the Value of Housing Quality." *Journal of the American Statistical Association* 65, 532–48.

———. 1972. "Housing Market Discrimination, Homeownership, and Savings Behavior." *American Economic Review* 62, 263–77.

Kasarda, J. D. 1989. "Urban Industrial Transition and the Underclass." *Annals of the American Academy of Political and Social Science* 501(1), 26–58.

———. 1993. "Inner-City Concentrated Poverty and Neighborhood Distress: 1970 to 1990." *Housing Policy Debate* 4, 253–302.

Katz, B., ed. 1993. *The "Underclass" Debate: Views from History.* Princeton, N.J.: Princeton University Press.

———. 2004. "A Progressive Agenda for Metropolitan America." In M. Green, ed., *What We Stand For.* New York: New Market Press.

Kingsley, G. T., and K. L. S. Pettit. 2003. *Concentrated Poverty: A Change in Course.* Washington, D.C.: Urban Institute.

Kirschenman, J., and K. Neckerman. 1991. "'We'd love to hire them, but . . . ': The Meaning of Race for Employers." In C. Jencks and P. E. Peterson, eds., *The Urban Underclass.* Washington, D.C.: Brookings Institute.

Kiska, T. 1984, May 10. "Federal Judge Rejects Defense Attempt to Sequester Jury in Chin Case." *Detroit Free Press.*

Kissane, R., and S. Clampet-Lundquist. 2005, August 13–16. "Friends, Jobs, and Moving to Opportunity." *Annual Meeting of the American Sociological Association.*

Kling, J., J. Ludwig, and L. Katz. 2005. "Neighborhood Effects on Crime for Female and Male Youth: Evidence from a Randomized Housing Voucher Experiment." *Quarterly Journal of Economics* 120, 87–130.

Knoll, F. R. 1974. "Casework Services for Mexican-Americans." In D. Hartman, ed., *Immigrants and Migrants: The Detroit Ethnic Experience.* Detroit: Wayne State University Press.

Kresnak, J. 1980. "City Police: A Past of Racism." In Scott McGehee and Susan Watson, eds., *Blacks in Detroit: A Reprint of Articles from the Detroit Free Press December 1980.* Detroit: Detroit Free Press.

Kusmer, K. L. 1976. *A Ghetto Takes Shape: Black Cleveland 1870–1930.* Urbana: University of Illinois Press.

Lamarre, L. 1981, May 22. "Latinos Accuse New Detroit." *The Detroit News.*

Lawrence, C. R. 1977. "Segregation 'Misunderstood': The Milliken Decision Revisited." *University of San Francisco Law Review* 12, 15–56.

Lee, A. M., and N. D. Humphrey. 1943. *Race Riot.* New York: Dryden Press.

Lee, J. 1995, May 20. "How to Achieve Racial Harmony." Workshop presentation at the Second Annual Model of Racial Unity Conference, Detroit.

Leibowitz, A. 1983. "The Refugee Act of 1980: Problems and Congressional Concerns." *Annals of the American Academy of Political and Social Science* 467(1), 163–71.

Lemieux, T. 2006. "Postsecondary Education and Increasing Wage Inequality." *American Economic Review* 96, 195–99.

Lewis, D. 1969. "Black Consciousness and Voting Behavior of Blacks in Detroit: 1961–1968." MA thesis, Wayne State University.

Lewis, O. 1966, October. "The Culture of Poverty." *Scientific American.*

Light, I. 1972. *Ethnic Enterprise in America.* Berkeley: University of California Press.

———. 1980. "Asian Enterprise in America." In S. Cummings, ed., *Self Help in America: Patterns of Minority Economic Development.* Port Washington, N.Y.: Kennikat Press.

Light, I., and S. Gold. 2000. *Ethnic Economies.* San Diego: Academic Press.

Local Spiritual Assembly of the Baha'is of Detroit (LSA). 1998, May 2. Conference program. Fourth Model of Racial Unity Conference, Detroit.

Locke, H. 1969. *The Detroit Riot of 1967.* Detroit: Wayne State University Press.

Logan, J., and B. Stults. 2011. "The Persistence of Segregation in the Metropolis: New Findings from the 2010 Census." Census brief prepared for Project US2010. Retrieved from http://www.s4.brown.edu/us2010/Projects/reports.htm.

Logan, J. and B. Stults. 2010. "Separate and Unequal." Census brief prepared for Project US2010. Retrieved from http://www.s4.brown.edu/us2010/Projects/authors_su.htm.

Lowry, J. H. 2005. *Realizing the New Agenda for Minority Business Development.* Boston: Boston Consulting Group.

Ludwig, J., J. B. Liebman, J. Kling, G. J. Duncan, L. F. Katz, R. C. Kessler, et al. 2008. "What Can We Learn about Neighborhood Effects from the Moving to Opportunity Experiment?" *American Journal of Sociology* 114, 144–88.

Magnusson, P. 1983, July 1. "Federal Officials May Intercede in Chin Slaying Case." *Detroit Free Press.*

Mahaffey, M. 2002, June 21–23. "Letter, Maryann Mahaffrey to Ronald Hwang." Paper presented at the Rededication to Justice: Vincent Chin's 20th Year Remembrance, Detroit.

"Make New Bethel a Freedom Shrine." 1969, April 19. *Michigan Chronicle.*

McGraw, B. 1986, February 12. "Verdict Voided in Chin Killing." *Detroit Free Press.*

———. 1987, February 24. "Trial of Vincent Chin's Assailant Moved to Ohio Due to Publicity." *Detroit Free Press.*

McMillian, F.1983, May 7. "Slain Son's Mother 'Won't Rest in Peace.'" *Michigan Chronicle.*

———. 1983, May 14. "Chin Case Protestors Assail Bill Cahalan." *Michigan Chronicle.*

Meek, W. 1973, November 10. "Romney: System Will Not Let Young Help Detroit." *Detroit Free Press.*

Marable, M. 1983. *How Capitalism Underdeveloped Black America: Problems in Race, Political Economy and Society.* Boston: South End Press.

Martelle, S. 2008. December. "Staying in Focus." *Hour Detroit.*

Massey, D., and N. Denton. 1993. *American Apartheid: Segregation and the Making of the Underclass.* Cambridge: Harvard University Press.

Massey, D., and A. Gross. 1991. "Explaining Trends in Racial Segregation, 1970–1980." *Urban Affairs Quarterly* 27, 13–35.

Mast, R. H. 1994. *Detroit Lives: Conflicts in Urban and Regional Development.* Philadelphia: Temple University Press.

Mauer, M. 1990. *Young Black Men and the Criminal Justice System: A Growing Problem.* San Francisco: Center on Juvenile and Criminal Justice.

Mayor's Committee on Race Relations. 1926. *Report.* Detroit: Bureau of Governmental Research.

McDonald, J. F. 1981. "The Direct and Indirect Effects of Housing Segregation on Employment Opportunities for Blacks." *Annals of Regional Science* 15, 27–38.

McGraw, Bill. 1986, May 2. "NAACP Lawyer: Dearborn Bigoted." *Detroit Free Press.*

———. 2008, September 5. "The Rise and Fall of Kwame Kilpatrick." *Detroit Free Press.* Retrieved June 30, 2011, from http://www.freep.com/article/20080905/News01//809050448/-1/newsso101/the-rise-fallKwame-Kilpatrick.

Meier, B. 2006, November 11. "Quarterback Turned Politician Calls Own Number as Lobbyist." *New York Times.*

Mendenhall, R. 2005. "Black Women in *Gautreaux's* Housing Desegregation Program: The Role of Neighborhoods and Networks in Economic Independence." Northwestern University.

Meyer, Z. 2007, August 30. "Apartments to Pay in Discrimination Case." *Detroit Free Press.*

Michigan Civil Rights Commission. 1969. *Toward Equality: Two-Year Report of Claims Activity, 1968–1969.* Lansing: Michigan Department of Civil Rights.

———. 1971, November 13. News for release. Civil Rights Commission, Detroit.

———. 2007. *One Michigan at the Crossroads: An Assessment.* Lansing.

Michigan Department of Civil Rights. 2008. *Annual Report 2006.* Lansing: Michigan Department of Civil Rights.

Michigan Department of Education. 1968. "Ranking of Michigan Public High School Districts by Selected Financial Data 1967–1968." State Board of Education Report, Lansing.

———. 2004. "Ranking of Michigan Public High School Districts by Selected Financial Data 2003–2004." State Board of Education Report, Lansing.

———. 2008. "MEAP Test Scores by School District." Lansing.

———. 2009. MEAP downloadable data files, fall 2008.

———. 2010. "92 Lowest Achieving Schools Identified; and Latest 'Top-to-Bottom' School Rankings Released." Retrieved February 15, 2012, from http://www.michigan.gov/mde/0,1607,7–140—242163—,00.html.

Michigan Employment Security Commission, U.S. Department of Labor. 1967. Annual *Current Population Survey.* Washington, D.C.

"Michigan Reader Sends Petition." 1983. *East/West: The Journal of Chinese Americans,* April 13.

Michigan Roundtable for Diversity and Inclusion. N.d.-a. "About Us." Retrieved July 5, 2011, from http:www.miroundtable.org/aboutus.htm.

———. N.d.-b. Records. Box 1, Michigan Roundtable for Diversity and Inclusion, Bentley Historical Library, University of Michigan.

———. 2006, November 28. "59th Annual Humanitarian Tribute." Box 1, Michigan Roundtable for Diversity and Inclusion, Bentley Historical Library, University of Michigan.

———. 2008, November 6. "61st Annual Humanitarian Tribute." Box 1, Michigan Roundtable for Diversity and Inclusion, Bentley Historical Library, University of Michigan.

Michigan State Board of Education. 1972a. "Metropolitan One-Way Student Movement and Reassignment Plan." Report submitted to Judge Stephen Roth, Library of Michigan, Lansing.

———. 1972b. "Metropolitan School District Reorganization Plan." Report submitted to Judge Stephen Roth, Library of Michigan, Lansing.

Miller, J. 1992. *Hobbling a Generation: Young African American Males in the Criminal Justice System.* Baltimore: National Center on Institutions and Alternatives.

"Milliken Asks for Probe of Crockett." 1969, April 3. *Detroit Free Press.*

Model of Racial Unity. 1995, May 20. Conference program. Second Annual Model of Racial Unity Conference, Detroit.

———. 1996, May 18. Conference brochure. Third Annual Model of Racial Unity Conference, Detroit.

———. 1998a, August. Newsletter.

———. 1998b. Conference report. Fourth Model of Racial Unity Conference, Detroit.

———. 1998c, May 2. "The History of the Model of Racial Unity, Inc.," in the conference program. Fourth Model of Racial Unity Conference, Detroit.

———. 1999a, January. Newsletter.

———. 1999b. Conference report. Fifth Model of Racial Unity Conference, Detroit.

———. 2000. Sixth Model of Racial Unity Conference.

Mollison, A. 1968, June 1. "Will Detroit's Next Mayor be a Negro?" *Detroit Scope.*

Moon, E. L. 1994. *Untold Tales, Unsung Heroes: An Oral History of Detroit's African-American Community, 1918–1967.* Detroit: Wayne State University Press.

Moore, T., and A. Laramore. 1990. "Industrial Change and Urban Joblessness: An Assessment of the Mismatch Hypothesis." *Urban Affairs Quarterly,* 25, 640–58.

Morant, G. 1987, March 26. Interview by Richard W. Thomas. Inner City Sub-Center, Detroit.

Moss, P., and C. Tilly. 1996. "'Soft' Skills and Race: An Investigation of Black Men's Employment Problems." *Work and Occupations* 23, 252–76.

National Advisory Commission on Civil Disorders. 1968. *Report.* Washington, D.C.: Government Printing Office.

National Association for the Advancement of Colored People, Education Committee. 1963. Series V, Box 21, Wayne State University Archives.

National Center for Chronic Disease Prevention and Health Promotion. 2009. Youth Risk Behavior Surveillance System. Retrieved February 15, 2012, from http://www.cdc.gov/HealthyYouth/yrbs/index.htm.

National Center for Education Statistics. 2009. "The Nation's Report Card: Trial Urban District Assessment Mathematics 2009."

Neill, W. J. V. 2004. *Urban Planning and Cultural Identity.* New York: Routledge.

Nevers, L. 2006. *Good Cops, Bad Verdict: How Racial Politics Convicted Us of Murder.* Detroit: LAN Publications.

New Detroit. 1968. *Progress Report, April, 1968.* Detroit: Metropolitan Fund.

———. 1969. *The New Bethel Report: The Law on Trial.* Detroit: New Detroit Board of Trustees.

———. 1981. "Hispanic Leadership Development Project." *New Detroit Now* 12, 6.

———. 1982. "Anti-Racism." 1982. *Fifteen Years of Progress*, 3.

———. 1983a. "Latino Caucus Progress Report."

———. 1983b. "Progress Report."

———. 1985. "Hispanic Affairs Annual Report."

———. 1988. "Hispanic Affairs Annual Report."

———. 1988–89. "Annual Report 1988–89."

———. 1992, Fall. "Giving Voice to the Unheard: First Urban Coalition Reaches Twenty-five Years." *New Detroit Now.*

———. 1999. "1999 Multi-Cultural Immersion Program Fact Sheet." *The Coalition.*

Nichols, B. 2002. "Historical Consciousness and the Viewer: Who Killed Vincent Chin?" In P. X. Feng, ed., *Screening Asian Americans*. Piscataway, N.J.: Rutgers University Press.

"1960s–1970s: Focus: HOPE Emerges as Advocate for Minorities and Poor." N.d. Retrieved February 13, 2012, from http://www.focushope.edu/page.aspx?content_id=124&content_type=level2.

"The Officers." 1992, November 17. *Detroit Free Press.*

Oguntoyinbo, L. 1999a, June 3. "Mayor: Killing Not Racial." *Detroit Free Press.*

———. 1999b, July 6. "Program Aims to Keep Peace for Merchants." *Detroit Free Press.*

Ong, P. M. 1981. "Factors Influencing the Size of the Black Business Community." *Review of Black Political Economy* 11, 313–19.

Operation Get-Down. 1986. "History of Operation Get Down." 15th anniversary dinner brochure. Operation Get Down, Detroit.

———. 1987, February. Newsletter.

Orr, L., J. Feins, R. Jacob, E. Beecroft, L. Sanbonmatsu, L. Katz, et al. 2003. *Moving to Opportunity Interim Impacts Evaluation.* Washington, D.C.: U.S. Department of Housing and Urban Development.

Osinio, C. 2005, September 19. "Mayor Rekindles Tensions between Detroit and Suburbs." *USA Today.* Retrieved March 30, 2011, from http://www.usatoday.com/news/nation/2005-09-19-detroit-mayor_x.htm?csp=34.

Pangborn, M. 2002, June 21–23. "Message from the ACJ President." Paper presented at the Rededication to Justice: Vincent Chin's 20th Year Remembrance, Detroit.

Parker, B. 1987, February 24. Interview by Richard W. Thomas. Operation Get Down, Detroit.

Peach, C. 1996. "Does Britain Have Ghettos?" *Transactions of the Institute of British Geographers* 21, 216–35.

Perlstein, R. 2008. *Nixonland: The Rise of a President and the Fracturing of America.* New York: Scribners.

Philpott, T. L. 1978. *The Slum and the Ghetto: Neighborhood Deterioration and Middle Class Reform, Chicago, 1880–1930.* New York: Oxford University Press.

Pop, S., and M. Steider. 1970. *Exploratory Study of the Mexican-American Community.* Detroit: Wayne State University.

Race Relations Alert. 1993. "Issues and Mayoral Candidates Heat Up at a Race Relations Council's Candidates Forum." *Race Relations Alert.*

"Racial Unity Conference, May 20 at Cobo Hall." 2000, May 10–16. *Michigan Chronicle.*

Ransack, J. 1980. "City police: A Port of Racism." *Detroit Free Press.*

Raphael, S., and M. Stoll. 2002. "Modest Progress: The Narrowing Spatial Mismatch between Blacks and Jobs in the 1990s." Brookings Institution.

"Reader Angry over Injustice." 1983, April 6. *East/West: The Journal of Chinese Americans.*

Reyes, A., and A. White. 1995, May 20. "Racism from an Indigenous People's Point of View." Workshop presentation at the Second Annual Model of Racial Unity Conference, Detroit.

Reynolds, P., and S. White. 1996. *The Entrepreneurial Process: Economic Growth, Employment, Women, and Minorities.* Westport, Conn.: Quorum Books.

Rich, W. C. 1989. *Coleman Young and Detroit Politics.* Detroit: Wayne State University Press.

Richards, E., and A. Hetzner. 2011, March 29. "Choice Schools Not Outperforming MPS." *Journal Sentinel.*

Ricketts, E. R., and R. Mincy. 1990. "Growth of the Underclass: 1970–1980." *Journal of Human Resources* 25, 137–45.

Ricketts, E. R., and I. V. Sawhill. 1988. "Defining and Measuring the Underclass." *Journal of Policy Analysis and Management* 7, 316–25.

Riddle, D. 1998. "HUD and the Open Housing Controversy of 1970." *Michigan Historical Review* 24(2), 1–36.

Robertson, A. 2008, February 28. "Mayor Won't resign." *WWJ AM Detroit.* Retrieved from http://www.wwj.com/Mayor-Won-t-Resign/1735255.

Robinson, G. 2005. *Survey of School Choice Research.* Marquette, Wisc.: Institute for Transformation of Learning, Marquette University.

Rochelle, L. N.d. "Kwame Kilpatrick." Retrieved March 30, 2011, from http://www.answers.com/topic/kwame-kilpatrick.

Rodriguez, C. 2007, October 15. "Many Metro Blacks Feel Isolated in Suburbs." *The Detroit News.*

Roger, C. "Few Cops Convicted of 2nd Degree Murder." 1992, November 18. *Detroit Free Press.*

Romney, G. 1970. Statement of the Honorable George Romney, Secretary of Housing and Urban Development. U.S. Senate Select Committee on Equal Educational Opportunity.

Roscigno, V. J. 2000. "Family/School Inequality and African American/Hispanic Achievement." *Social Problems* 47, 266–90.

Rosenbaum, J. 1995. "Changing the Geography of Opportunity by Expanding Residential Choice: Lessons from the Gautreaux Program." *Housing Policy Debate* 6(1), 231–70.

Rosenbaum, J., L. Reynolds, and S. DeLuca. 2002. "How Do Places Matter? The Geography of Opportunity, Self-Efficacy, and a Look Inside the Black Box of Residential Mobility." *Housing Studies* 17(1), 71–82.

"Roundtable Responds to Vincent Chin Case." 1983, Fall. *GDRTNCCJ Newsletter.* Box 1, Michigan Roundtable for Diversity and Inclusion Records, Bentley Historical Library, University of Michigan.

Rouse, C. E., and L. Barrow. 2006. "U.S. Elementary and Secondary Schools: Equalizing Opportunity or Replicating the Status Quo?" *Future of Children* 16(1), 89–108.

Rubinowitz, L. S., and J. Rosenbaum. 2000. *Crossing the Class and Color Lines: From Public Housing to White Suburbia.* Chicago: University of Chicago Press.

Ruggles, P., and W. P. Marton. 1986. "Measuring the Size and Characteristics of the Underclass: How Much Do We Know?" Urban Institute, Washington, D.C.

Salas, G., and I. Salas. 1974. "The Mexican Community in Detroit." In D. Hartman, ed., *Immigrants and Migrants: The Detroit Ethnic Experience.* Detroit: Wayne State University Press.

Sander, W. 2006. "Educational Attainment and Residential Location." *Education and Urban Society* 38, 307–26.

Sarafa, M. 1999, May 22. "Don't Make Race the Issue in Killing." *Detroit Free Press.*

Saulny, S. and N. Bunkley. 2008, September 5. "Detroit's Mayor Will Leave Office and Go to Jail." *New York Times.* Retrieved March 30, 2011, from http://query.nytimes.com/gst/fullpage.html ?res=9D01EFD91239F936A3575AC0A96E9C8B63andscp=3andsq=kwame+kilpatrickandst=nyt.

Schaefer, J. "Sergeant Beats Charge in Slaying." 1992, December 24. *Detroit Free Press.*

Schaefer, J., and M. L. Elrick. 2008, January 24. "Kilpatrick, Chief of Staff Lied under Oath, Text Messages Show." *Detroit Free Press.* Retrieved March 30, 2011, from http://www.freep.com/Article/20080124/NEWS05/801240414/Kilpatrick%E2%80%94chief-of%20staff-lie.

Schmidt, P. 2006, November 17. "Michigan Overwhelmingly Adopts Ban on Affirmative-Action Preferences." *Chronicle of Higher Education.*

Schuman, H., C. Steeh, and L. Bobo. 1985. *Racial Attitudes in America: Trends and Interpretations.* Cambridge: Harvard University Press.

Sengstock, M. D. 1983. "Detroit's Iraqi-Chaldeans: A Conflicting Conception of Identity." In S. Y. Abraham and N. Abraham, eds., *Arabs in the New World: Studies on Arab American Communities.* Detroit: Wayne State University Center for Urban Studies.

———. 1999. *Chaldean Americans: Changing Conceptions of Ethnic Identity.* New York: Center for Migration Studies.

Serrin, W. 1969, January 12. "Mayor Hubbard Gives Dearborn What It Wants—and Then Some." *New York Times Magazine.*

Sheffield, H. 1983, April 30. "As I See It." *Michigan Chronicle.*

Shlay, A. B. 1993. "Family Self-Sufficiency and Housing." *Housing Policy Debate* 4(3), 457–496.

Shogan, R., and T. Craig. 1964. *The Detroit Race Riot: A Study in Violence.* Philadelphia: Clinton Books.

Sieh, M. 2008, March 15. "Detroit's Mayor Kwame Kilpatrick Used N-Word in State of the City Speech." Retrieved October 16, 2009, from http://blog.syracuse.com/metrovoices/2008/03/watch_the_video.html.

Sigelman, L., and S. Welch. 1991. *Black American Views of Racial Inequality.* Cambridge: Cambridge University Press.

Skendzel, E. A. 1980. *Detroit's Pioneer Mexicans: A Historical Study of the Mexican Colony in Detroit.* Grand Rapids: Littlefield Press.

Smith, S. E. 1999. *Dancing in the Street: Motown and the Cultural Politics of Detroit.* Cambridge: Harvard University Press.

"Sorority Explores Black/Arab Relations." 2001, December 5. *Michigan Chronicle.*

Spilerman, S. 1970. "The Causes of Racial Disturbances: A Comparison of Alternative Explanations." *American Sociological Review* 35, 627–49.

———. 1971. "The Causes of Racial Disturbances: Tests of an Explanation." *American Sociological Review* 36, 427–42.

Staples, R. 1975. "White racism, Black Crime, and American Justice: An Application of the Colonial Model to Explain Race and Crime." *Phylon* 36, 14–22.

Stein, H. 2008. "Racial-Preference Ballots Go National." *City Journal.*

Sternberg, L. N.d. "Detroit Mayor Kwame Kilpatrick's Track Record and Timeline." Retrieved October 16, 2009, from http://detroit.about.com/od/governmentpolitics/i/Kilpatrickrec.htm.

Stevens, A. 2008, September 5. "Kwame Kilpatrick: Mayor of Detroit." Retrieved October 16, 2009, from http://citymayors.com/mayors/detroit_mayor.html.

Stolberg, M. M. 1998. *Bridging the River of Hatred: The Pioneering Efforts of Detroit Police Commissioner George Edwards.* Detroit: Wayne State University Press.

Stoll, M. 2007. "Spatial Mismatch and Job Sprawl." In R. Bullard, ed., *The Black Metropolis in the Twenty-first Century.* New York: Rowman and Littlefield.

Sugrue, T. 1996. *The Origins of the Urban Crisis: Race and Inequality in Post-war Detroit.* Princeton, N.J.: Princeton University Press.

Swickard, J. 1984, September 19. "Ebens Gets 25-Year Sentence." *Detroit Free Press.*

———. 1984, November 16. "Student Sorry for Depiction of Chin Slaying." *Detroit Free Press.*

Takaki, R. 1983, September 21. "Who Really Killed Vincent Chin?" *San Francisco Examiner.*

Tang, I. A.-B. 1995. *Not in Vain: The Politics of Anti-Asian Violence since the Death of Vincent Chin.* Austin: University of Texas.

Taylor, C. S. 1990. *Dangerous Society.* East Lansing: Michigan State University Press.

Taylor, D., S. Wright, F. Moyhaddan, and R. Lalonde. 1990. "The Personal/Group Discrimination Discrepancy: Perceiving My Group, but Not Myself to Be a Target for Discrimination." *Personality and Social Psychology Bulletin* 16(2), 254–62.

Taylor, P. 1987, March 26. Interview by Richard W. Thomas. Detroit.

Tefera, A., E. Frankenberg, G. Siegel-Hawley, and G. Chirichigno. 2011. *Integrating Suburban Schools.* Los Angeles: The Civil Rights Project, UCLA Graduate School of Education and Information Studies.

Tempest, R. 1973, November 8. "Police Glum, but Accept Young." *Detroit Free Press.*

"Tense Verdict Not Guilty." 2000, May 23. *Detroit Free Press.*

Thomas, J. M. 1995, May 20. "Social Justice in the City." Workshop presentation at the Second Annual Model of Racial Unity Conference, Detroit.

———. 1997. *Redevelopment and Race: Planning a Finer City in Postwar Detroit.* Baltimore: Johns Hopkins University Press.

Thomas, R. W. 1987a. *The State of Black Detroit: Building from Strength—the Black Self-Help Tradition in Detroit.* Detroit: Detroit Urban League.

———. 1987b. "Looking Forward: The Detroit Experience after the riots of 1943 and 1967." In J. Benyon and J. Solomos, eds., *The Roots of Urban Unrest.* New York: Pergamon.

———. 1992. *Life for Us Is What We Make It: Building Black Community in Detroit, 1915–1945.* Bloomington: Indiana University Press.

———. 1993. *Racial Unity: An Imperative for Social Progress.* Ottawa: Association of Baha'i Studies.

———. 1995, May 20. "Unifying Racially Polarized Groups." Workshop presentation at the Second Annual Model of Racial Unity Conference, Detroit.

———. 2002. *Bridging Racial Divides in Michigan's Urban Communities: Historical Analysis of Selected Organizational and Group Efforts.* East Lansing: Institute for Public Policy and Social Research and Urban Affairs Programs at Michigan State University.

Thompson, H. 2001. *Politics, Labor Race in a Modern American City.* Ithaca: Cornell University Press.

Thompson, J. E. 2005. *Dudley Randall, Broadside Press, and the Black Arts Movement in Detroit, 1960–1995.* Jefferson, N.C.: McFarland.

Tiebout, C. 1956. "A Pure Theory of Local Public Expenditures." *Journal of Political Economy* 64, 416–24.

Tiggs, L., and D. Tootle. 1993. "Underemployment and Racial Competition in Local Labor Markets." *Sociological Quarterly* 34, 279–98.

Trent, K. 2001, December 19. "Sharing Differences Brings Us Closer." *The Detroit News.*

Turner, M. 2008. "Residential Segregation and Employment Inequality." In J. Carr and N. Kutty, eds., *Segregation.* New York: Routledge.

Turner, M., M. Fix, and J. Struyk. 1991. *Opportunities Denied, Opportunities Diminished: Racial Discrimination in Hiring.* Washington, D.C.: Urban Institute Press.

Turner, M., and S. Ross. 2005. "How Racial Discrimination Affects the Search for Housing." In X. Briggs, ed., *The Geography of Opportunity.* Washington, D.C.: Brookings Institution Press.

Turner, M., S. Ross, G. Galster, and J. Yinger. 2002. *Discrimination in Metropolitan Housing Markets: National Results from Phase 1 HDS 2000.* Washington, D.C.: Urban Institute.

Turner, M., R. M. Struyk, and J. Yinger. 1991. *The Housing Discrimination Study.* Washington, D.C.: Urban Institute.

Turner, M., and R. Wrenk. 1993. "The Resistance of Segregation in Urban Areas: Contributing Causes." In T. Kingsley and M. Turner, eds., *Housing Markets and Residential Mobility.* Washington, D.C.: Urban Institute.

Tyson, R. 1980. "Long Struggle Led to Firm Power Base: Blacks in Detroit." In S. McGehee and S. Watson, eds., *Blacks in Detroit: A Reprint of Articles from Detroit Free Press.* Detroit: Detroit Free Press.'

Tyson-Walker, Joyce. 1983, March 18. "Men Charged In '82 Slaying Get Probation." *Detroit Free Press.*

Umemoto, K. 1984. "Blacks and Koreans in Los Angeles: The Case of La Tasha Harlin and Soon Ja Du." In J. Jennings, ed., *Blacks, Latinos, and Asians in Urban America: Status and Prospects for Politics Activism.* Westport, Conn.: Praeger.

U.S. Bureau of the Census. 1963. *1960 Census of Population and Housing Characteristics of the Population.* Washington, D.C.: Government Printing Office.

———. 1972. *1970 Census of Population and Housing: Census Tracts Final Reports.* Washington, D.C.: Government Printing Office.

———. 1973. *1970 Census of Population and Housing Characteristics of the Population.* Washington, D.C.: Government Printing Office.

———. 1980. *Census of Population and Housing Summary File 4.* Washington, D.C.: Government Printing Office.

———. 1990. *Population and Housing Summary File 4.* Washington, D.C.: Government Printing Office.

———. 1992. 1990 Census Summary File 3. State of Michigan.

———. 1993. 1990 Census of Population: Social and Economic Characteristics, Michigan.

———. 2000. *Geographic Areas Reference Manual.* Washington, D.C.: Government Printing Office.

———. 2002. 2000 Census Summary File 3. State of Michigan.

———. 2004. *2000 Census of Population and Housing Summary File 4.* Washington, D.C.: Data User Services Division.

———. 2006a. 2002 Survey of Business Owners: Black Owned Firms.

———. 2006b. 2002 Survey of Business Owners: Hispanic Owned Firms.

———. 2008. *2007 American Community Survey (Three Year Estimates).* Washington, D.C.: Government Printing Office.

———. 2009a. American Community Survey 2006–2008, 3 Year Survey. Retrieved from http://factfinder.census.gov.

———. 2009b. American Community Survey Demographic and Housing Estimates: 2006–2008, Detroit City.

———. 2009c. *2008 American Community Survey (Three Year Estimates)*. Washington, D.C.: Government Printing Office.

———. 2010. 2005–2009 American Community Survey: Five Year Estimates. Retrieved from Factfinder.census.gov.

———. 2011a. Census 2010-PL94 Redistricting Data. Retrieved from http://factfinder2.census.gov.

———. 2011b. 2007 Survey of Business Owners (SBO). Company Statistics Series: Statistics for All U.S. Firms by Geographic Area, Industry, Gender, Ethnicity and Race. Retrieved from factfinder.census.gov.

———. 2011c. 2010 Census Redistricting Data 94-171 Summary Files. Retrieved from factfinder.census.gov.

U.S. Bureau of Labor Statistics. 2010. Local Area Unemployment Statistics Information.

U.S. Commission on Civil Rights. 1973. *Understanding Fair Housing: A Report of the Commission*. Washington, D.C.: Government Printing Office.

U.S. Department of Housing and Urban Development. 1973. *Housing in the Seventies*. Washington, D.C.: Government Printing Office.

U.S. Department of Housing and Urban Development. 2009. 2007 American Housing Survey. Metropolitan Data Set. Retrieved from http://factfinder2.census.gov.

U.S. Department of Housing and Urban Development. 2011. Moving to Opportunity for Fair Housing Demonstration Program: Final Impacts Evaluation. Retrieved December 15, 2011, from http://www.huduser.org/portal/publications/pubasst/MTOFHD_summary.html.

"Vincent Chin: The Outcome Made Life Cheap and Justice Elusive." 1983, April 24. *Detroit Free Press*.

Walker, J. 1998. *The History of Black Business in America: Capitalism, Race, Entrepreneurship*. New York: Macmillan Library Reference.

Warren, D. I. 1972. "Mass Media and Racial Crisis: A Study of the New Bethel Church Incident in Detroit." *Journal of Social Issues* 28(1), 111–31.

Weeks, J., and J. Spielberg Benitez. 1979. "The Cultural Demography of Midwestern Chicano Communities." In S. A. West and J. Macklin, eds., *The Chicano Experience*. Boulder, Colo.: Westview Press.

Welch, S., L. Sigelman, T. Bledsoe, and M. Combs. 2001. *Race and Place*. Cambridge: Cambridge University Press.

"What People Write about Crockett." 1969, June. *Tuebor*.

"White Ex-Officer Guilty in Black Motorist's Death." 1998, March 8. *CNN.com*. Retrieved February 18, 2011, from http://www.cnn.com/US/9803/19/police.beating/index.html.

Widick, B. J. 1972. *Detroit: City of Race and Class Violence*. Chicago: Quadrangle Books.

Wilger, R. J. 1988. *Black-White Residential Segregation in 1980*. Ann Arbor: University of Michigan.

Williams, C. 1995, May 20. "Personal Recovery from Racism." Workshop presentation at the Second Annual Model of Racial Unity Conference, Detroit.

Wilson, D. 1983a, April 2. "Trying to Defuse a Powder Keg." *Michigan Chronicle*.

———. 1983b, May 7. "Potential Pitfalls En Route to Coalition of Blacks, Hispanics." *Michigan Chronicle*.

Wilson, F. D. 1975. "The ecology of a black business district." *Review of Black Political Economy* 5, 535–75.

Wilson, W. J. 1987. *The Truly Disadvantaged: The Inner City, the Underclass, and Public Policy.* Chicago: University of Chicago Press.

———. 1999. *The Bridge over the Racial Divide: Rising Inequality and Coalition Politics.* Berkeley: University of California / Russell Sage Foundation.

Wimberly, M. 1991, January 23. "Black Detroiters: Arab/Chaldeans Aren't Our Enemies." *Michigan Chronicle.*

Winfrey, L. 1969, March 31. "Two Charged after Slaying of Policeman Outside Church." *Detroit Free Press.*

Woodard, M. D. 1997. *Black Entrepreneurs in America: Stories of Struggle and Success.* New Brunswick, N.J.: Rutgers University Press.

Wooley, J. T., and G. Peters. 2008. Richard Nixon, Statement about a national program for minority business enterprise, March 5th 1969. *The American Presidency Project.* Santa Barbara, Calif.

Wu, F. H. 2002. *Yellow: Race in America beyond Black and White.* New York: Basic Books.

Yinger, J. 1995. *Closed Doors, Opportunities Lost: The Continuing Costs of Housing Discrimination.* New York: Russell Sage Foundation.

Young, C. 1976. Jimmy Carter Campaign: Remarks by Mayor Coleman A. Young. Mayor Coleman A. Young Speeches, Charles H. Wright Museum Archives and Research Library, Detroit.

———. 1977a, August 28. Speech at Police Academy Graduation Class. Mayor Coleman A. Young Speeches, Charles H. Wright Museum Archives and Research Library, Detroit.

———. 1977b, August 28. Speech at Firefighters Graduating Class. Mayor Coleman A. Young Speeches. Charles H. Wright Museum Archives and Research Library, Detroit.

———. 1978, July 20. Welcoming remarks to NAACP. Mayor Coleman A. Young Speeches. Charles H. Wright Museum Archives and Research Library, Detroit.

———. 1980, October 19. Jimmy Carter Campaign: Remarks by Mayor Coleman A. Young. Mayor Coleman A. Young Speeches, Charles H. Wright Museum Archives and Research Library, Detroit.

———. 1984, August 22. Speech to Booker T. Washington Business Association. Mayor Coleman A. Young Speeches. Charles H. Wright Museum Archives and Research Library, Detroit.

Young, C., and L. Wheeler. 1994. *Hard Stuff: The Autobiography of Mayor Coleman Young.* New York: Viking Press.

Young, H., and J. Harding. 1971. "Negro Entrepreneurship in Southern Economic Development." In E. M. Epstein and D. R. Hampton, eds., *Black Americans and White Business* .Encino, Calif.: Dickers.

Zahirovic-Herbert, V., and G. Turnbull. 2008. "School Quality, House Prices and Liquidity." *Journal of Real Estate Finance and Economics* 37(2), 113–30.

Zhou, M., and S. Kim. 2007, May. "After-School Institutions in Chinese and Korean Immigrant Communities: A Model for Others?" *Migration Information Source,* 1–12.

Zia, H. 2002a, June 21–23. Eulogy for Mrs. Lily Chin, 1920–2002. Presented at the Rededication to Justice: Vincent Chin's 20th Year Remembrance, Detroit.

———. 2002b, June 21–23. Statement presented at the Rededication to Justice: Vincent Chin's 20th Year Remembrance, Detroit.

Zurowich, D., and C. Stoehl. 1983, April. "A Suburb Grows Up." *Monthly Detroit.*

Index

Abernathy, Ralph, 41
Aboose, Lubna, 196
Abonyi, Malvina Hauk, 201
Adams, Charles G., 55, 122
affirmative action, 113–14, 228–29, 230–31
Akrawi, Jamal, 192
Aldridge, Dan, 47
Algiers Motel incident, 1, 40–41, 53, 56
Ali, Muhammad, 25
Alkema, Robert, 279
Allen, Roy, 15, 16
American Citizens for Justice (ACJ), 161–64, 166–67, 169–74, 179
American Civil Liberties Union (ACLU), 38, 145, 162, 179, 193–94
Amsden, Ted, 289
Angelo, Frank, 9
Anthony, Wendell, 61, 126
anti-Arab racism. *See* Chaldean community; black/ Middle Eastern relations
anti-Asian racism. *See* racism
Aramaki, Ron, 289
Arbulu, Augin, 217
Arcand, Robert, 283–84
Archer, Dennis W., 120–27, 128, 129, 132, 135, 191–92, 285
Austin, Richard, 94, 95–98, 99, 100, 121
auto industry, 155–56, 164–66, 170–71, 178, 180, 200, 237, 240, 263
Automobile Club of Michigan (AAA), 276–80
Avignone, Jack, 280

Baba, Marietta Lynn, 201
Badillo, David A., 200, 201
Baha'i community, 282–83, 285, 289–90, 296
Bailey, Corado, 142
Bailey, Ruby, 142
Bakke decision (*Regents of the University of California v. Bakke*), 114
Ballenger, John, 34
Baltimore Housing Mobility Program, 304–5
Bannon, John, 188
Batchelor, Michael B., 56

Bates, Ted, 143
Baxter, Willie, 267
Beatty, Christine, 129–30, 132
Beck, Mary, 95
Berkowitz, William R., 83
Beydoun, Nassar, 186, 195
Black Enterprise, 25
Black Panther Party, 23–24, 47
Black Slate, 126
Black Star Co-op, 15
black suburbanization, 139–40, 147, 240–41, 262, 312–17
Black United Front, 47
Black Unity Day Rally, 8
black/Latino relations, 123–24, 139, 199–219; socio-economic differences, 206–16, 219, 248–57
black/Middle Eastern relations, 181–98, 217, 283
Black, Harold, 241
Blalock, Hubert M., Jr., 204
Blanchard, James, 121, 171
Blanchard, Paula, 272
Blaque, Taurean, 27
Bledsoe, Harold E., 31
Bledsoe, Tomothy, et al., 151
Bobb, Robert, 298–299, 300
Bolkosky, Sidney, 289
Bonds, Bill, 61
Booker T. Washington Businessmen's Association, 14, 16
Booker, David, 19
Boone, T. S., 33
Boskin, Joseph, 82–83
Boyd, Gwendolyn E., 197
Bradley, Tom, 164
Breakthrough, 7
Brown v. Board of Education, 69, 74, 79
Brown, Gary, 129–30
Brown, Hayward, 53–54
Browne, Ernest, 113
Buckman, Sharlonda, 299
Budzyn, Walter, 54–65
Butler, Charles W., 105, 267
Byrd, Connie, 196

Cabbil, Lila, 284–85
Cahalan, William, 161–62
Campbell, James, 12–13
Campbell, Sharon N., 286
Capeci, Dominic J., 33
capitalism, 22–23
Carter, Jimmy, 109–10, 113, 114
Cavanagh, Jerome, 7, 8, 11–12, 37, 38–39, 41, 45, 46, 265
Chaldean community, 15, 182–89, 283, 284. *See also* black/Middle Eastern relations
Chaldean Society, 7
Chan, Liza, 161, 162–64, 173
Chang, Marira, 161
Charlie Rum, 171–72
Cheatio, Imad Hussein, 194–95
Chin, Hing, 158–59
Chin, Lily, 157–61, 163–64, 166, 167, 169, 172–73, 175–77, 179–80
Chin, Vincent, 155–70, 292
Chrysler Corporation, 12, 107
Cisneros, Henry, 302
City Wide Citizen Action Committee (CCAC), 14–18
Civil Rights Act, 36, 114, 277
Cleage, Albert B., Jr., 9, 13, 14, 15, 16, 93, 96, 97–98
Clinton, Bill, 121, 128
Cleage, Henry, 38
Cobo Hall incidents, 41–42, 53
Cockrel, Ken, 53
Coleman, Trevor W., 193–94
Colvin, Sara, 291
Comerica Park, 125
Committee to End Police Brutality, 32
Community Relations Bureau (CRB), 36–37
Connerly, Ward, 230
Conyers, John, 11–12, 13, 38, 47, 95, 107, 281
cost of living, 261
Cost of Segregation, 295
Costello, Thomas, 295
Cotillion Club, 14, 16
Council of Baptist Ministers, 14, 15
Crockett, George, 43–49
Crockett, George, III, 57, 60, 62–64, 96, 121
Coughlin, Charles, 290
Cunningham, William, 274–75, 277, 278, 279–80
Czapski, Michael, 44

Darity, William, 89
Davis, John P., 31, 32
Davis, Sammy, Jr., 25
Davis, Willie, 172
Dearden, John F., 266
Deeb, Edward, 187, 190
Del Rio, James, 43, 47

Dent, Raffael, 194
Denton, Nancy, 226
desegregation conflicts, 67–80
Deskins, Donald, 87
Detroit Commission on Community Relations, 4, 5, 50, 290
Detroit Common Council, 4, 8, 32, 97
Detroit Council of Organizations (DCO), 15–18
Detroit Free Press, 9, 36, 43, 48, 49, 55, 58, 60–61, 96, 97, 102–4, 127, 130, 132, 156–57, 297
Detroit Housing Commission, 4
Detroit Industrial Mission, 12
Detroit Interracial Committee, 4, 34, 290
Detroit Lions, 125–26
Detroit News, 47–48, 124, 142, 188, 262
Detroit Police Department, 29–66, 100–101, 104–5, 108–9, 110–12, 117
Detroit Police Officers Association (DPOA), 42, 43, 49, 59
Detroit Public Schools, 68–79, 129, 183, 211–13, 237, 298–300
Detroit Roundtable of Catholics, Jews and Protestants. *See* Michigan Roundtable for Diversity and Inclusion
Detroit Scope, 94
Detroit suburbs: Birmingham, 128–29; Bloomfield Hills, 128–29, 262; Dearborn, 5–6, 141, 144–46, 147, 276–79; Oakland County, 147–49, 152, 153; Southfield, 141, 146–50, 192; Warren, 6, 7, 141–44, 147, 265
Detroit Task Force for Justice, 43
Detroit Tigers, 125
Detroit Urban League (DUL), 6, 9, 11, 13, 39
Detroiter, 125
Dickerson, Brian, 186
Diggs, Charles C., Jr., 38, 40, 47
Diggs Taylor, Anna, 168–69, 172–73
Dillard, Angela D., 38
Dingell, John, 155, 165
Ditto, Frank, 18
Doss, Larry, 25
Douglas, Freddie, 54, 56–57
Douglas, Walter, 187–88, 217
Douglass, James, 185, 187
Dragovic, Ljubisa, 57, 192
DunCombe, Trudy, 120

East/West, 159–60, 167
Ebens, Ronald, 155–69, 172–76
Ebony, 120
economic restructuring, 221–38
education, theories of, 67–68, 305–6, 310–11. *See also* Detroit Public Schools
Edwards, George, 33, 37, 38–40
Elsheick, Jumana, 189

employment discrimination, 81–91, 221, 223, 225
Engler, John, 281
Episcopal Society for Culture and Racial Unity, 270

Fair Housing Center of Metropolitan Detroit, 314–17
Farley, Reynolds, 141
Fields, Kim, 27
Fine, Sidney, 3, 8, 12, 37, 39, 138, 199
Fischer, Mary J., 228
Fletcher, Ralph, 56
Focus: HOPE, 186, 273, 274–81, 296
Ford Motor Company, 6, 99, 106, 230
Ford, Gerald, 110
Ford, Henry, II, 12, 18, 106, 113
Four Tops, 25
Franklin, C. L., 44–45, 46
Fraser, Douglas, 113, 171
Freeman, Lorenzo, 13
Freiji, Maha, 196–97
Fried, Henry, 31

Gaddis, Mildred, 129
Garrett, James S., 16–18, 37
Garvey, Marcus, 23
Gautreaux v. Chicago Housing Authority, 301–2, 303
Gaye, Marvin, 25
General Motors, 12, 96, 165
Georgakas, Dan, and Marvin Surkin, 41–42, 49
Giles, Ronald, 132
Gilman, Leonard, 161, 169
Gordon, Leonard, 266–68
Gore, Al, 126, 128
Grace, Robert, 45
Granholm, Jennifer, 133
Greater Detroit Board of Commerce, 11
Green, Malice, 54–66, 117–18, 192
Green, Patricia, 58, 66
Green, Rose Mary, 63
Gribbs, Roman S., 50, 95–96, 276
Grimshaw, Allen, 83
Groner, David, 133–34
Gross, Andrew B., 242–43
Group of Advanced Leadership (GOAL), 38
Guardians, 47, 52
gun ownership, 7, 8, 49, 265

Harlan, Carmen, 131
Hankerson, Barry L., 23–24, 25
Harmony Project, 194–95
Harper, Jim, 171
Harper, Shannon, 231
Harrison, Paul, 283
Harrison, Susan, 283
Hart, William L., 111

Henderson, Erma, 94, 160, 161
Hendrix, Freeman, 128–29
Henry, Milton R., 13, 45
Hermalin, Albert I., 141
Herman, Max, 86
Hersch, Joni, 204
Hesburgh, Theodore M., 140
Hersey, John, 40–41
Hewitt, Ron, 125, 126
Hill, Gill, 128
Hispanic Detroiters. *See* black/Latino relations
Hoekenga, Daniel, 163
Holzer, Harry J., 224
Hood, Nicholas, 97
Hoover, J. Edgar, 99
House Committee on Un–American Activities, 99, 102
Houston, Charles H., 31–32
Hubbard, Orville L., 5–6, 144
Hudson, Joseph L., Jr., 11, 12–13, 15, 271
Hunter, Gary, 190
Hurst, Lorraine, 196
Hwang, Roland, 178

Iacocca, Lee, 166
Ihlanfeldt, Keith R., 82
index of dissimilarity, 137, 319
Inner City Organizing Committee, 13
Inner-City Sub-Center (ICSC), 9, 18–21, 23, 27
Inner City Voice, 14
Inouye, Karen, 176
Interfaith Emergency Council (IEC), 15, 268–71
Interreligious Foundation for Community Development, 15

Jackson, Jesse, 293
James, Jesse, 31
Jargowsky, Paul A., 226–27
Jiraki, Kalil, 57
Johnson, Arthur, 13, 18, 34, 35, 36, 268
Johnson, Lyndon B., 39, 81
Johnson, Patrick, 272
Joiner, Charles W., 278–79
Josaitis, Eleanor, 274–75, 281
Joseph, Larry, 188

Kain, John F., 82, 87, 223–24, 300
Karenga, Maulana Ron, 20
Kasarda, John D., 226
Kaufman, Charles, 156–68
Keith, Damon J., 13, 105–6, 107
Kennedy, Robert F., 36
Kerner Commission Report, 2, 84, 85, 91, 152–53, 266, 268

Khoury, Edward, 163–64, 167
Kilpatrick, Bernard, 127
Kilpatrick, Carolyn Cheeks, 127–28
Kilpatrick, Kwame, 127–35
King, Martin Luther, Jr., 37, 197, 267, 275
King, Rodney, 55, 57, 58, 62, 118
Knight, Gladys, 26; and the Pips, 25
Knoll, Faustina Ramirez, 201
Knowles, John, 188
Knox, Robert, 57
Knox, Stanley, 59, 62
Krichbaum, Dan, 295

Lang, Winston, 161, 188
Latin Americans for Social and Economic Development (LASED), 199
Latinos. *See* black/Latino relations
Lee, Cherylene, 179
Lee, Elis Choy, 160
Lee, James, 283
Lee, Wen Ho, 178
Lee, Henry, 163
Lessnau, Robert, 54, 57, 58
Levin, Carl, 121, 281
Levin, Sander, 281
Lewis, Lyn, 65
Lobsinger, Donald, 7
Love, Barbara, 285
Lucas, William, 272

Madison, Joseph, 144
Mahaffy, Maryann, 124, 178, 281
Maida, Adam, 281
Malcolm X, 14, 19, 23, 24, 25
Malcolm X (film), 58, 65
Malcolm X Society, 9–11
Marshall, Robert, 37
Marshall, Thurgood, 39
Mason, Patrick, 89
Massey, Douglas, 226, 228, 242–43
Matsui, Robert, 171
Mauer, Marc, 235
Mayne, Joseph Q., 290–91
McClendon, James J., 30, 31–32
McClendon, Mary, 190
McClinton, Robert, 161
McIlwain, Toni, 194–95
McPhail, Sharon, 121–24, 129
Meisner, Mort, 61
Meriwether, Heath, 126
Messigner, Frances, 24
Metropolitan Detroit Religion and Race Conference, 266–68

Michigan Chronicle, 14, 16–18, 42, 46, 51, 55, 94–95, 98, 105, 110–11, 160
Michigan Civil Rights Commission, 41, 50–51, 88, 153–54
Michigan Roundtable for Diversity and Inclusion, 290–96
Middle Eastern Detroiters: *See* black/Middle Eastern relations; Chaldean community
migration theory, 298
Millender, Robert, 94
Miller, Jerome G., 235
Milliken v. Bradley, 71, 73–74
Milliken, William, 45, 46
Milner, Ron, 25
Mincy, Ronald, 227
Mineta, Norman, 166
minority business ownership theories, 215
Mirchandani, Haresh, 57
Miriani, Louis, 35
Model of Racial Unity conferences, 282–89, 296
Mondale, Walter, 166
Mosley, Leon, 33
Moss, Phillip, 89
Moss, Tom, 52
Motown Record Company, 22
Moving to Opportunity program (MTO), 303–4
Moy, Charles, 167
Murphy, Daniel, 272
Murphy, Sheila, 42
Myrdal, Gunnar, 267

NAACP, 16, 64, 113, 124, 132, 160, 189–90, 193–94; vs. police brutality, 30–36, 38, 39, 46–47, 66; vs. residential discrimination, 144–45; vs. school segregation, 68–71
National Guard, 2, 10
National Rifle Association, 7
Naylor, Michael, 290
Neill, William J. V., 126–27
Nelthorpe, Harold, 129–30
Nevers, Larry, 54–61, 63, 65–66
New Bethel Church incident, 43–49, 53, 96
New Detroit, Inc. (NDI), 9, 10, 11, 13, 14, 15, 16, 18, 19, 25, 26, 46, 124, 186, 188, 271–74, 296; relations with Hispanics, 217–18, 271–72, 274
Nguzo Saba (Seven Principles of Blackness), 20
Nichols, Bill, 176–77
Nichols, John, 51, 54, 100–104
1943 riot, 4, 12, 33, 66, 186, 265, 290
1967 disorder: historical background, 4–7, 11, 12, 29–40; white vs. black perspectives on, 2–3, 9, 12, 27, 83

Nitz, Michael, 156–69, 173
Nixon, Richard M., 229

Olsen, Samuel H., 37–38
O'Neill, Tip, 166
Operation Get-Down (OGD), 9, 18, 23–27

Page, Clarence, 123
Pangborn, Mominic, 178
Parker, Bernard, 23–24, 25, 27
Parks, Rosa, 38, 177
Parrish, Gail, 123
Patrick, William T., Jr., 13, 46
Patterson, L. Brooks, 122, 128–29
Peach, Ceri, 203
Peek, Lonnie, 188
Peek, Susan, 188
Pelham, Alfred, 38–39
Pelham, Joseph, 268
Perry, Jimmie, 162
Philpot, Thomas Lee, 203
Porter, Herman A., 291
Porter, Kalvin, 190–93, 195, 198

Race Relations Council of Metropolitan Detroit
    (RRCMD), 123
racism: anti-Asian, 155–80; anti-Middle Eastern: *see*
    black/Middle Eastern relations; institutional, 2–4,
    27, 60, 97–98, 112, 115, 184, 265, 276
Randall, Dudley, 182
Ravitz, Mel, 281
Reading, Richard, 30, 32
Reagan, Ronald, 110, 114–15, 118, 167
Republic of New Africa, 9, 13, 44–45, 182
residential segregation, 68–80, 81–90, 137–54, 183,
    205–6, 222, 226, 239–42, 244–48, 306, 313,
    316–17
Reskin, Barbara, 231
Reuter, Eugene, 38
Reuther, Walter, 102
Reyes, Angie, 284
Reynolds, William Bradford, 166–67
Richmond v. Crosen, 229–30
Ricketts, Erol R., 227
Riegle, Donald, 166, 171
Roberson, Dalton, 62
Roberts, Roy, 78
Robinson, Gloria, 125, 126
Roche, James, 12, 18
Rochester Street Massacre, 52, 53
Rogell, Michael, 282
Romney, George W., 2–3, 11, 41, 103–4, 143
Roscigno, Vincent J., 211

Rosen, Gerald, 57
Ross, Diana, 107
Roth, Stephen, 71
Roundtree, Bill, 161
Rueppel, Carol, 61
Rumor Control Center, 8–9
Russell, Nipsey, 25
Rutstein, Nathan, 285
Rydstedt, Ruth, 289

Saperstein, Bruce, 163–64
Sarafa, Michael, 187, 190–91
Saunders, Neil, 44–45
Sawhill, Isabel V., 227
Schineider, Tom, 59
Schrupp, Clifford C., 314
Scott, Cynthia, 37–38, 39
Sedler, Robert, 145
Sengstock, Mary, 188–89
Shallal, Jane, 290
Shapero, Nate S., 292
Sheffield, Horace, 160–61, 268
Sheffield, Horace L., III, 185–86, 194
Shimoura, James, 165, 170, 172–73, 174
Shine, Neal, 281
Sigelman, Lee, 151
Simmons, Russell, 129
Simon, Howard, 145
Sjoquist, David J., 82
Skendzel, Eduard Adam, 200, 203–4
Smith, Gerald L. K., 290
Smith, Roger, 272
Smith, Suzanne E., 22–23
Smith, William French, 166
Smyrna, David F., 273
Snyder, Rick, 80
Sojourner Housing riot, 33
"spatial mismatch," 81–82, 87, 90, 223–24, 237–38,
    300–301
"spatial mobility," 297–317
Spicher, Theodore, 37–38, 39
Spinners, 25
Staples, Robert, 234
Steinberg, Martha Jean (the Queen), 61
Stempler, Marvin R., 145
Stokes, Carl, 94
Stokes, Chuck, 290
Stoll, Michael, 82
Stop the Robberies, Enjoy Safe Streets (STRESS), 49–
    54, 100, 104, 117, 135
Strong, Charles P., 23, 24
Sugrue, Thomas J., 86
Surkin, Marvin, 41–42, 49

Takaki, Ronald, 164–65
Tang, Irwin Ai-Bong, 177
Tannian, Philip, 107
Taylor, Darnell, 61–62
Taylor, Paul, 19–23
Thomas, June M., 127, 282, 284
Thomas, Richard, 282, 284
Thomas, Oliver, 283
Tiebout, Charles M., 306
Tilly, Chris, 89
Time, 129, 133, 297
Tindal, Robert, 14, 94
Toneye, L. Rod, 289
Townsend, Lynn, 12
Trade Union Leadership Council, 14, 16
Trent, Kim, 197
Tso, James, 174
Tuebor, 44
Turner, Margery Austin, et al., 152
Turner, Tom, 50
12th Street, 2, 3, 5, 10–11, 12, 36, 116, 292; 12th
    and Clairmount, 83, 86

UAW (United Auto Workers), 16, 33, 106, 166, 230
UHURU, 38
Ujamaa Club, 21–22

Vann, Edgar, 64–65
Vargas, Horatio, 218
Vaughn, Jackie, III, 46, 281
Veterans Memorial Hall incident, 42–43, 53

Wakabayashi, Ron, 174
Wallace, George, 42, 144
Warren, Donald I., 49
Washington, Lawrence, 268
Watkins, Ethel, 4–5
Watson, JoAnn, 119, 189
Watson, Susan, 58
Watts riot, 270
Welch, Susan, 151West Central Organization (WCO),
    13
Wheeler, Heaster, 193

white flight, 7–8, 22, 27, 93, 94, 96, 116, 142, 183,
    200, 239, 262, 276, 277
White, Andrea, 284
White, Horace, 31
White, Hugh, 12–13
White, Laurence, 289
White, Winifred, 289
Whitten, Charles, 24
Who Killed Vincent Chin?, 176–77
Wilger, Robert James, 242
Wilkerson, Martha, 33
Williams, Amos, 130
Williams, Clarence, 283, 285
Wilson, William Julies, 187
Wimberly, Michael, 189
Wolverine Bar Association, 16, 120
Wonder, Stevie, 25, 127
Wong, George, 165
Wong, Vickie, 155–56, 157
Woodcock, Leonard, 106
Worobec, Richard, 44, 50
Wright, Barbara Ann, 192
Wright, Charles, 218
Wright, Genarda, 196
Wu, Frank, 165
Wurtsmith, Frank J., 291
Wynn, Obie, 107

Yan, Victor J., 162
Yang, Rebecca, 227
Yee, Kin, 161
Yono, Jerry, 187
Young, Coleman: background, 99, 119, 120; early career,
    33, 42, 45, 98, 99–100; election as mayor, 10, 54, 66,
    94, 100–105, 199–200; mayoral administration, 60,
    64, 105–19, 120, 121, 124, 125, 126; post-mayoral
    legacy, 128, 129, 132, 134–35; relations with the
    Carter Administration, 109–10, 229; relations with
    Dennis Archer, 121–22; relations with Detroit Police
    Department, 55, 59, 104–5, 108–9, 111–12, 117–18

Zia, Helen Y., 160, 167, 169–71, 176–79
Zoma, Nabil, 185, 187